D0629645

JESUS THROUGH THE CENTURIES

MARY THROUGH THE CENTURIES

JESUS THROUGH THE CENTURIES
MARY THROUGH THE CENTURIES

BY

JAROSLAV PELIKAN

WITH A NEW PREFACE
BY THE AUTHOR

HISTORY BOOK CLUB
NEW YORK

Preface to the History Book Club Edition
Jesus Through the Centuries and *Mary Through the Centuries*

This History Book Club edition brings together into a single volume, for the first time, my *Jesus Through the Centuries*, originally published in 1985, and *Mary Through the Centuries*, which first appeared in 1996. In these two books I have dealt with the two historical figures who, among all who have ever lived, certainly qualify most for the overworked buzzword "iconic," having surely been the subjects of more icons than all other biblical and postbiblical personages put together.

My career as a scholar and writer of history spans approximately six decades now, since I received my Ph.D. in 1946, and it divides itself, though not quite neatly, into three almost equal parts. The first third was spent in researching literally thousands of primary texts in different languages from the various periods of the history of the Christian tradition, and editing and translating many of them, "making deposits into the account," as I used to say; books and monographs on different periods represented a preliminary probing of the subject. The second third of my professional career as a historian was largely devoted to writing *The Christian Tradition: A History of the Development of Doctrine*, which eventually came to five volumes and was published from 1971 to 1989; it has since appeared, or is now in the process of appearing, in several translations, including French and Chinese, Russian and Romanian. Having thus documented at considerable length—counting the numerous abbreviations, it has been estimated (though not by me!) as having come to a total of nearly a million words—the history of one of the most shattering explosions in the history of the human spirit, I have for the past two decades or so been charting the history of the cultural "fallouts" from that explosion, in fields of thought and expression that include music, philosophy, literature, rhetoric, and constitutional law. My first full-length study of such a fallout was *Jesus Through the Centuries: His Place in the History of Culture*, which was first published exactly twenty years ago, in 1985, to which then *Mary Through the Centuries* was a natural sequel.

The very phenomenon of secularization in culture and education has served in a curious way to accentuate the subtitle "his place in the history of culture." For images and titles and metaphors that could be taken for granted in an earlier age had now lost their meaning, and therefore the only way to understand them historically was to see how inseparable they have been from the person of Jesus. That was uniquely true of the sign of the Cross—the German words for "to bless" is *segnen*—but it ran through art and poetry and even science. An extensive and gratifying correspondence with readers of widely varied background and educational level suggests that even with the ruthless necessity of selecting and abridging, *Jesus Through the Centuries* has apparently provided many thousands of readers in many languages with a new introduction to their own collective memory. In this as in so many other respects, Johann Wolfgang von Goethe was articulating that collective memory when he said, less than two weeks before he died: "Beyond the grandeur and the moral elevation of Christianity, as it sparkles and shines in the Gospels, the human mind will not advance."

Goethe was also the spokesman for the memory of "Mary through the centuries" when, in the climactic conclusion of his poetic drama *Faust* he had "Doctor Marianus" (the scholastic nickname of the Franciscan theologian Duns Scotus) invoke the authority of Mary as "Virgin, Mother, Queen, Goddess." Therefore these words are not, or at any rate not primarily, addressed to an unspecified Feminine Principle, but to "the Eternal Feminine, *das Ewig-Weibliche.*" A cultural amnesia produces in modern readers, as one of its most dangerous symptoms, a tone-deafness to these accents. Because of this tone-deafness, many otherwise well-informed readers of Goethe's *Faust* miss completely the close ties between its conclusion and the conclusion of the greatest of its predecessors in the Western literary canon, Dante's *Divine Comedy.* Here again it is the Virgin Mary in whom the work achieves its climax and summation, in words that are put into the mouth of (and taken largely from the writings of) the medieval mystic Bernard of Clairvaux, an earlier "Doctor Marianus."

In many ways, therefore, it makes literary and historical sense to bring these two histories together into a single volume. As even her most fervent enthusiasts acknowledge, Christian language about the

Blessed Virgin Mary in the Orthodox and Catholic traditions has let itself get into great difficulties whenever it has made her an object of devotion in her own right rather than, in Dante's phrase, as "the face that most resembles Christ's," who was her Son and her Lord and Redeemer. And in the Protestant traditions, on the other hand, the violent act of separating loyalty to Jesus Christ from the celebration of Mary of which it has so long been an essential partner has led not to the glorification of Him alone, as was intended, but to Christological chaos instead of Christological confession.

It also makes historical sense to package these two-books-in-one with my most recent volume in this genre, *Whose Bible Is It? The History of the Scriptures Through the Ages*, published in 2005. For the histories both of the study of the figure of Jesus and of the interpretation of his Mother are, of course, an indispensable component of that larger account. At the same time, a fundamental element in the history of Jesus and a significant element in the history of Mary has been central to the history of the Bible: the relation between the Jewish way and the Christian way of reading their Scriptures. Here in *Jesus Through the Centuries* I asked twenty years ago: "Would there have been such anti-Semitism, would there have been so many pogroms, would there have been an Auschwitz, if every Christian Church and every Christian home had focused its devotion on icons of Mary not only as Mother of God and Queen of Heaven but as the Jewish maiden and the New Miriam, and on icons of Christ not only as Pantocrator but as *Rabbi Jeshua bar-Joseph*, Rabbi Jesus of Nazareth, the Son of David, in the context of the history of a suffering Israel and a suffering humanity?"

In a real sense, I could not have begun answering that momentous question, for myself or for my readers, without going on to write both *Mary Through the Centuries* and *Whose Bible Is It?* As I have discovered (or rediscovered) by rereading all three of them together in recent weeks, they do belong together and each is enlightened and enriched by the other two. I hope that the readers of all of them will agree.

JESUS THROUGH THE CENTURIES

His Place in the History of Culture

To the Benedictines
of Saint John's Abbey
Collegeville, Minnesota

nihil amori Christi praeponere

Contents

Contents

Illustrations

Initial crosses: *Introduction, Russian Orthodox; 1, Passover; 2, Alpha
and Omega; 3, Light and Life; 4, Labarum of Constantine; 5, Universe; 6,
Golgotha; 7, Byzantine; 8, Monogram of Charlemagne; 9, Right Hand of*

Our Lord; 10, Christus Noster; 11, Cross of Peter; 12, Branch; 13, The Evangelists; 14, Crusaders; 15, Latin cross; 16, Fleur-de-lis; 17, Jerusalem; 18, Rainbow.

Preface

I think I have always wanted to write this book. Having described, in *The Christian Tradition*, the history of the significance of the person and work of Jesus Christ for the faith and teaching of the Christian church, I am turning here to the other half of the story: his place in the general history of culture.

Clemenceau once remarked that war was entirely too important a matter to be left to the military. So also, Jesus is far too important a figure to be left only to the theologians and the church. And the invitation to deliver the William Clyde DeVane Lectures at Yale, public lectures in an academic setting, gave me just the opportunity I needed to write the book I had always wanted to write. The audiences at the lectures represented both town and gown—all ages, social backgrounds, educational levels, and religious persuasions. That is as well the kind of audience for whom the book is intended. Therefore I have sought, in citing my sources, to make use, if at all possible, of generally available editions, adopting and adapting earlier translations (including my own) without a pedantic explanation each time; biblical quotations are usually from the Revised Standard Version.

I have been greatly aided by listeners and students, colleagues and critics, to all of whom I am pleased to express my thanks. Special thanks are due my editors, John G. Ryden and Barbara Hofmaier, for bringing a sensitive ear and an impeccable taste to the improvement of my manuscript and for saving me from inelegancies and howlers.

The dedication is the expression of my fraternal devotion to my *fratres* at the Abbey of Saint John the Baptist in Collegeville, Minnesota, of whose Benedictine family I am proud to be an adopted son.

A Personal Preface to *Jesus Through the Centuries* for the Year 2000

Some of my friends and colleagues have suggested to me, only half-facetiously, that reissuing this book as we near the year 2000 really calls for it also to be retitled, perhaps as *Jesus Through the Millennia*—or, altogether facetiously, even as *Jesus at Y2K*. Several others, however, have been urging that I use this preface for a more serious as well as a more personal purpose.

In the original publication of 1985 I had largely avoided the personal and confessional tone, except at a few places. There have now been several editions in English, including *The Illustrated Jesus Through the Centuries* in 1997, together with translations of *Jesus Through the Centuries* into many languages, bringing the number of copies in circulation to well over a hundred thousand. Therefore the appearance of this edition provides me with a welcome opportunity to reflect yet again, and much more in the form of (if this is a permissible neologism) an "autobiobibliography" this time, on the book and on its Subject, in the New Testament's formula, "Jesus Christ the same yesterday and today and for ever" (Heb. 13:8). I must acknowledge that I have found these recommendations to be quite compelling the more I have thought about them, and I have decided to follow their advice.

To begin with the most obvious change that has taken place in "the real world" since 1985—a change that has been reflected also in the publishing history of this book—Slavic Europe is now no longer dominated by a totalitarian and atheistic ideology that had tried to ignore even the "yesterday" of that New Testament formula and had officially declared the "today and for ever" to be obsolete, indeed an "opium of the masses." Because Slavic Europe is where my own family traditions and spiritual roots lie, the revolution that overthrew the Revolution has had special importance for me, not only as a person but as an author. The appearance of this edition of *Jesus Through the Centuries* simultaneously marks for me the fiftieth anniversary of my first book, *From Luther to Kierkegaard* (Saint Louis, 1950). (My earlier University of Chicago Ph.D. dissertation of 1946 has never appeared in print as a monograph, only as articles or as chapters in later books.) *From Luther to Kierkegaard* of a half-century ago and many of the books that followed it have been translated not only into practically all of the languages of Western Europe but into several Asian languages as well—yet never into any of the Slavic tongues, and that for the obvious reasons.

Now with the collapse of the Communist regimes, *Jesus Through the Centuries* has been published as the first of my works to be turned into several Slavic languages, including Croatian, Slovak, and Polish, although the Croatian version was, at least initially, the victim of yet another war in the Balkans. These translations into Slavic languages using the Latin alphabet have been followed by others, and now by a projected Russian translation of all five volumes of *The Christian Tradition: A History of the Development of Doctrine* (Chicago, 1971–89), beginning with volume 2, *The Spirit of Eastern Christendom (600–1700)*, as *Duch Vostočnogo Christianstva*, for which I have had the pleasure of writing a new preface addressed particularly to my Eastern Orthodox fellow-believers in Russia. Because I had already been calling him "Ježiš Kristus" in Slovak before I ever learned to call him "Jesus Christ" in English, the appearance of these Slavic translations of *Jesus Through the Centuries* and then of my other books is, I hope, a justifiable source for some sense of gratification, if not—considering the state of that part of the world, which does seem to be "the same yesterday and today," though not, please God, "for ever"!—for any feelings of triumphalism.

Meanwhile, the various historical developments that I had examined in various chapters of this book have, over the past decade and a half, become subjects for further research projects in their own right, many of which I might never have undertaken and completed if I had not launched them here. Above all, the companion volume to this one, my *Mary Through the Centuries* of 1996, based on lectures that were the last course I gave at Yale, grew out of my deepening awareness of the remarkable persistence with which, "through the centuries," the ancient and perennial question of the Gospels, "What think ye of Christ?" (Matt. 22:42) has necessarily entailed a consideration of his Mother in turn. And the continuing efforts of individual Christians and of churches in every continent and "through the centuries" to find formulas for expressing and confessing what they believed and taught about him are at the core of the multivolume set of *Creeds and Confessions of Faith in the Christian Tradition*, which Valerie R. Hotchkiss and I are now editing; when, *Deo volente*, we have completed it in the next year or so, it will come out under the imprint of Yale University Press.

Chapter 5 of *Jesus Through the Centuries*, "The Cosmic Christ," deals with the fourth century in the Greek-speaking Orthodox Christian East, as this was represented above all by "the three Cappadocians" (Basil of Caesarea, Gregory of Nazianzus, and Gregory of Nyssa), to whose thought I was finally able to give a full-length exposition in my Gifford Lectures at Aberdeen, which appeared as *Christianity and Classical Culture* in 1993. More recently, this exposition has led me still further, to probe a fascinating case study of the relation between Christianity and classical culture and of "the cosmic Christ" in the creation narratives of Plato and the Bible, as I traced their historical interactions in the Jerome Lectures at Ann Arbor and Rome, which became *What Has Athens to Do with Jerusalem? "Timaeus" and "Genesis" in Counterpoint* (1997), developing some of the thoughts set forth here in Chapter 3, "The Light of the Gentiles." The ideas in Chapter 7, "The True Image," were much more fully fleshed out in my Andrew W. Mellon Lectures, given at the National Gallery of Art in 1987 (for the twelve-hundredth anniversary of the restorations of the icons after iconoclasm by the Second Council of Nicaea in 787) and published in 1990 by Princeton University Press in the United States and by Yale University Press in the United Kingdom as *Imago Dei: The Byzantine Apologia for Icons*. A combination of the "sacred philology" of the Renaissance discussed in Chapter 12, "The Universal Man," with the "biblical humanism" of the Reformation discussed in Chapter 13, "The Mirror of the Eternal," inspired *The Reformation of the Bible / The Bible of the Reformation* (which I prepared with Valerie R. Hotchkiss and David Price, as a book and a library exhibition in Dallas, New Haven, New York, and Cambridge, in 1996).

Nor have I, despite my personal loyalties, confined my historical scholarship to the Christian mainstream and the Orthodox tradition.

In fact, the four final chapters of *Jesus Through the Centuries*, dealing with modern criticisms of the Orthodox tradition and substitutes for it, have each led me into deeper investigations. Thus in "Jefferson and His Contemporaries," the afterword I wrote in 1989 to the audacious abridgment of the Gospels now called *The Jefferson Bible: The Life and Morals of Jesus of Nazareth*, by Thomas Jefferson, the theme was the curious Enlightenment blend of rationalism and moralism as keys to its interpretation of the figure of Jesus, as I had first tried to expound it here on the basis of Jefferson's thought in Chapter 15, "The Teacher of Common Sense." The next chapter, "Poet of the Spirit," was the presupposition for my introduction to the sesquicentennial facsimile version of the first edition of Ralph Waldo Emerson's dithyrambic first book, *Nature,* in 1985. At the end of that chapter I also addressed one of the most profound images of Christ in all of literature, the Legend of the Grand Inquisitor in F. M. Dostoevsky's *The Brothers Karamazov,* on which I have now been invited to prepare an essay for a forthcoming symposium. Representing the sharpest possible contrast with Dostoevsky's image of the Prisoner, Leo Tolstoy's highly individual-istic picture of Christ and of Christianity, whose repercussions in the thought and action of his disciple Mahatma Gandhi, and then of Gandhi's disciple Martin Luther King, occupy me here in Chapter 17, "The Liberator," took substantial form of its own in a lecture I entitled "Russia's Greatest Heretic," delivered at and published by Seton Hall University in 1989. It was at least in part because of the "universal vision" expressed in my conclusion to this book in Chapter 18, "The Man Who Belongs to the World," that I was invited by my late friend Clifton Fadiman to prepare *The World Treasury of Modern Religious Thought,* which was published with his gracious foreword in 1990.

Although I have therefore, I believe, the right to cite these later chap-ters, as well as the subsequent publications growing out of them, as evidence that I am by no means tone-deaf to other Christologies than the Orthodox, even to those of Jefferson, Emerson, and Tolstoy, I do feel obliged to express my dismay that, in the fifteen years since the original appearance of *Jesus Through the Centuries,* there sometimes seems to be an even greater divide than ever separating what Chris-tians and the Christian Church believe, teach, and confess about Jesus Christ from what at least some New Testament scholars feel qualified to state about him on the basis of their speculations and hypotheses. That dismay has its roots in my ever-stronger conviction that sound

faith and sound scholarship are not antithetical but mutually supportive. My disclaimers in this book and elsewhere about any qualifica-
tions of my own as a card-carrying New Testament scholar—which I
usually summarize in the formula "I do not study what the New Testament *meant,* but what it *has been taken to mean!*"—have not managed
to protect me over the past fifteen years from vast volumes of commu-
nications by every available technological means, soliciting (or de-
manding) my comments about this or that hypothesis concerning Jesus
that has been floated by one or another radical critic. If my response to
such importunity has sometimes been less than Christlike, as I must
admit that it has, my impatience has been evoked by a viewpoint that
claims, on the basis of the principle that historical events become clearer
the farther we are removed from them, to be able to come at the first
century from the vantage point of the twentieth, with little or no attention to the centuries that intervened, which are the centuries about
which (or "through" which) I wrote this book. I believe that the Church
did get it right in its liturgies, councils, and creeds about Jesus Christ;
but I have never required that my readers (or my students) agree,
merely that they take this seriously, if only to reject it.

By hindsight it seems clear to me that all of that is certainly part of
what I meant when I said in the opening sentence of my original preface: "I think I have always wanted to write this book." It can also be
taken to be the meaning of what the historian who has been my scholarly inspiration and my theological bête noire during my lifetime, Adolf
von Harnack of the University of Berlin, marking the previous turn of
a century exactly one hundred years ago, made the opening sentence
of his lectures, *What Is Christianity?* [*Das Wesen des Christentums*] of
1899/1900: "The great English philosopher, John Stuart Mill, once commented that mankind can hardly be too often reminded that there was
once a man named Socrates. That is correct, but it is even more important to remind mankind that a man named Jesus Christ once stood in
their midst."

It still is, even in the third millennium.

Introduction
The Good, the True, and the Beautiful

*From his fulness have we all re-
ceived, grace upon grace.*

Regardless of what anyone may personally think or believe about him, Jesus of Nazareth has been the dominant
figure in the history of Western culture for almost twenty
centuries. If it were possible, with some sort of supermagnet, to pull up out of that history every scrap of metal
bearing at least a trace of his name, how much would be
left? It is from his birth that most of the human race dates
its calendars, it is by his name that millions curse and in his name
that millions pray.

"Jesus Christ is the same yesterday and today and for ever. Do not
be led away by diverse and strange teachings" (Heb. 13:8–9). With
these words the anonymous (and still unknown) author of the first-
century document that has come to be called the Epistle to the Hebrews admonished his readers, who were probably recent converts
from Judaism to Christianity, to remain loyal to the deposit of the
authentic and authoritative tradition of Christ, as this had come down
to them through the apostles of the first Christian generation, some
of whom were still living.

"The same yesterday and today and for ever" eventually came to
have a metaphysical and theological significance, as "the same" was
taken to mean that Jesus Christ was, in his eternal being, "the image
of the unchangeable God, and therefore likewise unchangeable."[1] But

for the purposes of this book, it is the historical, not the metaphysical or theological, import of this phrase that must chiefly engage our attention. For, as will become evident in great and perhaps even confusing detail before this history of images of Jesus through the centuries is finished, it is not sameness but kaleidoscopic variety that is its most conspicuous feature. Would we not find it more accurate to substitute for the first-century formula "the same yesterday and today and for ever" the twentieth-century words of Albert Schweitzer? "Each successive epoch," Schweitzer said, "found its own thoughts in Jesus, which was, indeed, the only way in which it could make him live"; for, typically, one "created him in accordance with one's own character." "There is," he concluded, "no historical task which so reveals someone's true self as the writing of a *Life of Jesus.*"[2]

This book presents a history of such images of Jesus, as these have appeared from the first century to the twentieth. Precisely because, in Schweitzer's words, it has been characteristic of each age of history to depict Jesus in accordance with its own character, it will be an important part of our task to set these images into their historical contexts. We shall want to see what it was that each age brought to its portrayal of him. For each age, the life and teachings of Jesus represented an answer (or, more often, *the* answer) to the most fundamental questions of human existence and of human destiny, and it was to the figure of Jesus as set forth in the Gospels that those questions were addressed. If we want to comprehend the answers these previous centuries found there, we must penetrate to their questions, which in most instances will not be our own questions and in many instances will not even be explicitly their own questions. For, in the provocative formula of Alfred North Whitehead,

> When you are criticizing [or, one may add, interpreting] the philosophy of an epoch, do not chiefly direct your attention to those intellectual positions which its exponents feel it necessary explicitly to defend. There will be some fundamental assumptions which adherents of all the variant systems within the epoch unconsciously presuppose. Such assumptions appear so obvious that people do not know what they are assuming because no other way of putting things has ever occurred to them. With these assumptions a certain limited number of types of philosophic systems are possible.[3]

During the past two thousand years, few issues if any have so persistently brought out these "fundamental assumptions" of each epoch as has the attempt to come to terms with the meaning of the figure of Jesus of Nazareth.

For that very reason, however, the converse of the relation between what Whitehead calls "the philosophy of an epoch" and its picture of Jesus will also hold true: the way any particular age has depicted Jesus is often a key to the genius of that age. We who seek, whether as professional or as amateur students of history, to understand and appreciate any segment of the past are continually frustrated not only by the inaccessibility of many of the most revealing monuments of that experience (since only small fragments, and not necessarily the most representative ones, have come down to us), but also by our lack of a proper antenna for picking up the signals of another time and place. We cannot, and we must not, trust our own common sense to give us the right translation of the foreign languages of the past—all of whose languages are by definition foreign, even when the past speaks in English. A sensitivity to that frustration is the necessary prerequisite, but it may also become the occupational disease, of the historian, who can end up despairing of the effort and becoming a victim of what has been called "the paralysis of analysis."

One element of any method for coping with such frustration must be to inquire after instances of continuity within the change and variety, and if possible to find issues or themes that document both the change and the continuity at the same time. The point can be illustrated by reference to a field of historical research far removed from the concerns of this book. Without interruption since the days of the Hebrew Bible and of Homer, olive oil has been a major constituent of the diet, the pharmacopoeia, and the trade of the peoples surrounding the Mediterranean Sea, so that one of the most distinguished of contemporary social and economic historians, Fernand Braudel, is able to define the Mediterranean geographically as the "region [that] stretches from the northern limit of the olive tree to the northern limit of the palm tree. The first olive tree on the way south marks the beginning of the Mediterranean region and the first compact palm grove the end."[4] But even a comparison of Homer and the Hebrew Bible will show some of the variety in both the literal and the metaphorical use of olive oil. If, therefore, one were to study its history as condiment and cosmetic, culture and commodity, one would probably be able to discover many of the continuities—and many of the discontinuities—in the past three millennia of the Mediterranean world.

Similarly, the history of the images of Jesus illustrates the continuities and the discontinuities of the past two millennia simultaneously. Arthur O. Lovejoy, founder of the history of ideas as a distinct discipline in modern American scholarship, used it to illustrate only the discontinuities. "The term 'Christianity,' " he wrote in *The Great Chain of Being*, "is not the name for any single unit of the type for which the historian of specific ideas looks." For Lovejoy saw the history of Christianity as not such a single unit at all, but rather as "a series of facts which, taken as a whole, have almost nothing in common except the name." Although he was willing to acknowledge, as that series of facts obliged him to acknowledge, that the one thing they did hold in common was "the reverence for a certain person," the person of Jesus Christ, he went on to add that his "nature and teaching . . . have been most variously conceived, so that the unity here too is largely a unity of name."[5] Yet Lovejoy would also have been obliged to acknowledge that each of the almost infinite—and infinitely different—ways of construing that name has been able to claim some warrant or other somewhere within the original portrait (or portraits) of Jesus in the Gospels. And so there is continuity in this history, yes; but no less prominent a characteristic of the ways of describing the meaning of Jesus Christ has been their discontinuity.

One consequence of the discontinuity is the great variety and unevenness in the concepts and terms that have been used to describe this meaning, from the most naive and unsophisticated to the most profound and complex. According to the Gospels, Jesus prayed, "I thank thee, Father, Lord of heaven and earth, that thou hast hidden these things from the wise and understanding and revealed them to babes" (Luke 10:21). These words have served to remind theologians and philosophers that "man's discernment is so overwhelmed that it is hindered from attaining the mysteries of God, which have been 'revealed to babes alone.' "[6] But the words of Jesus in the very next verse make the declaration "All things have been delivered to me by my Father; and no one knows who the Son is except the Father, or who the Father is except the Son and any one to whom the Son chooses to reveal him" (Luke 10:22). It took centuries of speculation and controversy by some of the most "wise and understanding" minds in the history of thought to probe the implications of that declaration.[7]

The outcome was a metaphysical tradition that, from Augustine to Hegel, interpreted the Trinity as the most profound of all the mysteries of being. Some of the images to be described here, therefore, will be quite clear and simple, others rather subtle and difficult to grasp; but chapters about both must be part of the history. In a favorite metaphor of the church fathers, the Gospels are a river in which an elephant can drown and a gnat can swim. For some of the same reasons, moreover, the images in later chapters of the book will often be considerably more diffuse than earlier ones; for the second millennium of this history is the period during which the prestige of institutional Christianity gradually declined in Western society. But it was, paradoxically, a period in which, far beyond the borders of the organized church, the stature of Jesus as an individual increased and his reputation spread.

Whatever blurring of his image the welter of portraits of Jesus may create for the eyes of a faith that wants to affirm him as "the same yesterday and today and for ever," that very variety is a treasure trove for the history of culture, because of the way it combines continuity and discontinuity. Nor is the portrait of Jesus in any epoch confined to the history of faith, central though it is for that history. It is, of course, appropriate (or, in the familiar terminology of the *Book of Common Prayer*, "meet, right, and salutary") that the history of faith, and specifically the history of the faith in Jesus Christ, should form the subject matter for scholarly research and exposition in its own right. The rise of the history of Christian doctrine at the beginning of the nineteenth century as a historical discipline in its own right— distinct from the history of philosophy, from the history of the Christian church, and from doctrinal theology, though continually related to all three of these fields—forms an important chapter in the history of modern scholarship.[8] But a narrative of the complex evolution of the doctrine of Christ, defined as "what the church of Jesus Christ believes, teaches, and confesses on the basis of the word of God,"[9] does not even begin to exhaust the history of the meaning that Jesus has had for the development of human culture. For, in the words of the Gospel of John, "from his fulness [*plērōma*] have we all received, grace upon grace" (John 1:16)—a fulness that has proved to be inexhaustible as well as irreducible to formulas, whether dogmatic or antidogmatic. To borrow the distinction of Werner Elert, alongside the "dogma of Christ" there has always been the "image of Christ."[10]

Jesus through the Centuries is a history of the "image [or images] of Christ."

This is, then, neither a life of Jesus nor a history of Christianity as a movement or an institution. The invention of a genre of biographical literature known as the *Life of Jesus* is, strictly speaking, a phenomenon of the modern period, when scholars came to believe that by applying the methodology of a critical historiography to the source materials in the Gospels they would be able to reconstruct the story of his life; Albert Schweitzer's *Quest of the Historical Jesus* remains the standard account of the growth of that literature from the eighteenth to the twentieth century. Naturally, the reconstructions of the life of Jesus in any period, beginning with the reconstructions in the Gospels themselves, will serve as indispensable artifacts of this history of Jesus through the centuries. But we shall be concerned here with more than the history of ideas, whether theological ideas or nontheological ideas— or, for that matter, antitheological ideas. For example, the efforts to portray the person of Jesus in visual form are likewise "artifacts" for our story. They will perform that function not only when, as in the Byzantine empire of the eighth and ninth centuries and again in the Reformation of the sixteenth century, the legitimacy of such efforts became a subject of intense discussion, with far-reaching implications for the history of art and aesthetics as well as for the history of European politics East and West. But in each chapter the portrayals of Christ in such works of art as roadside crosses in Anglo-Saxon Northumbria or Carolingian miniatures or Renaissance paintings will also provide us with the raw material for a cultural history of Jesus, and we shall usually concentrate on one example of such portrayals. Similarly, we shall throughout the book be drawing over and over upon works of literature, from the Old English *Dream of the Rood* through the *Divine Comedy* to Dostoevsky's tale of the Grand Inquisitor in *The Brothers Karamazov,* in order to assess the impact of Jesus on culture.

Yet the term *culture* in the subtitle "His Place in the History of Culture" does not refer here exclusively to what has now come to be called "high culture," seen as what poets, philosophers, and artists create. Would it not be ironic if the one who was attacked by his contemporaries for associating with the outcasts of polite and respectable society were to be interpreted solely on the basis of his contribution to the enhancement and beautification of the life and thought of the rich and educated classes? As *culture* is used here, however, it has almost the significance it has in anthropology, including as it does the life of society and of the state no less than literature, philosophy, and the fine arts. For we shall also be paying attention to the political, social, and economic history of the interpretation of Jesus, and we must incorporate into our recital instances of the ongoing practice of invoking the name of Jesus to legitimate political activity, as this practice becomes visible in the history of both radical and reactionary movements.

The most inclusive conceptual framework for this range of images is provided by the classical triad of the Beautiful, the True, and the Good, which has itself played a significant role in the history of Christian thought.[11] Corresponding to that classical triad, though by no means identical with it, is the biblical triad of Jesus Christ as the Way, the Truth, and the Life, as he is described as having identified himself in the Gospel of John (John 14:6). This formula from the Gospel of John became the motif for a striking image of Jesus in the Archiepiscopal Chapel at Ravenna: "EGO SUM VIA VERITAS ET VITA."[12] As one ancient Christian writer had put it in an earlier century, "He who said 'I am the Way' . . . shapes us anew to his own image," expressed, as another early author had said, in "the quality of beauty";[13] Christ as the Truth came to be regarded as the fulfillment and the embodiment of all the True, "the true light that enlightens every man" (John 1:9); and Christ as the Life was "the source" for all authentic goodness.[14] The Ravenna mosaic, therefore, summarized Christ as the Way, the Truth, and the Life, and at the same time it epitomized Christ as the Beautiful, the True, and the Good.

In a set of public lectures delivered at the University of Berlin in the academic year 1899–1900, that university's most renowned scholar, Adolf von Harnack, undertook to answer the question "What is Christianity?" The book that came out of his lectures has achieved a circulation of well over one hundred thousand copies in the original version, has been translated into more than a dozen languages, and is still in print both in German and in English.[15] Harnack's introduction opens with words that can well form the conclusion of this introduction:

The great English philosopher, John Stuart Mill, once commented that "mankind can hardly be too often reminded that there was once a man named Socrates." That is correct; but it is even more important to remind mankind that a man named Jesus Christ once stood in their midst.[16]

The images in this book represent a series of such reminders "through the centuries."

1
The Rabbi

A light for glory to
thy people Israel.

The study of the place of Jesus in the history of human culture must begin with the New Testament. This is not simply for the self-evident reason that all representations of him since the first century have been based—or, at any rate, have claimed to be based—on the New Testament, although of course they have. But we shall not understand the history of those subsequent representations unless we begin by considering the nature and literary form of the sources that have come down to us in the four Gospels. For the presentation of Jesus in the New Testament is in fact itself a representation: it resembles a set of paintings more closely than it does a photograph.

Even without settling all the thorny problems of authorship and of dating, we must recognize that in the several decades between the time of the ministry of Jesus and the composition of the various Gospels, the memory of what he had said and done was circulating among the various Christian congregations, and probably beyond them, in the form of an oral tradition. Thus the apostle Paul, writing to one such congregation at Corinth in about the year 55 C.E. (hence about twenty years or so after the life of Jesus), was able to remind them that during his visit to Corinth a few years before, probably in the early fifties, he had orally "delivered to you as of first importance what I also received" still earlier, thus perhaps in the forties, con-

cerning the death and resurrection of Jesus (1 Cor. 15:1–7) and the
institution of the Lord's Supper (1 Cor. 11:23–26). But it is noteworthy
that, except for the words of the institution of the Lord's Supper
themselves, Paul does not in any of his epistles quote the exact words
of any of the sayings of Jesus as we now have them in the Gospels.
Nor does he mention a single event in the life of Jesus—again except
for the institution of the Lord's Supper—between his birth and his
death on the cross. From the writings of Paul we would not be able
to know that Jesus ever taught in parables and proverbs or that he
performed miracles or that he was born of a virgin. For that information we are dependent on the oral tradition of the early Christian
communities as this was eventually deposited in the Gospels, all of
which, in their present form at any rate, probably appeared later than
most or all of the epistles of Paul.

Everyone must acknowledge, therefore, that Christian tradition had
precedence, chronologically and even logically, over Christian Scripture; for there was a tradition of the church before there was ever a
New Testament, or any individual book of the New Testament. By
the time the materials of the oral tradition found their way into written
form, they had passed through the life and experience of the church,
which laid claim to the presence of the Holy Spirit of God, the selfsame
Spirit that the disciples had seen descending upon Jesus at his baptism
and upon the earliest believers on the fiftieth day after Easter, in the
miracle of Pentecost. It was to the action of that Spirit that Christians
attributed the composition of the books of the "new testament," as
they began to call it, and before that of the "old testament," as they
referred to the Hebrew Bible. Because the narrative of the sayings of
Jesus and of the events of his life and ministry had come down to
the evangelists and compilers in this context, anyone who seeks to
interpret one or another saying or story from the narrative must always ask not only about its place in the life and teachings of Jesus,
but also about its function within the remembering community. Although there is no warrant for the extreme skepticism of those who
maintain that the historical figure of Jesus, if indeed there even was
one, is irretrievably lost behind the smoke screen of the preaching of
the early Christian church, it is necessary nevertheless to begin with
the caution that every later picture of Jesus is in fact not a picture
based on an unretouched Gospel original, but a picture of what in
the New Testament is already a picture.

It is obvious—and yet, to judge by much of the history of later centuries, including and especially the twentieth century, it is anything but obvious—that according to the earliest portrayals Jesus was a Jew. Therefore the first attempts to understand and interpret his message took place within the context of Judaism, and it is likewise there that any attempt to understand his place in the history of human culture must begin. Although the New Testament was written in Greek, the language that Jesus and his disciples spoke was Aramaic, a Semitic tongue related to Hebrew but by no means identical with it.[1] For the use of Hebrew was by this time largely restricted to worship and scholarship, while the spoken tongue among Palestinian Jews was Aramaic, and in many instances Greek in addition. Meanwhile, many of the Jews of the Diaspora, in places like Alexandria, apparently could not even speak Aramaic, much less Hebrew, but only Greek, and are therefore sometimes called Hellenists.[2] There are Aramaic words and phrases, transliterated into Greek, scattered throughout the Gospels and the other books of the early Christian community, reflecting the language in which various sayings and liturgical formulas had presumably been repeated before the transition to Greek became complete in Christian teaching and worship. These include such familiar words as Hosanna, as well as the cry of dereliction of Jesus on the cross, *"Eloi, Eloi, lama sabachthani?"* "My God, my God, why hast thou forsaken me?" which in the original Hebrew of Psalm 22 would have been *"Eli, Eli, lama azavtani?"*[3]

There are, among these Aramaic words that appear in the New Testament, at least four titles for Jesus, which can provide a convenient set of labels for our consideration of the Jewish idiom and Jewish framework of reference in which the earliest followers of Jesus spoke about him: Jesus as *rabbi* or teacher; Jesus as *amen* or prophet; Jesus as *messias* or Christ; and Jesus as *mar* or Lord.

The most neutral and least controversial of these titles is probably *rabbi,* together with the related *rabbouni.*[4] Except for two passages, the Gospels apply the Aramaic word only to Jesus;[5] and if we conclude, as we seem to be justified in concluding, that the title "teacher" or "master" (*didaskalos* in the Greek New Testament) was intended as a translation of that Aramaic name, it seems safe to say that it was as a rabbi that Jesus was known and addressed by his immediate followers and by others. Yet the Gospels, by a superficial reading at any rate, usually seem to be accentuating the differences, rather than the

similarities, between Jesus and the other rabbis as teachers. As the
scholarly study of the Judaism contemporary or nearly contemporary
to Jesus has progressed, however, both the similarities and the differences have become clearer. On the one hand, scholars of the relation between the Gospels and rabbinic sources have, as their "first
basic observation," come to the conclusion that "Jewish material has
been taken over by the Christian tradition and ascribed to Jesus"; on
the other hand, the comparison has shown that many passages that
sound like borrowings from the rabbis are in fact "something new in
distinction from Judaism."[6] A good illustration of both characteristics
is the anecdote with which, in the story line of the Gospel of Luke,
the preaching ministry of Jesus as rabbi is reported to have been
launched (Luke 4:16–30).

Luke tells us that after the baptism of Jesus and his temptation by
the devil, which taken together are an inauguration into his ministry
according to Matthew and Mark as well, he "came to Nazareth, where
he had been brought up, and he went to the synagogue, as his custom
was, on the sabbath day. And he stood up to read." Following the
customary rabbinical pattern, he took up a scroll of the Hebrew Bible,
read it, presumably provided an Aramaic translation-paraphrase of
the text, and then commented on it. The words he read were from
the sixty-first chapter of the Book of Isaiah:

> The Spirit of the Lord is upon me,
> because he has anointed me to preach good news to the poor.
> He has sent me to proclaim release to the captives
> and recovering of sight to the blind,
> to set at liberty those who are oppressed,
> to proclaim the acceptable year of the Lord.

But instead of doing what a rabbi was normally expected to do, which
was to provide an exposition of the text that compared and contrasted
earlier interpretations and then applied the text to the hearers, he
proceeded to declare: "Today this scripture has been fulfilled in your
hearing." Although the initial reaction even to this audacious declaration was said to be wonderment "at the gracious words which
proceeded out of his mouth," his further explanation produced the
opposite reaction, and everyone was "filled with wrath."

Behind the many such scenes of confrontation between Jesus as
rabbi and the representatives of the rabbinical tradition, the affinities
are nevertheless clearly discernible in the very forms in which his

teachings appear in the Gospels. One of the most familiar forms is that of question and answer, with the question often phrased as a teaser. A woman had seven husbands (in series, not in parallel); whose wife will she be in the life to come? Is it lawful for a devout Jew to pay taxes to the Roman authorities? What must I do to inherit eternal life? Who is the greatest in the kingdom of heaven?[7] In the Gospel narratives the one who puts each of these questions acts as a kind of straight man. Sometimes, in the so-called controversy dialogues, it is an opponent of Jesus who is the straight man; at other times it is one of his followers. This sets up the opportunity for Rabbi Jesus to drive home the point, often by standing the question on its head. There is an old story about a rabbi who was asked by one of his pupils: "Why is it that you rabbis so often put your teaching in the form of a question?" To which the rabbi answered: "So what's wrong with a question?" A striking illustration of such rabbinic pedagogy in the Gospels, and one that is pertinent to several of the issues of affinity and difference with which we are dealing here, is the following story:

> And when he entered the temple, the chief priests and the elders of the people came up to him as he was teaching, and said, "By what authority are you doing these things, and who gave you this authority?" Jesus answered them, "I also will ask you a question; and if you tell me the answer, then I also will tell you by what authority I do these things. The baptism of John [the Baptist], whence was it? From heaven or from men?" And they argued with one another, "If we say, 'From heaven,' he will say to us, 'Why then did you not believe him?' But if we say, 'From men,' we are afraid of the multitude; for all hold that John was a prophet." So they answered Jesus, "We do not know." And he said to them, "Neither will I tell you by what authority I do these things." (Matt. 21:23–27)

To the writers of the New Testament, however, the most typical form of the teachings of Jesus was the parable: "All this," Matthew tells us, "Jesus said to the crowds in parables; indeed he said nothing to them without a parable" (Matt. 13:34). But this word "parable" (*parabolē* in Greek) was taken from the Septuagint, where it had been used by the Jewish scholars who translated the Hebrew Bible into Greek to render the Hebrew word *mashal*. Thus here, too, the evangelists' accounts of Jesus as a teller of parables make sense only in the setting of his Jewish background. Recent interpretations of his parables on the basis of that setting have fundamentally altered conventional explanations of the point being made in many of these comparisons between the kingdom of God and some incident from human life, often rather homely in its outward appearance.[8] One example is the familiar parable of the prodigal son (Luke 15:11–32), which in some ways might better be called the parable of the elder brother. For the point of the parable as a whole—a point frequently overlooked by Christian interpreters, in their eagerness to stress the uniqueness and particularity of the church as the prodigal younger son who has been restored to the father's favor—is in the closing words of the father to the elder brother, who stands for the people of Israel: "Son, you are always with me, and all that is mine is yours. It was fitting to make merry and be glad, for this your brother was dead, and is alive; he was lost, and is found." The historic covenant between God and Israel was permanent, and it was into this covenant that other peoples, too, were now being introduced. This parable of Jesus affirmed both the tradition of God's continuing relation with Israel and the innovation of God's new relation with the church—a twofold covenant.

That oscillation between tradition and innovation, between describing the role of Jesus as a rabbi and attributing to him a new and unique authority, made it necessary to find additional titles and categories to describe his ministry. Of these, the next one up on the scale was the title of prophet, as in the acclamation that appears in the story of Palm Sunday, "This is the prophet Jesus from Nazareth of Galilee" (Matt. 21:11). Probably the most intriguing version of this designation is, once again, in Aramaic: "The words of the *Amen*, the faithful and true witness, the beginning of God's creation" (Rev. 3:14). Ever since the Hebrew Bible, the word Amen had been the formula of affirmation to conclude a prayer; for example, in the mighty chorus of the recitation of the law in the closing charge of Moses to the people of Israel, each verse concludes: "And all the people shall say, 'Amen' " (Deut. 27:14–26). Amen continued to perform that function in early Christianity. Thus Justin Martyr, describing the liturgy of the second-century Christian community for his pagan Gentile readers, says that at the end of the prayers, "all the people present express their assent by saying 'Amen.' " "This word 'Amen,' " Justin explains, "corresponds in the Hebrew language to 'So let it be!' "[9]

But a further extension of the meaning of Amen becomes evident for the first time in the New Testament in the best-known message (or compilation of messages) in the Gospels, the so-called Sermon on the Mount. There it appears as what grammarians call an asseverative particle: *"Amēn legō hymin,* Truly, I say to you." It is used as such some seventy-five times throughout the four Gospels, but exclusively in the sayings of Jesus, to introduce an authoritative pronouncement. As the one who had the authority to make such pronouncements, Jesus was a prophet. Despite our English usage, the word *prophet* does not mean here only or even chiefly one who *foretells,* although the sayings of Jesus do contain many predictions, but one who *tells forth,* one who is authorized to speak on behalf of Another. That is the basis of the title in the Book of Revelation, "the Amen, the faithful and true witness"; and that is also why the Amen-formula begins to make its appearance in the Sermon on the Mount, which is a document of the oscillation, even in the earliest pictures of Jesus, between rabbinic tradition and prophetic innovation.

The comparisons that both Jewish and Christian scholars have made between the method of interpretation at work in the Sermon on the Mount and the literature of rabbinic Judaism have documented that oscillation. For it is in the Sermon on the Mount that, after the introductory pronouncements called the Beatitudes, Jesus is quoted as asserting: "Think not that I have come to abolish the law and the prophets; I have come not to abolish them but to fulfil them. For truly [*amēn*], I say to you, till heaven and earth pass away, not an iota, not a dot, will pass from the law until all is accomplished" (Matt. 5:17–18). That ringing affirmation of the permanent validity of the law of Moses as given to the people of Israel on Mount Sinai is followed by a series of specific quotations from the law. Each of these quotations is introduced with the formula "You have heard that it was said to the men of old"; and each such quotation is then followed by a commentary opening with the magisterial formula *"But I say to you."*[10] The sense of the commentary is an intensification of the commandment, to include not only its outward observance but the inward spirit and motivation of the heart. All these commentaries are an elaboration of the warning that the righteousness of the followers of Jesus must exceed that of those who followed other doctors of the law (Matt. 5:20).

In confirmation of the special status of Jesus as not only rabbi but also prophet, the conclusion of the Sermon on the Mount reads: "And when Jesus finished these sayings, the crowds were astonished at his teaching, for he taught them as one who had authority, and not as their scribes. When he came down from the mountain, great crowds followed him" (Matt. 7:28–8:1). Then there come several miracle stories. As a recent study has noted, in such stories "Matthew has sought to make an important point that once more recalls the function of miracle in the rabbinic tradition: to lend authority to Jesus' activity, and especially to his interpretation of the Law."[11] The New Testament does not attribute the power of performing miracles only to Jesus and his followers, for Jesus defends himself against the accusation of being in conspiracy with Beelzebul, prince of devils, by retorting: "And if I cast out demons by Beelzebul, by whom do your sons cast them out?" (Matt. 12:27). But it does cite the miracles as substantiation of his standing as rabbi-prophet. (It should be noted, in relation to our examination of Aramaic titles, that there are also Aramaic formulas by which Jesus performs some of the miracles: *"Ephphatha,* that is, 'Be opened,' " to heal a deaf man; and *"Talitha cumi,* which means, 'Little girl, I say to you, arise,' " to raise a child from the dead.)[12]

The identification of Jesus as prophet was a means both of affirming his continuity with the prophets of Israel and of asserting his superiority to them as *the* prophet whose coming they had predicted and to whose authority they had been prepared to yield. In the Pentateuch (Deut. 18:15–22) the God of Israel tells Moses, and through him the people, that he "will raise up a prophet from among you," to whom the people are to pay heed. In the context, this is the authorization of Joshua as the legitimate successor of Moses; but already within the New Testament itself, and then at greater length in later Christian writers such as Clement of Alexandria around the year 200, the promise of the prophet to come is taken as a reference to Jesus, who had the same name as Joshua.[13] He is portrayed as the one prophet in whom the teaching of Moses was simultaneously fulfilled and superseded, as the one rabbi who both satisfied the law of Moses and transcended it. For, in the words of the Gospel of John (John 1:17), "The law was given through Moses; grace and truth came through Jesus Christ." To describe such a revelation of grace and truth, the categories of rabbi and prophet, while necessary, were not sufficient. Studies of the descriptions of Jesus in the Jewish tradition after the age of the New Testament have shown that it sought to accommodate him within those categories, but in its disputes with Judaism Christianity insisted that he had broken out of that entire categorial system. And so, by the time Islam came along to identify him as a great prophet, greater in many ways than Moses but still a prophet who had acted as a forerunner to Mohammed, that was, for such anti-Muslim Christian apologists as John of Damascus in the eighth century, not adequate and therefore not even accurate.[14] Consequently, the potential significance of the figure of Jesus as a meeting ground between Christians and Jews, and between Christians and Muslims, has never materialized.

For the rabbi and the prophet both yielded to two other categories, each of them likewise expressed in an Aramaic word and then in its Greek translation: *Messias*, the Aramaic form of "Messiah," translated into Greek as *ho Christos*, "Christ," the Anointed One;[15] and *Marana*, "our Lord," in the liturgical formula, *Maranatha*, "Our Lord, come!" translated into Greek as *ho Kyrios* and quoted by the apostle Paul and in a very early liturgical prayer.[16] The future belonged to the titles "Christ" and "Lord" as names for Jesus, and to the identification of him as the Son of God and the second person of the Trinity. It was not merely in the name of a great teacher, not even in the name of the greatest teacher who ever lived, that Justinian built Hagia Sophia in Constantinople and Johann Sebastian Bach composed the *Mass in B-Minor*. There are no cathedrals in honor of Socrates. But in the process of establishing themselves, *Christ* and *Lord*, as well as even *Rabbi* and *Prophet*, often lost much of their Semitic content. To the Christian disciples of the first century the conception of Jesus as a rabbi was self-evident, to the Christian disciples of the second century it was embarrassing, to the Christian disciples of the third century and beyond it was obscure.

The beginnings of the transformation, what Dix has labeled the "de-Judaization of Christianity,"[17] are visible already within the New Testament. For with the decision of the apostle Paul to "turn to the Gentiles" (Acts 13:46) after having begun his preaching in the synagogues of the Mediterranean world, and then with the sack of Jerusalem by the Roman armies under Titus and the destruction of the temple in the year 70 C.E., the Christian movement increasingly became Gentile rather than Jewish in its constituency and in its outlook. In that setting, as we shall have several occasions to note in this and in subsequent chapters, the Jewish elements of the life of Jesus grew increasingly problematical and had to be explained to the Gentile readers of the Gospels. The writer of the Gospel of John, for instance, found himself obliged to account for the jars of water changed by

Jesus into wine at the wedding in Cana by stating that they were intended to be used "for the Jewish rites of purification" (John 2:6), which any Jewish reader would have been expected to know without being told. And the Book of the Acts of the Apostles can be read as a kind of "tale of two cities": its first chapter, with Jesus and his disciples after the resurrection, is set in Jerusalem, for "he charged them not to depart from Jerusalem"; but its last chapter, and thus the book as a whole, reaches its climax with the final voyage of the apostle Paul, in the simple but pulse-quickening sentence "And so we came to Rome."

The apostle Paul often appears in Christian thought as the one chiefly responsible for the de-Judaization of the gospel and even for the transmutation of the person of Jesus from a rabbi in the Jewish sense to a divine being in the Greek sense. Such an interpretation of Paul became almost canonical in certain schools of biblical criticism during the nineteenth century, especially that of Ferdinand Christian Baur, who saw the controversy between Paul and Peter as a conflict between the party of Peter, with its "Judaizing" distortion of the gospel into a new law, and the party of Paul, with its universal vision of the gospel as a message about Jesus for all humanity.[18] Very often, of course, this description of the opposition between Peter and Paul, and between law and gospel, was cast in the language of the opposition between Roman Catholicism (which traced its succession to Peter as the first pope) and Protestantism (which arose from Luther's interpretation of the epistles of Paul). Luther's favorite among those epistles, the letter to the Romans, became the charter for this supposed declaration of independence from Judaism.

Since then, however, scholars have not only put the picture of Jesus back into the setting of first-century Judaism; they have also rediscovered the Jewishness of the New Testament, and particularly of the apostle Paul, and specifically of his Epistle to the Romans. They have concluded, in the words of Krister Stendahl, that "in this letter Paul's focus really is the relation between Jews and Gentiles, not the notion of justification or predestination and certainly not other proper yet abstract theological topics." For such a reading of the epistle, moreover, "the climax of Romans is actually chapters 9–11, i.e., his reflections on the relation between church and synagogue, the church and the Jewish *people*—not 'Christianity' and 'Judaism,' not the attitudes of the gospel versus the attitudes of the law."[19] Chapters 9–11 of the Epistle to the Romans are Paul's description of his struggle over that relation between church and synagogue, concluding with the prediction and the promise: "And so all Israel will be saved"— not, it should be noted carefully, converted to Christianity, but *saved*, because, in Paul's words, "as regards election they are beloved for the sake of their forefathers. For the gifts and the call of God are irrevocable" (Rom. 11:26–29).

"It is stunning to note," Stendahl has observed, "that Paul writes this whole section of Romans (10:18–11:36) without using the name of Jesus Christ." Yet if one accepts this reading of the mind of Paul in Romans, his many references to the name of Jesus Christ in the remainder of the epistle acquire a special significance: from "descended from David according to the flesh . . . , Jesus Christ our Lord," in the first chapter to "the preaching of Jesus Christ," which "is now disclosed and through the prophetic writings is made known to all nations," in the final sentence of the final chapter. The Jesus Christ of the Epistle to the Romans is, as Paul says of himself elsewhere, "of the people of Israel . . . , a Hebrew born of Hebrews" (Phil. 3:5). The very issue of universality, which has been taken to be the distinction between the message of Paul and Jewish particularism, was for Paul what made it necessary that Jesus be a Jew. For only through the Jewishness of Jesus could the covenant of God with Israel, the gracious gifts of God and his irrevocable calling, become available to all people in the whole world, also to the Gentiles, who thus "were grafted in their place to share the richness of the olive tree," the people of Israel (Rom. 11:17).

During later centuries it repeatedly became necessary to return to this theme, even as many other ways of portraying Jesus were developed that came to make more sense to those centuries than did the picture of him as Rabbi. But no one can consider the topic of Jesus as Rabbi and ignore the subsequent history of the relation between the synagogue and the church, between the people to whom Jesus belonged and the people who belong to Jesus. It is important, in considering that history, to take to heart the recent reminder that "we have no license to judge the distant past on the basis of our present perception of events of more recent times."[20] Nevertheless, the religious, moral, and political relations between Christians and Jews do run like a red line through much of the history of culture. Even as we heed the warning against rashly judging the quick and the dead, since ultimately there is another Judge who will do so and who will judge us as well, we who live in the twentieth century do have a unique responsibility to be aware of that red line, above all as we study the history of the images of Jesus through the centuries.

One such image from the twentieth century, Marc Chagall's *White Crucifixion*, has made this point forcefully. The crucified figure in Chagall's painting wears not a nondescript loincloth, but the *tallith* of a devout and observant rabbi. His prophecy, "They will put you out of the synagogues; indeed, the hour is coming when whoever kills you will think he is offering service to God" (John 16:2), is seen as having been fulfilled, in a supreme irony, when some who claimed to be his disciples regarded the persecution of Jews as service to God. And the central figure does indeed belong to the people of Israel, but he belongs no less to the church and to the whole world—precisely because he belongs to the people of Israel.

For the question is easier to ask than it is to answer, and it is easier to avoid than it is to ask in the first place. But ask it we must: Would there have been such anti-Semitism, would there have been so many pogroms, would there have been an Auschwitz, if every Christian church and every Christian home had focused its devotion on icons of Mary not only as Mother of God and Queen of Heaven but as the Jewish maiden and the new Miriam, and on icons of Christ not only as Pantocrator but as *Rabbi Jeshua bar-Joseph*, Rabbi Jesus of Nazareth, the Son of David, in the context of the history of a suffering Israel and a suffering humanity?

2

The Turning Point of History

When the time had fully come,
God sent forth his Son, born of
woman, born under the law.

The contemporaries of Jesus knew him as a rabbi, but this was a rabbi whose ministry of teaching and preaching had as its central content "the gospel of God: 'The time is fulfilled, and the kingdom of God is at hand; repent, and believe in the gospel' " (Mark 1:14–15). Many of his early followers found it unavoidable to describe him as a prophet, but further reflection led them to specify what was distinctive about his prophetic mission: "In many and various ways God spoke of old to our fathers by the prophets; but in these last days he has spoken to us by a Son, whom he appointed the heir of all things, through whom also he created the world. He reflects the glory of God and bears the very stamp of his nature, upholding the universe by his word of power" (Heb. 1:1–3).

"The time is fulfilled . . . in these last days": it is obvious from these and other statements of the early generations of Christian believers that as they carried out the task of finding a language that would not collapse under the weight of what they believed to be the significance of the coming of Jesus, they found it necessary to invent a grammar of history. Categories of the cosmos and of space, and not only categories of history and of time, were pressed into service for this task; and before the task was finished, the followers of Christ had managed to transfigure the systems of metaphysics that they had inherited from Greek philosophy. "But," as Charles Norris Cochrane, one of the most provocative and profound analysts of this process, has suggested, "the divergence between Christianity and Classicism was in no respect more conspicuously or emphatically displayed than with regard to history." "In a very real sense indeed," he concludes, "it marked the crux of the issue between the two."[1] It likewise marked the crux of the issue between the church and the synagogue. Calling itself the new Israel and the true Israel, the church appropriated the schema of historical meaning that had arisen in the interpretation of the redemption of Israel accomplished by the exodus from Egypt, and adapted this schema to the redemption of humanity accomplished by the resurrection of Jesus Christ from the dead.

Like every other portrait in the history of the depictions of Jesus, then, this one had its origins in Jewish tradition. In language redolent of Ezekiel, Daniel, and later Jewish apocalyptic writings, one of his early followers, who heard Jesus call himself "the first and the last," that is, the Lord of history, declared:

> Then I turned to see the voice that was speaking to me, and on turning I saw seven golden lampstands, and in the midst of the lampstands one like a son of man, clothed with a long robe and with a golden girdle round his breast; his head and his hair were white as white wool, white as snow; his eyes were like a flame of fire, his feet were like burnished bronze, refined as in a furnace, and his voice was like the sound of many waters; in his right hand he held seven stars, from his mouth issued a sharp two-edged sword, and his face was like the sun shining in full strength. (Rev. 1:12–20)

Except for some details (such as the shoes instead of "feet like burnished bronze"), Albrecht Dürer's *Vision of the Seven Candlesticks*, with its "sense of fantastic unreality," in which "the three-dimensionality of space is stressed and denied at the same time,"[2] looks almost as though it could have served as the basis for these words of the Apocalypse, rather than the other way around. The majestic figure in Dürer's woodcut truly is the Lord of history, sovereign over heaven and earth, over eternity and time, and is both "the Alpha and the Omega, the beginning and the end."[3]

From contemporary Jewish sources we know that the proclamation of Jesus himself about the kingdom of God, as well as such proclamations of his followers about him, resounded with the accents of

Albrecht Dürer, *Vision of the Seven Candlesticks*, woodcut, c. 1498, from the *Apocalypse*.

Jewish apocalypticism, the fervid expectation that the victory of the God of Israel over the enemies of Israel, so long promised and so often delayed, was now at last to break. The generation to which Jesus, and before him John the Baptist, addressed that proclamation was, we are told, a generation standing on tiptoes "in expectation" (Luke 3:15). The Book of Acts describes the disciples of Jesus, even after the events of Good Friday and Easter, as inquiring of him just before he withdrew his visible presence from them, "Lord, will you at this time restore the kingdom to Israel?" to which Jesus replies, "It is not for you to know about times or seasons which the Father has fixed by his own authority" (Acts 1:6–7).

It would, however, be too easy an evasion of the deepest problems connected with the Jewish and the early Christian expectation of the coming kingdom of God to leave it at that. For particularly in the twentieth century, New Testament scholarship has forced consideration of the place that apocalyptic expectation held not only for the hearers of Jesus but in the message of Jesus himself.[4] Repeatedly in the message of Jesus the call for repentance and the summons to ethical change took as its ground the promise of the Parousia: that the coming of the Son of Man in the clouds of glory would soon put an end to human history and would usher in the new order of the kingdom of God. Specifically, the moral teachings of the Sermon on the Mount, such as the command about turning the other cheek, which have so often seemed (except, of course, to Tolstoy) to be an utterly impractical code of ethics for life in the real world, came as the announcement of what his followers were to do in the brief interim between his earthly ministry and the end of history. "You will not have gone through all the towns of Israel," Jesus said to his disciples according to Matthew, "before the Son of man comes"; and all three of the Synoptic Gospels quote him as saying near the end of his ministry, "Truly, I say to you, this generation will not pass away till all these things take place. Heaven and earth will pass away, but my words will not pass away."[5]

But that generation did not live to see it all: the Son of Man did not come, and heaven and earth did not pass away. It has even been suggested that "the whole history of 'Christianity' down to the present day, that is to say, the real inner history of it, is based on the delay of the Parousia, the non-occurrence of the Parousia, the abandonment of eschatology."[6] What did this disappointment of the apocalyptic hope of the Second Coming mean for the promise "My words will not pass away"? How could, and how did, the person of Jesus retain hold on an authority whose validity had apparently depended on the announcement of the impending end of history? Twentieth-century scholars have sought to identify a crisis brought on by the disappointment as the major trauma of the early Christian centuries and the source for the rise of the institutional church and of the dogma about the person of Jesus. Somewhat surprisingly, however, this hypothesis of a trauma caused by the "delay of the Parousia" finds very little corroboration in the sources of the second and third centuries themselves. What those sources disclose instead is the combination, side by side in the same minds, of an intense apocalyptic expectation that history will end and of a willingness to live with the prospect of a continuance of human history—both of these finding expression in an increasing emphasis on the centrality of Jesus.

The North African thinker Tertullian, the first important Christian writer to use Latin, may serve as an illustration of such a combination at the end of the second century.[7] Warning his fellow believers against attending the degrading shows and spectacles of Roman society, Tertullian urged them to wait for the greater spectacle of the great day coming, when the victorious Christ would return in triumphal procession like a Roman conqueror and would lead in his train, as prisoners, the monarchs and governors who had persecuted his people, the philosophers and poets who had mocked his message, the actors and other "ministers of sin" who had ridiculed his commandments. "And so," he wrote elsewhere, "we never march unarmed. . . . With prayer let us expect the angel's trumpet."[8] Yet this same Tertullian could declare, in response to the charge of treason against the Roman empire: "We also pray for the emperors, for their ministers and for all in authority, for the welfare of the world, for the prevalence of peace, *for the delay of the final consummation.*"[9] Such statements about the Roman emperors were in some sense a preparation for the rise, in the fourth century, of the notion of a Christian Roman emperor, reigning in the name and by the power of Jesus Christ; but in the present context we must address the assertion that Christians were praying for the postponement of the second coming of Jesus Christ.

For that assertion of Tertullian represents nothing less than a new understanding of the meaning of history, an understanding according to which Jesus was not simply going to be the end of history by his second coming in the future, as a naive and literalistic apocalypticism had viewed him, but already was the Turning Point of History, a history that, even if it were to continue, had been transformed and overturned by his first coming in the past. Tertullian is likewise remembered as a major figure in the history of the development of the dogmas of the Trinity and of the person of Christ, anticipating in his theological formulas much of the ultimate outcome of the debates that were to occupy the third and fourth centuries. During those centuries, however, it was not only the theological and dogmatic significance of Jesus as the Son of God that was worked out in the clarification of the dogma of the Trinity, but also the cultural significance of Jesus as the hinge on which history turned and therefore as the basis both for a new interpretation of the historical process and for a new historiography.

The new interpretation of the historical process began with the history of Israel, whose principal goal was now taken to be the life, death, and resurrection of Jesus. That made itself evident in the interpretation—and the manipulation—of the *prophetic* tradition of the Jewish Scriptures. Describing the exodus of the children of Israel from captivity, the prophet Hosea had said, speaking in God's name, "When Israel was a child, I loved him, and out of Egypt I called my son" (Hos. 11:1); but in the hands of the Christian evangelist, these words became a prediction of the flight to Egypt by the Holy Family to escape the murderous plot of King Herod (Matt. 2:15). The so-called enthronement psalms identified God as the true king of Israel, even when Israel had earthly kings like David, and Psalm 96 declared, "The Lord reigns!"; but Christian philosophers and poets added to the text an explicit reference to the cross of Christ, so that it now became "The Lord reigns *from the tree*," words which they then accused the Jews of having expunged.[10] Christians ransacked the Hebrew Bible for references to Christ, compiling them in various collections and commentaries.[11] The prophets of Israel had found their aim, and their end, in Jesus.

So it was as well with the *kingdom* of Israel, which Christians saw as having now become the authentic kingdom of God, over which the Crucified reigned "from the tree." Israel had been changed into a kingdom with the reign of King Saul; but "when he was rejected and laid low in battle, and his line of descent rejected so that no kings should arise out of it, David succeeded to the kingdom, whose son

Christ is chiefly called." King David, who "was made a kind of start-ing-point and beginning of the advanced youth of the people of God," established Jerusalem as the capital of his kingdom; yet even as king of that "earthly Jerusalem," he was "a son of the heavenly Jerusalem." He received the promise that "his descendants were to reign in Je-rusalem in continual succession."[12] But David as king had looked beyond himself and his own kingdom to the kingship of Jesus Christ, declaring in Psalm 45, which, according to the Christian reinterpre-tation of history, had been addressed to Christ as king:

> Your throne, O God, endures for ever and ever.
> Your royal scepter is a scepter of equity;
> You love righteousness and hate wickedness.
> Therefore God, your God, has anointed you
> [in the Greek of the Septuagint, *echrisen se*, has made you Christ]
> with the oil of gladness above your fellows.
>
> (Ps. 45:6–7)

Thus David had called him God in the first line, and then had identified him as both king and Christ, the authentic king anointed to be "much superior to, and differing from, those who in days of old had been symbolically anointed."[13] A review of the entire history of the divided kingdoms of Judah and Israel on the basis of what "the providence of God either ordered or permitted" showed that although the kings beginning with Rehoboam, the son of Solomon, did not "by their enigmatic words or actions prophesy what may pertain to Christ and the church," they did nevertheless point forward to Christ. For when the divided kingdoms were eventually reunited under one prince in Jerusalem, this was intended to anticipate Christ as the one and only king; and yet their kingdom no longer possessed any au-thority and sovereignty of its own, for "Christ found them as tribu-taries of the Romans."[14]

The history of the changes and successive forms of the *priesthood* of Israel also made sense, according to the Christian argument, only when viewed from the perspective of Jesus as its turning point. The Levitical priesthood of Aaron had been temporary, nothing more than a shadow, whose substance had now at last appeared in the true high priest, Jesus Christ; for "he holds his priesthood permanently, be-cause he continues for ever" (Heb. 7:24). The threat and prophecy addressed to Eli the high priest (1 Sam. 2:27–36), "I will raise up for myself a faithful priest, who shall do according to what is in my heart and in my mind," was not fulfilled in the priesthood and the priests of Israel, all of whom had been temporary, but had "come to pass through Christ Jesus" as the eternal high priest.[15] Although in the New Testament itself the term *priest* does not ever refer explicitly to the ministers of the Christian church, nor even to the apostles of Jesus in their ministry, but only to Christ himself as priest or to the priests of the Old Testament or to all believers as priests, the church soon took over the term for its ordained clergy.[16] The history of priesthood, therefore, was seen as having begun with the shadowy figure of Melchizedek, who "offered bread and wine," and then as acquiring a definite form with Aaron, the brother of Moses; but it all led to Jesus Christ, from whom, in turn, it led to the priesthood of the New Testament church and to the sacrifice of the Mass.[17]

Thus the entire history of Israel had reached its turning point in Jesus as prophet, as priest, and as king.[18] After the same manner, he was identified as the turning point in the entire history of all the nations of the world, as that history was encapsulated in the history of the "mistress of nations," the Roman empire. Although this was in fact a leitmotiv of the third, fourth, and fifth centuries, the most massive and most influential monument of that identification was what the author himself called in his preface his "great and arduous task," Augustine's *City of God*.[19] For this task of locating Jesus within world history, as indeed for the entire enterprise of interpreting the person and the message of Jesus to the Gentile world, the New Testament, as a book written chiefly by Jewish Christians, offered far less explicit guidance than it did for the specification of his locus within the history of Israel. But it did speak of his having come only in the fulness of time.[20]

Echoing this Pauline language, one early Christian writer, in an attempt to explain why God had waited so long, divided the history of the world into two "times" or "epochs," on the basis of the "pattern" that was both disclosed and established in Jesus.[21] Others, too, made an effort to establish some connection between the coming of Jesus and the history of Rome, beginning as early as the first chapters of the Gospel of Luke, with their language about "the decree [that] went out from Caesar Augustus that all the world should be enrolled" and about "the fifteenth year of the reign of Tiberius Caesar."[22] But the catalyst for a thoroughgoing examination of that connection was the accusation that the substitution of Christ for the gods of Rome had brought their wrath and punishment down upon the city and had caused Rome to fall. For, Augustine contended, "not only before Christ had begun to teach, but even before he was born of the Virgin," the history of Rome was characterized by the "grievous evils of those former times," evils that had, moreover, become "intolerable and dreadful" not when Rome suffered military defeat but when it achieved military victory.[23] Indeed, "when Carthage was destroyed and the Roman republic was delivered from the great reason for its anxiety, then it was that a host of disastrous evils immediately resulted from the prosperous condition of things," above all the concentration of the "lust of rule" in the hands of the "more powerful few," while the "rest, worn and wearied" were subjected to its yoke.[24] It was not defeat and depression that Rome could not handle, but prosperity and victory. Therefore the expansion of the Roman empire, which accusers were blaming Christ for having reversed, was not automatically of any obvious benefit to the human race; for, in an oft-quoted maxim of Augustine, "If justice has been abolished, what is empire but a fancy name for larceny [grande latrocinium]?"[25]

On the other hand, the many undoubtedly great achievements of Rome could be traced, according to Augustine, to what the Roman historian Sallust had identified as its ambition and its "desire for glory" and prestige, which functioned as a restraint on vice and immorality.[26] The God who had acted and become known in Christ made use also of these qualities in carrying out the purposes of history, which were the result not of luck or fortune or the power of the stars, but of an "order of things and times, which is hidden from us, but thoroughly known to [God, who] . . . rules as lord and appoints as governor."[27] This concept of an "order of things and times," what the Bible called a "series of generations," Augustine vigorously defended against the theory that history repeats itself, that "the same temporal event is reenacted by the same periodic revolutions" and cycles.[28] And the clinching argument against the theory of cycles in history was the life and person of Jesus Christ: Because "Christ died for our sins once and for all, and, rising from the dead, dies no more," it also had to be true that Plato had taught in the Academy at only one point in history, not over and over again "during the countless cycles that are yet to be."[29] It was the consideration of the life, death, and resurrection of Christ, as an event that was single and unrepeatable and yet at the same time as a message and "mystery announced from the very beginning of the human race,"[30] that made it possible for Christopher Dawson to call Augustine, with only slight exaggeration, "not only the founder of the Christian philosophy of history," but "actually the first man in the world to discover the meaning of time."[31]

Time and history were, then, crucial for Augustine—crucial in the literal sense of *crucialis*, as pertaining to the *crux Christi*, the cross of Christ (a usage of the word *crucialis* for which there is not any classical or even patristic precedent, our English word being apparently a coinage of Sir Francis Bacon):[32] the history of the cross of Christ was both his work for redemption and his example for imitation.[33] But the events of the life of Jesus, seen as the turning point of history, did not affect merely the interpretation of that history; they were also responsible for a revitalized and transformed interest in the writing of history. Although Augustine not only composed many different kinds of literature but in his *Confessions* even created a literary genre for which there is no genuine precedent, classical or Christian, he himself never put his hand to narrative history, except perhaps for one or two of his works of controversy which did have marks of such history. But two Greek Christian authors from the century before Augustine, Eusebius of Caesarea and Athanasius of Alexandria, may serve as documentation for this new historiography, inspired by the person of Jesus Christ. That they happened to be on opposing sides of the great debate of the fourth century touching the relation of the person of Jesus Christ to the Godhead makes their common contribution to historiography all the more noteworthy.

Although Eusebius has sometimes been accused of excessive optimism and even of dishonesty,[34] his work as a historian of the first three centuries makes him indispensable to any understanding of the period: if one were to take any modern church history of that period and delete from it the data that come from Eusebius, only bits and pieces would be left. As the author of two books intended to be an apologia for the Christian message, *The Preparation of the Gospel* and *The Demonstration of the Gospel*, and as the principal historian of earlier apologias during those preceding centuries, Eusebius was critical of his predecessors for concentrating on "arguments" rather than on "events."[35] In his *Ecclesiastical History* he set out to rectify that imbalance, and to do so concretely in the way that he would write history in the light of the life of Jesus.

In the preface to the work he stated two objections made by pagan critics of Christ and Christianity: that Christ was "a recent arrival in human history," and that the nation of Christ was "hidden away in some corner of the world somewhere," in short, that Christ was both "novel and outlandish." His answer to these objections was, first and foremost, to describe the history of Jesus himself.[36] According to Eusebius, this history extended all the way to the beginnings of the human experience, for all those to whom God had appeared could be called Christians "in fact if not in name."[37] But the history also extended forward into the author's own time; for like the historians of classical antiquity, Eusebius concentrated on contemporary events. Yet there was this fundamental difference: according to Eusebius the decisive event in the history he was narrating had not been in his own lifetime, but had taken place in the life of Jesus Christ. As one scholar has put it, "his interest was directed toward grasping, on the basis of the plan of God for the world, the universal-historical implications of the entry of Jesus into the world."[38] To set forth these implications, he presented not arguments but events: he wrote a historical account whose turning point was the "principate of Augustus," when Jesus Christ was born.[39]

The contemporary and sometime adversary of Eusebius, Athanasius bishop of Alexandria, is remembered chiefly for his works of dogmatic and polemical theology. Yet in many ways the most influential book he ever wrote dealt with dogmatics and polemics only incidentally. It was *The Life of Antony,* a biography of the founder of Egyptian Christian monasticism, which even the harshest critics of Athanasius are compelled to admire.[40] Apparently the work was written at least partly for a Western readership and was translated during the author's own lifetime from Greek into Latin, in which form it seems to have played a part in Augustine's conversion.[41] For our present purposes *The Life of Antony* stands as a prime example of the new historiography and new biography inspired by the life of Jesus in the Gospels.

To be sure, there are many affinities between it and various pagan Greek biographies. The well-known *Parallel Lives* of Plutarch presents some similarities, although the differences are far more striking. One of the most meticulous studies of the literary form of the Greek *Lives of the Saints,* that of Karl Holl, has pointed especially to the biographies of Posidonius and of Apollonius of Tyana as models.[42] Although the purpose of the book is to present Antony as the embodiment of an ideal, that does not prevent Athanasius from describing his life in concrete terms as an existential struggle, and a struggle that never ends until death. Throughout, it is an effort to describe Antony's life as "the work of the Savior in Antony."[43] It is clear that Antony chose the monastic life because here he was able to obey the teachings of Jesus the most effectively.[44] *The Life of Antony* is replete with miracle stories, as well as detailed in its recital of the sermons against heresy that Antony delivered. Johannes Quasten, our leading historian of early Christian literature, has accurately summarized the place of Athanasius's *Life of Antony* in the history of biography:

> There cannot be any doubt that the ancient classical model of the hero's [*Vita*] as well as the newer type of the *Vita* of the sage served as inspiration for Athanasius. But it remains his great achievement that he recast these inherited expressions of popular ideals in the Christian mold and disclosed the same heroism in the imitator of Christ aided by the power of grace. Thus he created a new type of biography that was to serve as a model for all subsequent Greek and Latin hagiography.[45]

Such a medieval biography as Bede's *Life of Cuthbert* is an outstanding example of the tradition established by *The Life of Antony*; as a recent study has observed, "It is commonplace to observe that a holy man like Cuthbert imitated the lives of Christ and the saints, but we tend to forget the reality and the implications of such imitation when we talk about biography."[46] The life of Jesus in the Gospels was a turning point both for the life of Cuthbert (the life that he lived) and for *The Life of Cuthbert* (the life that Bede wrote).

Eventually the very calendar of Europe, which then became the calendar for most of the modern world, evolved into a recognition of this view of the significance of the figure of Jesus as the turning point of history, the turning point both of history as process and of history as narrative. As we have noted, Christian historians from Luke to Eusebius and beyond retained the Roman system of dating events by the reigns of the emperors. The dates of the imperial reigns were in turn cited according to a chronology, computed from the legendary date of the founding of Rome by Romulus and Remus, as A.U.C., *Ab Urbe Condita* (the actual title of the work of Livy which we now call *The History of Rome*). The persecutions of the church under the emperor Diocletian, who ruled from 284 to 305, led some Christian groups to date their calendars from the so-called Age of the Martyrs. For example, the fourth-century *Index to the Festal Letters of Athanasius* is arranged according to the Egyptian calendar of months and days within each year, but it identifies the year of the first *Festal Letter* as "the forty-fourth year of the Diocletian Era," that is, A.D. 327.[47] This is a calendrical system still retained by the Christian Copts of Athanasius's Egypt and by the Christians of Ethiopia.

But in the sixth century a Scythian monk living in Rome, Dionysius Exiguus ("Little Denis"), proposed a new system of reckoning. It was to be named not for the pagan myth of the founding of Rome by Romulus and Remus, nor for the persecutor Diocletian, but for the incarnation of Jesus Christ, specifically for the day of the annunciation of his birth to the Virgin Mary by the angel Gabriel, 25 March, in the year 753 A.U.C. For reasons that seem still to be somewhat obscure, Dionysius Exiguus miscalculated by four to seven years, producing the anomaly by which it is sometimes said that Jesus was born in 4 B.C. Such trifles aside, however, Dionysius's identification of "the Christian era" gradually established itself, even though the process of establishing it required many centuries, and is now universal.[48] Henceforth the dates of history and biography are marked as A.D. and B.C., according to "the years of Our Lord." Even the life of an Antichrist is dated by the dates of Christ; biographies of his enemies have to be written this way, so that we speak of Nero as having died in A.D. 68 and of Stalin as having died in A.D. 1953. In this sense at any rate, and not only in this sense, everyone is compelled to acknowledge that because of Jesus of Nazareth history will never be the same.

3

The Light of the Gentiles

He did not leave himself without
witness.

"Nothing is so incredible," Reinhold Niebuhr has said, "as an answer to an unasked question."[1] He went on to use that epigram as a basis to divide human cultures into those "where a Christ is expected" and those "where a Christ is not expected." But the disciples of Jesus, in their effort to explain the meaning of his message and work to their world during the first three or four centuries, carried out their mission on the growing assumption that there was no culture "where a Christ is not expected" and that therefore, in his person and in his teaching, in his life and in his death, Jesus represented the divine answer to a question that had in fact been asked everywhere, the divine fulfillment of an aspiration that was universal, in short, what one of the earliest of them called "the ground for hoping that [all of humanity] may be converted and win their way to God," through Jesus the Christ, "our common name and our common hope."[2]

In addressing the message of that common hope to the Gentile world, they sought to discover in Greco-Roman culture the questions to which that common name of Jesus Christ was the answer; as had been prophesied of him in his infancy,[3] he was

thy salvation
which thou hast prepared in the presence of all peoples,

a light for revelation to the Gentiles,
and for glory to thy people Israel.

By analogy with the techniques that seemed to be working so successfully, beginning with the New Testament, in using the Hebrew Bible to interpret Jesus as the glory of the people of Israel, there were discovered several methods for interpreting him also as the light for revelation to the Gentiles. These methods may usefully be grouped under three headings: non-Jewish prophecies of a Christ; Gentile anticipations of the doctrine about Jesus; and pagan foreshadowings or "types" of the redemption achieved by his death.

While messianic hope and messianic prophecy had been the peculiar feature of the history of the Jewish people, they were not the exclusive possession of Israel. "Even in other nations," Augustine said, "there were those to whom this mystery was revealed and who were also impelled to proclaim it."[4] Job, Jethro the father-in-law of Moses, and Balaam the prophet were three such "Gentile saints," spoken of in the Hebrew Bible, with whose existence both the rabbis and the church fathers had to come to terms.[5] Armed with such biblical warrant, Christian apologists found in Gentile literature other evidence of messianic prophecy that pointed forward to Jesus.

Perhaps the most dramatic and almost certainly the most familiar was the prophecy of the Roman poet Vergil in the fourth of his *Eclogues*.[6] It predicted the breaking in of a "new order of the ages"; for "now the virgin is returning [*jam redit et virgo*]," and "a new human race is descending from the heights of heaven." What would bring about this change would be "the birth of a child [*nascenti puero*], with whom the iron age of humanity will end and the golden age begin." His birth would achieve a transformation of human nature; for

Under your guidance, whatever vestiges remain of our ancient wickedness,
Once done away with, shall free the earth from its incessant fear.

There would even be changes in nature:

For your sake, O child, the earth, without being tilled,
Will freely pour forth its gifts.
. . . .
Your very cradle shall pour forth for you
Caressing flowers. The serpent too shall die.

And therefore:

Assume your great honors, for the time will soon be at hand,
Dear child of the gods, great offspring of Jove!
See how it totters—the world's vaulted might,
Earth, and wide ocean, and the depths of heaven,
All of them, look, caught up in joy at the age to come!

It is not surprising that these words—which are translated here
from Latin into as neutral, that is, nonbiblical, an English as possible—
should have been seized upon by early Christians as evidence for a
messianic hope also outside the boundaries of the people of Israel.
They seemed especially close to the prophecies in the Book of Isaiah,
but they appeared to echo other biblical accents as well: they anticipated "a new heaven and a new earth"; they looked forward to a
new human race, one whose citizenship would be of heaven, not of
earth; they predicted the abolition of the ancient and hereditary blight
of wickedness that clung to human nature in this fallen world; they
even described the crushing of the serpent, the old evil foe of humanity, as the consolation given to Adam and Eve in the Garden of
Eden had promised—all of this brought about by the coming of the
wondrous Virgin and by the birth of the divine Child, who would be
the very progeny of the Most High.[7]

As was perhaps appropriate (though somewhat ironically so) for a
poem written to celebrate the emperor Augustus, the *Fourth Eclogue*
was claimed as a prophecy of Jesus by the emperor Constantine, in
a Good Friday *Oration to the Saints* delivered perhaps in 313; he quoted
Vergil in a Greek translation and provided a Christian commentary
on the *Eclogue*, line by line.[8] Although Jerome was not prepared to
accept the messianic interpretation of Vergil, Augustine, like Constantine, maintained that "it is of [Christ] that this most famous poet
speaks."[9] A setting of the Mass of Saint Paul, sung at Mantua until
the end of the Middle Ages, contained the legend that the apostle
had visited the grave of Vergil in Naples and had wept over not having
come soon enough to find him alive.[10] But the most unforgettable
application of the *Fourth Eclogue* to the coming of Jesus is in the twenty-
second canto of the *Purgatorio*,[11] where Dante quotes the verses of
Vergil in Italian translation,

Secol si rinova;
torna giustizia e primo tempo umano,
e progenie scende da ciel nova,

and then adds a salute to Vergil:

Per te poeta fui, per te cristiano
[Through you I became a poet, through you a Christian].

The standing of Vergil's *Fourth Eclogue* as a prophecy about Jesus
was enhanced for his Christian interpreters by his reference to the
authority of the Greco-Roman prophetess Cuma, the Cumean Sibyl;
Vergil spoke of her also in the *Aeneid* as she "sang frightening riddles
[*horrendas canit ambages*]."[12] There were several collections of visions
and sayings of the various Sibylline oracles, one of the most important
of which was destroyed by a fire in the Capitol in the year 83 B.C.E.
That provided an irresistible opportunity over the next several centuries for various groups—pagan, Jewish, and Christian—to tamper
with the new collections of oracles, and entire books of Christian (or
Christianized) sayings were interpolated into them.

"Instead of calling Jesus the Son of God," wrote one of the most
important early critics of Christianity, "it would be better to give that
honor to the Sibyl." But the Christians were using the Sibyls to back
up their claims about Jesus as the Son of God, and we know from
the same source that Christians were quoting the Sibylline Oracles,.
albeit in a heavily doctored version.[13] They cited them as prophetic
books with an authority derived from their inspiration by the Holy
Spirit, which deserved to be equated with the authority of the Hebrew
Bible itself.[14] The Sibyl was "at once prophetic and poetic."[15] In the
Oration to the Saints Constantine also appealed to the Sibyl, finding
in her a poem whose first letters spelled the Greek words "Jesus
Christ, Son of God, Savior, cross,"[16] which in turn were an acrostic
for *ichthys,* the Greek word for fish, a symbol of Christ[17]—all of this
predicted, so it was assumed, by a pagan Roman prophetess (though
actually, of course, by some anonymous Christian forger).

In addition to providing this supposedly ancient Roman prophecy
of the coming of Christ, and even of his very name, the Sibylline
tradition was especially useful as a source of verification concerning
the coming of Christ to judgment at the end of the world. For already
in their unalloyed pagan form, the sayings of the Sibyl had apparently
contained threats and warnings about a divine punishment to come.
In Jewish and then especially in Christian hands, these threats became
both more extensive and more explicit. To substantiate the prophecy
of the creed that Jesus was to come a second time as judge of the
quick and the dead, apologists for the Christian creed quoted the
Sibyl's prophecy that everything changeable and corruptible was going

to be destroyed by God in the Last Judgment, and quoted her as proof
that God was the source of famines, plagues, and all other dire punishments.[18] Especially in this function as a prophecy of the second
coming of Christ to judge the quick and the dead, the oracles of the
Sibyl enjoyed wide favor both in the theology and in the folklore of
the Middle Ages, but also in medieval art, especially in the Italian art
of the late Middle Ages and the Renaissance.[19]

This reached its artistic climax when, along the left and right walls
of the Sistine Chapel, Michelangelo's ceiling frescoes depicted five of
the Sibyls and five of the prophets of the Old Testament in alternating
figures. Despite differences of emphasis that Charles de Tolnay sees
in Michelangelo's treatment of them, "the correlation of Prophets and
Sibyls," he suggests, "reverts to an old literary and artistic tradition,"
in which "Sibyls had always been depicted as predicting the advent
and passion of Christ."[20] Although de Tolnay argues that "Michelangelo conceived the Sibyls as a contrast to the Prophets," both their
size and their placement by Michelangelo can be taken to mean that
he was in substantial agreement with the tradition in depicting the
Delphic Sibyl and the prophet Isaiah as occupying jointly the position
of witnesses who predicted the first and second comings of Christ.
As such a prediction about Christ, the sayings of the Sibyl were
permanently enshrined in the words of the "Dies irae" of Thomas of
Celano, sung at countless Requiem Masses (at least until the Second
Vatican Council):

> Dies irae, dies illa,
> solvet saeclum in favilla,
> teste David cum Sibylla.

> The day of wrath, that dreadful day
> Shall the whole world in ashes lay,
> As David and the Sibyl say.

A second method for portraying Jesus as the light of the Gentiles
was to find in Gentile thought anticipations of the Christian doctrines
about him. The most complete formulation of this method comes from
Clement of Alexandria at the end of the second century. He had read,
widely if not always deeply, in classical Greek literature, especially
in Homer and Plato, but he consistently saw himself as a faithful pupil
of Jesus, the divine Tutor, whom he described in his book *Paidagogos*,
or *Tutor*, as follows:

> Our Tutor is like God his Father, whose Son he is—sinless, blameless, and with a soul devoid of passion; God in the form of man, stainless, the minister of his Father's will, the Word [Logos] who is God, who is in the Father, who is at the Father's right hand, and with the form of God is God. He is to us a spotless image; to him we are to try with all our might to assimilate our souls.[21]

That is as explicit and as complete a confession of what came to be acknowledged as the orthodox faith about Jesus in his relation to God as can be found in any thinker of the time. And again:

> Where he came from and who he was, he showed by what he taught and by the evidence of his life. He showed that he was the herald, the reconciler, our saviour, the Word, a spring of life and peace flooding over the whole face of the earth. Through him, to put it briefly, the universe has already become an ocean of blessings.[22]

Or, as Eric Osborn has paraphrased the latter passage, "The Lord, despised in his humility, was divine Word, true God made known, equal to the Lord of all things. He took flesh and acted out the drama of man's salvation."[23]

But at the same time, as Osborn points out, "this high and lyrical enthusiasm [about the person of Jesus] is combined with a Platonism in which the Son is the highest excellence, most perfect, holy, powerful, princely, regal and beneficent."[24] For this devout and orthodox advocate of the person of Jesus was, at the same time and without any final sense of contradiction, an advocate of Platonic philosophy, to which he assigned a high and holy mission. "Before the advent of the Lord [Jesus]," he maintained, "philosophy was necessary to the Greeks for righteousness." It could perform this role because one and the same "God is the cause of everything that is good"—of the revelation of Christ given in the Old and in the New Testament, of course, but also of the illumination given to the Greeks in their philosophy. "Perhaps," he was willing to suggest, "philosophy was given to the Greeks [by God] directly and primarily," although not permanently, but "until the Lord should call the Greeks." The apostle Paul had said, in the Epistle to the Galatians, that the law of Moses was a kind of tutor or "custodian until Christ came." In somewhat the same way, Clement maintained, "philosophy was a preparation, paving the way for the one who is perfected in Christ," in short, "a tutor to bring the Hellenic mind to Christ."[25] In sum, as Henry Chadwick puts it, for Clement "both the Old Testament and Greek philosophy are alike tutors to bring us to Christ and are both tributaries of the one great river of Christianity."[26]

Most scholarly commentators on this passage from Clement, whether they have commended him or condemned him, have concentrated on what he says about philosophy, often not noting with equal care that philosophy was intended, according to him, "to bring the Hellenic mind *to Christ*": "the real philosophy" as the Greeks had discovered it would lead to "the true theology" as Christ had disclosed it.[27] Among the many philosophical anticipations of the Christian doctrine of Christ to which Clement and other early Christian philosophers laid claim, the most important is probably the *Timaeus* of Plato, with its description of how the creation of the world had been accomplished. The statements in the *Timaeus* about the creator as "father" and about the three levels of divine reality were, for Clement, evidence for "nothing else than the Holy Trinity."[28] This dialogue is, with the *Laws*, one of the two great works of his last years, and it was also to be for many centuries the best known of the Platonic dialogues in the Latin Middle Ages.[29] In it Plato declared that "the maker and father of this universe it is a hard task to find, and having found him, it would be impossible to declare him to all mankind." But he asserted that the most fundamental of all questions, "which, it is agreed, must be asked at the outset of inquiry concerning anything," was: "Has it always been, without any source of becoming; or has it come to be, starting from some beginning?" To which Plato replied: "It [the universe] has come to be; for it can be seen and touched and it has body, and all such things are sensible." The main body of the dialogue described the emergence of order from chaos as having been achieved by the action of creation. The creator, "being without jealousy . . . desire[d] that all things should come as near as possible to being like himself"; "this is," he added, "the supremely valid principle of becoming and of the order of the world."[30] Such "becoming" took place through the action of an intermediary agent of creation, less than the supreme God but more than creatures, the Demiurge, who brought order and rationality out of primal chaos and thus gave "form" to "matter."

Clement quoted extensively from the *Timaeus* of Plato, including several of the passages just cited, as proof that "the philosophers, having heard so from Moses, taught that the world was created."[31] Since he was sure that it was from Moses that Plato had learned this,

Clement found it legitimate to interpret the *Timaeus* on the basis of the first chapters of Genesis—which meant, at the same time of course, to interpret Genesis on the basis of Plato. The key to that interpretation was Jesus as the Son of God; for Plato had said in the *Timaeus* that it was possible to understand God only on the basis of the "descendants" of God, and Jesus had said the same: "No one knows the Father except the Son and any one to whom the Son chooses to reveal him."[32] Therefore the Demiurge of Plato's *Timaeus* was the creating Word of God of the Genesis story and the prologue to the Gospel of John, according to which all things had come to be through the Word or Logos of God. As the preexistent Demiurge and Logos, the Word and the Reason of God, Jesus had brought order and rationality out of primal chaos, and man in his rationality was created, according to both Genesis and *Timaeus*, in the image of God; for, Clement explains, Jesus himself was "the Image of God as the divine and royal Logos, the man who could not suffer; and the image of that Image is the human mind," human reason patterned after divine Reason, which was Jesus Christ.[33]

A third technique for identifying Jesus as the light of the Gentiles no less than as the glory of the people of Israel was to look in classical history and literature for persons and events that could be interpreted as "types" and prefigurings of Jesus and of redemption through him. "A type," according to the definition of Origen of Alexandria in the third century, "is a figure that came before us in the [Old Testament] fathers, but is fulfilled in us." For example, when Joshua conquers Jericho, this deed of the first Joshua, the son of Nun, foreshadows the redemption accomplished by the second Joshua, Jesus, the son of Mary; for in Aramaic and in Greek the two names are the same.[34] Thus "as Moses lifted up the [bronze] serpent in the wilderness, so must the Son of man be lifted up [on the cross], that whoever believes in him may have eternal life."[35]

In his presentation of the arguments for Jesus to a rabbi named Trypho (who may have been the well-known Rabbi Tarphon mentioned in the Mishnah), Justin Martyr maintained that wherever wood or a tree appeared in the Old Testament, this could be a type or figure of the cross. But when he turned to present the arguments for Jesus to a Roman emperor, Antoninus Pius, he drew upon non-Jewish sources and examples to set forth the case for the cross as "the greatest symbol of the power and rule" of Jesus.[36] In the *Timaeus*, invoking what Iris Murdoch has called one of "the most memorable images in European philosophy,"[37] Plato had taught that in the creation of the universe the Demiurge had "split [the soul-stuff] into two halves and [made] the two cross one another at their centers in the form of the letter Chi."[38] Repeating the standard charge of Jewish and Christian apologists that Plato had borrowed from the Hebrew Bible, Justin insisted that Plato, misunderstanding Moses "and not apprehending that it was the figure of the cross," had nevertheless said that the Logos, "the power next to the first God, was placed crosswise in the universe."[39]

Among the examples of the cross in Justin's catalogue, one of the most intriguing is his symbol of the cross as a mast, without which it would be impossible to traverse the sea. For that symbolism, of which sailors have been reminded throughout Christian history, provided the interpreters of the person of Jesus to the Gentiles with the occasion for discovering at the very fountainhead of classical literature a "type" of the cross to correspond to the pole on which Moses had lifted up the bronze serpent, the story of Odysseus at the mast.[40] The story is taken from book 12 of Homer's *Odyssey*,[41] where Odysseus addresses his companions, relaying the instructions of the divine Circe:

> First of all she tells us to keep away from the magical
> Sirens and their singing and their flowery meadow, but only I,
> she said, was to listen to them, *but you must tie me hard in*
> *hurtful bonds, to hold me fast in position upright against the*
> *mast,* with the ropes' end fastened around it; but if I
> supplicate you and implore you to set me free, then you must tie
> me fast with even more lashings.

Although some of the early Christian writers, including Justin and Tertullian, repeated Plato's criticisms of Homer,[42] even Tertullian was obliged to acknowledge him as "prince of poets, the very billow and ocean of poetry."[43] Once again, however, it was Clement of Alexandria who made the most effective and profound use of the image of Odysseus at the mast as a foreshadowing of Jesus. Circe's instructions to Odysseus and his band were twofold: to avoid the allurements of the Sirens by stopping up their ears, and to tie Odysseus to the mast so that he alone would hear the call of the Sirens but would triumph over it. Both parts applied to Christian believers. They were to avoid sin and error "as we would a dangerous headland, or the threatening Charybdis, or the mythic Sirens"; as Odysseus ordered his helmsman,[44]

> You must keep her clear from where the smoke and the breakers
> are, and make hard for the sea rock lest, without your knowing,
> she might drift that way, and you bring all of us into disaster.

But they could do this because of Jesus, the Logos and Word of God, the Christian Odysseus:

> Sail past their music and leave it behind you, for it will bring about your
> death. But if you will, you can be the victor over the powers of destruction.
> Tied to the wood [of the cross], you shall be freed from destruction. The
> Logos of God will be your pilot, and the Holy Spirit will bring you to anchor
> in the harbor of heaven.[45]

During the Byzantine period various Christian commentaries on both the *Iliad* and the *Odyssey* carried out this image and in the process helped to protect the ancient classics against the misplaced zeal of religious bigotry.[46] And a fourth-century Christian sarcophagus, made of marble and now preserved in the Museo delle Terme in Rome, shows Odysseus at the mast, which rises to the yardarm to form a cross.[47] As a later Byzantine sermon was to put it, "O man, do not fear the loudly roaring waves in the sea of this life. For the cross is the pattern of a strength that cannot be broken, so that you may nail your flesh to that unlimited reverence for the Crucified One and so with great pain arrive at the haven of rest."[48] The story of Odysseus at the mast became a permanent component of the Gentile "types of Christ."

In using the Hebrew Bible and the Jewish tradition to explain the meaning of Jesus, Christians had applied all three of these methods— foreshadowings of the cross, anticipations of doctrine, and prophecies of the coming of Christ—to their interpretation of Moses. His description of the binding and sacrifice of Isaac became one of the most pervasive figures of redemption: God, like Abraham, had willingly offered his own first-born Son as a sacrifice.[49] Moses' narrative of the creation of the world through the word of God was fundamental to the Christian identification of Jesus as the Logos or Word of God who had been with God forever and who interpreted the will of God to the world of creatures.[50] And his prophecy that another prophet, Joshua-Jesus, was to arise as his legitimate successor gave Christians a basis for declaring that "Moses prophetically, giving place to the

Logos as the perfect Tutor, predicts both the name and the office of the Tutor."[51]

When they addressed the message of Jesus to the Gentiles, on the other hand, Socrates performed a function similar to that of Moses.[52] He was himself a type and forerunner of Christ. The divine Logos, the same that was to appear in Jesus, had been active in Socrates, denouncing the polytheism and devil-worship of the Greeks. As one who "lived reasonably, viz., in accordance with the Logos [*meta Logou*]," Socrates was "a Christian before Christ," and like Christ he was put to death by the enemies of reason and the Logos. "Socrates," Justin said, "was accused of the very same crimes as we are" and as Jesus was.[53] The teachings about Jesus Christ could likewise justly lay claim to Socrates as one who had anticipated Christian doctrine, preeminently the Christian doctrine of life eternal. For while the New Testament had asserted that Jesus "abolished death and brought life and immortality to light through the gospel," most early Christian thinkers (except for a few such as Tatian of Syria) did not take this to mean that there had not been any awareness of immortality before him.[54] On the contrary, quoting the Book of Psalms and Plato's *Republic* on the Final Judgment, Clement could conclude, "It follows from this that the soul is immortal," a doctrine on which Scripture and philosophy were agreed.[55]

But Socrates and Plato could also serve the interpreters of Christ as the source for prophecy about Jesus—not only, as in the case of Vergil, about the birth of the Child, but even about his death on the cross. In the course of listing various pagan prophecies about creation, the Sabbath, and other biblical themes, Clement came to one prophecy in which, he said, "Plato all but predicts the history [*oikonomia*] of salvation." This remarkable passage is from the dialogue between Socrates and Glaucon in book 2 of Plato's *Republic*.[56] Drawing a distinction between righteousness and unrighteousness, Glaucon postulates that, instead of beings who are both righteous and unrighteous, as most of us are most of the time, there would arise one unrighteous man who is entirely unrighteous and one righteous man who is entirely righteous. Let this one "righteous man, in his nobleness and simplicity, one who desires, in the words of Aeschylus, to be a good man and not merely to give the impression of being a good man," now be accused of being in fact the worst of men. Let him, moreover, "remain steadfast to the hour of death, seeming to be unrighteous and yet being righteous." What will be the outcome? The answer, for whose gruesomeness Glaucon apologizes in advance to Socrates, must be (and, to preserve once again the neutrality of language, this translation is that of Gilbert Murray) nothing other than the following: "He shall be scourged, tortured, bound, his eyes burnt out, and at last, after suffering every evil, shall be impaled or crucified."[57]

As Paul, the apostle of Jesus Christ, had said to the Greeks about "the Unknown God," so the successors of Paul went on to say to the Greeks and to all the Gentiles about "the Unknown Jesus": "What therefore you worship as unknown, this I proclaim to you."[58]

4
The King of Kings

The kingdom of the world has be-
come the kingdom of our Lord and
of his Christ, and he shall reign
for ever and ever.

X P P Even before Jesus was born, the Gospels inform us, the
X angel of the annunciation told his mother: "The Lord God
will give to him the throne of his father David, and he
will reign over the house of Jacob for ever; and of his
kingdom there will be no end" (Luke 1:32–33). After his
birth there came wise men from the East, asking, "Where is he who
has been born king of the Jews?" (Matt. 2:2) The entry into Jerusalem
on Palm Sunday reminded his followers of the words of the prophet,
"Behold, your king is coming to you, humble and mounted on an
ass" (Matt. 21:5). When he died on the cross on the last day of that
same week, Pontius Pilate had placed over his head an inscription in
three languages: "Jesus of Nazareth, the King of the Jews" (John
19:19). The last book of the New Testament, employing a title that
had also been claimed by earthly monarchs, hailed him as "Lord of
lords and King of kings" (Rev. 17:14).

And yet Pontius Pilate could ask him (John 18:37), "So you are a
king?"

Pilate's question could be, and has been, answered in many different ways. For the title "king" did not remain on the cross; it moved
out into the world of nations and of empires. And the cross itself

moved out to decorate the crowns and flags and public buildings of empires and of nations—as well as the graves of those who died in their wars: as Augustine said, "That very cross on which he was derided, he has now imprinted on the brows of kings."[1] Before the entire process of the enthronement of Jesus as King of kings was finished, it had transformed the political life of a large part of the human race. As we shall see repeatedly in later chapters, much of the "divine right of kings" and of the theory of "holy war" rested on the presupposition that Jesus Christ was King, and so did much of the eventual rejection both of all war and of the divine right of kings. To trace the historical variations and permutations of the kingship of Jesus in its interaction with other political themes and symbols is to understand a large part of what is noble and a large part of what is demonic in the political history of the West: even the Nazi swastika, though older than Christianity in its form, was used as an obscene parody of the cross of Christ, as is evident from its very name, *Hakenkreuz.* "So you are a king?"—Pilate's question has continued to be a very good question indeed.

Accompanying the image of Jesus as King of kings was the expectation that he was about to establish his kingdom here on earth, in which the saints would rule with him for a thousand years; the classic statement of that expectation was the twentieth chapter of the Book of Revelation. The prophecy of Daniel about the four kingdoms that would perish from the earth (Dan. 7:17–27) was now to be fulfilled, and the fourth of the kingdoms was the Roman empire.[2] Declaring that Christ "shall destroy temporal kingdoms and introduce an eternal one," several writers of the early church went on to describe in great detail the changes both in human life and in nature itself that the coming of Christ as King would accomplish.[3] In substantiation of this millenarian hope for the coming kingdom, the writer of the Apocalypse heard voices in heaven shouting: "The kingdom of the world has become the kingdom of our Lord and of his Christ, and he shall reign for ever and ever" (Rev. 11:15). Yet we should note, as various exponents of the millenarian hope themselves did, that this literal expectation of the reign of Christ was by no means universal among Christians even in the second century. Thus Irenaeus admitted that there were some, with whom he did not agree, who interpreted it all as an allegory of eternal life in heaven, while Justin Martyr acknowledged that although he "as well as many others" held to a literal expectation of the earthly kingdom of Christ, there were "many who belong to the pure and pious faith and are true Christians [who] think otherwise."[4]

Both the millenarians and the antimillenarians, moreover, would have answered Pilate's question by saying with Justin that "truly Christ is the everlasting King."[5] Coming as it did from the representative of Tiberius Caesar, Pilate's question was to be echoed many times in the following centuries by the representatives of other Caesars. It is clear, for example, from the account (which has been shown to be authentic) of the martyrdom of seven men and five women at Scillium in North Africa in the year 180 that the title "King of kings" when applied to Jesus meant, to the Christian martyrs and to their pagan persecutors alike, an opposition to Caesar's claims to be supreme king.[6] Thus the representatives of Caesar asked Polycarp of Smyrna at about the same time: "What harm is there in saying 'Caesar is Lord [*Kyrios Kaisar*],' and offering incense and saving your life?" But he replied, according to *The Martyrdom of Polycarp:* "For eighty-six years I have been the servant [of Jesus Christ], and he never did me any injury. How then can I blaspheme my King who saved me?"[7] A similar story told in *The Martyrdom of Ignatius,* which—if it is authentic—may be even earlier, has Ignatius telling the emperor Trajan to his face, "I have Christ the King of heaven [within me], . . . May I now enjoy his kingdom."[8]

Alongside such pledges of allegiance to Jesus as the heavenly King over all earthly kings, however, there stand the repeated reassurances by the apologists for Christianity that this did not make the followers of Jesus disloyal to their earthly kings. "When you hear that we are looking for a kingdom," they said to the Roman emperor himself, "you suppose, without making any further inquiry, that we are speaking about a human kingdom." In fact, they insisted, they were not speaking about a political kingdom at all, but about a kingdom "that is with God." For if it had been a this-worldly and a political kingdom, they would not have hesitated to make the political compromises necessary to buy their safety by denying Christ. Rather, Jesus Christ was "the King of glory," who made an ultimate claim upon human life. In response to that ultimate claim, "we render worship to God alone, but in other things we gladly serve you, acknowledging you as kings and rulers."[9] They cited as evidence of their loyalty the prayers "for the safety of our princes" that were being offered in

Christian worship "to the eternal, the true, the living God, whose favor, beyond all others, they must themselves desire. . . . We pray for security to the empire, for protection to the imperial house." What they refused to do was to treat the emperor as divine, to say "Kyrios Kaisar," and to swear by his "genius."[10] The kingdoms of this present age had been established by God, not by the devil as some heretics maintained, and therefore were worthy of obedience under God.[11] In short, "as far as the honors due to kings and emperors are concerned," the command was obedience, but obedience short of idolatry: "Render therefore to Caesar the things that are Caesar's, and to God the things that are God's."[12] But since Caesar, even when he called himself lord, was only king and emperor while Jesus was King of all kings and Lord of all lords, not simply one in a series of lords,[13] there was nothing due to Caesar that was not due also, and first, to God.

Thanks to the careful work of recent social and political historians of late antiquity, we are beginning to understand better the complex of political, social, economic, psychological, and ideological factors that, along with the religious factors, underlay the Roman persecutions of Christians.[14] Nevertheless, as those scholars have also shown, it does remain necessary to conclude that the image of Jesus as King and Lord repeatedly came into conflict with the sovereignty of Caesar as king and lord. Christians did not look upon Jesus as the leader of a political revolution "from below" that would mean the end of the empire and its replacement by still another political system. And yet, despite the sincerity of their protestations that they prayed for the delay of the end of the world and for the health of the empire, they were all awaiting the second coming of Christ, which would "from above" bring the end of the world and therefore of the empire. The continuance of the Roman empire was the final obstacle to the end; for when Rome fell, the world would fall.

One of them summarized this complex position with simple eloquence:

> Do you think that [Jesus] was sent [by God], as might be supposed, to establish some sort of political sovereignty [*tyrannis*], to inspire fear and terror? Not so. But in gentleness and meekness has He sent him, as a king would send a son who is himself a king. He sent him, as [God] sending God. . . . And He will send him [again] in judgment, and who shall endure his presence? . . . [Therefore] Christians are not distinguished from the rest of humanity either in locality or in speech or in customs. For they do not dwell off somewhere in cities of their own, neither do they use some

different language, nor do they practice an extraordinary style of life. . . .
But while they dwell in cities of Greeks and barbarians as the lot of each
is cast, . . . the constitution of their citizenship is nevertheless quite amazing
and admittedly paradoxical. They dwell in their own countries, but only
as sojourners. . . . *Every foreign country is a fatherland to them, and every fath-*
erland is a foreign country.[15]

That is one of the reasons behind the circumstance, which later students of Rome have sometimes found to be so puzzling, that it was
some of the "best" emperors, the best morally and the best politically,
like Marcus Aurelius and Diocletian, who also instituted some of the
fiercest persecutions of the Christians. Because Jesus was King, Christians could be provisionally loyal to Caesar; but because Jesus was
King, they could not give Caesar the measure of loyalty that the best
Caesars demanded, and perhaps even needed, for the Roman empire
to be, as Vergil had said it would be, *imperium sine fine,* "the empire
that will never end."[16]

One eventuality that these various Christian schematizations of
history and politics did not envisage was the possibility that Caesar
himself might acknowledge the sovereignty of Christ as King of kings.
"The Caesars too would have believed in Christ," Tertullian asserted,
"if Christians could have been Caesars"; but that was a contradiction
in terms.[17] Yet that moral contradiction became a political reality in
the fourth century, when the emperor Constantine I became a Christian, declaring his allegiance to Jesus Christ and adopting the cross
as his official military and personal emblem.

The question of the "sincerity" of Constantine's conversion to Christ
is a modern issue, both in the sense that it has been widely debated
in modern times and in the sense that it represents a modern—indeed,
an anachronistic—way of putting the matter. To his contemporaries
it was not a serious question: the contemporary *Life of Constantine* by
the court theologian and historian Eusebius of Caesarea is an encomium of the emperor cast in the form of a saint's life. But in the historiography of the nineteenth and twentieth centuries that account
has been fundamentally challenged, and Eusebius has even been
rejected as "the first thoroughly dishonest historian of antiquity"; for
in fact Constantine could be characterized, on the basis of the figure
of Napoleon, as "a great man of genius, who in his politics had no
sense of moral concern and who viewed the religious question completely and exclusively in the light of political utilitarianism."[18] On

the other hand, the "documents leave no doubt that . . . Constantine regarded himself as a Christian."[19] And so it is perhaps safest to suggest, with Ramsay MacMullen, that Constantine's spirit passed "not instantaneously from paganism to Christianity but more subtly and insensibly from the blurred edges of one, not truly itself, to the edges of the other," apparently without going through the center of either.[20]

Although Constantine himself may not have referred to the name of Jesus Christ very often until the 320s, at least in the surviving documents, that name did dominate the two most important Christian historical reconstructions of the events of the preceding decade, specifically of the so-called Battle of the Milvian Bridge of 28 October 312: that of Lactantius, tutor in Constantine's household, who died in 320; and that of Eusebius, who completed his *Life of Constantine* between the death of the emperor in 337 and his own death in 340. According to Lactantius, on the eve of the battle "Constantine was directed in a dream to cause a heavenly sign to be delineated on the shields of his soldiers, and so to proceed to battle. He did as he had been commanded" and marked on their shields the Chi-Rho.[21] It seems clear, then, that according to Lactantius's version of the events of 312, Constantine hitched his wagon to the star of Jesus Christ, was victorious through the victory of Christ, and from now on would exercise his own kingly authority through the eternal and indestructible kingship of Jesus.

At the hands of Eusebius, this historical and theological interpretation of Constantine's victory and kingship as an achievement of Christ the Victor and King through the sign of his cross became a full-blown theology of history and an apologia for the idea of a Christian Roman empire.[22] "Thus then the God of all, the Supreme Governor of the whole universe, by his own will appointed Constantine . . . to be prince and sovereign": this is how Eusebius begins his account. Eusebius reports Constantine's having narrated to him under oath many years later that on 27 October 312, as he was praying, he "saw with his own eyes the trophy of a cross of light in the heavens above the sun, and bearing this inscription, CONQUER BY THIS [*Toutō nika*]." The entire army of Constantine, moreover, also witnessed the heavenly apparition and "were struck with amazement." Only after that, according to Eusebius, did the dream come. "Then in his sleep the Christ of God appeared to him with the same sign which he had seen in the heavens, and commanded him to make a likeness of that sign which he had seen in the heavens, and to use it as a safeguard in all engagements with his enemies." And that was just what he did. "The emperor," Eusebius concludes, "constantly made use of this sign of salvation as a safeguard against every adverse and hostile power, and commanded that others similar to it should be carried at the head of all his armies."

In the version of Constantine's victory that Eusebius presents in his *History,* on the other hand, Eusebius reports that after the Battle of the Milvian Bridge Constantine ordered "a trophy of the Savior's passion, . . . the savior sign of the cross," to be placed in the hand of his own statue, which was to be erected in Rome to celebrate the victory, with the following inscription in Latin: "By this savior sign, the true test of bravery, I saved and freed your city from the yoke of the tyrant, and restored the senate and the Roman people, freed, to their ancient fame and splendor." Rome had passed into the protection of Christ. For Constantine, this successor of the Roman Caesars, Jesus the crucified King had become not only Christus Victor, but the very restorer of the traditional honor of the senate and the Roman people.[23]

Constantine returned the favor. "As a thank offering to his Savior for the victories he had obtained over every foe,"[24] he convoked the first ecumenical council of the church at a city named for *Nikē* (Victory), Nicea in Bithynia, for the purpose of restoring concord to church and empire. The fundamental question creating discord was the relation between the Godhead and Jesus as the Son of God: in the formulation of one modern scholar, "Is the divine that has appeared on earth and reunited man with God identical with the supreme divine, which rules heaven and earth, or is it a demigod?"[25] The answer of the Council of Nicea, and of all subsequent Christian orthodoxy, to that question was to declare that Jesus as the Son of God was "begotten not created, one in being [*homoousios*] with the Father."[26] That dogmatic formula was, according to Eusebius, the result of a direct personal intervention by Constantine himself in the deliberations of the council, when "our emperor, most beloved by God, began to reason [in Latin, with a Greek translation then supplied by an interpreter] concerning [Christ's] divine origin, and His existence before all ages: He was virtually in the Father without generation, even before He was actually begotten, the Father having always been the Father, just as [the Son] has always been a King and a Savior."[27]

Once the Council of Nicea had accepted these formulas, they became the law not only for the church but for the empire. To the church of Alexandria Constantine wrote that "the fearful enormity of the blasphemies which some were shamelessly uttering concerning the mighty Savior, our life and hope," had now been condemned and suppressed; "for that which has commended itself to the judgment of three hundred bishops cannot be other than the doctrine of God."[28] Therefore "whatever is determined in the holy assemblies of the bishops," Constantine wrote to all the churches in all his provinces, "is to be regarded as indicative of the divine will." He then issued an edict against heretics on that basis, forbidding them to gather and confiscating their church buildings and places of assembly.[29] That edict treated Christian dissenters far more harshly than it did pagans, to whom Constantine extended what was a remarkable measure of tolerance, forbidding anyone "to compel others" to accept Christianity.[30] It "served as the basis for all subsequent legislation on heresy by the Christian emperors."[31] The foundation of this legislation was the affirmation of the Nicene Creed that Jesus Christ as Lord and Son of God was one in being with the Father, and that "of his kingship there will be no end." Only those who conformed to that "apostolic discipline" of the Nicene Creed, as the *Theodosian Code* of the Roman law was to call it, would have the right to hold political office within the Christian empire. (Since this was still the law in the Holy Roman Empire of the sixteenth century, it was the political, though not the theological, reason why the Protestant Reformers made such a point of their loyalty to the orthodoxy of the trinitarian creeds.) As a result of the events of the fourth century, it was necessary, for the next thousand years and more, to accept Christ as the eternal King if one wanted to be a temporal king.

Yet that did not of itself settle the question of political sovereignty, for it was possible to draw the lines of connection between the eternal kingship of Christ and the temporal kingship of earthly rulers in several different patterns. Beginning already in the century of Constantine and in his two cities of Rome and Constantinople, the definition of Jesus Christ as King produced divergent political theories. One theory was the one with which Constantine himself seems to have been operating, or certainly it was the theory that evolved during the next two or three centuries in Byzantine Christendom, finding its climax in the career and thought of the emperor Justinian the Great. The remark of Eusebius that when Constantine the emperor entertained the bishops of the church at a banquet during the Council of Nicea, "one might have thought that this was a foreshadowing of the kingdom of Christ"[32] may tell even more than the author intended. Christ had promised his disciples that he would eat and drink with them anew in the kingdom of his Father (Matt. 26:29). The setting of this promise in the Gospel accounts of the institution of the Lord's Supper meant to most interpreters that, at each commemoration of the Lord's Supper, Christ through the celebrating priest was the host and the communicants were the guests, thus foreshadowing the eternal kingdom of Christ. But at Constantine's banquet the kingdom of Christ was foreshadowed when the divinely ordained emperor was the host and the bishops were the guests.

So it was also in the political order. Constantine's language in addressing bishops and clergy was properly deferential, but behind the deference was the firm hand of one who knew where the real power lay. As Eusebius put it at the conclusion of his *History*, the emperors—and not only Constantine—"had God, the universal King, and the Son of God, the Savior of all, as their Guide and Ally . . . against the haters of God."[33] God the Father as King of the universe had conferred authority on Jesus, to whom, as he said just before his ascension, "all authority in heaven and on earth has been given" (Matt. 28:18). That authority was transmitted to the emperor, beginning with Constantine; for Christ the King had elected to exercise his sovereignty over the world through the emperor, to whom he had appeared in visions. The emperor was "crowned by God [*theostephēs*]," a belief reflected in the Byzantine ceremony of coronation.[34] As early as 454, the patriarch of Constantinople performed the ritual of coronation for the emperor Leo I. But in Byzantium this did not come to mean, as it was taken to mean in the Latin West, that the authority of the emperor was derivative from that of the pope or even from that of the church. On the contrary, at the consecration of the patriarch the Byzantine emperor would declare: "By the grace of God and by our imperial power, which proceeds from the grace of God, this man is appointed patriarch of Constantinople." The emperor Justinian was Melchizedek, king and priest at the same time.[35] In a mosaic on the south

gallery of Hagia Sophia in Constantinople there is a graphic presentation of this political theology. Christ the King is enthroned at the
center, and his position makes it clear that he is Lord of all. On either
side of him stand the emperor Constantine IX Monomachus and the
empress Zoe, with no priestly intermediaries, for their sovereignty
comes directly to them from his sovereignty. (The line was, however,
sometimes less clearly drawn in political reality than it was in political
theology; for Constantine was Zoe's third husband, and the mosaic
is a palimpsest, on which his image has replaced that of his predecessor.) It was, moreover, to become evident in the iconoclastic controversy that even this authority had its limits: the emperor could rule
in the name of Christ the King, but he had better not lay hands on
the images of Christ the Image of God.

The dedication of the rebuilt city of Byzantium as Constantinople,
often called New Rome, on 11 May 330 was the result, among other
things, of Constantine's resolve to reunite his empire and of his wish
to establish a truly Christian capital to replace the pagan capital of
Old Rome. But when the capital left Rome for Constantinople, there
was much of the aura of Rome that it could not export. That aura
devolved, as it had already been doing, on the bishop of Rome. In
452 Pope Leo I confronted Attila, king of the Huns, at Mantua, and
persuaded him not to lay siege to Rome; he also saved the city from
other barbarian conquerors.[36] In that setting, the political implications
of the authority of Christ the King came to mean something quite
different in Old Rome from what they meant in New Rome. When
Jesus Christ before his ascension declared, "All authority in heaven
and on earth has been given to me," he went on to give his "great
commission" to the apostles as the first bishops. To one of them,
moreover, namely to Peter as the first pope, he had already entrusted
the authority to "bind and loose"—to bind and loose sins, but also,
so the interpretation eventually ran, to bind and loose political
authority.[37]

The coronation of Charlemagne as emperor by Pope Leo III on
Christmas Day in the year 800 at Saint Peter's in Rome became the
model of how political sovereignty was believed in the West to have
passed: from God to Christ, from Christ to the apostle Peter, from
Peter to his successors on the "throne of Peter," and from them to
emperors and kings. Therefore when Emperor Henry IV had defied
the authority of Pope Gregory VII, it was not to the king but to the

apostle Peter himself that the pope, at the Lenten Synod of 1076, addressed the bull excommunicating Henry and deposing him from the imperial throne. That theory of the political kingship of Christ was to be opposed, both in the name of the autonomy of the political order and in the name of the eternal kingship of Christ, by various thinkers of the later Middle Ages, including Dante Alighieri. Curiously, the act of legitimizing this papalist theory of political authority was eventually attributed to the emperor Constantine. The eighth-century forgery that came to be called *The Donation of Constantine* represented him as conferring on the pope imperial authority and jurisdiction in perpetuity, in gratitude for what Christ had done for him through Pope Sylvester I, who cured him of leprosy. Christ was King, the church was a monarchy, the pope was a monarch, and it was by his authority that earthly monarchs exercised their authority. Christ had said to his disciples that the two swords in their hands were "enough" (Luke 22:38), and so they proved to be: Peter and his successors had both the "spiritual sword" of ecclesiastical governance and the "temporal sword" of political governance, even though they might exercise the latter through the instrumentality of secular rulers.[38]

"So you are a king?" Pilate had asked Jesus, and in the inscription he placed on the cross he had called him one. But even when they celebrated the kingship of Jesus in the triumphalism of the Byzantine emperor or of the Roman bishop, those who professed obedience to him were obliged to consider the fuller implications of that encounter between Jesus the King and Pontius Pilate the king's procurator, as recorded in the eighteenth chapter of the Gospel of John, an encounter that provoked quite another question from Pilate as well:

> Pilate entered the praetorium again and called Jesus, and said to him, "Are you the King of the Jews?" . . . Jesus answered, "My kingship is not of this world. . . ." "So you are a king?" said Pilate. Jesus answered, "You say that I am a king. For this I was born, and for this I have come into the world, to bear witness to the truth. Every one who is of the truth hears my voice." Pilate said to him, "What is truth?" (John 18:33–38)

That latter question of Pilate has likewise called forth a great variety of answers through the centuries, all of them suggested by the figure of Jesus.

5

The Cosmic Christ

All things were created through him and for him. He is before all things, and in him all things hold together.

 In the first of a series of lectures called *Science and the Modern World*, one of the wisest men of the twentieth century, Alfred North Whitehead, came to speak about the scientific and philosophical belief that "every detailed occurrence can be correlated with its antecedents in a perfectly definite manner, exemplifying general principles." "Without this belief," he continued, "the incredible labours of scientists would be without hope. It is this instinctive conviction, vividly poised before the imagination, which is the motive power of research:—that there is a secret, a secret which can be unveiled." And then he put this fundamental question: "How has this conviction been so visibly implanted on the European mind?" His answer was:

When we compare this tone of thought with the attitude of other civilizations when left to themselves, there seems but one source for its origin. It must come from the medieval insistence on the rationality of God, conceived of as with the personal energy of Jehovah and with the rationality of a Greek philosopher.[1]

The epitome of that insistence and of that combination of beliefs— the "personal energy of Jehovah" plus the "rationality of a Greek philosopher"—was the medieval and Christian doctrine of Jesus Christ as the incarnate Logos.

By the fourth century it had become evident that of all the various "titles of majesty for Christ" adapted and adopted during the first generations after Jesus,[2] none was to have more momentous consequences than the title Logos, consequences as momentous for the history of thought as were those of the title King for the history of politics. Indeed, one Christian philosopher of that century could speak about "the titles of the Logos, which are so many, so sublime, and so great,"[3] thus attaching all the other titles as predicates to this one. To this day, people who have, as Ben Jonson said of Shakespeare, "small Latin, and less Greek" can often recite the opening words of the Gospel of John, *En archē ēn ho Logos;* and near the beginning of Goethe's *Faust* the aged philosopher Faust is sitting in his study pondering that very text and trying out several different translations for it: "Im Anfang war das Wort/der Sinn/die Kraft/die Tat": In the beginning was the word/the mind/the power/the deed.[4] The term Logos can have any and all of those meanings, and many other meanings besides, such as "reason" or "structure" or "purpose."

The chief monument of the fourth-century consideration of Jesus as the Logos was the dogma of the Holy Trinity, as enshrined in the Nicene Creed. Through most of Christian history, the doctrine of the Trinity has been the unquestioned—and unquestionable—touchstone of truly orthodox faith and teaching. It has given its outline to systematic theologies like the *Institutes* of John Calvin, to catechisms, and to sermons. Christian worship and hymnody, from the *Gloria Patri* of the Latin liturgy to the nineteenth-century hymn "Holy, Holy, Holy," by Bishop Reginald Heber, often gave better expression to faith in the Trinity than did theology; even Calvin thought that the Nicene Creed was better sung than said. The development of trinitarian dogma is an important chapter, one may safely say the most important single chapter, in the history of the development of Christian doctrine, and it must bulk large in any account of that history. But the identification of Jesus as Logos also made intellectual, philosophical, and scientific history. For by applying this title to Jesus, the Christian philosophers of the fourth and fifth centuries who were trying to give an account of who he was and what he had done were enabled to interpret him as the divine clue to the structure of reality (metaphysics) and, within metaphysics, to the riddle of being (ontology)—in a word, as the Cosmic Christ.

It is likewise from the fourth century that we have another kind of monument to the interpretation of Jesus as the Cosmic Christ. A Christian sarcophagus from that century, which belongs to the Lateran Museum in Rome, presents a striking depiction of his sovereignty over the universe. Between two elaborately carved scrolls at the center of the marble frieze along the side of the sarcophagus is the seated figure of Christ enthroned, raised higher than the figures on either side of him. His left hand holds a scroll, and his right hand is raised in the gesture of blessing and of authority. Beneath his feet is a personification of the cosmos. "He must reign," the apostle Paul declared, "until he has put all his enemies under his feet. The last enemy to be destroyed is death" (1 Cor. 15:25–26). And again, in words that sound like a hymn:

> He is the image of the invisible God, the first-born of all creation; for in him all things were created, in heaven and on earth, visible and invisible, whether thrones or dominions or principalities or authorities—all things were created through him and for him. He is before all things, and in him all things hold together. He is the head of the body, the church; he is the beginning, the first-born from the dead, that in everything he might be preeminent. For in him all the fulness of God was pleased to dwell. (Col. 1:15–19)

On a fourth-century sarcophagus intended to affirm victory over death as "the last enemy," through the one who was "the first-born from the dead," it was this cosmic dimension both of his victory and of his lordship that took visible shape, just as it was this same dimension that was taking conceptual shape at the very same time in the doctrine of the Trinity.

The opening words of the Gospel of John, "In the beginning was the Word," were evidently meant to be a paraphrase of the opening words of the Book of Genesis, "In the beginning God created the heavens and the earth. . . . And God said." That was, at any rate, how the early Christians were reading the two texts side by side.[5] Because the speaking of God (which is one way to translate Logos) made the world possible, it was also the speaking of God that made the world intelligible: Jesus Christ as Logos was the *Word of God* revealing the way and will of God to the world. As the medium of divine revelation, he was also the agent of divine revelation, specifically of revelation about the cosmos and its creation. His "credibility" was fundamental to all human understanding.[6] Therefore when, in the fourth century, Basil of Caesarea set about to interpret the meaning of the cosmos,

Christ Seated above a Personification of the Cosmos, fourth-century Roman sarcophagus, Museo Laterano, Rome.

he began with the story of creation in six days as recorded in the Book of Genesis and proceeded to expound it in his *Hexaemeron*—a curious mixture of theology, philosophy, science, and superstition—which was soon thereafter taken over and paraphrased in Latin by Ambrose of Milan.

As we have already seen, many early Christian thinkers brought to their interpretation of the biblical account of creation an understanding of the origins of the universe that had been profoundly shaped by the *Timaeus* of Plato, a use of Plato's cosmology that received significant reinforcement for Christians from their belief that Plato had read the Book of Genesis and that in the *Timaeus* he had perceived, however dimly, that the structure of the cosmos was cruciform.[7] From its very beginning, therefore, the Christian view of creation, even of creation through the Logos who was to become incarnate in Jesus, was what later generations were to call a "mixed doctrine," that is, one on which both divine revelation and human reason had something to say. The interaction between the two ways of knowing, whether it was seen as harmony or as contradiction, has helped to shape the history not only of theology but of philosophy and of science, well into the nineteenth and twentieth centuries.[8] For most of these fourth-century fathers, what bound together the religious-theological cosmogony of the Nicene Creed ("We believe in one God, Maker of heaven and earth and of all that is—visible and invisible") and the philosophical-scientific cosmology of Plato and of Platonism (as formulated by the *Timaeus* and its commentators, including its Christian commentators) was the further affirmation of the content of the Logos doctrine (though the term Logos itself did not appear in the Nicene Creed) when it declared that "through the one Lord Jesus Christ, the Son of God, all things were made." That affirmation, however, also drew the line where the two ways of perceiving cosmic reality diverged.

The test case for the relation between them was the definition of creation as "creation out of nothing [*creatio ex nihilo*]."[9] That definition was directed against the idea that matter was eternal, hence coeternal with the Creator.[10] Although "the philosophers of Greece have made much ado to explain nature," the best they could manage, in such works as the *Timaeus*, was "some imagination, but no clear comprehension" of that "hidden doctrine" of the Book of Genesis, which had been revealed by the Word of God to and through Moses.[11] To consider the universe in the light of divine wisdom rather than of worldly wisdom, therefore, meant to recognize that "the Word of God pervades the creation" from the very beginning and to the very present.[12] And the Word that God spoke, as well as the One to whom God spoke the words, "Let *us* make man in *our* image," was none other than "his Co-operator, the one through whom [God] created all orders of existence, the one who upholds the universe by his word of power," Jesus Christ the Logos seen as "the second person" of the Trinity and as the Cosmic Christ.[13]

To put this in the succinct formula of a fourth-century Latin interpreter of Greek Christian thought, "It is the Father to whom all existence owes its origin. In Christ and through Christ he is the source of all. In contrast to all else he is self-existent."[14] It was necessary in such a definition to clarify whether the Word that God spoke at creation, the Logos now present in Jesus, could say, in the words of the Book of Proverbs, "The Lord *created* me at the beginning of his work."[15] For then the Logos would be the first among creatures, but nevertheless still only a creature and part of the order of creation. There were, according to Christian orthodoxy, only these two possibilities: either creature or Creator. It was the conclusion of the bitter debates over the doctrine of the Trinity during the fourth century that the Logos as the Word of God spoken at the creation had been with God from before the creation, from eternity, and was therefore coeternal, "one in being [*homoousios*] with the Father." In the celebrated exposition of creation in book 11 of his *Confessions* Augustine, asking, "How, O God, didst thou make heaven and earth?" replied that it was in that Word which God spoke eternally and by which all creatures were spoken eternally: "In this Beginning, O God, hast thou made heaven and earth—in thy Word, in thy Son, in thy Power, in thy Wisdom, in thy Truth, wondrously speaking and wondrously making."[16]

But "Logos of God" when applied to Jesus Christ meant far more than "Word of God," more even than divine revelation; there were many other Greek vocables that would have sufficed to express that much and no more, and several of them were being used in the New Testament and in other early Christian literature. Employing the specific name Logos implied in addition to this that what had come in Jesus Christ was also the *Reason and Mind of the cosmos*. To be "without logos [*alogos*]" had meant, also in classical Greek, to be without reason or contrary to reason;[17] those second-century Christian heretics who were opposed to the use of the Logos doctrine—and to the Gospel of John because it contained that doctrine—had therefore been dubbed "the Alogoi," and those fourth-century thinkers who denied the eternity of the Logos were accused of teaching that God had once been *alogos,* insane.[18] "There never was a time when God was without the Logos," orthodox thought insisted, "or when he was not the Father."[19] As these Christian philosophers pondered the deeper connotations of this identification of Jesus as eternal Logos, the cosmological import of Logos as Reason in the framework of the doctrine of creation became apparent.

Asking the rhetorical question "In what then does the greatness of man consist?" one of them answered that it consisted "in his being in the image of the Creator." Then he analyzed the connotations of that doctrine for the relation of Christ to the creation:[20]

> If you examine the other points by which the divine beauty is expressed, you will find that in them too the likeness in the image [of God] which we present is perfectly preserved. The Godhead is mind and word; for "in the beginning was the Word," and the followers of Paul have "the mind of Christ" which "speaks" in them. Humanity too is not far removed from these; for you see in yourself word and understanding, which are an imitation of that authentic Mind and Word [namely, Christ as Logos].

There was, therefore, an analogy between the Logos of God, which had become incarnate in Jesus, and the logos of humanity, which was incarnate in each person and perceptible to each person from within. But since the Logos of God, related to the Father as word was to mind, was the divine Demiurge, through whom all of the cosmos had come into being, it followed that "this name [Logos] was given to him because he exists in all things that are."[21]

From this description of the relation between the cosmos as the creation of God and the Logos as the Reason of God there followed two implications for the theory of knowledge. On the one hand, the identification of the Logos as the Reason and Mind of the cosmos acted to countervail the tendency, which had seemed endemic to the Christian movement from the very beginning, to revel in the paradox of faith in Christ to the point of glorifying the irrational. Tertullian never said (or, to be accurate, never quite said) what is often attributed to him, *Credo quia absurdum,* "I believe it because it is absurd." But he did say, "The Son of God died; this is by all means to be believed, because it makes no sense [*quia ineptum est*]. And he was buried and rose again; this fact is certain, because it is impossible."[22] "After possessing Christ Jesus," he said elsewhere, "we want no curious disputation, no inquiries after enjoying the gospel! What does Athens have to do with Jerusalem?"[23]

Taken by themselves as literal and authoritative, as they have sometimes been in the history of Christian literalism and anti-intellectualism in all generations, such sentiments would have brought an end to philosophical thought and would have aborted scientific investigation, both of which depend on the assumption that there is a rational order in the cosmos. But by the latter half of the fourth century it had become possible for those who still accepted the paradox of faith in Christ to affirm nevertheless the validity of the rational process and to appeal to the evidence of "our very eyes and the law of nature."[24] For a creation that had been carried out by God the Father through his eternal Son the Logos could not be arbitrary or haphazard, nor could it be "conceived by chance and without reason"; but it had to have "a useful end."[25] A corollary of this affirmation of the rationality of the cosmos was a rejection of the special form of arbitrariness and chance represented in antiquity by the dominance of astrology.[26] It was a fundamental difference between humanity and other creatures that, having been created in the image of God and by a special action of the creating Logos, even the human body must be *logikos*, "capable of speech" or "suited to the use of reason" or in any case "mirroring forth the presence of the creating Logos."[27]

This confidence of fourth-century Christian philosophers that the divine Reason disclosed in Christ had endowed human reason with a capacity for penetrating the workings of created nature was, however, restrained from presumption by the other pole of the dialectic: a profound sense, also based on the revelation in Christ, of the limitations that had been placed upon human capacity for understanding ultimate reality. As happened so often, it was a Christian heretic who served as the catalyst for a fundamental insight: Eunomius, one of the ablest of fourth-century Christian philosophers, is quoted by more than one of his orthodox opponents as having claimed that he could know the essence of God as well as God himself did. We need not necessarily accept the historical accuracy of such quotations to recognize that, by contrast, his orthodox opponents made a point of declaring that there was much about God that they could not know.

For an investigation of creatures, it was enough to know their "names" in order to understand their "essences," but "the uncreated nature [of God] alone, which we acknowledge in the Father and in the Son and in the Holy Spirit, transcends all significance of names."[28] For "the Deity cannot be expressed in words"; "we sketch It by Its attributes" and so "obtain a certain faint and feeble and partial idea concerning It," so that "our best theologian" was one who spoke about God on the basis of these fragments of knowledge that were available.[29] The outcome was what can be called a "biblical positivism," as expressed in the motto of Hilary of Poitiers: "God is to be believed insofar as he speaks of himself [*Ipsi de Deo credendum est*]."[30] And God had spoken decisively in the Logos, incarnate in the historical flesh of Jesus Christ. Thus the cosmos was reliably knowable and at the same time it remained mysterious, both of these because the Logos was the Mind and Reason of God.

Because the Logos incarnate in Jesus was the Reason of God, it was also possible to see the Logos as the very *Structure of the universe.* Following the pattern, familiar by now, of combining the biblical account of creation in the Book of Genesis with the Platonic doctrine of the preexistence of the Forms, Basil of Caesarea provided a graphic description of that structure:

> Before all those things which now attract our notice existed, God, after casting about in his mind and determining to bring into being that which had no being, imagined the world such as it ought to be, and created matter in harmony with the form which he wished to give it. . . . He welded all the diverse parts of the cosmos by links of indissoluble attachment and established between them so perfect a fellowship and harmony that the most distant, in spite of their distance, appeared united in one universal sympathy.[31]

That harmony, binding together the atom and the galaxy, was expressed in a cosmic *systēma,* all of it brought about by the "magnificence of the Creator-Logos."[32] The concept of harmony in the universe expressed in the Greek word *systēma* also hovered over one of the most powerful of the New Testament statements we have quoted about the Cosmic Christ, as the one through whom, in Basil's phrase, "all things have their continuance and constitution," the one who had "primacy over all created things," in whom "everything in heaven and on earth was created," and in whom moreover "all things are held together [or: are made into a cosmic system, *synestēken*]."[33]

The identification of the Creator-Logos in Jesus as the foundation for the very structure of the universe and the belief that "the Logos of God is in the whole universe" had its basis in the even more fundamental identification of the Logos as the *Agent of creation out of nothing,* or, to use a term that was common to biblical and philosophical language, out of nonbeing.[34] The Creator could be described as "the one who is [ho ōn]," while creatures had their being by derivation from the Creator and participation in the Creator and they could not "be of themselves."[35] In the fullest sense, therefore, only the Creator could be said "to be." For the same reason, using the name Father for God was *not* a figure of speech. It was only because God was the Father of the Logos-Son that the term father could also be applied to human parents, and when it was used of them it *was* a figure of speech. As the Father of the Logos, God was, according to the New Testament, "the Father, from whom every family in heaven and on earth is named," and in human families both the parents and the children were an "imitation" of their divine prototypes.[36] That was also why the Logos could not be a creature, not even the primary creature; for all creatures had been brought out of nonbeing, and as the agent who had brought them out of nonbeing the Creator-Logos must "have being" in the full and nonmetaphorical sense of the word.[37]

Therefore it was the Logos as the Reason of the universe who "structures it into a cosmos of order."[38] Having been created out of nonbeing through this structuring Logos, the cosmos manifested in its "order and providence" the ordering presence of "the Logos of God who is over all and who governs all."[39] The universe was not "absurd" or "bereft of the Logos [alogos]," but it made sense because of the Logos. Conversely, however, its hold on reality was derived from its hold on the Logos, without whom it would slip back into the nonbeing out of which the Logos had originally brought it in creation. In sum,

> The one who is good cannot grudge anything. Therefore God does not grudge even being, but wants everything to be, so as to manifest steadfast love. God saw that all created nature, if left to its own principles, was in flux and subject to dissolution. To prevent this and to keep the universe from disintegrating back into nonbeing, God made all things by the eternal Logos of God itself and endowed the creation with being. . . . God guides [the universe] by the Logos, so that by the direction, providence, and ordering of the Logos, the creation may be illumined and enabled to abide always securely.[40]

Because sin was a turning of the eyes away from God and from the Logos, sinners were threatened with falling back into the abyss of nonbeing out of which the creating action of the Logos had called them.

To meet and to overcome this threat, the Logos, as the *Savior of the cosmos*, became incarnate in Jesus Christ, who suffered and died on the cross and rose from the dead victorious over sin, death, and hell. This was necessary because the world that the Logos had fashioned was now a fallen world. It was characteristic of the Greek Christian philosophers of the fourth and fifth centuries that, by contrast with the later Christian individualism manifest especially in Western thought, they always viewed humanity and the cosmos in close proximity. As this was the case, first of all, in the very understanding of creation through the Logos, so it had to be also in the diagnosis of the human predicament and in the prescription of the divine cure through the selfsame Logos, now incarnate in Christ. Not only, therefore, did "all things hold together" in Christ the Logos as the Structure of the cosmos, but it would also be in the Logos as Savior that "the universe itself is to be freed from the shackles of mortality and enter upon the liberty and splendor of the children of God."[41]

One reason for a greater emphasis on the Cosmic Christ in the thought of the Greek East than in that of the Latin West must be sought in the ideas about being and creation through the Logos that we have just been reviewing in the writings of Athanasius and other fourth-century Eastern thinkers. For it is possible to draw a distinction between those philosophical theologies that have interpreted death as the result of guilt and sin and those philosophical theologies that have tended to see death as the consequence of transiency and impermanence; neither emphasis exists utterly without echoes of the other, but the distinction is clear. If sin was defined as a relapse into the nothingness out of which the creating Logos had taken humanity, it was appropriate to describe the plight of the human soul as "imagining evil for itself" and therefore as supposing that "it is doing something" when, by committing the sin that is nonbeing, "it is in fact doing nothing."[42] Such a soul was deceived into believing that this nonbeing was the "only true reality" and that the reality of God was "nonbeing." This total reversal of the created metaphysical polarity between being and nonbeing was the meaning of the fall. For, in the formula of Athanasius, "humanity is by nature subject to transiency [*phthartos*], inasmuch as it is made out of what is not."[43] The adjective *transient* with its cognates was of decisive importance. For it put the understanding of sin and the fall into the context of the transiency and decay to which not only human nature but the cosmos itself was subject, by virtue of its having been created out of nothing. The fall both of humanity and of the world was a loss of the tenuous hold on true being and therefore a fall into the abyss. In the case of humanity, it was all the more tragic because only Adam and Eve, and not any of the other creatures on earth, had been created in the image of God, that is, in the image of the divine Logos.[44] Despite many statements to the contrary, this view of the human condition did concentrate on death as corruptibility and transiency rather than on death as guilt and the "wages of sin" (Rom. 6:23).

The corollary of this view of the human fall in the context of the cosmic fall was an understanding of the saving activity of Jesus the Logos that applied it not only to the expiation of the guilt caused by sin against the law and will of God, but to the repair of the fracture in being caused by alienation from the God who was defined as "the one who is"—thus not only to guilt but also to ontology.[45] By becoming incarnate in Jesus, the Logos had enabled human beings to transcend themselves and, in a pregnant phrase of the New Testament, "to become partakers in the divine nature" (2 Pet. 1:4). "The Logos of God has become human," one Greek father after another would say, "so that you might learn from a human being how a human being may become divine."[46] The original creation in the image of God, in which true human greatness consisted,[47] had been brought about through the Logos; that creation would now achieve not only restoration but consummation and perfection through the same Logos: his incarnation would achieve our deification. And the whole cosmos would have its proper share in that consummation; for "the establishment of the church is a re-creation of the world," in which "the Logos has created a multitude of stars," a new heaven and a new earth.[48]

From the ascription of the creation of the universe to Jesus the Logos it also followed, by a necessary inference, that the Logos was not only the beginning but the end, the *Goal of the cosmos*.[49] He was Omega as well as Alpha. When it was transposed into the key of Christian philosophy, this teaching was what had become of the primitive Christian expectation of the imminent end of the world and the immediate coming of Christ to judgment. The observation that time moved along in sequence should lead to the recognition that time would also have an end, just as it had had a beginning. Thus, "as we suppose the power of the divine will to be a sufficient cause to the things that are, for their coming into existence out of nothing, so too we shall not repose our belief on any improbability in referring the re-formation of the world to the same power."[50]

Underlying this vision of Logos as the telos of the universe was the outline of the drama of world history and of cosmic history quoted earlier from the fifteenth chapter of 1 Corinthians. Jesus had come as true man to be the Second Adam; "for as by a man came death, by a man has come also the resurrection of the dead." This he did as the "first fruits," and after him would come life for "those who belong to Christ." And "then comes the end, when he delivers the kingdom to God the Father. . . . For [Christ] must reign until he has put *all* his enemies under his feet. The last enemy to be destroyed is death. . . . that God may be all in all" (1 Cor. 15:20–28). But could the God who had come in Christ ever truly be "all in all" if there still were anywhere in the cosmos any illness beyond the reach of his healing love? If, according to the Gospel of John (John 1:9), the Logos was "the true light that enlightens every man," could there be any abyss so dark that the light which had now come into the world and had now shone in the Logos could not penetrate it? As the Word of God, the Logos had spoken in creation, and spoken in the prophets of Israel, and spoken again—and decisively—in the life and teachings of Jesus. As the Reason of God, the Logos made sense out of the madness of the world and the power of evil. As the Structure of the cosmos, the Logos held forth the promise that there could be a "system" and a connection between the disparate elements of the universe as it was experienced. As the Savior of the cosmos, the Logos had not snatched humanity out of the goodness of the created order, but had transformed the created order into a fit setting for a transformed humanity. And as the Goal of the cosmos, the Logos represented the hope that even the devil could finally be restored to wholeness in "the restitution of all things [*apokatastasis tōn pantōn*], and with the re-formation of the world humanity also shall be changed from the transient and the earthly to the incorruptible and the eternal."[51]

Yet lest we forget—and sometimes they do seem to have forgotten, though more often they remembered[52]—all of these metaphysical constructs of fourth-century Christian philosophers about the preexistent Word and Logos were supposed to find their religious and moral focus, and even their intellectual justification, in the historical figure of Jesus in the Gospels, in "the humble Word [*sermo humilis*]" and in "the glory of his passion" on the cross.[53] "In the beginning was the Word": this could have been said, and had been said, by many thinkers who had never heard of Jesus of Nazareth. But what made this portrait of the Logos as Cosmic Christ special was the declaration that the Word had become flesh in Jesus and that in Jesus the incarnate Word had suffered and died on the cross.[54] Yet if that declaration was true, there was ultimately no way to avoid declaring as well that nothing short of the cosmos was the object of the love that had come through him. For the Gospel of John, which opened with the Logos doctrine, went on to affirm, in its best-known verse: "God so loved the world that he gave his only Son, that whoever believes in him should not perish but have eternal life" (John 3:16). The "whoever" could indeed be taken to mean each individual, one at a time; but the Greek word for "world" in this passage was still *kosmos*.

6

The Son of Man

Behold the Man!

It is evident from the Gospels that Jesus' favorite designation for himself was "the Son of Man," which occurs about seventy times in the Synoptic Gospels and eleven or twelve times in the Gospel of John.[1] In the Hebrew Bible the term was sometimes a way of referring to humanity, with the meaning "mortal man."[2] But by the first century C.E. its usage within Judaism had acquired apocalyptic connotations, which it also carries in many of the sayings of Jesus: "As the lightning comes from the east and shines as far as the west, so will be the coming of the Son of man.... All the tribes of the earth will mourn, and they will see the Son of man coming on the clouds of heaven with power and great glory" (Matt. 24:27, 30). In Christian usage after the New Testament the title almost immediately regained its original significance, particularly because it came to be used to refer to the human nature of Jesus, in parallel with the term "Son of God," which referred to his divine nature.[3]

Thus it was that although Jesus had from the very beginning been seen by his followers as the disclosure of the mystery of the nature of divinity, it was only as their reflection on him deepened that they came to recognize what it fully meant that he was at the same time the revelation of the mystery of the nature of humanity, and that, in the formula of the Second Vatican Council, "only in the mystery of the incarnate Word does the mystery of man take on light."[4] Logically it might seem that it should have been the other way around: diagnosis should have preceded prescription. If the logic of Christian catechisms and sermons or of books on doctrinal theology from every historical period is any guide, the doctrine of the creation and fall of man must come first, to be followed by the doctrine of the person and work of Christ as the divine answer to the human predicament. But historically that was not how it developed, for the position of Jesus as the Son of God, the Logos, and the Cosmic Christ had to be clarified first, before there could come a mature understanding of the human predicament. Rather than making the punishment fit the crime, Christian thought had to gauge the magnitude of the human crime by first taking the measure of the one on whom the divine punishment of the cross had been imposed and thus (shifting to the original metaphor of salvation as health) making the diagnosis fit the prescription. "Long before [Christianity] had achieved its final triumph by dint of an impressive philosophy of religion," Harnack has said, "its success was already assured by the fact that it promised and offered salvation."[5] But it became "an impressive philosophy of religion" when it drew from its gospel of salvation through Jesus Christ the necessary implications for a doctrine of man.

The grim painting *Light* by the powerful twentieth-century American artist Siegfried Reinhardt documents this thesis that the dimensions of the human predicament become fully clear only in the light of its redemption. The crucified Christ, the *Ecce Homo*, appears at the top of the painting, but the light from which the work takes its name is revealed in the figure of the risen Christ, standing out in third dimension from the dark figure on the cross. He shakes his crown of thorns, as though it were a tambourine, and demands attention. But he does not get it. Violating all the rules of unity in painting, the two other figures are both facing away—one of them lost in her ecstasy, the other blowing his saxophone in the opposite direction. It is not only that in their self-indulgence they choose to ignore Jesus the light of the world. Rather, it is his very appearing that, for the first time, reveals to them their true condition. Both the misery and the grandeur have now become visible through the coming of that light. For, in the words of the Gospel of John, "This is the judgment, that the light has come into the world, and men loved darkness rather than light, because their deeds were evil. For every one who does evil hates the light, and does not come to the light, lest his deeds should be exposed" (John 3:19–20).

The definition of how it was that the coming of the light should have proved to be the revelation of darkness,[6] the identification of the crime, and the clarification of the diagnosis—all of this was the historic achievement of Augustine of Hippo, who died a century after the basic statement of the orthodox doctrine of Christ as the Second Person of the Trinity, "God from God, Light from Light," at the Council of Nicea. First Nicea had to determine what Jesus the Light *was* before Augustine could determine why He *had to be* what He was. The historical reasons for this sequence are complex, not least among them the intellectual and religious development of Augustine himself. But within and behind those historical reasons is a reason that is to be found within the human predicament itself, a reason formulated with characteristic precision and verve by a faithful disciple of Augustine who was born almost twelve centuries after Augustine died, the French scientist and Christian philosopher Blaise Pascal: "The knowledge of God without that of man's misery causes pride. The knowledge of man's misery without that of God causes despair. The knowledge of Jesus Christ constitutes the middle course, because in him we find both God and our misery.... [both misery and] grandeur."[7] Pascal was saying that it is easy for any view of human nature to recognize either misery or grandeur, but that combining them in one view and drawing from that combination the necessary philosophical and psychological consequences has proved to be far more difficult. For Pascal, and for Augustine before him, the combination was made possible by "the knowledge of Jesus Christ." In seeking to understand this chapter in the history of the images of Jesus, it may be helpful as well to call upon a distinction formulated by the nineteenth-century thinker Friedrich Schleiermacher, who declared that "if men are to be redeemed [in Jesus Christ], they must both be in need of redemption and be capable of receiving it"; to assert either the need or the capability without asserting the other was "heresy."[8] It was the genius of Augustine's picture of Jesus Christ as the key to both the grandeur and the misery of humanity that he managed to hold together that which made Christ and redemption possible and that which made Christ and redemption necessary. Thus "the pride of man may be cured through the humility of God" in the person and life of Jesus Christ.[9]

While much of what Augustine said about the human predicament and human misery was his own special insight, he was, in the use of the figure of Jesus to define the *grandeur* of humanity, attaching himself to what had preceded him in the thought of the second, third, and fourth centuries, as this had been summarized for example by Gregory of Nyssa: "In what then does the greatness of humanity consist, according to the doctrine of the church? Not in its likeness to the created world, but in its being in the image of the nature of the Creator."[10] In the fullest sense of the word, the true image of God for Gregory of Nyssa and for his successors was the man Jesus. Yet when the Word was made flesh in the man Jesus, this was human flesh and not any other kind of flesh, because humanity had been created in the image of God and the incarnation in Christ renewed that very image.[11] Although Augustine had, in the course of his controversies over original sin, sometimes spoken as though the image of God had been altogether obliterated through the fall of Adam, he made it clear upon further reflection near the end of his life that the doctrine of the fall must not be interpreted "as though man had lost everything he had of the image of God."[12]

For if the image of God had been totally destroyed by sin and the fall, there would have been no point of contact between human nature as such and the incarnation of the Logos in the truly human nature of Jesus.[13] Jesus was, then, not only the image of divinity, but the image of humanity as it had originally been intended to be and as through him it could now become; he was in this sense the "ideal man." By sending him, God had proved how deeply he loved humanity; for "he who did not spare his own Son but gave him up for us all, will he not also give us all things with him?" (Rom. 8:32). "But," as Augustine explained those words of Paul, "God loves us, such as we shall be, not such as we [now] are."[14] The contours of this future condition were already visible now, not in our empirical humanity but in the humanity of Jesus, the Word made flesh; and as it viewed that prospect, empirical human nature was filled with yearning and with a desire to press forward toward that ideal. Thus "Christ Jesus is the Mediator between God and men, not insofar as he is divine but insofar as he is human," as not only the source but also the "goal of all perfection."[15] He was both Alpha and Omega.

The human Jesus had not always held this position of importance in the thought of Augustine, even in his thought as a Christian. Thus in his early treatise *The Teacher*, he had said that to gain wisdom "we do not listen to anyone speaking and making sounds outside ourselves. We listen to Truth which presides over our minds within us, though of course we may be bidden to listen by someone using words." That inner teacher was called "Christ," who thus did not have to be the truly human person in the Gospels to perform this function, but seemed to act in some Platonic fashion as the recollection of a truth hidden deep within the soul.[16] The same emphasis is evident elsewhere, in his familiar words, "What then do you wish to know? I desire to know God and the soul. Nothing more? Nothing whatever."[17] He eventually became far more critical of the Platonic doctrine of recollection, and he acknowledged that he had had difficulty making the transition from the "immutability of the Logos, which I knew as well as I could and about which I did not have any doubts at all" (and which one did not have to be a Christian to accept) to the full meaning of the words of the Gospel of John, "The Logos was made flesh," which, Augustine confessed, he had come to understand "only somewhat later."[18] But once he did understand these words, the Logos made flesh, whose humility was made known in the narratives of the Gospels, dominated his language about Christ, in his expositions of the Psalms, which were for him the voice of Christ,[19] and in his exposition of the Gospel of John, whose teaching about the Logos as preexistent and incarnate and yet "lowly" made it the most "sublime" of the four Gospels.[20]

It was likewise from the portrait of the preexistent and incarnate Logos in the Gospel of John that Augustine, in the same years in which he was expounding that Gospel, developed the most sublime of his own psychological insights into the content of the image of God: the definition of the image as an image of the Trinity. He investigated the various "footprints of the Trinity," the ways in which the human mind by its very structure as single and yet possessing relationship within itself, as one and yet three, could be interpreted as a reflection of the relation between Father, Son, and Holy Spirit.[21] This has inspired one twentieth-century writer and literary critic, Dorothy L. Sayers, to explore the "creative imagination" as reflected in writing and in the arts and to find its analogies with the trinitarian "creative image," the structure of the Trinity as reflected in the historic Christian creeds and in the thought of Augustine.[22]

One of these "footprints of the Trinity," according to Augustine, was the trinity of being, knowledge, and will, capacities that were distinct within the mind and yet were one mind: "for I am, and I know, and I will."[23] Again, "when I ... love anything, there are three

realities involved: myself, and the beloved, and the love itself."[24]
Perhaps the most profound of the analogies was that of "memory,
understanding [*intelligentia*], and will," which "are not three lives but
one life, not three minds but one mind" and yet were not identical.[25]
Augustine freely conceded the inadequacy, and obviously sensed the
artificiality, of all such constructs, including the very language of the
ecclesiastical doctrine of the Trinity itself (which was necessary if faith
was not to remain altogether silent, but could not pretend to provide
an accurate description of the mystery of the inner life of God).[26] But
this much was certain: Jesus Christ was for the thought of the Catholic
Augustine the key to the mystery of the Trinity, and through it the
key to the mystery of the human mind.

Profound and provocative though this exploration of the psychological analogies to the Trinity in the human mind may have been,
Augustine's most important contribution to the history of human
psychology came in his doctrine of sin, his investigation, to use our
earlier terminology, of what had made Christ necessary rather than
of what had made Christ possible, of the *misery* rather than of the
grandeur of humanity. Walter Lippmann was referring above all to
Augustine's doctrine of sin when, in his column for 30 October 1941,
four months after the German invasion of the Soviet Union and five
weeks before Pearl Harbor, he was moved to reflect on the presence
within human nature of what he called "ice-cold evil":

> The modern skeptical world has been taught for some 200 years a concep-
> tion of human nature in which the reality of evil, so well known to the
> ages of faith, has been discounted. Almost all of us grew up in an envi-
> ronment of such easy optimism that we can scarcely know what is meant,
> though our ancestors knew it well, by the satanic will. We shall have to
> recover this forgotten but essential truth—along with so many others that
> we lost when, thinking we were enlightened and advanced, we were merely
> shallow and blind.[27]

In that thoughtful tribute to the Augustinian tradition of the "ages
of faith" Lippmann was joined during those very years by Reinhold
Niebuhr, whose Gifford Lectures, *The Nature and Destiny of Man* (delivered in 1939 and published in 1941–43), were an effort at a critical
restatement of Augustinian anthropology.

What role did the figure of Jesus play in Augustinian anthropology?
The most fundamental component in any answer to that question is
to be sought in an assessment of his *Confessions* and of its form and

tone.[28] For in its literary structure it is, from the first sentence to the last, one long prayer, which is of course why it is called a confession, defined as accusation of oneself and praise of God.[29] The principal literary inspiration for the prayer comes from the Latin Psalter, which Augustine seems to have known by heart and from which he could, as a kind of contrapuntal virtuoso, spin out rhapsodic cadenzas.[30] But because he read the Psalms as the voice of Christ, the principal religious inspiration for his *Confessions* was his awareness of the grace of God which he had come to know in Christ through the Catholic Church.

It was, then, "in the permissive atmosphere of God's felt presence" and grace that he wrote the prayer of the *Confessions*.[31] Even though there is inevitably a certain amount of self-deception in any such memoir, Augustine could speak with as much candor as he did in the *Confessions* because the sin he was confessing was the sin that God in Christ had forgiven.[32] He was expressing the "sacrifice of my confessions" in the presence of a God whose eye could penetrate into even the most closed of hearts and had penetrated even into his, and to whom therefore it was not possible to lie. But he was also expressing the "confession of a broken and contrite heart" in the presence of a God whose grace "through Jesus Christ our Lord" had granted him deliverance from the power of sin, and to whom therefore it was not necessary to lie. It was Christ, as "our very Life" who "bore our death," to whom, Augustine said, "my soul confesses, and he heals it, because it had sinned against him."[33] And in a series of apostrophes to Christ scattered throughout the *Confessions*, Augustine gave devotional expression to what he asserted and defended elsewhere as dogma: that Jesus Christ was the Son of God, the source of grace, the ground of hope, and the worthy object of prayer, adoration, and confession.[34]

Standing then in the presence of God in Christ and probing both his own soul and his own memory, Augustine in the *Confessions* focused his attention on various sins of his youth, at least two of which have achieved considerable psychological notoriety. One of these, described at the beginning of book 3, was being "in love with loving" but not knowing the true nature of love.[35] As T. S. Eliot paraphrases Augustine's words,[36]

To Carthage then I came
Burning burning burning burning

O Lord Thou pluckest me out
O Lord Thou pluckest
burning.

If lust is defined, in keeping with both the Hebrew Bible and the New Testament, not as natural sexual desire but as the tendency to regard another person as primarily a sex object, Augustine's probing of the hidden fires of sexuality begins to seem considerably less quaint than it may appear at first.[37] Alongside the undeniable extremes to which he often went in his language about sexual desire, even about sexual desire within the boundaries of matrimony, he was at the same time rejecting the heretical notion that "marriage and fornication are two evils, of which the second is worse," and substituting for it the orthodox Catholic principle that "marriage and continence are two goods, of which the second is better," which, whatever modern readers may think of it, did have warrant both in the teachings of Jesus himself and in those of the apostle Paul, as well as in those of noble pagans of late antiquity.[38] The clinching argument in favor of the holiness of marriage came for Augustine from some other words of the apostle Paul: "Husbands, love your wives, as Christ loved the church and gave himself up for it. . . . This is a great sacrament [*magnum sacramentum*], and I take it to mean Christ and the church."[39] Marriage was a sacrament of Christ and the church.

The other sin mentioned in the *Confessions* that has provoked great psychological interest is the famous anecdote of the pear tree, with which book 2 closes.[40] "Rum thing to see a man making a mountain out of robbing a peartree in his teens," commented Justice Holmes on this story.[41] But as a close reading of the entire passage will show, Augustine's recollection of the incident provided him with an opportunity to probe the mysterious depths of the motivation of evil acts. The pears were not particularly attractive to him, nor did he find them very good to eat; he did not need them. What he did need was to steal them, and having satisfied that need, he threw them to the pigs. Even though he might not have done it without the company of his peer group who egged him on, it was not their companionship but the theft itself that he loved. When, in summarizing the incident, he speaks of having "become to myself an unfruitful land," he is, in his characteristic allegorical fashion, echoing the story of the Garden of Eden and of what an English poet and theologian steeped in Augustine was to call

> the fruit
> Of that forbidden tree, whose mortal taste
> brought death into the world, and all our woe,
> With loss of Eden, till one greater Man
> Restore us, and regain the blissful seat.[42]

It was that "greater Man," Jesus Christ, in whose "fruits" the soul, liberated from the tyranny of irrational sin, could now "rejoice."[43] Therefore he was the Second Adam, through whom the grace of God had prevailed over the sin and death that had come upon humanity through the First Adam.[44]

While Augustine's theory about the misery of humanity was thus in one sense highly personal and downright autobiographical, he rejected indignantly any suggestion that he was only extrapolating from his personal views and experiences and generalizing these into a universal condition.[45] Rather, he was seeking to take account of what already was, empirically speaking, recognizable as a universal condition. For if, as some people seemed to think, every human being was exactly poised between good and evil and thus faced the very same choice that Adam and Eve had faced,[46] how was one to account for the statistical regularity with which every human being managed to make the same choice that Adam and Eve had made, in favor of sin and against the good?[47] This was not to deny that there could be "on earth righteous men, great men—brave, prudent, chaste, patient, pious, merciful"; yet even they could not be "without sin."[48] Who was more holy than the saints and apostles? "And yet the Lord [Jesus] prescribed to them to say in their prayer, 'Forgive us our debts.' "[49]

There was only one unqualified exception to the rule, Jesus Christ as the Mediator between a righteous God and a sinful humanity; and he was, to use a cliché that in this case is not a cliché at all, the exception that proves the rule.[50] For it was his status as the sinless Savior that proved the necessity of salvation, and anyone who denied the universality of sin was obliged, for the sake of consistency, to deny the universality of the salvation and mediation accomplished in him. This was for Augustine the decisive argument in his analysis of the human condition. For all "ordinary" people, death was not only universal but involuntary: there might be some choice about whether to die at this time or at that time, but no choice about whether to die or not to die. The exception was Jesus Christ, who was not mortal by nature but who "died for mortals" and therefore was the only one who could say of himself: "I lay down my life, that I may take it again. No one takes it from me; I lay it down of my own accord."[51] Augustine's most influential insight into human nature and psychology, the idea of original sin, was therefore not only a way of speaking about the misery of humanity, but a means of recognizing and praising the uniqueness of Jesus.

Despite the sensitivity and frankness of the introspection at work in the *Confessions*, it seems safe to say that he would not have come to this insight without the illumination of Christ, reasoning backward from the cure to the diagnosis. Further substantiation for that hypothesis comes from his use of the Virgin Birth.[52] The assertion that Jesus was born of the Virgin Mary without a human father appears in the Gospels of Matthew and Luke, though without any specific explanation of its significance; but it is absent from the other two Gospels, as well as from the epistles of Paul, whose statement that Christ was "born of woman" meant that Jesus was fully and truly human,[53] but did not imply anything one way or the other about human paternity. It remained for Augustine, together with his mentor Ambrose, to draw from the Virgin Birth the conclusion that since Jesus "alone could be born in such a way as not to need to be reborn," all those who were born in the normal way, as the result of the sexual union of their parents, were in need of being reborn in Christ through baptism.[54] The statement of the Psalmist, "Behold, I was brought forth in iniquity, and in sin did my mother conceive me," was spoken in the awareness of forgiveness through the "selfsame faith" in Christ that was now confessed by the Catholic Church.[55] That was why Augustine entitled the treatise just quoted *On the Grace of Christ and Original Sin*; for he found the knowledge of the grace of Christ unintelligible without the knowledge of original sin, but he also saw that the knowledge of original sin was unbearable without a knowledge of the grace of Christ.

Jesus was the only unqualified exception that Augustine would grant to the rule of the universality of original sin. There was, however, one other exception that he had to consider: Mary the Virgin Mother of Jesus. After rejecting the contention that various other saints, both male and female, had been totally sinless, Augustine continued: "We must except the Holy Virgin Mary, concerning whom I wish to raise no question when it touches the subject of sins, *out of honor to the Lord*; for from him we know what abundance of grace for overcoming sin in every particular was conferred upon her who had the merit to conceive and to bear him who undoubtedly had no sin."[56] The outcome of that additional exception was to have a profound effect not only on devotion and theology, but on art and literature for the next fifteen centuries. It took almost exactly a thousand years before a church council (the Council of Basel in 1439) would define the doctrine that among mortals Mary alone had been conceived without sin, and even that council was found not to have had the right to define it. Thus it was only in 1854 that Pope Pius IX made the doctrine binding that, "in view of the merits of Christ Jesus, the Savior of the [entire] human race," which included her, Mary had been permitted to become an exception to the universality of original sin.[57] But long before it became a dogma, the immaculate conception of Mary was the subject quite literally of thousands of paintings and poems, in which, with infinite variations on the theme, Augustine's phrase "out of honor to the Lord" found expression in the use of the figure of Mary as a means of celebrating the figure of Jesus: the familiar theme of late medieval painters, the coronation of the Virgin, for example, shows her receiving the crown from her divine Son. Conversely, whenever devotion or speculation glorified Christ as Lord and King in such a way as to lose touch with the Man of Nazareth, Mary would become a substitute for him—human, compassionate, accessible. And then the devotion to her and the speculation about her were no longer being carried on "out of honor to the Lord."

"Know thyself" was a motto carved on the temple of the oracle at Delphi. As the linking of the Delphic oracle and the prophet Isaiah suggests,[58] others before Augustine had applied that axiom, often attributing it to Socrates, to the need for a self-understanding in the light of Christ, and Etienne Gilson is certainly correct in speaking about what he calls "Christian Socratism"; but it is significant that he refers in that context above all to the "profound psychological speculations of Saint Augustine."[59] Those speculations had grown out of Augustine's existential needs, but they had led him to Jesus, "the humble Word," and to "the glory of his passion."[60] Here alone it was that he was able to confront, to understand, and to articulate those needs, for the Jesus of Augustine was the key to what humanity was and to what, through Jesus, it could become. As he said in the opening words of the *Confessions:*

> Great art thou, O Lord, and greatly to be praised. . . . And man desires to praise thee, for he is a part of thy creation—man, who bears about with him his mortality, the witness of his sin. . . . Thou hast made us for thyself,

and restless is our heart until it comes to rest in thee. . . . I call upon thee, O Lord, in my faith, which thou hast given me, which thou hast inspired in me through the humanity of thy Son.

7

The True Image

He is the image of the invisible
God.

The victory of Jesus Christ over the gods of Greece and Rome in the fourth century did not, as both friend and foe might have expected, bring about the demise of religious art;[1] on the contrary, it was responsible over the next fifteen centuries for a massive and magnificent outpouring of creativity that is probably without parallel in the entire history of art. How and why did that happen? How could Jesus have evolved from the very antithesis of all representations of the divine in images to become their most important concrete inspiration—and eventually their principal theoretical justification?

In the Ten Commandments of Moses, whose permanent validity Christians also accepted,[2] the prohibition of religious art as idolatrous was explicit and comprehensive: "You shall not make for yourself a graven image, or any likeness of anything that is in heaven above, or that is in the earth beneath, or that is in the water under the earth" (Ex. 20:4). Quoting such prohibitions from the Hebrew Bible as well as the opinions of such pagan thinkers as Cicero that "the deities which men worshiped were false," the followers of Jesus claimed to be joining themselves both to Judaism and to the best in classical paganism when they rejected images, but they chided enlightened pagans for their elitism and inconsistency in allowing the "vulgar and ignorant" to keep their images.[3] What was more, they went beyond

Judaism in denouncing as well the very notion of religious architecture: "The God who made the world and everything in it, being Lord of heaven and earth, does not live in shrines made by man."[4] They took the prohibition of images to apply not only to the idolaters who worshiped them but even to the artists who made them, who were practicing a "deceptive art," and they celebrated those "who refuse to look at any temples and altars."[5] Thus in contradistinction to paganism and in some ways even to Judaism, they claimed, in the name of the revelation of the divine that had come in Jesus, to be proclaiming a God who transcended all efforts of human hands to devise sacred images; for it was the rational soul that was the "image of God."[6] There were neither sacred images nor sacred places; not even the places where Jesus had been born and buried were possessed of any special holiness.[7]

Thanks to archaeological research at Dura Europos, carried on during the twentieth century, we know now, to an extent that previous generations of scholars did not, that the absolute prohibition of images in the law of Moses did not deter the Judaism contemporary with early Christianity from making holy pictures and exhibiting them in its places of worship. "The Dura Synagogue," according to Carl Kraeling, was "with its decorations one of the finest and most fitting monuments of ancient Judaism," and "the paintings of Dura can properly be called forerunners of Byzantine art."[8] Kraeling distinguished the work of two Jewish artists in the synagogue at Dura; one of them he characterized as a "Symbolist," which is not so surprising, but the other was a "Representationalist." It has even been suggested that "illustration archetypes [of the Dura frescoes] illuminated Greek copies of Biblical materials: translations like the Septuagint; Greek paraphrases of separate books or scripture sections; or other Greek literary types, such as epics or tragedies or histories, composed by Hellenistic Jews on Biblical themes."[9] Yet in the conclusion of his work Kraeling warns:

> A close study of the literary tradition indicates that the Christians, having adopted the Bible of the Jewish people, had to grapple with the selfsame prohibition of the use of images that had so much preoccupied the Jews of the post-Maccabean period, and found no easy solution. Even after Palestinian Judaism had found the way toward a more liberal interpretation of the Biblical commandment, Christian writers were still taking a conservative position in their discussion of it.[10]

Despite the intriguing and undeniable parallels between the artistic practice of early Christianity and that of Hellenistic Judaism, whether in Palestine or in the Diaspora, therefore, we may not explain the Christian development simply as an adaptation of the Jewish. Doing that would oversimplify the special qualities and the special problems of both. For early Christianity, those special qualities and special problems were clearly the ones associated with the life and person of Jesus. Although it had confronted these problems from the very beginning,[11] it was only with the challenge to the use of images in the eighth and ninth centuries that the orthodox Byzantine interpreters of the person and message of Jesus were compelled to articulate a comprehensive philosophical and theological aesthetic based on the person of Christ, an aesthetic within which the legitimacy of drawing images of the divine would take its proper place.[12]

Fundamental to any consideration of the issues in the aesthetics of Byzantine iconography was the unanimous affirmation of the New Testament and the fathers of the early church that, in a special and unique sense, "the image of God is his Logos, the genuine Son of Mind, the divine Logos, the archetypal light of light," as Clement of Alexandria had put it in an elaboration on the theme suggested by the Epistle to the Colossians;[13] for, in the formula of Vladimir Lossky, "it is in the context of the Incarnation (say rather: it is by the fact, by the event of the Incarnation) that the creation of man in the image of God receives all its theological value."[14] If, following Whitehead, as noted in the introduction to this book, we should look in any controversy of the past for the "fundamental assumptions which adherents of all the variant systems within the epoch unconsciously presuppose,"[15] the assumption that Jesus Christ was uniquely the image of God was shared by the proponents of both major alternatives in the controversies of the eighth and ninth centuries over images. But from this theological asssumption concerning Jesus Christ they drew conclusions about religious art that were diametrically opposed.

The earliest application of this assumption to the question of religious art came from the opponents of images.[16] Constantia, the sister of the emperor Constantine, wrote to Eusebius of Caesarea requesting an image of Christ. He replied: "I do not know what has impelled you to command that an image of our Savior be drawn. Which image of Christ do you want? Is it to be a true and unchangeable one, portraying his countenance truly, or is it to be the one which he assumed on our behalf when he took on the appearance of the 'form of a slave'?"[17] The alternatives as formulated by Eusebius bear careful consideration in their implications for iconography. In his bemusement at Constantia's interest in an image of Christ, Eusebius apparently could not imagine that anyone would be interested in an image of that countenance which Christ "assumed on our behalf when he took on the appearance of the 'form of a slave,' " for that was transitory and not permanently relevant—even though, presumably, an eyewitness in Jerusalem who saw Jesus in the flesh during the first century could have drawn such a picture of him or even, technology permitting, could have photographed him. But that would not have been "a true image" of the one who was himself the True Image. For Eusebius, a "true" image of that Image would have to be unchangeable, for only that would "portray his countenance truly." And such an image was, by definition, impossible. Thus the demands of the authentic doctrine of the person of Christ precluded, for Eusebius, any attempt at an image.

Eusebius became the "coryphaeus and acropolis"[18] for the iconoclasts of the eighth and especially of the ninth century, because he had put the issue of Christ as image at the center of the debate on the question of images. In applying the concept of Christ as Image to the issue, the iconoclasts invoked the authority of the councils of the fourth and fifth century, at which the status of Christ as the Image of the Father had been definitively formulated. The only way an image of Christ could be a true image was in the same way that Christ himself was the True Image of the Father. The Council of Nicea in 325 had formulated the meaning of the status of Christ as the true image of the Father within the Holy Trinity by declaring that he was "one in being" with the one whom he imaged.[19] Therefore, according to Emperor Constantine V, an icon of Christ could not be a true image of him unless it too was "one in being" with him, in the same way that Christ the Son of God was one in being with the Father.[20] Obviously, no work of art made by human hands—nor even, for that matter, the images supposedly made without hands, by angels[21]— could ever hope to meet such a qualification. The only image of Christ that could be said to be "one in being" with Christ in the same sense that Christ was one in being with the Father was the Eucharist, which contained the real presence of the body and blood of Christ. According to Constantine, the bread of the Eucharist was truly "an image of his body, taking the form of his flesh and having become a type of his body."[22] "It has been laid down for us," the iconoclasts taught, "that Christ *is* to be portrayed in an image, but only as the holy teaching transmitted by divine tradition says: 'Do this in remembrance of me.' Therefore it is evidently not permitted to portray him in an image or to carry out a remembrance of him in any other way, since this portrayal [in the Eucharist] is true and this way of portraying is sacred."[23] Thus the Eucharist, as an image that everyone had to agree was one in being with its original, precluded every other so-called image of Christ.

After the Council of Nicea in 325, the most important church council was that held at Chalcedon in 451, at which the relation between the divine nature and the human nature in Christ was set down in a formula that has continued for fifteen centuries to be the definition of orthodox belief about the person of Jesus.[24] On the basis of the formulas of Chalcedon, the opponents of images insisted that Christ, as the True Image of God, was "beyond description, beyond comprehension, beyond change, and beyond measure," since such transcendence was characteristic of God.[25] They seem to have held that this rule applied even to the miracles and to the sufferings of Christ in the days of his flesh, which it was "illegitimate to portray in images."[26] Whatever the status of Christ "before the passion and the resurrection" may have been, however, latter-day artists in any case had no right to attempt to portray him now; for now "the body of Christ is incorruptible, having inherited immortality," and that was beyond the competence of any artistic representation.[27] Invoking the orthodox dogma of Christ, formulated by Chalcedon, as consisting of two natures, divine and human, in a single person, they put their opposition to images of Christ in the form of a disjunctive syllogism. Either those who painted images of Christ were portraying his deity by an icon, or they were not: if they were, they violated its essential nature as being beyond description and circumscription; if they were not, they were separating the two natures of Christ and thus dividing his single person. In either case they were guilty of blasphemy and heresy against the person of Christ as this had been defined by the orthodox church councils, particularly those of Nicea and Chalcedon. As the emperor Constantine V, perhaps the most profound theoretician among the iconoclasts, put it, "if someone makes an image of Christ, . . . he has not really penetrated the depths of the dogma of the inseparable union of the two natures of Christ" as formulated by those two councils.[28]

Underlying these aspersions on the artistic portrayal of Jesus Christ appears to have been a deep-seated aversion to the material and physical aspects of his person: "It is degrading and demeaning to depict Christ with material representations. For one should confine oneself to the mental observation [of him] . . . through sanctification and righteousness."[29] By focusing the gaze of the viewer on these "degrading and demeaning" qualities of the man Jesus, the portrayal of him in an image inevitably diverted the attention from what was important about him, his transcendent rather than his immanent qualities. As the defenders of the gospel against the Greeks had long been able to quote the best of the Greeks in insisting, the requirement both of the Platonic tradition and of the Gospel of John, "God is spirit, and those who worship him must worship in spirit and truth," was being violated whenever the outward physical picture was substituted for the spirit and whenever the deception of the icon replaced the truth.[30] The Christian opponents of images in Byzantium during the eighth and ninth centuries, therefore, had behind them a distinguished history—Jewish, Greek, and Christian—of the struggle to extricate the divine from the unworthy physical representations of the divine. Jesus Christ himself was the True Image, every other image was false.[31]

"We join you in declaring that the Son is the Image of God the Father," the defenders of the icons said to the iconoclasts.[32] That was, in Whitehead's phrase, the fundamental assumption presupposed by all the adherents of all the variant systems of the epoch. But the Jesus Christ who was the True Image was the one who had been made human, and thus physical and material, by his incarnation and birth from the Virgin Mary, and therefore a Christian icon was not an idol but an image of the Image: such was in essence the case for a Christian art.[33] The logical implication of the view of Christ set forth in the orthodox tradition, as this was being cited by the iconoclasts, was a justification for the representation of Christ in pictures. This case for images in Christian art was set into the context of a total theory of images, which was yet another illustration of the artful combination of biblical and philosophical perspectives, of Hebrew and Greek language, to which we have pointed several times. All reality, both divine and human, participated one way or another in what might be called a great chain of images. For it was mistaken to charge that images were a novelty recently invented by those who were seeking to smuggle idolatry back into the churches. Who invented images? "God himself was the first" to do so, John of Damascus replied.[34] *God was the first and the original image-maker of the universe.*

In the most fundamental sense of the word *image*, the Son of God was uniquely the Image of God, "the living Image, who is his image in his very nature, who is the image of the invisible Father differing in no way from him" except by being the Son rather than the Father.[35] As the Epistle to the Colossians said, "He is the image of the invisible God" (Col. 1:15). The worship of the Son of God was therefore not idolatrous, because, in the oft-quoted formula of Basil of Caesarea, "the honor paid to the image [the Son] passes over to the prototype [the Father]."[36] All the other images in the chain of images had the right to be called "image" by some sort of participation in this primal and eternal image-making within the Holy Trinity. Even the Holy Spirit was, in turn, the image of the Son, since "no one can say 'Jesus is Lord' except by the Holy Spirit" (1 Cor. 12:3). Quite apart from human history, therefore, there was, in the very life of the Godhead, an image-making and an image-manifesting, which expressed the mystery of the eternal relation of Father, Son, and Holy Spirit. In this sense, the Son of God before the incarnation was not only "the image of the invisible God," but "the invisible image of the invisible God," unknown and unknowable except as he chose to make himself known and visible.

In a secondary and derivative sense, image could be taken to refer to the "images and paradigms in God of the things that are to be produced by him." Because God was absolute and unchangeable, with "no variation" (James 1:17), he did not, as the Artist-Maker of the cosmos, create the particulars of the empirical world directly. Instead, creation consisted in the designing of these images and paradigms, which could be called the "predeterminations [*proorismoi*]" of the empirical world.[37] Before any particular reality came into being as such, it had, as image, been predetermined within the "counsel [*boulē*]" of God, and in that sense it already possessed reality. That reality preceding the empirical was best exemplified in the work of a human architect, who, "before a house is constructed, already images in his mind the scheme and plan of what it is to be." For the tradition of Christian Neoplatonism expressed by the philosophers of the fourth century, these images of an empirical world yet to be were produced by and through the Logos, the cosmic Christ, since "all things were made through him, and without him was not anything made that was made" (John 1:3). God created the world we see through the Logos, his Image, who in turn called into being the Platonic forms, the images from which that world would come.

Although the entire created world was in this sense an image of God, or perhaps more precisely an image of the Image of God, the human creature had a special claim to that honorific title. For in the creation story of the Book of Genesis, the God of Israel was said to have created man in his own image. What is more, he had done so after taking counsel with himself: "Let us make man in our image, after our likeness" (Gen. 1:26). Whatever these Hebrew plurals in Genesis may have meant originally, Christian interpreters had, almost "in the beginning," taken them to refer to a counsel between the Father and the Son within the mystery of the Trinity;[38] and Augustine had even used them as the basis for his provocative hypothesis, discussed earlier, that the very image of God in man was itself trinitarian in structure.[39] For the image of God the Creator in man the creature was an example of an image "by imitation," mirroring forth in the structure of human life and thought the nature of God the image-maker. Thus the God who in the law on Sinai prohibited the making of images had himself made such an image in the very creature who was then forbidden to become an image-maker; and the polemic against images in early Christian thought had often been based on this very argument, that a living God could not have wood and stone as a fitting image, but only the rational soul of his supreme creature.[40] Hence the command not to make images was based not on a degraded view of images, but on an exalted one: because a proper image of God could only be something as noble as the human mind, it demeaned both God the image-maker and man the image to attempt to substitute for it some less worthy picture.

In addition to these usages of the word *image,* which we may call metaphysical, there were historical usages. Because of the way the human mind was constructed, it could not perceive spiritual reality except through the use of physical images. It could not describe even "creatures" that were nonphysical, such as angels, except by employing "physical" language.[41] The Bible itself had accommodated its ways of speaking to this characteristic of human thought and language, presenting its sublime content by means of simple and even homely analogies. For by no mental acrobatics was it possible to go around such analogies to a purely intellectual and spiritual vision of God; rather, "ever since the creation of the world his invisible nature, namely, his eternal power and deity, has been clearly perceived in the things that have been made" (Rom. 1:20). In these visible realities of the empirical and historical world, therefore, there were images of the transcendent being of God, and it was unavoidable to use these temporal realities as metaphors for the eternal reality, as the images and symbols for the Trinity itself showed.

As biblical usage likewise made clear, historical images of this kind could move in either direction within time, describing either "the things that are yet to be in the future" or "the things that have already happened in the past." According to the Christian way of reading it, the Hebrew Bible was filled with images and anticipations of what was to be fulfilled with the coming of Jesus. They were real in and of themselves: Israel did cross the Red Sea during the exodus from Egypt, on a date that historical research was, at least in principle, capable of fixing. But at the same time they were images of what was to come: the crossing of the Red Sea was a "type" of Christian baptism. On the other hand, there were likewise images that were intended to serve as "monuments of past events, of some wondrous achievement or of some virtue, for glory and honor and remembrance." A book of history written as a memorial of past events was such an image, whose purpose it was to inform later generations about what had happened and thus to instruct them about virtue and vice. Non-literary images in memory of historical events and personages were intrinsically no different from books; they were, in fact, "books for the illiterate," differing from the Bible only in form but not in content.[42]

Between these two categories of images, the metaphysical and the historical, however, there was a great gulf fixed. So long as there was such a gulf, the only possible justification for religious art was the didactic one represented by the phrase "books for the illiterate." Idolatry was the vain attempt of the human worshiper to cross the gulf, by pretending that an artistic, historical image mounted on the wall or held in the hand was in fact a cosmic and metaphysical image with some genuine affinity to the First Principle of the universe. The prohibition of graven images in the Second Commandment was the divine assertion and restraint preserving the gulf. But that gulf—indeed, every gulf, including the very separation between the visible and the invisible, between time and eternity—had been bridged when the Logos became flesh. The incarnation of the cosmic and metaphysical Logos in the this-worldly and historical person of Jesus of Nazareth supplied what one can only call the missing link in the great chain of images. The fallacy of misplaced concreteness, by which idolatry had correctly intuited an identity of images in the abstract but had falsely executed it in the concrete, had now been replaced by the concrete events of the life of Jesus as described in the Gospels, as recounted by John of Damascus in what sounds like a catalogue raisonné of Byzantine icons:

> Because the one who by excellency of nature transcends all quantity and size and magnitude, who has his being in the form of God, has now, by taking upon himself the form of a slave, contracted himself into a quantity and size and has acquired a physical identity, do not hesitate any longer to draw pictures and to set forth, for all to see, him who has chosen to let himself be seen: his ineffable descent from heaven to earth; his birth from the Virgin; his baptism in the Jordan; his transfiguration on Mount Tabor; the sufferings that have achieved for us freedom from suffering; the miracles that symbolized his divine nature and activity when they were performed through the activity of his [human] flesh; the burial, resurrection, and ascension into heaven by which the Savior has accomplished our salvation—describe all of these events, both in words and in colors, both in books and in pictures.[43]

Thus the God who had prohibited religious art as the idolatrous effort to depict the divine in visible form had now taken the initiative of depicting himself in visible form, and had done so not in metaphor or in memorial but in person and, quite literally, "in the flesh." The metaphysical had become historical, and the cosmic Logos who was the true image of the Father from eternity had now become a part of time and could be portrayed in an image of his divine-human person as this had carried out the events of salvation history. The creation of Adam and Eve in the image of God had been an anticipation of the coming of Jesus the Second Adam and of Mary the Second Eve, so that the depiction of Christ and of his Mother could be at the same time the description of the true image of God in humanity. The image portrayed him in the individual specificity of his unique person, not as humanity in the abstract. Nevertheless, the humanity of Jesus depicted in the icons, and by derivation the humanity of his saints and of all who had been made alive in him, was a humanity suffused with the presence of divinity: it was, in this sense, the "deified" body of Christ that was being portrayed, and the most characteristic Eastern Orthodox way of speaking about the salvation granted in Christ has been to call it "deification" (*theōsis* in Greek, *obozhenie* in Russian).[44] The iconography of the icon (to resort deliberately to an almost unavoidable tautology) was well designed to carry out both of these themes simultaneously: specificity and deification, and therefore what one of the most profound twentieth-century interpreters of icons, Evgenii Nikolaevich Trubetskoi, has called "theory of colors" or "contemplation in images."[45]

An icon of Christ Pantocrator, Christ the All-Sovereign, which is probably to be dated to the sixth century and was probably produced at Constantinople, embodies that very combination of specificity and deification. It belongs to that small but important group preserved at the Monastery of Saint Catherine on Mount Sinai. One of the consequences of the thoroughness with which the iconoclasts carried out their task is the small number of preiconoclastic icons still in existence.[46] Among these Christ Pantocrator holds a special place, now that it has been found under the layers of later paint that had covered it. This is a specific human face, but in it, as André Grabar has said, "the artist achieves an effect of aloofness and timelessness, a pictorial expression of the divine nature." And yet, he continues, the artist has managed to use "abstracting features along with more naturalistic ones" so subtly that he "has been able to convey pictorially the dogma of the two natures of Christ, the divine and the human."[47] "The all-sovereign God, the Logos [*ho Pantokratōr Theos Logos*]" had long been one of the titles for Christ.[48] By depicting the indissoluble union between the timeless nature of the All-Sovereign and the historical nature of Jesus of Nazareth, this Byzantine icon of Christ Pantocrator succeeded in conceptualizing the one who was the embodiment not only of the True in his teaching and of the Good in his life, but of the Beautiful in his form as "the fairest of the sons of men" (Ps. 45:2).

Within that triad of the Beautiful, the True, and the Good, invoked in the introduction to this book as a way of expressing the many facets of the meaning of Jesus for human culture, it was the Beautiful that took by far the longest time to evolve. One of Augustine's early books, since lost except for his occasional references to it, was called *On the Beautiful and the Fitting*.[49] In one of the most memorable passages of his *Confessions* he exclaimed: "Too late have I loved Thee, Thou Beauty

ever ancient, ever new, too late have I come to love Thee!"[50] Yet if
Augustine may be said to have a theory of the Beautiful, it is worked
out the most successfully in his analysis of language and its meaning,
in connection with his aesthetic of signs,[51] and in his treatise *On Music*,
both of which were to shape medieval aesthetic theory and practice
in the Latin West for a thousand years.

But for the Christian justification of religious art, it was only with
the ninth century and in the Greek East that an exploration and
application of the deeper significance of the person of Jesus appeared.
As the iconoclasts saw with great clarity, the Beautiful was (and is)
the most subtle and the most dangerous of the triad: the dangers of
identifying the Holy with the True (intellectualism) and with the Good
(moralism) have manifested themselves repeatedly in the history of
Judaism and of Christianity, but it is noteworthy that both the Second
Commandment itself and the message of the Hebrew prophets singled out the identification of the Holy with the Beautiful as the special
temptation to sin. The formulation of an aesthetic that came to terms
with the reality of this temptation called for philosophical and theological sophistication. In addition, of course, there had to have been
an inspiration for religious art, an inspiration of more than a flatly
didactic sort, before there could be any such aesthetic justification;
and a sophisticated philosophical-theological challenge to religious
art was necessary before any sophisticated defense of it was possible.
All of this—the inspiration and the challenge and the justification—
was eventually provided by the person of Jesus, who came to be seen
as both the ground of continuity in art and the source of innovation
for art, and thus, in a sense that Augustine could not have intended,
as a "beauty ever ancient, ever new."

8
Christ Crucified

Far be it from me to glory except in the cross of our Lord Jesus Christ, by which the world has been crucified to me, and I to the world.

The followers of Jesus came very early to the conclusion that he had lived in order to die, that his death was not the interruption of his life at all but its ultimate purpose.[1] Even by the most generous reading, the Gospels give us information about less than a hundred days in the life of Jesus; but for the last two or three days of his life, they provide a detailed, almost hour-by-hour scenario. And the climax of that scenario is the account of Good Friday and of his three hours on the cross. The Apostles' Creed and the Nicene Creed recognized this when they moved directly from his birth "from the Virgin Mary" to his crucifixion "under Pontius Pilate." What was said of the thane of Cawdor in *Macbeth* was true preeminently of Jesus: "Nothing in his life / Became him like the leaving it."[2]

It was above all the apostle Paul who formulated this distinctive place of the death on the cross. "Far be it from me," he said, "to glory except in the cross of our Lord Jesus Christ, by which the world has been crucified to me, and I to the world" (Gal. 6:14). But the gospel of the cross pervades the New Testament and early Christian literature. Christ was the "Lamb of God, who takes away the sin of

the world" (John 1:29). The prophecy of the fifty-third chapter of the
Book of Isaiah about the suffering servant who was "wounded for
our transgressions, bruised for our iniquities" was taken to refer to
Jesus on the cross.[3] The use of the sign of the cross, as a mark of
identification and a means of warding off the power of demons, is
not mentioned as such in the New Testament; but it appears very
early in Christian history, and when it is mentioned it is already being
taken for granted. Tertullian declares that "at every forward step and
movement, at every going in and out . . . in all the ordinary actions
of daily life, we mark upon our foreheads the sign," and the sign of
the cross became the prime evidence for the existence of an unwritten
tradition that everyone observed even though it was not commanded
in the Bible.[4] Those who did not belong to the church could not help
noticing the practice. The emperor Julian, whom Christians called
"the Apostate" because he had forsaken the Christianity of his childhood, complained to the Christians in the fourth century: "You adore
the wood of the cross and draw its likeness on your foreheads and
engrave it on your housefronts";[5] when, in one of the most widely
read novels to come out of World War II, a ship was torpedoed and
was sinking, one of the crew noticed another "crossing himself, and
remembered that he was a Roman Catholic";[6] and on 15 March 1897,
Gustav Mahler, while visiting Moscow, observed that its people were
"incredibly bigoted. Every two steps there's an icon or a church, and
every passer-by stops, beats his breast, and makes the sign of the
cross as is customary in Russia."[7] (The "customary" way of doing so
in Russia is, of course, from the right shoulder to the left, rather than
from the left to the right as in the West, and aficionados of spy stories
will recall that many a Western operative whose Russian accent was
impeccable blew his cover when, at table, he made the sign of the
cross the wrong way.)

As Mahler observed in czarist Russia, the sign of the cross of Jesus
Christ pervaded the culture and folklore of the nations of medieval
Europe—their literature, music, art, and architecture—as no other
symbol had. To lend at least some coherence to this welter of cruciform
impressions in the culture of the Middle Ages, it may be useful to
draw upon a distinction that comes from the apostle Paul. "We preach
Christ crucified," he wrote, "the power of God and the wisdom of
God" (1 Cor. 1:23–24). For although ultimately there is, as Augustine
saw in explaining these words, no clear division in biblical usage

between the power of God and the wisdom of God, the distinction does help.[8]

As the power of God, the sign of the cross was a talisman against evil. Medieval lives of the saints, both Eastern and Western, are replete with stories of its wondrous powers. In one of the apocryphal *Acts* of the apostles, for example, making the sign of the cross over a locked door causes it to open miraculously for the apostles to enter; and in one of the *Martyrdoms*, it is successful in silencing the barking of a dog.[9] Augustine reports that a woman in Carthage, suffering from cancer of the breast, "was instructed in a dream to wait for the first woman who would come out of the baptistery after being baptized, and to ask here to make the sign of Christ [the sign of the cross] upon her lesion. She did so and was cured immediately."[10] Remaclus, a Christian missionary in the seventh century, made the sign of the cross over a spring dedicated to pagan gods, driving out the gods and instantly purifying the water.[11] An "ordeal of the cross [*judicium crucis*]" became, in medieval legal practice, a way of settling disputes; thus an eighth-century code prescribes: "If a woman claims that her husband has never remained with her [i.e., that the marriage has never been consummated], let them go out to the cross; and if it be true, let them be separated."[12] Especially frequent in several folk literatures are accounts of how the cross provided a cure for diseases and wounds. The sight of a cross could break a fever or quiet hysteria. We have reports of hemorrhages on the battlefield or in knightly combat, which no tourniquet could stanch but which the cross succeeded in stopping. Sometimes it was even successful in raising the dead. And in the folklore of the Slavs and the Transylvanians the crucifix had special power against vampires, graphically described in *Dracula*, the novel and the film.

As that last example suggests, there was a close connection between these uses of the cross (many of which, to say the least, certainly bordered on the magical) and the ancient and medieval belief in the presence and power of demons. In a familiar epigram from Shirley Jackson Case, "the sky hung low in the ancient world."[13] The description continues:

> Traffic was heavy on the highway between heaven and earth. Gods and spirits thickly populated the upper air, where they stood in readiness to intervene at any moment in the affairs of mortals. And demonic powers, emerging from the lower world or resident in remote corners of the earth,

were a constant menace to human welfare. All nature was alive—alive with supernatural forces.

If anything, medieval Christianity reinforced that belief in demonic powers, but it also provided various charms to break their spell: holy water, relics, incantations, the consecrated host of the Eucharist, and, above all, the sign of the cross. These became vehicles for the power of God against the demons. Among them, the cross simultaneously could serve as a magical amulet and, because of its inseparable association with the crucifixion of Jesus, could act as a reminder, more or less effective as the case might be, that the power against demons and diseases was not resident in the amulet or the gesture, but was in fact the power of God, of that God who had come in the life and death of Jesus to break the power of evil.

A special case was the power available in the relics of the true cross. These were unknown in the first three centuries, but references to them begin to appear in the 350s.[14] Although Eusebius of Caesarea, our most important source of information about Constantine and his family, makes no mention of it at all, the discovery of the cross in Jerusalem was attributed to Saint Helena, mother of the emperor Constantine, in several different versions of the legend. In a chamber under the present Church of the Holy Sepulcher she was said to have found not one cross, but three. By divine inspiration she resolved to determine which cross was authentic by applying each one to a dead body: the one that raised the man from the dead would be the true cross.[15] After she had discovered the cross, the chronicler Socrates Scholasticus tells us,

> the emperor's mother erected over the place of the sepulcher a magnificent church.... There she left a portion of the cross, enclosed in a silver case, as a memorial for those who might wish to see it. The other part she sent to the emperor, who, *being persuaded that the city would be perfectly secure where that relic should be preserved*, privately enclosed it in his own statue ...at Constantinople.... Moreover, the nails with which Christ's hands were fastened to the cross (for his mother, having found these also in the sepulcher, had sent them) Constantine took and had made into bridle-bits and a helmet, which he used in his military expeditions.[16]

But these two portions of the true cross, one in Jerusalem and one in Constantinople, were not to be the only ones. As early as 350 we find Cyril of Jerusalem asserting to those who would deny the crucifixion: "The whole world has since been filled with pieces of the wood of the cross."[17] We have references to such pieces of wood in Cappadocia and in Antioch during the second half of the fourth century, and by the beginning of the fifth century in Gaul; at the middle of that century the patriarch Juvenal of Jerusalem sent one to Pope Leo I in Rome. Pope Gregory I, who died in 604, presented one to the queen of the Lombards, Theodelinde, and to Recared I, king of the Visigoths, who became a Catholic. Helena's discovery (or, as it was called in Latin and then, with an unintentional irony in English, the "invention") of the cross became a day on the church calendar of the Middle Ages in the Carolingian era and was observed on 3 May (until it was abolished for the Latin rite during the Second Vatican Council, in 1960). The true cross itself was captured by the Persians in the seventh century and recovered by the emperor Heraclius, but in the twelfth century it was carried into battle by the bishop of Bethlehem and lost—except, of course, for all those fragments, with which, to use the words of Cyril of Jerusalem, the "whole world" was indeed filled in the Middle Ages, until, as the waggish saying had it, it would have been possible to rebuild the entire city of Jerusalem with the pieces of the true cross.

As the report in the *Ecclesiastical History* of Socrates makes clear, the cross was believed to be "the power of God" not only to ward off disease and other such perils, but above all in battle. Nor was this power restricted to the true cross: after his victory at the Milvian Bridge, Constantine had ordered a banner of the cross to be carried at the head of each of his armies when it went into battle. *Ho nikopoios stauros*, "the victory-granting cross," as Eusebius called it, became a military insignia on both land and sea.[18] With some help from the celebrated "Greek fire" (apparently a compound of sulphur, saltpeter, and naphtha, though the recipe is still a Byzantine secret) and with the tactical expertise of Byzantine military science, the cross did grant victory; and the strategic location of the city of Constantinople protected it against invaders for a millennium. In the West, too, the cross was thought to be a source of protection in war, and at the end of the eleventh century it became the central symbol of the expeditions to Palestine that acquired the name *crusades:* "to take the cross" meant to go off on a crusade.

The cross was believed to possess all of this victorious power because it had been the instrument for the greatest victory of them all, the cosmic victory of the power of God over the power of the devil in the death and resurrection of Jesus. "The word of the cross is called the power of God," John of Damascus said, "because the might of God, that is, his victory over death, has been revealed to us through it."[19] The earliest versions of the idea had described this victory as a trick that God had played on the devil, death, and sin, the alliance of enemies who had held humanity in thrall. In one of the most striking—and one of the most problematical—of images for the trick, the devil with his allies was depicted as a giant fish that had devoured every human being since Adam. When the humanity of Christ was cast into the pool, the fish took it to be yet another victim to be swallowed up. But hidden within this bait of the human nature of Christ was the hook of his divine nature, so that when the devil gobbled up the man Jesus in his death on the cross, he was impaled on the divinity. He had to regurgitate the humanity of Jesus, and with it all those whom Jesus had taken as his own; and death and the devil, who had taken the human race, were now themselves taken. Through the cross, therefore, liberation and victory had come.

In a more subtle and sophisticated form, this theory of the cross became the metaphor of *Christus Victor,* which Gustaf Aulén made the title of a controversial book on the meaning of the cross. Here, in what Aulén does not hesitate to call the "classic" theory of how the cross saves, the cross became the sign of God's invasion of enemy territory and of the "wondrous battle [*mirabile duellum*]" by which Jesus Christ had accomplished the salvation of the human race.[20] Shedding the cruder aspects of the earlier metaphor of deception, the theme of Christus Victor nevertheless retained the interpretation that the enemies of God and man were the ones with whom Christ on the cross had to contend. The death of Christ on the cross was therefore his capitulation to those enemies and to their power, before which he made himself weak. But he took those enemies into the grave with him. In the resurrection Christ was set free from their power, but they remained behind in the grave. Although this interpretation of the cross as the power of God was more prominent in the Greek East than in the Latin West, it was never lost even in the West; and, according to Aulén, the Reformation revived it. Thus the so-called Easter Cantata (Cantata 4), "Christ lag in Todesbanden," of Johann Sebastian Bach is a celebration of Christus Victor; and in Bach's *Saint John Passion,* the dying words on the cross, "It is finished!" become the occasion for an alto aria to exclaim:

Der Held aus Juda siegt mit Macht
Und schliesst den Kampf:
"Es ist vollbracht!"

Lo, Judah's Lion wins with might
And now victorious ends the fight:
"It is finished!"

As the act of divine power manifest in Christus Victor, the cross was interpreted as the enactment, in the arena of the cosmos and of world history, of the dramatic battle between God and the enemies of God over the future of humanity.[21] Whatever its theological advantages or disadvantages may have been, this theory of the atonement had the advantage, in relation to the art and music of the Middle Ages, of being able to connect the cross with the resurrection as two parts of a single action. In the liturgical music of the Middle Ages, that connection took the form of setting Good Friday and Easter into the greatest possible contrast: Good Friday was the only day in the church year when the sacrifice of the Mass was not celebrated, because on that day it was the original sacrifice of the cross on Calvary that was to be commemorated.[22] Following a tradition that went back at least to Origen in the first half of the third century,[23] medieval art depicted the crucifixion as having taken place on the very place where the skull of Adam was buried; and the processions and the liturgical drama of the Middle Ages kept the motif of Christus Victor alive even when Latin theology was no longer able to deal with it adequately because of its preoccupation with interpreting the death of Christ as an act of satisfaction.[24]

One of the greatest early poems in the English language, *The Dream of the Rood*, has the tree of the cross describe the "young Hero" who would ascend it for his combat with death and, succumbing in the combat, would nevertheless prevail. Already in the sixth century, the poet Venantius Fortunatus had put the dramatic interpretation of the cross into two Latin poems that were to become a standard part of medieval Lenten music and poetry.[25] One of them he was moved to write when, in 569, the Byzantine emperor Justin II sent a fragment of the true cross to Rhadegund, the Frankish queen. It served as the processional hymn for the arrival of that fragment:

Vexilla regis prodeunt,
Fulget crucis mysterium.

The royal banners forward go,
The cross shines forth with mystic glow.

The other poem made Christus Victor even more explicit:

Pange, lingua, gloriosi proelium certaminis
et super crucis tropaeo dic triumphum nobilem,
qualiter redemptor orbis immolatus vicerit.

Sing, my tongue, the glorious battle,
Sing the ending of the fray.
Now above the cross, the trophy,
Sound the loud triumphant lay;
Tell how Christ, the world's redeemer,
As a victim won the day.

Another ancient literary device that could likewise be adapted to the sign of the cross was the *carmen figuratum,* or figured poem. It combined poetic and visual forms by varying the length of the poetic lines to lay out a prescribed shape, which could then be supplemented with other figures. The cross lent itself very conveniently to such treatment. Of such poems on the cross, the best known was that of the ninth-century scholar and author Rabanus Maurus, *De laudibus sanctae crucis* (The Praises of the Holy Cross), in which the dominant theme celebrated by the "praises" was that of Christus Victor.[26] Most of its verses are cast in the form of square "grids," each formed by a number of letters equal to the number of lines in the text of that verse, a method that permitted crosses with arms of equal length to be superimposed on the text. A further elaboration could then be the arrangement of the traditional symbols for the four evangelists—a man for Matthew, a lion for Mark, an ox for Luke, and an eagle for John (Rev. 4:6–10)—in the form of a cross on the page.

Being the symbol of the power of God, the cross also served as the sign of the wisdom of God, which, as "the foolishness of God" in the Pauline formula, was wiser than any vaunted human wisdom (1 Cor. 1:25). "As the wisdom of the world is foolishness to God," Tertullian had said, "so also the wisdom of God is foolishness in the world's esteem."[27] In seeking to celebrate the cross as wisdom, the Christian writers and artists of the Middle Ages often took pains to revel first in its "foolishness." That was the valid point behind the formula quoted earlier and often misattributed to Tertullian, "I believe it because it is absurd," and especially behind the language of heightened paradox in such statements of Augustine as this:

Rabanus Maurus, *De laudibus sanctae crucis*, ninth century, Vienna Nationalbibliothek, Cod. Vindob. 652, fol. 20v.

> The deformity of Christ forms you. If he had not willed to be deformed, you would not have recovered the form which you had lost. Therefore he was deformed when he hung on the cross. But his deformity is our comeliness. In this life, therefore, let us hold fast to the deformed Christ.[28]

From the legislation of Constantine forbidding the continuation of its use as the means of capital punishment, it is clear that the Christians never forgot, in their celebration of the cross as the "royal banner," that it was in the first instance an instrument of torture, a gallows, and therefore, in the language of the New Testament (1 Cor. 1:23), a stumbling block and an offense.[29] It was above all the mystery of the cry of dereliction on the cross, in the words from the psalm, "My God, my God, why hast thou forsaken me?" that evoked their awe and consternation.[30] The beginning of wisdom, therefore, was the acceptance of that mystery: the one whom they believed to be "one in being with the Father" had been—whatever sense anyone might, or might not, be able to make of it all—forsaken by his Father on the cross.

When they spoke of the cross as wisdom, it was often to cite Jesus on the cross as an example of patience and charity even in the midst of suffering: "For to this you have been called, because Christ also suffered for you, leaving you an example, that you should follow in his steps. He committed no sin; no guile was found on his lips. When he was reviled, he did not revile in return; when he suffered, he did not threaten; but he trusted to him who judges justly" (1 Pet. 2:21–23). One of the most widely read books in the Middle Ages was the *Moralia* of Pope Gregory I, composed at the end of the sixth century; it was a massive exposition of the Book of Job, which considered the sufferings of that "Gentile saint" of the Old Testament in such a way as to direct attention through them to the exemplary sufferings of Jesus. An eighth-century writer defined a Christian simply as "one who imitates and follows Christ in all things."[31] And in an epic of seven books about Paradise lost and Paradise regained (a work that poses no threat to the greatness of John Milton, but that embodies much of medieval piety and emotion), which abbot Odo of Cluny composed in the ninth century, Christ, who had come to save the world from pride, "teaches this especially by all the things that he does in utmost humility, saying, 'I am meek, all of you learn this from me.' "[32]

This continuing emphasis on the imitation of Christ's example as the foundation of true wisdom was never, however, the whole of the content of wisdom. Christ was not simply one of the saints to be followed; the wisdom of his cross was more than an example. Deeper reflection on the meaning of the cross led to a consideration of how it was possible to justify the ways of God to man. The very shape of the cross symbolized its comprehension of all the ways of God, the vertical and the horizontal bars representing the height and the breadth of the universe, and their point of convergence where the head of Christ was laid representing the unification and ultimate harmony of all in Christ crucified.[33] For the cross was, on the one hand, the most evident of all proofs for the power of evil in the world; as Pope Gregory the Great reminded a colleague in the midst of his suffering, Jesus had said to his captors in the Garden of Gethsemane, "This is your hour, and the power of darkness."[34] But the cross was at the same time the supreme proof that the will and way of God would eventually prevail, regardless of what human plans might conspire to do. As Joseph had said to his brothers in Egypt, so by the wisdom of God in the cross it could be said now for the whole world: "You meant evil against me; but God meant it for good, to bring it about that many people should be kept alive, as they are today."[35] True wisdom, the wisdom of the cross, consisted in the ability to hold both of these together, neither ignoring the presence and power of evil, as a superficial optimism was tempted to do, nor allowing the presence and power of evil to negate the sovereignty of the one God, as a fatalistic dualism tended to do.[36] Thus the providence of God, which the Christian philosopher Boethius had been able to define in relation to fate (without any reference to the Bible or to Christ) as "the divine type itself, seated in the Supreme Ruler, which disposes all things," became, in the hands of the Christian philosopher-theologian Thomas Aquinas, a part of his examination of the activity of God in relation to the world, an examination whose ultimate foundation was the unmerited love of God.[37]

The wisdom of the cross was, then, the disclosure not only of human morality but of divine love. Placing this at the center of his description of what Christ had done by his life and his death, Peter Abelard, in a sermonic essay entitled "The Cross," emphasized that the love of God in Christ lay beyond "our own power to share in the passion of Jesus by our suffering and to follow him by carrying our own cross."[38] Therefore he insisted that it was unfair to accuse him of teaching that Christ had only provided an example for our imitation, as though such imitation were possible for the powers of an unaided human nature to achieve. On the contrary, the fundamental meaning of the wisdom of the cross was that contained in the words of Jesus in the Gospel of John: "Greater love has no man than this, that a man lay down his life for his friends" (John 15:13). Such love had its ground and origin only in God; but from God it came to humanity, and it did so through the cross. For "by the faith which we have concerning Christ, love is increased in us, through the conviction that God in Christ has united our nature to himself and that by suffering in that nature he has demonstrated to us the supreme love of which he speaks." Nowhere else but in Jesus and in his cross was the true nature of love visible. The purpose of the cross, therefore, was to bring about a change in sinners, to thaw their frozen hearts with the warmth of the sunshine of divine love. Christ did not die on the cross to change the mind of God (which, like everything about God, was unchangeable), as some pious language about the cross that Abelard was criticizing seemed to imply, but "to reveal the love [of God] to us or to convince us how much we ought to love him 'who did not spare even his own Son' for us."[39] True love was self-sacrificing love, and God had demonstrated it uniquely by giving up his own Son to the death of the cross. This exhibited the authentic nature of love and the depth of divine love, thus making human love, even self-sacrificing human love, possible.

Abelard's critics found such language about the wisdom of the cross not so much incorrect as inadequate. Of course Christ crucified was an example of patience, everyone would agree; and no one would deny that the cross of Christ was the supreme revelation of the love of God, and indeed of the very definition of love, whether divine or human. The question was whether this language exhausted the wisdom of the cross or whether a more profound consideration of the cross would lead to some other way of thinking and speaking about it. That other way found its definitive formulation in one of the most influential works of medieval thought, *Why God Became Man (Cur deus homo)* by Anselm of Canterbury. More than any other treatise between Augustine and the Reformation on any other doctrine of the Christian faith, Anselm's essay has shaped the outlook not only of Roman Catholics, but of most Protestants, many of whom have paid him the ultimate compliment of not even recognizing that their version of the wisdom of the cross comes from him, but attributing it to the Bible itself.[40]

Anselm's *Why God Became Man* belongs to a consideration of the theme of the "wisdom of the cross" for another reason as well. In it he develops his argument, as he says, "as though Christ did not exist [*remoto Christo*]," claiming to proceed by reason alone. The underlying presupposition of Anselm's thought was the consistency of God and the universe, which God did not violate by arbitrary acts, for such acts would undermine the moral order of the universe itself.[41] Anselm's term for that moral order was "rightness [*rectitudo*]." Rightness consisted in rendering to each a due measure of honor. Although created for participation in such rightness, the human race had refused to give God due honor and had fallen into sin. This God could not simply overlook or forgive by fiat, without thereby violating "rightness" and moral order; such was the demand of divine justice, which Anselm could have defined as "God taking himself seriously." Yet both human wisdom and divine revelation made it clear that God was a God not only of justice, but of mercy, who declared: "I have no pleasure in the death of the wicked, but that the wicked turn from his way and live" (Ezek. 33:11).

Such was the divine dilemma to which the wisdom of the cross provided a resolution, according to Anselm's reasoning. For the justice of God, having pronounced that violation of the moral will was worthy of death, clashed with the mercy of God, which desired life rather than death. The one who was guilty of the sin, man, could not pay the penalty except by being lost forever; the one who wanted to forgive, God, could not do so except by undercutting the moral order of the universe. Only a being able to pay the penalty (by being human) but capable of making a payment that was of infinite worth (by being divine) could simultaneously carry out the imperatives of divine mercy and satisfy the demands of divine justice. The payment, moreover, had to be voluntary, and could not be made by someone who owed it on his own behalf, for that would not avail for others. Therefore God had to become a man, and moreover had to die on the cross, so as to achieve the ends of divine mercy and yet to render satisfaction to divine justice and thus uphold "rightness." His death on the cross made it, one may say, morally possible for God to forgive.

As with the metaphor of Christus Victor, our interest here is not in the theological adequacy or inadequacy of Anselm's doctrine of satisfaction, but in its bearing on the cultural significance of the portrait of Jesus as "Christ crucified." If that metaphor gave expression to the dramatic accents of literature and art, this metaphor embodied themes that came from the structure and the practice of both church and society in the Western Middle Ages. The term *satisfaction* as a description of the act that had taken place on the cross came from the penitential practice and the canon law of the church: a sinner who was truly contrite for his sin, and who confessed that sin and was absolved, nevertheless had to make restitution of what the sin had taken away. So it was also on a cosmic scale with the sin of the entire human race, and the death of Christ on the cross was such an act of restitution and reparation, to which human acts of satisfaction then attached themselves. The ecclesiastical system of satisfaction, moreover, may have contained echoes of civil law as well, in which, according to the ancient Germanic requirement of *wergild*, one was obliged to make good for a crime in accordance with the standing of the injured party in society. Since in this case God was the injured party, only a *wergild* paid by one who was both God and man would have been adequate. By arriving at this definition *remoto Christo*, Anselm could set it forth as a "wisdom of the cross" that was pertinent to the total human situation and that could be perceived by human reason as well as through divine revelation. "Therefore," he said, "we have clearly come to Christ, whom we confess to be both God and man and to have died on our behalf."[42]

At every level of its culture, therefore, medieval society, whether Eastern or Western, was pervaded by the sign of the cross, both literally and figuratively. Thus regardless of the historical credence anyone may be prepared to give the statement of Cyril of Jerusalem quoted earlier, that "the whole world has been filled with pieces of the wood of the cross," we may see in the Middle Ages the fulfillment of another statement, which is apparently more modest but is actually more extravagant, in the first paragraph of the first book written by Cyril's older contemporary, Athanasius of Alexandria, when he was about twenty-two: "The power of the cross of Christ has filled the world."[43]

9

The Monk Who Rules the World

They left everything and followed him.

 "If any man would come after me, let him deny himself and take up his cross and follow me" (Mark 8:34): these words of Jesus in the Gospels had been, from the very beginning, a summons to the discipline and self-denial of discipleship for all who strove to follow him.[1] But early in the sixth century they became the charter of Western Christian monasticism, which denied the world for the sake of Christ—and then went on to conquer the world in the name of Christ, the Monk who ruled the world.

This saying also shaped the image of Jesus as the perfect Monk, who had the right to issue such a summons because he himself obeyed it unconditionally. For he in a unique sense had denied himself and had taken up his cross. Neither enemy nor friend could succeed in deflecting him from this denial of himself and of the world. When the Tempter offered him "all the kingdoms of the world and the glory of them" (as though these were the Tempter's own to give), he indignantly refused (Matt. 4:8–10); when the spectators of his miracles "were about to come and take him by force to make him king, Jesus withdrew" summarily (John 6:15); and when the prince of the apostles sought to dissuade him from taking up his cross, Jesus rebuked him with some of the harshest words in the Gospels (Matt. 16:23), "Get behind me, Satan!" Although there are passages contrasting his way of life with that of the more ascetic John the Baptist (Luke 7:31-35), the fundamental imperatives of the monastic life were no less fundamental to the portrait of Jesus in all four Gospels. Yet by his denial of the world he had conquered the world and established his everlasting kingdom, in which he invited his followers to share by also denying the world, taking up their own cross, and following him.

Thus the monks began by patterning themselves after Christ. But by the time they were finished they were likewise patterning Christ after themselves. "Christ the Monk" is a motif carried out in many monastic manuscripts and altarpieces of the Middle Ages, as well as in modern adaptations of this monastic tradition. A twentieth-century example is the statue entitled *Pax Christi,* "the Peace of Christ." In it Christ is represented as dressed in the loosely hanging folds of the cowl now associated with the religious habit of a Benedictine monk (although originally there was no special habit for Benedictine monks),[2] and with sandals on his feet. His face is fully bearded, with bushy eyebrows, but otherwise is stylized. He is holding the book of the Gospel in his left hand, engraved with a cross at the center and with four circles for the four evangelists. With his right hand he is pronouncing the *Pax* or benediction. And yet both his garb and the book of the Gospel make it clear that he is at the same time pronouncing the summons to deny the world, take up the cross, and follow him, for only in obedience to that summons can there be the *Pax Christi.* Even for those who do not, or cannot, forsake society to enter the cloister, the summons stands as both a challenge and a promise.

Christian monasticism is, in a sense, older than Christianity, for there were both hermits and monastic communities in the Jewish as well as in the pagan environment where Christianity grew.[3] All three forms of monasticism—pagan, Jewish, and Christian—had their beginnings in the Egyptian desert. In the Egyptian desert dwelled the Therapeutae, a Jewish monastic community described by Philo, the Jewish theologian of Alexandria and contemporary of Jesus, in his treatise *On the Contemplative Life.*[4] So closely did the Therapeutae resemble the early Christian monastic communities that the fourth-century Christian historian Eusebius interpreted Philo's description as the account of a Christian group in the first century and used it to prove the apostolic antiquity of Christian monasticism.[5] And just a century ago some historians were still so struck by the resemblance that they sought to expose Philo's treatise as a Christian forgery from

Pax Christi, sculpture from Saint John's Abbey, Collegeville, Minnesota,
author's collection.

the third century, a theory that was "adopted by a majority of scholars."[6] Nowadays everyone accepts the authenticity and the Philonic
authorship of *On the Contemplative Life,* which has received further
corroboration from the descriptions of Jewish monasticism in the Dead
Sea Scrolls. Therefore the treatise stands today as evidence for the
existence in Egypt of ascetic impulses that antedate Christian
asceticism.

Christian asceticism in Egypt was to find its most abiding expression
in the life and work of Saint Antony of Egypt, who lived from the
middle of the third century to the middle of the fourth, and in the
influential *Life of Antony* prepared after Antony's death by his friend,
Athanasius, bishop of Alexandria. The biography, though composed
by Athanasius in Greek, seems to have been written at least in part
for Western readers, and soon after its appearance it was translated
into Latin for them.[7] One of its Western readers, later in that same
century, appears to have been Augustine.[8] He went on to establish
a monastic community of his own and to write for it a letter that was
eventually to become the basis of the so-called *Rule of St. Augustine*
(although the *Rule* as such was apparently not written out by Augustine himself but by one of his pupils).[9] Yet by far the most influential document of Western asceticism, and one of the most influential
documents of Western civilization, is the *Rule of Saint Benedict of Nursia,* written about a century later. It provides eloquent testimony for
an interpretation of monasticism as a way of understanding the meaning of the life and person of Jesus, and therefore for identifying the
image of Jesus as the Monk who ruled the world. For it was the
central purpose of Benedict's *Rule* to teach novice monks how to
"renounce themselves in order to follow Christ," how to "advance
in the ways [of Christ] with the Gospel as our guide," and, by per-
severing in the monastic life, how to "share by patience in the passion
of Christ and hereafter deserve to be united with him in his kingdom"—in a single formula, "not to value anything more highly than
the love of Christ [*nihil amori Christi praeponere*]."[10] The love of Christ,
moreover, modified one of the basic impulses that had originally led
to the rise of monasticism. "Deep in the monastic consciousness is
solitude," writes a historian of Western asceticism. But, he continues,
"you discover to your vexation that deep in the Christian consciousness, ran the axiom that you must receive strangers as though they
were Christ, and they really might be Christ." Therefore, quoting the

Gospel (Matt. 25:35), Benedict specified in his *Rule:* "All guests coming to the monastery shall be received as Christ."[11]

Benedict was, in short, defining the life of the monk as a participation in the life of Christ. All three of the special monastic virtues that constituted the vows of the monk—poverty, chastity, and obedience—were based on Christ as their model and their embodiment. In a scene that was to become a commonplace in monastic biographies throughout the Middle Ages, Antony just happened to be in church when "the Gospel was being read, and he heard the Lord saying to the rich man, 'If you would be perfect, go, sell what you possess and give to the poor, and you will have treasure in heaven; and come, follow me.' And Antony, as though . . . the passage had been read on his account, went out immediately from the church and gave the possessions of his ancestors to the villagers."[12] Similarly, Antony's successful defense of his chastity was interpreted as his "struggle against the devil, or rather this victory was the Savior's work in Antony."[13] And the virtue of obedience to the abbot, which was fundamental to Benedict's *Rule*, found its warrant in the position of the abbot as one who is "esteemed to supply the place of Christ in the monastery, being called by his name," and in the example of Christ, who came not to do his own will, but the will of God, who had sent him.[14] Even when the name of Jesus was not explicitly mentioned, therefore, the way of life followed by the monk was seen as the *vita evangelica*, the way of life prescribed by the Gospel, as this had been first practiced and then enjoined by Christ. Everything the monk did was, in one way or another, the practical application of the *vita evangelica*.

Although the ascetic impulse had been present in the Christian movement from the beginning, having been articulated for example by the apostle Paul (1 Cor. 7:1–7), it is no coincidence that it should have risen to prominence, in the life of monks such as Antony, precisely at the time when the church was making its peace with the Roman empire and with the world. Part of the price the church paid for that peace was the necessity of coming to terms with those who could not, or at any rate did not, take its message with utmost seriousness, but who were willing to go along with being Christians much as they had been willing to go along with being pagans, just as long as it did not cost them too much. Now that it was easier to be a nominal Christian than to be a nominal pagan, the multitudes who began to crowd into the church were not looking to become "athletes" for Christ; but that was precisely the term that Athanasius used to describe Antony the ascetic, who underwent rigorous training in order to be able to compete and win in Christ's contest against the devil, the world, and the flesh.[15] These monastic athletes, as one scholar has put it, "were not only fleeing from the world in every sense of the word, they were fleeing from the worldly church."[16] Interpreted in this way, the monasticism of the fourth and fifth centuries was a protest, in the name of the authentic teaching of Jesus, against an almost inevitable by-product of the Constantinian settlement, the secularization of the church and the lowering of the standards of discipleship set in the Gospels.

Thus there was introduced into the life and teaching of the church a double standard of discipleship, based on a bifurcation of the ethical demands of Jesus into "commandments," which "imply necessity" and which were taken to be binding upon everyone, and "counsels of perfection," which were "left to choice" and which ultimately were binding only upon the monastic athletes.[17] "If you would be perfect," Jesus had said in the Gospel, "go, sell what you possess and give to the poor"; in the same chapter he had also spoken of those "who have made themselves eunuchs for the sake of the kingdom of heaven" (Matt. 19:21, 12). Neither of those was a commandment setting down what was necessary for salvation, but rather a counsel of perfection; and to make that clear, he had explicitly appended the proviso to the statement about renouncing marriage for the sake of the kingdom of heaven: "He who is able to receive this, let him receive it." To be sure, the medieval church defined matrimony as a sacrament, a sacred sign through which the grace of God was communicated, while it never made either celibacy or monastic vows such a sacrament— although holy orders or ordination to the priesthood, which in the West (though not in Byzantium) presupposed celibacy, was one of the seven sacraments. Nevertheless, the Sermon on the Mount demanded "perfection" of its hearers (Matt. 5:48); and the meaning of perfection was increasingly to be sought not in the family life and daily work of the Christian believer within society, but in the life of the monk and the nun, to whom the word *religious* applied in a strict sense as a technical term.

Yet this protest against a secularized church became a means of conquering that church, as well as of conquering the world with which

the church had made its peace. The most striking mark of this monastic conquest in the Byzantine church was the requirement of celibacy
for the bishop. At councils involving the entire church, including the
first such council at Nicea in 325, representatives of the East consistently opposed the efforts of Western churchmen to make celibacy a
requirement for all parish clergy: married men could be ordained,
although ordained men could not enter into marriage.[18] As late as the
fourth century, even some bishops in the East were married and
remained married after assuming episcopal office; for example, Gregory of Nazianzus, who came to be known as "the Theologian" and
who eventually became patriarch of Constantinople, was the son of
Gregory the Elder, bishop of Nazianzus, who was already a priest
when his son was born.[19] But beginning in that century, the legislation
of the Eastern provinces of the church began to specify that while
parish clergy could remain married, bishops had to be celibate. As
incorporated into the civil law in the *Code of Justinian,* this legislation
barred the father of a family from election to the episcopate, permitting it for a married man without children but only on the condition
that he and his wife separate.[20] As the so-called Trullan Synod of the
Eastern Church in 692 was to specify, this usually meant that she
entered a convent.[21]

In effect, this combination of rules—celibacy required for bishops,
but marriage permitted for parish clergy—granted the monks a virtual
monopoly on the episcopate of the Eastern churches. A fifteenth-
century Greek archbishop was to put it this way:

> [Monasticism] is endowed with such prestige and standing that practically
> the entire church seems to be governed by monks. Thus if you make diligent
> inquiry, you will hardly find anyone who has been promoted to the sacred
> hierarchy from the world [apparently including the secular clergy as part
> of the "world"]; for this has been allotted to the monks. And you know
> that if some are appointed to the holy offices [of bishop or patriarch], it is
> stipulated by the church that they should first put on the monastic habit.[22]

Ordinarily, therefore, a bishop or a patriarch came from the monastic
life. If an unmarried parish priest or a widower was chosen for the
office, he would, at least since the eighth century, take monastic vows
before being consecrated. And when—as in the notorious case of the
scholar Photius, who was selected as the patriarch of Constantinople
in 858—the choice fell on a layman, the result was that "the monastic
world all but unanimously refused allegiance to the new Patriarch."[23]

During the conflicts over the icons in the century preceding Photius's election, Byzantine monks had played an important, indeed eventually a decisive, role, as supporters of images and as agitators, stirring up the populace against the enemies of the images, including the most highly placed enemies, the emperor and the patriarch. Significantly, it was after the iconoclastic controversies that it became a rule for the patriarch-elect or bishop-elect to be a monk, or to become one. Those who had fled from the world that was in the church acquired dominion over the church that was in the world.

The dominant position of the monk in Eastern Orthodoxy continued to make itself visible in the two best-known literary descendants of Eastern Orthodoxy in the nineteenth century, Dostoevsky and Tolstoy. For the figure of Father Zossima in *The Brothers Karamazov* is the embodiment and the advocate of the monastic ideal of Byzantium and Russia, which had reached its climax in the *starets*, or elder:

> How surprised men would be if I were to say that from these meek monks, who yearn for solitary prayer, the salvation of Russia will perhaps come once more! For they are in truth made ready in peace and quiet "for the day and the hour, the month and the year." Meanwhile, in their solitude, *they keep the image of Christ fair and undefiled*, in the purity of God's truth, from the times of the fathers of old, the apostles and the martyrs. And when the time comes they will show it to the tottering creeds of the world. That is a great thought. That star will rise out of the East.[24]

Tolstoy, too, whose rejection of Russian Orthodoxy was far more radical than was Dostoevsky's, nevertheless emerges as the "authentic Greek monk."[25] Thus T. G. Masaryk, who regarded the discourses of Father Zossima in *The Brothers Karamazov* as "the essential portion of the book," went on to observe that Dostoevsky and Tolstoy, in spite of the drastic differences of belief and of ideology between them, had a "similarity of views" in their acceptance of the "ascetic ideal of the monk," which they shared with "their ecclesiastical environment."[26]

In the Latin West, the career of Jesus the Monk in the development of monasticism throughout the Middle Ages is the history of successive movements of reform. Each of them was intent on bringing rejuvenation to the monastic ideal; on achieving, through such a rejuvenation of the monastic ideal, the renewal of the church and the papacy; and on redeeming and purifying medieval society through such a renewal of church and papacy. The intellectual and institutional evolution of these reform movements during the almost exactly one thousand years between Benedict of Nursia (who founded the monastery of Monte Cassino in about 529) and Martin Luther (who entered the monastery of the Augustinian Hermits at Erfurt in 1505) is a story of inestimable importance for the history of Europe and of the world.[27] Over and over, it was the primitive model of Christ as Monk, and of the monk as the imitator of this model, that animated these reform movements. There is in some ways a depressing repetition of pattern, as each monastic reform in its turn protests against decline and stagnation in the monasteries, sets up new administrative and disciplinary structures to reverse the downward trend, prevails for a century or two, and then proves itself vulnerable to the same tendencies of stagnation and decline: Benedict of Aniane in the Carolingian period; Odo of Cluny and the Cluniac reform movement a century or so later; about a century after that the monastic reformation that began at Citeaux, which through the powerful life and Christocentric thought of Saint Bernard spread the Cistercian message throughout Europe; then the friars of the twelfth and thirteenth centuries in their new dedication to renewal; and, in reaction to the Protestant Reformation and under the inspiration of an intensified Christ-mysticism in sixteenth-century Spain, the Society of Jesus.

In each instance, however, it bears noting not only that reform once again became *necessary*, but that reform was once again *possible*, as the transforming power of the ideal represented by the figure of Jesus the Monk reasserted itself and as Jesus returned yet once more "and drove out all who sold and bought in the temple" (Matt. 21:12)—at least temporarily.

Through these reform movements within medieval monasticism, the monastic conquest of the church sought to make itself ever more complete. As early as the beginning of the fourth century, regional synods in Spain were requiring celibacy of parish clergy, and by the end of that century a series of popes and councils had made the requirement universal. It was, however, only several centuries later, when monasticism came into a dominant position within the organizational structure of the Western Church, that it was possible to begin enforcing the requirement with rigor and consistency. That enforcement is associated with the work of Hildebrand, the eleventh-century reformer and monk (although some scholars contend that he was not, technically, a monk) who was the gray eminence of the papacy for a quarter-century before finally becoming pope in his own right in 1073, when he took the name Gregory VII.[28] His training under the influence of the Order of Cluny, with its dedication to rooting out the corruptions that had infected Benedictine monasticism, inspired him in his program for the reform of the church. The Cluniac reform had convinced him that the way to bring the church and the papacy into conformity with the will of Christ was by restoring the monastic life to its original ideals, and then applying those ideals to the life of the church as a whole. A basic component of that program of reform was the strict enforcement of clerical celibacy, which may be defined, in a formula recently adopted by Pope John Paul II, as an imitation of Jesus Christ by which "a priest is a man who lives alone so that others should not be alone."[29] In the social and political setting of the eleventh century, it was a means of securing the economic independence of the priest and bishop from secular authorities—and therefore their dependence on the church and the papacy. Yet it is evident from the letters of Pope Gregory VII that he saw in this administrative reform of the priesthood and the episcopate something far more than this: nothing less than a spiritual renewal of the church's dedication to Christ.

And that new dedication and dependence was in turn a means for the reconquest of the world for Christ. The charter of Christian monasticism, the words of Jesus about denying oneself, taking up the cross, and following him, appear in the Gospel of Matthew just a few verses after the charter of the papacy, the words of Jesus to Peter: "I tell you, you are Peter [*Petros*], and on this rock [*petra*] I will build my church, and the powers of death shall not prevail against it. I will give you the keys of the kingdom of heaven, and whatever you bind on earth shall be bound in heaven, and whatever you loose on earth shall be loosed in heaven" (Matt. 16:18–19). Quoting those words, Gregory VII set the terms for Christ's reconquest of the world and of the empire:

> Now then tell me, are kings an exception to this rule? Do they not also belong to the sheep which the Son of God has entrusted to the blessed Peter? Who, I ask, can regard himself as excluded from the power of Peter in this universal grant of authority to forbid and to allow, except perhaps for someone who declines to bear the yoke of the Lord [Jesus], who subjects himself instead to the burden of the devil, and who refuses to be counted among the sheep of Christ?[30]

And in the famous confrontation with the emperor Henry IV at Canossa in 1077 (where the emperor's tactics may have won the battle, but the pope's strategy probably won the war), Gregory VII, having been addressed by the emperor as "Hildebrand, at present not pope but false monk," reaffirmed the authority of Christ to bind and loose sins by granting absolution to Henry. Hildebrand the monk had conquered not only the church and the papacy, but the empire and the world, in the name of Jesus the Monk.

Perhaps the most remarkable such conquest, however, was to come just over half a century later, when a Cistercian abbot was elected pope as Eugenius III in 1145. He was a disciple of Bernard, the abbot of Clairvaux, celebrated for his fervent mystical devotion to Christ as the Bridegroom of the Soul. To his son in Christ who had now become his father in Christ, Bernard addressed one of the most moving treatises in the history both of medieval monasticism and of the medieval papacy, *On Consideration*.[31] Drawing upon the monastic distinction between the contemplative life and the active life, Bernard admonished his former pupil not to allow the administrative details of the papacy to deflect him from what was primary in the church: the person of Jesus Christ. The pope should not, he urged, become the successor of Constantine, but of Peter. For the monastic ideals of contemplation and study were not irrelevant to the governance of the church, but central to it. The subsequent use of Bernard's treatise by church reformers of every stripe in the fifteenth and sixteenth centuries is a documentation of how the monastic ideal of denying the world for Christ did indeed conquer the world for Christ.[32]

One of the most lasting of monastic conquests for Christ was the work of medieval missions. The Christianization of the barbarian Germanic, Slavic, and Eurasian tribes who came into Europe was almost completely the achievement of monks. As Lowrie J. Daly has said,

> What is most evident in the history of the conversion of the barbaric peoples is the great missionary feat which the monks accomplished. Whether it was a mission sent from Byzantium or one setting out from Rome, whether it came from Celtic Ireland or from the recently converted English lands, the missionaries were monks. The tremendous achievement of winning the Teutonic and Slavic peoples to Christianity and then to civilization was brought about by the continual self-sacrifice and heroic labors of hundreds of monks in all parts of Europe.[33]

Protestant scholars have likewise acknowledged that the name of Jesus Christ would have remained largely unknown in Europe and in the Americas "but for the monks."[34] Thus the "apostles to the Slavs," Saints Cyril and Methodius in the ninth century, were Byzantine monks; and by designating them as "joint patron saints of Europe" together with Saint Benedict, Pope John Paul II has once again recognized the decisive contribution of monks, both Western and Eastern, in the mission and expansion of Christianity. Conversely, the abolition of the monastic orders by the sixteenth-century Reformers must certainly be reckoned as a major reason for the (almost, though not quite) total loss of the missionary imperative in most of Protestantism for more than two centuries.[35]

There is no indication that Benedict envisaged a missionary role for his monks when he founded Monte Cassino. There is likewise nothing in the *Rule*, not even the proviso that a portion of each day be given over to "sacred reading,"[36] that would have led inevitably to another of the great conquests of Benedictine monasticism, its dominance of European scholarship for centuries; for "no judgment either favorable or unfavorable as to the worth of learning or of the study of letters is to be found in the *Rule* of St. Benedict."[37] One may perhaps begin to comprehend how completely Christ the Monk conquered the scholarly world of the Middle Ages by checking, in the standard modern editions, how many works of antiquity even exist for us today only because they were copied by monks in some medieval scriptorium. And that applies to the works not only of the church fathers and Christian saints, but of classical and pagan authors. The almost idolatrous devotion of many medieval monks to scholarship, described in Umberto Eco's *Name of the Rose*, is summarized near the end of that book in the apocalyptic exclamation of the protagonist, William of Baskerville, after a holocaust has destroyed all the books of the abbey: "It was the greatest library in Christendom. Now the Antichrist is truly at hand, because no learning will hinder him any more."[38] Antichrist was restrained by that monastic library because the library represented the claims of Christian discipleship upon the mind, what an essay by Etienne Gilson once called "The Intelligence in the Service of Christ the King."[39]

Dedicated missionaries and scholars though they were, the monks never forgot—or, as we said of the fourth century, did sometimes forget, but were insistently reminded every time they did forget— that their service to this King was above all to be carried out in the worship of the mystery of Christ and in the imitation of the example of Jesus. *Opus Dei*, "the work of God," was and is the Benedictine term for the prayer and the liturgical service of the monastery, not for any of the other activities of the community or the individual monk. Although Benedict himself was a layman and did not found a monastic order consisting of men who were ordained to the priesthood, ordination of monks has become the pattern over and over, with the consequence that the "active life" in missions, parishes, and classrooms threatened to crowd out the "contemplative life." Then it was necessary to point out to monastic communities again what their primary "mission" was: in the formula of the *Rule of Saint Benedict* quoted earlier, "not to value anything more highly than the love of Christ."[40] It was in carrying out that mission that Benedictine monasticism became in the Middle Ages—and would become again in the twentieth century, at such abbeys as Saint John's in the United States, Solesmes in France, and Beuron and Maria Laach in Germany—the principal agent for the renewal and reform of the liturgy, of liturgical art, and of sacred music, with consequences that are evident, since the Second Vatican Council, in every Roman Catholic parish in the world.

Throughout this discussion of Jesus the Monk there has been no explicit reference to the one person in the Middle Ages, indeed in all of history, who most completely figured forth the ideal of the conquest of the world by Christ through the denial of the world for Christ: Saint Francis of Assisi, in whom, as Dante said, "a sunrise broke again upon the world [*nacque al mondo un sole*]."[41] The reason for that omission is that an entire chapter, "The Divine and Human Model," will be devoted to Francis as the *alter Christus*. It is nevertheless with Francis of Assisi as monk that this chapter, too, must close, because it is above all the picture of Saint Francis that everyone must irresistibly call to mind upon hearing the saying of Jesus, "If any man would come after me, let him deny himself and take up his cross and follow me" (Mark 8:34).

10

The Bridegroom of the Soul

My beloved is mine and I am his.

Jesu, Lover of my soul,
Let me to Thy bosom fly,
While the nearer waters roll,
While the tempest still is high.

Charles Wesley wrote this familiar English hymn soon after the conversion of his brother John in 1738, when his heart had been "strangely warmed" through a reading of Martin Luther's "Preface to the Epistle to the Romans." Since then, as the hymnologist John Julian has said, "its popularity increases with its age, and few collections are now found from which it is excluded."[1] Nevertheless, as Julian goes on to note, "the opening stanza of this hymn has given rise to questions which have resulted in more than twenty different readings of the first four lines. The first difficulty is the term *Lover* as applied to our Lord," which various revisions have bowdlerized to "Jesus, Refuge of my soul" or to "Jesus, Saviour of my soul." A few years earlier, Count Nikolaus von Zinzendorf, founder of the Moravian Church at Herrnhut (from which Wesley derived some of his inspiration, perhaps also for this poem), had written the no less popular hymn "Seelenbräutigam, O du Gottes Lamm!"[2]

The case for the legitimacy of calling Jesus "Lover of my soul" or "Bridegroom of the Soul" stands or falls with the legitimacy, both psychological and religious, of the total mystical enterprise, and then with the assessment of the particular subspecies of it usually labeled

"Christ-mysticism."[3] By a working definition, mysticism may be identified as "the immediate experience of oneness with Ultimate Reality."[4] It is, though not a universal phenomenon, at least one that is widely distributed across most of the races of the globe and most of the religions of humanity. In some religions, notably in Hinduism and then in Buddhism as it drew upon its Hindu sources, mysticism stands very close to the center of the normative understanding of the religious tradition that has come from its principal interpreters, so that the distinction between mysticism and religion becomes difficult to identify. In other religions, for example in certain strains of Confucianism, the mystical elements, if any, seem to be considerably more elusive.

In Christianity, Christ-mysticism is what emerged when the figure of Jesus of Nazareth became the object of mystical experience, mystical thought, and mystical language. Standing as he did in the line of succession of the prophets of Israel, Jesus in his own message has sometimes been interpreted as the very antithesis of much that would ordinarily be called mystical. For, in the epigrammatic distinction of Abraham Joshua Heschel, whose scholarship included research both into the prophets of Israel and into the great Jewish mystics, "what is important in mystical acts is that *something happens,* what is important in prophetic acts is that *something is said.*"[5] Nevertheless, the prophetic literature of the Hebrew Bible, from the inaugural vision of Isaiah to the apocalyptic raptures of Ezekiel and Daniel, is replete with what sounds very much like mystical experience, mystical thought, and mystical language. In postbiblical Judaism, moreover, these elements have frequently assumed a dominant role.[6]

Although the mystical tradition within Judaism cannot be ignored, it is nonetheless appropriate to observe that the rise of Christ-mysticism was most closely associated not with this tradition, but with what, quoting Gregory Dix, we called earlier "the de-Judaization of Christianity." And it has not been in its Jewish gardens but in its Greek gardens that the church has cultivated the most delicate—and the most dangerous and problematical—flowers of Christ-mysticism. For much of the vocabulary of mysticism, even as employed in devotion to the person of Jesus, has come from Neoplatonic sources.[7] The understanding of the way to a relation with Ultimate Reality as an ascent (*anagōgē*), as well as the classic enumeration of the three steps of that mystical ascent as purification (*katharsis*), illumination (*ellampsis*), and union (*henōsis*), can all be traced to Proclus, the great systematizer of Neoplatonism in the fifth century C.E.; and through him much of it goes back to Plotinus, and ultimately even to Plato himself. Although both Plotinus and Proclus were critics of Christianity, they also owed much to it; and, in turn, their Christian opponents shared much of their Neoplatonism with them, especially these very elements of the mystical vision.

Therefore it did not come as a shock when, in the sixth century, there appeared a corpus of Greek writings that seemed to have blended Christian and Neoplatonic elements almost indiscriminately and that bore the name of Dionysius the Areopagite. This Dionysius was, in the report of the Acts of the Apostles, the only man named together with the women who "joined and believed" at Athens in response to the preaching of the apostle Paul; by the second century he seems to have been known as the first bishop of the Christian church at Athens; in the sixth century he suddenly produced this massive collection of Christian Neoplatonic speculations; and in the ninth century he came to be identified with Saint Denis, patron saint of France and third-century bishop of Paris.[8] Certified as it was with such impressive and all-but-apostolic credentials, the thought of Pseudo-Dionysius was accepted as authentic almost without dissent in the sixth century, and it retained its authoritative position, again almost without dissent, for an entire millennium, not being seriously challenged until the fifteenth and sixteenth centuries.

What place does the person of Jesus occupy in the mystical schema expounded by these pseudonymous writings of Dionysius the Areopagite? The answer is not easy. For while, in the words of a leading historian of Byzantine thought, "undoubtedly Dionysius . . . mentions the name of Jesus Christ and professes his belief in the incarnation," it must be acknowledged that "the structure of his system is perfectly independent of his profession of faith. 'Jesus' is for him . . . 'the principle, the essence . . . of all holiness and of all divine operation,' " but not in any central or decisive sense the son of Mary and the man of Nazareth.[9]

Whatever may have been the status of Jesus in the Christian Neoplatonic mysticism of Pseudo-Dionysius, however, the subsequent history of the Christ-mysticism inspired by it manifests a complex and subtle synthesis between Neoplatonic and biblical elements. The achievement of that synthesis was the historic accomplishment of

Maximus Confessor in the seventh century, who began his work in Constantinople but spent much of his life as an exile in the West.[10] By the time Western Europe had begun to come of age, that is, in the age of Charlemagne in the ninth century, mystical thought and imagery represented that synthesis; and it should be noted that both Maximus Confessor and Pseudo-Dionysius were translated from Greek into Latin during the Carolingian era and were thus made available to the West. From that ninth-century importation into the West of a literature that was Neoplatonic and Christian, Dionysian and Maximian—all at the same time—has come much of the Christ-mysticism of the Middle Ages and since.

Although Pseudo-Dionysius was undoubtedly the source for much of it, a major inspiration of Christ-mysticism was the interpretation of the Song of Songs (or Song of Solomon) as a Christian allegory. As most scholars would agree today, be they Jewish or Roman Catholic or Protestant, the Song was originally a poem celebrating the love between man and woman. But throughout its history it has in fact been read allegorically, and it may even be that it came into the Jewish canon that way. Defending its canonicity at the council of Jamnia in 90 C.E., which stabilized the canon of the Hebrew Bible, the celebrated Rabbi Aqiba declared: "The whole world is not worth the day on which the Song of Songs was given to Israel, for all the Scriptures are holy, but the Song of Songs is the Holy of Holies." From this interpretation comes the rule promulgated by the rabbis: "He who trills his voice in chanting the Song of Songs in the banquet house and treats it as a sort of song has no part in the world to come."[11]

Whether or not the allegorizing of the Song preceded its canonical status within Judaism is a matter of dispute among scholars; but by the time Christian interpreters took on the task of understanding it, it was definitely an allegory, and so it remained until modern times. As Jean Leclercq has noted, the Song of Solomon was "the book which was most read, and most frequently commented [upon] in the medieval cloister," more even than the four Gospels. And while, to use Leclercq's distinction, a scholastic commentary on the book "speaks mostly of God's relations with the entire Church, . . . the monastic commentary's object is rather God's relations with each soul, Christ's presence in it, the spiritual union realized through charity."[12] The earliest full-length Christian commentary on it we have comes from Origen in the third century, followed by that of Gregory of Nyssa in the fourth century; but the greatest commentary comes from Bernard of Clairvaux in the twelfth century, consisting of eighty-six sermons covering the first two chapters and the beginning of the third.[13]

As read through the eyes of Bernard's allegorization, the Song became an account of Jesus as the Bridegroom of the Soul. "By inspiration from above [Solomon] sang the praises of Christ and his church, the grace of holy love, and the sacraments of eternal marriage; and at the same time he gave expression to the deepest desires of the holy soul."[14] And therefore, he declared, *Ipsum saltem hominem homo hominibus loquor:* "As a human being, I speak of him as a human being to other human beings."[15] That declaration took him through all the successive stages of the life and humiliation of Jesus in the Gospels, "all the cares and bitter experiences of my Lord"—his infancy, labors, preaching, prayer, fasting, cross, and burial—as a commentary on the words of the Song (1:13), "My beloved is to me a bag of myrrh."[16] As the myrrh was an allegory for his suffering, so the lilies celebrated in the Song represented the glory and the blessings in "all the events in his life."[17] And so the "kiss" of which the Song speaks is "the man Christ Jesus," whose mouth gives the kiss; and through his human nature humanity receives the kiss.[18] "He it is," Bernard says, "whose speech, living and powerful, is to me a kiss . . . the imparting of joys, the revelation of secrets."[19] The soul responds to the summons of its Bridegroom and follows him into the chamber of his love. His love for the soul, as expressed in the cross, becomes the source and the object of the soul's love for him: "It is this which attracts my affection more sweetly, which requires it more justly, which retains it by closer ties and a more vehement force."[20] The end of this exchange of love between the soul and the Bridegroom of the Soul was the achievement of the union celebrated in the words of the soul-bride (Song of Solomon 2:16):

My beloved is mine and I am his,
he pastures his flock among the lilies.

As an earlier commentary on this verse had put it, "This done, the two are united: God comes to the soul, and the soul in turn unites itself with God. For she says, 'My beloved is mine and I am his, he pastures his flock among the lilies.' [I am] his who has transformed our human nature from the realm of shadowy appearances to that of ultimate truth."[21]

The mystical concept of ascent provided the framework for one of the masterpieces of medieval Christ-mysticism, *The Soul's Journey into God (Itinerarium mentis in Deum)* by Bonaventure.[22] The mind begins where it is, among the visible creatures of the sensible world. But as it ponders those creatures, it is filled with awe and reverence and aspires to rise higher. Its contemplation of itself, because of "the mirror of our mind," fills it with a longing for more and higher experience of God.[23] Held back as it is by its sins, it yearns for forgiveness and grace. Blinded as it is by the night of the world, a night both of its own making and of the evil that surrounds it, it strains for the eternal light. By successive stages, then, the mind moves from creature to Creator. To do this, the mystic must recognize not only the power of intellect, but also its limitations, and must acknowledge the primacy of will, of desire, of love. For each of these stages of the mystical ascent or *itinerarium*, according to Bonaventure, the "ladder" of the human nature of Jesus is decisive.[24] We rise from his feet to the wounds in his side to his head, once crowned with thorns and now crowned with glory. In the language of the Song of Songs, Jesus invites the soul to come to him and to abide with him. "If an image is an expressed likeness," Bonaventure argued, then "in Christ, the Son of God, who is the image of the invisible God by nature," humanity could "reach something perfect."[25]

Thus the three stages of mystical ascent—purification, illumination, and union—were easily adaptable to this imagery of Christ as Bridegroom of the Soul. Before the soul could even dare to hope for the object of its longing, it must be purged of its impurity and receive the forgiveness of sins. But it must be purified as well of its preoccupation with its own carnal self, with matter and the things of sense. Because of the inborn carnality of all human beings, "God the Word became flesh [*Verbum caro factum est*]," that is to say, became, quite literally, "carnal." For only thus could he "draw to the saving love of his sacred flesh all the affections of carnal men who were unable to love otherwise than in a carnal manner, and so by degrees to draw them to a pure and spiritual affection."[26] Jesus moved from infancy through to manhood, in order to grant this purification to every age of human life:[27] thus, in a perfect synthesis, Bernard blended the first step of the mystical ascent, purification, with the Gospel narrative of the human life of Jesus.

The second step of the mystical ascent was illumination, and this too lent itself to the use of the familiar biblical metaphor of Jesus the Light. This is well exemplified in the words of Julian of Norwich, whom David Knowles called "in qualities of mind and heart, one of the most remarkable—perhaps the most remarkable—Englishwoman of her age."[28] For Julian, "the light is God, our Maker, Father, and Holy Ghost in Christ Jesus our Saviour."[29] The suffering and cross of Jesus become a way of overcoming what she called the "darkness of sin" and the "blindness" of the soul.[30] For, she said, the darkness of sin "hath no manner of substance nor particle of being" and is not a reality in its own right but the absence of light, as evil is the absence of good and does not exist as such. Because the soul does not know this of itself, it lives in the darkness as though it were real. Only with the coming of the light that is Jesus and with the revelation of his suffering, does the power of this unreal darkness become evident and thereby lose its hold.[31] The natural lights of the natural world lose their hold as well when his light overwhelms them all. As another English mystic, Robert Herrick,[32] put it,

And these mine eyes shall see
All times, how they
Are lost i' th' Sea
Of vast Eternitie.

Where never Moone shall sway
The Starres; but she,
And Night, shall be
Drown'd in one endlesse Day.

And after purification and illumination will come union. Here it was especially the language of the Gospel of John that lent itself to the uses of Christ-mysticism. "Abide in me, and I in you," Jesus says to the disciples in that Gospel (John 15:4); and in his high-priestly prayer on the night of his betrayal he implored his Father for his followers, "that they may all be one; even as thou, Father, art in me, and I in thee, that they also may be in us" (John 17:21). When such sayings of Jesus were combined with the words of the Song of Songs quoted earlier, "My Beloved is mine and I am his," the eternal union between Jesus and the Father in the mystery of the holy and indivisible Trinity became the ground for what Protestant devotion came to call the *unio mystica*, "the mystical union" between Bridegroom and bride, between Christ and the soul.

Without imposing an artificial rigidity upon it, it is even possible to read the *Divine Comedy* of Dante Alighieri as a celebration of these three stages—not, of course, as though its three *cantiche* of *Inferno*, *Purgatorio*, *Paradiso* corresponded to purification, illumination, and union, for they do not (since none of the three is possible in hell); but the three themes mark the steps of the soul's ascent, and thus of the poet's ascent. The *Purgatorio*'s recitation, one by one, of the means by which each of the seven mortal sins is purged away through penance and the grace of Christ is an almost clinical analysis of what the mystics meant by the *via purgationis*. Thus in canto 17, with many echoes from Augustine, sin is traced to a disordering, "through excess or through deficiency," of the love with which and for which the human heart was created.[33] Purgation, then, consists in the reordering of love in accordance with the will of God. The illumination sought by Christ-mysticism is proclaimed in the very opening lines of the *Paradiso*:

> La gloria di colui che tutto move
> per l'universo penetra e risplende
> in una parte più e meno altrove.
> Nel ciel che più della sua luce prende
> fu' io.

As John Sinclair translates these words, "The glory of Him who moves all things penetrates the universe and shines in one part more and another less. I was in the heaven that most receives His light." And in the closing canto of the *Paradiso* this "luce etterna che sola in te sidi" overpowers the poet's mind. Leaving behind the claims of intellect, he turns instead, as mystics like Bonaventure had said one must, to the will and to its desire, which bring him to harmony and union with divine Love:

> ma già volgeva il mio disio e 'l velle,
> sì come rota ch' igualmente e mossa,
> l'amor che move il sole e l'altre stelle,

which Sinclair renders: "But now my desire and will, like a wheel that spins with even motion, were revolved by the Love that moves the sun and the other stars."

The themes of purification, illumination, and mystical union with Christ the Bridegroom of the Soul also shaped the depictions of the lives of the saints in both literature and art. Many of these appeared in the *Lives* of female saints, both during the Middle Ages and in the age of Counter-Reformation and Baroque.[34] The thirteenth-century Franciscan saint Margaret of Cortona, "the new Magdalene," is an especially striking example, for her revelations and mystical experiences resulted from a conversion to Christ that followed the tragic death of a young nobleman with whom she had been living for nine years outside the sacrament of matrimony. Her official biography in the *Acts of the Saints* tells us that "she heard Jesus Christ calling her in a sweet manner," and that, "lifted up to the extremes of ecstasy, she lost all consciousness and motion."[35] That experience has been vividly portrayed in Giovanni Lanfranco's *Ecstasy of Saint Margaret of Cortona* from about 1620, in which "the saint, lost in the utter transport of ecstasy and held up by the angels," has her gaze fixed on "Christ upon a throne of clouds, borne by angels."[36] On the basis of the iconography as well as of the hagiography, it does not seem exaggerated to see "more than a suggestion of a sublimated erotic experience" in "the excited movement of the rumpled draperies and the swift, flickering play of light and dark" in Lanfranco's depiction of her "vehement emotions."[37]

The attitude of medieval mystics and thinkers toward these tendencies in Christ-mysticism was by no means naive or uncritical, and many of them sought to curb the potential dangers. The most obvious of these dangers, as evidenced both by Christian art and by Christian mystical commentaries on the Song of Songs, was eroticism. The Song is, after all, still a love poem, and a very explicit love poem at that, even if one reads it as an allegory; and the allegory can easily revert to the very eroticism it is intended to transcend.[38] In many of the poems of the troubadours, as their editor has put, "the worship of the lady suggests a kind of literary mariolatry; but the love celebrated, for all its refinement, was adulterous."[39] Thus lyrics addressed to the Blessed Virgin Mary and lyrics addressed to a sweetheart often became interchangeable, with the devotional lines being used to conceal—or, rather, to conceal and thus to reveal—the poet's true desire for his lady love. The word "soul" is feminine in most of the languages of Europe: *psychē* in Greek, *anima* in Latin and its descendants, *Seele* in German, *dusha* in the Slavic tongues. That made it all the easier to transpose the metaphors about the Bridegroom of the Soul into highly charged sexual images. Nor does the insistence upon the identity of Jesus the Crucified as the Bridegroom protect against such images. Julian was careful, when she declared that "our sensuality is only in the second Person, Christ Jesus," to put such statements into the context of a fully developed doctrine of the Trinity.[40] But in some hymns and prayers addressed to Christ Crucified (for example, those of the Moravian Church at Herrnhut), the wound in his side became the object of a veneration and yearning for union that acquired strikingly sexual overtones. The line from emotion to sentimentality was easy to cross, and so was the line from love as the *agapē* of Christ to love as *erōs* for Christ; it was just as easy to cross both lines at once.

Also easy to cross, especially in the later Middle Ages, was the line separating Christ-mysticism from pantheism.[41] The yearning for union with the divine frequently seemed to become a yearning for the obliteration of the distinction between Creator and creature. Jewish mysticism had frequently addressed this problem, but for Christ-mysticism the temptation would appear to have been even more insidious. For the very orthodoxy invoked against such tendencies has at its center the dogma that in the person of Jesus, as Bonaventure put it, "there is joined the First Principle with the last, . . . the eternal with temporal man."[42] This could be taken to mean that in him the distinction between Creator and creator had been transcended, perhaps even obliterated. The goal and the achievement of Christ-mysticism had been formulated in the words of the New Testament: "We are God's children now; it does not yet appear what we shall be, but we know that when he appears we shall be like him, for we shall see him as he is" (1 John 3:2). That could be interpreted as a promise that the creaturely state of the soul, now captive in the prison of the body, would be sloughed off when the soul would fly "from the alone to the Alone." Various mystics of the fifteenth century were accused, especially by more orthodox mystics, of harboring an eschatology in which everything, having come from God, would be reabsorbed into God.[43]

Likewise implicit in many strains of Christ-mysticism, already in the Middle Ages and even more in Pietist Protestantism, was individualism; in the words of one extreme critic, "in the midst of its struggle for unselfish love, mysticism proves to be the most refined form, the acme of egocentric piety."[44] As we noted earlier, the scholastic tradition of mystical commentaries on the Song of Songs read it as an exposition of the relation between Christ and the church, just as one rabbinical tradition saw it as an allegory of the relation between God and the people of Israel. But in the monastic tradition, it often became instead an allegory of Christ and the individual soul. "My beloved is mine and I am his" became a way of describing my very own private relation to Jesus, and his relation to me, to the exclusion, or at least the diminution, of others. A well-known sentimental religious song has expressed this individualism quite unabashedly:

I come to the garden alone,
While the dew is still on the roses.
And the voice I hear,
Falling on my ear,
The Son of God discloses.
And He walks with me and He talks with me,
And He tells me I am His own.
And the joys we share, as we tarry there,
None other has ever known.

Whether sentimental or sublime, Christ-mysticism has repeatedly been the supreme instance of how, within the classic triad of the Good, the True, and the Beautiful, it has been the Beautiful that has been able to portray him the most effectively—and the most seductively. Responding to the deepest yearnings of the human spirit for transcendent meaning and authentic fulfillment, the experience of purification, illumination, and union with the "Beautiful Savior" has succeeded in ennobling every natural sensibility and elevating it into a means of grace: nothing need be profane, everything can be sacramental. But in the process, it sometimes proved all too tempting to lose sight of the Good and the True in the blinding light of the Beautiful, or "to dissolve historical events into religious experience," with the real danger of "not an abandonment of the dogma of the Incarnation of the Son of God, but an underestimation of it," producing "a morass of spiritualizing exposition which has no legitimate ground in historical reality."[45] Cutting itself loose as it does from the strict grammatical sense of the biblical text, a mystical exegesis is especially vulnerable on this count. But as this issue arose in the Christ-mysticism of the High Middle Ages, so it was in the same era that there appeared a new subjectivity that stood the whole issue on its head. For the figure who was the apex of the development of Christ-mysticism was at the same time the fountainhead for a new appreciation of the Historical Jesus of Nazareth as the Divine and Human Model.

11

The Divine and Human Model

*Take my yoke upon you, and learn
from me.*

If a public opinion poll were to ask a representative group of informed and thoughtful people "Which historical figure of the past two thousand years has most fully embodied the life and teachings of Jesus Christ?" the person mentioned most often would certainly be Francis of Assisi.[1] That answer might, if anything, be even more frequent if the people polled were not affiliated with any church. And it is probably also the answer that many of his own contemporaries would have given to such a question—or, at any rate, those who lived within a century or so after him. For in Francis of Assisi the imitation of the life of Jesus and the obedience to his teachings (which were, at least in principle, binding on every believer) attained such a level of fidelity as to earn for him the designation, eventually made official by Pope Pius XI, of "the second Christ [*alter Christus*]."[2]

There was little in his early life to suggest that Giovanni di Bernardone would ever assume any such place in history. Born in 1181 or 1182 to a merchant family in Assisi, he aspired to the rank of knight, and to a chivalric career. Instead, he was converted to be a chevalier of the cross of Christ and the "herald of the great King."[3] The reasons for any conversion are generally more complicated than the later explanations provided by the convert or the convert's followers. So it had been been with Paul and Augustine, and so it was with Francis.

From the documents of the life of Francis, which have been subjected to meticulous study, it is evident that his transformation was not one single moment of blinding incandescence, but a gradual movement away from his old manner of life to a new understanding of himself and of his mission in the world. It is no less evident that at the center of this transformation was the person of the historical Jesus as the Divine and Human Model. At prayer one day, Francis beheld the figure of the crucified Christ, and the vision stayed with him all his life. He understood the vision to mean that Christ was summoning him personally in the words of the Gospel, so familiar through the centuries of monastic history, "If any man would come after me, let him deny himself and take up his cross and follow me" (Matt. 16:24).[4]

That was what Francis did. "From that time on," his official biography reports, he "developed a spirit of poverty, with a deep sense of humility, and an attitude of profound compassion."[5] The summons of Christ to take up the cross and follow him included the specific instruction to "go and repair my house [the church], which is in total disrepair." At first Francis interpreted this command in a literal sense, undertaking to repair several church buildings in the vicinity that needed restoring. But gradually it dawned on him that the church to whose rebuilding Christ had called him was not merely this sanctuary or that parish church, but nothing less than the very church of Christ on earth. The central content of that mission was disclosed to Francis on 24 February 1209—a date marked by his followers every year, along with other anniversaries of his life. On that day Francis perceived the words of Jesus, at the first sending of the twelve apostles during his earthly ministry (as distinct from the sending after the resurrection reported in Matt. 28:19–20), to have been spoken also to him: "Preach as you go, saying, 'The kingdom of heaven is at hand.' Take no gold, nor silver, nor copper in your belts" (Matt. 10:7, 9).[6] Despite the austerity of that requirement—or, to be utterly precise, because of its austerity—Francis almost immediately began to attract followers, who wanted to share this radically evangelical way of life: first there were five, then there were twelve; but by 1221 there were at least three thousand. The small Church of Saint Mary of the Angels (Santa Maria degli Angeli), popularly called Portiuncula, near Assisi, was one of the buildings that Francis restored. It then became, in the words of Bonaventure, "the place where St. Francis founded the Order of Friars

Minor by divine inspiration.'"[7] (It would also be the place where Francis died on 3 October 1226.)

Like Benedict and other monastic founders throughout the Middle Ages, Francis prepared a monastic rule for his small band of followers. It was approved by Pope Innocent III soon after its composition, thus in 1209 or 1210. The pope's approval was not, however, written down anywhere. Moreover, the first *Rule* itself has not survived in a written form, and we are dependent on various (and sometimes conflicting) accounts of what it contained. It does appear from all accounts that in it Francis avoided lengthy prescriptions of structure or conduct for the order, preferring to "use for the most part the words of the holy Gospel."[8] But that explanation omits the decisive factor in the way the order was organized and governed: the personality of Francis himself. The sources that survive compel us to the conclusion that his must have been an almost magical presence. It was this that drew followers from various regions and from many different walks of life. They came because of the magnetic pull of Francis, and they came because of the authority of the Gospel of Jesus—and these two reasons were one in their eyes. For Francis was devoted to what his first biographer, Thomas of Celano, would call "the humility of the incarnation" of Christ.[9]

That devotion to Christ took the form of a deliberate conformity to the details of his life "in all things." So literal and total was the conformity that followers of Francis in subsequent generations evolved a special literary form, the double biography. The widely read *Parallel Lives* of Plutarch had treated the great men of Greece and of Rome side by side, for example Alexander the Great and Julius Caesar, comparing and contrasting them and drawing a moral lesson. The double biography of Jesus and Francis carried this method several steps further. In both instances, the existing sources—the four Gospels and the original *Lives of Francis*—were quite fragmentary and, as biographies, less than satisfying to a disciple who wanted to know everything possible about the Master. The way to satisfy this yearning was to fill in the gaps from the parallel life; for because Francis had been the most perfect among all the imitators of Christ, it was possible to know more about either one by studying the life of the other.

By far the most dramatic evidence of the parallel between the lives of Jesus and of Francis came near the end of the life of Francis, in

September 1224. As was his wont, he had gone on retreat to Alvernia (La Verna in Italian), a mountain between Arezzo and Florence, where a chapel to Saint Mary of the Angels had been built for the Franciscans a few years earlier. Following the example of Christ in the desert before his temptation (Matt. 4:2), who had in turn followed the example of Moses (Ex. 34:28), Francis spent forty days on the mountain. On or about the feast of the Exaltation of the Cross, 14 September, he had a vision. He beheld an angel, a seraph with six wings (Isa. 6:1–13), and between the wings of the seraph Francis suddenly descried the figure of the crucified Christ. He was overwhelmed by the vision, and then, in the words of his biographer Bonaventure,

> as the vision disappeared, it left his heart ablaze with eagerness and impressed upon his body a miraculous likeness. There and then the marks of nails began to appear in his hands and feet, just as he had seen them in the vision of the Man nailed to the Cross. His hands and feet appeared pierced through the center with nails. . . . His right side seemed as if it had been pierced with a lance and was marked with a livid scar which often bled.[10]

From the statement of the apostle Paul, which the disciples of Francis were to recall, "I bear on my body the marks [Greek, *stigmata*] of Jesus" (Gal. 6:17), these markings were called "stigmata."[11] In the *Paradiso* Dante has Thomas Aquinas—who was a Dominican, not a Franciscan—call them "the final seal [*l'ultimo sigillo*]."[12]

Francis appears to have been the first person in history to have undergone a stigmatization, but there have been other instances of it since, perhaps as many as three hundred having been fairly well authenticated according to one census.[13] Nowadays only the most incurably skeptical would question the historical accuracy of the reports that Francis actually did bear the marks in his limbs and side. At least some of the more recent cases have also been verified fully, sometimes even by physicians who were not themselves believers. Whether such cases are attributable to a miracle or to autosuggestion is, however, quite another question. There are, after all, cases on record of devout Muslims on whose bodies have appeared the marks of the wounds incurred by the prophet Mohammed in battle. It does seem arbitrary to attribute these to autosuggestion and then to claim a miracle in the case of all the Christians who have had a similar experience. Whatever the right answer to this dilemma may be, almost everyone would agree that the stigmatization of Francis represents a special case, in many ways one of a kind. The reason for its uniqueness is, basically, the uniqueness of Francis himself as "the second Christ": if it was fitting for anyone ever to bear in his body the stigmata of the sufferings of Christ, Francis was the one to whom it ought to have happened. He himself, it is clear, did not take the stigmata as an occasion for self-esteem; indeed, he even imitated Christ (Matt. 16:20) in keeping his special identity a secret.[14] Nor did he, for that matter, regard them as the primary form of his imitation of Christ. That place of honor, or of lack of honor, belonged rather to poverty.

Poverty had always been a prominent feature of the kingdom of God as Jesus had perceived it, lived it, and proclaimed it.[15] "Foxes have holes, and birds of the air have nests," the Gospel of Matthew has Jesus say, "but the Son of man has nowhere to lay his head" (Matt. 8:20). With the development of Christian monasticism, as we have noted earlier, poverty became the mark of those athletes of Christ who strove to carry out more fully the counsels of perfection that exceeded the competence of workaday believers out in the world. Together with lifelong chastity and obedience, the vow of poverty was required by the *Rule* of every monastic order—required of the individual, that is, but not necessarily of the order itself. Throughout the Middle Ages that distinction had been a source of difficulty and of corruption. Monasteries acquired vast holdings of land, their libraries expanded, and their treasures of gold and jewels made them rivals of the great noble houses of Europe. Satirists and moralists enjoyed contrasting this with the saying of the disciples in the Gospel, "Lo, we have left everything and followed you" (Mark 10:28).

Francis made a radical break with the ambiguities of this monastic tradition. The second written version of his *Rule* described his followers, in the words of the New Testament, as "strangers and pilgrims in this world," who were detached from the tyrannical hold that material possessions exerted over those who owned them.[16] The ground of this detachment was the literal imitation of the example of Christ and the strict observance of his teaching. Poverty was not merely the absence of property, but was a positive good, "the Queen of the Virtues," because of its identification with Christ and with Mary.[17] One of the early legends of Francis, popularized in several paintings, described him as searching for poverty in the woods, when he met a woman who asked him what he was doing there. Upon his explanation, "I have gone forth to look for poverty, for I have cast away riches, and I will go on seeking and calling her until I meet her," the woman let it be known to him that her name was *Paupertas*, Lady Poverty. He resolved to make her his bride, and the marriage was performed by Christ himself.

It would, however, be a grave error to interpret the Franciscan detachment from material wealth as the expression of a hatred for the material and natural world. Quite the opposite: Francis of Assisi was responsible for the rediscovery of nature, and he introduced into medieval Christianity a positive enjoyment of the natural realm for which there were few precedents. It was, Chesterton has said, as if Europe had first been obliged to pass through a tunnel of purgation, in which it was cleansed of the degrading nature-worship it had inherited from both its classical and its barbarian origins, so that then, in Francis, "man has stripped from his soul the last rag of nature-worship, and can return to nature."[18] In his familiar *Canticle of Brother Sun*, the first significant work in the history of Italian vernacular literature, Francis sang,

> All praise be yours, my Lord, through all that you have made,
> And first my lord Brother Sun,
> Who brings the day.

The moon was his sister, the wind his brother; and, in a stanza said to have been added at his last hour, "Sister Death," too, was a gift from God.[19] Many of the most familiar hymns of praise to God for nature, including the well-known "All Things Bright and Beautiful" by Cecil Frances Alexander, are reworkings of this Franciscan material.

In a paradoxical form, that attitude of regard for the created world is evident also in the way Francis thought and spoke about the human body. At one level, his aspersions on the physical side of human nature went to lengths that almost anyone would find excessive. He mingled ashes with his food to keep it from being too palatable, and he "would hurl himself into a ditch full of ice" when he felt sexually tempted.[20] Yet even these extremes of ascetic self-denial were part of a total view of the world and of life. All of them belonged to his commitment as a follower of Christ and a bearer of the cross, for he reminded himself of the words of the apostle Paul: "Those who belong to Christ Jesus have crucified the flesh with its passions and desires. If we live by the Spirit, let us also walk by the Spirit" (Gal. 5:24–25). The purpose of all these acts of self-mortification was to discipline the body for the sake of a higher goal. There are more than superficial similarities between ascetics like Francis and present-day athletes, who set their faces grimly, strain every muscle, bend every nerve, and punish their bodies—all to win. "They do it to receive a perishable wreath," Francis could have said with the apostle, "but we an imperishable. I pommel my body and subdue it" (1 Cor. 9:25, 27).

A direct corollary of discovering nature and of identifying the sufferings of his body with the sufferings of Christ was a new and deeper awareness of the humanity of Christ, as disclosed in his nativity and in his sufferings. It was, so the followers of Francis believed, as if "the Child Jesus had been forgotten in the hearts of many," but "was brought to life again through his servant St. Francis."[21] If Jesus were now finally to be taken with utmost seriousness, he had to have an authentic image here within human history. Therefore both the beginning of the human life of Jesus Christ and its end found new forms of expression through the life and work of Francis. The celebration of Christmas had come rather late in the development of the Christian calendar, after the other festivals had already been established.[22] Its growing importance was probably related to the increasing emphasis of the fifth and sixth centuries on the true and complete humanity of Jesus. Francis, according to Thomas of Celano, "observed the birthday of the Child Jesus with inexpressible eagerness over all other feasts, saying that it was the feast of feasts."[23] As his principal contribution to the observance of this festival, Francis in 1223 set up a *presepio* or crèche at the Umbrian village of Greccio, where midnight Mass was celebrated on Christmas Eve in that year, with Francis, as the deacon of the Mass, preaching "about the birth of the poor King, whom he called the Baby of Bethlehem in his tender love."[24]

Important though this theme of Franciscan faith in Christ was for the history of art and the history of devotion, the most lasting impression he left in both areas came through his concentration on the Jesus of the cross. He made his own the New Testament determination "to know nothing except Jesus Christ and him crucified" (1 Cor. 2:2). Throughout his life Francis identified himself with the events of the suffering of Christ—so much so that it would probably be possible to reconstruct almost the entire Gospel history of the Passion from the individual scenes in which Francis has been depicted as a participant. "Christ hung upon his Cross, poor and naked and in great pain," Bonaventure writes, "and Francis wanted to be like him in everything."[25] Francis strove to conform himself to Christ and to imitate him perfectly in life and in death. So reciprocal was the relation between the contemporary perception of Francis and the image of Christ that the story of the friar with the stigmata led to a deeper awareness of his Divine and Human Model. The Christ of Francis was not one in whom the presence and power of the divine had anesthetized his human nature so that the pain of the cross left him unaffected. Rather, as the New Testament had said, "we have not a high priest who is unable to sympathize with our weaknesses, but one who in every respect has been tempted as we are, yet without sinning" (Heb. 4:15). The experience of Francis as the second Christ, and specifically of his conformity to the cross, served to endow painting and poetry with a new realism, as they struggled to give form to the fundamental conviction that in the suffering and death of Jesus on the cross both the mystery of divine life and the mystery of human life had become manifest.

Yet it was not conformity to Christ in his crucifixion, but conformity to Christ in his poverty, that proved to be the most controversial item on the Franciscan agenda. Both by his own actions in relation to Lady Poverty and by the language of his instructions to his followers, Francis had made clear his own strict construction of the vow of poverty.[26] Christ, the Virgin Mary, and the apostles had abstained from all ownership of money and property; therefore absolute poverty was essential to the perfection of the Gospel. Following the death of Francis, one party among his followers, which came to be called the Spirituals, insisted that this strict construction was the only acceptable one, since the *Rule* and the *Testament* of Francis were divinely inspired. Combining this insistence with a denunciation of the church and its institutions for its compromises with secularism, some of them came to see themselves as the forerunners of a new "spiritual church," in which the purity of the Gospel, as announced by Francis the "angel with an eternal Gospel" (Rev. 14:6), would be restored and absolute poverty would prevail. The more moderate party among the followers of Francis, sometimes called Conventuals, refrained from posing such a radical antithesis between the institutional church and the "spiritual church." They found their most balanced interpreter in Bonaventure—theologian, philosopher, mystical writer, and Franciscan saint—whose normative reinterpretation of the *Rule* and authorized *Life* of Francis, intended to supplant all the preceding *Lives*, made Franciscanism acceptable to the church and made Bonaventure, as he is often called, the "second founder of the Friars Minor."

This controversy over poverty had some unlooked-for political consequences. Nothing would seem to be more otherworldly and apolitical—indeed, downright idealistic—than the doctrine that because Christ, Mary, and the apostles had practiced total poverty, it was incumbent on the church to obey their example and to abstain from owning anything. Yet by one of those curious ironies with which history, and perhaps especially the history of the church, is fraught, this otherworldly position formed an alliance with various radical secularists of the fourteenth century, who were asserting the authority of the state over against that of the church. The eminent Franciscan philosopher and theologian William of Ockham attacked Pope John XXII for modifying the requirements of the *Rule* and *Testament* of Francis on poverty. During the ensuing conflict, Ockham found political asylum at the court of the Holy Roman Emperor, Louis of Bavaria, who was engaged in a struggle with the papacy over the relative prerogatives of church and state. Taking over some of Ockham's arguments and adapting them in a manner that was in fact quite un-Franciscan and that Ockham, as a devoted churchman and (so he insisted) an orthodox Catholic, had not intended, the emperor and his supporters cast themselves in the role of liberators of the true church from the burdens of property and power. In the process, then, this image of Jesus made a contribution to the formulation of the founding principles and "secular values" of modern political philosophy.[27] This was a long distance indeed from the Francis of the stigmata and his quest for the simplicity of the life set forth in the Gospels.

Even amid the political turbulence of the later Middle Ages, that quest for the authenticity of the Gospels continued to exercise its hold upon human hearts and lives. Although historians have sometimes tended to emphasize the political battles of the time to the exclusion of everything else, the Franciscan dedication to Christ as the Divine and Human Model was in many ways a more universal, as well as a more abiding, theme. Early in the fifteenth century there appeared a book entitled *The Imitation of Christ*, which is said to have achieved a greater circulation than any book in history save the Bible itself. The book, which was anonymous, is generally attributed to the Rhenish mystic Thomas à Kempis, who died in 1471. Whoever the author of the book may have been, the central figure of the book is unquestionably Jesus Christ. "Ever put before thee," it admonished (in a sixteenth-century English translation), "the image of the crucifix"; and it exclaimed, quite in the spirit of Francis: "Would God we had naught else to do, but only to praise our Lord Jesus Christ with all our heart."[28] In its very first chapter it announced, "Let our sovereign study be—in the life of Jesu Christ." That study was the foundation both of an accurate self-knowledge and of a true recognition of the reality of God. Nor was it enough to know the church's doctrines or the sayings of the Bible, "for whoever will understand the words of Christ plainly and in their full savour must study to conform all his life to his life." Once again, the Franciscan glorification of Jesus as the Divine and Human Model was asserting itself as an alternative to the smugness of conventional religion.

And it goes on doing so. During 1926, the seven-hundredth anniversary of the death of Francis, two million pilgrims came to Assisi. Most of them were, of course, devout members of the church, who believed, as had Bonaventure and Francis himself, that loyalty to the institutional church and the imitation of Christ were not at all incompatible, but mutually supportive and ultimately identical. On the other hand, Francis has also become the patron saint, whatever his own original intention may have been, of that growing number in the modern world who become more devoted to Jesus as they become more alienated from the church, who find an irreconcilable conflict betweeen ecclesiastical Christianity and the permanently relevant teaching of the Gospels—or, as they have often phrased it, between the religion *of* Jesus and the religion *about* Jesus. Homes in which no religious pictures or icons appear, where there is not even so much as a cross, will nevertheless often have a plaque, sometimes rather sentimentalized, with the familiar *Prayer of Saint Francis:* "Lord, make me an instrument of your peace." And the interpretation of Francis that has had the widest influence in modern times has not been the official one of the church, based on Bonaventure's, but that of Paul Sabatier, who believed that the original message of Francis had been expurgated by his later disciples, notably Bonaventure, in order to make him acceptable to church authorities.[29] Present-day scholars may be less skeptical than Sabatier was about the orthodox version of Francis, but even they have had to rely on his researches and editions to argue against him.

That ambiguity runs through the entire history of Francis and of

Christ Militant ("Ego sum via, veritas, et vita"), sixth-century mosaic, The Archiepiscopal Chapel, Ravenna. See p. 7.

Marc Chagall, *The White Crucifixion*, 1938, The Art Institute of Chicago. See p. 20.

Michelangelo, Sistine Chapel ceiling: *Delphica*, 1509–10. See p. 38.

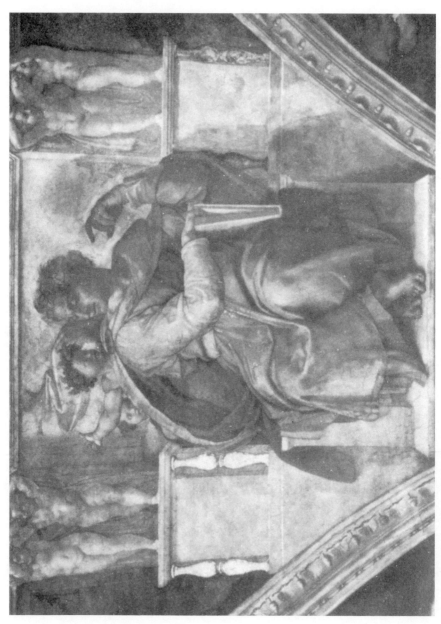

Michelangelo, Sistine Chapel ceiling: *Isaiah*, 1509–10. See p. 38.

Christ Enthroned between the Emperor Constantine IX Monomachus and the Empress Zoe, eleventh-century mosaic, south gallery, Hagia Sophia, Constantinople. See pp. 54–55.

Siegfried Reinhardt, *Light*, 1959, author's collection. See p. 72.

Bust of Christ Pantocrator, sixth-century encaustic icon, The Monastery of Saint Catherine, Sinai. See p. 93.

Giovanni Lanfranco, *The Ecstasy of Saint Margaret of Cortona*, 1618–20, Galleria Pitti, Florence. See p. 130.

Giotto, *The Dream of Pope Innocent III*, 1297, upper basilica of Saint Francis, Assisi. See p. 143.

El Greco, *The Savior*, c. 1610–14, Museo del Greco, Toledo. See p. 148.

Lucas Cranach the Younger, *The Last Supper* (Memorial to Joachim of Anhalt), 1565, Dessau-Mildensee. See p. 162.

William Blake, *Christ Appearing to the Apostles after the Resurrection*, c. 1795, Yale Center for British Art. See p. 198.

the Franciscan spirit. It is the theme of one of the oldest of the innumerable legends about Saint Francis, enshrined in a painting attributed to Giotto. After receiving the revelation of Christ that called him from his former way of life to the life of the Gospel, Francis came to Rome to obtain the pope's sanction, required for founding a new religious order. As has been noted, Francis received this sanction, albeit only orally, in 1209 or 1210. But, at least according to the legend and Giotto's picture, it happened in a remarkable way. Although Pope Innocent III was deeply touched by the sanctity of Francis and by the power of his evangelical commitment, he withheld any response to the application for approval until he could consult the princes of the church, the cardinals. Various members of this body expressed misgivings about Francis, particularly about the evident parallels between the preachments of various heretical movements abroad in the land and his message of radical poverty in obedience to Christ the Divine and Human Model. Others were more positive in their reactions.

Ultimately, of course, the decision was up to the pope himself. The following night Pope Innocent III had a dream (which is why one of the names for Giotto's mural was *The Dream of Pope Innocent III*). Two figures dominate the fresco—Francis on the left and Pope Innocent on the right. The pope, attended by two watchmen, is asleep on a sumptuous canopied bed. He is, even in his sleep, wearing a miter, the symbol of his episcopal office, as well as an elegant cape. Francis, the subject of the pope's dream, is, by contrast, attired in the coarse habit that became his trademark, with a cord about his waist and with bare feet. His left arm is akimbo, but with his right he is holding up a building, the venerable Basilica of Saint John Lateran, which had been donated to the church by Emperor Constantine I and was the seat of authority for the pope as bishop of Rome. The church was tilted at a dangerous angle, and was, in Innocent's dream, in danger of falling over until this young man came to its rescue. On the basis of the vision in the dream, the pope granted the request and confirmed the first *Rule*.

The contrast could not have been more striking. Here was the most powerful man ever to occupy the Throne of Saint Peter, whom the earliest *Life of Francis* called "a famous man, greatly learned, renowned in discourse, burning with zeal for justice in the things that the cause of the Christian faith demanded."[30] He had just turned thirty-seven when he became pope in 1198, and for almost two decades he piloted the Bark of Peter with a sound instinct for just what it needed. A man of blameless character and great eloquence, he had believed before his election that the pope, as the successor of Peter, was the one to whom Christ had addressed his words: "On this rock I will build my church" (Matt. 16:18). After his election, he strove to live up to what he had believed about the papacy, and he succeeded. The pope, he believed, was "less than God but more than man," mediating between them. At the greatest church council of the Middle Ages, held in 1215 at the Lateran, he was hailed as "lord of the world [*dominus mundi*]." The continuity of the church, without which, historically speaking, there would be no Gospel—and no Francis of Assisi—and the presence and power of Christ became visible, almost tangible, in the pontificate of Pope Innocent III. And on the other side of Giotto's picture is the simple figure of the young man from Assisi, in his late twenties at the time. His eyes are lifted to heaven, and seemingly without any strain he has taken on one shoulder the entire weight of the Lateran—and of the world. Giotto's painting and subsequent history join to compel the question, though not to answer it:

Now which of the two was truly the "Vicar of Christ"?

12

The Universal Man

*As the truth is in Jesus, be re-
newed in the spirit of your minds,
and put on the new nature.*

 "The Discovery of the World and of Man" and "The De-
velopment of the Individual" were two major themes of
the Renaissance of the fourteenth, fifteenth, and sixteenth
centuries, as formulated by its most celebrated modern
interpreter, Jacob Burckhardt:

In the Middle Ages both sides of human consciousness—that which was
turned within as that which was turned without—lay dreaming or half awake
beneath a common veil. The veil was woven of faith, illusion, and childish
prepossession, through which the world and history were seen clad in strange
hues.... [But in the Italian Renaissance] the *subjective* side ... asserted itself
...: man became a spiritual *individual*, and recognized himself as such. Observe the expressions *uomo singolare* and *uomo unico* for the higher and highest
stages of individual development.[1]

Burckhardt does not say that this change was due to a rejection of
the authority of the figure of Jesus; interestingly, he just does not
refer in this context to the figure of Jesus at all.

Ironically, however, the very concept and name Renaissance (*ri-
nascimento*), whatever the ultimate origins of the idea may have been,
had come into the vocabulary of European civilization principally
through the teachings of Jesus.[2] "Truly, truly, I say to you," the
Gospel of John has him declare to Nicodemus, "unless one is born

anew [*renatus* in the Vulgate], he cannot see the kingdom of God" (John 3:3). And near the end of the Book of Revelation attributed to the same apostle John, Jesus, "who sat upon the throne, said, 'Behold, I make all things new' " (Rev. 21:5). Although they often set the "new birth" of the Renaissance into contrast with the supposed "Gothic" or barbarian decadence of the Middle Ages, the humanists of the Renaissance yielded to no exponent of medieval theology in their admiration for Jesus and their devotion to him. In fact, Erasmus of Rotterdam, citing the passage from the Gospel of John just quoted, made the identification of the Renaissance with the person of Jesus altogether explicit. "What else is the philosophy of Christ," he asked in the preface to his edition of the Greek New Testament in 1516, "which He Himself calls a 'rebirth [*renascentia*],' than the restoration of [human] nature to the original goodness of its creation?"[3] Dante's *Vita Nuova* may be seen as sounding the same theme of renewal and "new life." Therefore, in the apt formula of Konrad Burdach, "the Renaissance, which establishes a new concept of humanity, of art, and of literary and scholarly life," arises "not in opposition to the Christian religion," as so much of modern historiography since Burckhardt has imagined, "but out of the full vitality of a religious revival."[4] Hence the very title Universal Man, which has come to be known, even in popular magazines, as the slogan of the Renaissance,[5] and which the humanists not only employed but strove to embody, may well serve as a summary of the place that Renaissance thought and art accorded to Jesus, as the only one who could be called *uomo singolare* and *uomo unico* in the strict and total sense. For "the Universal Man" had been his title in the Christian tradition all along,[6] and in the Renaissance it came into its own.

The effort to see the Renaissance as a naturalistic revolt against such traditional and medieval ideas of Christ as the doctrine of the incarnation and the concept of the two natures, divine and human, seems to have become almost canonical among certain nineteenth-century historians of Renaissance art. For the origins of this interpretation, as for so much of the origins of both the history of ideas and the history of aesthetics in the nineteenth century, we must look to Goethe. His essay on Leonardo da Vinci's *Last Supper*, written in German in 1817 and published in English translation only four years later, characterized Leonardo's portrayal of Jesus as "the boldest attempt to adhere to nature, while, at the same time, the object is supernatural," with the result that "the majesty, the uncontrolled will, the power and might of the Deity" were not expressed.[7] In his widely influential book *The Renaissance. Studies in Art and Poetry*, Walter Pater, acknowledging his debt to Goethe, set forth his own conclusion that "though [Leonardo da Vinci] handles sacred subjects continually, he is the most profane of painters." Therefore Pater sought to interpret Leonardo's *Last Supper*, dealing though it did with one of the most sacred of subjects, as a painting in which the institution of the Lord's Supper by Jesus on the night in which he was betrayed provided "merely the pretext for a kind of work which carries one altogether beyond the range of its conventional associations." The inspiration of the work was an aestheticist naturalism far removed from the themes conventionally associated with the image of Jesus:

> Here was another effort to lift a given subject out of the range of its traditional associations. Strange, after all the mystic developments of the middle age, was the effort to see the Eucharist, not as the pale Host of the altar, but as one taking leave of his friends. . . . Vasari pretends that the central head was never finished. But finished or unfinished, or owing part of its effect to a mellowing decay, the head of Jesus does but consummate the sentiment of the whole company—ghosts through which you see the wall, faint as the shadows of the leaves upon the wall on autumn afternoons. This figure is but the faintest, the most spectral of them all.[8]

More recently, however, historians of Renaissance art have come to interpret this supposed naturalism more subtly and more profoundly. Thus a monograph by the art historian Leo Steinberg on how Renaissance painters portrayed the sexuality of Jesus has taken a subject that could have lent itself to sensationalism, but has instead related this theme to the central motifs in the doctrine of the incarnation as "the centrum of Christian orthodoxy." It argues that unlike many of its predecessors in Christian history, "Renaissance culture not only advanced an incarnational theology (as the Greek Church had also done), but evolved representational modes adequate to its expression." Therefore, it concludes, "we may take Renaissance art to be the first and last phase of Christian art that can claim full Christian orthodoxy."[9] Although it would be possible to take issue with this interpretation of the theological implications of the Byzantine icons, the case is far stronger for this interpretation of the Renaissance Christ, an interpretation in which art history and intellectual history come together.

One of the many Renaissance portraits of Jesus as Universal Man to combine magnificently several of the motifs and "images" that we have been discussing throughout this book is *The Savior* by Kyriakos Theotokopoulos, whom posterity calls El Greco. The model for the portrait was a Jewish young man in Toledo, for El Greco wanted to take seriously the Jewishness of Jesus. It is clear that he had learned the style of the portrait from the masters of the Italian Renaissance, specifically from his teacher Titian. But what sets this portrait apart from many others of the period is another quality: "The light of his paintings almost has nothing in common with daylight. It represents a type of 'supernatural explosion of color,' as René Huyghe describes it. . . . It has been described as 'a kind of spiritual experience emanating from the eye of the faith-filled soul of El Greco.' "[10] This Jesus is indeed a historical figure, and he is indeed Jewish; but he has been pictured in a way that also stands in the tradition of the Byzantine icon, as the Jesus of the Transfiguration. And all of this has been suffused with the spirit of the Spanish Christ-mysticism of the sixteenth century, in whose atmosphere El Greco worked. The result is a remarkable synthesis of several artistic, mystical, and theological traditions—a synthesis that makes its presence felt throughout the Renaissance perspective on Jesus as the Universal Man.

A representative spokesman for this Renaissance view of the Universal Man was Donato Acciaiuoli, a humanist and statesman who belonged to one of the most eminent families of Florence. In a sermon preached on 13 April 1468, dealing with the same subject as da Vinci's painting, he set his exposition of the Eucharist apart from the "many subtle investigations which the [scholastic] doctors have made concerning its matter, its form, its efficient cause and its final cause, and how the substance of the bread and the wine is transformed into the most true body of Christ." But it would be a serious anachronism to read such a polemic against the philosophical theology of scholasticism as a rejection of the orthodox doctrine of the incarnation of the Son of God in the man Jesus. On the contrary, Acciaiuoli reaffirmed that doctrine with sincerity and vigor even as he broke with the scholastic version (or, as he would have it, distortion and unnecessary complication) of it:

> Our Savior Jesus Christ, my beloved fathers, having so greatly benefited human nature by first assuming this flesh of ours and then through all the course of his life in teaching the people and spreading his doctrines among

readers, in freeing the weak and raising the dead, in taking away sins and in most holy works, gave himself as a most singular example of every kind of virtue.

Therefore the Eucharist was for Donato, as Trinkaus has put it, "the most important mode by which Christ reinforces faith in his doctrine, as it is a commemoration of the divine Incarnation by which and through which Christ became the great teacher of mankind." In his reverence for Jesus as "the teacher and exemplar," Donato Acciaiuoli joined himself to the Franciscan revival (or, perhaps better, "renaissance") of the Gospel portrait and to the Jesus who had been celebrated earlier in the same century by the *Imitation of Christ*. It is, then, "difficult and essentially arbitrary either to separate the humanists' views of human nature from their peculiar approaches to religion [above all, their picture of Jesus], or on the other hand to do the reverse."[11]

Dante Alighieri, whose place in the history of Christ-mysticism has been examined earlier, occupies an important place also in the history of the Renaissance image of Jesus. Champions of the Middle Ages and of the Renaissance may dispute over which of them has a more proper claim upon Dante; but for our present purposes it is necessary only to point out, as Jacob Burckhardt himself acknowledged, that "in all essential points" of his systematic interpretation of the Italian Renaissance "the first witness to be called is Dante," perhaps most eloquently in Burckhardt's exposition of the very ideal of *l'uomo universale*, the Universal Man.[12] Yet to a degree that Burckhardt did not adequately appreciate, Dante's inspiration for that ideal, as well as for both his poetry and his politics, was inseparable from the person of Jesus.

That inspiration makes its presence felt in the very title of Dante's first book, the *Vita Nuova*. The "new life" of which it speaks refers in the first instance to Dante's own youth, as the poet's use of the very same phrase in the *Divine Comedy* to describe his early years indicates.[13] But reducing its meaning to that alone does much less than complete justice to the phrase itself and to the argument of the work, with its subtle images and its multilayered plays on words. Thus in the *Vita Nuova* Dante introduces a young woman named Giovanna (Joan), the sweetheart of his "first friend," Guido Cavalcanti; her nickname was Primavera (Spring). But Dante is told here that Giovanna is called Primavera because, as the forerunner of Beatrice, "prima verrà [she will come first]." In a sense, then, her name is derived from her nickname, and she is called Giovanna in honor of John the Baptist, who likewise came first as the one sent to announce the coming of Christ.[14] Beatrice herself, therefore, as the very incarnation of love, is, in Singleton's phrase, "an analogy and a metaphor of Christ."[15]

If that is what Beatrice is "already in the *Vita Nuova*," then she becomes "in the *Commedia*, a symbol of theology, learning illuminated by grace, even the Christian faith."[16] Near the end of the *Purgatorio* she promises Dante that he will be "with me forever a citizen of that Rome where Christ is a 'Roman,' " that is, of Paradise.[17] The *Paradiso* is throughout a panorama of how that promise is to be fulfilled. As the poet's "sweet and dear guide,"[18] Beatrice has the function of leading him—and the reader—to Christ and to the Mother of Christ, who are always inseparable and sometimes well-nigh indistinguishable. In the words of Beatrice to Dante that follow, Mary is "the rose in which the divine Word was made flesh," but like all the other flowers in the divine "garden," she, too, "blossoms under the rays of Christ," not finally of her own powers.[19] She is "the fair flower which I always invoke morning and evening," to whom angelic love itself sings that it will continue to "circle around you, Lady of Heaven, until you follow your Son and make even the highest sphere more divine by entering it."[20] It is amid the strains of a hymn to the Queen of Heaven, the *Regina coeli*, that Peter and the church triumphant receive their "treasure" of "victory, under the exalted Son of God and of Mary."[21] On the basis of such scenes as the final three cantos, describing the Empyrean with Bernard of Clairvaux and the Virgin, some eminent Dante scholars have suggested that the focus of the *Paradiso* is on Mary rather than on Christ, who seems by the end of the poem to have become so transcendent as to be inaccessible. After having given "Beatrice a place in the objective process of salvation . . . , an element which disrupts the doctrine of the church," Dante appears to have fused Beatrice and Mary into a prototype of Goethe's "eternal Feminine" and a substitute for Jesus Christ.[22] But if that is the impression of some scholars, it was not the intention of the poet.[23] For even while he is transported by the rhapsody to Mary, he describes her countenance as "the face that most resembles Christ."[24] With her eyes she directs the poet's attention to "the eternal Light," by which she too is illumined, and to eternal Love, by which she too has been saved and sustained, the Light and the Love that have come solely through Jesus, the Universal Man, the Son of God and the Son of Mary.[25]

Dante also drew on the figure of Jesus for his political theory. He was, as a Ghibelline, a supporter of the rights of the empire against the temporal claims of the papacy. The theological justification for those claims was the commission of Christ to Peter, granting him the keys of the kingdom of heaven, so that "whatever [*quodcunque*]" he would bind and loose here on earth, be it in church or state, would also be bound and loosed in heaven (Matt. 16:18–19). But Dante insisted that Christ had not intended this "whatever" to be taken "absolutely" and indiscriminately, but had meant that it "must be related to a particular class of things," namely, the authority to grant absolution and forgiveness.[26] Although the biblical doctrine of the creation of a single humanity in the image of God implied that a single world government would be best, this did not mean that the papacy should have both spiritual and temporal authority or that it should function as such a world government.[27] For man was created for a twofold goal: "the bliss of this life . . . and the bliss of eternal life."[28] The bliss of eternal life was the gift and achievement of Christ and of his suffering; but in the very midst of the suffering the same Christ had declared to Pontius Pilate: "My kingship is not of this world" (John 18:36).

According to Dante, this was not to be taken, as a later secularism would contend, "as if Christ, who is God, were not lord of this world"; rather, it meant that "as an example for the Church," he would not exercise dominion over the kingdoms of this world.[29] It would, then, be fair to Dante's position in the *De Monarchia* to say that what was at issue for him was the relation between two sets of sayings of Jesus, both of them authoritative, and the familiar hermeneutical problem of deciding which sayings were to be interpreted in the light of which. It was, he was arguing, most faithful to the will of God as articulated in the life and teachings of Jesus to let the church be the church and the empire be the empire, and not to subordinate the essential character of either one to the other. Moreover, as Kantorowicz has tellingly observed,

> A duality of goals does not necessarily imply a conflict of loyalties or even an antithesis. There is no antithesis of "human" versus "Christian" in the work of Dante, who wrote as a Christian and addressed himself to a Chris-

tian society, and who, in the last passage of the *Monarchy,* said clearly that "after a certain fashion [*quodammodo*] this mortal blessedness is ordained toward an immortal blessedness."[30]

For that, too, his highest authority was the revelation that had come in Jesus Christ.

Nevertheless, most Renaissance scholars would probably concur in the judgment that "if we try to assess the positive contributions of humanist scholarship to Renaissance theology, we must emphasize above all their achievements in what might be called sacred philology."[31] "Sacred philology" in this sense participated in the more general "revival of antiquity," as Burckhardt calls it, in which the humanists of the Renaissance were caught up. "Had it not been for the enthusiasm of a few collectors of that age," Burckhardt suggests, "who shrank from no effort or privation in their researches, we should certainly possess only a small part of the literature, especially of the Greeks, which is now in our hands."[32] The zeal for the literature of classical antiquity was more than nostalgia or acquisitiveness, though both of these were undoubtedly present. It was grounded in the conviction that a major source for the superficiality and the superstition of the present was an ignorance of the classical past and that therefore a recovery of that past would serve as an antidote. "Ad fontes!" was the watchword: "Back to the sources!"

Although these classical "sources" were in both Latin and Greek, with Cicero being perhaps the most important single author, the great innovation introduced by Renaissance humanism was the new interest in the study of Greek. Petrarch received a manuscript of Homer from Nicholas Sygeros of Constantinople and cherished it, but never learned to read it, so that it was, he said in a letter to the donor, "certainly a pleasure, though no advantage, to regard the Greeks in their own dress."[33] This touching story may serve as a reminder that the *Iliad* and the *Odyssey* had been largely unknown in the Middle Ages, except as background for the *Aeneid*. But when refugee Greek scholars came to the West from Constantinople, clutching manuscripts of their classics, they helped to stimulate a knowledge of Greek authors.[34] The list of such authors, however, included not only the classical Greek philosophers, poets, and dramatists, but the Greek church fathers and hymnographers.[35] Above all, the one Greek text that everyone was eager to learn to read was the Greek New Testament. For just as the Greek of Homer and Plato had been largely unknown through much of the Middle Ages, so also most of the leading medieval theologians and preachers had not been able to handle the original text of the New Testament with any authority. Even Augustine's knowledge of biblical and patristic Greek was shaky. Exegetical genius though he was, he could not draw independent philological judgments of his own or make use of the Greek Christian scholars for whom the original language of the New Testament had been their mother tongue. This circumstance was to result in "a 'splendid isolation' that would have momentous consequences for the culture of the Latin church."[36] Thomas Aquinas, too, was dependent on the Latin translation of the Bible, and sometimes on its mistranslations, for his interpretations. For example, he followed his predecessors in applying the words of Ephesians 5:32 about marriage, "This is a great mystery," translated in the Vulgate as "Sacramentum hoc magnum est," as a biblical proof text that matrimony was one of the seven sacraments of the church.[37]

The reappropriation of the Greek New Testament by Western scholars in the fifteenth and sixteenth centuries brought on a systematic philological review of all such proof texts. The pioneer in this campaign was the Italian scholar Lorenzo Valla, who was "among the most original and influential Italian Humanists."[38] In a satirical *Encomium of Saint Thomas Aquinas,* he called for a return from scholasticism to an authentic Christian antiquity represented by Augustine and other church fathers, but above all by the New Testament.[39] Valla's *Annotations on the New Testament* was not a comprehensive and systematic commentary on the Gospels and epistles, but consisted of intermittent grammatical and philological notes on various texts. He attacked the simplistic equation of the original Greek word *mystērion* with the Latin *sacramentum,* for the term did not refer to the ritual actions of the church instituted by Christ, but to the truth that God had previously hidden and had now revealed in Christ. Similarly, the summons with which the preaching of Jesus began did not say, as medieval misreading had supposed, "Do penance [*Poenitentiam agite*]," but "Repent," that is, "Turn your mind around"; and the salutation of the angel to the Virgin Mary, *kecharitōmenē* in Greek, did not mean "full of grace [*gratia plena*]," as the Ave Maria had it, but "highly favored."[40]

Although Valla's application of sacred philology to the Greek texts of the Gospels evoked controversy in his own time and, together with the Reformers' use of such philology, helped to provoke the Council of Trent into making the Latin Vulgate the official version of the Bible, it was not Valla, but his even more celebrated colleague Erasmus of Rotterdam, who elevated the recovery of the original message of Jesus, on the basis of the Greek sources, into a comprehensive program of church reform and theological renaissance. He did so in 1505, when he published Valla's *Annotations on the New Testament*, with a preface of his own that has been called "Erasmus' Inaugural Lecture as Professor-at-large to Christendom."[41] Theology, he insisted, had to be founded on grammar. "Ad fontes!" indeed: a knowledge of the New Testament in the original Greek was essential for an interpreter of the message of the Gospels. The original Greek New Testament had to be freed of the mistranslations in the Vulgate, the misinterpretations imposed upon it by later theologians, and the corruptions of the text introduced by copyists. To that end Erasmus in 1516 published his most important book, *Novum instrumentum*, the first printed edition of the Greek New Testament to be issued, which revolutionized forever the image of Jesus in Western culture. Its most obvious impact may have come through the Protestant Reformation, but the study of the Greek New Testament was by no means confined to Protestants. For not only Roman Catholic humanists like Valla and Erasmus, but the dominant Roman Catholic churchman of Spain, Cardinal Ximénez, archbishop of Toledo and founder of the University of Alcalá, fostered such study, producing a sumptuous edition of the Bible in several languages, the *Complutensian Polyglot* in six volumes; its New Testament was printed already in 1514, two years before the *Novum instrumentum*, but it did not circulate until after that of Erasmus.

Although Erasmus is best remembered for his Greek New Testament and for his works of satire, particularly *The Praise of Folly* of 1509, he was, also in these works, engaged in his lifelong vocation: to use sacred philology as a means of discovering, and of recovering, *philosophia Christi*, "the philosophy of Christ." In *The Praise of Folly* he called upon the popes to take seriously their title as "vicars of Christ" and "to imitate His poverty, tasks, teachings, crosses, and indifference to comfort"; for it was obvious from a reading of the Gospels that "the entire teaching of Christ inculcates nothing but meekness, tolerance, and disregard for one's own life."[42] Most eloquently of all, he expounded this *philosophia Christi* in his *Enchiridion militis Christiani*

(Handbook of the Christian Knight), published in 1503. Its central theme was: "Make Christ the only goal of your life. Dedicate to Him all your enthusiasm, all your effort, your leisure as well as your business. And don't look upon Christ as a mere word, as an empty expression, but rather as charity, simplicity, patience and purity—in short, in terms of everything he has taught us." For Jesus was "the sole archetype of godliness."[43]

The authentic Jesus, then, was the Jesus of the Gospels, whose life and teachings were to be studied on the basis of the original sources in the Greek New Testament. In the conclusion of the *Enchiridion* Erasmus defended the combination of *philosophia Christi* and Christian humanism against "certain detractors who think that true religion has nothing to do with the humanities [*bonae literae*]" or with "a knowledge of Greek and Latin."[44] But it was precisely through the humanistic study of the Gospels, using the same literary methods and philological scholarship that Erasmus's fellow humanists were applying to other texts of classical antiquity, that the reader could discover the meaning of the Gospels and thus learn the "words of life" spoken by Jesus, which "flowed from a soul that was never for a moment separated from the divinity and that alone restores us to everlasting life."[45] The Gospels were the key to knowing Jesus. At the same time, however, the converse also applied: Jesus was the key to knowing the meaning of the Gospels and of the Bible as a whole. Instead of "remaining content with the bare letter," even if this was textually sound and grammatically correct, the reader should "pass on to the more profound mysteries," which were available only through the person of Jesus. For "no one knows the Son except the Father and any one to whom the Son chooses to reveal him."[46]

In his effort to disentangle the person and message of Jesus from the complications that the scholastic theologians had imposed upon them, Erasmus harked back to the "Christian Socratism" of various early Christian writers. The maxim "Know thyself" was one that ancient classical writers had "believed to have been sent from heaven," but a Christian was to accept it because it agreed with the message of the Bible and the teaching of Jesus. As "the author of wisdom and Himself Wisdom in person, the true Light, who alone shatters the night of earthly folly," Jesus Christ had taught that "the crown of wisdom is that you know yourself."[47] His message, therefore, was a revelation from God himself, without which there would be "folly" and darkness. And yet Erasmus could also make the appeal: "The way of Christ is the most sensible and logical one to follow. . . . When you abandon the world for Christ, you do not give up anything. Rather, you exchange it for something far better. You change silver into gold, and rocks into precious gems."[48] And, in keeping with this Christian Socratism, he could "recommend the Platonists most highly" among all the classics, because "not only their ideas but their very mode of expression approaches that of the Gospels."[49] For that harmony with the best that had been thought and known everywhere was what made Jesus the Universal Man.

This apparent equation of the *philosophia Christi* with pagan philosophy persuaded Martin Luther that Erasmus was not serious in his espousal of the biblical message, but was essentially a skeptic, "an Epicurus," and a moralist. Because so many historians of the Reformation and historians of Christian doctrine have been the products of the Lutheran heritage, they have tended to follow Luther in this judgment. But in doing so they have not only misread Erasmus but borne false witness against him. As one interpreter of Erasmus has well said, "the fool's part, mistaken for pagan frivolity in serious times, has betrayed Erasmus."[50] For when he died on 12 July 1536, Erasmus, faithful to the end to the *philosophia Christi* and to the church founded by Jesus the Universal Man—not as the church was, but as Jesus had intended it to be—received the sacraments of that church, the chrism of anointing and the food for his final journey in the *viaticum*, and died with a prayer to Jesus on his lips, which he repeated over and over: "*O Jesu misericordia*, O Jesus, have mercy; *Domine libera me*, Lord deliver me."[51]

13

The Mirror of the Eternal

He who has seen me has seen the
Father.

 The Reformation broke out as an appeal from the authority of the institutional church to the authority of the historical Jesus. On 31 October 1517 Martin Luther, Augustinian friar and doctor of theology at the University of Wittenberg, posted ninety-five theses, challenging all comers to debate. The first of those theses read: "In the Name of Our Lord Jesus Christ. Amen. When our Lord and Master Jesus Christ said, 'Repent [*Poenitentiam agite*]' (Matt. 4:17), he willed the entire life of believers to be one of repentance."[1] This appeal to the message of Jesus in the Gospels was a direct application of the sacred philology and New Testament scholarship of Christian humanists like Valla and Erasmus to the sacramental life of the church. Before his life had ended, Martin Luther in his work as a theologian and interpreter of the Bible had ranged over not only the Gospels but most of the books of Old and New Testament alike. In particular, it was the epistles of the apostle Paul that became his focus, especially in the debates over the doctrine of justification by faith. Luther became the Reformer when, as he described in the *apologia pro vita sua* written just a year before his death, he was pondering the meaning of Paul's words in Romans 1:17: "In [the gospel] the righteousness of God is revealed through faith for faith; as it is written, 'The righteous shall live by faith.' "[2] He was deeply puzzled over the question of how it could be the content of the gospel of Christ, as "good news," that God was a righteous judge, rewarding the good and punishing the evil: Did Jesus really have to come to reveal that terrifying message? Then he suddenly broke through to the insight that the "righteousness of God" of which Paul spoke in this text was not the righteousness by which God *was* righteous in himself (passive righteousness), but the righteousness by which, for the sake of Jesus Christ, God *made* sinners righteous (active righteousness) through the forgiveness of sins in justification. When he discovered that, Luther said, it was as though the very gates of Paradise had been opened for him.

For the understanding of Luther and the Reformation as a chapter in the history of the church and the history of theology, therefore, it is certainly appropriate to concentrate on his work as an interpreter of the apostle Paul—though not perhaps with as much neglect of his work on other parts of the Bible as characterizes many discussions of him. But what Luther and the other Reformers learned from the apostle Paul was above all "to know nothing except Jesus Christ and him crucified" (1 Cor. 2:2). Justification by grace through faith was the restoration of the right relation with God accomplished by God through the life, death, and resurrection of Jesus: that was the central affirmation of the Reformation. In a characteristic phrase of Luther, Jesus was the "Mirror of the fatherly heart [of God], apart from whom we see nothing but a wrathful and terrible judge."[3] For John Calvin likewise, "Christ is the Mirror wherein we must, and without self-deception may, contemplate our own election."[4] "Let Christ," said Calvin's Zurich colleague Heinrich Bullinger in an official confession of the Reformed Church, "be the Mirror in which we contemplate our predestination."[5]

"Mirror" was, then, "a key metaphor" in Reformation thought.[6] And therefore the way the Reformers interpreted the figure of Jesus as the Mirror of the Eternal was central both to the religious achievements of the Reformation and to its cultural contributions. At the same time, it is obvious that the Reformers all found different reflections in that Mirror. They would all have agreed in principle with what we have seen to be the universal Christian consensus that Jesus, as the Mirror of the Eternal, was the revelation of the True, the Beautiful, and the Good (though they might not always have regarded such abstract philosophical terminology as very congenial). Yet it was only on his significance as Mirror of the True that they would have found substantial agreement: Christ was the true revelation of what Luther called "the hidden God [*Deus absconditus*]," and the source of divine Truth as this had been set down in the Scriptures. Calvin was no less persuaded than Luther that for the true knowledge of God it was necessary to look to the revelation that had come in Jesus, the Mirror of the True. Quoting the words of the New Testament, "the light of the knowledge of the glory of God in the face of Jesus Christ" (2 Cor. 4:6), he explained that "when [God] appeared in this, his image, he, as it were, made himself visible; whereas his appearance had before been indistinct and shadowed."[7]

As Karl Holl has said, referring not only to Luther but to the entire Reformation movement of the sixteenth century, "the Reformation, in fact, enriched all areas of culture."[8] Principal among these were, on the one hand, literature, art, and music, inspired by Jesus as Mirror of the Beautiful, and, on the other hand, the political order, illumined by Jesus as Mirror of the Good. All of these areas experienced revival and renewal throughout Reformation Europe, and no one of the Reformation churches had a monopoly on any of them. Nevertheless, a sharp difference appears between the two main Reformers, Luther and Calvin, and between the two principal Reformation traditions, Lutheran and Reformed, on the definitions of Jesus as Mirror of the Beautiful and as Mirror of the Good; for Calvin and his followers were suspicious of the idolatrous possibilities in the former, while Luther and his followers proved to be extremely hesitant about the political implications of the latter. The cultural and social relevance of these differences over the precise meaning of Jesus as Mirror, which is certainly not unrelated to the theological differences over doctrine, has had an even more far-reaching importance in the history of the past four centuries.

Although Luther's principal theological contribution was certainly his doctrine of justification, his most important literary achievement was no less certainly his translation of the New Testament into German, which he accomplished in a period of eleven weeks from the middle of December 1521 to the beginning of March 1522. Eventually, of course, he would translate the entire Bible, but it was his first rendition of the New Testament that made history; with various revisions, it was to go through about one hundred separate editions in his own lifetime, and innumerable ones since. Even those who regarded his theology with indifference or with alarm had to concede that he was a linguistic genius; indeed, several of his theological enemies during the next two decades were to pay him the ultimate linguistic compliment of borrowing from him extensively for their own translations of the Bible into German.[9] Heinrich Bornkamm is not exaggerating when, in commenting on the 1521 translation of the New Testament, he speaks of "the difference between the eaglelike flight of Luther's language and the diction of his medieval predecessors," and therefore concludes that Luther was "entirely dependent on himself for the task of pouring the New Testament into a true mold of the German language." He adds that "a wonderful providence had placed Luther, the greatest sculptor of the German language," into just the right time and place to make his historic contribution to the creation of modern German.[10] Latin had truly achieved the status of a world language only when Jerome's Vulgate translation of the Bible had opened a new chapter in the history of the language.[11] So also the various Reformation translations of the Bible into the vernacular, with Luther's in the vanguard, became turning points for their languages in turn—a process that has continued, with additional languages, ever since.

In Luther's translation of the Gospels, as well as in his sermons on the Gospels that have been preserved (they number one thousand or more), both the teachings and the life of Jesus were set forth in vivid detail.[12] Spurning the traditional methods of allegorical interpretation, even for the Old Testament but especially for the New, because they made the Bible into a "nose of wax" that anyone could distort in any direction, he applied himself instead to reconstructing the history of the Jesus of the Gospels and making him live for his hearers.[13] The comment of Heinrich Heine that Luther, "who could scold like a fishwife, could also be as gentle as a sensitive maiden"[14] is nowhere more apt than in Luther's translation and paraphrases of the Gospels and in the narratives he based on those texts for his preaching. Far from transposing the language of the Gospels into the key of the Pauline epistles—as he might have been expected to do and as some scholars claim he did—he endeavored to allow each evangelist, or rather Jesus according to each evangelist, to speak in a distinctive accent. For even though he insisted that "the notion must be given up that there are four Gospels and only four evangelists," since there was in reality a single Gospel,[15] he constantly drew comparisons and contrasts between the way the several Gospels handled particular subjects.[16]

The outcome was a depiction of Jesus marked by such freshness of language that Jesus became a sixteenth-century contemporary. To hearers who cooed sentimentally over the Infant Jesus and clucked over his poverty, "If only I had been there! How quick I would have been to help the Baby!" Luther retorted: "Why don't you do it now? You have Christ in your neighbor."[17] The familiar admonition of the Sermon on the Mount to consider the lilies of the field and the birds of the air (Matt. 6:26–27) became at Luther's hands a discourse about how Jesus

> is making the birds our schoolmasters and teachers. It is a great and abiding disgrace to us that in the Gospel a helpless sparrow should become a theologian and a preacher to the wisest of men . . . , as if he were saying to us: "Look, you miserable man! You have house and home, money and property. . . . Yet you cannot find peace."[18]

The enemies of Jesus sound very much like the enemies of Martin Luther, and the reader sometimes needs to be reminded that the original language of the Gospels was not German but Greek. In Calvin's exegesis, too, as in Luther's, the scenes of the Gospel story acquired directness and challenging force, as becomes visible for example in his vivid exposition of the encounter between Jesus and the woman at the well.[19]

The literary power with which Luther was able to make Jesus a contemporary was an expression of his conception of Jesus as Mirror of the Beautiful. In painting, Luther strove to infuse into the religious art of the later Middle Ages his understanding of what the authentic message of the Gospels was: it was specifically the humanity of Jesus that was the Mirror of the Eternal. Therefore when he criticized medieval painters of the Virgin Mary, it was not for doing violence to the literal meaning of the Gospels by picturing her in modern dress and in a contemporary setting, but for depicting her in such a way "that there is found in her nothing [lowly] to be despised, but only great and lofty things"; what they should have done was, as she herself had said in the Magnificat, to show "how the exceeding riches of God joined in her with her utter poverty."[20] Albrecht Dürer shared Luther's ideas and reflected them in his art; his biographer speaks of "a conversion—both in subject matter and in style" brought about in

Dürer's faith and life through his acceptance of Luther's teachings, as a consequence of which "the man who had done more than any other to familiarize the Northern world with the true spirit of pagan Antiquity now practically abandoned secular subject matter except for scientific illustrations, traveler's records and portraiture."[21]

In keeping with this willingness of Luther to use painting as a means of achieving contemporaneity with the Christ of the Gospels as Mirror of the Eternal, Lucas Cranach the Younger several times portrayed the events of the Gospels as though Martin Luther had been present personally when they happened. The most successful of Cranach's paintings in this genre was probably *The Last Supper*, executed for the Church of Saint Mary in Dessau-Mildensee and dedicated in 1565. As in countless paintings before, Jesus is shown instituting the Lord's Supper, and the twelve disciples seated around the table are dressed as sixteenth-century German burghers, including Judas with his thirty pieces of silver. But suddenly, there in the midst of the group at table are the unmistakable faces of Martin Luther, of his colleague at Wittenberg, Philip Melanchthon, and of the prince of Anhalt. Quite unabashedly, then, the events of the first century have been transported into the sixteenth.

Perhaps nowhere has the contemporaneity of Luther's renditions of the Gospels come through more dramatically and convincingly than in the settings of the Gospel accounts of the suffering and death of Jesus in the *Saint Matthew Passion* and *Saint John Passion* of Johann Sebastian Bach. As one of the most profound historians of the modern spirit has observed, the true significance of Luther and the Reformation "cannot be fully appreciated merely on the basis of works of dogmatics. Its documents are the writings of Luther, the church chorale, the sacred music of Bach and Handel, and the structure of community life in the church."[22] One of the planks in the Reformation platform for the renewal of church life was, along with the translation of the Bible into the vernacular and the revitalization of preaching on the basis of such translations, the composition of vernacular hymns for congregational singing. Some Reformation groups objected to the creation of new songs, preferring to rely on paraphrases of "God's hymnbook," the Psalter, and producing such masterworks as the *Geneva Psalter* and the *Bay Psalm Book*. But Luther was "not of the opinion that the gospel should destroy and blight all the arts, as some of the pseudo-religious claim." He would, he added, "like to see all the arts, especially music, used in the service of Him who gave and made them."[23] Taking up and developing the style of hymns and chorales that had arisen during the later Middle Ages, he gave them new life, and the Lutheran chorale, as it reached its pinnacle in the work of such poets and composers as Paul Gerhardt, became one of the Reformation's principal cultural monuments.

It was the genius of Bach that he brought together, already in the cantatas and then on a larger scale in the *Passions*, these two Reformation elements: the text of the Gospel in Luther's translation and the Lutheran chorale. As a result, hearers could experience the meaning of the life and death of Jesus as Mirror of the Eternal with unmatched freshness and power. In the words of Nathan Söderblom,

> The Passion music, which was created within the church and which experienced a new depth, a new richness, and a new intensity in the sixteenth century, constitutes in its way the most important addition that has ever been made to the sources of revelation in the Old and New Testament. If you ask about a fifth Gospel, I do not hesitate to name the interpretation of salvation history as it reached its acme in Johann Sebastian Bach. The *Saint Matthew Passion* and *Mass in B Minor* give deep insight into the mystery of the passion and salvation.[24]

Bach was the fifth evangelist.

It would, however, violate both historical honesty and ecumenical integrity to concentrate on Jesus as the Mirror of the Eternal in these Protestant cultures while ignoring the transforming presence of his person in the religious and cultural revival fostered during the sixteenth century by the Catholic Reformation. The presence of Christ was the central theme of one of the masterpieces of the Catholic Reformation in Spain, *The Names of Christ* by Luis de León. As is evident from its very title, the book presents itself as a continuation and expansion of the treatise *On the Divine Names* of Pseudo-Dionysius the Areopagite, which had played such an influential role in the history of medieval Christ-mysticism. Luis de León seems to have concluded that now it was time to become explicit about the "Christ" in Christ-mysticism, and to specify the meaning of his names. "The names which Scriptures give to Christ," he says in book 1, "are numerous, like his virtues and attributes."[25] Throughout the remainder of this treatise, the author exploits his knowledge of Hebrew to analyze various names mentioned in various texts of the Hebrew Bible, basically ten in number, that can appropriately be used for Jesus.

"Jesus' spirit," he writes, "penetrates and changes" the human soul and the human personality; for "in Jesus Christ, as in a deep well, as in a vast ocean, we find a treasure of Being."[26] That treasure had brought "beauty" and "virtue" through "the new laws given to us by Jesus."[27] It was the purpose and the fulfillment of human life to find the treasure and to live in obedience to the "new laws."

The Christ-mysticism voiced by Luis de León achieved even greater heights both of spirituality and of literary power in the poems of Saint John of the Cross, whom many historians and literary critics regard as the finest poet in the Spanish language. Like Dante, he was both a poet and a philosopher, one who had been schooled in the thought of Thomas Aquinas, striving to resolve the tensions between intellect and will, between the knowledge of God and the love of God. The resolution came for him in the person of Jesus as Mirror of the Eternal, who was simultaneously the ground for the knowledge of God and the revelation of the love of God. In his *Songs of the Soul* (*Canciones de el alma*) he explored "the path of spiritual negation,"[28] which, as we have seen, had been the philosophical foundation for the Greek-speaking Christian Neoplatonists of the fourth century as they explored the meaning of the Cosmic Christ. But knowledge of Christ, even this profound knowledge through negation, was not sufficient of itself: love of Christ had to follow. Therefore in the madrigal "Of Christ and the Soul," he used the predicament of a young lover, "with love in his heart like a ruinous wound," as a metaphor for the mystical love between the soul and Christ.[29] The two themes of knowledge and love converged in his ballad "On the Incarnation,"[30] where Saint John of the Cross rehearsed a conversation between Jesus and his heavenly Father about the mystical earthly bride whom the Father had found for him. "Perfect love" would be fulfilled in the union between Jesus and this bride. But at the same time Jesus says to God the Father:

> How better blazon your might,
> sweet reason and deep mind?
> I'll carry word to the world,
> news of a novel kind:
> news of beauty and peace,
> of sovereignty unconfined.

Thus the mind and reason of God, the divine Logos, and the love and will of God, the divine Bridegroom, were present together in Jesus, the Mirror of the Eternal.

With the fundamental ideas in this image of Jesus as the Mirror of the Beautiful (if not always with its language) Luther might have had little difficulty, for he often used similar metaphors himself. But when it came to defining Jesus as the Mirror of the Good for the political order, Luther drew the line against seeking to make the person and message of Jesus contemporary or relevant in any direct way. Some of the radical Reformers of the sixteenth century, in their redefinition of the demands of "discipleship," called for the transformation of the entire social, economic, and political system. Nothing less than that was necessary, they believed, to bring society into conformity with the will of God announced in the law of the Bible, as that law had been fundamentally recast in the teachings of Jesus, which were summarized in the Sermon on the Mount. In his sermons of 1530–32 expounding the entire Sermon on the Mount, Luther attacked those "who have failed to distinguish properly between the secular and the spiritual, between the kingdom of Christ and the kingdom of the world." They had not recognized that in the Sermon on the Mount Jesus "is not tampering with the responsibility and authority of the government, but he is teaching his individual Christians how to live personally, apart from their official position and authority." For "there is no getting around it, a Christian has to be a secular person of some sort."[31] As such, the Christian was not to attempt to use the teachings of Jesus or the laws of the Bible to govern the state. That was best done on the basis not of revelation but of reason, by the legislation of "the mirror of the Saxons [*Sachsenspiegel*]," not by the decrees of Jesus, the Mirror of the Eternal. Jesus forbade taking oaths, the government required it; and both were right, each in the proper sphere. One did not have to be a Christian to rule justly, and the interpreter of the message of the Gospels did not, as such, have any special insight into the specifics of what it meant to rule justly. Therefore, politically involved though he and his Reformation undoubtedly were—when he died in 1546, he was engaged in mediating a conflict between princes—Luther did not, as an expositor of the Gospels, evolve a "Christian politics," for that was not why Jesus Christ had come to earth.

For the articulation of a Christian politics in the age of the Reformation, and one that would, especially in the English-speaking world, fundamentally redefine the nature of government, we must look not to Wittenberg but to Geneva. For, apart from such doctrinal issues as double predestination and the nature of the presence of the body

and blood of Christ in the Lord's Supper, the principal difference
between Luther's Reformation and Calvin's Reformation should be
sought here in the definition of the political and social significance of
the image of Jesus as the Mirror of the Good. Calvin was not as content
as was Luther to trust secular rulers to find their own guidance in
reason and legal tradition, important though these were as components of sound rule. He acknowledged in the concluding chapter of
his *Institutes* "that Christ's spiritual Kingdom and the civil jurisdiction
are things completely distinct."[32] But he went on in the very next
paragraph to assert:

> Civil government has as its appointed end, so long as we live among men,
> to cherish and protect the outward worship of God, to defend sound doc-
> trine of piety and the position of the church, to adjust our life to the society
> of men, to form our social behavior to civil righteousness, to reconcile us
> with one another, and to promote general peace and tranquillity.[33]

Magistrates, therefore, were to "submit to Christ the power with
which they have been invested, *that He [Jesus Christ] alone may tower
over all.*"[34] "The president and judge of our elections," he urged in
keeping with this, was to be God. God had laid down in his law how
the state and society were to function, and how magistrates were to
govern in achieving those ends. It was, therefore, at his insistence
that the ruling magistracy of Geneva, the Council of Two Hundred,
pledged on 2 February 1554 "to live according to the Reformation,
forget all hatreds, and cultivate concord." "To live according to the
Reformation" implied, moreover, that they would seek to bring the
laws of Geneva into harmony with the word and will of God, as
mirrored in the law of the Scriptures and above all in the person and
message of Jesus, so that, as Calvin said in the *Institutes*, Jesus Christ
"alone may tower over all."

But if the government was to achieve such a faithfulness to Christ
as the Mirror of the Good, it was essential that the word of God be
preached and taught in all its truth and purity and be applied concretely to the total life of the individual and of society. In principle,
to be sure, the Reformation idea of the universal priesthood of all
believers meant that not only the clergy but also the laity, not only
the theologian but also the magistrate, had the capacity to read, understand, and apply the teachings of the Bible. Yet one of the contributions of the sacred philology of the biblical humanists to the
Reformation was an insistence that, in practice, often contradicted

the notion of the universal priesthood: the Bible had to be understood on the basis of the authentic original text, written in Hebrew and Greek, which, most of the time, only clergy and theologians could comprehend properly. Thus the scholarly authority of the Reformation clergy replaced the priestly authority of the medieval clergy. Functionally, therefore, the quest for a form of government that would embody the will that God had revealed for society in Jesus Christ the Mirror led to a system that has often been called "theocracy." John T. McNeill has sought to clarify in what sense it was, and in what sense it was not, theocratic:

> The word "theocracy" is often applied to the Geneva of Calvin's time, but the word is now ambiguous to most minds. Many [including, one could add, many clergy] confuse "theocracy," the rule of God, with "hierocracy," the rule of the clergy. . . . Calvin wished the magistrates, as agents of God, to have their own due sphere of action. But so intense was his consciousness of vocation, and so far did his mental energy outstrip that of his political associates, that he ultimately gained ascendancy to the point of mastery.[35]

It was, moreover, thanks to Calvin's understanding of civil government and of its duty to shape society on the basis of the law of Christ that when his followers finally established a society in which it was possible to carry out that duty, the underlying assumption of that society was that the law of Christ did have a message, and often a very specific and concrete message, for both rulers and ruled. The election sermons of Puritan divines in colonial New England were based on that assumption.[36] "It is better," John Cotton declared, "that the commonwealth be fashioned to the setting forth of God's house, which is his church, than to accommodate the church to the civil state."[37] And, as one scholar has commented on Cotton's statement, "every Puritan would have agreed."[38] One of the few not to agree with this assumption was Roger Williams, who denied the continuity between biblical "government," either in the kingdom of Israel or in the kingdom of God proclaimed by Jesus, and the "rule of the saints" claimed by Puritanism.[39] In many ways, as a later chapter on Jesus the Liberator will suggest, it was Abraham Lincoln who, during the conflict over slavery, found the fallacy in the traditional assumption.[40] And the decisive authority for this was, also according to Lincoln, the person of Jesus as the Mirror of the Eternal, who thus provided, in two of the traditions that could be traced to the Reformation, both the justification of "theocracy" and its most telling refutation.

14
The Prince of Peace

To us a Child is born, to us a Son
is given; and his name will be
called Prince of Peace.

One of the *Names of Christ* to which Luis de León, in the spirit of the Catholic Reformation, devoted his treatise under that title was "Prince of Peace," derived from the words of the prophet Isaiah (Isa. 9:6): "To us a Child is born, to us a Son is given; . . . and his name will be called . . . Prince of Peace."[1] There was reason enough in the age of the Reformation, which was also the age of the Wars of Religion, to emphasize once again that Jesus, as Prince of Peace, called upon his followers in every age to seek the ways of peace and not of war. One of the last of the Reformation leaders, John Amos Comenius (Jan Amos Komenský), who with his Moravian church and nation had suffered the consequence of the Wars of Religion, insisted that Jesus Christ was

the only real deliverer from all slavery of soul and body (John 8:32–36). For *the way of peace they knew not* at all, who about the kings of the earth, instead of a sceptre, have gathered spears, swords, wheels, halters, crosses, flames, and headsmen, so making them rather to be feared than loved. Is this what was taught by the best of Teachers? Does this proceed from the teachings of Him who commended to His followers nought but love, and affection, and mutual help?[2]

That was a very good question to put to all the descendants of the Reformation, regardless of their denomination, in 1667, exactly one hundred fifty years after Luther's Ninety-five Theses. For because the Reformation was raising anew so many of the questions that had seemed to be settled forever, it compelled reconsideration also of the question of war: "Is this," as Comenius asked, "what was taught by the best of Teachers?"

The Reformation answered the question of what the person and teaching of Jesus meant for the problem of war, as it answered most other questions, with a spectrum of theories, some of them reflecting historic views of war and some presenting new variations and new alternatives. The standard threefold typology of theories about "Jesus and war" across that spectrum may conveniently serve to organize the variety: the doctrine of "just war," the theory of a "crusade," and the ideology of Christian pacifism.[3] For each of these Jesus provided fundamental justification.

Perhaps the most widely circulated sixteenth-century defense of the doctrine of just war as what "the best of Teachers" had taught about war was a treatise by Luther on the subject. It was addressed to the question, in Luther's words,

> Whether the Christian faith, by which we are accounted righteous before God, is compatible with being a soldier, going to war, stabbing and killing, robbing and burning, as military law requires us to do to our enemies in wartime? Is this work sinful or unjust? Should it give us a bad conscience before God? Must a Christian only do good and love, and kill no one, nor do anyone any harm?[4]

Luther's answer was consistent both with his theology and with his political theory. The distinction described earlier between the two kingdoms, the spiritual kingdom of Christ and the earthly kingdom of this world, together with the corresponding distinction between the public office and the private person, gave him the framework within which to resolve the contradiction between the absolute ethic of love as announced by Jesus and the concrete duties of political life and even of military service. Absolute love was incumbent on the follower of Jesus as a person; but it was not to be the norm by which to regulate the duties of the public office that the same follower of Jesus might occupy, and such duties were therefore not subject to the same imperatives. Hence the coming of Jesus and of his new ethic of the kingdom of God did not, according to Luther, overthrow the structures of political authority in human society, not even such structures as the office of the soldier to wage war.

The nature of both kingdoms was, according to Luther, set forth in the words of Jesus to Pontius Pilate (which Dante had also used in *De Monarchia*): "My kingship is not of this world; if my kingship were of this world, my servants would fight" (John 18:36). These words implied, on the one hand, that Christ did not want to interfere with the kingdoms of this world and with their structures, since his kingship belonged to another order, and that therefore military action was not an appropriate means of defending the kingdom of Christ. But they meant as well, according to Luther's reading of them, "that war was not wrong" in and of itself, since Jesus was saying, on the other hand, that in the kingdoms that did belong to this world it was appropriate for his "servants" as citizens to fight. Similarly, as both Calvin and Luther argued,[5] John the Baptist did not tell the soldiers who came to him with the question "And we, what shall we do?" that it was their duty, in the name of love, to renounce their sinful office of fighting and killing; he only "said to them, 'Rob no one by violence or by false accusation, and be content with your wages' " (Luke 3:14). In short, according to Luther, "he praised the military profession, but at the same time he forbade its abuse. Now the abuse does not affect the office." The coming of Christ meant, therefore, the introduction of a radically new imperative, the imperative of suffering love; but that imperative was not addressed to Pilate and the other officers of the Roman empire of his day, nor to soldiers, be they pagan or Christian, whose task it was to go on obeying the imperatives of their public office.[6]

An even more adroit and skillful exegesis enabled Luther to cope with another saying of Jesus that appeared to be applying the radical love ethic to prohibit the use of force by his disciples. When Peter, in the garden of Gethsemane, sought to protect Jesus against his captors by striking one of them with a sword, Jesus reproved him, saying, "Put your sword back into its place; for all who take the sword will perish by the sword" (Matt. 26:52). On the face of it, those words of Jesus did seem to forbid the use of the sword, also adding the threat that such use would ultimately bring a similar violence upon the perpetrators of any such violence. Thus the commandment of Jesus would appear to be an extension and further application of the words addressed by the Lord to the people of Israel in Deuteronomy (Deut. 32:35), as quoted by the apostle Paul (Rom. 12:19): "Beloved, never avenge yourselves, but leave it to the wrath of God; for it is written, 'Vengeance is mine, I will repay, says the Lord.' " But in the light of Luther's doctrine of the two kingdoms, the warning in the words of Jesus really meant that "the sword" was "a godly estate," through which that vengeance which was God's sole prerogative would be carried out: "All who take the sword [as private persons rather than in the faithful execution of a public office] will perish by the sword," a sword to be wielded by the incumbents of a public office—be they executioners or soldiers, pagans or Christians. "Hence," Luther concluded, "it is certain and clear enough that it is God's will that the temporal sword and law be used for the punishment of the wicked and the protection of the upright"; it could, moreover, be used also by Christians.[7]

As for the prohibition of Jesus in the Sermon on the Mount, "Judge not" (Matt. 7:1), it, too, was to be taken in the light of the declaration "Vengeance is mine" (Rom. 12:19).[8] Rather than prohibiting war and the use of force, the imperative of Jesus made it incumbent upon his followers to respect established political order. They were to do so, moreover, even when rulers were unjust and oppressive. For "if this king keeps neither God's law nor the law of the land, ought you to attack him, judge him, and take vengeance on him?" That was precisely what Jesus was forbidding in the Sermon on the Mount. Luther read the ethic of Jesus, therefore, as a condemnation of revolution, but not as a condemnation of war. For revolution was by definition an act of injustice, but war could be an instrument of justice. Thus the mainstream of the Reformation, whether Lutheran or Calvinist or Anglican, in its understanding of the implication of the love ethic of Jesus for the problem of war, attached itself to the medieval "just war" tradition of Augustine and Thomas Aquinas.[9]

Augustine had denounced Roman militarism, with its glorification of armed violence, and had used war as evidence that human beings could be far more cruel and bloodthirsty than wild animals.[10] Nevertheless, he had, somewhat reluctantly, conceded that there could be "just wars," made necessary by human wrongdoing; but he added that one must, even in these cases, "lament the necessity of just wars" rather than glory in them.[11] He elaborated his views in a letter to the Christian governor of the province of Africa, who had sought his counsel about various of his political duties, including the waging of war. "Peace should be the object of your desire," Augustine warned, and therefore "war should be waged only as a necessity, and waged only that God may by it deliver men from the emergency and preserve them in peace." The priority of peace over war was fundamental for Augustine: "Peace is not sought in order to kindle war, but war is waged in order to obtain peace." A "just war" was one whose purpose and intent it was to achieve peace. From this it followed that "even in waging war" a follower of Christ was to "cherish the spirit of a peacemaker." And the clinching argument for this interpretation of war and peace came from Jesus, who had said in the Beatitudes of the Sermon on the Mount (Matt. 5:9): "Blessed are the peacemakers."[12] In his consideration of war, Thomas Aquinas quoted many of these same sayings of Jesus and other New Testament passages, and he also proceeded from the distinction between private person and public office. Thus he systematized Augustine's definition of just war by specifying three conditions necessary to make a war just: the one who wages the war must have the authority to do so; there must be a "just cause"; and the war must be carried on with the "right intention" of advancing the good and achieving the peace. The sayings of Jesus such as the word of the Sermon on the Mount, "Do not resist evil" (Matt. 5:39), were indeed the ultimate authority for the follower of Jesus as a private person; "nevertheless, it is sometimes necessary for the common good for a man to act otherwise" in the execution of a public office.[13] Later followers of Thomas would add a fourth condition (and one that has become important in recent discussion of nuclear war): that the war be carried on *"debito modo,* with appropriate [and thus appropriately limited] means."[14]

In their explanation of how there could be a just war in the light of the unqualified way Jesus had condemned violence and the unequivocal way he had exalted peace, Reformers such as Luther repeated much of the medieval doctrine of Augustine and Aquinas, while adding their own perspectives on the ethical and political meaning of the Gospels. There was, however, one aspect of the treatment of war in medieval theology on which Luther broke radically with his predecessors: the idea of a crusade. As a solution for the moral ambiguity of war that went beyond the tragic necessity implied in the Augustinian idea of just war, the crusade imprinted the sacred sign of the cross of Jesus on the cause of "Holy Peace and Holy War."[15] "To take the cross" meant to go off to war against the Turk in Palestine, wearing a cross of red cloth on the shoulder of one's outer garment. While there is serious inconsistency between the accounts given by our several sources on the sermon preached by Pope Urban II at the Council of Clermont on 27 November 1095, it does seem clear that he promised remission of sins and indulgences to those who took the cross. He seems, moreover, to have described the death of those who, after taking the cross, fell in battle against the Turkish infidels as a kind of participation in the sufferings and death of Christ. In the event, as Runciman has put it, this "Crusading fervour" in the name of Jesus "always provided an excuse for killing God's enemies" and led to pogroms against Jews; it even led to what he calls "the great betrayal of Christendom," the sack of Christian Constantinople by Christian Crusaders on the Fourth Crusade in 1204, a "crime against humanity" and "an act of gigantic political folly," as well as a flagrant negation of the teachings of the very One in whose name they had gone forth and whose cross they bore.[16]

By the period of the Reformation, the atmosphere had changed drastically; as one historian has put it, albeit with some exaggeration, "in the sixteenth century the idea of a Crusade falls into oblivion."[17] It is more precise to say, with another scholar, that "the idea of the crusade continued to haunt the imagination of western princes until the seventeenth century."[18] What fell into virtual oblivion was the practical possibility of a Crusade to Palestine to free the Holy Land from the infidel, for now the infidel had become a clear and present danger to Christian Europe itself. In 1453, Constantinople, the capital of the Byzantine empire, which had been the victim of Western Christian aggression in 1204, fell to the Ottoman Turks, who during the next three-quarters of a century threatened central Europe: Belgrade surrendered to them in 1520, Vienna was in danger, and in 1526 at the battle of Mohacs the army of Hungary and its king, Louis II, fell before the superior might of the Turkish armies. Thanks to the recent invention of printing, a vast propaganda literature on the Turkish peril spread over central Europe, with some calling for compromise and appeasement and others for war and even for a revival of the Crusade—directed this time not against the Turks who had taken Palestine, but against the Turks who had pointed a dagger at the very heart of Western Christendom. All of this came at the very time that the Reformation seemed to be pointing its own dagger at Christendom, dividing the Christian forces just when they needed to unite against the common enemy. The coincidence of the two threats was the occasion for the convoking of the diet of the Holy Roman Empire at Augsburg in 1530, where the Augsburg Confession presented the case for the Lutheran Reformation.

That confession made it the official position of the Reformation party that, since "all government in the world and all established rule and laws were instituted and ordained by God," it was perfectly legitimate for Christians to "punish evildoers with the sword" and to "engage in just wars." Specifically, it declared that Emperor Charles V, "His Imperial Majesty, may in salutary and godly fashion imitate the example of David in making war on the Turk."[19] But the parallel between the Holy Roman Emperor and the ancient king of Israel did not make the emperor a theocratic ruler, who governed and waged war in the name of Jesus. The reason given for approving war against the Turk was, therefore, not the Crusade ideal of a holy war against the enemy of the cross of Christ; rather it was that, as the "incumbent of a royal office," Charles V, like King David of Israel, had the right, indeed the obligation, of "the defense and protection of [his] subjects." Luther's treatise of 1526 on the Turkish war took the same position. It was mistaken to preach a Crusade and to urge "the emperor, as guardian of the church and defender of the faith," to take arms against the Turks; on the contrary, taking arms against the Turks would be the duty of the rulers of Europe, "whether they themselves were Christians or not," in keeping with their calling in the world to govern.[20] In its validation of war against the Turks, the mainstream of the Reformation rejected the Crusade ideal but insisted on the just war theory: such a war was legitimate on account of the Jesus who had acknowledged that Pontius Pilate and Caesar possessed an authority that came from God (John 19:11), not on account of the Jesus whose crucifixion under Pontius Pilate had placed authority into the hands of his disciples and his church (Matt. 28:19–20).

Curiously, the nearest analogue to the Crusade ideal in the Reformation era did not come from either Roman Catholicism or mainline Protestantism, but from one of the left-wing leaders of the Radical Reformation, Thomas Muentzer.[21] He was convinced that "Christ the Son of God and his apostles" had established a pure faith, but that it had been corrupted immediately thereafter, so that "the precious Stone Jesus Christ," on whom the church was to have been built, had been "completely trampled" by his false disciples. Muentzer, in what his editor has correctly called "one of the most remarkable sermons of the Reformation Era," preached on 13 July 1524, announced the vengeance of that precious Stone Jesus Christ, which was "about to fall and strike these schemes of [mere] reason and dash them to the ground." For Jesus had warned: "Do not think that I have come to bring peace on earth; I have not come to bring peace, but a sword" (Matt. 10:34). He had, moreover, "commanded in deep gravity, saying: 'Take these enemies of mine and strangle them before my very eyes' (Luke 19:27)." And why did the Prince of Peace, whom Muentzer himself here called "the gentle Son of God," issue such a bloodthirsty command?

> Ah, because they ruin Christ's government for him. . . . Now if you want to be true governors, you must begin government at the roots, and, as Christ commanded, drive his enemies from the elect. For you are the means to this end. Beloved, don't give us any old jokes about how the power of God should do it without your sword. Otherwise may it rust away for you in its scabbard!

The summons of Jesus was a call for nothing less than Christian revolution, a new kind of holy war.[22] Muentzer was captured and put to death the following year; but his spirit would live on, through the radical political apocalypticism of the Fifth Monarchy Men who emerged from English Puritanism in the seventeenth century, and then through the efforts of some twentieth-century Christians in Eastern Europe and in the Third World, for whom Muentzer and other Christian revolutionaries have become, quite literally, church fathers and authentic voices for what one exponent of liberation theology has called "a christology of revolutionary praxis."[23]

Muentzer's theology of holy war ended in the debacle of the Peasants' War; Luther's theory of just war ended in the catastrophe of the Thirty Years' War. Neither holy war nor just war, moreover, constituted a new answer to the dilemma of Jesus and war, as formulated by Comenius: "Is this what was taught by the best of Teachers?" The only truly new answer of the sixteenth and seventeenth centuries to that dilemma (an answer which, they insisted, was actually very old) came, first from Erasmus, then from certain Anabaptists, Quakers, and other peace groups of the Radical Reformation, who bore witness to an understanding of the person and message of Jesus by which holy war was not holy and just war was not just.[24] Although they often invoked arguments from reason and from universal human morality in their attacks on war, it was theology and specifically Christology—a Christology of life and praxis rather than principally a Christology of doctrine—that constituted the heart of their argument.[25]

The foundation of that argument was the definition of the essence of Christianity as "discipleship."[26] "In the ninth chapter of Matthew," the Anabaptists declared in a disputation with the Swiss Reformed at Zofingen, "Christ came to Matthew the tax collector and said to him, 'Follow me' [Matt. 9:9]." Reviving the New Testament call for a drastic break with the past as the condition for authentic discipleship, they rejected such external criteria of discipleship as participation in the outward rituals of the institutional church and recitation of its creedal formulas. These external criteria and so-called means of grace must be subordinated to the person of Jesus; for "Christ himself is the means, whom no one can truly know except by following him in his life." Although there were some striking affinities between Anabaptism and medieval monasticism, as the Protestant critics of both were quick to point out—one of Luther's favorite epithets for the Anabaptists was "the new monks"—such a following of Christ in radical discipleship went even beyond the conception of following that had been at work in the *Imitation of Christ* and other monastic works of devotion. For in the Anabaptist theology of discipleship, Jesus was both example and exemplar: of course an example of how to live a godly life in strict conformity to the demands of the law and will of God, but also an exemplar of the way such a life under God worked itself out concretely in the world. And that way was "the way of the cross," on which the disciple followed Jesus into death and through death into life.[27] Some of the most profoundly stirring documents to come out of the Reformation anywhere are the accounts of the martyrdom of Anabaptists, who, as one of their enemies put it, "marched to the scaffold as though they were going to a dance," because they saw the scaffold and the execution pyre as an opportunity to participate, through the way of the cross, in the life and death and resurrection of Jesus.

The primary imperative of such a definition of discipleship was a total resignation to the will of God in obedience to Jesus and in imitation of him, what Anabaptists came to call "passivity" or "yieldedness." By sharp contrast with the revolutionary activism of a Thomas Muentzer, the evangelical Anabaptists believed themselves to be summoned to a yielded life of total dependence on God, the kind of life Christ himself had lived. They were not to try to reshape the external world and the civil order into a Christian society in conformity with the will of Jesus, but were to become the "little flock" to which Jesus had addressed himself (Luke 12:32), a genuine community of committed disciples and the true church. Therefore, by a sharp contrast with Luther's way of interpreting the secularity of the Christian life, they called upon the true disciples of Jesus to separate themselves drastically from the world and from the worldly life. By means of his doctrine of the two kingdoms, Luther had distinguished between the duties of the Christian as citizen and the duties of the Christian as disciple. Both were necessary, according to Luther's reading of the Gospels; but Jesus in passages like the Sermon on the Mount was talking only about the latter, meanwhile leaving undisturbed the external structures of government and citizenship, such as military service, in which his disciples were to participate fully. On the basis of their own distinction between the kingdom of Christ and the kingdoms of this world, Anabaptists attacked Luther's distinction as an evasion both of the full cost of discipleship and of the way of the cross to which it led: Jesus was the Prince of Peace.

It was into the context of that image of Jesus that the pacifist Anabaptists put their interpretation of war and of the use of force, a succinct statement of which appears in their Seven Articles of 1527, commonly known as the Schleitheim Confession:

> We are agreed as follows concerning the sword: The sword is ordained of God outside the perfection of Christ. It punishes and puts to death the wicked, and guards and protects the good. In the [Old Testament] Law the sword was ordained for the punishment of the wicked and for their death, and the same [sword] is [now] ordained to be used by the worldly magistrates. In the perfection of Christ, however, only the ban is used for a warning and for the excommunication of the one who has sinned, without putting the flesh to death—simply the warning and the command to sin no more.[28]

Despite the conventional accusations against it in the polemics of its opponents, this position is anything but anarchy. Echoing the words of the New Testament which had been the traditional legitimation of government, "Let every person be subject to the governing authorities. For there is no authority except from God, and those that exist have been instituted by God," the Anabaptists acknowledged that God had instituted government, which, as a later verse said, "does not bear the sword in vain" (Rom. 13:1–4). They were not intent on overthrowing the governing authorities, but on supporting them. What they opposed was the idea that the followers of Christ could themselves be magistrates and wield the sword. For government had been instituted "outside the perfection of Christ," and those who now lived "in the perfection of Christ" invoked the disciplinary measures of the ban and excommunication, not the sword, as the means of carrying out the will of God.

It was a similar concept of "the perfection of Christ" that provided the next stage in the history of Christian pacifism. The Society of Friends, in England and then in America, worked out a theologically more elaborate formulation of the case against Christian participation in war. This was the achievement of Robert Barclay, the principal systematic theologian and apologist of the Quaker movement. Barclay was prepared to acknowledge that for "the present magistrates of the Christian world" war was not "altogether unlawful"; for they were still "far from the perfection of the Christian religion." "But," he went on, "for such whom Christ has brought hither, it is not lawful to defend themselves by arms, but they ought over all to trust to the Lord." For they had been led by the Spirit of Christ to see the fundamental inconsistency between warfare and "the law of Christ." True obedience to the law of Christ demanded of the Quakers that they not wage war, but "suffer ourselves to be spoiled, taken, imprisoned, banished, beaten, and evilly entreated, without any resistance, placing our trust only in GOD, that he may defend us, and lead us by the way of the cross unto his kingdom." It did not matter that the majority of those who claimed to be followers of Christ were willing to wield the sword and go to war, because it was not by the way of the majority, but by "the way of the cross" of Jesus, the Prince of Peace, that God would "lead us unto his kingdom."[29]

The image of Jesus as Prince of Peace was not, however, a prominent theme of Christian iconography in the period of the Reformation. The reason for this was, in part, that many of the exponents of Christian pacifism were also critical of the use of images in the church. But it is also intrinsically more difficult to dramatize the figure of Jesus as Prince of Peace. For one *Ninth Symphony* in the nineteenth century, there are dozens of compositions like the *Marche militaire* and the *1812 Overture*. The most effective representations of the Prince of Peace have been achieved by an unintentional irony. Thus an illustration for the last masterpiece of Italian Renaissance literature, Torquato

Engraving from Torquato Tasso's *Jérusalem Délivrée*, Beinecke Rare Book and
Manuscript Library, Yale University.

Tasso's *Jerusalem Delivered*, might appear to be a depiction of the catalogue quoted earlier from Comenius's *Angel of Peace*: "spears, swords, wheels, halters, crosses, flames, and headsmen." In fact it carries out the motif of such descriptions of the Crusaders as this:

> Some shirts of mail, some coats of plate put on,
> Some don'd a cuirass, some a corslet bright,
> An hawberk some, and some a habergeon,
> So every one in arms was quickly dight,
> His wonted guide each soldier tends upon,
> Loose in the wind waved their banners light,
> Their standard royal towards heaven they spread,
> The cross triumphant on the Pagans dead.[30]

"The cross triumphant" was sacred to all Christians, pacifists as well as Crusaders. But Christian pacifism saw it as triumphing *over* armor and weapons, not *through* them: Jesus the Prince of Peace had seized the sword by the blade and torn it from the hands of the soldiers, lifting it to the sky hilt-high to make the sign of the cross.

It is noteworthy, in relation to the total history of the images of Jesus, that several of those who attacked the traditional use of the figure of Jesus to justify war were at the same time carrying on a vigorous campaign against the traditional dogmas about the person of Jesus Christ. Some of the Anabaptists, such as David Joris, became Antitrinitarians, and some of the Quaker emphases on reason and the "inner light" did lead to a repudiation of Christian orthodoxy. Those who defended both the doctrine of just war and the doctrine of the two natures in Christ professed to find inconsistency in the practice of invoking, as a divine authority against war, a Jesus Christ to whom meanwhile many of his traditional divine prerogatives were being systematically denied. For if Jesus as Lord did indeed have the absolute right to command such radical obedience, to prohibit even fighting in self-defense, and to abrogate the fundamental demands of state and society, he must be vastly more than many of the simplistic christological formulas of Anabaptists and Quakers confessed him to be.

Such an argument undoubtedly carried a great deal of validity. And yet—the copies of the Gospels being read by both sides contained a parable of Jesus that contrasted saying the right thing and doing the right thing in quite another fashion: "What do you think? A man had two sons; and he went to the first and said, 'Son, go and work in the vineyard today.' And he answered, 'I will not'; but afterward he repented and went. And he went to the second and said the same; and he answered, 'I go, sir,' but did not go. Which of the two did the will of his father?" (Matt. 21:28–31).

15

The Teacher of Common Sense

The true light that enlightens
every man.

During the Age of Reason, the Enlightenment of the seventeenth and eighteenth centuries, the orthodox Christian image of Jesus Christ came in for severe attack and drastic revision. Among the efforts of this period to deal with him, the best known are the early attempts at a biography of Jesus, what Albert Schweitzer (or rather his English translator) called "the quest of the Historical Jesus." But the Enlightenment's quest of the Historical Jesus was made possible, and made necessary, when Enlightenment philosophy deposed the Cosmic Christ.[1]

In 1730 there appeared in London the first volume of *Christianity as Old as the Creation, or, The Gospel, a Republication of the Religion of Nature,* by Matthew Tindal. If we judge by the literally hundreds of replies he evoked, Tindal might seem to have been attacking the gospel of Jesus Christ. In fact he was—or, at any rate, he thought he was—defending it, and in the only way he believed to be open to him now, which was to equate the essence of the gospel with reason and natural religion and to identify the essential Jesus as the Teacher of Common Sense. One of the factors he cited in support of the argument that a new understanding of Jesus had become necessary was the disappearance of miracle as a proof for the uniqueness of his person and the validity of his message. Throughout most of the history of Christianity it had seemed possible to argue on the basis of the supposedly incontestable historical evidence for miracles. Any question about the credibility of the miracle stories in the Bible could be dismissed as, in effect, "a denial either that there is any divine power or that it intervenes in human affairs."[2] Jesus had "procured authority for himself by means of miracles," whose purpose it was "that he should be believed in."[3] Many of the defenders of Christianity were, of course, aware all along of the ambiguity of such proofs, which were an argument in a circle: the historical credibility of the miracle stories was based on the theological doctrine of the divine nature of Jesus, which was in turn validated by the presumed scientific and philosophical possibility of miracles. But the argument in a circle worked, though only so long as the circle remained unbroken. Conversely, once the circle was broken, it was broken in several places—scientific-philosophical, historical, and theological—but not in all of them at the same time. We must look at each of them in turn, and at its implications for the image of Jesus.

Although the perception of Jesus as the Logos and Cosmic Christ had been one of the philosophical sources of modern scientific thought, the scientific thought of the seventeenth and eighteenth centuries gradually eroded it. Isaac Newton provides the most important evidence for this change. The ancient "negative theology" of the Greek fathers persisted in Newton: "As a blind man has no idea of colors," he said at the conclusion of his most famous book, "so we have no idea of the manner by which the all-wise God perceives and understands all things." But he also declared his conviction, as an article of sound natural philosophy, which could "discourse of [God] from the appearances of things," that "this most beautiful system of the sun, planets, and comets" was not to be attributed to some "blind metaphysical necessity," but "could only proceed from the counsel and dominion of an intelligent and powerful Being," who governed all things, "not as the soul of the world, but as Lord over all."[4] There was, he asserted elsewhere, "nothing of contradiction" in acknowledging that as the First Cause, God could "vary the laws of Nature" (thus apparently allowing for the miraculous) and yet at the same time in assuming that the world "once formed . . . may continue by those laws for many ages" (thus apparently precluding the miraculous).[5] In his writings on theology and biblical interpretation Newton accepted as trustworthy the miracle stories of the Bible, especially the accounts of miracles attributed to Jesus, but the miracles did not lead to the orthodox image of the Cosmic Christ. For he rejected the traditional doctrines of the Trinity and the person of Christ as incompatible both with reason and with Scripture, and, like John Milton, taught a subordination of Jesus to the Father that earned for him the epithet "Arian."[6]

It remained only to rule the miracles themselves out of court as inadmissible evidence. "There is not to be found in all history," David Hume asserted, "any miracle attested by a sufficient number of men, of such unquestioned good-sense, education, and learning, as to secure us against all delusion in themselves."[7] Reflecting the Enlightenment habit of undercutting all of historic Christianity by attacking Roman Catholicism, he referred to various alleged miracles, past and present, "Grecian, Chinese, and Roman Catholic," but was silent about the miracles in the Gospels, preferring to consider the miracles reported in the Pentateuch. Asserting that not reason but faith was the foundation of "our most holy religion," he concluded with the argument that faith was itself the greatest miracle, and indeed the only miracle:

> On the whole, we may conclude that the Christian Religion not only was at first attended with miracles, but even at this day cannot be believed by any reasonable person without one. Mere reason is insufficient to convince us of its veracity: And whoever is moved by Faith to assent to it, is conscious of a continued miracle in his own person, which subverts all the principles of his understanding, and gives him a determination to believe what is most contrary to custom and experience.

In such a context the miracles of Jesus had lost all power to prove who he was. For, as Goethe was to have Faust say, "The miracle is faith's most cherished child [*Das Wunder ist des Glaubens liebstes Kind*]," rather than the other way around.[8]

Miracle was, therefore, an issue both for science (usually called natural philosophy) and for history. In Edward Gibbon's examination of five historical causes for the victory of Christianity in the Roman empire, miracles constituted the third cause. Gibbon used the issue of miracles to describe the way "credulity" and "fanaticism" had prevailed in the Christian movement of the first three centuries. "The duty of an historian," he observed a bit archly, "does not call upon him to interpose his private judgment in this nice and important controversy" over whether or not miracles had continued after the apostolic age. And, even more coyly, he closed the chapter with a consideration also of the miracles of the apostolic age, above all the miracles performed by Jesus himself. "How shall we excuse the supine inattention of the Pagan and philosophic world to those evidences which were presented by the hand of Omnipotence, not to their reason, but to their senses?" Gibbon asked. For, he continued, "during the age of Christ, of his apostles, and of their first disciples, the doctrine which they preached was confirmed by innumerable prodigies. . . . The Laws of nature were frequently suspended for the benefit of the church." Then, focusing on the most spectacular miracle of all, he facetiously accused the classical writers of having "omitted to mention the greatest phenomenon to which the mortal eye has been witness since the creation of the globe . . . , the praeternatural darkness of the Passion," when the sun was obscured for three hours on Good Friday while Jesus hung on the cross.[9]

In the same spirit Gibbon forbore to list the commanding moral and religious authority of the figure of Jesus Christ as one of his five "secondary causes of the rapid growth of the Christian church," but cited, as "an obvious but satisfying answer" to the whole question, that the triumph of Christianity (or, as he called it later, the "triumph of barbarism and religion") "was owing to the convincing evidence of the doctrine itself, and to the ruling providence of its great Author." Consideration of that answer, however, lay beyond "the duty of an historian." Instead, he subjected early Christianity to a searching, and in many ways devastating, historical analysis. In later chapters he did discuss the rise and development of the doctrine of the Trinity, including especially the confession that Christ was "one in being with the Father," and the history of the doctrine of the incarnation.[10] But it was only in connection with the theological controversies over the person and the natures of Christ that he said anything significant about the life of Jesus at all, and then he disposed of it in one paragraph:

> The familiar companions of Jesus of Nazareth conversed with their friend and countryman, who, in all the actions of rational and animal life, appeared of the same species with themselves. His progress from infancy to youth and manhood was marked by a regular increase in stature and wisdom; and, after a painful agony of mind and body, he expired on the cross. He lived and died for the service of mankind; . . . the tears which he

shed over his friend and country may be esteemed the purest evidence of his humanity.[11]

Now it may be true, as one twentieth-century scholar has suggested, that calling "the unique attractiveness of the central figure of Christianity as presented in the Synoptic Gospels . . . a primary factor in the success of Christianity" is only "a product of nineteenth-century idealism and humanitarianism."[12] Yet that does not mean that the history of the life and death, the teachings and miracles, the preexistence and exaltation, of Jesus did not figure prominently in the triumph of the Christian movement. But Gibbon the historian was not dealing with that history.

Other historians of Gibbon's time were less hesitant. Indeed, the effort to reconstruct the biography of Jesus from the data in the Gospels was about to become, at the very time when Gibbon published his first volume in 1776, an overriding preoccupation of scholars and other literati in many lands. For in 1778 the German philosopher and literary critic Gotthold Ephraim Lessing published, as the last of seven *Wolfenbüttel Fragments* by an anonymous author, a treatise bearing the title *Concerning the Intention of Jesus and His Teaching*. That publication set off a debate over the authentic message and purpose of Jesus that has continued now for two centuries and shows no sign of relenting. The author of the treatise, as of the six previously published *Fragments*, was Hermann Samuel Reimarus, who at his death had left behind a massive work entitled *Apology for the Rational Worshipers of God*. In it he defended a Deistic philosophy of religion, with many affinities to Tindal's, against the traditional Christian doctrine of Creator and creation, and he insisted that the Jesus of the Gospels "taught no new mysteries or articles of faith or undertook to teach them." For "if Jesus himself had wished to expound this strange doctrine of three different persons in one divine nature . . . , would he have kept silent about it until after his resurrection?"[13] It was not to miracles, which were "unworthy of notice," or to the disclosure of so-called mysteries like the Trinity that the success of Jesus and his message was to be attributed, but to purely natural motives and causes, "a reason which operates and has operated at all times so naturally, that we need no miracle to make everything comprehensible and clear. That is the real mighty wind (Acts 2:2) that so quickly wafted all the people together. This is the true original language that performs the miracles."[14]

The controversy aroused by Lessing's publication of Reimarus belongs, of course, to the history of theology and of New Testament scholarship, but it extended far beyond theological circles and is therefore relevant also to our study of the place of Jesus in the history of culture. A century after Lessing, another German man of letters and, as Leander Keck has called him, "ex-theologian," David Friedrich Strauss, once again focused attention on Reimarus in defense of his own exposition of the concept of "myth" as a means of finding the elusive figure within and behind the Gospel accounts.[15] Strauss's *Life of Jesus*, first published in 1835–36, obtained an international circulation, popular at least as much as academic, when it was translated into English (anonymously) by a scholarly young Englishwoman named Mary Ann Evans, who went on in 1854 to translate Ludwig Feuerbach's *Essence of Christianity* as well; she is better known by her nom de plume of George Eliot.[16] As her biographer notes of her translation of Strauss, "few books of the nineteenth century have had a profounder influence on religious thought in England."[17] And it was the audacity of Reimarus that had prepared the way for Strauss to have that profound influence, first in Germany and then in England and America.

As the thought of Lessing and the interest of George Eliot in Strauss's *Life of Jesus* suggest, the quest of the Historical Jesus was not confined to the German biblical and theological scholars whose names form the table of contents of Albert Schweitzer's *Quest*. Even for the theologians, moreover, as Otto Pfleiderer has noted, "the examination of the literary details of the Gospels" became so dominant "that the interest in the supreme problems of the evangelical history seemed to have been almost lost sight of."[18] But in the latter part of the eighteenth century and the early part of the nineteenth, the quest of the Historical Jesus became at least as much the vocation of other intellectuals than theologians and New Testament scholars. In a search for new ways to understand reality, to validate morality, and to organize society, now that the old orthodoxy had been discredited, they undertook to reinterpret the major classics of Western culture in a manner that would make their abiding message available to a new age. If metaphysical unity with God in the Trinity and miraculous revelation from on high no longer constituted credentials for the message of Jesus, the harmony between his message and the best of human wisdom everywhere could. Where others had perceived in part, he "saw life steadily and saw it whole" (as Matthew Arnold was to say of Sophocles); but his way of doing so stood in continuity with the rest of human experience.

Enlightenment scholars searching for the Historical Jesus were, therefore, engaged at the same time in what might be called the quest of the historical Homer and the quest of the historical Socrates, as well as in a quest of the historical Moses. Less than two decades after the publication of Reimarus's essay on the Jesus of the Gospels, Friedrich August Wolf, one of the pioneers of modern classical scholarship, wrote his *Prolegomena ad Homerum*. In it he argued that Homer was not the name for an individual poetic genius who composed the *Iliad* and the *Odyssey*, but for a multiplicity of sources now collected into those epic poems. Wolf's method bore certain analogies to the techniques being employed by other scholars to identify the multiplicity of sources collected into the Pentateuch, but also to the effort to sort out various strata by sifting through the Gospels. Other scholars of the time were addressing themselves yet once more to the perennial Socratic problem; but, as Jaeger says, "Schleiermacher was the first to express the full complexity of this historical problem in a single condensed question." In a formulation suggestive of the problem of the relation between the Synoptic Gospels and the Gospel of John, to which he was to address himself in his own later *Lectures on the Life of Jesus*, Schleiermacher, translator of Plato into German, asked: "What *can* Socrates have been, in addition to all Xenophon says he was, without contradicting the characteristic qualities and rules of life that Xenophon definitely declares to have been Socratic—and what *must* he have been, to give Plato the impulse and the justification to portray him as he does in the dialogues?"[19]

The parallels between Socrates and Jesus had been drawn in the second and third centuries, as we have seen earlier. And again in the Enlightenment these parallels were, to be sure, of more than purely literary importance. Both Socrates and Jesus were outstanding teachers; both of them urged and practiced great simplicity of life; both were regarded as traitors to the religion of their community; neither of them wrote anything; both of them were executed; and both have become the subject of traditions that are difficult or impossible to harmonize. Yet the study of the parallel went even beyond those striking similarities. For the thinkers of the Enlightenment took Socrates as evidence for the presence, beyond the limits of alleged biblical revelation, of a wisdom and moral power that must have come from the God whom Jesus called Father. If, as the prologue to the Gospel of John asserted, the Logos-Word that became incarnate in Jesus of Nazareth was "the true light that enlightens every man" (John 1:9), whether Jew or Christian, Greek or heathen, Socrates made it extremely difficult to restrict the revealing activity of God—perhaps even the saving activity of God—to the history of the people of Israel and of the church. And if the true God had spoken and acted through Socrates, that meant that divine truth was universal. If it was universal, then both Socrates and Jesus must themselves have taught that it was.

On the other hand, even those who were prepared to concede the force of the parallelism were also concerned to identify the superiority and distinctiveness of the person and teaching of Jesus—if only it were possible to find out what his true person and authentic teachings were, behind the veil of the apostles and evangelists. Joseph Priestley, scientist and scholar, took up the question of disentangling the historical Jesus from the sources about him by writing a long book entitled *The Corruptions of Christianity* and by compiling *A Harmony of the Gospels*. In another work, a longish pamphlet of sixty pages dealing with the similarities and differences between Jesus and Socrates, he strove to do justice to the philosophical greatness and moral stature of Socrates, but came down on the side of the essential superiority of Jesus:

> In comparing the characters, the moral instructions, and the whole of the history, of Socrates and Jesus, it is, I think, impossible not to be sensibly struck with the great advantage of revealed religion, such as that of the Jews and the christians, as enlightening and enlarging the minds of men, and imparting a superior excellence of character. This alone can account for the difference between Socrates and Jesus, and the disciples of each of them; but this one circumstance is abundantly sufficient for the purpose.[20]

For Priestley, Jesus was no longer the Cosmic Christ or the Second Person of the Trinity, but he was a divinely inspired teacher, in a way that even Socrates was not.

Priestley's *Socrates and Jesus Compared*, as well as his other works of theology and biblical scholarship, had a profound influence on a man who was certainly the most eminent of all the many participants in the quest of the historical Jesus (even though Schweitzer does not so much as mention his name): Thomas Jefferson, third president of the United States. Nor was Jefferson's curiosity about the problems of

Jesus and the Gospels merely one of the seemingly infinite number of scholarly and scientific hobbies in which his capacious and penetrating intellect engaged; rather, Jefferson concerned himself with these problems during most of his adult life. He was convinced, as Daniel Boorstin has noted, that "purified Christianity could promote moral health in the actual setting of eighteenth-century America."[21] Therefore it was simultaneously as a statesman and as a philosopher that he was functioning when he undertook to discover (or rediscover) such a purified Christianity, and the results of his discovery went into his formulation of the American tradition.

Writing in his middle forties, he avowed that "from a very early part of [his] life" he had experienced the "difficulty of reconciling the idea of Unity and Trinity" in traditional Christian doctrine. In his judgment, such doctrines as the Trinity were not needed to account for Jesus of Nazareth, who was "a man, of illegitimate birth, of a benevolent heart, [and an] enthusiastic mind, who set out without pretensions of divinity, ended in believing them, and was punished capitally for sedition by being gibbeted according to the Roman law." Nor was it enough simply to reject the dogmatic and liturgical tradition of orthodox Christianity or to restore the message of the Bible. Jefferson was convinced that the purified Christianity he sought, the authentic message of Jesus, was not to be automatically equated with the total content of the Gospels, and that therefore it was necessary to extract that message from the present form of the texts. Out of that conviction came two separate attempts at what he himself called "abstracting what is really his from the rubbish in which it is buried, easily distinguished by its lustre from the dross of his biographers, and as separable from that as the diamond from the dung hill."[22]

The first such attempt was carried out while Jefferson was president, in February 1804. Working in the White House—as he admitted later, "too hastily"—he completed the task in "2. or 3. nights only at Washington, after getting thro' the evening task of reading the letters and papers of the day." As is evident from the photograph of an early facsimile of its first page, in an imitation of Jefferson's hand, the outcome bore the title *The Philosophy of Jesus of Nazareth*. The subtitle asserted that this had been "extracted from the account of his life and doctrines as given by Mathew, Mark, Luke, & John," and that what he was presenting was "an abridgement of the New Testament for the use of the Indians unembarrassed with matters of fact

The Philosophy

of Jesus of Nazareth
extracted from the account of
his life and doctrines as given by
Mathew, Mark, Luke, & John.

being an abridgement of
the New Testament
for the use of the Indians
unembarrassed with matters of fact
or faith beyond the level of their
comprehensions.

Title page of Thomas Jefferson's *Philosophy of Jesus of Nazareth*, holograph facsimile, Thomas Jefferson Papers, University of Virginia Library.

or faith beyond the level of their comprehensions." Whether he actually meant native Americans by the term "Indians" or was referring to his political opponents, he did take it upon himself to clip from two printed copies of the English New Testament those sayings which he recognized to be authentic, since they were, as he himself said, "easily distinguished" from the "rubbish" of the Gospel writers.

Long after leaving the presidency, Jefferson returned to his New Testament research and, probably in the summer of 1820, completed work on a much more ambitious compilation, entitled *The Life and Morals of Jesus of Nazareth Extracted textually from the Gospels in Greek, Latin, French & English.* The text is in four parallel columns in the four languages, pasted together in the order that Jefferson had outlined in a preliminary table of contents. What is omitted is in many ways even more revealing than what is included. Both the beginning and the end of the Gospel story have disappeared. The prologue of the Gospel of John is gone, and so are the accounts of the annunciation, the virgin birth, and the appearance of the angels to the shepherds. The account closes with a conflation of the first half of John 19:42 with the second half of Matthew 27:60: "There laid they Jesus and rolled a great stone to the door of the sepulchre, and departed." There is no mention of the resurrection. In *The Philosophy of Jesus,* Luke 2:40 appears in full, "And the child grew, and waxed strong in spirit, filled with wisdom; and the grace of God was upon him." But in *The Life and Morals of Jesus of Nazareth,* Jefferson took the trouble to expunge, in all four languages, the final words, "and the grace of God was upon him."[23] As the editor of Jefferson's version of the Gospel puts it, rather gently but no less effectively, "Although many distinguished biblical scholars have been daunted by the challenge of disentangling the many layers of the New Testament, the rationalistic Jefferson was supremely confident of his ability to differentiate between the true and the false precepts of Jesus."[24]

The Jesus who emerged from this method of differentiating between the true and the false was the Teacher of Common Sense, or, in Jefferson's words, "the greatest of all the Reformers of the depraved religion of his own country." The content of his message was a morality of absolute love and service, which was not dependent either upon the dogmas of the Trinity and the two natures in Christ or finally even upon the claim that he had a unique inspiration from God, but authenticated itself to his hearers by its intrinsic worth. But as one study of Jefferson has noted, Jefferson has "a concept of self-evident truths that accords well with his general training, his known reading and recommendations, and the language he used both in and of the Declaration [of Independence]"; but the "truths" he enumerated as "self-evident" were at once "more specific" and "more confusing" than those being propounded as such by some of his contemporaries.[25] Evidently, one source both of the specificity and of the confusion was his understanding of the "philosophy" and "morals" contained in the message of Jesus as the Teacher of Common Sense. Many of these elements of the Enlightenment image of Jesus are tersely summarized in the well-known letter of Jefferson's colleague Benjamin Franklin, writing a few weeks before his death to Ezra Stiles, president of Yale College:

> As to Jesus of Nazareth, my opinion of whom you particularly desire, I think the system of morals and religion, as he left them to us, the best the world ever saw or is likely to see; but I apprehend it has received various corrupting changes, and I have, with most of the present dissenters in England, some doubts as to his divinity, tho' it is a question I do not dogmatize upon, having never studied it, and think it needless to busy myself with it now, when I expect soon an opportunity of knowing the truth with less trouble. I see no harm, however, in its being believed, if that belief has the good consequence, as probably it has, of making his doctrines more respected and better observed.[26]

It is probably correct to suggest that "few other Americans of his time could have said" this,[27] but for Franklin and Jefferson that message of common sense was enough, and *Poor Richard's Almanak* can be read as a compilation of it. But for many others, it was either too much or too little—or perhaps both.

16
The Poet of the Spirit

You are the fairest of the sons of men; grace is poured upon your lips.

 When Shakespeare had Hamlet say, "There are more things in heaven and earth, Horatio, / Than are dreamt of in your philosophy,"[1] he could have been anticipating the rebuke issued by much of nineteenth-century thought and literature to its predecessors of the eighteenth century: by reducing mystery to reason and by flattening transcendence into common sense, the rationalism of the Enlightenment had dethroned superstition only to enthrone banality. What the nineteenth century substituted for such rationalism was, in René Wellek's words, the "attempt, apparently doomed to failure and abandoned by our time, to identify subject and object, to reconcile man and nature, consciousness and unconsciousness by poetry which is 'the first and last of all knowledge.' "[2] Wellek was defining Romanticism, in response to Lovejoy's effort to show that "the word 'romantic' has come to mean so many things that, by itself, it means nothing."[3] For our present purposes we may characterize as "Romantic" the effort of various nineteenth-century writers and thinkers to go beyond the quest of the Historical Jesus to a Jesus who—(to use Wellek's formula) by identifying subject and object and by reconciling man and nature, consciousness and unconsciousness—could be called the Poet of the Spirit.

As if to announce the end of the eighteenth century, the leading German interpreter of this Romantic version of faith in Christ, Friedrich Schleiermacher, quoted in the preceding chapter, issued his *On Religion. Speeches to Its Cultured Despisers* in 1799.[4] He went on, in 1806, to publish a kind of Platonic dialogue about Christ entitled *Christmas Eve Celebration* and, in 1819, to become "the first person to lecture publicly on the topic of the life of Jesus," making this the subject of academic lectures at the University of Berlin five times between 1819 and 1832, although the book to come out of student notes on the lectures did not appear until 1864.[5] Schleiermacher's most abiding achievement was a systematic theology entitled *The Christian Faith* and published in 1821–22.[6] Among English writers, probably the most profound as well as the most important of the transmitters of German Romanticism was Samuel Taylor Coleridge, who died in the same year as Schleiermacher.[7] Coleridge's *Aids to Reflection* of 1825 and his posthumously published *Confessions of an Inquiring Spirit* articulated in philosophical and theological prose some of the ideas to which he gave voice in his poetry, especially after 1810 or so, as he found himself moving closer to historic Christian beliefs. Coleridge was, in turn, a major force in the intellectual and spiritual development of Ralph Waldo Emerson, who belonged to the next generation and who was probably the most influential thinker in nineteenth-century America.[8] While acknowledging Lovejoy's corrective suggestion "that we should learn to use the word 'Romanticism' in the plural,"[9] we may nevertheless perhaps be permitted the generalization that each of these three—a German, an Englishman, and an American—stands in his own individual way as a spokesman for the literary and philosophical spirit of the Romanticism of the nineteenth century, and that each of them sought the incarnation of that spirit in the person of Jesus.

Like the rationalists, they all found it impossible to accept the Gospel stories of the miracles of Jesus as literal historical truth. Rather than explaining them away, however, they endeavored to incorporate them into a more comprehensive world view.[10] As Coleridge put it, "what we now consider as miracles in opposition to ordinary experience" would, with further insight, be seen "with a yet higher devotion as harmonious parts of one great complex miracle, when the antithesis between experience and belief would itself be taken up into [the] unity of intuitive reason."[11] Both the eighteenth-century attack of the Enlightenment on the notion of miracles as violations of natural law and the theological apologetics in defense of miracles had missed the point; for on both sides, in the phrase of Emerson's first book, published in 1836, "the savant becomes unpoetic," through the failure to realize "that a guess is often more fruitful than an indisputable affirmation, and that a dream may let us deeper into the secret of nature than a hundred concerted experiments."[12]

In this search for a "unity of intuitive reason" that would go beyond the antitheses between nature and miracle or between experience and belief, Jesus was, they recognized, the crucial problem and, they believed, the source for a solution to the problem as well. What has been called "Coleridge's ever-changing attitude toward Christ" was the endeavor to break out of the dilemmas formulated by the eighteenth century.[13] Similarly, in his lectures on the *Life of Jesus*, Schleiermacher discarded as not very helpful "the contrast between the supernatural and the natural that we include in the term 'miracle' on the basis of scholastic terminology."[14] Miracles were important as a "sign" and "mighty work," in which not the suspension of the laws of nature, but the "significance" was the primary component. Confronted by the Gospel accounts of the miracles, therefore, the biographer of Jesus had to relate them to the central themes of his life and work:

> The more the deed can be understood as a moral act on the part of Christ and the more we can establish a comparison between Christ's way of accomplishing a given result and that employed by other people, the more we can comprehend the acts as genuine constituents of the life of Jesus. The less we can understand them as moral acts on Christ's part and the less at the same time we can discover analogies, the less we shall be able to form a definite idea of the account and understand the facts on which it is based.[15]

On that basis Schleiermacher felt able to classify the miracle stories under various categories and to deal with the historical content in each of them.

The central content of the biography of Jesus, in Schleiermacher's *Life*, was the "development" in him of a "God-consciousness" that was, in comparison with the God-consciousness of others, on the one hand, "perfect" and therefore unique in degree, but, on the other hand, not fundamentally different in kind.[16] Understandably, the discussion of this theme follows immediately upon a consideration of the problems inherent in the orthodox dogma of the two natures, divine and human, and the treatment of the God-consciousness of Jesus may be seen as a substitute for that dogma. Thus the *Life of Jesus* formed a transition in Schleiermacher's own development from the somewhat dithyrambic picture of Jesus in the last of his *Speeches on Religion* of 1799 to the fully articulated and far more subtle portrait in *The Christian Faith* of 1821–22. In the *Speeches* Schleiermacher insisted that what was distinctive about Jesus was neither "the purity of his moral teaching" nor even "the individuality of his character, the close union of high power with touching gentleness," both of which were present in every great religious teacher; but "the truly divine element is the glorious clearness to which the great idea he came to exhibit attained in his soul": namely, "that all that is finite requires a higher mediation to be in accord with the Deity, and that for man under the power of the finite and the particular, and too ready to imagine the divine itself in this form, salvation is only to be found in redemption."[17] This Poet of the Spirit was thus the fulfillment of the theme announced near the opening of the *Speeches:*

> As a human being I speak to you of the sacred secrets of humanity according to my views—of what was in me as with youthful enthusiasm I sought the unknown, of what since then I have thought and experienced, of the innermost springs of my being which shall for ever remain for me the highest, however I be moved by the changes of time and humanity.[18]

By the time he wrote *The Christian Faith* two decades later, Schleiermacher had come to define Jesus as the "archetype [*Urbild*]" of authentic humanity in its relation to, and consciousness of, God: in Jesus Christ, he said there, "the archetype must have become completely historical . . . and each historical moment of this individual must have borne within it the archetypal."[19]

Because such "God-consciousness" and divine inspiration had been manifested with special force in artists and poets, the aesthetic experience provided the most appropriate categories for interpreting the figure of Jesus. In his early work on the life and teachings of Jesus, *The Spirit of Christianity and Its Fate,* Hegel defined "truth" as "beauty intellectually represented," and he therefore saw "the spirit of Jesus" as "a spirit raised above morality."[20] Jesus had, of course, been an inspiration to artists, poets, and musicians since the beginnings of Christianity. What sets much of the nineteenth century apart from that universal tradition is the effort to make this poetic and artistic understanding of him supersede the dogmatic, the moral, and even the historical. William Blake's powerful poem, *The Everlasting Gospel*, which he never finished, resembled other attempts of the time to rediscover the authentic Jesus who had been buried under tradition and dogma: Blake's Jesus, as the embodiment of what he calls the "poetic," denounced in his words and violated in his deeds the conventionalities of gentle and genteel religion. This was the restatement of an essentially apocalyptic picture of Jesus—the very feature of the message of the Gospels on which, along with the miraculous, the Enlightenment had foundered.[21] In Blake's case, moreover, the phrase "poetic and artistic understanding" of Jesus takes on special meaning, because Blake created a series of portraits of Jesus in which the antithesis between nature and supernature is transcended. Thus in *Christ Appearing to the Apostles after the Resurrection*, painted just before the transition from the eighteenth century to the nineteenth, the light surrounding the central figure clearly belongs to another order of reality than the natural, and yet the wounds in the hands and the side of Christ are there to prove the identity between the Risen One and the Historical Jesus, whom the disciples had known as part of the natural world. Because of the wounds and because of "the opposition between the one young apostle who regards the risen Christ with adoration while the others bow before Him as if He were an idol," it is, as Martin Butlin suggests, "tempting to see this more specifically as showing Doubting Thomas."[22] And, it may be added, Doubting Thomas had in many ways become the patron saint of the Enlightenment.

For it was a hasty and superficial conclusion from the scientific discovery of the natural world to suppose that now all mystery had been exorcised from it. If the mystery of faith did not make sense to the Doubting Thomases among the children of the eighteenth century, then perhaps the mystery of beauty could. In a famous (and sometimes ridiculed) passage that has been called "an image impatient with all possibility of loss . . . less an image than a promise of perpetual repetition,"[23] Emerson articulated that mystery of beauty:

> Standing on the bare ground—my head bathed by the blithe air and uplifted into infinite space—all mean egotism vanishes. I become a transparent eyeball; I am nothing; I see all; the currents of the Universal Being circulate

through me; I am part or parcel [particle] of God. . . . I am the lover of uncontained and immortal beauty.[24]

For, as he went on to say a little later, "The ancient Greeks called the world *kosmos*, beauty. Such is the constitution of all things, or such the plastic power of the human eye, that the primary forms, as the sky, the mountain, the tree, the animal, give us a delight *in and for themselves*." Thus Emerson sought, as he said in one of his earliest lectures, to "look upon Nature with the eye of the Artist," for in that way he could "learn from the great Artist whose blood beats in our veins, whose taste is upspringing in our own perception of beauty."[25] The presence, within and beneath human consciousness, of a sense of the mystery of beauty constituted Emerson's version of what the medieval scholastics had called the *analogia entis*, the analogy of being between Creator and creature, which now had become an aesthetic *analogia Naturae*, an analogy of Nature.

More even than it had in Schleiermacher's lectures on the life of Jesus or in the Romanticism of the young Hegel's treatment of Christian beginnings, the sort of aestheticism articulated by Emerson shaped the presentation of the biography of Jesus published in 1863 by Emerson's French contemporary, Ernest Renan, which has been called, perhaps a bit hyperbolically, "the most famous and enduring work upon the subject ever written."[26] More than sixty thousand copies of the book were sold in the first six months. Renan's *Vie de Jésus* was a celebration of what he himself called "the poetry of the soul—faith, liberty, virtue, devotion," as this had been voiced by Jesus, the Poet of the Spirit.[27] "This sublime person," he said, "who every day still presides over the destiny of the world, we may call divine," not in the sense in which that word had been employed by the orthodox dogma of the two natures, but because "his worship will constantly renew its youth, the tale of his life will cause endless tears, his sufferings will soften the best hearts."[28] Renan was writing as a historian; he had been appointed a professor in the Collège de France in 1862, although he was forced to resign his professorship in 1864. As a historian, however, he invoked the aesthetic mystery as an antidote to the ravages of a rationalistic historical skepticism. It was, he urged, necessary for the historian to understand how a faith "has charmed and satisfied the human conscience," but equally necessary not to believe it any longer, since "absolute faith is incompatible with sincere history." But he consoled himself with the belief that "to abstain from attaching one's self to any of the forms which captivate the adoration of men, is not to deprive ourselves of the enjoyment of that which is good and beautiful in them."[29] So it was to be with Jesus.

Many of the efforts to cast the person of Jesus in such a mold, including Renan's, came to grief on the moral question. Try though they did, they could not bring together the True, the Good, and the Beautiful, or connect their fundamental category of an aesthetic appreciation of Jesus to the prophetic earnestness that had been unmistakably present in his summons to discipleship. For Emerson, the crisis came in the conflict over slavery during the decades before the outbreak of the Civil War, a time that his biographer, echoing the title of the first volume of Winston Churchill's history of World War II, has called "The Gathering Storm."[30] He had attempted, in the first of the *Essays: Second Series* of 1844, entitled "The Poet," to bring together the True, the Good, and the Beautiful. "The Universe," he said there, "has three children, born at one time." "Theologically," he continued, they had been called "the Father, the Spirit and the Son," but "we will call [them] here the Knower, the Doer and the Sayer." "These stand respectively," he explained, "for the love of truth, for the love of good, and for the love of beauty." "The three are equal," he added in an obvious allusion to a trinitarian dogma that he rejected. It was the task of the poet to be the sayer and the namer, and to represent beauty. In that task he stood in continuity with God. "For the world is not painted or adorned, but is from the beginning beautiful; and God has not made some beautiful things, but Beauty is the creator of the universe." As Jesus was the Poet of the Spirit, so now the poet was to be the new Second Person of the Trinity, through whom the Beauty that was the creator of the universe would shine through, manifesting its essential unity with Truth and Goodness. But at the end of the essay Emerson lamented: "I look in vain for the poet whom I describe. . . . Time and nature yield us many gifts, but not yet the timely man, the new religion, the reconciler, whom all things await."[31] Emerson closed his poem, "Give All to Love," published in his *Poems* of 1847,[32] with the lines:

Heartily know,
When half-gods go,
The gods arrive.

But in place of the "half-god" Jesus who had gone, no "god," no new Poet of the Spirit, had arrived to unite the Good, the True, and the Beautiful.

Nor was it only the morality of Jesus that could not be accommodated in the Romantic reaction to the Enlightenment. Despite the valiant efforts of both Schleiermacher and Renan, the Historical Jesus did not quite suit its categories. As Karl Barth put it, "Jesus of Nazareth fits extremely badly into this theology.... The historical in religion, the objective element, the Lord Jesus, is a problem child [*Sorgenkind*] to the theologian, a problem child that ought throughout to be accorded respect and that somehow does receive respect, but a problem child nevertheless."[33] In this criticism Barth was echoing the comments of David Friedrich Strauss, who noted that although the title of Schleiermacher's lecture course was *The Life of Jesus*, in fact "he uses the name 'Christ' virtually throughout" rather than "Jesus."[34] The same criticism was repeated by Albert Schweitzer.[35] Strauss was objecting in part to Schleiermacher's effort, especially in *The Christian Faith*, to combine a critical historical study of the Jesus of the Gospels with an affirmative attitude toward the Christ of church dogma, a task that Strauss regarded as impossible and essentially dishonest. But also for Karl Barth, who carried out that very task in a way unmatched by anyone else in the twentieth century, the Romantic portrait of Jesus, as represented by Schleiermacher, was a brilliant failure.

In turn, however, Barth was hostile to the enterprise of apologetics at work in Strauss and in Schleiermacher's *Speeches On Religion*, whose subtitle makes clear that it was addressed "to the cultured among [religion's] despisers." For the sake of that appeal to the cultured despisers, the Schleiermacher of the *Speeches* was prepared to cut and trim, to adjust and omit, even if this meant overlooking or distorting central elements of the Christian tradition. "Even the distinctive artistic style of the *Speeches* is to be understood as 'apologetic' in this [reductionistic] sense," Barth charged, "in which Schleiermacher—as he himself said once, more as one playing music than as one presenting arguments—accommodated himself to the language" of his hearers. Barth concluded:

> As an apologist for Christianity, he played upon it as a virtuoso does upon his violin, [selecting] those tones and ways of playing that, even if they

did not have to sound delightful, could at least sound acceptable, to his hearers. Schleiermacher does not speak as a responsible servant of the matter [of Christian revelation], but, in true virtuoso style, as a free master of it.[36]

And the Historical Jesus, the "problem child," was, for Barth, the crucial instance of this tendency.

From within the privileged sanctuary of the church and of its dogmatic theology, one may certainly raise serious questions about the foreshortening of the doctrinal perspective on the person of Jesus Christ in such reductionistic apologetics. But the appeal of these portraits of Jesus to large sections of the populace in the nineteenth century appears incontestable, especially at a time when the traditional Christ of church and of dogma no longer spoke to them. Romanticism, in the sense of the word being employed here, arose at least in part out of the very crisis of faith connected with the quest of the Historical Jesus. In its concrete performance as an outlook on the past and as a method for understanding the past, moreover, the Romanticism of the nineteenth century demonstrated that it had an antenna far more sensitive to the signals of that past than the Rationalism that sought to lay exclusive claim to the title "historical." For example, it is difficult to see how our present awareness of the culture and thought of the Middle Ages could have developed as it did if it had not been for the pervasive force of Romanticism, just at the time when medieval studies came into prominence as a field of study. In 1845, Philip Schaf, a leading example of Romanticism in American theology, published his *Principle of Protestantism*, which articulated his theory of historical development and included the Reformation in the theory.[37] In the same year, John Henry Newman, who is sometimes associated with Romanticism, published his own epoch-making *Essay on Development*, which has played a major part in both the "rediscovery of tradition" and the "recovery of tradition."[38] Romanticism was able to do far greater justice than much of modern Existentialism to the depth and complexity of the past and thus to make that past live—at least for audiences that shared Romantic presuppositions.

On graduation evening, Sunday, 15 July 1838, Ralph Waldo Emerson, at the invitation of the senior class of the Harvard Divinity School, delivered an address that was to scandalize New England and bar him from returning to Harvard for almost thirty years.[39] In it he attacked "historical Christianity" for having "dwelt . . . with noxious exaggeration about the *person* of Jesus" when, in truth, "the soul knows no persons." Instead of urging that "[you] live after the infinite Law that is in you, and in company with the infinite Beauty which heaven and earth reflect to you in all lovely forms," it demanded that "you must subordinate your nature to Christ's nature; you must accept our interpretations, and take his portrait as the vulgar draw it." That was a violation of the imperative to "every man to expand to the full circle of the universe," with "no preferences but those of spontaneous love."

But it was also a violation of the authentic portrait of Jesus. "His doctrine and memory" had suffered a grave "distortion" already in his own time, and even more in "the following ages." The tropes in which he spoke were taken literally, and "the figures of his rhetoric have usurped the place of his truth." The church could not tell the difference between prose and poetry, and those who professed to be his orthodox followers threatened their theological adversaries, saying, "This was Jehovah come down out of heaven. I will kill you, if you say he was a man." Of course "he spoke of miracles," but only because "he felt that man's life was a miracle . . . and he knew that this daily miracle shines as the character ascends." In the mouths of the theologians and prelates, however, "the word Miracle . . . gives a false impression; it is Monster," instead of being "one with the blowing clover and the falling rain." The outcome of such a distortion was conventional Christian preaching. "I once heard a preacher," Emerson said, "who sorely tempted me to say I would go to church no more. Men go, thought I, where they are wont to go, else had no soul entered the temple in the afternoon." Such preachers, he said, "do not see that they make his gospel not glad, and shear him of the locks of beauty and the attributes of heaven."

How different was the true message of Jesus as Poet of the Spirit. "A true conversion, a true Christ, is now, as always, to be made by the reception of beautiful sentiments." Those beautiful sentiments were not confined to the Jesus of the Gospels, but they had achieved their pinnacle there—precisely because they were universal:

> Jesus Christ belonged to the true race of the prophets. He saw with open eye the mystery of the soul. Drawn by its severe harmony, ravished with its beauty, he lived in it, and had his being there. Alone in all history he estimated the greatness of man. One man was true to what is in you and

me. He saw that God incarnates himself in man, and evermore goes forth anew to take possession of his World. He said, in this jubilee of sublime emotion, "I am divine. Through me, God acts; through me, speaks. Would you see God, see me; or see thee, when thou also thinkest as I now think."

Therefore, Emerson went on to say, "it is the office of a true teacher to show us that God is, not was; that He speaketh, not spake." Otherwise, "the true Christianity—a faith like Christ's in the infinitude of men—is lost." He concluded by expressing the hope that "that supreme Beauty which ravished the souls of those Eastern men" of the Bible "shall speak in the West also," showing "that the Ought, that Duty, is one thing with Science, with Beauty, and with Joy." Therefore, he urged the neophyte minister of Jesus Christ, "Yourself a newborn bard of the Holy Ghost, cast behind you all conformity, and acquaint men at first hand with Deity." For that was to be truly faithful to the person and message of Jesus, Poet of the Spirit.

But the poetic treatment of the person of Jesus could also move in quite another direction, not to a denial of the historic faith of Orthodoxy about him but to an affirmation of it. One of the most effective examples is the scene in Dostoevsky's *Crime and Punishment* in which Raskolnikov demanded that Sonia read to him the story of the resurrection of Lazarus.[40] He had kissed her foot, explaining: "I did not bow down to you, I bowed down to all the suffering of humanity." Then he picked up the Russian New Testament and asked her to find the account of Lazarus. "Read!" he cried out to her plaintively, and then repeated it more urgently, but she hesitated. Gradually he understood that she combined a reluctance to read it to him with "a tormenting desire to read and to read to him," and that made him even more insistent. As she read the verses of the eleventh chapter of the Gospel of John, it was as though she were "making a public confession [*ispoviedovala*]." At first, Sonia's reading of the Gospel story "passionately reproduced the doubt, the reproach and censure" of those who had refused to accept Christ. But when she came to the miracle of the raising of Lazarus, she was "cold and trembling with ecstasy [*drozha i cholodeja*], as though she were seeing it before her very eyes." As the candle guttered, it cast its dying light on "the murderer and the harlot who had so strangely been reading together the holy book," whom Dostoevsky clearly sees as this new Magdalene and this new Lazarus. And the result was that Raskolnikov knew he must confess to her his murder of the old pawnbroker. When he finally did, she told him what he must do: "Go at once, this very minute. . . . Kiss the earth which you have defiled!" Precisely because Sonia knew that the Gospel story was true, it was through the history of Jesus' miracle of the raising of Lazarus that Raskolnikov came to an authentic awareness of himself and to a sense of kinship with the earth, to what René Wellek, in his definition of Romanticism quoted earlier, calls a reconciliation of man and nature, consciousness and unconsciousness, subject and object. The full poetic meaning of this reconciliation and identification with Christ becomes evident from an unused entry in Dostoevsky's notebook for the novel:[41]

> Now, kiss the Bible, kiss it, now read.
> [Lazarus come forth.]
> [And later when Svidrigaylov gives her money]
> "I myself [was] a dead Lazarus, but Christ resurrected me."
> N.B. Sonia follows him to Golgotha, forty steps behind.

And that Christ, too, was the Poet of the Spirit.

17

The Liberator

There is neither Jew nor Greek,
there is neither slave nor free,
there is neither male nor female;
for you are all one in Christ Jesus.
For freedom Christ has set us free;
stand fast, therefore, and do not
submit again to a yoke of slavery.

It is sometimes difficult to see in the Jesus of both Rationalism and Romanticism just why he was ever crucified, so accommodated had his image become to the spirit of the times. For example, one of the most widely read books ever written in the English language, Charles Monroe Sheldon's *In His Steps*, first published in 1896, was an idealized description of the success in business and in society that awaited an American community in which everyone decided to follow seriously in the footsteps of Jesus. Surely an example of such eminent practicality, a teacher of such convincing rationality, a figure of such incandescent beauty ought to have appealed to the first century as much as to the eighteenth or nineteenth.

Yet the same nineteenth-century Russian writer whose narrative in *Crime and Punishment* of Sonia and Raskolnikov reading together the Gospel story of the raising of Lazarus gave such vivid expression to the perception of Jesus as Poet of the Spirit also expressed, perhaps more profoundly than anyone before or since, the meaning of Jesus the Liberator, as one whom the first century—or any other century of human history—was bound to reject. Dostoevsky did this in Ivan Karamazov's vision of the Grand Inquisitor.[1] Christ returned to earth and was welcomed by the people as he blessed them with his presence and his miracles. But once again he was arrested—this time by orders of the Grand Inquisitor, the cardinal-archbishop of Seville and defender of the faith—and confronted by this spokesman for an institutional Christianity that had finally succeeded in correcting all the mistakes he made while he was on earth. In the well-known woodcut by William Sharp, the two stand in dramatic contrast. The gaunt form of the aged Inquisitor, in clerical garb, is illumined, as he faces Jesus the Prisoner. The face of Jesus is not visible, for he is turned toward the Inquisitor with his back to the viewer; yet it is the darkened figure of the Prisoner, not the illumined figure of the Inquisitor, that dominates the picture. For Jesus the Prisoner was in fact Jesus the Liberator, as the Inquisitor acknowledged when he rehearsed the three questions that Satan, "the wise and dread spirit, the spirit of self-destruction and non-existence," had addressed to Jesus during the temptation in the wilderness. "For in those three questions the whole subsequent history of mankind is, as it were, brought together into one whole, and foretold, and in them are united all the unresolved historical contradictions of human nature."

The first of Satan's questions, "If you are the Son of God, command these stones to become loaves of bread" (Matt. 4:3), presented the choice between turning the stones into bread, so that "mankind will run after thee like a flock of sheep, grateful and obedient," and "some promise of freedom which men in their simplicity and their natural unruliness cannot even understand"; "for nothing has ever been more insupportable for a man and a human society than freedom." Jesus chose to be the Liberator rather than the Bread King, but in that he was mistaken. The freedom he offered was only for the elite. Ever since that mistake, his followers had been coming to the powers of the earth in both church and state, to "lay their freedom at our feet, and say to us, 'Make us your slaves, but feed us.' " When the Inquisitor had finished his commentary on the temptation of Jesus,

he waited some time for his Prisoner to answer him. . . . But [Jesus] suddenly approached the old man in silence, and softly kissed him on his bloodless aged lips. That was all his answer. The old man shuddered. His lips moved. He went to the door, opened it, and said to him: "Go, and

William Sharp, woodcut, *The Grand Inquisitor*, from Fyodor Dostoevsky's *Brothers Karamazov* (Modern Library edition).

come no more. . . . come not at all, never, never!" And he let Him out into the dark alleys of the town. The Prisoner went away.

And, Dostoevsky (or, at any rate, Ivan Karamazov) implies, he never came back again.

Alongside the conventional portraits of Jesus as the pillar of the status quo in state and church, there had been a continuing tradition of describing him, in his own time and in every age that was to follow, as the Liberator. So it apparently was that many of his own contemporaries had seen him, as the one who challenged every social system and called it to account before the judgment of God. But it was above all in the nineteenth and twentieth centuries that the first-century Prophet who had preached the justice of God as it was directed against all the oppressors of humanity became Jesus the Liberator. And Jesus the Liberator became—and in our time has become and is—a political force that overthrows empires, even so-called Christian empires. The charter and the agenda of liberation in Jesus Christ were formulated in what has been called the Magna Charta of Christian liberty, the epistle of Paul to the Galatians: "There is neither Jew nor Greek, there is neither slave nor free, there is neither male nor female; for you are all one in Christ Jesus. . . . For freedom Christ has set us free; stand fast, therefore, and do not submit again to a yoke of slavery."[2] Neither Jew nor Greek; neither slave nor free; neither male nor female—each in its historical turn, these three captivities have originally been justified in the name of Christ the Creator and Lord as belonging to the natural order and to natural law, but they have finally been challenged, and have eventually been overcome, in the name of Jesus the Liberator.

From the seventeenth to the nineteenth century, the most persistent test case for the complicated dilemma of the relevance of Jesus the Liberator to the social order was the debate over slavery.[3] Both sides appealed to the text of the Bible and the authority of the person of Jesus. Both sides, as Abraham Lincoln said in the Second Inaugural of 4 March 1865, "read the same Bible, and pray to the same God; and each invokes his aid against the other." As he pointed out there, moreover, "it may seem strange that any men should dare to ask a just God's assistance in wringing their bread from the sweat of other men's faces." But he added, quoting the commandment of Jesus in the Sermon on the Mount, "let us judge not, that we be not judged" (Matt. 7:1). It was above all his awareness that "since man is finite he can never be absolutely sure that he rightly senses the will of the infinite God" that made "Abraham Lincoln in a real sense the spiritual center of American history."[4] To an abolitionist like James Russell Lowell, editor of the *Anti-Slavery Standard* and distinguished New England man of letters, the authority of Jesus for the situation was less equivocal.[5] Facing the implications of the war with Mexico for the future of slavery, he spoke out against the injustice both of slavery and of the war, in a poem of 1845 that was to become, for the next hundred years and more, a battle hymn of the Social Gospel:

> Once to every man and nation
> Comes the moment to decide,
> In the strife of truth with falsehood,
> For the good or evil side;
> Some great cause, God's new Messiah,
> Offering each the bloom or blight,
> And the choice goes by for ever
> 'Twixt that darkness and that light.

> By the light of burning martyrs
> Jesus' bleeding feet I track,
> Toiling up new Calvaries ever
> With the cross that turns not back;
> New occasions teach new duties,
> Time makes ancient good uncouth;
> They must upward still, and onward,
> Who would keep abreast of truth.

On the one hand, therefore, Robert Sanderson, an Anglican bishop in the seventeenth century, had declared that Christians "must not acknowledge any our supreme Master, nor yield our selves to be wholly and absolutely ruled by the will of any . . . but only Christ our Lord and Master in heaven." But on the other hand, he could, in the very same sermon, reject any interpretation of the supreme lordship of Christ over all earthly masters that proceeded "as if Christ or his Apostle had any purpose . . . to slacken those sinews and ligaments . . . which tie into one body . . . those many little members and parts, whereof all humane societies consist," and that included the sinews of slavery.[6]

The juxtaposition of those two statements in the same sermon about what it meant, and what it did not mean, to call Jesus the Liberator would be easy to duplicate over and over from the literature of the debate over slavery. The tension they represent was not unique to the modern period, however, for it seems to have been present in the Gospel portraits of Jesus themselves. Among those who claimed to be followers of Christ there had long been an uneasiness about the institution of slavery. They recognized that because of his coming "slavery had been deprived of any claim to be an inner necessity derived from the structure of human nature."[7] Augustine articulated this uneasiness when he declared it to have been the original intention of the Creator "that his rational creature should not have dominion over anything but the irrational creation—not man over man, but man over the beasts." Slavery, therefore, was not a natural institution created by God, but was a result of the fall of the human race into sin.[8] Yet in a fallen world, where it was necessary to accept the imperfections of all human institutions, slavery, too, had to be tolerated, and the authority of Christ the Liberator could not be invoked to justify overthrowing it by revolutionary force. The most compelling testimony for such social conservatism was found in the epistle of Paul to Philemon. In it the same apostle who announced the Magna Charta "There is neither slave nor free" informed Philemon, a slaveholder, that he was sending Onesimus, a runaway slave, back to him, in order "to do nothing without your consent"; but he expressed the hope that Philemon "might have him back for ever, no longer as a slave but more than a slave, as a beloved brother," which John Knox takes to mean that Onesimus might become a Christian evangelist.[9] Although, in Bishop Lightfoot's words, "the word 'emancipation' seems to be trembling on his lips,"[10] Paul declined to compel Philemon to set Onesimus free as a matter of Christian duty (Philem. 14–16), and he did not address (one way or the other) the general question of the Christian attitude toward slavery as an institution.

Those who continued to find that institution tolerable could thus lay claim to the letter of what the New Testament had said: certainly it was not, strictly speaking, against the law, either in the Old Testament or in the New, to have ownership of another human being.[11] As on the question of paying taxes to Caesar (Matt. 22:21), so here, the New Testament appeared to have taken it for granted that there would be slavery in the society. It had even used it as an analogy for the relation of the believer to the lordship of Christ, as well as for the relation of the sinner to the lordship of the devil.[12] It was, consequently, no more legitimate to employ the sayings of Jesus as a weapon against slavery than it was to use his language about the kingdom of

God as the basis for denouncing all earthly kingdoms as usurpations. Yet the spirit of the epistle to Philemon, if not the letter, did call the institution of slavery into question, and new occasions did teach new duties. Even though the church "allowed [the institution of slavery] to endure," therefore, it "was fully conscious of the inconsistency between this institution and the inner freedom and equality which was the Christian ideal."[13] It was only a matter of time—though, in the event, a long time indeed—before the recognition of that inconsistency between the toleration of slavery and the proclamation of Jesus as Liberator produced decisive action.

The rediscovery of Jesus the Liberator was not confined to the debate over slavery, nor to British and American thought. Perhaps the most widely celebrated such rediscovery in the nineteenth century was that of Lev Tolstoy. In his novel *Resurrection*, whose uncensored version was published two decades later than *The Brothers Karamazov*, the same contrast between the Liberator and an inquisitor appears, once again in a prison, where a visitor "was startled to see a large picture of the Crucifixion, hanging in an alcove. 'What's that here for?' he wondered, his mind involuntarily connecting the image of Christ with liberation and not with captivity."[14] The message of Tolstoy's *Resurrection* was that the teachings of Jesus were intended to be taken literally. The final chapter of the novel was a commentary on portions of the Gospels, above all on the commandments of the Sermon on the Mount, in which the protagonist "pictured to himself what this life might be like if people were taught to obey these commandments." The excitement and the ecstasy that came over him, "as happens to vast numbers who read the Gospels," convinced him that "it is man's sole duty to fulfil these commandments, that in this lies the only reasonable meaning of life." In that realization, "it was as though, after long pining and suffering, he had suddenly found peace and liberation."[15]

"When the novel *Resurrection* appeared in 1899," a scholarly monograph by the Soviet literary historian G. I. Petrov has observed, "it was the occasion for displeasure and embarrassment in the government and in the higher circles of the church."[16] Tolstoy's radical Christianity drew the excommunication of the Russian Orthodox Church, but his reinterpretation of the message of Jesus also drew the devoted attention of many thousands from both within and beyond Russia as well as Orthodxy. They made pilgrimages to Yasnaya Polyana to visit the prophet of a new Christianity, and they wrote to him from all over the world. Even George Bernard Shaw corresponded with him about his own "theology," although Tolstoy found offensive Shaw's flippancy in treating the gospel, since "the problem about God and evil is too important to be spoken of in jest."[17] In his novels, as Isaiah Berlin has put it, "Tolstoy perceived reality in its multiplicity, as a collection of separate entities round and into which he saw with a clarity and penetration scarcely ever equalled." But in his philosophy and theology, "he believed only in one vast, unitary whole," which he finally formulated as "a simple Christian ethic divorced from any complex theology or metaphysic . . . , the necessity of expelling everything that does not submit to some very general, very simple standard: say, what peasants like or dislike, or what the gospels declare to be good," two standards that were often the same for Tolstoy.[18] "Do not resist one who is evil. But if any one strikes you on the right cheek, turn to him the other also" (Matt. 5:39): Tolstoy's radical views about the literal application of these words of Jesus seemed to most prophets of liberation and champions of the oppressed to be the height of impracticality, a capitulation to injustice, indeed "the opium of the masses."

One exception was a young Indian-born barrister in South Africa, who came under the powerful influence of Tolstoy's religious and ethical philosophy. Tolstoy's book *The Kingdom of God Is within You*, he was to write later, "overwhelmed me. It left an abiding impression on me. Before the independent thinking, profound morality, and the truthfulness of this book, all [other Christian] . . . books . . . seemed to pale into insignificance."[19] He went on to found a Tolstoyan commune in South Africa in 1910, the year of Tolstoy's death. Tolstoy wrote a letter (in English) to his admirer in South Africa on 7 September 1910, just two months before he died. Except for short personal notes to friends and family, it was to be his final epistle, almost a religious-philosophical last will and testament:

> The longer I live, and especially now when I feel keenly the nearness of death, I want to tell others what I feel so particularly keenly about, and what in my opinion is of enormous importance, namely what is called non-resistance, but what is essentially nothing other than the teaching of love undistorted by false interpretations. . . . This law has been proclaimed by all the world's sages, Indian, Chinese, Jewish, Greek and Roman. I think it has been expressed most clearly of all by Christ. . . . The whole of Christian civilisation, so brilliant on the surface, grew up on [an] obvious, strange,

sometimes conscious but for the most part unconscious misunderstanding and contradiction [of the authentic teachings of Jesus the Liberator]. . . . For 19 centuries Christian mankind has lived in this way. . . . There is such an obvious contradiction that sooner or later, probably very soon, it will be exposed and will put an end either to the acceptance of the Christian religion which is necessary to maintain power, or to the existence of an army and any violence supported by it, which is no less necessary to maintain power.[20]

"Your British, as well as our Russian" government, with their nominal allegiance to the lordship of Jesus Christ, would have to face this contradiction and its consequences.

The name of Tolstoy's Indian disciple and correspondent in South Africa was Mohandas K. Gandhi. His philosophy of what Erik Erikson has aptly termed "militant non-violence" was a blending of elements from traditional Hinduism, which he had initially rejected but on which he eventually looked more favorably, and elements from Christianity, or more specifically from the teachings of Jesus. Tolstoy's interpretations had helped him to understand the authentic message of Jesus, within and behind the traditional Christianity he and his Indian countrymen had learned from the missionaries. And so "a gathering of economists found themselves lectured to ('perhaps you will treat my intrusion as a welcome diversion from the trodden path') on—Jesus."[21] By the time Gandhi died a martyr on 30 January 1948, history had fulfilled Tolstoy's dying prophecy. "Your British" and "our Russian" empires, both of which had claimed to embody Christian values in their governments, had been overthrown by forces claiming to be champions of liberation and of nonviolence, though certainly not of traditional Christian belief in the message of Jesus the Liberator.

Yet Gandhi continued to have many disciples for his gospel of nonviolence in the spirit of Jesus the Liberator. They were to learn that following in the footsteps of Jesus the Liberator, and in the footsteps of Mahatma Gandhi, might temporarily lead them, as it had Gandhi himself, to triumphant processions like the one on Palm Sunday (Matt. 21:1-11). But eventually it would take them to the confrontations with the establishment that immediately followed the triumph.[22] And there would be some whose path of following Jesus the Liberator (to borrow Sheldon's title) "in his steps" took them the full distance from Palm Sunday to Good Friday, as the way of triumph became the way of the cross and the imitation of Christ took the form of being quite literally, in the words of the New Testament, "made conformable unto his death."[23] One of these was Martin Luther King, Jr., who, like Gandhi, was martyred by an assassin's bullet, on 4 April 1968.

Radical conformity to the life of Jesus, and even to his death, and revolutionary obedience to his imperatives were not alien to the particular traditions out of which Martin Luther King came. Both as a black American and as an American Baptist who believed himself to stand as well in the spiritual lineage of the sixteenth-century Continental Anabaptists, he was descended from forebears who had historically always been a despised minority and who had often been obliged to learn the "cost of discipleship" by suffering oppression and even death. Like many Protestant leaders, he came from a family of ministers, and in later years he would often recall having heard the stories and sayings of the Gospels in church and home long before he learned to read them in school. His eventual decision as an undergraduate to follow his father and his grandfather into the Christian ministry took him to theological seminary and then to graduate school. His academic studies developed in him the theological, philosophical, and moral principles that were to mold his life, shape his message, determine his public career, and bring him to his death.

While many of the books he studied as a seminarian and graduate student were the standard titles that most Protestant students of theology at that time were reading—his dissertation dealt with the doctrine of God in the thought of Paul Tillich and Henry Nelson Wieman— one name stands out on his reading list that was absent from most of the others: Mohandas K. Gandhi, whose death in 1948 coincided with Martin Luther King's matriculation in the seminary. Gandhi, while employing the instruments of nonviolence in his battle for the liberation of India from colonialism under the British empire, had expressed the hope that it would be through American blacks "that the unadulterated message of nonviolence will be delivered to the world." One influential black Christian in America who owed much to Gandhi was Howard Thurman.[24] Thurman reached through the philosophy of Gandhi, but beyond it, to the message of Jesus, upon which Gandhi had drawn, to portray Jesus as the Liberator especially of those who had been denied opportunity and fulfillment. But it was Mordecai Johnson, another leading black preacher and thinker, whose sermon at Crozer Theological Seminary in Philadelphia brought the young theological student face to face with the thought of Gandhi as an eminently workable contemporary system. Johnson, he recalled, aroused in him the conviction that Gandhi was "the first person in history to live the love ethic of Jesus above mere interaction between individuals." Years later, in his last book, he was still citing Gandhi against the "nihilistic philosophy" and hatred that threatened to make his revolution "bloody and violent." "What was new about Mahatma Gandhi's movement in India," King declared, "was that he mounted a revolution on hope and love, hope and nonviolence."[25]

That interpretation of the teaching of Jesus as a love ethic that repudiated violence and went beyond individualism represented the intellectual and moral foundation of King's thought and action. For it had to be action as well as thought. The Sermon on the Mount, which he had studied in the seminary as a biblical text, became for him in the mature years of his ministry a textbook for social and political activism. As he would later reminisce,

> When I went to Montgomery as a pastor, I had not the slightest idea that I would later become involved in a crisis in which nonviolent resistance would be applicable. I neither started the protest nor suggested it. I simply responded to the call of the people for a spokesman. When the protest began, my mind, consciously or unconsciously, was driven back to the Sermon on the Mount, with its sublime teachings on love, and to the Gandhian method of nonviolent resistance.[26]

Gandhi and the Sermon on the Mount were his continuing inspiration. The accents of the Sermon on the Mount, as he had learned through these experiences to interpret it, ring out in all his speeches and public documents. The most profound of these documents is probably his "Letter from Birmingham Jail," completed on 16 April 1963, in which he voiced the prophetic hope that "one day the South will know that when these disinherited children of God sat down at lunch counters, they were in fact standing up for what is best in the American dream and for the most sacred values in our Judeo-Christian heritage."[27]

This sounded naive to all of his critics and even to some of his supporters, as well as to the main body of the scholarly and theological interpreters of the teachings of Jesus and the Sermon on the Mount, who had by this time achieved something of a consensus that the message of Jesus was a "consistent eschatology." But King's interpretation of the Sermon on the Mount was in fact a carefully thought out and highly sophisticated strategy. In 1959, he and his wife, Coretta Scott King, made a pilgrimage to India, the land of Gandhi, where they saw some of the concrete results that had been attained by the "naive" Mahatma. Through "militant nonviolence" Gandhi had accomplished a liberation that the repeated Indian rebellions before him, going back to the Sepoy Mutiny of 1857 and beyond, had been unable to attain. "I left India," King reported, "more convinced than ever before that nonviolent resistance is the most potent weapon available to oppressed people in their struggle for freedom." "It was," he added, speaking of Gandhi's historic achievement, "a marvelous thing to see the results of a nonviolent campaign."[28]

In his own series of nonviolent campaigns over the next decade, Martin Luther King put that philosophy to the test. Even many of his followers, both black and white, urged that the time for nonviolence had passed, that the message of liberation in the Sermon on the Mount could not succeed as a "weapon available to oppressed people in their struggle for freedom." Repeatedly he acknowledged that he was finding their arguments increasingly persuasive, their impatience more appealing, their strategies of direct action more tempting. Yet each time he ended up reaffirming his fundamental commitment to the practicality of the teachings of the Sermon on the Mount as a political program for the liberation of American blacks. At the heart of this program was the vision of human society as a "beloved community."[29] He described this community at length especially in his book *Stride toward Freedom*.[30] It was to be a society in which—within the standard triad of justice, power, and love—the historic definition of justice would gradually become a reality through the moderation of power by love. He knew it would not happen all of a sudden, and he was realistic enough to recognize that there would be many individuals whom the evangelical imperatives of love would not change; only law, and the enforcement of law, could do that. But he had learned from Gandhi that "mere interaction between individuals" was not, despite centuries of Christian interpretation, the deepest meaning of "the love ethic of Jesus." Rather, the love ethic would have to penetrate and reform the structures of society itself and, through those structures, create a context of love and justice to which, through power, even the recalcitrant would have to conform.

When an eminent scholar of black literature in America was asked why Martin Luther King had not become a Marxist and why those who followed him had accepted his philosophy of nonviolence, he unhesitatingly replied: "Because of the overpowering force of the figure of Jesus." That was also the reason in many cases for the positive response, painfully slow in coming though it was, that King's message called forth in white Christians. Obviously there remained a large group who did not respond that way, and Martin Luther King, Jr., became their victim, as he had long known he might. But in his death he carried out what he knew in his life, that he had been called to follow in the footsteps of Another. And so, when he accepted the Nobel Peace Prize in December 1963, he repeated, yet one more time, the commands and the promises of Jesus in the gospel of liberation as enunciated in the Sermon on the Mount:

> When the years have rolled past and when the blazing light of truth is focused on this marvelous age in which we live, men and women will know and children will be taught that we have a finer land, a better people, a more noble civilization, because these humble children of God were willing to "suffer for righteousness' sake."

Despite all its ambiguity, theological no less than political, such a reading of the message of Jesus continues to inspire the campaign for human liberation. Especially in the Third World, Jesus the Liberator is being pitted against all the Grand Inquisitors, whether sacred or secular. But now he is seen as inverting his original statement (Matt. 4:4) to read that man shall not live by the word of God alone but by bread as well, as sanctioning not only militant nonviolence but direct action, as not only blessing a spiritual poverty that awaits supernatural goods in the life to come but leading the poor of this world to natural goods in this life and in this world. This is what Casalis calls a "christology of revolutionary praxis."[31] The contrast between this picture of Jesus the Liberator and earlier pictures of Jesus the Liberator may perhaps become visible if we compare the two versions in the New Testament of one of the Beatitudes. As the advocates of a nonpolitical interpretation of Christ the Liberator have always pointed out, the more familiar version in the Gospel of Matthew reads, "Blessed are the poor in spirit, for theirs is the kingdom of heaven" (Matt. 5:3). Yet the theology of liberation is based on the reminder that in the Gospel of Luke Jesus cries out, "Blessed are you poor . . . , but woe to you that are rich!" (Luke 6:20, 24).[32] But if Dostoevsky's legend of the Grand Inquisitor was the most profound portrayal of Jesus the Liberator, it was the American War between the States that evoked not only Lincoln's recognition of the ambiguity in citing Jesus as an authority for specific political action, but also the most stirring summons to live and die in the name of Jesus the political Liberator. In February 1862, Julia Ward Howe, drawing upon Romantic imagery of Jesus, published "The Battle Hymn of the Republic":

In the beauty of the lilies Christ was born across the sea,
With a glory in his bosom that transfigures you and me;
As he died to make men holy, let us die to make men free,
While God is marching on.

18

The Man Who Belongs to the World

Both in Jerusalem, and in all Ju-
daea, and in Samaria, and unto
the uttermost part of the earth.

 Nazareth was what is known in colloquial English as a
hick town, an insignificant village. It almost sounds like
a proverbial saying when in the Gospel of John Nathanael
asks (John 1:46), "Can anything good come out of Nazareth?" Thus Jesus of Nazareth was a villager and a provincial. Whatever may be the historical status of the story
of his flight to Egypt as an infant with his parents, he never as an
adult traveled beyond the borders of the Levant. As far as we can
tell, he did not command either of the world languages of his time,
Latin and Greek, although both are said by the Gospel of John to
have appeared in the inscription on his cross (John 19:20). The only
reference to his having written anything in any language, when he
stooped to write with his finger on the ground, comes in a passage
of dubious textual authenticity, which most manuscripts include
somewhere in the Gospel of John (John 8:6, 8). He spoke of how "the
rulers of the Gentiles lord it over them, and their great men exercise
authority over them" (Matt. 20:25), but as of a phenomenon belonging
to a world far removed from his own. And even when, in an appearance after the resurrection, he is represented by the author of the
Acts of the Apostles as having referred to the outside world, it was
as a provincial might, dividing the world into the immediate environs

220

and everything that was elsewhere: "Ye shall be witnesses unto me both in Jerusalem, and in all Judaea, and in Samaria—and unto the uttermost part of the earth."[1] Therefore his cosmopolitan detractors in the Roman empire were able to sneer that he had put in his appearance "in some small corner of the earth somewhere," and not (to borrow a modern phrase that seems appropriate) out here in the real world.[2]

Jesus of Nazareth may have been a provincial, but Jesus Christ is the Man Who Belongs to the World. By a geographical expansion shattering anything that either his cosmopolitan detractors within paganism or, for that matter, the author of the Book of Acts within Christianity could have imagined, his name has moved out far from that "small corner of the earth somewhere" and has come to be known "unto the uttermost part of the earth." In the words of the paraphrase of Psalm 72 by Isaac Watts,

> Jesus shall reign where'er the sun
> Does his successive journeys run,
> His kingdom stretch from shore to shore
> Till moons shall wax and wane no more.
> People and realms of every tongue
> Dwell on his love with sweetest song.[3]

When that hymn was published in 1719, the most dramatic growth in the extension of his influence ever known was just beginning. Because of that quantum increase, the best-known history of Christian expansion in English devoted three of its seven volumes to the nineteenth century alone, calling it *The Great Century.*[4] The sun never sets on the empire of Jesus the King, the Man Who Belongs to the World.

Not coincidentally, the great century of Christian missionary expansion was also in many ways the great century of European colonialism.[5] As in past centuries of Christian conversion, the missionary and the military sometimes went hand in hand, each serving the purposes of the other, and not always in a manner or a spirit consonant with the spirit of Christ. The medieval method of carrying on Christian missions was often to conquer the tribe in warfare and then to subject the entire enemy army to baptism at the nearest river.[6] That pattern continued to appear in modern missions, despite the many differences between their methods. Consequently, although Jesus himself had lived in the Near East, it was as a religion of Europe that his message came to the nations of the world and the islands of the sea—a religion of Europe both in the sense of a religion *from* Europe and, often, a religion *about* Europe as well. Indeed, at the end of the "great century" and on the eve of the First World War, the provocative aphorism was coined, apparently by Hilaire Belloc: "The Faith is Europe and Europe is the Faith."[7]

The identification of Europe and "the faith" implied, on the one hand, that those who accepted European economic, political, and military domination and who adopted European civilization thereby came under pressure to undergo conversion to the European faith in Jesus Christ. It likewise implied, however, that faith in Jesus Christ must be on European terms, take them or leave them, and that the forms it took—organizational, ethical, doctrinal, liturgical—must be, with as much adaptation as necessary but as little adaptation as possible, the ones it had acquired in its European configuration.

Although it has become part of the conventional wisdom in much of contemporary anticolonialist literature, both Eastern and Western, it is an oversimplification to dismiss the missions as nothing more than a cloak for white imperialism. Such an oversimplification ignores the biographical, religious, and political realities running through the history of Christian missions during the "great century" and long before, as missionaries have, in the name of Jesus, striven to understand and learned to respect the particularity of the cultures to which they have come. It should be noted, in addition, that there was historically a sharp difference on this count between the missionary methods of the Eastern and the Western churches. When Constantine-Cyril and Methodius came as Christian missionaries to the Slavs in the ninth century, they translated not only the Bible, but the Eastern Orthodox liturgy into Slavonic.[8] By contrast, when Augustine had come to the English in 597, he had brought with him not only the message of the gospel and the authority of the See of Rome, but the liturgy of the Latin Mass, and he had made the acceptance of this a condition of conversion to faith in Christ.[9] While Greek-speaking missionaries like Cyril and Methodius did not teach their Slavic disciples to read Greek, Western missionaries had to provide the nations they converted with the rudiments of Latin and the means of learning it. In the Carolingian period, "the use of Latin was everywhere and irrevocably narrowed down to liturgy and the written word," and Latin became a "purely artificial language." Nevertheless, it was also the "sole medium of intellectual life" and could become again, incidentally to the process and quite unintentionally, a way of access to the heritage of pre-Christian Roman culture and classical Latin literature.[10]

The most celebrated instance of the Christian understanding and respect for a native culture, however, was in the work of a Roman Catholic rather than of an Eastern Orthodox missionary, the Jesuit Matteo Ricci, in China. He has been called by a modern English historian of Chinese culture "one of the most remarkable and brilliant men in history."[11] The first generation of Jesuits, under the leadership and inspiration of Francis Xavier, made the mission to China a major item on their agenda. But in carrying out the mission, the Jesuits had followed the medieval pattern of the Western church, introducing the Roman Catholic liturgy of the Mass, forbidding any of the Chinese vernaculars in worship, and enforcing the use of Latin. With Ricci's arrival at Macau in 1582, that strategy underwent drastic revision. Ricci adopted the monastic habit of a Buddhist monk, then the garb of a Confucian scholar, and became a renowned authority both in the natural sciences and in the history and literature of China.

This erudition enabled him to present the person and message of Jesus as the fulfillment of the historic aspirations of Chinese culture, in much the way that Jesus had been presented by the early fathers as the culmination of the Greco-Roman faith in the Logos and by the New Testament as the fulfillment of the Jewish hope for the Messiah. The Chinese, Ricci maintained, "could certainly become Christians, since the essence of their doctrine contains nothing contrary to the essence of the Catholic faith, nor would the Catholic faith hinder them in any way, but would indeed aid in that attainment of the quiet and peace of the republic which their books claim as their goal."[12] Already in his lifetime and even more in the years of the "rites controversy" over the legitimacy of "accommodationism" that followed his death in 1610, Ricci was accused of having compromised the uniqueness of the person of Christ. But the upsurge of interest in his work has made it clear, on the basis of such theological works in Chinese as *The True Meaning of the Lord of Heaven* of 1603, that Ricci was and remained an orthodox Catholic believer, whose very orthodoxy it was that impelled him to take seriously the integrity of Chinese traditions.[13] Although with a less dramatic involvement in native thought and culture than Ricci's, both Roman Catholic and Protestant missionaries in the nineteenth century often managed to combine a commitment to evangelization in the name of Jesus with a deep (and ever deepening) respect for the native culture and indigenous traditions of the nations to which they had been sent.

As in the past, Christian missions in the nineteenth and twentieth centuries have involved many social changes as well as changes in religious affiliation. Perhaps the most important of these changes for the future cultural development of the nations was the close association between the missions and the campaign for world literacy. A monument to the importance of that achievement for the history of the Slavs is the very alphabet in which most Slavs write, which is called Cyrillic, in honor of Saint Cyril, the ninth-century "apostle to the Slavs," who, with his brother Methodius, is traditionally given credit for having invented it, using Greek uncial script, plus some letters from Hebrew, because of the complexity of Slavic phonemes. Not only among the Slavs in the ninth century, but also among the other so-called heathen in the nineteenth century, the two fundamental elements of missionary culture for more than a millennium have therefore been the translation of the Bible, especially of the New Testament, and education in the missionary schools. In one after another of the nations of Africa and of the South Seas, Christian missionaries found, upon arriving, that none of the native languages had been committed to writing, and that therefore it was necessary, for the sake of the translation of the word of God, to reduce one or more of those languages to written form. In many cases, therefore, the first efforts ever at a scientific understanding of the language, by native or foreigner, came from Christian missionaries. They compiled the first dictionaries, wrote the first grammars, developed the first alphabets. Thus it came about that the first important proper name to have been written in many of these languages must have been the name of Jesus, with its pronunciation adapted to their distinctive phonic structure, just as it had been in all the languages of Europe. The Protestant missionary Bible societies, especially the British and Foreign Bible Society and the American Bible Society, owed their origins to Christian missions in the nineteenth century. During the nineteenth and twentieth centuries, they have put at least the Gospels, and sometimes the rest of the New Testament and of the entire Bible, into more than a thousand additional languages, which averages out to more than five new languages per year.[14]

The schools founded by Protestant missionary societies and by Roman Catholic religious orders have been closely associated with this enterprise and often functioned as the centers for both the translation of the Gospels and the linguistic study undergirding it.[15] At the same time, they taught the children of Christian converts, and any other children who would come, the Western language and the Western-Christian culture of the church that had sent the missionaries. This often led to an ambivalence about the native culture, which the teachers in the missionary schools wanted to master in the name of Christ, and felt obliged to exorcise also in the name of Christ. Because the indigenous legends and practices were seen as permeated with the spirit and the superstition of heathenism, such schools did not regard it as part of their mission to propagate them; and yet they had to learn them, if not always to teach them, in order to teach the message of Jesus. In the memoirs of Asian and African leaders who were graduates from these schools it has become almost obligatory, as part of an attack upon white Christian colonialism, to express bitterness and recrimination about the loss of native roots that came as a by-product of missionary education and of imperialist schools both in the mission field and in the home country. Jawaharlal Nehru, for example, was educated at Harrow and Cambridge, becoming, in his own eloquent English phrase, "a queer mixture of the East and West, out of place everywhere, at home nowhere" and sensing a profound alienation between himself and the religion of the common people of India—an alienation from which he never quite recovered.[16] Nehru could have been speaking for several generations in many nations, some of them committed Christians and others merely deracinated Asians or Africans, who were "out of place everywhere, at home nowhere." Thus it was with a grim literalness that there was fulfilled, in the life of entire cultures and not only of individual families, the alienation described by the saying of Jesus in the Gospels: "I have come to set a man against his father, and a daughter against her mother, and a daughter-in-law against her mother-in-law; and a man's foes will be those of his own household" (Matt. 10:35–36).

So it was that Jesus was seen as a Western figure, and in the early religious art of the "younger churches" he often continued to be represented as he had been in the evangelical and pietist literature of the missionary movements in Europe, England, and America. Beginning already with Ricci and even earlier, however, Christian art in the mission field recognized the need to present the figure of Jesus

Monika Liu Ho-Peh, *The Stilling of the Tempest*, probably 1950s.

in a form that was congenial to his new audience. Ricci, therefore, adapted to his purposes in China a picture from the engravings prepared by one Anthony Wierix, representing Christ and Peter after the resurrection (John 21), which he altered to depict Peter's walking on the water (Matt. 14).[17] A similar theme appears in *The Stilling of the Tempest* by Monika Liu Ho-Peh, an artist with a Chinese surname and a Christian name taken from that of Augustine's mother. Here a Chinese Jesus, standing in the prow of the boat, rebukes the waves and commands, "Peace! Be still!" (Mark 4:39), as his terrified Chinese disciples—most of them bearded, as in Western art, but with Oriental features—strain at the oars and tug at the flapping sails. The dangers of a storm at sea were familiar to the missionaries and to their congregations, and a miracle that demonstrated the sovereignty of Jesus over the forces of nature spoke to their condition.

Yet evangelicals and pietists, too, early recognized, sometimes far more explicitly in the mission field than at home, that it was not enough to bring pictures of Jesus, even pictures of Jesus with native features, or words about Jesus, even words about Jesus in the native vernaculars, to the non-Christian world. It had not been enough in the days of Jesus, either, and so he had come as a healer and not only as a teacher. Similarly, the mission of his followers in the second and third centuries had been one of help and healing, not of evangelization alone. For the word "salvation"—*sotēria* in Greek, *salus* in Latin and its derivative languages, *Heil* in German and its cognate languages—meant "health." As Harnack has noted,

> Into this world of craving for salvation the preaching of Christianity made its way. Long before it had achieved its final triumph by dint of an impressive philosophy of religion, its success was already assured by the fact that it promised and offered salvation—a feature in which it surpassed all other religions and cults. It did more than set up the actual Jesus against the imaginary Aesculapius of dreamland. *Deliberately and consciously it assumed the form of "the religion of salvation or healing," or "the medicine of soul and body," and at the same time it recognized that one of its chief duties was to care assiduously for the sick in body.*[18]

That trenchant description of the full range of the gospel of salvation through Jesus could apply as easily to the nineteenth and twentieth centuries as to the second and third. In the third century, Origen described Jesus, "the Logos and the healing power [*therapeia*] within him," as "more powerful than any evils in the soul."[19] And the closing chapter of the New Testament depicted the city of God, with the throne of Jesus Christ the Lamb of God and the tree of life, and explained that "the leaves of the tree were for the healing of the nations" (Rev. 22:2).

In an age in which the healing of the nations from the ravages of hunger, disease, and war has become the dominant moral imperative, Jesus the Healer has come to assume a central place. It was an emblem of the central place of Jesus when, under the terms of the Geneva Convention of 1864 for the Amelioration of the Condition of the Wounded and Sick of Armies in the Field, the international organization created to carry out that moral imperative took the name "Red Cross Society"; its symbol, based on a reversal of the colors of the Swiss flag, is a red cross on a white background. Yet the connection between evangelization in the name of Jesus and the mission of help and healing has also been an issue for debate, especially in the twentieth century. This debate, too, comes as a commentary on the literal meaning of a word in the Gospels: "Whosoever shall give you a cup of water to drink in my name, because ye belong to Christ, verily I say unto you, he shall not lose his reward."[20] It has almost seemed that in every epoch there were some who were primarily interested in naming the name of Christ, clarifying its doctrinal and theological meaning, and defending that meaning against its enemies—but who named the name without giving the cup of water. Yet it has seemed possible for others to give the cup of water, to provide the healing, and to improve the social lot of the disadvantaged—but to do so without explicitly naming the name of Christ. Does that saying of Jesus mean that each of these ways of responding to his summons is only a partial obedience to this dual command? In the answer to this question, much of the debate over the primary responsibility of Christ's disciples in the modern world has concentrated on the disjunction between the two components of the imperative.

A growing feature of the debate has been the stress on cooperation rather than competition between the disciples of Jesus and those who follow other ancient Teachers of the Way. Those followers of Jesus who advocate such cooperation insist that they are no less committed to the universality of his person and message than are the advocates of the traditional methods of conquest through evangelization. But the universality of Jesus, they have urged, does not establish itself in the world through the obliteration of whatever elements of light and truth have already been granted to the nations of the world. For whatever the proximate and historical sources of that truth may have been, its ultimate source is God, the same God whom Jesus called Father; else the confession of the oneness of God is empty. Criticism of many of the elements of historic Christianity, especially of its dogmatism and cultural imperialism, led to the suggestion that it had much to learn, as well as much to teach, in its encounter with other faiths. Jesus was indeed the Man Who Belongs to the World, but he was this because he made it possible to appreciate more profoundly the full scope of the revelation of God wherever it had appeared in the history of the world, in the light of which, in turn, his own meaning and message acquired more profound significance. In the paradoxical formula of Archbishop Nathan Söderblom's Gifford Lectures of 1931, "the uniqueness of Christ as the historical revealer, as the Word made flesh, and the mystery of Calvary," which are an "essentially unique character of Christianity," compel the affirmation that "God reveals himself in history, outside the Church as well as in it."[21] The most complete statement of that position was the thought-provoking and massive report, *Re-thinking Missions: A Layman's Inquiry after One Hundred Years*, published in 1932 by a Commission of Appraisal representing seven American Protestant denominations.

Having carried out an extensive survey of world missions, particularly in Asia and in Africa, the authors of this "laymen's inquiry" reviewed, in seven volumes of data, the state of evangelization and Christian world service, recommending far-reaching revisions not only of specific strategy but of underlying philosophy. They concluded that the stress upon the particularity of Jesus and the absoluteness of his message had been, though perhaps necessary, a temporary element in the program of the missions. As one historian of missions has summarized the position of *Re-thinking Missions*,

> The task of the missionary today, it was maintained, is to see the best in other religions, to help the adherents of those religions to discover, or to rediscover, all that is best in their own traditions, to cooperate with the most active and vigorous elements in the other traditions in social reform and in the purification of religious expression. The aim should not be conversion—the drawing of members of one religious faith over into another or an attempt to establish a Christian monopoly. Cooperation is to replace aggression. The ultimate aim, so far as any can be descried, is the emergence of the various religions out of their isolation into a world fellowship in which each will find its appropriate place.[22]

So drastic a revision of the traditional Christian understanding that "there is salvation in no one else than [Jesus], for there is no other name under heaven [than the name of Jesus] given among men by which we must be saved" (Acts 4:12) would inevitably evoke vigorous discussion and extensive controversy, especially coming as it did just when the theology of Karl Barth was emphasizing again the uniqueness of Jesus and the centrality of his claims.

Such proposals for the redefinition of the universality of Jesus came also at a time when scholars in the West were giving new attention to the languages and cultures of other religious traditions. Not surprisingly, many of those scholars have had ties, of family or education or both, to Christian missions. Sons and daughters of Protestant missionaries, as well as many of the missionaries themselves, took the lead in explaining Eastern cultures to Europe and America. The researches into scholarly linguistics that had originally been the necessary preparation for the translation of the Gospels into more than a thousand tongues now became a bridge that carried Western travelers in the opposite direction as well. In 1875, the eminent German-born Indologist Friedrich Max Müller, professor at Oxford, began the publication of the monumental *Sacred Books of the East*, which eventually came to fifty-one volumes. This series opened up the riches of the Eastern religious sages, particularly those of India, to readers who could not study the original sources. At about the same time, in connection with the World's Columbian Exposition held at Chicago in 1893 to commemorate the four-hundredth anniversary of Columbus's discovery of the New World, there was held a world parliament of religions, whose purpose it was to draw the religious implications of the discovery that the human race was not exclusively European and therefore not exclusively Christian, but global and universal. Despite the phenomenal successes of Christian missions during the nineteenth and twentieth centuries, it seems incontestable that the percentage of Christians in the total world population is continually declining, and therefore it seems inconceivable that the Christian church and the Christian message will ever conquer the population of the world and replace the other religions of the human race. If Jesus is to be the Man Who Belongs to the World, it will have to be by some other way.

Perhaps the most remarkable document to come out of this deepening sense of a new universalism was not *Re-thinking Missions* of

1932, but a decree published a third of a century later, on 28 October
1965, the Declaration on the Relationship of the Church to Non-Christian Religions, *Nostra aetate*, of the Second Vatican Council. In a series
of succinct but striking paragraphs, the decree described the religious
quest and the spiritual values at work in primitive religion, in Hinduism, in Buddhism, and in Islam; and in a historic affirmation the
council declared:

> The Catholic Church rejects nothing which is true and holy in those reli-
> gions. She looks with sincere respect upon those ways of conduct and of
> life, those rules and teachings which, though differing in many particulars
> from what she holds and sets forth, nevertheless often reflect a ray of that
> Truth which enlightens all men (John 1:9). Indeed, she proclaims and must
> ever proclaim Christ, "the way, the truth, and the life" (John 14:6), in
> whom men find the fullness of religious life, and in whom God has rec-
> onciled all things to Himself.[23]

The two passages from the Gospel according to John quoted in the
decree clearly identify the issue. For it is in that Gospel that Jesus
speaks of himself as "the way, the truth, and the life" and says that
no one comes to the Father except through him. And yet that same
Gospel provided the epigraph for the universalism of the Enlightenment's portrait of Jesus; for the Gospel of John declares in its prologue that the Logos-Word of God, incarnate in Jesus, enlightens
everyone who comes into the world. By citing the authority of both
passages, the Second Vatican Council sought to affirm universality
and particularity simultaneously and to ground both of them in the
figure of Jesus.

A special issue at the Second Vatican Council and throughout Christianity, especially since the Second World War, was the relation between Christianity and its parent faith, Judaism. The Holocaust took
place in what had been nominally Christian territory; moreover, the
record of the churches in opposing it was not the noblest page in
Christian history. Among both Roman Catholics and Protestants in
Germany there were those who, as the New Testament says about
the apostle Paul's involvement in the martyrdom of Stephen, were
"consenting to the death" of the Jews (Acts 8:1), and many more who
were (as it seems now, by hindsight) blindly insensitive to the situation. The Second Vatican Council "deplores," it declared, "the hatred,
persecutions, and displays of anti-Semitism directed against the Jews
at any time and from any source," which would appear to include

the official sources of the church's past.[24] And it condemned any attempt to blame the death of Jesus "upon all the Jews then living, without distinction, or upon the Jews today," insisting that "the Jews should not be presented as repudiated or cursed by God."

This rethinking of the relation between Christianity and Judaism was partly the consequence of the worldwide horror over the Holocaust, but partly it also came through a deepening of Christian understanding and reflection. The result was the most basic Christian reconsideration of the status of Judaism since the first century. Ironically, the years of Nazi anti-Semitism and the Holocaust in Germany had also been the years in which Christians developed the new awareness of the Jewishness of Jesus, the apostles, and the New Testament, an awareness that receives expression in the language of the Vatican Council. It was in 1933, the beginning of the Nazi era in Germany, that there appeared, also in Germany, the first volume of one of the most influential biblical reference works of the twentieth century, the multivolume *Theological Dictionary of the New Testament* edited by Gerhard Kittel.[25] Probably the most important scholarly and theological generalization to be drawn from the hundreds of articles in the Kittel *Dictionary* has been that the teaching and language of the New Testament, including the teaching and language of Jesus himself, cannot be understood apart from their setting in the context of Judaism. It was once again in the Gospel of John, despite the hostility of some of its language about Jews, that Jesus, speaking as a Jew to a non-Jew, was described as saying: "We [Jews] worship what we know, for salvation is from the Jews" (John 4:22). Directly he went on to say, in the very next verse: "But the hour is coming, and now is, when the true worshipers [which, of course, refers to both Jews and Gentiles] will worship the Father in spirit and truth." Once again the theme is universality-with-particularity, as both of these are grounded in the figure of Jesus the Jew.

By a curious blend of these currents of religious faith and scholarship with the no less powerful influences of skepticism and religious relativism, the universality-with-particularity of Jesus has thus become an issue not only for Christians in the twentieth century, but for humanity. The later chapters of this book show that as respect for the organized church has declined, reverence for Jesus has grown. For the unity and variety of the portraits of "Jesus through the centuries" has demonstrated that there is more in him than is dreamt of in the philosophy and Christology of the theologians. Within the church, but also far beyond its walls, his person and message are, in the phrase of Augustine, a "beauty ever ancient, ever new,"[26] and now he belongs to the world.

Notes

INTRODUCTION: THE GOOD, THE TRUE, AND THE BEAUTIFUL

1. Athanasius, *Discourses against the Arians* 1.10.36.
2. Albert Schweitzer, *The Quest of the Historical Jesus*, trans. William Montgomery (1956; New York: Macmillan, 1961), p. 4; translation herein revised.
3. Alfred North Whitehead, *Science and the Modern World* (1925; New York: Mentor Editions, 1952), pp. 49–50.
4. Fernand Braudel, *The Mediterranean and the Mediterranean World in the Age of Philip II*, trans. Sian Reynolds, 2 vols. (New York: Harper and Row, 1972), 1:168.
5. Arthur O. Lovejoy, *The Great Chain of Being: A Study of the History of an Idea* (Cambridge, Mass.: Harvard University Press, 1936), p. 6.
6. John Calvin, *Institutes of the Christian Religion* 3.2.34, ed. John Thomas McNeill, 2 vols. (Philadelphia: Westminster Press, 1960), 1:581.
7. See, for example, Athanasius, *On Luke 10:22*; Gregory of Nyssa, *Against Eunomius* 2.4. See also p. 41.
8. Jaroslav Pelikan, *Historical Theology: Continuity and Change in Christian Doctrine* (New York: Corpus Books, 1971), pp. 33–67: "The Evolution of the Historical."
9. Jaroslav Pelikan, *The Christian Tradition: A History of the Development of Doctrine*, 4 vols. to date (Chicago: University of Chicago Press, 1971–), 1:1.
10. Werner Elert, *Der Ausgang der altkirchlichen Christologie* (Berlin: Lutherisches Verlagshaus, 1957), pp. 12–25: "Christusbild und Christusdogma."
11. See Jaroslav Pelikan, *Fools for Christ: Essays on the True, the Good, and the Beautiful* (Philadelphia: Muhlenberg Press, 1955).
12. On this image in relation to analogous ones at Ravenna, see Spiro K. Kostof, *The Orthodox Baptistery of Ravenna* (New Haven: Yale University Press, 1965), pp. 67–68.
13. Gregory of Nyssa, *Against Eunomius* 2.10; Augustine, *On the Trinity* 6.10.11.
14. Augustine, *Tractates on the Gospel of John* 22.8.
15. Agnes von Zahn-Harnack, *Adolf von Harnack*, 2d ed. (Berlin: Walter de Gruyter, 1951), pp. 181–88.
16. Adolf Harnack, *What Is Christianity?* trans. Thomas Bailey Saunders (1900; New York: Harper Torchbooks, 1957), p. 1; translation herein revised. Quotation is from

John Stuart Mill, *On Liberty,* chap. 2, in *The English Philosophers from Bacon to Mill,* ed. Edwin A. Burtt (New York: Modern Library, 1939), p. 967.

1. THE RABBI

1. For a brief but helpful review of the problem, see Matthew Black, "The Recovery of the Language of Jesus," *New Testament Studies* 3 (1956–57): 305–13; also his longer monograph, *An Aramaic Approach to the Gospels and Acts,* 3d ed. (Oxford: Clarendon Press, 1967).
2. Acts 6:1; 9:29.
3. Mark 15:34; the version in Matt. 27:46 differs somewhat, and the textual variants of the transliterations in both passages differ still further.
4. See, in general, Eric M. Meyers and James F. Strange, *Archeology, the Rabbis, and Early Christianity* (Nashville: Abingdon Press, 1981).
5. The exceptions occur in Matt. 23:7–8 and in John 3:26.
6. Rudolf Bultmann, *The History of the Synoptic Tradition,* trans. John Marsh (New York: Harper and Row, 1963), pp. 125–26.
7. Matt. 22:23–33; Matt. 22:15–22; Mark 10:17–22; Matt. 18:1–6.
8. See, for example, William Oscar Emil Oesterley, *The Gospel Parables in the Light of Their Jewish Background* (New York: Macmillan, 1936).
9. Justin Martyr, *First Apology* 65.4.
10. Matt. 5:21–48; italics mine.
11. Howard Clark Kee, *Miracle in the Early Christian World: A Study in Sociohistorical Method* (New Haven: Yale University Press, 1983), p. 188.
12. Mark 7:34; 5:41.
13. Acts 3:22–23; 7:37; Clement of Alexandria, *The Tutor* 1.7.
14. Pelikan, *Christian Tradition* 2:209–10, 238–40.
15. John 1:41; 4:25.
16. 1 Cor. 16:22; *Didache* 10.6.
17. Gregory Dix, *Jew and Greek. A Study in the Primitive Church* (New York: Harper and Brothers, 1953), p. 109.
18. See Peter C. Hodgson, *The Formation of Historical Theology* (New York: Harper and Row, 1966).
19. Krister Stendahl, *Paul among Jews and Gentiles* (Philadelphia: Fortress Press, 1976), p. 4; italics in original.
20. Robert L. Wilken, *John Chrysostom and the Jews* (Berkeley and Los Angeles: University of California Press, 1983), p. 162.

2. THE TURNING POINT OF HISTORY

1. Charles Norris Cochrane, *Christianity and Classical Culture: A Study of Thought and Action from Augustus to Augustine* (Oxford: Clarendon Press, 1944), p. 456.
2. Erwin Panofsky, *The Life and Art of Albrecht Dürer,* 4th ed. (Princeton: Princeton University Press, 1955), pp. 56–57.
3. Rev. 21:6; 1:8.
4. Two of the most profound attempts to address that problem are Amos Wilder, *Ethics and Eschatology in the Teaching of Jesus,* rev. ed. (New York: Harper, 1950), and Rudolf Otto, *The Kingdom of God and the Son of Man,* trans. Floyd V. Filson and Bertram Lee Wolff (London: Lutterworth, 1938).
5. Matt. 10:23; Matt. 24:34; Mark 13:30; Luke 21:32.
6. Schweitzer, *Quest of the Historical Jesus,* p. 360.

7. Jaroslav Pelikan, "The Eschatology of Tertullian," *Church History* 21 (1952): 108–22.
8. Tertullian, *On Spectacles* 30; *On Prayer* 29.
9. Tertullian, *Apology* 39; italics mine.
10. Ps. 96:10; italics mine. Justin, *Dialogue with Trypho* 73.1; Venantius Fortunatus, *Carmina* 2.7.
11. Irenaeus, *Proof of the Apostolic Preaching*; Cyprian, *Testimonies*.
12. Augustine, *City of God* 16.43; 17.20; 17.4.
13. Augustine, *City of God* 17.16; Eusebius, *Ecclesiastical History* 1.3.14–15.
14. Augustine, *City of God* 17.20–23.
15. Augustine, *City of God* 17.5–6.
16. Pelikan, *Christian Tradition* 1:25–26.
17. Fred L. Horton, Jr., *The Melchizedek Tradition: A Critical Examination of the Sources to the Fifth Century A.D. and in the Epistle to the Hebrews* (Cambridge: Cambridge University Press, 1976).
18. Eusebius, *Ecclesiastical History* 1.19; Augustine, *City of God* 17.4; John Calvin, *Institutes of the Christian Religion* 2.15, McNeill ed., 1:494–503.
19. Peter Brown, *Augustine of Hippo. A Biography* (London: Faber and Faber, 1969), pp. 299–312.
20. Eph. 1:10; Gal. 4:4.
21. *Epistle to Diognetus* 9.
22. Luke 2:1; 3:1; Eusebius, *Ecclesiastical History* 1.5.2.
23. Augustine, *City of God* 2.18–19.
24. Augustine, *City of God* 1.30.
25. Augustine, *City of God* 4.3–4.
26. Sallust, *Catilina* 7; Augustine, *City of God* 5.12–13.
27. Augustine, *City of God* 4.33; 5.1; 5.11.
28. Augustine, *City of God* 16.10; 12.18.
29. Augustine, *City of God* 12.13; Origen, *Against Celsus* 4.67.
30. Augustine, *City of God* 7.32.
31. Christopher Dawson, "St. Augustine and His Age," in *St. Augustine*, ed. Martin C. D'Arcy (New York: Meridian Books, 1957), p. 69.
32. See *Oxford English Dictionary*, s.v. "crucial."
33. Augustine, *On the Creed* 9.
34. Martin Werner, *Die Entstehung des christlichen Dogmas* (Bern: Paul Haupt, 1941), pp. 112–13. See also p. 50.
35. Eusebius, *The Preparation of the Gospel* 1.3.6–7.
36. I have adapted here some of the material in my book *The Finality of Jesus Christ in an Age of Universal History* (London: Lutterworth, 1965), pp. 48–56.
37. Eusebius, *Ecclesiastical History* 1.4.6.
38. C. F. Georg Heinrici, *Das Urchristentum in der Kirchengeschichte des Eusebius* (Leipzig: Verlag der Dürr'schen Buchhandlung, 1894), p. 21.
39. Eusebius, *Ecclesiastical History* 4.26.7, quoting Melito of Sardis.
40. Eduard Schwartz, *Zur Geschichte des Athanasius* (Berlin: Walter de Gruyter, 1959), p. 286, n. 3.
41. See p. 112.
42. Karl Holl, "Die schriftstellerische Form des griechischen Heiligenlebens," *Gesammelte Aufsätze zur Kirchengeschichte*, 3 vols. (1928; reprint, Darmstadt: Wissenschaftliche Buchgesellschaft, 1964), 2:249–69.
43. Athanasius, *Life of Antony* 7.
44. Athanasius, *Life of Antony* 1–2.

45. Johannes Quasten, *Patrology*, 3 vols. to date (Westminster, Md.: Newman Press, 1951–), 3:43.
46. Judith H. Anderson, *Biographical Truth: The Representation of Historical Persons in Tudor-Stuart Writing* (New Haven: Yale University Press, 1984), pp. 21–22.
47. See the translation and helpful table prepared by Archibald Robertson, *Nicene and Post-Nicene Fathers of the Church* 4:502–03.
48. Bruno Krusch, *Studien zur christlichen-mittelalterlichen Chronologie: Die Entstehung unserer heutigen Zeitrechnung*, 2 vols. (Berlin: Akademie der Wissenschaften, 1938), 2:59–87.

3. THE LIGHT OF THE GENTILES

1. Reinhold Niebuhr, *The Nature and Destiny of Man*, 2 vols. (New York: Charles Scribner's Sons, 1941–43), 2:6.
2. Ignatius, *Ephesians* 10.1; 1.2.
3. Luke 2:32; Prosper of Aquitaine, *The Call of All Nations* 2.18.
4. Augustine, *City of God* 18.47.
5. Judith Baskin, *Pharaoh's Counsellors: Job, Jethro, and Balaam in Rabbinic and Patristic Tradition* (Chico, Calif.: Scholars Press, 1983).
6. Vergil, *Eclogues* 4.5–52.
7. Compare Isa. 61:17 (Rev. 21:1); Phil. 3:20; Isa. 53:5; Gen. 3:15; Isa. 7:14; Isa. 9:6.
8. Constantine, *Oration to the Saints* 19–21.
9. Jerome, *Epistles* 53.7. Augustine, *City of God* 10.27; Augustine, *Epistles* 137.3.12.
10. Domenico Comparetti, *Vergil in the Middle Ages*, trans. E. F. M. Benecke (London: George Allen and Unwin Ltd., 1966), p. 98, n. 6.
11. Dante, *Purgatorio* 22.70–73.
12. Vergil, *Aeneid* 6.99.
13. Origen, *Against Celsus* 7.56; 7.53.
14. Theophilus, *To Autolycus* 2.9; Lactantius, *Divine Institutes* 1.6.
15. Clement of Alexandria, *Exhortation to the Greeks* 2.
16. Constantine, *Oration to the Saints* 18.
17. Augustine, *City of God* 18.23.
18. Justin Martyr, *I Apology* 20; Clement of Alexandria, *Exhortation to the Greeks* 8.27.4.
19. A. Rossi, "Le Sibille nelle arti figurative italiane," *L'Arte* 18 (1915): 272–85.
20. Charles de Tolnay, *The Sistine Ceiling*, vol. 2 of his *Michelangelo* (Princeton: Princeton University Press, 1945), pp. 46, 57.
21. Clement of Alexandria, *Tutor* 1.2.
22. Clement of Alexandria, *Exhortation* 10.110.
23. Eric Osborn, *The Beginning of Christian Philosophy* (Cambridge: Cambridge University Press, 1981), p. 219.
24. Osborn, *Beginning of Christian Philosophy*, p. 219.
25. Clement of Alexandria, *Stromata* 1.5; Gal. 3:24.
26. Henry Chadwick, *Early Christian Thought and the Classical Tradition* (New York and Oxford: Oxford University Press, 1966), p. 40.
27. Clement of Alexandria, *Stromata* 5.9; italics mine.
28. Clement of Alexandria, *Stromata* 5.14.
29. Raymond Klibansky, *The Continuity of the Platonic Tradition during the Middle Ages*, 2d ed. (Millwood, N.J.: Kraus International Publications, 1982).
30. Plato, *Timaeus* 28–29; all translations of *Timaeus* by Francis Macdonald Cornford, *Plato's Cosmology* (London: Routledge and Kegan Paul, 1937).
31. Clement of Alexandria, *Stromata* 5.14.

32. Clement of Alexandria, *Stromata* 5.13.84, quoting *Timaeus* 40 and Luke 10:22.

33. Clement of Alexandria, *Stromata* 5.14.

34. Compare Henri de Lubac, *Histoire et esprit. L'intelligence de l'Ecriture d'après Origène* (Paris: Aubier, 1950), pp. 144–45.

35. John 3:14–15; Augustine, *Tractates on the Gospel of John* 12.11.

36. Justin Martyr, *I Apology* 55; *Dialogue with Trypho* 86.

37. Iris Murdoch, *The Fire and the Sun: Why Plato Banished the Artists* (Oxford: Clarendon Press, 1977), p. 87.

38. Plato, *Timaeus* 36B.

39. Justin Martyr, *I Apology* 60.

40. Hugo Rahner, "Odysseus am Mastbaum," *Zeitschrift für katholische Theologie* 65 (1941): 123–52; an English summary appears in his *Greek Myths and Christian Mystery*, trans. Brian Battershaw (New York: Harper and Row, 1963), pp. 371–86.

41. Homer, *Odyssey* 12.158–64, trans. Richmond Lattimore (New York: Harper and Row, 1967); italics mine.

42. Justin Martyr, *II Apology* 10; Tertullian, *Apology* 4.

43. Tertullian, *To the Nations* 1.10.

44. Homer, *Odyssey* 12.219–21.

45. Clement of Alexandria, *Exhortation* 12.118.4.

46. Karl Krumbacher, *Geschichte der byzantinischen Literatur*, 2d ed. (Munich: C. H. Beck, 1897), pp. 529–30, 538.

47. Josef Wilpert, *I sarcofagi cristiani antichi*, 2 vols. (Rome: Pontificio istituto di archeologia cristiana, 1919), vol. 1, pl. 24.

48. Quoted in Rahner, *Greek Myths and Christian Mystery*, p. 381; translation herein slightly revised.

49. David Lerch, *Isaaks Opferung christlich gedeutet: Eine auslegungsgeschichtliche Untersuchung* (Tübingen: J. C. B. Mohr, 1950).

50. George Leonard Prestige, *God in Patristic Thought* (London: SPCK, 1956), pp. 117–24.

51. Deut. 18:15–22; Clement of Alexandria, *Tutor* 1.7.

52. Adolf von Harnack, "Sokrates und die alte Kirche," *Reden und Aufsätze*, 2 vols. (Giessen: Alfred Töpelmann, 1906), 1:27–48; Geddes MacGregor, *The Hemlock and the Cross: Humanism, Socrates, and Christ* (Philadelphia: Lippincott, 1963).

53. Justin Martyr, *I Apology* 5, 46; *II Apology* 10.

54. 2 Tim. 1:10; Jaroslav Pelikan, *The Shape of Death: Life, Death, and Immortality in the Early Fathers* (New York: Abingdon Press, 1961).

55. Clement of Alexandria, *Stromata* 5.14.

56. Plato, *Republic* 2.360–61; translation, except for the final quotation, is my own.

57. Gilbert Murray, *Five Stages of Greek Religion* (Boston: Beacon Press, 1951), p. 157, and his footnote on the Greek verb *anaschindyleō*.

58. Acts 17:23; Clement of Alexandria, *Stromata* 5.12.

4. THE KING OF KINGS

1. Augustine, *On the Psalms* 76.7.

2. Justin Martyr, *I Apology* 31.

3. Irenaeus, *Against Heresies* 5.26.2; 5.33–34 (quoting Papias).

4. Irenaeus, *Against Heresies* 5.35.1; Justin Martyr, *Dialogue with Trypho* 80; see Richard Patrick Crosland Hanson, *Allegory and Event* (Richmond, Va.: John Knox Press, 1959), pp. 333–56.

5. Justin Martyr, *Dialogue with Trypho* 135.

6. *Martyrum Scillitanorum Acta* 6, in *The Acts of the Christian Martyrs*, ed. Herbert Musurillo (Oxford: Clarendon Press, 1972), pp. 86–89.
7. *Martyrdom of Polycarp* 8–9.
8. *Martyrdom of Ignatius* 2.
9. Justin Martyr, *I Apology* 11; 51; 17.
10. Tertullian, *Apology* 30–32; 1 Tim. 2:2.
11. Irenaeus, *Against Heresies* 5.24.1; Rom. 13:1, 4, 6.
12. Tertullian, *On Idolatry* 15; Matt. 22:21.
13. 1 Cor. 8:4–6; see the comments of Augustine, *City of God* 9.23.
14. See above all William Hugh Clifford Frend, *Martyrdom and Persecution in the Early Church: A Study of a Conflict from the Maccabees to Donatus* (Oxford: Blackwell, 1965).
15. *Epistle to Diognetus* 7, 5; italics mine.
16. Vergil, *Aeneid* 1.279.
17. Tertullian, *Apology* 21.
18. Jacob Burckhardt, *Die Zeit Constantins des Grossen* (Vienna: Phaidon, n.d.), p. 242.
19. Hermann Doerries, *Constantine the Great*, trans. Roland H. Bainton (New York: Harper Torchbooks, 1972), pp. 229–30.
20. Ramsay MacMullen, *Constantine* (New York: Dial Press, 1969), p. 111.
21. Lactantius, *On the Manner in Which the Persecutors Died* 44; *Divine Institutes* 4.26–27; *Epitome* 47.
22. Eusebius, *Life of Constantine* 1.24–31.
23. Eusebius, *Ecclesiastical History* 9.9.10–11.
24. Eusebius, *Life of Constantine* 1.6–7.
25. Adolf Harnack, *Grundrisz der Dogmengeschichte*, 4th ed. (Tübingen: J. C. B. Mohr, 1905), p. 192.
26. For a fuller exposition of the issues and alternatives, see Pelikan, *Christian Tradition* 1:172–225.
27. Theodoret, *Ecclesiastical History* 1.11–12.
28. Socrates, *Ecclesiastical History* 1.9.
29. Eusebius, *Life of Constantine* 3.20, 64–65.
30. Eusebius, *Life of Constantine* 2.56–60.
31. Hermann Doerries, *Constantine and Religious Liberty*, trans. Roland H. Bainton (New Haven: Yale University Press, 1960), p. 110.
32. Eusebius, *Life of Constantine* 3.15.
33. Eusebius, *Ecclesiastical History* 10.9.4.
34. Frank Edward Brightman, "Byzantine Imperial Coronations," *Journal of Theological Studies* 2 (1901): 359–92.
35. Gen. 14:18; Ps. 110:4; Heb. 7:1–17.
36. C. Lepelley, "S. Léon . . . et la cité romaine," *Revue des sciences religieuses* 35 (1961): 130–50.
37. Matt. 16:18–19; see Pelikan, *Christian Tradition* 4:81–84.
38. See Walter Ullmann, *Medieval Papalism: The Political Theories of the Medieval Canonists* (London: Methuen, 1949).

5. THE COSMIC CHRIST

1. Alfred North Whitehead, *Science and the Modern World* (1925; New York: Mentor Books, 1952), p. 13.
2. Ferdinand Hahn, *Christologische Hoheitstitel: Ihre Geschichte im frühen Christentum* (Göttingen: Vandenhoeck und Ruprecht, 1963).
3. Gregory of Nazianzus, *Orations* 36.11.

4. Goethe, *Faust* 1224–37.
5. Gregory T. Armstrong, *Die Genesis in der alten Kirche* (Tübingen: J. C. B. Mohr, 1962).
6. Gregory of Nyssa, *On the Making of Man* 25.2.
7. See pp. 40–42 above.
8. Jaroslav Pelikan, "Creation and Causality in the History of Christian Thought," in *Issues in Evolution*, ed. Sol Tax and Charles Callender (Chicago: University of Chicago Press, 1960), pp. 329–40.
9. Pelikan, *Christian Tradition* 1:35–37; 3:290–91.
10. Gregory of Nyssa, *On the Making of Man* 24.
11. Basil of Caesarea, *Hexaemeron* 1.2; 3.8. Gregory of Nyssa, *On the Making of Man* 8.4.
12. Basil of Caesarea, *Hexaemeron* 6.1; 9.2.
13. Basil of Caesarea, *Hexaemeron* 9.6; Gen. 1:26 (italics mine); Heb. 1:2–3.
14. Hilary of Poitiers, *On the Trinity* 2.6.
15. Prov. 8:22 (italics mine); Athanasius, *Discourses against the Arians* 2.18–82.
16. Augustine, *Confessions* 11.3.5–11.9.11.
17. In Plato's *Theaetetus* 203 the word occurs twice, once in each of these senses.
18. Epiphanius of Salamis, *Against All Heresies* 51.3; Gregory of Nyssa, *The Great Catechism* 1.
19. Gregory of Nazianzus, *Theological Orations* 3.17.
20. Gregory of Nyssa, *On the Making of Man* 16.2; 5.2 (John 1:1; 1 Cor. 2:16; 2 Cor. 13:3).
21. Gregory of Nazianzus, *Theological Orations* 4.20.
22. Tertullian, *On the Flesh of Christ* 5.
23. Tertullian, *On Prescription against Heretics* 7.
24. Gregory of Nazianzus, *Theological Orations* 2.6.
25. Basil of Caesarea, *Hexaemeron* 1.6.
26. Basil of Caesarea, *Hexaemeron* 6.5–7.
27. Gregory of Nyssa, *On the Making of Man* 8.8.
28. Gregory of Nyssa, *Against Eunomius* 2.3.
29. Gregory of Nazianzus, *Theological Orations* 4.17.
30. Jaroslav Pelikan, *Development of Christian Doctrine: Some Historical Prolegomena* (New Haven: Yale University Press, 1969), pp. 129–31; Hilary, *On the Trinity* 4.14.
31. Basil of Caesarea, *Hexaemeron* 2.2.
32. Gregory of Nazianzus, *Orations* 38.10–11.
33. Basil of Caesarea, *On the Holy Spirit* 7; Col. 1:15–17.
34. Rom. 4:17; Athanasius, *The Incarnation of the Word* 42.
35. Athanasius, *Discourses against the Arians* 3.63; *Defense of the Nicene Definition* 3.11.
36. Athanasius, *Discourses against the Arians* 1.23; 3.19–20 (Eph. 3:14–15).
37. Athanasius, *Discourses against the Arians* 1.25.
38. Athanasius, *Against the Heathen* 45.
39. Athanasius, *To the Bishops of Egypt* 15.
40. Athanasius, *Against the Heathen* 41.
41. Athanasius, *Discourses against the Arians* 2.63 (Col. 1:17; Rom. 8:21).
42. Athanasius, *Against the Heathen* 7–8.
43. Athanasius, *The Incarnation of the Word* 5.
44. Gregory of Nyssa, *On the Making of Man* 5.2; 30.34.
45. Cf. Pelikan, *Christian Tradition* 1:344–45; 2:10–16.
46. Clement of Alexandria, *Exhortation to the Greeks* 1.8.4; Athanasius, *The Incarnation of the Word* 54.3.
47. Gregory of Nyssa, *On the Making of Man* 16.2.

48. Gregory of Nyssa, *Sermons on the Song of Songs* 13.
49. Basil of Caesarea, *Hexaemeron* 1.3; 3.6.
50. Gregory of Nyssa, *On the Making of Man* 23.1, 5.
51. Gregory of Nyssa, *On the Making of Man* 22.5.
52. Gregory of Nazianzus, *Orations* 39.13; 45.26.
53. Erich Auerbach, " 'Sermo Humilis' and 'Gloria Passionis,' " in *Literary Language and Its Public in Late Latin Antiquity and in the Middle Ages*, trans. Ralph Manheim (New York: Pantheon, 1965), pp. 27–81.
54. Augustine, *Confessions* 7.18.24–25.

6. THE SON OF MAN

1. From the vast literature, see Carl H. Kraeling, *Anthropos and Son of Man* (New York: Columbia University Press, 1927).
2. So, for example, in Ps. 8:4 (cf. Heb. 2:6–9), and above all in Ezekiel, where it appears some ninety times as a designation for the prophet himself.
3. For a very early instance of the parallel, see Ignatius, *Epistle to the Ephesians* 20.2.
4. "Pastoral Constitution on the Church in the Modern World: *Gaudium et Spes*" 22, in *The Documents of Vatican II*, ed. Walter M. Abbott (New York: America Press, 1966), p. 220.
5. Adolf von Harnack, *The Mission and Expansion of Christianity in the First Three Centuries*, trans. James Moffatt, 2 vols. (London: Williams and Norgate, 1908), 1:108.
6. See the discussion of this by Augustine, *Tractates on the Gospel of John* 12.13.
7. Blaise Pascal, *Pensées* 526, 431.
8. F. D. E. Schleiermacher, *The Christian Faith*, trans. H. R. Mackintosh and J. S. Stewart (Edinburgh: T. and T. Clark, 1928), p. 98.
9. Augustine, *Enchiridion* 108.
10. Gregory of Nyssa, *On the Making of Man* 16.2.
11. On Augustine's view of image and renewal, cf. Gerhart B. Ladner, *The Idea of Reform: Its Impact on Christian Thought and Action in the Age of the Fathers* (Cambridge, Mass.: Harvard University Press, 1959), pp. 185–203.
12. Augustine, *Retractations* 1.25.68; 2.24.2.
13. Augustine, *Reply to Faustus the Manichean* 24.2.
14. Augustine, *On the Trinity* 1.10.21.
15. Augustine, *Ten Homilies on the First Epistle of John* 4.5–6; 10.6; *Tractates on the Gospel of John* 82.4; *Confessions* 10.43.68.
16. Augustine, *The Teacher* 38.
17. Augustine, *Soliloquies* 2.7.
18. Augustine, *On the Trinity* 12.15.24; *Confessions* 7.18.24–25.
19. William S. Babcock, "The Christ of the Exchange: A Study in the Christology of Augustine's *Enarrationes in Psalmos.*" Ph.D. diss., Yale University, 1971.
20. Augustine, *Tractates on the Gospel of John* 36.1–2.
21. Augustine, *On the Trinity* 12.4.4.
22. Dorothy Leigh Sayers, *The Mind of the Maker* (New York: Harcourt, Brace, 1941), pp. 33–41.
23. Augustine, *Confessions* 13.11.12.
24. Augustine, *On the Trinity* 9.2.2.
25. Augustine, *On the Trinity* 10.11.17–12.19.
26. Augustine, *On the Trinity* 7.4.7; 15.12.43–44.
27. Ronald Steel, *Walter Lippmann and the American Century* (Boston: Little, Brown, 1980), pp. 390–91.

28. On the *Confessions*, see especially Peter Brown, *Augustine of Hippo*, pp. 158–81, and the literature cited there.

29. Augustine, *Confessions* 6.6.9.

30. See Georg Nicolaus Knauer, *Die Psalmenzitate in Augustins Konfessionen* (Göttingen: Vandenhoeck und Ruprecht, 1955).

31. Albert C. Outler, "Introduction" to Augustine, *Confessions* (Philadelphia: Westminster Press, 1955), p. 17.

32. Augustine, *Confessions* 2.7.15.

33. Augustine, *Confessions* 5.1.1; 7.21.17; 4.12.19.

34. One of the most notable of these apostrophes is found at the end of book 10, *Confessions* 10.43.68–70.

35. Augustine, *Confessions* 3.1.1.

36. T. S. Eliot, "The Waste Land," 307–11, in *Collected Poems 1909–1935* (New York: Harcourt, Brace, 1936).

37. Compare C. Klegeman, "A Psychoanalytic Study of the *Confessions* of St. Augustine," *Journal of the American Psychoanalytic Association* 5 (1957): 469–84.

38. Augustine, *On the Good of Marriage* 8; Matt. 19:12; 1 Cor. 7:1–5; E. R. Dodds, *Pagan and Christian in an Age of Anxiety* (Cambridge: Cambridge University Press, 1965), pp. 29–30.

39. Augustine, *On Marriage and Concupiscence* 1.21.23–1.22.24; *On Continence* 22–23. (The Latin translation of Eph. 5:25–32 has "sacrament" for "mystery.")

40. Augustine, *Confessions* 2.4.9–2.10.18.

41. Oliver Wendell Holmes, Jr., to Harold J. Laski, 5 January 1921, *Holmes-Laski Letters: The Correspondence of Mr. Justice Holmes and Harold J. Laski, 1916–35*, ed. Mark DeWolfe Howe, 2 vols. (Cambridge, Mass.: Harvard University Press, 1953), 1:300.

42. Milton, *Paradise Lost* 1.1–5.

43. Augustine, *Confessions* 13.26.39–40.

44. Augustine, *On the Spirit and the Letter* 6.9.

45. Augustine, *On Marriage and Concupiscence* 2.12.25.

46. Augustine, *On Nature and Grace* 7.8.

47. Augustine, *On the Spirit and the Letter* 1.1.

48. Augustine, *On the Forgiveness of Sins* 2.13.18.

49. Augustine, *Against Two Letters of the Pelagians* 3.5.14–15.

50. Augustine, *On Perfection in Righteousness* 21.44; 12.29.

51. John 10:17–18; Augustine, *Tractates on the Gospel of John* 47.11–13; *On the Psalms* 89.37.

52. See Pelikan, *Christian Tradition* 1:286–90.

53. Gal. 4:4; Irenaeus, *Against Heresies* 3.22.1.

54. Augustine, *Enchiridion* 14.48.

55. Augustine, *On the Grace of Christ and Original Sin* 2.25.29; Ps. 51:5.

56. Augustine, *On Nature and Grace* 36.42; italics mine.

57. Pelikan, *Christian Tradition* 4:38–50.

58. See p. 38 above.

59. Basil of Caesarea, *Hexaemeron* 9.6; Etienne Gilson, *L'esprit de la philosophie médiévale*, 2d ed. (Paris: Libraire Philosophique J. Vrin, 1944), pp. 218–19.

60. See p. 242, n. 53 above.

7. THE TRUE IMAGE

1. Origen, *Against Celsus* 7.65–67; Arnobius, *The Case against the Pagans* 1.38–39.

2. Irenaeus, *Against Heresies* 4.16.4.

3. Lactantius, *Divine Institutes* 2.2–4.
4. Acts 17:24; Arnobius, *Case against the Pagans* 6.3–5.
5. Tertullian, *On Idolatry* 4; Clement of Alexandria, *Exhortation to the Greeks* 4.
6. Origen, *Against Celsus* 7.65.
7. Gregory of Nyssa, *Epistles* 2.
8. Carl H. Kraeling, *The Synagogue*, 2d ed., foreword by Jaroslav Pelikan (New York: KTAV Publishing House, 1979), p. 384.
9. Harold R. Willoughby, review of *The Synagogue*, by Carl H. Kraeling. *Journal of Near Eastern Studies* 20 (January 1961): 56.
10. Kraeling, *Synagogue*, p. 399.
11. For a perceptive essay, see Hans von Campenhausen, "The Theological Problem of Images in the Early Church," in *Tradition and Life in the Church*, trans. A. V. Littledale (Philadelphia: Fortress Press, 1968), pp. 171–200.
12. For some suggestive ideas, see Gervase Mathew, *Byzantine Aesthetics* (New York: Viking Press, 1964).
13. Col. 1:15; Clement of Alexandria, *Exhortation to the Greeks* 10.
14. Vladimir Lossky, *In the Image and Likeness of God*, trans. John Erickson and Thomas E. Bird, introd. John Meyendorff (Tuckahoe, N.Y.: Saint Vladimir's Seminary Press, 1974), p. 136.
15. Whitehead, *Science and the Modern World*, pp. 49–50.
16. On the fourth-century consideration of the problem, see Georges Florovsky, "Origen, Eusebius, and the Iconoclastic Controversy," *Church History* 19 (1950): 77–96.
17. Eusebius, *Epistle to Constantia*, quoting Phil. 2:7.
18. Nicephorus, *Greater Apology for the Holy Images* 12.
19. See pp. 52–53 above.
20. Nicephorus, *Refutation of the Iconoclasts* 1.15.
21. John of Jerusalem, *Against Constantinus Cabalinus* 4.
22. Nicephorus, *Refutation of the Iconoclasts* 2.3.
23. Theodore of Studios, *Refutation of the Poems of the Iconoclasts* 1.10.
24. Pelikan, *Christian Tradition* 1:263–66.
25. John of Jerusalem, *Against Constantinus Cabalinus* 4.
26. John of Damascus, *On the Images* 3.2.
27. Nicephorus, *Refutation of the Iconoclasts* 3.38.
28. Nicephorus, *Refutation of the Iconoclasts* 1.42; 2.1.
29. Theodore of Studios, *Refutation of the Poems of the Iconoclasts* 1.7.
30. John 4:24; cf. Origen, *On First Principles* 1.1.4.
31. Nicephorus, *Refutation of the Iconoclasts* 3.18.
32. Nicephorus, *Refutation of the Iconoclasts* 3.19.
33. Theodore of Studios, *Refutation of the Poems of the Iconoclasts* 1.16.
34. John of Damascus, *On the Images* 3.26.
35. What follows is a summary and interpretation especially of John of Damascus, *On the Images* 1.9–13; 3.18–23.
36. Basil, *On the Holy Spirit* 18.45.
37. Pseudo-Dionysius the Areopagite, *On the Divine Names* 1.5.
38. Justin Martyr, *Dialogue with Trypho* 62.
39. Augustine, *On the Trinity* 7.6.12.
40. Origen, *Against Celsus* 7.65. See p. 41 above.
41. Gregory of Nazianzus, *Theological Orations* 2.31.
42. John of Damascus, *On the Images* 1.
43. John of Damascus, *On the Images* 3.8.
44. Pelikan, *Christian Tradition* 2:10–16.

45. Evgenii Nikolaevich Trubetskoi, *Icons: Theology in Color*, trans. Gertrude Vahar (New York: Saint Vladimir's Seminary Press, 1973).

46. Cf. Ernst Kitzinger, "The Cult of Images before Iconoclasm," *Dumbarton Oaks Papers* 7 (1954): 85–150.

47. André Grabar, *Early Christian Art: From the Rise of Christianity to the Death of Theodosius*, trans. Stuart Gilbert and James Emmons (New York: Odyssey Press, 1968), "Catalogue," p. 15.

48. Clement of Alexandria, *Tutor* 3.7.

49. See Augustine, *Confessions* 4.13.20.

50. Augustine, *Confessions* 10.27.38.

51. Augustine, *On Christian Doctrine* 2.1.1–2.

8. CHRIST CRUCIFIED

1. See the highly revealing Emmaus pericope, Luke 24:13–35, summarizing the "Gospel of the forty days."

2. Shakespeare, *Macbeth* 1.4.7.

3. Isa. 53:5; Acts 8:26–39; cf. also Matt. 8:17.

4. Tertullian, *The Chaplet* 3; Basil of Caesarea, *On the Holy Spirit* 27.66.

5. Julian, *Against the Galileans* 194D, Loeb Classical Library ed., 3:373.

6. Nicholas Monsarrat, *The Cruel Sea* (1951; New York: Giant Cardinal ed., 1963), p. 319.

7. Gustav Mahler to Anna von Mildenburg, 15 March 1897, in *Selected Letters of Gustav Mahler*, ed. Knud Martner (New York: Farrar, Straus, Giroux, 1979), p. 215.

8. Augustine, *On the Trinity* 7.1.1.

9. *Acts of Andrew and Matthew* 19; *Martyrdom of Nereus and Achilleus* 13.

10. Augustine, *City of God* 22.8.

11. Heriger of Lobbes, *Life of Remaclus* 12.

12. This example and others in J. F. Niermeyer, *Mediae Latinitatis Lexicon Minus* (Leiden: E. J. Brill, 1976), s.v. "crux."

13. Shirley Jackson Case, *The Origins of Christian Supernaturalism* (Chicago: University of Chicago Press, 1946), p. 1.

14. See the careful discussion by Henri Chirat, *New Catholic Encyclopedia*, s.v. "Cross, Finding of the Holy," with full documentation of the several references and legends.

15. Sulpicius Severus, *Chronicle* 2.34.4.

16. Socrates Scholasticus, *Ecclesiastical History* 1.17; italics mine.

17. Cyril of Jerusalem, *Catechetical Lectures* 4.10; 10.19; 13.4.

18. Eusebius, *Life of Constantine* 1.41.

19. John of Damascus, *The Orthodox Faith* 4.11.

20. Gustaf Aulén, *Christus Victor: An Historical Study of the Three Main Types of the Idea of Atonement*, trans. A. G. Hebert, introd. Jaroslav Pelikan (New York: Macmillan, 1969), pp. 4–7.

21. Athanasius, *On the Incarnation* 29.1.

22. William J. O'Shea, *The Meaning of Holy Week* (Collegeville, Minn.: Liturgical Press, 1958).

23. Origen, *Commentary on Matthew* 27:32.

24. Karl Young, *The Drama of the Medieval Church*, 2 vols. (Oxford: Clarendon Press, 1933).

25. Frederic James Edward Raby, ed., *The Oxford Book of Medieval Latin Verse* (Oxford: Oxford University Press, 1959), pp. 74–76.

26. See the prejudiced but succinct account of Max Manitius, *Geschichte der lateinischen*

Literatur des Mittelalters, 3 vols. (Munich: C. H. Beck'sche Buchhandlung, 1911–31), 1:295–96.

27. Tertullian, *Against Marcion* 2.2.
28. Augustine, *Sermons* 44.6.6.
29. Sozomen, *Ecclesiastical History* 1.8.
30. Matt. 27:46; Mark 15:34; Ps. 22:1. See Pelikan, *Christian Tradition* 1:245–46, for some representative statements.
31. Priminius, *Scarapsus* 13.
32. Odo of Cluny, *Occupatio* 5.559–62; Matt. 11:29.
33. John of Damascus, *The Orthodox Faith* 4.11.
34. Luke 22:53; Gregory the Great, *Epistles* 6.2.
35. Gen. 50:20; see the comments of Cassian, *Conferences* 3.11.
36. Compare Augustine, *Against Two Letters of the Pelagians* 3.9.25.
37. Boethius, *The Consolation of Philosophy* 4.6.; Thomas Aquinas, *Summa Theologica* I.q.23.a.4.
38. Abelard, *Sermons* 12.
39. Abelard, *Commentary on Romans* 2; Rom. 8:32.
40. See Pelikan, *Christian Tradition* 3:106–57; 4:23–25, 156–57, 161–63.
41. Gerald Phelan, *The Wisdom of Saint Anselm* (Latrobe, Pa.: Saint Vincent's Archabbey, 1960), pp. 30–31.
42. Anselm, *Why God Became Man* 2.15.
43. Athanasius, *Against the Heathen* 1.

9. THE MONK WHO RULES THE WORLD

1. See, for a second-century example, Irenaeus, *Against Heresies* 4.5.4.
2. See Benedict of Nursia, *Rule* 55.
3. Mervin Monroe Deems, "The Sources of Christian Asceticism," in *Environmental Factors in Christian History,* ed. John Thomas McNeill et al. (Chicago: University of Chicago Press, 1939), pp. 149–66.
4. See the edition and discussion, still useful, by Frederick Cornwallis Conybeare, *Philo: About the Contemplative Life, or the Fourth Book of the Treatise concerning Virtues* (Oxford: Clarendon Press, 1895).
5. Eusebius, *Ecclesiastical History* 2.17.
6. Hugh Jackson Lawlor and John Ernest Leonard Oulton, eds., *The Ecclesiastical History,* by Eusebius, 2 vols. (London: SPCK, 1954), 2:67.
7. Gérard Garitte, *Un témoin important du texte de la Vie de S. Antoine par S. Athanase* (Brussels: Palais des Académies, 1939). See also p. 31 above.
8. Augustine, *Confessions* 8.6.15.
9. See John Compton Dickinson, *The Origins of the Austin Canons and Their Introduction into England* (London: SPCK, 1950), pp. 255–72.
10. Benedict, *Rule* 4; prologue.
11. Owen Chadwick, *The Making of the Benedictine Ideal* (Washington, D.C.: Saint Anselm's Abbey, 1981), p. 22; Benedict, *Rule* 53.
12. Athanasius, *Life of Antony* 2; Matt. 19:21.
13. Athanasius, *Life of Antony* 7.
14. Benedict, *Rule* 2, 5; John 6:38.
15. Athanasius, *Life of Antony* 12.
16. Adolf von Harnack, "Das Mönchtum. Seine Ideale und seine Geschichte," in *Reden und Aufsätze* 1:101.

17. The distinction is trenchantly summarized in Thomas Aquinas, *Summa Theologica* II-1.q.108.a.4.
18. Socrates Scholasticus, *Ecclesiastical History* 1.11.
19. Gregory of Nazianzus, *Orations* 12, on the occasion of his assuming the position of bishop-coadjutor of Nazianzus.
20. *Corpus Iuris Civilis: Codex Justinianus* 1.3.47; *Novellae* 6.1; 123.1.
21. Trullan Synod, canon 48.
22. Symeon of Thessalonica, *On the Priesthood*.
23. Francis Dvornik, *The Photian Schism. History and Legend* (Cambridge: Cambridge University Press, 1948), pp. 63–64; it should perhaps be added that it was not only because he had been a layman.
24. Fyodor Dostoevsky, *The Brothers Karamazov*, bk. 6, "The Russian Monk," chap. 3, "Conversations and Exhortations of Father Zossima"; italics mine.
25. Harnack, "Das Mönchtum," p. 111.
26. Thomas Garrigue Masaryk, *The Spirit of Russia*, 3 vols. (London: George Allen and Unwin, 1967–68), 3:15, 204.
27. The chapters "The Religious Orders" and "Fringe Orders and Anti-Orders" in Richard W. Southern, *Western Society and the Church in the Middle Ages*, vol. 2 of The Pelican History of the Church (Harmondsworth: Penguin Books, 1970), pp. 214–358, occupy nearly half of that small book.
28. See especially Walter Ullmann, *The Growth of Papal Government in the Middle Ages: A Study in the Ideological Relation of Clerical to Lay Power*, 2d ed. (London: Methuen, 1962), pp. 262–309.
29. *Be Not Afraid! André Frossard in Conversation with Pope John Paul II*, trans. J. R. Foster (New York: Saint Martin's Press, 1984), p. 150.
30. Gregory VII to Bishop Hermann of Metz, 15 March 1081, in *Das Register Gregors VII*, ed. Erich Caspar, 2 vols. (Berlin: Weidmann, 1920–23), 2:544.
31. Elizabeth T. Kennan, "The 'De Consideratione' of St. Bernard of Clairvaux in the Mid-Twelfth Century: A Review of Scholarship," *Traditio* 23 (1967): 73–115.
32. See Pelikan, *Christian Tradition* 3:300; 4:71.
33. Lowrie J. Daly, *Benedictine Monasticism. Its Formation and Development through the 12th Century* (New York: Sheed and Ward, 1965), pp. 135–36.
34. Kenneth Scott Latourette, *A History of the Expansion of Christianity*, 7 vols. (New York: Harper and Brothers, 1938–45), 2:17; 3:26.
35. Jaroslav Pelikan, *Spirit versus Structure* (New York: Harper and Row, 1968), pp. 52–56.
36. Benedict, *Rule* 48.
37. Jean Leclercq, *The Love of Learning and the Desire for God: A Study of Monastic Culture*, trans. Catharine Misrahi (1961; New York: Mentor Omega Books, 1962), p. 31.
38. Umberto Eco, *The Name of the Rose*, trans. William Weaver (New York: Harcourt Brace Jovanovich, 1983), p. 491.
39. *Modern Catholic Thinkers*, ed. Aloysius Robert Caponigri (New York: Harper and Brothers, 1960), pp. 495–506.
40. Benedict, *Rule* 4; cf. Colman J. Barry, *Worship and Work* (Collegeville, Minn.: Liturgical Press, 1956), p. 85.
41. Dante, *Paradiso* 11.50.

10. THE BRIDEGROOM OF THE SOUL

1. John Julian, *A Dictionary of Hymnology*, 2d ed. (1907; New York: Dover Publications, 1957), pp. 590–91.

2. Julian, *Dictionary of Hymnology*, p. 1038.

3. It will be evident that I owe much to the discussion of David Knowles, *The English Mystical Tradition* (New York: Harper and Brothers, 1961), pp. 1–38.

4. I am adopting here the definition in my article "Mysticism," *Encyclopaedia Britannica*, 14th ed.

5. Abraham Joshua Heschel, *The Prophets* (New York: Harper and Row, 1963), p. 364; italics in original.

6. Gershom Gerhard Scholem, *Major Trends in Jewish Mysticism* (Jerusalem: Schocken Publishing House, 1941).

7. Jean Daniélou, *Platonisme et théologie mystique: Essai sur la doctrine spirituelle de saint Gregoire de Nysse* (Paris: Aubier, 1944).

8. Acts 17:34; Eusebius, *Ecclesiastical History* 3.4.11; 4.23.3; Hilduin of Saint Denis, *Vita Dionysii*.

9. John Meyendorff, *Christ in Eastern Christian Thought* (Washington, D.C., and Cleveland: Corpus Books, 1969), p. 81.

10. See Jaroslav Pelikan, "Introduction" to *Maximus Confessor*, Classics of Western Spirituality (New York: Paulist Press, 1985), pp. 1–13.

11. Marvin H. Pope, *Song of Songs. A New Translation with Introduction and Commentary*, The Anchor Bible (Garden City, N.Y.: Doubleday, 1977), pp. 18–19.

12. Leclercq, *Love of Learning*, pp. 90–91.

13. See the masterful treatment in Etienne Gilson, *The Mystical Theology of Saint Bernard*, trans. Alfred Howard Campbell Downes (London: Sheed and Ward, 1940).

14. Bernard, *Canticles* 1.4.8.

15. Bernard, *Canticles* 22.1.3.

16. Bernard, *Canticles* 43.3.

17. Bernard, *Canticles* 70.7.

18. Bernard, *Canticles* 2.2.3.

19. Bernard, *Canticles* 2.1.2.

20. Bernard, *Canticles* 20.2.

21. Gregory of Nyssa, *Sermons on the Song of Songs* 6.

22. Etienne Gilson, *The Philosophy of St. Bonaventure*, trans. Illtyd Trethowan and F. J. Sheed (New York: Sheed and Ward, 1938).

23. Bonaventure, *The Soul's Journey into God* 2.13, ed. Ewert Cousins, Classics of Western Spirituality (New York: Paulist Press, 1978), p. 77.

24. Bonaventure, *Journey* 4.2, Cousins ed., p. 88.

25. Bonaventure, *Journey* 6.7, Cousins ed., pp. 108–09.

26. Bernard, *Canticles* 20.6.

27. Bernard, *Canticles* 66.10.

28. Knowles, *English Mystical Tradition*, p. 135.

29. Julian of Norwich, *The Revelations of Divine Love* 83, trans. James Walsh (New York: Harper and Brothers, 1961), p. 206.

30. Julian of Norwich, *Revelations* 72, Walsh ed., p. 186.

31. Julian of Norwich, *Revelations* 27, Walsh ed., pp. 91–92.

32. Robert Herrick, "Eternitie," in *The Oxford Book of English Mystical Verse*, ed. D. H. S. Nicholson and A. H. E. Lee (Oxford: Clarendon Press, 1917), pp. 20–21.

33. Dante, *Purgatorio* 17.96.

34. For a general introduction, marred by an uncritical use of such terms as "passionate hallucinations," see Henry Osborn Taylor, *The Mediaeval Mind. A History of the Development of Thought and Emotion in the Middle Ages*, 4th ed., 2 vols. (London: Macmillan, 1938), 2:458–86.

35. *Acta Sanctorum*, February (Paris: Victor Palme, 1865), 3:308.

36. Mariella Liverani, "Margherita da Cortona: Iconographia," in *Bibliotheca Sanctorum*, 12 vols. (Rome: Istituto Giovanni XXIII nella Pontificia Università Lateranense, 1961–69), 8:772.
37. John Rupert Martin, *Baroque* (New York: Harper and Row, 1977), pp. 102–03.
38. See the detailed account of "Interpretations of the Sublime Song" in Pope, *Song of Songs*, pp. 89–229.
39. Thomas G. Bergin, *Dante* (New York: Orion Press, 1965), p. 46.
40. Julian of Norwich, *Revelations* 58, Walsh ed., pp. 159–60.
41. Friedrich von Hügel, *The Mystical Element of Religion as Studied in Saint Catherine of Genoa and Her Friends*, 4th ed., 2 vols. (London: J. M. Dent and Sons, 1961), 2:309–40.
42. Bonaventure, *Journey* 6.5, Cousins ed., p. 107.
43. Pelikan, *Christian Tradition* 4:63–68.
44. Anders Nygren, *Agape and Eros*, trans. Philip S. Watson (Philadelphia: Westminster Press, 1953), p. 650.
45. Hanson, *Allegory and Event*, p. 283.

11. THE DIVINE AND HUMAN MODEL

1. Most of the relevant texts are collected in *St. Francis of Assisi: Writings and Early Biographies*, ed. Marion Alphonse Habig (Chicago: Franciscan Herald Press, 1972).
2. Pius XI, Encyclical *Rite Expiatis* (30 April 1926).
3. Thomas of Celano, *First Life of Saint Francis* 7.16, Habig ed., p. 242.
4. Francis of Assisi, *Rule of 1221* 1, Habig ed., p. 31.
5. Bonaventure, *Major Life of Saint Francis* 1.6, Habig ed., p. 639.
6. Thomas of Celano, *First Life* 9.22, Habig ed., pp. 246–47.
7. Bonaventure, *Major Life* 2.8, Habig ed., pp. 645–46.
8. Thomas of Celano, *First Life* 13.32, Habig ed., p. 254.
9. Thomas of Celano, *First Life* 30.84, Habig ed., p. 299.
10. Bonaventure, *Major Life* 13.3, Habig ed., p. 731.
11. Thomas of Celano, *First Life* 4.98, Habig ed., p. 312.
12. Dante, *Paradiso* 11.107.
13. *Dictionnaire de Théologie Catholique*, 15 vols. (Paris: Libraire Letouzey et Ane, 1903–50), s.v. "stigmatisation."
14. Thomas of Celano, *First Life* 4.95–96, 9.113; Habig ed., pp. 310, 326.
15. Leander E. Keck, "The Poor among the Saints in Jewish Christianity and Qumran," *Zeitschrift für die neutestamentliche Wissenschaft* 57 (1966): 54–78.
16. Francis, *Rule of 1223* 6, Habig ed., p. 61; Heb. 11:13; 1 Peter 2:11.
17. Francis, *Rule of 1221* 9, Habig ed., p. 39; Bonaventure, *Major Life* 7.1, Habig ed., p. 680.
18. Gilbert Keith Chesterton, *Saint Francis of Assisi* (Garden City, N.Y.: Doubleday, 1931), p. 51.
19. Francis, *The Canticle of Brother Sun*, Habig ed., pp. 130–31.
20. Thomas of Celano, *First Life* 19.51, 16.42; Habig ed., pp. 272, 264.
21. Thomas of Celano, *First Life* 30.86, Habig ed., p. 301.
22. Oscar Cullmann, "The Origins of Christmas," in *The Early Church*, ed. A. J. B. Higgins (Philadelphia: Westminster Press, 1956), pp. 17–36.
23. Thomas of Celano, *Second Life of St. Francis* 151.199, Habig ed., p. 521.
24. Bonaventure, *Major Life* 10.7, Habig ed., p. 711.
25. Bonaventure, *Major Life* 14.4, Habig ed., p. 739.
26. Francis, *Rule of 1221* 8, *Rule of 1223* 6; Habig ed., pp. 38, 60.

27. Alan Gewirth, *Marsilius of Padua and Medieval Political Philosophy* (New York: Columbia University Press, 1951), pp. 78–85, 295–96.
28. Thomas à Kempis, *Imitation of Christ* 1.25 (London: Everyman's Library, 1910), pp. 56–57.
29. A. G. Little, "Paul Sabatier, Historian of St. Francis," in *Franciscan Papers, Lists and Documents* (Manchester: University of Manchester, 1929), pp. 179–88.
30. Thomas of Celano, *First Life* 13.33, Habig ed., p. 255.

12. THE UNIVERSAL MAN

1. Jacob Burckhardt, *The Civilization of the Renaissance in Italy*, trans. Samuel George Chetwynd Middlemore, 2 vols. (1929; New York: Harper Torchbooks, 1958), 1:143 and n. 1; italics in original.
2. Harold Rideout Willoughby, *Pagan Regeneration* (Chicago: University of Chicago Press, 1929), pp. 287–88.
3. Erasmus, *Paracelsis*, in *Christian Humanism and the Reformation: Selected Writings of Erasmus*, ed. John C. Olin (New York: Fordham University Press, 1975), p. 100.
4. Konrad Burdach, "Sinn und Ursprung der Worte Renaissance und Reformation," *Reformation Renaissance Humanismus*, 2d ed. (Berlin and Leipzig: Gebrüder Paetel, 1926), p. 83.
5. *Webster's Third New International Dictionary of the English Language Unabridged*, s.v. "Renaissance" (quoting *Horizon Magazine*).
6. See Pelikan, *Christian Tradition* 2:75–90.
7. Goethe, "Observations on Leonardo da Vinci's celebrated picture of The Last Supper," in *Goethe on Art*, ed. John Gage (Berkeley and Los Angeles: University of California Press, 1980), p. 192.
8. Walter Pater, *The Renaissance. Studies in Art and Poetry: The 1893 Text*, ed. Donald H. Hill (Berkeley and Los Angeles: University of California Press, 1980), pp. 93–95.
9. Leo Steinberg, *The Sexuality of Christ in Renaissance Art and in Modern Oblivion* (New York: Pantheon, 1983), pp. 71–72.
10. *Treasures of the Vatican* (New Orleans: Archdiocese of New Orleans, 1984), p. 57.
11. Charles Trinkaus, *In Our Image and Likeness: Humanity and Divinity in Italian Humanist Thought*, 2 vols. (Chicago: University of Chicago Press, 1970), 2:644–50.
12. Burckhardt, *Civilization of the Renaissance* 1:151; see also 1:147.
13. Dante, *Purgatorio* 30.15.
14. Dante, *Vita Nuova* 24, in Mark Musa, *Dante's "Vita Nuova": A Translation and an Essay* (Bloomington: Indiana University Press, 1973), p. 52.
15. Charles S. Singleton, *An Essay on the "Vita Nuova"* (Cambridge, Mass.: Harvard University Press, 1949), p. 112.
16. Bergin, *Dante*, p. 85.
17. Dante, *Purgatorio* 32.101–02.
18. Dante, *Paradiso* 23.34.
19. Dante, *Paradiso* 23.71–74.
20. Dante, *Paradiso* 23.106–08.
21. Dante, *Paradiso* 23.133–39.
22. Ernst Robert Curtius, *European Literature and the Latin Middle Ages*, trans. Willard R. Trask (Princeton: Princeton University Press, 1973), pp. 372–73.
23. For a careful discussion, see Etienne Gilson, *Dante and Philosophy*, trans. Vaid Moore (New York: Sheed and Ward, 1949), pp. 1–82.
24. Dante, *Paradiso* 32.85–86.

25. Dante, *Paradiso* 33.43; 33.145.
26. Dante, *On World-Government or De Monarchia* 3.8, trans. Herbert W. Schneider (New York: Liberal Arts Press, 1957), p. 64.
27. Dante, *De Monarchia* 1.8, Schneider ed., p. 11.
28. Dante, *De Monarchia* 3.16, Schneider ed., p. 78.
29. Dante, *De Monarchia* 3.15, Schneider ed., p. 77.
30. Ernst H. Kantorowicz, *The King's Two Bodies: A Study in Mediaeval Political Theology* (Princeton: Princeton University Press, 1957), p. 464.
31. Paul Oskar Kristeller, *Renaissance Thought: The Classic, Scholastic, and Humanistic Strains* (New York: Harper Torchbooks, 1961), p. 79.
32. Burckhardt, *Civilization of the Renaissance*, 1:196.
33. Petrarch to Nicholas Sygeros, 10 January 1354, in *Letters from Petrarch*, ed. Morris Bishop (Bloomington: Indiana University Press, 1966), p. 153.
34. Deno J. Geanakoplos, *Greek Scholars in Venice: Studies in the Dissemination of Greek Learning from Byzantium to Western Europe* (Cambridge, Mass.: Harvard University Press, 1962).
35. See Pelikan, *Christian Tradition* 4:76–78.
36. Peter Brown, *Augustine of Hippo*, p. 271.
37. Thomas Aquinas *Summa Theologica* 3.44; Pelikan, *Christian Tradition* 3:212; 4:295.
38. Charles Trinkaus, "Introduction" to Valla in *The Renaissance Philosophy of Man*, ed. Ernst Cassirer et al. (Chicago: University of Chicago Press, 1948), p. 147.
39. Hanna Holborn Gray, "Valla's *Encomium of St. Thomas Aquinas* and the Humanist Conception of Christian Antiquity," in *Three Essays* (Chicago: University of Chicago Press, 1978), pp. 23–40.
40. On all these passages, see Pelikan, *Christian Tradition* 4:308–09.
41. E. Harris Harbison, *The Christian Scholar in the Age of the Reformation* (New York: Charles Scribner's Sons, 1956), p. 85.
42. Erasmus, *The Praise of Folly*, in *The Essential Erasmus*, ed. John Patrick Dolan (New York: New American Library, 1964), pp. 157, 165.
43. Erasmus, *Enchiridion* 2.4, 2.6; Dolan ed., pp. 58, 71.
44. Erasmus, *Enchiridion*, conclusion, Dolan ed., p. 93.
45. Erasmus, *Enchiridion* 1.1, Dolan ed., p. 33.
46. Erasmus, *Enchiridion* 1.2, Dolan ed., p. 38; Luke 10:22.
47. Erasmus, *Enchiridion* 1.3, Dolan ed., pp. 42, 40. See p. 81 above.
48. Erasmus, *Enchiridion* 2.3, Dolan ed., pp. 56–57.
49. Erasmus, *Enchiridion* 1.2, Dolan ed., p. 36.
50. Marjorie O'Rourke Boyle, *Christening Pagan Mysteries: Erasmus in Pursuit of Wisdom* (Toronto: University of Toronto Press, 1981), p. 92.
51. Roland H. Bainton, *Erasmus of Christendom* (New York: Charles Scribner's Sons, 1969), p. 272.

13. THE MIRROR OF THE ETERNAL

1. Martin Luther, *Ninety-Five Theses* 1, in *Luther's Works: American Edition*, ed. Jaroslav Pelikan and Helmut Lehmann, 55 vols. (Saint Louis and Philadelphia: Concordia Publishing House and Fortress Press, 1955–), 31:25.
2. Luther, *Preface to Latin Writings*, in *Luther's Works* 34:336–37.
3. Luther, *Large Catechism* 2.3.65.
4. John Calvin, *Institutes of the Christian Religion* 3.24.5, ed. John Thomas McNeill, 2 vols. (Philadelphia: Westminster Press, 1960), 2:970.

5. *Second Helvetic Confession* 10. For other examples, see Pelikan, *Christian Tradition* 4:167, 230–31, 240–41.

6. Brian A. Gerrish, *The Old Protestantism and the New. Essays on the Reformation Heritage* (Chicago: University of Chicago Press, 1982), pp. 150–59.

7. Calvin, *Institutes of the Christian Religion* 2.9.1, McNeill ed., 1:424.

8. Karl Holl, *The Cultural Significance of the Reformation*, trans. Karl and Barbara Hertz and John H. Lichtblau (New York: Meridian Books, 1959), p. 151.

9. Michael Reu, *Luther's German Bible* (Columbus, Ohio: Lutheran Book Concern, 1934), pp. 180–81.

10. Heinrich Bornkamm, *Luther's World of Thought*, trans. Martin H. Bertram (Saint Louis: Concordia Publishing House, 1958), pp. 273–83.

11. Auerbach, *Literary Language and Its Public*, pp. 45–50.

12. A substantial number of these sermons, on the Gospels of Matthew and of John, can be found in volumes 21–24 of *Luther's Works*.

13. Jaroslav Pelikan, *Luther the Expositor. Introduction to the Reformer's Exegetical Writings* (Saint Louis: Concordia Publishing House, 1959), esp. pp. 89–108.

14. Heinrich Heine, *Religion and Philosophy in Germany*, trans. John Snodgrass (Boston: Beacon Press, 1959), p. 46.

15. Luther, *Preface to the New Testament*, in *Luther's Works* 35:357.

16. See, for only one example among many, *Sermons on the Gospel of John*, in *Luther's Works* 22:37–38.

17. *The Martin Luther Christmas Book*, ed. Roland H. Bainton (Philadelphia: Westminster Press, 1948), p. 38.

18. Luther, *The Sermon on the Mount*, in *Luther's Works* 21:197–98.

19. Calvin, *The Gospel According to St. John 1–10*, trans. Thomas Henry Louis Parker (Grand Rapids: Wm. B. Eerdmans, 1959), pp. 89–103.

20. Luther, *Magnificat*, in *Luther's Works* 21:323.

21. Panofsky, *Life and Art of Albrecht Dürer*, p. 199.

22. Wilhelm Dilthey, *Weltanschauung und Analyse des Menschen seit Renaissance und Reformation*, 7th ed. (Stuttgart: B. G. Teubner, 1964), p. 515.

23. Luther, *Preface to the Wittenberg Hymnal of 1524*, in *Luther's Works* 53:316.

24. Nathan Söderblom, *Kristi Pinas Historia* (Stockholm: Svenska Kyrkans Diakonistyrelses Bokförlag, 1928), pp. 430–31; translation provided by Conrad Bergendoff.

25. Luis de León, *The Names of Christ*, bk. 1, ed. Manuel Durán and William Kluback, Classics of Western Spirituality (New York: Paulist Press, 1984), p. 42.

26. Luis de León, *Names of Christ*, bk. 3, Durán-Kluback ed., pp. 303, 366.

27. Luis de León, *Names of Christ*, bk. 2, Durán-Kluback ed., p. 202.

28. *The Poems of St. John of the Cross*, ed. John Frederick Nims, 3d ed. (Chicago: University of Chicago Press, 1979), pp. 18–19.

29. *Poems of St. John of the Cross*, pp. 40–41.

30. *Poems of St. John of the Cross*, pp. 68–71.

31. Luther, *Sermon on the Mount*, in *Luther's Works* 21:105–09.

32. Calvin, *Institutes of the Christian Religion* 4.20.1, McNeill ed., 2:1486.

33. Calvin, *Institutes of the Christian Religion* 4.20.2, McNeill ed., 2:1487.

34. Calvin, *Institutes of the Christian Religion* 4.20.5, McNeill ed., 2:1490; italics mine.

35. John Thomas McNeill, *The History and Character of Calvinism* (New York: Oxford University Press, 1954), p. 185.

36. See Perry Miller, *Orthodoxy in Massachusetts 1630–1650* (Boston: Beacon Press, 1959), pp. 245–53.

37. H. Richard Niebuhr, *The Kingdom of God in America* (New York: Harper and Brothers, 1937), p. 80.

38. Winthrop S. Hudson, *The Great Tradition of the American Churches* (1953; New York: Harper Torchbooks, 1963), p. 49.

39. See Perry Miller, *Roger Williams: His Contribution to the American Tradition* (New York: Atheneum, 1953), p. 38.

40. Sidney E. Mead, *The Lively Experiment: The Shaping of Christianity in America* (New York: Harper and Row, 1963), pp. 72–89. See pp. 209–10 below.

14. THE PRINCE OF PEACE

1. Luis de León, *Names of Christ*, bk. 2, Durán-Kluback ed., pp. 212–39.

2. John Amos Comenius, *The Angel of Peace* 9, trans. Walter Angus Morison (New York: Pantheon Books, n.d.), p. 39; italics in original.

3. For a helpful examination, see Roland H. Bainton, *Christian Attitudes Toward War and Peace: A Historical Survey and Critical Re-evaluation* (New York: Abingdon Press, 1960).

4. Luther, *Whether Soldiers, Too, Can Be Saved*, in *Luther's Works* 46:95.

5. John Calvin, *Institutes of the Christian Religion* 4.20.11–12, McNeill ed., 2:1499–1501.

6. Luther, *Whether Soldiers, Too, Can Be Saved*, in *Luther's Works* 46:97.

7. Luther, *Temporal Authority: To What Extent It Should Be Obeyed*, in *Luther's Works* 45:87.

8. Luther, *Whether Soldiers, Too, Can Be Saved*, in *Luther's Works* 46:113.

9. Bainton, *Christian Attitudes Toward War and Peace*, pp. 136–47.

10. Augustine, *City of God* 3.14; 12.22.

11. Augustine, *City of God* 19.7.

12. Augustine, *Epistles* 189.2.

13. Thomas Aquinas, *Summa Theologica* 2.2.40.

14. John Courtney Murray, "Remarks on the Moral Problem of War," *Theological Studies* 20 (1959): 40–61, still an indispensable introduction.

15. Steven Runciman, *A History of the Crusades*, 3 vols. (Cambridge: Cambridge University Press, 1951–54), 1:83–92.

16. Runciman, *History of the Crusades* 3:7; 2:287; 3:130.

17. Hans Pfeffermann, *Die Zusammenarbeit der Renaissancepäpste mit den Türken* (Winterthur: Mondial Verlag, 1946), p. 63.

18. Aziz S. Atiya, "The Aftermath of the Crusades," in *A History of the Crusades*, ed. Kenneth M. Setton, 5 vols. (Madison: University of Wisconsin Press, 1955–75), 3:660.

19. *Augsburg Confession* 16.1–2; 21.1.

20. Luther, *On War against the Turk*, in *Luther's Works* 46:186–88.

21. See the balanced account of Eric W. Gritsch, *Reformer without a Church: The Life and Thought of Thomas Muentzer* (Philadelphia: Fortress Press, 1967).

22. Thomas Muentzer, "Sermon before the Princes" in *Spiritual and Anabaptist Writers*, ed. George Huntston Williams (Philadelphia: Westminster Press, 1957), pp. 50–53, 65–66.

23. George Casalis, *Correct Ideas Don't Fall from the Skies: Elements for an Inductive Theology*, trans. Jeanne Marie Lyons and Michael John (Maryknoll, N.Y.: Orbis Books, 1984), p. 114.

24. On the entire movement, see George Huntston Williams, *The Radical Reformation* (Philadelphia: Westminster Press, 1962).

25. Harold S. Bender, "The Pacifism of the Sixteenth-Century Anabaptists," *Church History* 24 (1955): 119–31.

26. Pelikan, *Christian Tradition* 4:313–22.

27. Ethelbert Stauffer, "The Anabaptist Theology of Martyrdom," *Mennonite Quarterly Review* 19 (1945): 179–214.

28. A convenient edition in English is that of Hans J. Hillerbrand, ed., *The Reformation* (New York: Harper and Row, 1964), pp. 235–38.

29. Bainton, *Christian Attitudes Toward War and Peace*, pp. 157–65.

30. Torquato Tasso, *Jerusalem Delivered* 1.72, trans. Edward Fairfax (Carbondale: Southern Illinois University Press, 1962), p. 21.

15. THE TEACHER OF COMMON SENSE

1. See Peter Gay, *The Enlightenment: An Interpretation*, 2 vols. (New York: Alfred A. Knopf, 1966–69), 1:256–321.

2. Augustine, *City of God* 10.18.

3. Augustine, *On the Profit of Believing* 14.32.

4. Isaac Newton, *Mathematical Principles of Natural Philosophy*, bk. 3, "The System of the World," General Scholium.

5. Newton, *Optics*, bk. 3, pt. 1.

6. Edwin A. Burtt, *The Metaphysical Foundations of Modern Science*, 2d ed. (1932; Garden City, N.Y.: Anchor Books, 1954), pp. 283–302.

7. David Hume, *Enquiry concerning Human Understanding*, sec. 10, pt. 2, in *The English Philosophers from Bacon to Mill*, ed. Edwin A. Burtt (New York: Modern Library, 1939), pp. 657–67.

8. Goethe, *Faust* 766.

9. Edward Gibbon, *The History of the Decline and Fall of the Roman Empire*, ed. John Bagnell Bury, 7 vols. (London: Methuen, 1896–1900), 2:28–31, 69–70.

10. Gibbon, *Decline and Fall* 2:335–87; 5:96–168.

11. Gibbon, *Decline and Fall* 5:97–98.

12. Arthur Darby Nock, *Conversion: The Old and the New in Religion from Alexander the Great to Augustine of Hippo* (Oxford: Oxford University Press, 1933), p. 210.

13. Hermann Samuel Reimarus, *Fragments*, trans. Ralph S. Fraser, ed. Charles H. Talbert (Philadelphia: Fortress Press, 1970), pp. 72, 95–96.

14. Reimarus, *Fragments*, p. 269.

15. Leander E. Keck, ed., *The Christ of Faith and the Jesus of History*, by David Friedrich Strauss (Philadelphia: Fortress Press, 1977), p. xxxiii.

16. David Friedrich Strauss, *The Life of Jesus Critically Examined*, 5th ed., introd. Otto Pfleiderer (London: Swan Sonnenschein, 1906).

17. Gordon Haight, *George Eliot: A Biography* (New York: Oxford University Press, 1968), p. 59.

18. Otto Pfleiderer, "Introduction" to English translation of Strauss, *Life of Jesus*, p. xxi.

19. Werner Jaeger, *Paideia: The Ideals of Greek Culture*, trans. Gilbert Highet, 3 vols. (New York: Oxford University Press, 1943–45), 2:21; italics in original.

20. Joseph Priestley, *Socrates and Jesus Compared* (Philadelphia: printed for the author, 1803), p. 48.

21. Daniel J. Boorstin, *The Lost World of Thomas Jefferson* (Boston: Beacon Press, 1960), p. 156.

22. Jefferson to William Short, 31 October 1819, in *Jefferson's Extracts from the Gospels*, ed. Dickinson W. Adams (Princeton: Princeton University Press, 1983), p. 388.

23. Adams, *Jefferson's Extracts*, p. 60; p. 135 and note (p. 300).

24. Adams, *Jefferson's Extracts*, pp. 27–28.

25. Garry Wills, *Inventing America: Jefferson's Declaration of Independence* (New York: Vintage Books, 1979), p. 191.
26. *Benjamin Franklin's Autobiographical Writings*, ed. Carl Van Doren (New York: Viking Press, 1945), p. 784.
27. Henry F. May, *The Enlightenment in America* (New York: Oxford University Press, 1976), pp. 128–29.

16. THE POET OF THE SPIRIT

1. Shakespeare, *Hamlet* 1.5.166–67.
2. René Wellek, "Romanticism Re-examined," in *Concepts of Criticism* (New Haven: Yale University Press, 1963), p. 221.
3. Arthur O. Lovejoy, *Essays in the History of Ideas* (New York: Braziller Press, 1955), p. 232.
4. Friedrich Schleiermacher, *On Religion. Speeches to Its Cultured Despisers*, trans. John Oman (1893; New York: Harper Torchbooks, 1958).
5. Jack C. Verheyden, "Introduction" to Friedrich Schleiermacher, *The Life of Jesus*, trans. S. Maclean Gilmour (Philadelphia: Fortress Press, 1975), p. xi.
6. Schleiermacher, *The Christian Faith*, trans. H. R. Mackintosh and J. S. Stewart (Edinburgh: T. and T. Clark, 1928).
7. Samuel Taylor Coleridge, *The Complete Works*, ed. W. G. T. Shedd, 7 vols. (New York: Harper, 1956).
8. *The Complete Essays and Other Writings of Ralph Waldo Emerson*, ed. Brooks Atkinson (New York: Modern Library, 1940).
9. Lovejoy, *Essays*, p. 235.
10. See J. Robert Barth, *Coleridge and Christian Doctrine* (Cambridge, Mass.: Harvard University Press, 1969), pp. 37–42.
11. Coleridge, *The Friend*, in *Works* 2:468.
12. Emerson, *Nature*, Atkinson ed., p. 37.
13. James D. Boulger, *Coleridge as Religious Thinker* (New Haven: Yale University Press, 1961), p. 175.
14. Schleiermacher, *Life of Jesus*, pp. 190–229.
15. Schleiermacher, *Life of Jesus*, p. 205.
16. Schleiermacher, *Life of Jesus*, pp. 87–122.
17. Schleiermacher, *On Religion*, p. 246.
18. *On Religion*, p. 3.
19. Schleiermacher, *Christian Faith*, chap. 90.
20. Georg Wilhelm Friedrich Hegel, *Early Theological Writings*, trans. T. M. Knox (Chicago: University of Chicago Press, 1948), pp. 196, 212.
21. Harold Bloom, *Blake's Apocalypse*, 2d ed. (Ithaca, N.Y.: Cornell University Press, 1970).
22. *The Paintings and Drawings of William Blake*, ed. Martin Butlin, 2 vols. (New Haven: Yale University Press, 1981), *Text*, pp. 175–76.
23. Harold Bloom, *Figures of Capable Imagination* (New York: Seabury Press, 1976), p. 50.
24. Emerson, *Nature*, Atkinson ed., pp. 6, 9; italics in original.
25. Ralph Waldo Emerson, *Early Lectures*, 3 vols. (Cambridge, Mass: Harvard University Press, 1961–72), 1:73.
26. John Haynes Holmes, "Introduction" to Ernest Renan, *The Life of Jesus* (1864; New York: Modern Library, 1927), p. 23.

27. Renan, *Life of Jesus*, p. 69.
28. Renan, *Life of Jesus*, pp. 392–93.
29. Renan, *Life of Jesus*, p. 65.
30. Gay Wilson Allen, *Waldo Emerson. A Biography* (New York: The Viking Press, 1981), pp. 570–92.
31. Emerson, *Essays: Second Series*, Atkinson ed., pp. 321, 338.
32. *Poems*, Atkinson ed., p. 775.
33. Karl Barth, *Die protestantische Theologie im 19. Jahrhundert* (Zurich: Evangelischer Verlag, 1947), pp. 385, 412–13.
34. David Friedrich Strauss, *The Christ of Faith and the Jesus of History*, trans. Leander E. Keck (Philadelphia: Fortress Press, 1977), p. 37.
35. Schweitzer, *Quest*, p. 67.
36. Barth, *19. Jahrhundert*, pp. 397–99.
37. James Hastings Nichols, *Romanticism in American Theology* (Chicago: University of Chicago Press, 1961), pp. 107–39.
38. Jaroslav Pelikan, *The Vindication of Tradition. The 1983 Jefferson Lecture in the Humanities* (New Haven: Yale University Press, 1984), pp. 3–40.
39. Emerson, *An Address*, Atkinson ed., pp. 67–84; italics in original.
40. Fyodor Dostoevsky, *Crime and Punishment* 4.4.
41. *The Notebooks for "Crime and Punishment,"* ed. Edward Wasiolek (Chicago: University of Chicago Press, 1967), p. 231.

17. THE LIBERATOR

1. Dostoevsky, *The Brothers Karamazov* 5.5.
2. Gal. 3:28; 5:1.
3. For a brief account, see John Francis Maxwell, *Slavery and the Catholic Church* (London: Barry Rose, 1975), esp. pp. 88–125.
4. Mead, *Lively Experiment*, p. 73.
5. See Julian, *Dictionary of Hymnology* 2:1684.
6. David Brion Davis, *The Problem of Slavery in Western Culture* (Ithaca, N.Y.: Cornell University Press, 1966), pp. 199–200.
7. Wilhelm Gass, *Geschichte der christlichen Ethik*, 3 vols. (Berlin: G. Reimer, 1881–87), 1:226.
8. Augustine, *City of God* 19.15.
9. John Knox, *Philemon among the Letters of Paul.* (Chicago: University of Chicago Press, 1935), pp. 46–56.
10. J. B. Lightfoot, *Saint Paul's Epistles to the Colossians and to Philemon* (London: Macmillan, 1900), p. 321.
11. Isaac Mendelsohn, *Slavery in the Ancient Near East: A Comparative Study* (New York: Oxford University Press, 1949).
12. Rom. 6:16; John 8:34; 2 Pet. 2:19.
13. Ernst Troeltsch, *The Social Teachings of the Christian Churches*, trans. Olive Wyon, 2 vols. (1931; New York: Harper Torchbooks, 1960), 1:133.
14. Lev Nikolaevich Tolstoy, *Resurrection*, pt. 1, chap. 41.
15. Tolstoy, *Resurrection*, pt. 3, chap. 28.
16. G. I. Petrov, *Otluchenie L'va Tolstogo od Tserkvi* (The separation of Lev Tolstoy from the church) (Moscow: Isdatyelstvo "Znanie," 1978), p. 28.
17. Tolstoy to Shaw, 9 May 1910, in *Tolstoy's Letters*, ed. R. K. Christian, 2 vols. (New York: Charles Scribner's Sons, 1978), 2:700.

18. Isaiah Berlin, "The Hedgehog and the Fox," *Russian Thinkers*, ed. Henry Hardy and Aileen Kelly (New York: Penguin Books, 1978), pp. 51–52.

19. Mohandas K. Gandhi, *An Autobiography: The Story of My Experiments with Truth*, trans. Mahadev Desai (Boston: Beacon Press, 1957), pp. 137–38.

20. Tolstoy to Mohandas K. Gandhi, 7 September 1910, *Letters* 2:706–08.

21. Erik Erikson, *Gandhi's Truth: On the Origins of Militant Non-Violence* (New York: Norton, 1969), p. 281.

22. Matt. 21:12–17; Matt. 23.

23. Phil. 3:10.

24. Howard Thurman, *Jesus and the Disinherited* (New York: Abingdon-Cokesbury Press, 1949).

25. Martin Luther King, Jr., *Where Do We Go from Here: Chaos or Community?* (Boston: Beacon Press, 1968), p. 44.

26. Martin Luther King, Jr., *Stride toward Freedom* (New York: Harper and Brothers, 1958), p. 101.

27. David Levering Lewis, *King: A Critical Biography* (1970; reprint, Baltimore: Penguin Books, 1971), p. 191.

28. Lewis, *King*, p. 105.

29. Kenneth L. Smith and Ira G. Zepp, Jr., *Search for the Beloved Community: The Thinking of Martin Luther King, Jr.* (Valley Forge, Pa.: Judson Press, 1974).

30. King, *Stride toward Freedom*, pp. 102–06, 189–224.

31. Casalis, *Correct Ideas Don't Fall from the Skies*, p. 114.

32. Gustavo Guttierez, *A Theology of Liberation: History, Politics, and Salvation* (Maryknoll, N.Y.: Orbis Books, 1973).

18. THE MAN WHO BELONGS TO THE WORLD

1. Acts 1:8.

2. Eusebius, *Ecclesiastical History* 1.4.2.

3. See Julian, *Dictionary of Hymnology* 1:601, and the account given there of the place of this hymn in the history of missions to the South Seas.

4. Kenneth Scott Latourette, *A History of the Expansion of Christianity*, 7 vols. (New York: Harper and Brothers, 1939–45).

5. Arthur Schlesinger, Jr., "The Missionary Enterprise and Theories of Imperialism," in *The Missionary Enterprise in China and America*, ed. John K. Fairbank (Cambridge, Mass.: Harvard University Press, 1974), pp. 336–73.

6. Karl Holl, "Die Missionsmethode der alten und die der mittelalterlichen Kirche," in *Gesammelte Aufsätze zur Kirchengeschichte*, 3 vols. (1928; reprint, Darmstadt: Wissenschaftliche Buchgesellschaft, 1964), 3:117–29.

7. Hilaire Belloc, *Europe and the Faith* (New York: Paulist Press, 1921), p. viii.

8. Francis Dvornik, *Byzantine Missions among the Slavs* (New Brunswick, N.J.: Rutgers University Press, 1970), pp. 107–09.

9. Venerable Bede, *Ecclesiastical History of the English People* 22.

10. Auerbach, *Literary Language and Its Public*, pp. 120–21.

11. Joseph Needham, *Science and Civilization in China, Introductory Considerations*, 2d ed., 2 vols. (Cambridge: Cambridge University Press, 1961), 1:148.

12. As quoted in Jonathan D. Spence, *The Memory Palace of Matteo Ricci* (New York: Viking Press, 1984), p. 210.

13. I know *True Meaning* only in the anonymous French translation, *Entretiens d'un lettre chinois et d'un docteur européen, sur le vraie idée de Dieu*, in *Lettres édifiantes et curieuses* 25 (1811): 143–385.

14. This material has been gathered in *The Book of a Thousand Tongues*, ed. Eric M. North (New York: Harper and Brothers, 1938).

15. For only one example among many, see P. Yang Fu-Mien, "The Catholic Missionary Contribution to the Study of Chinese Dialects," *Orbis* 9 (1960): 158–85.

16. Jawaharlal Nehru, *Toward Freedom: Autobiography* (Boston: Beacon Press, 1958), pp. 236–50.

17. Spence, *Memory Palace*, pp. 59–92.

18. Harnack, *Mission and Expansion* (see chap. 6, n. 5), p. 108; italics in original.

19. Origen, *Against Celsus* 8.72.

20. Mark 9:41.

21. Nathan Söderblom, *The Living God: Basic Forms of Personal Religion* (Boston: Beacon Press, 1962), pp. 349, 379.

22. Stephen Neill, *A History of Christian Missions* (Baltimore: Penguin Books, 1964), p. 456.

23. *Documents of Vatican II*, pp. 660–68.

24. *Documents of Vatican II*, pp. 666–67.

25. On the ironies of its appearance, see Robert P. Ericksen, *Theologians Under Hitler: Gerhard Kittel, Paul Althaus, and Emanuel Hirsch* (New Haven: Yale University Press, 1985).

26. Augustine, *Confessions* 9.27.38.

Index of Proper Names

Aaron, and Israelitic priesthood, 27–28

Abelard, Peter, on the cross, 105–06

Abraham, Christian use of, 43

Acciaiuoli, Donato, on Jesus, 148–49

Adams, Dickinson W., on Thomas Jefferson's research into the Gospels, 192 n. 24

Aeschylus, quoted on righteousness, 44

Alexandria: Diaspora Jews in, 11; letter of Constantine to, 53

Allen, Gay Wilson, on Emerson, 200 n. 30

Alvernia (La Verna), 136

Ambrose of Milan: *Hexaemeron* on the cosmos, 61; on Virgin Birth, 80

American Bible Society, 224

Anabaptists: and orthodox doctrine of Christ, 180; on peace and war, 175–78

Anhalt, prince of, 162

Anselm of Canterbury, on the wisdom of the cross, 106–08

Antoninus, Pius, and Justin, 41–42

Antony: *Life* of, 31–32; as monastic founder, 112; poverty and chastity, 113–14

Apollonius of Tyana, *Life* of, 31

Apostles' Creed, on life of Jesus, 95

Aqiba, rabbi, on Song of Songs, 125

Arnold, Matthew, quoted, 187–88

Assisi. *See* Francis of Assisi

Athanasius: on becoming divine, 68; as biographer of Antony, 30–32, 112, 114; calendar, 32–33; on Christ as un-changeable, 1; on humanity as subject to transiency, 67–68; on the power of the cross, 108; on universe as cosmos of order, 66

Athens: Dionysius as bishop of, 124

Atiya, Aziz S., on Crusade ideal in the sixteenth century, 173 n. 18

Attila, and Leo I, 55

Auerbach, Erich, on Latin, 222–23 n. 10

Augsburg, diet of Holy Roman Empire at, 173–74

Augsburg Confession, on war, 174

Augustine of Hippo: on the Beautiful, 7, 93–94, 233; *City of God*, 28; *Confessions*, 30, 76–79; conversion of, 133; on creation, 62; on the cross and kings, 47; on the cross and miracles, 97; echoes of, in Dante, 129; on the historical figure of Jesus, 70; on human nature, 73–82; on image of God as image of the Trinity, 5, 75–76, 90; on Israel and its history, 26–27; knowledge of Greek, 153; on language, 94; on Mary, 80–81; on miracle, 183; and monasticism, 112; *On Music*, 94; on paradox, 102–04; and Platonism, 75; on revelation, 35; on Rome and its history, 29–30; on sin, 76–81; on slavery, 211; *The Teacher*, 74–75; on Vergil, 36; on war, 171–72; on wisdom and power, 96–97

Augustine of Kent, mission to England, 222

Index of Biblical References

MARY THROUGH THE CENTURIES

Her Place in the History of Culture

To Martha and Anne Therese

Each in her own special way Mulier Fortis (Proverbs 31:10 Vg)

Contents

Attributed to Saint Luke the icon painter, *Our Lady of Częstochowa, Queen of Poland*. (Photo courtesy of the Polish Institute of Arts & Sciences of America, Inc., New York City)

Preface

Already while I was planning and writing my *Jesus Through the Centuries*, which Yale University Press published in 1985, I was simultaneously planning a companion volume on Mary. In spite of the obvious chronological precedence of the Mother over the Son, however, both the relative amounts of the material dealing with them throughout history and the absolute difference in their theological importance required that the book about the Mother be published second—and that it be slightly shorter. In both books, the number of images and metaphors, leitmotivs and doctrines—and therefore, even after combining two (or more) of these into one as I have throughout, the number of chapters—could have been proliferated almost at will. But, as I did in *Jesus Through the Centuries*, I wanted to present, in roughly chronological order, a series of distinct but related vignettes of the Virgin both in their continuity and in their development across various cultures and "through the centuries."

This book has been made possible by the invitation of President Richard C. Levin of Yale University to return to the podium of the William Clyde DeVane Lectures in the autumn of 1995 for my final semester of teaching as a professor at Yale, concluding fifty years in the classroom here and elsewhere. I am pleased as well to acknowledge the stimulation and insight, and in some cases the bibliographical suggestions, that came from the students who took the DeVane Lectures as a course. My thanks are due also to my editors at Yale University Press, John G. Ryden, Judy Metro, and Laura Jones Dooley, and to the many readers, known and unknown, who have commented on the manuscript in whole or in part at various stages of its development.

In most cases I have quoted, or sometimes adapted, the Authorized ("King James") Version of the English Bible, except as indicated, where I am translating a translation, for example, "The Woman of Valor" in the title of chapter 6, as a rendering of *mulier fortis* from the Vulgate (abbreviated "Vg") of Proverbs 31:10, the Latin title that I am also pleased, in the Dedication, to award to my beloved daughters-in-law. Translations of other works are sometimes borrowed or adapted from existing versions and sometimes are my own.

Mary Through the Centuries

Russian school, twelfth century, *The Virgin of the Great Panagia* (called *The Virgin Orant of Jaroslavl*). Tretyakov Gallery, Moscow. (Scala / Art Resource, N.Y.)

Introduction
Ave Maria, Gratia Plena

Hail Mary, full of grace: the Lord is with thee.
—Luke 1:28 *(Vg)*

The second sentence of the Introduction to *Jesus Through the Centuries*, the companion volume to this book, posed the question: "If it were possible, with some sort of supermagnet, to pull up out of that history [of almost twenty centuries] every scrap of metal bearing at least a trace of his name, how much would be left?"[1] The same question may be appropriately asked also about Mary. There are, on one hand, many fewer such scraps of metal bearing the name Mary. But on the other hand, she has provided the content of the definition of the feminine in a way that he has not done for the masculine; for in a distinction of linguistic usage about which it may be necessary to remind present-day readers, it was "man" as humanity rather than merely "man" as male that he was chiefly said to have defined—to the point that some speculative thinkers were willing to portray him as androgynous. Even in the absence of reliable statistical data, however, it is probably safe to estimate that for nearly two thousand years "Mary" has been the name most frequently given to girls at baptism, and, through the exclamation "Jesus, Mary, and Joseph" (or just "Ježiš Mária!" as I used to hear it in Slovak from my father's Lutheran parishioners during my childhood), and above all through the *Ave Maria*, which has been repeated literally millions of times every day, the female name that has been pronounced most often in the Western world. Almost certainly she has been portrayed in art and music more than any other woman in history. To mention only one example for now, not only did Giuseppe Verdi compose an *Ave Maria* in 1889 (as well as a *Stabat Mater* in 1897); but Arrigo Boito's adaptation of Shakespeare's *Othello* for Verdi's opera in 1887 followed Gioacchino Rossini's opera *Otello* of 1816 in adding an *Ave Maria* to Shakespeare's text for Desdemona to sing just before her death.[2] It came in anticipation of the question Othello asked Desdemona in Shakespeare's play before he strangled her, "Have you pray'd to-night, Desdemona?"[3]

The Virgin Mary has been more of an inspiration to more people than any other woman who ever lived. And she remains so in the twentieth century, despite its being conventionally regarded as secularistic by contrast with previous so-called ages of faith. The last empress of Russia, Alexandra, who at her marriage to the czar had converted from Hessian Protestantism to Russian Orthodoxy, wrote a few weeks after the October Revolution: "An uncultured, wild people, but the Lord won't abandon them, and the Holy Mother of God will stand up for our poor Rus."[4] It was only a coincidence, but a striking one, that two years later, in 1919, the powerful icon *The Virgin of the Great Panagia*, shown here, was discovered in the Convent of the Transfiguration (*Preobraženie*) at Jaroslavl. Rose Fitzgerald Kennedy, in speaking near the end about all the tragedies she had endured in her long life, said that she had constantly found inspiration and consolation above all in "the Blessed Mother," who had not lost her faith in God even when her Son had been "crucified and reviled."[5] One of our most sensitive commentators on current affairs, the Hispanic-American man of letters Richard Rodriguez, has suggested that "the Virgin of Guadalupe symbolizes the entire coherence of Mexico, body and soul. . . . The image of Our Lady of Guadalupe (privately, affectionately, Mexicans call her La Morenita—Little Darkling) has become the unofficial, the private flag of Mexicans."[6] For the portrayal of the Virgin Mary in this Mexican image, as another twentieth-century writer has suggested, "contains the . . . basic themes of liberation."[7]

Secularistic or not, this century has, for example, witnessed a continuation, and probably an acceleration, of the phenomenon of apparitions of Mary, for which the nineteenth century became almost a golden age.[8] The Mariological scholar René Laurentin estimated some years ago that there had been well over two hundred of them since the 1930s, and they have continued unabated. Television reporters and print journalists, who sometimes seem to become interested in the phenomena of religious experience and expression only when they are politicized or bizarre or both, have managed to keep the public well informed about these sightings. In Bosnia-Herzegovina, which in 1914 was the fuse that ignited the First World War and which throughout the century has continued to be a venue for religious hatred and ethnic violence, the Virgin appeared in 1981, at Medjugorje, a Croatian-speaking village of 250 families.[9] Since then, more than twenty million pilgrims have visited it, despite the land mines and the sniper fire, and it has been given credit by no less an authority on such matters than the president of Croatia, Franjo Tudjman, for "the reawakening of the Croatian nation."[10] Nor is this phenomenon confined to Roman Catholic countries; in Orthodox Greece, for example, apparitions of the Virgin in the twentieth century have become a major force.[11]

Because, as was said just when the twentieth century was beginning, it was traditionally held that "in Mary, we see in the little that is told of her what a true woman ought to be,"[12] the twentieth century's dramatic upsurge of interest in the question of exactly "what a true woman ought to be" has likewise been unable to ignore her.[13] It has become a widely held historical consensus that "the theology of the Virgin Mary has not altered women's inferior status within the Church."[14] Indeed, one of the most articulate spokeswomen for the position that the modern woman cannot be truly free without a radical break from tradition, above all from religious tradition, has characterized the traditional picture of the Virgin Mary as follows: "For the first time in history, the mother kneels before her son; she freely accepts her inferiority. This is the supreme masculine victory, consummated in the cult of the Virgin—it is the rehabilitation of woman through the accomplishment of her defeat."[15] More ambivalently, advocates for the movement within the Christian thought of the late twentieth century that has come to be called "feminist theology" have also been striving— or, as one of them has put it, "desperately seeking"[16]—to come to terms with Mary as a symbol for "ultimate womanhood."[17] "The Mary myth," another of them has concluded, has "its roots and development in a male, clerical, and ascetic culture and theology. . . . The myth is a theology of woman, preached by men to women, and one that serves to deter women from becoming fully independent and whole human persons."[18] Conversely, Mary has also served advocates of Eastern Orthodoxy as a positive resource for the reinterpretation of the place of woman in Christian thought.[19]

One of the most important religious events of the twentieth century has been, and continues to be, the rise of the ecumenical movement. It began as a largely Protestant phenomenon with the heirs of the Reformation reexamining the issues that had begun to drive them apart almost from the beginning. At that stage, the question of Mary did not play a prominent role, except for the disputes between liberalism and fundamentalism over the historical accuracy of the biblical accounts of the Virgin Birth.[20] But with the participation of Eastern Orthodox and then of Roman Catholic partners in the conversation, the question became unavoidable, and eventually it came to be seen in significant ways as epitomizing many general issues that divide the churches: What is the legitimate role of postbiblical tradition in Christian teaching? What is the role of the saints, and above all of this saint, in Christian worship and devotion? And who has the authority to decide matters of Christian teaching? Thus twentieth-century explorations have made the history of Mary a major issue also for the ecumenical encounter, and a careful and candid review of the issue and its implications from Roman Catholic, Eastern Orthodox, Protestant, and even Jewish perspectives has illumined not only the ecumenical problem but the problem of Mariology.[21]

In the chapters that follow I shall try to show historically what Mary has meant, by following a roughly chronological order to box the compass of some of the provinces of life and realms of reality in which she has been a prominent force at various periods in history. It has been a process, as Hans Urs von Balthasar has put it, "that oscillates (from the Virgin Bride to the Mother of the Church, from the answering person to the Source of the race)."[22]

Jan Van Eyck, *The Annunciation*, c. 1430, detail of the Angel Gabriel. Gemäldegalerie, Staatliche Kunstsammlungen, Dresden. (Alinari/Art Resource, N.Y.)

1 Miriam of Nazareth in the New Testament

And in the sixth month the angel Gabriel was sent from God
unto a city of Galilee, named Nazareth, to a virgin
espoused to a man named Joseph, of the house of David;
and the virgin's name was Mary.—Luke 1:26–27

Because this book is not an inquiry into who Mary was in the first century but into what "through the centuries" she has been experienced and understood to be, biblical materials dealing with her have an essentially retrospective function here. In light of the subsequent development of devotion and doctrine, what did the Bible contribute to the portrait of the Virgin? That perspective applies with particular force to the subject of the next chapter, the allegorical and typological use of a Christianized Old Testament for its bearing on the question of Mary, where the problem of the original meaning of a passage, including the precise translation of the Hebrew text, will have to be quite secondary to the meaning that the passage acquired in Christian history through translation and exegesis. But the New Testament, certainly no less than the Old, has continually taken on new meanings in the course of the history of its interpretation, meanings that have sometimes been the consequence of what it did not say as much as of what it did. For to both Testaments we may apply the sage comment of a scholar of the Hebrew Bible who has illumined some special chapters in the history of its interpretation. "Just as a pearl results from a stimulus in the shell of a mollusk," Louis Ginzberg observed, "so also a legend may arise from an irritant in the scripture."[1] Whether as stimulus or irritant or inspiration, Scripture has dominated attention to the Virgin Mary though it has not always controlled it.

Nevertheless, the account of Mary in the New Testament is tantalizingly brief, and anyone who comes to consider the biblical references to Mary from the study of later development of devotion to her and of doctrine about her, as this book is doing, must be surprised or even shocked to discover how sparse they are. One interpreter early in this century, who was intent on maximizing the evidence as far as permissible (and perhaps a little farther), was compelled to acknowledge that "the reader of the gospels is at first surprised to find so little about Mary."[2] Or, as the leading Greek-English lexicon of the New Testament put it in identifying the first of the seven women bearing the name Maria in the New Testament, "Little is known about the life of this Mary."[3] Depending on what one includes, it could all be printed out on a few pages. If that were all there were to go on, this book would be short indeed! In fact, the contrast between the biblical evidence and the traditional material is so striking that it has become a significant issue in the ecumenical encounter between denominations.[4] Out of that encounter has come a volume jointly written by Roman Catholic and Protestant scholars entitled *Mary in the New Testament* and devoted to a book-by-book and topic-by-topic analysis of the possible references to Mary in the New Testament. Although the work has all the disadvantages of a book that has been not only jointly written but subjected to a series of votes, it has assembled the material in a convenient form. Even more surprisingly, it reflects a remarkable consensus across confessional lines, especially in its adherence to the historical-critical method of studying the Bible but even in its conclusions about individual passages of the New Testament. Pointing out that "in the course of centuries mariology has had an enormous development" (which is the business of this book), the authors of *Mary in the New Testament*, because of their focus, paid little attention to that development.[5]

For biblical scholarship, the fact that "in the course of centuries mariology has had an enormous development" may be something of a problem. But for historical scholarship, that development is also an enormous resource. To be sure, Mariology was not the only doctrine to have undergone such a development; in fact, it would be impossible to identify a doctrine that has not done so. The most decisive instance of the development of doctrine, and the one by which the fundamental issues of what could by now be called "the doctrine of development" have been defined, is the dogma of the Trinity. For the doctrine of the Trinity was not as such a teaching of the New Testament, but it emerged from the life and worship, the reflection and controversy, of the church as, in the judgment of Christian orthodoxy, the only way the church could be faithful to the teaching of the New Testament. It did so after centuries of study and speculation, during which many solutions to the dilemma of the Three and the One had surfaced, each with some passage or theme of Scripture to commend it. The final normative formulation of the dogma of the Trinity by the first ecumenical council of the church, held at Nicaea in 325, took as its basic outline the biblical formula of the so-called great commission of Christ to the disciples just before his ascension: "All power is given unto me in heaven and in earth. Go ye therefore, and teach all nations, baptizing them in the name of the Father and of the Son and of the Holy Ghost."[6] But into the framework of that New Testament formula the Nicene Creed had packed many other biblical motifs, as well as the portentous and non-biblical technical term for which it became known, suggested apparently by Emperor Constantine: "one in being with the Father [homoousios tōi patri]."[7] With characteristic acuity, therefore, John Courtney Murray once formulated the implications of this for the ecumenical situation: "I consider that the parting of the ways between the two Christian communities takes place on the issue of development of doctrine. . . . I do not think that the first ecumenical question is, what think ye of the Church? Or even, what think ye of Christ? The dialogue would rise out of the current confusion if the first question raised were, what think ye of the Nicene homoousion?"[8] If the Protestant churches acknowledged the validity of the development of doctrine when it moved from the great commission of the Gospel of Matthew to produce the Nicene Creed, as all of the mainline Protestant churches did and do, on what grounds could they reject development as it had moved from other lapidary passages of the Bible to lead to other doctrines?

From the apparently simple statements "This is my body" and "This is my blood" in the words of institution of the Lord's Supper,[9] for example, had come not only the resplendent eucharistic liturgies of Eastern Orthodoxy and the Latin Mass with all its concomitants, including the reservation of the consecrated Host and devotion to it, but the long and complicated history of the development of the doctrine of the real presence of the body and blood of Christ in the Sacrament, leading in the Western church to the promulgation of the doctrine of transubstantiation at the Fourth Lateran Council in 1215 and its reaffirmation by the Council of Trent in 1551.[10] If the First Council of Nicaea was a legitimate development and the Fourth Council of the Lateran an illegitimate development, what were the criteria, biblical and doctrinal, for discerning the difference? As it stood, the statement of Christ to Peter in the New Testament, "Thou art Peter, and upon this rock I will build my church; and the gates of hell shall not prevail against it,"[11] left more questions unanswered than answered. But by the time the development of doctrine had done its work on the passage, it had come to mean, in the formula of Pope Boniface VIII, that "to every creature it is necessary for salvation to be subject to the Roman pontiff."[12] To reject this development of doctrine on the argument that it was a development and that development was in itself unacceptable made it difficult for the biblical exegesis of the Reformation and post-Reformation periods to contend with those on the left wing of the Reformation who, sharing the insistence of the "magisterial Reformers" on the sole authority of Scripture, rejected the reliance on the trinitarian doctrine of Nicaea as a necessary presupposition and method for reading biblical texts.

For having thus developed out of Scripture, the trinitarian perspective had in turn become a way—or, rather, the way—of interpreting

Scripture. As it was systematized at least for the West chiefly by Augustine, this method of biblical exegesis was cast in the form of a "canonical rule [*canonica regula*]."[13] The several passages of the Bible that appeared directly to substantiate the dogma of the Trinity, such as above all the baptismal formula at the close of the Gospel according to Matthew and the prologue about the divinity of the Logos at the opening of the Gospel according to John,[14] mutually reinforced each other to form the biblical proof for church doctrine. Conversely, however, any passages that, taken as they stood, appeared to contradict church doctrine were subject to the "canonical rule" and required careful handling. When, several chapters after the solemn prologue, "And the Word was God," the Gospel of John had Jesus say of himself, "My Father is greater than I,"[15] Augustine had to bring his heaviest weapons into action. If the Protestant Reformers and their descendants were willing to hold still for such a manipulation of New Testament passages in the interest of upholding a doctrinal development that had come only in later centuries—and they were—what stood in the way of such manipulation when the passage in question was "This is my body" or "Thou art Peter, and upon this rock I will build my church"?

Perhaps nowhere, however, was the challenge of this dilemma more dramatically unavoidable than in the relation between the development of the doctrine of Mary and its purported foundation in Scripture. For some components of that doctrine, the foundation seemed relatively straightforward. Both the Gospel of Matthew and the Gospel of Luke left it unambiguously clear that it was as a virgin that Mary had conceived her Son.[16] But further reflection did produce the puzzling discrepancy that the rest of the New Testament remained so silent on the subject, if indeed it was so unambiguous and so essential. The epistles of Paul, the other epistles of the New Testament, and the preaching of the apostles as recorded in the Book of Acts—none of these contained a hint of the virginal conception. Because Matthew and Luke did both contain it, the other two Gospels were of special interest. Mark's Gospel opened with the adult ministry of Jesus and conveyed no information about his conception, birth, and infancy. John's Gospel opened far earlier than that, "In the beginning" when there was only God and the Logos. Yet in its first chapter, just before the celebrated formula "And the Word was made flesh, and dwelt among us,"[17] it carried an intriguing textual variant that was relevant to this issue. "As many as received him," it promised, "to them gave he power to become the sons of God, even to them that believe on his name, *which were born*, not of blood, nor of the will of the flesh, nor of the will of man, but of God."[18] But in some early Latin witnesses who were not without authority on other textual questions, the plural phrase "which were born," referring to the regeneration of believers by grace, was replaced by the singular "who was born" or "who was begotten," apparently referring to the virgin birth of Christ; and according to the New Jerusalem Bible, "there are strong arguments for reading the verb in the singular, 'who was born,' in which case the v[erse] refers to Jesus' divine origin, not to the virgin birth."[19] Beyond this variant, however, is the question of the biblical support for the idea of "virgin birth" as such. For the uncontested proofs from the Gospels of Matthew and Luke asserted only, strictly speaking, the virginal conception, leaving unaddressed the question of the manner of his birth, not to mention the question of the virginity of Mary after the birth. A related question, the identity of the "brethren" of Jesus spoken of several times in the New Testament, will engage us, at least briefly, at a later point.[20] Early creeds passed over such distinctions when they simply confessed that he was "born of the Virgin Mary."[21]

To summarize the biblical materials and simultaneously to prepare the ground for the development that followed, this chapter and the next, then, will look at some of the major themes of later thought about Mary asking what the adumbrations of these were seen to have been within the text of the New and Old Testaments. This book is not the place for an extended exegesis of these texts, but only for an identification of what the subsequent tradition took to be the evidence from the Bible, including that portion of it which Christians came to call the "Old" Testament, for the themes to follow. Some of this material can be considered rather briefly; other texts and topics will require more detailed exegetical grounding. In these chapters, therefore, the themes that are woven into the titles of the remaining chapters provide, roughly in the order of their appearance, an opportunity to review some of the principal biblical texts. As epigraphs for the chapters in turn, these passages from the two testaments will be emblematic of the dominance of Scripture.

Ave Maria. "Hail Mary, full of grace: the Lord is with thee," was, according to the Vulgate, the salutation of the angel Gabriel to Mary.[22] In reaction against that translation, and against the meaning with which it had been freighted when "full of grace" was taken to mean that Mary had not only been the object and the recipient of divine grace, but, possessing that grace in its fullness, also had the right to act as its dispenser, the Authorized Version of the Bible translated the salutation to read: "Hail, thou that art highly favored." The Greek passive participle being rendered by these conflicting translations was *kecharitōmenē*, whose root, the noun *charis* and its cognates, meant "favor" in general and, particularly in the New Testament and other early Christian literature, referred to "grace," seen as the favor and unearned generosity of God.[23] In the immediate context of the account of the annunciation, it does seem to have been referring first of all to the primary initiative of God in selecting Mary as the one who was to become the mother of Jesus and thus in designating her as his chosen one. In Martin Luther's Christmas hymn "Vom Himmel hoch da komm' ich her [From heaven above to earth I come]," which was to become the leitmotiv in each successive cantata of Johann Sebastian Bach's *Christmas Oratorio* of 1734– 35, another angel was presented as saying, to the shepherds of Bethlehem and through them to all the world, "Euch ist ein Kindlein heut' geborn,/Von einer Jungfrau auserkoren [To you this day is born a Child, from an *elect Virgin*]." That was a Reformation formulation for this designation of Mary as the chosen one—"predestined one," it would not be unwarranted to say, as, among others, the Second Vatican Council would say in 1964[24]—through whom the plan of God for the salvation of the world was set into motion.

This historic interconfessional dispute over the full implications of kecharitōmenē should not obscure the far more massive role played by the opening salutation, Ave/Hail, through the centuries. It came to open the prayer that has, it seems safe to estimate, ranked second only to the Lord's Prayer in the number of times it has been spoken over those centuries in Western Christendom: "Hail Mary, full of grace, the Lord is with thee. Blessed art thou among women, and blessed is the fruit of thy womb, Jesus. Holy Mary, Mother of God, pray for us sinners, now and in the hour of our death. Amen. [*Ave Maria, gratia plena, Dominus tecum, benedicta tu in mulieribus, et benedictus fructus ventris tui, Jesus. Sancta Maria, Mater Dei, ora pro nobis peccatoribus, nunc et in hora mortis nostrae. Amen.*]"[25] Its first sentence, as punctuated here, combined two biblical salutations in the Vulgate version.[26] Its second sentence was a petition that combined the postbiblical title Theotokos with later Mariological doctrine, according to which the saints in heaven interceded for believers on earth, and a fortiori that the Mother of God, being "full of grace" and therefore the Mediatrix, was in a position to intercede for them, which they in turn had the right to request from her directly. In a striking way, therefore, the *Ave Maria* epitomized not only the irony of Mary's having become a major point of division among believers and between churches but the dichotomy between the sole authority of Scripture and the development of doctrine through tradition; for even those who affirmed the absolute supremacy of biblical authority would nevertheless refuse to pray the impeccably biblical words of its first sentence.

The Second Eve. Because the chronological sequence of the composition of the books of the New Testament does not correspond to the order in which they appear in our Bibles as a collection of canonical books, the oldest written reference to Mary (though not by name) that appeared in the New Testament was not in any of the Gospels but in Paul's Epistle to the Galatians: "When the fulness of the time was come, God sent forth his Son, *made of a woman*, made under the law, to redeem them that were under the law, that we might receive the adoption of sons."[27] Most New Testament scholars would agree that "made of a woman" did not mean or even imply "but not of a man" (although it also did not exclude the idea of the virgin birth), but rather that it was a

Semitic expression for "human being," as in the statement "Man that is born of woman is of few days, and full of trouble."[28] (For that matter, Macbeth was to discover that the prophecy of the witches, "None of woman born shall harm Macbeth," did not preclude a human father— but also that it did not include a caesarean section!)[29] Thus the phrase in Galatians was taken from early times as a way of speaking about Jesus Christ as truly human, in opposition to the widespread Christian tendency (considered in chapter 3) of supposing that the way to ensure that he be regarded as more than human was to describe him as less than human. But associated with this New Testament point was one of the devices employed by the apostle Paul to make this same point about the true humanity of Christ, which he did on the basis of a special interpretation of the Old Testament. It was expressed in the verse "As by one man's disobedience many were made sinners, so by the obedience of one shall many be made righteous."[30] From that typology of speaking about the First Adam and then about Christ as the Second Adam it was a short step, albeit a step that the New Testament did not take, to speak about Mary as the Second Eve, and thus to extrapolate from Paul's words to say as well, "As by one [woman's] disobedience many were made sinners, so by the obedience of one shall many be made righteous," through the One to whom she gave birth. I shall examine in chapter 2 how it was that because Mary, the Second Eve, was the heir of the history of Israel, the history of the First Eve could be—or, as the early Christians saw it, had to be—read as a biblical resource and a historical source for providing more information about her.

The Mother of God. Even in the Gospels as they have come down to us, the relation between Jesus and John the Baptist was a complicated one. The evangelists did divulge that the ministry of John the Baptist had caused "all men" among his contemporaries to "muse in their hearts of John, whether he were the Christ, or not."[31] Nevertheless they were at pains to explain that John himself had identified Jesus as "the Lamb of God, that taketh away the sin of the world" and that, when challenged, he explicitly subordinated his historic mission to that of Jesus—and his person to that of the one "whose shoe's latchet I am not worthy to unloose."[32] This tendency was carried over from the relation between John and Jesus to the relation between Elizabeth and Mary. For in the account of what came to be known as the visitation, not only had John the unborn "babe leaped in my womb for joy," but Elizabeth "spake out with a loud voice, and said, Blessed art thou among women, and blessed is the fruit of thy womb. And whence is this to me, that the mother of my Lord should come to me?"[33]

If this verbal exchange between Mary and her "cousin [syngenis]" Elizabeth[34] were to be interpreted as having taken place in Aramaic or even to have employed some Hebrew, the title attributed by Elizabeth to Mary, "the mother of my Lord," which was hē mētēr tou kyriou mou in Greek, could conceivably be taken as a reference to Jesus Christ as Adōnai, "my Lord," the term used as a substitute for the ineffable divine name, JHWH. That was, at any rate, how from early times Christian inter- preters had seen the standard New Testament "Christological title of majesty"[35] kyrios, whether or not the Gospels or the apostle Paul had intended any such identification. And because, in the central affirma- tion of the faith of Israel, the Shema, "Hear, O Israel: the Lord our God is one Lord," repeated by Christ in the Gospels,[36] there already was the identification between "the Lord" and "our God" as one, the assembled bishops at the Council of Ephesus in 431 did not find it difficult to move from Elizabeth's formula of Mary as "the mother of my Lord" to Cyril's formula of Mary as Theotokos.

The Blessed Virgin. The chastity of Mary, in paradoxical combination with her maternity, was one of the elements held in common by the Gospel of Luke and the Gospel of Matthew. "And in the sixth month the angel Gabriel was sent from God unto a city of Galilee, named Nazareth, to a virgin espoused to a man named Joseph, of the house of David; and the virgin's name was Mary," Maria being one of the Greek forms of the Hebrew name Miryam, sister of Moses.[37] So began, in the first chapter of Luke's Gospel, the longest sustained account of Mary in the Bible.[38] In the next chapter, in the introduction to the story of the nativity, it was said that Joseph—and, according to many early Christian interpreters, Mary as well, though this was not made explicit[39]—was "of the house and lineage of David."[40] Although with fewer details, especially about Mary herself, Matthew's version paralleled that of Luke, also referring to her as a virgin and citing as evidence the prophecy of Isaiah that "a virgin [parthenos] shall be with child, and shall bring forth a son, and they shall call his name Emmanuel."[41]

It was Luke who in his first two chapters told the story of the exchange between Gabriel and Mary (the annunciation, from which the figure of Gabriel, as depicted by Jan Van Eyck, is shown here); of the exchange between Elizabeth, mother of John the Baptist, and Mary (the visitation), including the Magnificat, "My soul doth magnify the Lord" (which in some manuscripts was ascribed to Elizabeth rather than to Mary); of the coming of the shepherds (whereas Matthew uniquely had the coming of the Magi); and of the presentation of the infant Jesus in the temple, with Simeon's Nunc Dimittis, "Lord, now lettest thou thy servant depart in peace." So dominant was Mary's perspective in the way Luke narrated the story of the birth of Jesus that some early readers were driven to inquire where these details had come from, since they did not appear in other accounts. Luke's Gospel opened with words that some church fathers took as an explanation: "Forasmuch as many have taken in hand to set forth in order a declaration of those things which are most surely believed among us, even as they delivered them unto us *which from the beginning were eyewitnesses and ministers of the word; it seemed good to me also having had perfect understanding of all things from the very first,* to write unto thee in order."[42] Because it has usually been historians who have studied the structure and content of the Gospels, these introductory words have marked Luke as the historian among the evangelists.[43] He used about himself the Greek word parēkolouthēkoti, which meant that he had done historical research, more or less as his fellow historians did now. The sources on which he drew for that research were in part written, including the "many [who] have taken in hand to set forth in order a declaration of those things which are most surely believed among us," thus apparently including writers in addition to those who have been preserved in the pages of our New Testament. But the sources explicitly included the "eyewitnesses and ministers of the word," because Luke not only did not belong to the original twelve disciples and eyewitnesses but was not even a disciple of one of these; rather, according to tradition, he was a pupil and "the beloved physician" of the apostle Paul, who was "one born out of due time" in coming last to the band of the apostles.[44] When Luke undertook his research into the very beginnings of his narrative, as reflected in the first two chapters of his Gospel, who would have been the "eyewitnesses and ministers of the word" to whom he would have turned for what we today would call the "oral history" of those early events? The telling of the story in these chapters from the perspective of the Virgin Mary seemed to suggest her as primary among these original eyewitnesses and servants of the Gospel. In addition, although Luke, being a Gentile rather than a Jew, wrote, both in the main body of his Gospel and in the Book of Acts, a Greek that came closer to Attic standards than other parts of the New Testament and that sounded somewhat less like a translation, that quality was not present in these chapters, which in some respects did seem to be a translation from a Hebrew (or Aramaic) original. These considerations led early Christian writers to characterize the opening chapters of Luke's Gospel as the memoirs of the Virgin Mary—a characterization that has not commended itself to the historical-critical study of the Gospels. There even arose a tradition that Luke was the first painter of Christian icons, and the theme of Luke painting the icon of the Virgin became standard.[45]

The Mater Dolorosa. When the Apostles' Creed and the Nicene Creed, in their summary confessions about Jesus Christ as the Son of God, moved directly from his having been born of the Virgin Mary to his having suffered under Pontius Pilate without so much as mentioning his teachings or his miracles or his apostles, they were echoing, but also carrying at least one step further, the emphasis of the Gospels on his suffering and his crucifixion. Each Gospel, after its own fashion, shifted from the individual incidents and occasional glimpses of its previous narrative to a far more detailed preoccupation with the day-by-day and even hour-by-hour unfolding of the story of Christ's passion and death. From the perspective of the later history of interpretation the differences in their accounts of the passion were well illustrated by the compilation of "the seven words from the cross."[46]

Among these seven words, John provided the one most directly relevant here: "Woman, behold thy son! Behold thy mother!"[47] Homiletically if not theologically, "Behold thy mother" could easily become the charter for entrusting to the maternal care of Mary not only "the disciple whom Jesus loved," identified by the tradition though not by present-day scholarship as John the evangelist, but all the disciples whom Jesus loved in all periods of history, therefore the entire church past and present. As Origen of Alexandria had already put it in the first third of the third century, "No one can apprehend the meaning of [the Gospel of John] except he have lain on Jesus' breast and received from Jesus Mary to be his mother also. . . . Is it not the case that everyone who is perfect lives himself no longer, but Christ lives in him; and if Christ lives in him, then it is said of him to Mary, 'Behold thy son Christ.'"[48] But this scene also stirred the Christian imagination in more poignant ways; for, like the annunciation scene at the beginning of Christ's life, it seemed to provide a window into the inner life of the Virgin. From the beginning of Christ's life there also came the prophecy that would be seen as justification for such an exploration of the subjectivity of the Virgin when, as the Mater Dolorosa, she stood at the foot of the cross: "Yea, a sword shall pierce through thy own soul also."[49]

The Model of Faith in the Word of God. When the Epistle to the Hebrews, in its roll call of the saints throughout the history of Israel, rang the changes of those "of whom the world was not worthy," it introduced each name with the formula "By faith," after introducing this roster with its own definition: "Now faith is the substance of things hoped for, the evidence of things not seen."[50] And when the Epistle to the Romans defined that "faith cometh by hearing [*akoē*], and hearing by the word of God," and opened as well as closed its total message with the identification of "faith" as "obedience [*hypakoē*],"[51] it was summarizing a connection between obedience and faith, and between faith and the word of God, that had been especially prominent in the writings of the Hebrew prophets and in the teachings of Jesus. The differences between its declaration, so central to the Protestant Reformation, "that a man is justified by faith without the deeds of the law," and the declaration of the Epistle of James that "by works a man is justified, and not by faith only,"[52] would frustrate future attempts at harmonization, especially during the Reformation. But those differences did not detract from either the fundamental importance of faith to the entire New Testament message or the centrality of the doctrine of the word of God.

The one historical figure who played a major role in each of those New Testament pericopes—Hebrews, Romans, and James—was Abraham.[53] According to all three, he was what Romans called him, "the father of all them that believe."[54] But if there were to be a "mother of all them that believe," the prime candidate would have to be Mary, just as Eve was identified in the Book of Genesis as "the mother of all living."[55] The key statement by which Mary qualified for such a title was her response to the angel Gabriel, and through the angel to the God whose messenger Gabriel was: "Be it unto me according to thy word."[56] For without invoking the word "faith" explicitly, these words put into action the identification of faith with obedience, and by describing her obedience to the word of God made of her the model of faith. Indeed, beginning with Mary and moving backward through the history of Israel, it would be possible to devise a roll call of female saints—Eve and Sarah, Esther and Ruth, and many more—of whom she was an exemplar, just as it would be possible to begin with Mary and construct a similar roster of female saints since the New Testament era. And by its emphasis on faith such a roster could commend itself even to those heirs of the Protestant Reformation who have traditionally regarded with profound suspicion any such elitism among believers.

The Woman for All Seasons. Rosters of this kind would, of course, be a part, but only a small part, of all those who through the centuries have found in the Virgin Mary an object of devotion and a model of the godly life, for they shall occupy the balance of this book. As she was represented as predicting, "For, behold, from henceforth all generations shall call me blessed."[57] This was one of relatively few passages in the New Testament that seemed to envision a long period of many generations to come, along with the prophecy of Christ that "this gospel shall be preached in the whole world."[58] The content with which those successive generations would invest the title "blessed" would vary greatly through the centuries, but the striking quality would be the success with which, in all seasons, Mary's blessedness would be seen as relevant to men and woman in an equal variety of situations. And that has truly made her the Woman for All Seasons.

Marc Chagall, *The Pregnant Woman*, 1913. Stedelijk Museum, Amsterdam.

2 The Daughter of Zion
and the Fulfillment of Prophecy

He hath holpen his servant Israel, in remembrance of his mercy,
as he spake to our fathers, to Abraham, and to his seed for ever.
—Luke 1:54–55

I n a real sense, our inquiry into the witness of the New Testament to the Virgin Mary has been begging the question—and, in light of subsequent history, begging it falsely. For with their belief in the unity of the Bible, where "the New Testament is hidden in the Old and the Old becomes visible in the New [*Novum in Vetere latet, Vetus in Novo patet*]," and with the consequent ability to toggle effortlessly from one Testament to the other and from fulfillment to prophecy and back again, biblical interpreters throughout most of Christian history have had available to them a vast body of supplementary material to make up for the embarrassing circumstance that, as quoted earlier, "the reader of the gospels is at first surprised to find so little about Mary."[1] For the reader of the four Gospels was not reading only the Gospels, nor even only the New Testament, for information about Mary. Indeed, before there were the four Gospels, much less the entire New Testament, there was a Scripture, which Christians eventually came to call "Old Testament" and which, because of the centrality of typology and allegory, and because of the concept of prophecy and fulfillment, we are obliged to call a "Christian

Scripture."[2] The authors of the volume cited earlier, *Mary in the New Testament*, could content themselves with the reminder that "in some Roman Catholic mariology, there is a study of how Mary's role was foreshadowed in certain OT [Old Testament] passages, on the principle that, just as God prepared the way for His Son in the history of Israel, so too He prepared the way for the mother of His Son."[3] As the history of the development of biblical interpretation in the early church makes evident, moreover, it was not only, as this comment suggests, "some Roman Catholic mariology" but the entire patristic tradition East and West, that carried on such study of the foreshadowing of Mary in the Old Testament. Many of the rubrics considered in chapter 1 about the witness of the New Testament could just as easily find a place here; and as in that chapter, the attention required by the biblical material varies widely.

For our purposes, therefore, the evidence of the Bible is important not because of its contrast with subsequent tradition but precisely because of its anticipation of that tradition. Or, to put it the other way around and more accurately, the biblical evidence is interesting in the light of the way the subsequent tradition used it—or, as some might say, misused it. The rationale for the distinctive characteristic of this biblical evidence is to be found in the phrase from the Christmas Gospel, "of the house and lineage of David."[4] As it stood in the Gospel, this referred to Joseph, not to Mary, whose lineage was not traced in the genealogies provided by the Gospels of Matthew and Luke.[5] But it was also those same two Gospels that made a point of the virginal conception of Jesus and therefore of the conclusion that Joseph was only "supposed"[6] by some— but clearly not by the evangelists—to have been the father of Jesus. If "son of David" was in the language of the Gospels a way of affirming the continuity of Jesus Christ with Israel and the continuity of his kingship with that of his celebrated forefather, then his descent from David had to be through his only human parent, Mary, who must then also have been "of the house and lineage of David." That reasoning has provided the justification for the practice of going far beyond and behind the New Testament, by searching through the ancient Scriptures of Israel for prophecies and parallels, topics and typologies, that would enrich and amplify the tiny sheaf of data from the Gospels: Miriam, sister of Moses, of course, because of her name, but also Mother Eve; and then all the female personifications, above all in the writings carrying the name of King Solomon, particularly the figure of Wisdom in the eighth chapter of the Book of Proverbs and, among the books called Apocryphal or Deuterocanonical, in the Wisdom of Solomon (the name *Wisdom* being feminine, as is *Chokmah* in Hebrew, *Sophia* in Greek, *Sapientia* in Latin, and *Premudrost* in Russian) and the Bride in the Song of Songs, which was the longest and the most lavish portrait of a woman anywhere in the Bible. The process of appropriating this material for the purposes of Marian devotion and doctrine, which may be described as a methodology of amplification, was, on one hand, part of the much larger process of allegorical and figurative interpretation of the Bible, to which we owe some of the most imaginative and beautiful commentaries, in words and in pictures, in all of Medieval and Byzantine culture. It was, on the other hand, and almost against the intention of those who practiced it, a powerful affirmation that because Mary was, according to the reasoning summarized earlier, "of the house and lineage of David," she represented the unbreakable link between Jewish and Christian history, between the First Covenant within which she was born and the Second Covenant to which she gave birth, so that even the most virulent of Christian anti-Semites could not deny that she, the most blessed among women, was a Jew. Without explicit connection to the Virgin Mary, Marc Chagall's portrait of a pregnant woman exalted to heaven cannot help but convey this reminder.

The Black Madonna. One of the most impressive results of the Mariological interpretation of the Old Testament being discussed in this chapter was the application of the lush imagery of the Song of Songs to Mary. "*Nigra sum sed formosa* [I am black but comely]" were almost the first words of the Bride in the Song.[7] From those words came the biblical justification for the many portraits of Mary that have shunned the conventional representation of her as Italian or North European in favor of the Black Madonna. As it stood, the statement seemed to bespeak an all too widespread sense of contradiction between blackness and comeliness. But in his definitive commentary on the Song of Songs, Marvin Pope has convincingly shown on linguistic grounds that "Black am I *and* beautiful," not "but beautiful," is the correct translation of the Hebrew of this verse, which has also been preserved in the Greek of the Septuagint: *Melaina eimi kai kalē.* The grammatical conjunction was, of course, less important than the substantive connection. If, as I am presupposing throughout this book, the history of the interpretation of the Bible has not been confined to commentaries and sermons but has been the subject of the arts and of daily life, the Black Madonnas of Częstochowa and Guadalupe ("La Morenita—Little Darkling")[8] have expressed for countless millions, more eloquently than books could have, the exegetical intuition that, regardless of the translation, the Virgin was indeed black *and* beautiful. That also made her a special ambassador to that vast majority of the human race who were not white.

The Woman of Valor. I have already mentioned that the early Christians searched in the Jewish Scriptures, and specifically in the early chapters of Genesis, for prophecies that were fulfilled in the gospel. The most notable—notable enough to have eventually earned the name of first gospel or protevangel—was the promise of God after the fall of Adam and Eve. It was addressed to the serpent (taken by common consent to be the devil): "And I will put enmity between thee and the woman, and between thy seed and her seed; it shall bruise thy head, and thou shalt bruise his heel."[9] Irenaeus of Lyons, writing in the second half of the second century, expounded this text at great length to prove that Jesus was the seed of the woman and the Son of God, who as the Second Adam had withstood the assault of the tempter, conquering where the First Adam had been conquered, and who on the cross had been "bruised" by the serpent but had crushed him in the process.[10] On the basis of the best manuscripts it is the general agreement of modern students of the Vulgate text that Jerome, who was one of the few scholars in the first several centuries of Christian history to know Hebrew as well as Greek and Latin, translated this in the same sense as the King James Version just quoted (as it appears in the best critical edition of the Vulgate, published in 1986): "*Inimicitias ponam inter te et mulierem, et semen tuum et semen illius; ipsum conteret* caput tuum, et tu conteres calcaneum eius." But at some point in the transmission of the Latin text of the Vulgate, whether by mistake or by fraud or by pious reflection, that neuter "ipsum" corresponding to the neuter of "semen [seed]" was changed to a feminine: "Inimicitias ponam inter te et mulierem, et semen tuum et semen illius; ipsa conteret caput tuum, et tu insidiaberis calcaneo eius."[11] In poems and works of art throughout the Latin West, this translation inspired images of the humble Virgin triumphing over the proud tempter.[12]

And, in keeping with the appropriation of Old Testament language in the interest of amplifying the New Testament, she came to be seen as the divinely given answer to the question of the final chapter of the Book of Proverbs, which the Authorized Version rendered with "Who can find a virtuous woman?": "Mulierem fortem quis inveniet? [The woman of valor, who will find?]"[13] Mary as the Mulier Fortis was an extension and expansion of Mary as the Second Eve, who had entered the lists of battle as the First Eve had done but who, being fortis, had defeated the devil, conquering the conqueror. By extension, therefore, she could become the patron of victory. Her blessing was invoked by armies going into battle, particularly against those who were perceived to be the enemies of the faith, such as the Muslims. Her images were carried on banners and on the person of the warrior. As Tolstoy had Princess Marya Bolkonskaya in War and Peace (a character modeled after his mother) say at the end of a letter to her friend Julie, lamenting "this unfortunate war into which we have been drawn, God knows how and why": "Farewell, dear, good friend. May our divine Savior and His most Holy Mother keep you in their holy and almighty care. Marya."[14] And "our divine Savior and His most Holy Mother" were able also to keep soldiers in their holy and almighty care during battle, because Christ as Christus Victor and his Mother as Mulier Fortis could be not only gentle and humble but fierce and victorious. This was, once again, a picture of Mary that was, on the basis of this method of biblical interpretation, more evident in the Old Testament than in the New but that then could on that basis be found in the New Testament as well. It could also provide women of the Middle Ages with some sense of what they might be—and of what, by the election of God, they could be. For the most sensational Medieval answer to the question of Proverbs about the Woman of Valor was Joan of Arc.

The Leader of the Heavenly Choir. In spite of the use of Eve and of various female figures from the Solomonic writings, in many respects the most obvious prototype of Mary anywhere in the Old Testament had to be Miriam, sister of Moses and Aaron, for whom the Virgin was almost certainly named. The Hebrew name *Miryam* for the sister of Moses was rendered into Greek in several slightly divergent forms: *Maria, Mareia, Mariam, Mariamē*.[15] Both the form *Maria* and the form *Mariam* appeared in the Gospels, with the first being employed initially by Matthew and the second being employed initially by Luke. Except for the name itself, however, it would seem to be vain to look within the pages of the New Testament for any typology involving the mother of Jesus and the sister of Moses. But once it had become legitimate, indeed imperative, for Christian interpreters to invoke what we have been calling here the methodology of amplification, an imaginative interpreter of the Bible such as Augustine was drawn to the text from the history of the victory of the children of Israel over the armies of Pharaoh at the Red Sea, as described in the Book of Exodus: "And Miriam the prophetess, the sister of Aaron, took a timbrel in her hand; and all the women went out after her with timbrels and with dances. And Miriam answered them, Sing ye to the Lord, for he hath triumphed gloriously; the horse and his rider hath he thrown into the sea."[16] The powerful impact of that scene was heightened still further, in a stroke of musical and dramatic genius, by George Frideric Handel in his *Israel in Egypt*, when he switched the order of these verses 20 and 21 in the fifteenth chapter of Exodus with verse 1 in such a way that Miriam became the *choregos*, like the leader of the chorus in Aeschylus or Sophocles. But Marian devotion had, in effect, done just that long before, by applying the implications of the title Daughter of Zion to the typology of Mary and Miriam.

Ever-Virgin [Semper Virgo]. Although neither the writings of the apostle Paul nor the earliest Gospel, that of Mark, contained any reference to the virgin birth, that same biblical resource and historical source of Jewish Scripture did; or at any rate, it did in the Greek translation of it that had been prepared by the Jews of Alexandria during the century or two before the rise of Christianity, the Septuagint. From that source it came to the Gospels of Matthew and Luke, with Matthew quoting as authority the Greek translation of the prophecy of Isaiah: "Therefore the Lord himself shall give you a sign; Behold, a virgin [*parthenos* in the Septuagint] shall conceive, and bear a son, and shall call his name Immanuel."[17] The Greek *parthenos* was the translation of a Hebrew word that meant "young woman," not specifically "virgin," and the word was so quoted in the Greek New Testament. Mary asked the angel of the annunciation: "How shall this be, seeing that I know not a man?"[18] Three of the Gospels—Matthew, Mark, and John, but not Luke—did speak in later chapters about "brethren" of Christ,[19] as did the apostle Paul.[20] The apparently obvious and natural conclusion from this would seem to have been that after the miraculous conception of Jesus by the power of the Holy Spirit, Mary and Joseph went on to have other children of their own.

But that was not the conclusion that the vast majority of early Christian teachers drew. Instead, they came to call Mary Ever-Virgin, *Aeiparthenos, Semper Virgo*. To do this in the light of biblical materials about the "brethren" of Jesus, they had to resort to some elaborate biblical arguments. The biblical support for calling Mary Ever-Virgin, however, came not chiefly from the New Testament but from the Song of Songs: "A garden inclosed is my sister, my spouse; a spring shut up, a fountain sealed [*Hortus conclusus, soror mea sponsa, hortus conclusus, fons signatus*]."[21] Thus Jerome, after stringing together a series of texts from the Song of Songs, came to this verse, which he took to be a reference to "the mother of our Lord, who was a mother and a Virgin. Hence it was that no one before or after our Savior was lain in his new tomb, hewn in the solid rock."[22] An interesting process of creative biblical interpretation was going on here. For according to the Gospels at the other end of the story of the earthly life of Jesus Christ, the grave of Jesus was "a new sepulchre," belonging to Joseph of Arimathea, where no one had ever been buried before.[23] The Gospels said nothing about the later history of the sepulcher, after the resurrection of Jesus, just as they said nothing about the later history of the womb of Mary. But on the strength of the "*hortus conclusus*" of the Song of Songs, Jerome, who was arguably the greatest biblical scholar in the history of the Western Church, felt justified in concluding both that there would never be another person buried in the sepulcher and that there was never another person born of the Virgin. It is amusing, though not important, to note that in both cases the auxiliary role in the story belonged to a man bearing the name of Joseph.

The Face That Most Resembles Christ's. In the language of the Old Testament, "face" became almost a technical term for "person." This usage had appeared already in the story of creation, where, according to the Greek translation, "God formed the man of dust of the earth, and breathed upon his face [*prosōpon*] the breath of life, and the man became a living soul."[24] Throughout biblical language, and beyond it even in modern languages, "face to face" was a way of saying "person to person."[25] The benediction that Aaron was instructed to pronounce upon the people of Israel applied the concept to God: "The Lord bless thee, and keep thee: The Lord make his face shine upon thee, and be gracious unto thee: The Lord lift up his countenance upon thee, and give thee peace."[26] For the God of Israel, unlike the idols of the heathen, had neither form nor face to "shine upon" anyone, and the anthropomorphic ascription of a "face" to God could refer only to the special relation cemented in the covenant. When the New Testament sought to affirm the continuity of that covenant but at the same time its extension beyond the borders of the people of Israel, it spoke of how "the God who commanded the light to shine out of darkness, hath shined in our hearts, to give the light of the knowledge of the glory of God in the face of Jesus Christ."[27] The face of Jesus Christ, therefore, was seen as the divinely given answer to the prayer of the psalm "When thou saidst, See ye my face; my heart said unto thee, Thy face, Lord, will I seek."[28] And so it seemed to be a valid extension of this concept, and an application to it of the identification of Mary as Mediatrix, for Bernard of Clairvaux and then Dante Alighieri to speak about the face of the Virgin Mary as the one through which to view the face of Jesus Christ, through which in turn the face of God was visible.

Visions of the Virgin Mary. It was from the prominence of visions in the religious experiences and personal revelations described in the Old Testament that the biblical warrant for the apparitions of the Virgin Mary in ancient and modern times came. By visions and revelations of the Almighty, Abraham received the promise as well as the awesome command to sacrifice his son Isaac—and then the command "Lay not thine hand upon the lad."[29] The vision of the "bush that burned with fire, and was not consumed" provided the setting for the "towering text"[30] of God's self-disclosure as "I am that I am."[31] Similarly, "in the day that king Uzziah died," as the prophet Isaiah had reported, "I saw the Lord sitting upon a throne, high and lifted up."[32] Other prophets of Israel, too, had been the recipients of such visions at their inauguration into office or later in their prophetic careers.[33] For Ezekiel and Daniel, the reception of visions and the communication of their content to the people or their rulers had become the central and defining quality of their prophetic apocalypticism.[34] All that might have been expected to end with the New Testament; for it emphasized the uniqueness and finality of the revelation in Jesus Christ, as a result of which the stock prophetic formula "And the word of the Lord came" to the prophet, still used for John the Baptist, was no longer appropriate, because the Word of the Lord had come in the flesh, and "all the prophets and the law prophesied until John."[35] Nevertheless, and perhaps somewhat surprisingly, the visions that had begun in the Old Testament did not cease in the New. In fact, the apostle Peter was described in the Book of Acts as having appropriated the prophecy of Joel, "And it shall come to pass in the last days, saith God, I will pour out my Spirit on all flesh: and your sons and your daughters shall prophesy, and your young men shall see visions, and your old men shall dream dreams," as being fulfilled now in his generation.[36] In the same book of the New Testament, Peter required a heavenly vision of unclean and forbidden foods to cure him of his subservience to kosher laws.[37] His apostolic colleague and sometime adversary, Paul, received a vision of Jesus Christ on the road to Damascus that threw him to the ground, blinded him, and converted him to the "way" of the Christians whom he had been persecuting, a vision that was followed by others; and, as he said, he "was not disobedient unto the heavenly vision."[38]

Jesus Christ himself had such heavenly visions, according to the

Gospels, for he "beheld Satan as lightning fall from heaven."[39] During his agony in the Garden of Gethsemane, "there appeared an angel unto him from heaven, strengthening him" for the passion and death he was about to undergo.[40] More directly relevant to our concerns here are the visions attendant upon the birth of Jesus Christ from the Virgin Mary. The most important of these was the annunciation, but the others are also of great interest. It was by a vision in a dream that Joseph was dissuaded from "putting her away privily" when he discovered that Mary was pregnant with the child Jesus, by another vision that he was warned of the plot of Herod against the threat of the child who was "born king of the Jews" so that he took the child and Mary his mother to Egypt, and by yet another vision that he was told when it was safe to return with Jesus and Mary from Egypt to Nazareth.[41]

But by far the most abundant collection of visions anywhere in the New Testament appeared in the book that now stands last in the canon, and that has often been regarded in the subsequent tradition, whether accurately or inaccurately is not important here, as the last to have been written: the Book of Revelation, the Apocalypse of Saint John the Divine, attributed to the evangelist John. By the time the panorama of its visions had closed, the seer of the Apocalypse had viewed not only "one like unto the Son of Man,"[42] but angels and beasts and heavenly cities, all marching in dramatic procession across the screen of his frenzied and ecstatic sight. At about the halfway point of the visions came the following: "And there appeared a great wonder in heaven; a woman clothed with the sun, and the moon under her feet, and upon her head a crown of twelve stars."[43] Whether or not this was originally intended as a reference to the Virgin Mary, it comported so well with the developing ways of speaking and thinking about her that in the early Middle Ages, from the seventh to the ninth century in both East and West, it became clear that this "symbol of the woman who is the mother of the Messiah might well lend itself to Marian interpretation, once Marian interest developed in the later Christian community. And eventually when Revelation was placed in the same canon of Scripture with the Gospel of Luke and the Fourth Gospel, the various images of the virgin, the woman at the cross, and the woman who gave birth to the Messiah would reinforce each other."[44] It is worth remembering that some centuries later, by a somewhat similar process, some descendants of the Protestant Reformation had no compunction about identifying the "angel having the everlasting gospel" in the Book of Revelation with the person and ministry of Martin Luther.[45]

The Immaculate Conception. The intricate connection between the interpretation of the Bible and the development of doctrine, as briefly identified in the preceding chapter, has worked in both directions simultaneously, no less for Mariology than for other branches of theology. A doctrine about her would take a particular form because, in addition to the devotion to her and the speculation concerning her that were such fertile gardens for the growth of doctrine, some passage of Scripture from either the Old or the New Testament required consideration for its bearing on Marian teaching. Conversely, the growth of Marian teaching out of these various sources made it necessary to bring the exegesis of one or another passage, as that exegesis may originally have evolved independently of such teaching, into harmony with what Mary had come to mean. For in the Middle Ages, particularly after Peter Abelard's *Sic et Non* [*Yes and No*] had called attention to seeming contradictions in the tradition, the harmonization of biblical or other authoritative texts became one of the most important assignments of scholastic theology.[46] As it was anticipated by Cyprian of Carthage and then formulated by Ambrose of Milan and Augustine of Hippo, the standard Western interpretation of the words of David in the psalm "Behold, I was shapen in iniquity; and in sin did my mother conceive me,"[47] had generalized the statement from David to apply it to all humanity. But that interpretation appeared to collide with the increasingly transcendent valuation that was being placed on the unique holiness of the Virgin Mary. It was out of the need to harmonize these two imperatives that the doctrine of the immaculate conception finally emerged in Roman Catholicism.

The Assumption of the Mater Gloriosa. Of all the major privileges and attributes attaching to the person of Mary, none would seem to be more extraneous to the biblical account of her in the New Testament than the assumption, which was promulgated as a dogma of the church, binding on all believers, by Pope Pius XII on 1 November 1950, in the bull *Munificentissimus Deus*. But that depended on how one went about establishing biblical warrant. For the status of Mary as daughter of Zion and heir of the people of Israel meant that for her, just as for her divine Son, it was permissible and even mandatory to ransack the pages of the Old Testament for additional information about her. After the resurrection, Christ had appeared to the disciples at Emmaus, and "beginning at Moses and all the prophets, he expounded unto them in all the scriptures the things concerning himself,"[48] by a process that was taken to apply legitimately also to Mary. Thus the absence of New Testament information about what happened "when the course of her earthly life was run" was not a sufficient deterrent. Therefore the saying of the prophet Isaiah that the apostle Paul applied to the death and resurrection of Christ, "Death is swallowed up in victory,"[49] could in *Munificentissimus Deus* be extended to her. Part of what is being called here the methodology of amplification was based on the premise that because of her unique and supreme position among all humanity, as not only the highest of all women and the highest of all human beings but the highest of all creatures, "higher than the cherubim, more glorious than the seraphim," Mary came to be regarded as not unworthy of any of the honors and privileges that had, according to the Scriptures of both the Old and the New Testament, been conferred on others.

In addition, as the Byzantine descriptions of her dormition made clear,[50] two saints' lives of the Old Testament could, by following the methodology of amplification, be taken to supply additional data about how, when the course of an earthly life was run, someone could be and had been "assumed in *body and soul* to heavenly glory." They were the brief and enigmatic episode of Enoch in Genesis, and the dramatic episode of Elijah in 2 Kings: "And Enoch walked with God: and he was not; for God took him"; "And it came to pass . . . that, behold, there appeared a chariot of fire, and horses of fire, and parted them both asunder; and Elijah went up by a whirlwind into heaven. And Elisha saw it, and he cried, My father, my father, the chariot of Israel, and the horsemen thereof. And he saw him no more."[51] Jewish scholarship and devotion had seized upon both of these and amplified them. In apocryphal and apocalyptic literature Enoch's later destiny became a topic for speculation.[52] The figure of Elijah likewise became the subject of lore and legend.[53] At the Seder meal for Passover an empty place is still set for Elijah; and according to the New Testament, Elijah appeared with Moses at the transfiguration of Jesus.[54]

Now if these two men of God already in the Old Testament were deemed worthy of the special privilege of being taken up into heaven, with a chariot of fire and horses of fire, did not that constitute a form of biblical evidence also about Mary, who, by an a fortiori argument, could be seen as having been eminently more worthy of such special treatment? For if this way to heaven had already, in at least these two cases, been opened up for mere mortals, was one to say that the very Mother of God was less deserving of it than they had been? The story of Mary and Martha, the sisters of Lazarus, which would eventually serve as the Gospel pericope for the Feast of the Assumption, closed with the words, "Mary hath chosen that good part, which shall not be taken away from her"; this referred, of course, to the sister of Martha and Lazarus, but it seemed to many to fit the mother of Jesus even better.[55] By a similar transposition of reference, an Old Testament text such as "When he ascended up on high, he led captivity captive, and gave gifts unto men," which had been applied to the ascension of Christ, also seemed to suit the assumption of Mary, through which gifts had been distributed to humanity.[56] Or when Christ promised, "If any man serve me, let him follow me; and where I am, there shall also my servant be," there was no "man," indeed, no one among mortals, who had served him in so special a way as Mary had; and therefore, in accordance with his promise to her before his ascension, she had also followed him into heaven.[57]

This celebration of the Virgin Mary and the elaboration of such praises in her name coincided chronologically with the heyday of this method of allegorical and typological biblical interpretation. Conversely, the rejection of both the Marian celebration and the allegory came together, first in the Reformation and then in the Enlightenment and its aftermath. Looking back at both developments, in the Middle Ages and in the Reformation and Enlightenment, it is difficult to avoid the tough questions of loss and gain. For the allegorical and typological method had saved the Hebrew Bible from its enemies and detractors in the early Christian movement, who read it literally and rejected it. They were also often the ones who opposed the direction in which the interpretation of the Virgin Mary was moving. The vindication of the Jewish Scriptures as part of the Christian Bible coincided not only chronologically but logically with this picture of Mary. Vastly different though they seemed to be in their approach to the Bible, therefore, a fundamentalist literalism and a modernist historicism both yielded a two-dimensional perspective in the reading of the Bible. At the same time they also led to an impoverishment in the attitude toward Mary. Whether these went together is an intriguing historical question, which we can only begin to answer through the study of art, literature, and thought in subsequent chapters. In what follows, these and other Old Testament texts and this methodology of amplification will figure prominently as the depository from which the development of doctrine and devotion would take the language it needed to speak about Mary.

Toni Zenz, door for Saint Alban's Church, Cologne, 1958. (Bildquelle: Rheinisches Bildarchiv Köln)

3 The Second Eve and the Guarantee of Christ's True Humanity

As by one man's disobedience many were made sinners,
so by the obedience of one shall many be made righteous.
—Romans 5:19

In the second and third centuries after Christ, during the momentous age of cultural transition and spiritual-intellectual upheaval that historians call Late Antiquity, which falls somewhere between the Hellenistic age and the Byzantine and Medieval periods, the parallel between Mary and Eve was a primary focus for the consideration of two major issues of life and thought that continue to be perennial concerns in our era: the meaning (if any) of time and human history and the very definition of what it means to be human.[1]

A central contribution of the faith of Israel to the development of Western thought has been the interpretation of history. This is not to say that the question of the meaning of human history was absent from other cultures, for example from classical Greece. It was especially in the thought of Plato that this question received detailed attention. Book IV of Plato's *Laws* contains a profound analysis of the relative power of the several forces in history: "That God governs all things, and that chance [*tychē*] and opportunity [*kairos*] co-operate with Him in the governance of human affairs. There is, however, a third and less extreme view, that art [*technē*] should be there also."[2] Serious reflection on the interrelation of those three forces, as Constantine Despotopoulos has pointed out, could become the foundation for a far-ranging philosophy of history.[3] It is also the case that the historians of ancient Athens—above all Thucydides in the Funeral Oration of Pericles, but also Herodotus—carried on serious reflection of this kind as they pondered Greek history.[4]

Nevertheless, the coming of the faith of Israel and of the Hebrew Bible into the Greco-Roman world, which took place first through its translation into Greek at Alexandria by Hellenistic Jews and then more massively and more decisively through the mission and expansion of Christianity across the entire Mediterranean world, challenged and eventually transformed the prevailing views of the nature and purpose of the historical process. To go on saying with Plato's *Laws* "that God governs all things" came to mean something radically different when the historical "opportunity," or *kairos*, at issue was the exodus of the children of Israel from Egypt and the giving of the law to Moses at Sinai, or the life, death, and resurrection of Jesus Christ. For in one sense, the belief that "God governs all things" was, if anything, intensified when the word "God" was taken to refer neither to the gods of Mount Olympus nor to the One of Platonic philosophy but to the God of Abraham, Isaac, and Jacob, or to Father, Son, and Holy Spirit. In spite of their profound and fundamentally irreconcilable differences, Judaism and Christianity both viewed human history as a process in which divine governance was a matter of divine initiative. Moses did not use his own ingenuity to discover God while tending Jethro's flocks on the plains of Midian; rather, it was God who chose him, sought him out, called to him from the burning bush, and imposed on him the task of telling Pharaoh "Let my people go!"[5] Similarly, the New Testament was not the account of how the upward tendency of human history had finally attained to the level of the divine, as though human flesh had become the Word of God; on the contrary, "In the beginning was the Word, and the Word was with God, and the Word was God. And the Word was made flesh, and dwelt among us."[6] In a radical and transforming sense, then, history was viewed *from above*, as the record of the actions of the living God. As the New Testament put it,

"Every good gift and every perfect gift is from above, and cometh down from the Father of lights, with whom is no variableness, neither shadow of turning."[7]

But that is only half the story, for at the same time the Jewish and Christian traditions viewed that same history also from below, as the record of authentically human actions for which human beings with free will were to be held morally accountable. Amid the historical changes and upheavals of the Mediterranean world during the second and third century, the sensitive spirits of Late Antiquity were pondering whether there was a discernible meaning in human history. One of the noblest of these sensitive spirits, Marcus Aurelius, who died in the year 180, put that question of the age this way in Book XII of his *Meditations*, writing not in Latin (though he was emperor of Rome) but in Greek: "There is a doom inexorable and a law inviolable, or there is a providence that can be merciful, or else there is a chaos that is purposeless and ungoverned. If a resistless fate, why try to struggle against it? If a providence willing to show mercy, do your best to deserve its divine succour. If a chaos undirected, give thanks that amid such stormy seas you have within you a mind at the helm."[8] To the consideration of those three alternatives, as outlined by the philosopher-emperor Marcus Aurelius, Judaism, and then Christianity, brought a view of history as an arena in which both "a providence that can be merciful" and a human activity that can be responsible were at work, so that neither could be thought of apart from the other. That was the deepest meaning of the Hebrew word *berith*, covenant, in which both parties engaged to do certain things, even if one of them was the Creator of heaven and earth and the other was a human creature; and for the Christian version of this authentically human side of the historical dialectic, Eve and Mary were key players.[9]

There does seem to have been a practice in early Christianity of reading the first three chapters of Genesis as anticipating the coming of Christ. Therefore they may have cast the story of the temptation of Christ by the devil as a kind of midrash on the story of the temptation of Adam and Eve. The tempter said to Eve: "In the day ye eat thereof . . . ye shall be as gods."[10] And the tempter said to Christ, who "had fasted forty days and forty nights [and] was afterward an hungered": "If thou be the son of God, command that these stones be made bread."[11] In the Epistle to the Romans, the apostle Paul had drawn the parallel: "As by one man [namely, Adam] sin entered into the world, and death by sin. . . . much more the grace of God, and the gift by grace, which is by one man, Jesus Christ, hath abounded unto many."[12] In 1 Corinthians he developed the parallel and the contrast in greater detail: "And so it is written, The first man Adam was made a living soul; the last Adam was made a quickening spirit. . . . The first man is of the earth, earthy: the second man is the Lord from heaven."[13] But for the category of history from below, as the record of authentically human actions for which human beings were to be held accountable, that contrasting parallel between the First Adam as "of the earth, earthy" and the Second Adam, Christ as "the Lord from heaven," which has had such an important career in the history of ideas, also raised serious problems, to some of which we shall return in the second half of this chapter.

For many of those problems the contrasting parallel between Eve and Mary provided profound insight and an important corrective. Thus Irenaeus, bishop of Lyons, who was born probably in Asia Minor about A.D. 130 and who died about A.D. 200, strikingly formulated this parallel in both of his surviving writings: in a passage from his treatise *Against Heresies* (written in Greek but preserved largely in a Latin translation), but also in a work that was long thought to have been permanently lost but that was discovered only in this century, and in an Armenian translation, the *Epideixis*, or *Proof of the Apostolic Preaching*. Playing off against each other various elements in Genesis and in the Gospels, such as the Garden of Eden versus the Garden of Gethsemane and the tree of the knowledge of good and evil versus the tree of the cross, Irenaeus then came to the most innovative and most breathtaking of the parallels:

And just as it was through a virgin who disobeyed [namely, Eve] that mankind was stricken and fell and died, so too it was through the Virgin [Mary], who obeyed the word of God, that mankind, resuscitated by life, received life. For the Lord

[Christ] came to seek back the lost sheep, and it was mankind that was lost; and therefore He did not become some other formation, but He likewise, of her that was descended from Adam [namely, Mary], preserved the likeness of formation; for Adam had necessarily to be restored in Christ, that mortality be absorbed in immortality. *And Eve [had necessarily to be restored] in Mary, that a virgin, by becoming the advocate of a virgin, should undo and destroy virginal disobedience by virginal obedience.*[14]

Here was not only a parallel between the First Adam as "of the earth, earthy" and the Second Adam, Christ as "the Lord from heaven"—thus a contrast between the earthly and the heavenly—but a contrast between a calamitous disobedience by someone who was no more than human, Eve, and a saving obedience by someone who was no more than human, who was not "from heaven" but altogether "of the earth," Mary as the Second Eve. It was absolutely essential to the integrity of the two narratives that both the disobedience of Eve and the obedience of Mary be seen as actions of a free will, not as the consequences of coercion, whether by the devil in the case of Eve or by God in the case of Mary.

When it is suggested that for the development of the doctrine of Mary, such Christian writers as Irenaeus in a passage like this "are important witnesses for the state of the tradition in the late second century, *if not earlier*,"[15] that raises the interesting question of whether Irenaeus had invented the concept of Mary as the Second Eve here or was drawing on a deposit of tradition that had come to him from "earlier." It is difficult, in reading his *Against Heresies* and especially his *Proof of the Apostolic Preaching*, to avoid the impression that he cited the parallelism of Eve and Mary so matter-of-factly without arguing or having to defend the point because he could assume that his readers would willingly go along with it, or even that they were already familiar with it. One reason that this could be so might have been that, on this issue as on so many others, Irenaeus regarded himself as the guardian and the transmitter of a body of belief that had come to him from earlier generations, from the very apostles.[16] A modern reader does need to consider the possibility, perhaps even to concede the possibility, that in so regarding himself Irenaeus may just have been right and that therefore it may already have become natural in the second half of the second century to look at Eve, the "mother of all living,"[17] and Mary, the mother of Christ, together, understanding and interpreting each of the two most important women in human history on the basis of the other. With such moderns in mind, the parallelism was dramatically set forth by the German sculptor Toni Zenz in a metal door created in 1958 for the rebuilding of the Church of Sankt Alban in Cologne, which had been destroyed during World War II: in the lower left are Adam and Eve at the moment of the fall, in the upper right the Second Adam and the Second Eve at the moment of the crucifixion and redemption.

Once it was introduced into the vocabulary, this dialectic of Eve and Mary took on a life of its own. Because in Latin the name *Eva* spelled backwards became *Ave*, the greeting of the angel to Mary in the Vulgate as it was echoed by millions of souls in the prayer *Ave Maria*, there appeared to be a mystical Mariological significance in the very name. Less playfully and more profoundly, the elaborations upon the disobedience of Eve and the obedience of Mary produced extensive psychological comparisons between the two women. In those comparisons the negative interpretation of woman as embodied in Eve—vulnerable, irrational, emotional, erotic, living by the experience of the senses rather than by the mind and the reason, and thus an easy prey for the wily tempter—propagated the all-too-familiar stereotypes of misogynous slander that have so embedded themselves in the thought and language of so many nations, also but not only in the West. Modern polemical writers have combed the works of patristic and Medieval thinkers to find these stereotypes, and they have amassed a massive catalog that has by now passed from one book and article to another. It is not intended as a defense of the stereotypes, but it is intended as a necessary historical corrective, to point out that those same works of patristic and Medieval thinkers presented a counterpoise to the stereotypes, in their even more extensive interpretations of woman as embodied in Mary, the "Woman of Valor [*mulier fortis*]" who as the descendant and vindicator of the First Eve crushed the head of the serpent and vanquished the devil.[18] Historical justice requires that both poles of the dialectic be included. When, in *Paradise Lost*, John Milton, who was "an author unmistakably opposed to Catholicism and its veneration of Mary,"[19] nevertheless described how, in greeting Eve,

> . . . the Angel *Haile*
> Bestowed, the holy salutation us'd
> Long after to blest Marie, second Eve,[20]

he was quoting the angelic salutation "Ave Maria" and with it invoking the ancient parallel that is the theme of this chapter. But he did so, as a Puritan and Protestant, in a literary and theological context where the counterpoise of the Catholic portrait of Mary had largely been lost. Therefore Milton could have Adam, speaking after the fall, address an *Ave Maria* to the Virgin Mary in language that was clearly intended to make not only Eve but Mary know her proper place in the scheme of human history:

> . . . Virgin Mother, Haile,
> High in the love of Heav'n, yet from my Loines
> Thou shall proceed . . . .[21]

Milton's postmortem diagnosis of the psychology of the fall of Eve, step by painful step, is rightly celebrated as a flawed but brilliant character study. But when that autopsy of temptation is seen in the setting of the history of patristic and Medieval thought about the First and the Second Eve that had led up to Milton, it becomes clear that *Paradise Lost* emphasized one pole of the dialectic far more than the other. And the same has been true of many and lesser writers since Milton.

Returning to the categories of Marcus Aurelius and of Irenaeus (who were nearly contemporaries in the second century), the central theme of the thought of Irenaeus was, in the phrase of Marcus Aurelius, "a providence that can be merciful" and that had already proved itself to be merciful by bringing about a "recapitulation [*anakephalaiōsis*]" of human history, in which each successive stage of human sin had been restored by the successive stages of God's saving activity in Christ.[22] But the Stoic image of this "providence that can be merciful" often seemed to carry with it overtones of deterministic necessity, *anankē heimarmenē*, and to make free will problematical. That sort of deterministic necessity was by no means incompatible with profound insight into human motivation and psychology, as was evident not only from Marcus Aurelius but above all from Tolstoy.[23] In his famous second epilogue to *War and Peace*, Tolstoy attacked modern philosophies of history because of their lingering attachment to an untenable view of free will, concluding with the well-known axiom: "It is necessary to renounce a freedom that does not exist, and to recognize a dependence [that is, a determinism] of which we are not conscious."[24]

The theme of Mary as Second Eve likewise represented a critique of, and an alternative to, another view widely held in Antiquity and Late Antiquity: the cyclical theory of history, for which, as in the philosopher Porphyry, the metaphor of the wheel was the key. It was, in the formula of Charles N. Cochrane, a student of Herodotus, a "belief in the endless reiteration of 'typical' situations," to which, as for example in Augustine's *City of God*, the response was "the faith of Christians that, notwithstanding all appearances, human history does not consist of a series of repetitive patterns, but marks a sure, if unsteady, advance to an ultimate goal. As such, it has a beginning, a middle, and an end, *exortus, processus, et finis*."[25] For according to Augustine, the cyclical theory was right in discerning "repetitive patterns," but these did not negate the particularity of unrepeatable events and persons, which happened uniquely, once and only once: Adam and Eve did not continue to be created over and over again, and did not yield to the seductions of the tempter over and over again, and were not driven out of the garden over and over again. But by the process Irenaeus called recapitulation, a Second Adam did appear in the person of Jesus Christ, once and for all, to repair the damage done by the First Adam; and a Second Eve did come in the person of the Virgin Mary, as Irenaeus put it, "that a virgin, by becoming the advocate of a virgin, should undo and destroy virginal disobedience by virginal obedience"[26]—not repetition but recapitulation.

Yet the words of 1 Corinthians quoted earlier, "The first man is of

the earth, earthy: the second man is the Lord from heaven,"[27] identified
a second concept of Late Antiquity to which the figure of Mary provided an answer: the notion of "the divine man [ho theios anēr]," which,
when applied to the Christian understanding of the person of Jesus
Christ, led almost inescapably to the danger that "the second man
[who] is the Lord from heaven," because he was seen as *more* than
merely human, would come to be seen as *less* than completely human.
The tendency noted earlier that, in Louis Ginzberg's words, "just as a
pearl results from a stimulus in the shell of a mollusk, so also a legend
may arise from an irritant in the scripture,"[28] was at work already in the
earliest stages of Christian thought about Jesus Christ—and about Mary.
The most important evidence for that tendency was the apocryphal
Gospel, the *Protevangel of James*.[29] Although it was an apocryphal Gospel,—one that did not achieve official status as part of the canon of the
New Testament—it nevertheless "has dominated the development of
the Marian legend, providing much of the basic material for Mary's
biography."[30] Some of the legends about the Virgin contained in the
Protevangel of James were the inviolate virginity of Mary not only in conception but in birth, as well as the related idea that she gave birth to
Jesus without suffering birth pangs, and therefore the explanation that
the "brothers of Jesus" spoken of in the Gospels must have been the
children of Joseph the widower from his first marriage.[31] Although it is
not clear, there are grounds to suppose that some of these legends about
the Virgin Mary may implicitly have represented as well a hesitancy to
ascribe total humanity to her divine Son, as that hesitancy was already
being expressed in other sources nearly contemporary to the *Protevangel of
James*. Irenaeus, to whom we owe the first large-scale exposition of the
parallel between Eve and Mary, is likewise one of the sources from
whom we learn that such a hesitancy among the followers of the
Gnostic teacher Valentinus had led them to assert that Jesus had not
been "born" of the Virgin Mary in the usual sense at all, but had
"passed through Mary as water runs through a tube," not only without
birth pangs but without the involvement of the mother except in a

purely passive sense.[32] Christian art would eventually counter this tendency by its portrayals of the pregnant Mary.[33] It was likewise in
response to this Gnostic threat to the true humanity of Jesus, as well
as in defense of the unique position not only of Jesus but of Mary in
the history of salvation, that Irenaeus found this decisive role for the
Virgin.

The most important intellectual struggle of the first five centuries of
Christian history—indeed the most important intellectual struggle in
all of Christian history—took place in response to the question of
whether the divine in Jesus Christ was identical with God the Creator.[34]
For the answer to that challenge, too, was Mary, defined now as Theotokos and Mother of God.[35] Although that challenge to the full deity
of the Son of God had been present from the earliest times of the
Christian movement, as becomes clear from the iteration of the tempter's question "If thou be the Son of God"[36] by other doubters, the
special challenge in the second and third centuries was the one that
came from the opposite direction, questioning whether the divine man
was truly "man" in the fullest sense of that word or whether in one way
or another he needed to be shielded from the total implications of an
authentic humanity. Many movements of Christian thought and devotion in the second and third century that were eventually lumped together and condemned as "Gnostic" shared this outlook, which came
to be called "Docetism" from the Greek verb dokein, "to seem," meaning
that the humanity was "merely apparent"; conversely, the earliest
thinkers to be commended as "orthodox" were those who strove to
vindicate, against these "Docetic" and "Gnostic" tendencies, the fully
human dimension of the life and person of Jesus.

Although many individual incidents in the Gospels became battle-
grounds for this conflict—for example, the very idea of his eating and
drinking in a human fashion[37]—there were two junctures in his life on
which both sides concentrated, the nativity and the crucifixion: in the
words of the Apostles' Creed, "born of the Virgin Mary, suffered under
Pontius Pilate." Wolfgang Amadeus Mozart, in the last sacred composition he completed before his death, and certainly one of the most

exquisite and profoundly moving as well, set to music the affirmation that it had been these two events, "being truly born of the Virgin Mary [vere natum de Maria Virgine]" and "being truly sacrificed on the cross for mankind [(vere) immolatum in cruce pro homine]," that guaranteed both human salvation and the presence of "the true body [verum corpus]" in the Eucharist—and he did so by addressing another Ave to that "true body": Ave verum corpus.[38] The suffering and death on the cross was, to both sides, evidence of a nature that was, in Nietzsche's phrase, "human, all too human." Suffering was there regarded as unworthy of a truly divine nature; for by common consent (and, incidentally, without much explicit discussion), the divine nature was regarded as having the essential quality of being beyond the capacity for suffering or change, the quality defined by the Greek philosophical term apatheia, impassability, and incorporated into the Christian doctrine of God.[39] One of the leading Gnostic teachers, Basilides, was reported to have taken this revulsion at the idea of attributing suffering to the divine Christ so far that, on the basis of the report of the Gospels that on the way to Calvary the Roman soldiers "as they led [Christ] away, laid hold upon one Simon, a Cyrenian, coming out of the country, and on him they laid the cross, that he might bear it after Jesus,"[40] he claimed that Simon of Cyrene had been substituted for Jesus and crucified instead, sparing Christ the ignominy of the crucifixion and death.[41] Summarizing the response of an early Christian writer, Ignatius of Antioch, to such ideas, therefore, Virginia Corwin has said: "That the preaching of the cross and death of Christ continued to be a 'stumbling-block to unbelievers' (Eph. 18.1) need not surprise us, and Ignatius indicates why the docetic thinkers who were his opponents were repelled by it. In Ignatius' mind it was the final and incontrovertible proof that Christ truly became man and entered the scene of history."[42] It seems to have been at least partly with this controversy in view that so many versions of the early Christian creeds, including the Apostles' Creed and the Niceno-Constantinopolitan Creed, incorporated the phrase "under Pontius Pilate" into the recital of the sufferings of Christ, thereby identifying him as a truly human person and characterizing the suffering as a truly historical event that took place not in a mythical or Docetic "once upon a time" but at a particular place on the map and time in the history of the Roman empire.[43]

But Pontius Pilate was only one of the two dramatis personae mentioned in the creeds, and the second of them. The other, and the first mentioned, was the Virgin Mary; for the other decisive event on which the true humanity of Christ depended was that he was, as the Apostles' Creed said, "born of the Virgin Mary," a formula that appeared in various slightly differing permutations even more often than "under Pontius Pilate."[44] Here again, the Docetic campaign to shield him from the implications of being fully human had found various ingenious explanations, including the simile that at his birth he had passed through the body of Mary as water passes through a pipe, without affecting the medium and (more important) without being affected by the medium.[45] The response to this metaphor, and to the theory underlying it, was to emphasize his genuine birth from the Virgin Mary. For, as the founder of Christian Latin, Tertullian, put it, writing against Marcion, "All these illusions of an imaginary corporeality in [his version of Christ], Marcion adopted with this view, that his nativity also might not be furnished with any evidence from his human substance." To the contrary, Tertullian continued, "Since He was 'the truth,' He was flesh; since He was flesh, He was born. . . . He is no phantom."[46] The logic of the argument was clear, whether one accepted the substance of it or not: Salvation depended on the true and complete humanity of Christ in his life and death; that true and complete humanity depended in turn on his having been truly born; and his true birth in its turn depended on his having had a mother who was truly and completely human. And if, as the case argued by Irenaeus and others maintained, it was the voluntary and virginal obedience of Mary by which the voluntary and virginal disobedience of Eve was undone and set aright, Mary became, by that voluntary obedience, both the Second Eve and the principal guarantee of Christ's humanity.

As it was expounded in prose and especially in poetry, all of this frequently took the rhetorical form of saturation with dialectics and reveling in antithesis, as in the lines of a later British metaphysical poet of the Baroque period, Richard Crashaw, a Puritan who converted to Roman Catholicism:

Welcome, all wonders in one sight!
Eternity shut in a span!
Summer in Winter, Day in Night!
Heaven in earth, and God in man!
Great little One! whose all-embracing birth
Lifts Earth to Heaven, stoops Heaven to Earth—[47]

until the Virgin Mary could be seen as Our Lady of the Paradoxes: Virgin but Mother, Human Mother but Mother of God.

As herself a creature, she was as well the one through whom the Logos Creator had united himself to a created human nature.[48] In the striking formula of Gregory of Nyssa, contrasting the First Adam with the Second Adam, "the first time, [God the Logos] took dust from the earth and formed man, [but] this time he took dust from the Virgin and did not merely form man, but formed man around himself."[49] Although the Arianism that Athanasius combated is usually (and correctly) seen as the denial of the full and complete divinity of Christ, many earlier heresies about Christ—and, at least according to the charge of some interpreters,[50] Arianism itself—were guilty of denying his full and complete humanity. Beginning already with the teachings against which the later writers of the New Testament had directed their emphasis on the visibility and the tangibility of the human "flesh" of Christ, various early interpretations of the figure of Christ had striven to exempt him from the loathsome concreteness that flesh is heir to. And since nothing about human flesh was more concrete, and to many of them nothing was more loathsome, than the processes of human procreation and birth, they were especially intent on rescuing his humanity from an involvement in those processes. This inevitably made Mary the primary focus of their reinterpretations, as well as of the orthodox replies. Not only had some of the Gnostics said that Christ "received nothing from the Virgin,"[51] but (also according to the report of John of

Damascus, apparently quoting Irenaeus)[52] they had said that he passed through the body of Mary as "through a channel [dia sōlēnos]," that is, without being affected by the passive medium of his mother. This would appear to have been an exaggerated form of a notion, widespread in antiquity, that even in a normal conception and birth the mother functioned only as the "soil" for the child, which was produced by the "seed [sperma]" of the father.[53] In response to this Gnostic view of Mary, the earliest orthodox theologians had insisted that although Christ had been conceived in a supernatural manner without the agency of a human father, he was "truly [alēthōs] born," in the same manner as all other human beings are.[54] Even earlier, as has been noted in chapter 1, when the apostle Paul had wanted to assert that the Son of God, who had come "in the fulness of time," had participated in an authentic humanity, he said that he was "born of a woman,"[55] though apparently without implying thereby any explicit reference to the Virgin Birth or to the person of the Virgin Mary herself.

Having taken over the parallel from the Greeks, Western theologians were eventually able, as mentioned earlier, to take advantage of a verbal coincidence in the Latin language to play with the palindrome Ave/Eva. The First Eve had been, according to the etymology of the Book of Genesis, "the mother of all who live [matēr pantōn tōn zōntōn]," and therefore the Septuagint read: "And Adam called the name of his wife Life [Zōē]," rather than "Eve."[56] So the Second Eve, too, had become the new mother of all who believed and who lived through believing in her divine Son.

HIERVSALE

Epiphany and flight into Egypt, fifth-century mosaic. Santa Maria Maggiore, Rome. (Alinari/Art Resource, N.Y.)

4 The Theotokos, the Mother of God

And [Elisabeth] spake out with a loud voice, and said, . . .
And whence is this to me, that the mother of my Lord should come to me?
—Luke 1:42–43

Throughout history, and especially during the fourth and fifth centuries, the basic category for thinking about Mary was that of paradox: Virgin and Mother; Human Mother of One who is God, Theotokos.[1] For the most comprehensive—and, in the opinion of some, the most problematic—of all the terms invented for Mary by Eastern Christianity was certainly that title Theotokos. It did not mean simply "Mother of God," as it was usually rendered in Western languages (*Mater Dei* in Latin, and thence in the Romance languages, or *Mutter Gottes* in German), but more precisely and fully "the one who gave birth to the one who is God" (therefore *Bogorodica* and its cognates in Russian and other Slavic languages, and, more seldom but more precisely, *Deipara* even in Latin). Although the linguistic history of the title remains obscure, it does seem to have been a term of Christian coinage rather than, as might superficially seem to have been the case, an adaptation to Christian purposes of a name originally given to a pagan goddess.[2] The name appears in some manuscripts of the works of Athanasius.[3] Yet the textual evidence leaves ambiguous the question of how often Athanasius did use the title Theotokos for Mary.[4] In any event, it receives negative corroboration from its appearance, during the lifetime of Athanasius, in the attacks on the church by the emperor Julian "the Apostate," who criticized the superstition of the Christians for invoking the Theotokos.[5]

In the fifth century, the fear of mingling the divine and human natures in the person of Christ led Nestorius, patriarch of Constantinople, to stipulate that because it was only the human nature that had been born of her, Mary should be called not Theotokos, which gave the blasphemous impression that she had given birth to the divine nature itself and which therefore sounded like the title of the mother deities of paganism, but Christotokos, "the one who gave birth to Christ." In 431, slightly more than a century after the Christian religion had finally become a legal cult [religio licita] through the Edict of Milan, a council of Christian bishops met in the city of Ephesus—which had been the center of a flourishing devotion to the Greek goddess Artemis or Diana.[6] It was in Ephesus, in a scene graphically described in the Acts of the Apostles, that her devotees had rioted against Saint Paul and the other Christian apostles with the cry "Great is Diana of the Ephesians!"[7] There, assembled in the great double church of Mary, whose ruins can still be seen, they solemnly proclaimed that it was an obligation binding on all believers to call Mary Theotokos, making dogmatically official what the piety of orthodox believers had already affirmed, in the words of the first Anathematism of Cyril of Alexandria against Nestorius: "If anyone does not confess that Emmanuel is God in truth, and therefore that the holy virgin is the mother of God [Theotokos] (for she bore in a fleshly way the Word of God become flesh), let him be anathema."[8] It was, moreover, in honor of the definition by the Council of Ephesus of Mary as Theotokos that right after the council Pope Sixtus III built the most important shrine to Mary in the West, the Basilica of Santa Maria Maggiore in Rome; its celebrated mosaic of the annunciation and the epiphany gave artistic form to that definition.[9] A few centuries later John of Damascus would summarize the orthodox case for this special title: "Hence it is with justice and truth that we call holy Mary Theotokos. For this name embraces the whole mystery of the divine dispensation [to mystērion tēs *oikonomias*]. For if she who bore him is the Theotokos, assuredly he who was born of her is God and likewise also man. . . . The name [Theotokos] in truth signifies the one subsistence and the two natures and the two modes of generation of our Lord Jesus Christ."[10] And, as he argued elsewhere, that is what she was on the icons: Theotokos and therefore the orthodox and God-pleasing substitute for the pagan worship of demons.[11] At the same time, the defenders of the icons insisted that "when we worship her icon, we do not, in pagan fashion [*Hellēnikōs*], regard her as a goddess [*thean*] but as the Theotokos."[12]

That had come a long way even from the consideration of her as the Second Eve. It was probably the greatest quantum leap in the whole history of the language and thought about Mary, as we are considering it in this book. How and why could she have come so far so fast? At least three aspects of an answer to that historical question are suggested by the texts: the growth of the title Theotokos; in connection with the title, the rise of a liturgical observance called "the commemoration of Mary"; and, as a somewhat speculative explanation for both the title and the festival, the deepening perception that there was a need to identify some totally human person who was the crown of creation, once that was declared to be an inadequate identification for Jesus Christ as the eternal Son of God and Second Person of the Trinity.[13]

The origins of the title Mother of God are obscure. In spite of the diligence of Hugo Rahner and others,[14] there is no altogether incontestable evidence that it was used before the fourth century, despite Newman's categorical claim that "the title *Theotocos*, or Mother of God, was familiar to Christians from primitive times."[15] What is clear is that the first completely authenticated instances of the use of this title came from the city of Athanasius, Alexandria. Alexander, his patron and immediate predecessor as bishop there, referred to Mary as Theotokos in his encyclical of circa 319 about the heresy of Arius.[16] From various evidence, including the taunts of Julian the Apostate from a few decades later about the term Theotokos, cited earlier, it seems reasonable to conclude that the title already enjoyed widespread acceptance in the piety of the faithful at Alexandria and beyond. The history does not in any direct way corroborate the facile modern theories about the "mother goddesses" of Graeco-Roman paganism and their supposed significance for the development of Christian Mariology.[17] For the term Theotokos was apparently an original Christian creation that arose in the language of Christian devotion to her as the mother of the divine Savior and that eventually received its theological justification from the church's clarification of what was implied by the orthodox witness to him.

That justification was supplied by Athanasius, whose lifelong obsession it was to insist that to be the Mediator between Creator and creature Christ the Son of God had to be God in the full and unequivocal sense of the word: "through God alone can God be known," as the refrain of many orthodox church fathers put it. It did appear "inchoatively"[18] in his summary statement of "the scope and character of Holy Scripture," which "contains a double account [diplē epangelia] of the Savior: that he was God forever and is the Son, being Logos and Radiance and Wisdom of the Father; and that afterwards, taking flesh of a Virgin, Mary the Theotokos, for us, he was made man."[19] But the theological explanation of this "double account" went well beyond this summary statement of the creed. Most of the recent controversy about the theology of Athanasius has dealt with the question of whether he ascribed a human soul to Christ or whether he shared the "Logos-plus-flesh" schema of the incarnation, which came to be identified with the Apollinarist heresy.[20] That controversy has sometimes tended to obscure, however, his pioneering work in the elaboration of the "communication of the properties,"[21] the principle that, as a consequence of the incarnation and of the union of the divine and the human nature in the one person of Jesus Christ, it was legitimate to predicate human properties of the Logos and divine properties of the man Jesus, for example, to speak of "the blood of the Son of God" or "the blood of the Lord" or even (according to some manuscripts of the New Testament) "the blood of God."[22]

As Aloys Grillmeier has suggested, it was not until the debates over the term Theotokos in the first quarter of the fifth century "that the discussion of the so-called communicatio idiomatum in Christ began in earnest," even though language suggestive of it "had been employed since the apostolic age without further thought."[23] The place of Athanasius in its development seems, however, to be somewhat more important than Grillmeier made it. Grillmeier pointed to passages in which Athanasius "obviously regards the Logos as the real personal agent in those acts which are decisive for redemption, the passion and death of Christ," and he cited "expressions which describe the redemptive activity of the Logos according to the rules of the *communicatio idiomatum*." But in a long passage in his first *Oration Against the Arians*, Athanasius discussed in detail the question of the propriety of ascribing change and exaltation to the divine Logos, who could not be changed and did not need to be exalted. His answer was a paraphrase of the language of the New Testament about "Christ Jesus: who being in the form of God, . . . took upon him the form of a servant":[24] "As he, being the Logos and existing in the form of God, was always worshiped; so, being still the same though he became man and was called Jesus, he nevertheless has the whole creation under foot, and bending their knee to him in this name [Jesus], and confessing that the incarnation of the Logos and his undergoing death in the flesh has not happened against the glory of his Godhead, but 'to the glory of God the Father.'"[25]

Therefore when Athanasius spoke of the Logos "taking flesh of a Virgin, Mary the Theotokos,"[26] he was echoing the language of popular devotion; but he had already begun to provide the title with the very rationale that was to help defend it against attack half a century after his death. As Newman suggested in *The Arians of the Fourth Century*, the people were orthodox even when the bishops were not.[27] In his use of the Theotokos, as in his use of other titles and metaphors, Athanasius aligned himself with the orthodoxy of popular devotion and vindicated it. The idea of *lex orandi lex credendi*, that implicit in Christian worship there was a normative doctrinal content, which needed to be made explicit, seems to have been formulated shortly after the time of Athanasius,[28] but he evidently worked on the basis of some such idea.

The normative content of devotion also became evident in another context, when Athanasius used "the commemoration of Mary" to vindicate the orthodoxy of his doctrine. He did so in at least two of his writings. The more important of these is his epistle to Epictetus, which achieved wide circulation in Greek, Latin, Syriac, and Armenian in later centuries and was quoted in the decrees of both the Council of Ephesus in 431 and the Council of Chalcedon in 451.[29] It seems to have been called forth by the recrudescence, after the defeat of Arianism, of the ancient Docetic heresy, which denied the true and full humanity of Jesus or claimed that he did not have a genuinely human body.[30] Some were even going so far as to maintain that the body of Christ was of one essence [homoousion] with the Logos.[31] This new species of Docetism, about whose teachings scholars still do not agree, is often seen as a forerunner of the Apollinarist theology. In his response Athanasius argued on the basis of "the divine Scriptures" and of the decrees of "the fathers assembled at Nicaea" and accused the neo-Docetists of having outdone even the Arians: "You have gone further in impiety than any heresy. For if the Logos is of one essence with the body, that renders superfluous the commemoration and the office of Mary [perittē tēs Marias hē mnēmē kai hē chreia]."[32] And in his epistle to Maximus, combating the doctrine that the Logos had become man as a necessary consequence of his nature, Athanasius declared again: "If this were so, the commemoration of Mary would be superfluous."[33] Athanasius's theological point seems quite clear: Mary was again, as she had been to the anti-Gnostic fathers, the guarantee of the true humanity of Jesus Christ.[34]

What is less clear is the precise character of the "commemoration" to which Athanasius was referring. If the Greek word mnēmē meant no more than "memory," as it did in the New Testament and elsewhere,[35] then he would have been arguing that the remembrance of Mary, as enshrined for example in the creed or in memorial prayers, necessarily implied that the humanity of Christ took its beginning from her and had not preexisted from eternity. But mnēmē sometimes had a technical significance in the formation of the Christian calendar, referring to the anniversary of a saint or martyr.[36] Martin Jugie, in his early study of the first festivals devoted to Mary in both the East and the West, contended that the mnēmē of Mary referred to in early fifth-century documents was not the anniversary of her death or "dormition [koimēsis]"[37] but of her "nativity," which may have meant her entry into heaven.[38] In his later and massive study of the death and assumption of the Virgin he repeated, corrected, and amplified this argument.[39] For our purposes, however, this problem is secondary to the fundamental one. Is *tēs Marias hē mnēmē* a reference to some Mariological festival? There is some evidence to support the existence of a festival called the *mnēmē* of Mary and celebrated on the Sunday after Christmas,[40] but the evidence does not go back quite as far as Athanasius. Nevertheless, both that evidence and his language seem to make it plausible that such a commemoration of Mary was being kept already during his time and that his argument was based upon it.

He would then have been arguing that there was no justification for a festival commemorating the Virgin Mary the Theotokos if she had not played a part in the history of salvation. She belonged to the New Testament, not to the Old, and was not remembered, as the saints of ancient Israel were, as a prophet of the coming of Christ. Rather, she had a function or office, a *chreia*, as the chosen and commissioned one through whom alone the uncreated Logos received his created humanity. And that *chreia* or ministry was celebrated with grateful remembrance in the observance of the *mnēmē* or commemoration of Mary. The *chreia* was a given fact of the history of salvation, the *mnēmē* a given fact of Christian observance. Both the creed of the church and the calendar of the church, then, attested the doctrine that the human nature of Christ was a creature, just as they attested the doctrine that the divine nature of Christ was not a creature; and the sign of the bond between Christ the creature and mankind the creature was "the commemoration and the office of Mary," which would have been superfluous if the humanity of Christ had been some sort of component of his preexistence as the Logos of God. Although it is undeniable, from the evidence, that Athanasius never worked out as satisfactory a formula for the implications of the full and true humanity of the Lord as he did for those of his deity, it is equally clear that both aspects of the "double account"[41] were vouched for by the authority of the orthodox faith.

In the composition and identification of that authority, the worship and devotion of the church were seen as an important element of the definition of what Athanasius, in the conclusion of the Epistle to Epictetus, called "the confession of that faith which is both devout and orthodox [hē homologia tēs eusebous kai orthodoxous pisteōs]."[42] If Mary was Theotokos, as the language of Christian devotion declared she was, the relation between the divine and human in Jesus Christ had to be such as to justify this apparently incongruous term; hence the doctrine of the "communication of the properties." If Mary had the "office" of clothing the Logos in an authentic and therefore a created humanity, as in the "commemoration of Mary" the practice of Christian devotion declared she had, no aversion to flesh and blood could be permitted to vitiate the doctrine of the incarnation. To qualify as a dogma of the church, then, a doctrine had to conform not only to the apostolic tradition, as set down in Scripture and in such magisterial witnesses as the decrees of the Council of Nicaea, but also to the worship and devotion of the Catholic and apostolic church.

The creaturely status of Mary in relation to Christ indicated yet another line of development, the task of specifying more accurately the proper subject for predicates that had been misplaced by heresy. Most of the controversies in the fourth century dealt with the propriety of predications such as homoousios or Theotokos. But the literature of the controversies also suggested, or at least hinted at, a definition of heresy as misplaced predication, to which the eventual orthodox answer was a more precise specification of the subject. Only at the Council of Ephesus and beyond was this answer supplied, but by hindsight it may seen in an earlier stage of the development in the Arian controversy.

The Arian heresy, in the words of Henry Gwatkin, "degraded the Lord of Saints to the level of his creatures."[43] What it ascribed to Christ was more than it was willing to ascribe to any of the saints but less than it ascribed to the supreme Deity. The Arian doctrine concerning the saints is not easy to assemble from the fragments, though we know that the Thalia of Arius spoke of "the elect of God, the wise men of God, his holy sons."[44] There is some evidence that certain legends of the saints were handed down through Arian sources.[45] We are considerably better informed about the Arian view of the relation between Christ and the saints. According to the letter of the Arians to Alexander of Alexandria, the Logos was "a perfect creature of God, but not as one of the creatures,"[46] since he was the creature through whom God had made all the other creatures; therefore the "superiority" of this creature over all the other creatures was that he had been created directly whereas they had been created through him.[47] In his preexistence, then, the Logos was the perfect creature. But in his earthly career he *became* the perfect creature. Arianism seemed in its picture of the man Jesus Christ to have combined a denial of the presence of a human soul in him[48] with the doctrine of Paul of Samosata that he had made himself worthy of elevation to the status of "Son of God" by his "moral progress [*prokopē*]."[49] The Arians were reputed to have taught that God had elected him "because of his foreknowledge" that Christ would not rebel against him but would, "by his care and self-discipline [*dia epimeleian kai askēsin*]," triumph over his "mutable nature" and remain faithful.[50] Because the sonship of the Logos was a function of his perfect creaturehood and the sonship of the man Jesus was a consequence of his perfect obedience, the difference between his sonship and that of the saints was quantitative rather than qualitative, for by their own perfect obedience they could eventually attain to a participation in the same sonship.

Now this Arian doctrine of participation by the saints in the sonship of Christ had a counterpart in the Athanasian doctrine of participation through "divinization": "Because of our relationship to his body we, too, have become God's temple, and in consequence are made God's sons, in such a way that even in us the Lord is now being worshiped."[51] The sonship was due not in the first instance to the imitation of Christ by the saints but essentially to transformation by Christ, who, in the famous Athanasian formula, became human in order that the saints might become divine.[52] Athanasius contended that such a transformation and divinization was possible only because the Logos was Creator rather than creature. The Savior could mediate between God and humanity only because he himself was God. He was not promoted to a new status because he was the greatest of the saints but was restored to his eternal status after performing on earth the mission for which he had been sent into the flesh. Now the saints became sons of God, creatures in whom the Creator dwelt so fully that he could be worshiped in them. That status is what Arianism tried to make of Christ, a creature in whom the Creator dwelt so fully that God could be worshiped in him, the highest of the saints and therefore the mediator between God and humanity.

By drawing the line between Creator and creature and confessing that the Son of God belonged on God's side of that line, Nicene orthodoxy made possible and necessary a qualitative distinction between him and even the highest of saints, between his uncreated mediation and their created mediation.[53] Now that the subject of the Arian sentences was changed, what was to become of all the predicates? What we have seen so far in the Mariology of Athanasius would seem to indicate that, in a sense quite different from that implied by Harnack, "what the Arians had taught about Christ, the orthodox now taught about Mary,"[54] so that these creaturely predicates did not belong to Jesus Christ, the Son of God, but to the Virgin Mary, the Mother of God. The portrait of Mary in the *Letter to the Virgins* of Athanasius would fit the Arian description of the Son of God, who "was chosen because, though mutable by nature, his painstaking character suffered no deterioration." Athanasius spoke of her "progressing" and may even have been using here the word *prokopē*, moral progress, which the Arians had used of Christ.[55] Her progress, according to Athanasius, involved struggles with doubts and evil thoughts, but she triumphed over them and could thus become "the image" and "the model" of virginity for all those who strove for perfection, in short, the highest of the saints. The devotional language (Theotokos, "Mother of God") and the devotional practice (*mnēmē*, "commemoration") which, as we have noted earlier, lay behind the Mariology of Athanasius were the prime instance in all his thought of the doctrine that even a creature could become deserving of worship by virtue of the indwelling of the Creator. The hymn from which Athanasius may have been quoting the title Theotokos, the Greek original of the well-known Latin *Sub tuum praesidium*, was likewise the prime instance of such worship.[56]

It remained for further controversy to call forth further clarification of the doctrine, but in the light of that controversy we may see already in

Athanasius that it was a development by the specification of the subject. When the development did come, it came first and most fully in the Greek-speaking East, where the ascetical and devotional presuppositions of the doctrine of Mary were present long before they appeared in the West.

Rosemary Namuli, *Mary*, stone sculpture. East Africa. (Reprinted from Arno Lehmann, *Christian Art in Africa and Asia*, Concordia Publishing House, 1967)

5 The Heroine of the Qur'ān and the Black Madonna

Black am I and beautiful.
—Song of Songs 1:5 (translation by Marvin Pope)

Oe of the most profound and most persistent roles of the Virgin Mary in history has been her function as a bridge builder to other traditions, other cultures, and other religions. From the Latin word for "bridge builder" came the term *pontifex*, a priestly title in Roman paganism. In the form *pontifex maximus* it became one of the terms in the cult of the divine Roman emperor, and for that reason it was disavowed by Christian emperors already in the fourth century. Not long thereafter it was taken up by Christian bishops and archbishops, and it did not become an exclusive title for the bishop of Rome until considerably later.[1] But the concept of a *pontifex*, as distinct from the term, had far wider implications. Ultimately it applied to all those concepts and personalities whose fundamental message and significance could be expressed better by saying both/and than by saying either/or. One such was monasticism, which had appeared in several separate traditions and had manifested in them some striking similarities, as well as historic differences.[2] Efforts to cultivate exchange especially between Christian and Buddhist monasticism have made considerable headway in recent decades, and Thomas

Merton, Trappist monk and spiritual author, was engaged in such a "boundary journey" when he died in 1968.[3] Whenever the antitheses of either/or at all levels have threatened to erupt into a holocaust, there has been a desperate need to identify and to cultivate such bridge-building concepts and personalities.

Perhaps no antithesis has been more far-reaching in its implications than the relation between the rest of the world and what has been called "Islamdom" (as a counterpart to "Christendom"), which now numbers nearly one billion believers. And therefore this general need for bridge builders has taken on a special urgency and poignancy in the attempt to understand the religion of the prophet Muhammad and the message of the Qur'ān, concerning which the fundamental ignorance of otherwise well-educated Westerners is not only abysmal but frightening. The foundation of the Islamic faith came in a series of incandescent divine self-disclosures, beginning in about the year 610 and continuing to near the end of the prophet's life in 632.[4] These revelations are, to orthodox Muslim belief, the very voice of God. In them Muhammad was designated "a benevolence to the creatures of the world," whose message it was to say, "This is what has been revealed to me: 'Your God is one and only God.'"[5] Muhammad memorized many of these sayings, as did a multitude of his followers; other sayings seem to have been written down right away, in whatever medium was at hand. The collecting of the Qur'ān is attributed to Abū Bakr, the first caliph, and the standard version to 'Uthmān, the third caliph, who established the textual tradition at Medina as the normative one and who also fixed the sequence of the 114 chapters, or sūrahs, more or less from the longest to the shortest. Many Western scholars tend to think that the Qur'ān in its present form began to be set down in about 650 but that the text was not definitively fixed until the tenth century; normative Muslim doctrine teaches that it was all written at once.

For Western readers first coming to the Qur'ān, one of the most surprising sections has often been the sūrah numbered 19 in the canonical collection, which bore the title "Maryam: Mary."[6] For as the nineteenth of 114 sūrahs, this chapter was one of the longest in the Qur'ān. It was, moreover, the only sūrah to bear a woman's name, although sūrah 4 had the superscription "An-Nisā: The Women" and sūrah 60 was called "Al-Mumtahanah: The Woman Tried." But there was, for example, no sūrah named for Eve (who was, for Islam as for Judaism and Christianity, "the mother of all living"[7]), nor one named for Hagar, mother of Ishmael by Abraham and therefore in a real sense the founding mother of Islam. In the judgment of many scholars, sūrah 19 came from the Meccan period of the prophet's revelations, during which "references to Mary tend to emphasize the fact that she was the virgin mother of Jesus"; sūrah 3, by contrast, has often been assigned to the prophet's time in Medina, whose references to Mary "tend to focus on the negation of Jesus's divinity."[8] Sūrah 19 contained quotations, paraphrases, and adaptations from the Gospels of the New Testament, especially from the Gospel of Luke, which was, as mentioned earlier, the most detailed portrait of the Virgin Mary in the Christian Bible.[9] The parallels were important in their own right, but they became especially so when seen in connection with the differences between the Christian doctrine of Mary, as it had developed by the time of Muhammad in the early seventh century, and the Muslim portrait of her in the Qur'ān and in Islamic commentaries on the Holy Book.[10] For as Neal Robinson has pointed out, real parallels were being drawn not only between Muhammad and Jesus as part of the succession of prophets but between Muhammad and Mary as both bearers of the word of God.[11] As the Qur'ān says later, "And of Mary, daughter of 'Imran, who guarded her chastity, so that We breathed into her a life from Us, and she believed the words of her Lord and His Books, and was among the obedient."[12] In relation to the other materials about the history of Mary through the centuries and with the aid of commentators both Muslim and Western, then, what follows is a commentary on the portion of sūrah 19 dealing specifically with Mary.[13]

16. *Commemorate Mary in the Book.* These opening words followed upon a paraphrase of the account in the first chapter of the Gospel of Luke about the birth of John the Baptist, which seems to have been cast, as was the New Testament story, so as to emphasize the parallels between the birth of John the Baptist and the birth of Jesus: annunciation, miraculous divine

intervention, special mission for the about-to-be-born child.[14] But it is noteworthy that both in the New Testament and in the Qur'ān the annunciation of the miraculous birth of John was brought by the messenger of God to his father, Zechariah, whereas in Luke the annunciation by the angel of the birth of Jesus was addressed to his mother, Mary. In the Qur'ānic version, moreover, the name of Elizabeth, mother of John, did not even appear. Therefore, although the word of God to John the Baptist was "O John, hold fast to the Book,"[15] this section opened with the formula "Commemorate Mary in the Book," clearly assigning her a very special place in the historical plan of "Allah, most benevolent, most merciful." It may have been a reflection of postbiblical Christian Mariological spirituality and thought that the first narrative item in this commemoration of Mary was a report not contained in Luke or any of the other Gospels: "When she withdrew from her family to a place in the East and took cover from them." More likely, it would appear that at this point the commemoration of Mary brought echoes of the commemoration of Hagar, mother of Ishmael, in chapter 16 and again in chapter 21 of the Book of Genesis, the two accounts of her expulsion being rather difficult to harmonize; for Hagar did "take cover from" her family, that is, from Sarah and Abraham. It was to Ishmael, son of Abraham, that Islam looked as its founder, favored by God, who had promised about Ishmael, also in the Hebrew and Christian Scriptures and therefore both in the Jewish and in the Christian tradition, "I will make him a great nation."[16]

17. *We sent a spirit of Ours to her who appeared before her in the concrete form of a man. 18. "I seek refuge in the Merciful from you, if you fear Him," she said. He replied: "I am only a messenger from your Lord [sent] to bestow a good son on you."* And earlier: "The angels said: 'O Mary, indeed God has favoured you and made you immaculate, and chosen you from all the women of the world. So adore your Lord, O Mary, and pay homage and bow with those who bow in prayer.'"[17] This was the Qur'ān's version of the annunciation. In its basic outline it matched the account in the Gospel of Luke. There was an angelic messenger, identified in the New Testament as Gabriel but here less specifically as "the angels" or "a spirit of Ours." He identified himself as "only a messenger from your Lord." The content of the messenger's

announcement to her was, in the Qur'ān as in the Gospel, that she was to have a son. But here an interesting contrast asserts itself. In the Gospel, Gabriel said to Mary: "He shall be great, and shall be called the Son of the Highest: and the Lord God shall give unto him the throne of his father David: And he shall reign over the house of Jacob for ever; and of his kingdom there shall be no end."[18] Those words reflected, and formed a biblical foundation for, the Christian teaching that as "the Son of the Highest," Mary's Son occupied a unique position not only in human history but in the divine life itself, thus in the Holy Trinity. Because the single-minded concentration of the religion of the Qur'ān on the un-equivocal oneness of God excluded all such language about God's having a Son and therefore about there being a Trinity, that entire speech of Gabriel was encapsulated in the simple phrase "a good son." The angels said to Mary: "O Mary, God gives you news of a thing from Him, for rejoicing, (news of one) whose name will be Messiah, Jesus, son of Mary, illustrious in this world and the next, and one among the honoured, who will speak to the people when in the cradle and when in the prime of life, and will be among the upright and doers of good."[19] That was to say, the child to be born would be son of Mary, but not Son of God. The angelic message in Luke went on, moreover, to a prophecy that subsequent Christian interpreters were to find highly problematic, namely, that "the throne of his father David" would be his and that from that throne he would reign eternally. This prophecy and others like it in both the Old and the New Testaments figured prominently in the struggles during the second and third centuries over the question of whether Christ on his return would establish an earthly realm for a thousand years, struggles that have been reenacted repeatedly in Christian history, both at the end of the Middle Ages and in the twentieth century.[20] All of that, too, was absent from the Qur'ānic retelling, in which therefore Mary was not the Mother of the King and therefore would not be entitled, as she was in the Catholic tradition, to such a name as Queen.

20. *"How can I have a son," she said, when no man has touched me, nor am I sinful?"*
21. *He said: "Thus will it be. Your Lord said: 'It is easy for Me,' and that: 'We shall make him a sign for men and a blessing from Us.' This is a thing already decreed." Again, it is*

important to note in the first instance the fidelity of the Qur'ān to the New Testament version of the account of Mary's words: "How shall this be, seeing I know not a man?"[21]—which followed the standard language of the Hebrew Bible, going back to the early chapters of Genesis, in using the verb "to know" as a euphemism for sexual intercourse.[22] Such fidelity to the New Testament means that for the Qur'ān and for its loyal adherents, no less than for the Gospel and its loyal adherents, Mary was correctly identified by the oxymoron Virgin Mother. That aspect of Muslim Mariology went on to create both admiration and consternation in the Christian responses to Islam, both in the Byzantine East and in the Medieval West. Similarly, the statements "Your Lord said: 'It is easy for Me,'" and "That is how God creates what He wills. When He decrees a thing, He says 'Be,' and it is,"[23] represented the counterpart to the word of Gabriel in Luke: "With God nothing shall be impossible."[24] But again the omissions were, if anything, even more interesting, and more relevant to the consideration of the portrait of Mary. For in the Gospel, Gabriel answered Mary's question by explaining, "The Holy Ghost shall come upon thee, and the power of the Highest shall overshadow thee: therefore also that holy thing which shall be born of thee shall be called the Son of God."[25] All of that explanation was conspicuously eliminated in the Qur'ān. The one to be born, the angelic messenger said here, would be "a good son"—a good son of Mary, that is—but would in no traditional Christian sense "be called the Son of God," for that would have implied the Trinity and, in Muslim eyes, have negated biblical monotheism. Probably for the same reason, the promise of Gabriel to Mary, "The Holy Ghost shall come upon thee, and the power of the Highest shall overshadow thee," had likewise disappeared; for there was no Trinity, and hence no "Holy Ghost" in the orthodox trinitarian sense of that title.

22. *When she conceived him she went away to a distant place.* 23. *The birth pangs led her to the trunk of a date-palm tree. "Would that I had died before this," she said, "and become a thing forgotten, unremembered." 24. Then [a voice] called to her from below: "Grieve not; your Lord has made a rivulet gush forth right below you. Shake the trunk of the date-palm tree, and it will drop ripe dates for you. 26. Eat and drink, and be at peace. If you*

see any man, tell him: 'I have verily vowed a fast to Ar-Rahman and cannot speak to any one this day.'" All of this was entirely new in relation to the New Testament. Even more explicit in these verses than at the beginning of this pericope, moreover, was the aforementioned typology between Mary, mother of Jesus, and Hagar, mother of Ishmael. In two separate chapters of Genesis, which may have represented distinct original traditions but which have both been incorporated into the book as we have it, Hagar went "to a distant place," the first time when her pregnancy aroused the jealousy of Sarah and the second time after the birth of Isaac.[26] Her despairing cry was answered by a miraculous intervention of God. Because the Qur'ān was, by definition, a new revelation that came all at once in a blinding series of moments of divine authority, we can only speculate about the earlier stages of this typology between Hagar and Mary. But it does not seem to stretch historical and literary probability to draw an analogy with the typology between Eve and Mary discussed earlier.[27] For Hagar, too, was a founding mother, as Eve was; and Ishmael was the eponymous beginning of the people known as Ishmaelites. This entire construct, therefore, may be seen to have been an Islamic way of celebrating the special place of the Virgin Mary in the history of the dealings of "Allah, most benevolent, ever-merciful," with the world. As the "good son" of Mary, his mother, Jesus stood in the succession of the called servants of God—after Abraham, father of Ishmael, and after Moses; and before Muhammad. Therefore the opening words of this section of the nineteenth sūrah, "Commemorate Mary in the Book," were followed in later sections by "Commemorate Abraham in the Book" and then by "Commemorate Moses in the Book," "the Book" being the standard term in the Qur'ān for the Hebrew Scriptures.[28]

The relation of Mary to that succession took a surprising turn in the following verses: *27. Then she brought the child to her people. They exclaimed: "O Mary, you have done a most astonishing thing! 28. O sister of Aaron, your father was not a wicked person, nor your mother sinful!"* As it stood, the text identified Mary ("Maryam" in the superscription to this sūrah) with the "sister of Aaron" and sister of Moses, called "Miriam" in the Book of Exodus; in a similar way, the thirteenth-century Jewish polemic against Christianity, *Nizzahon*

Vetus, by means of the designation *Miriam m'gaddela nashaia*, conflated her with Mary Magdalene, perhaps with the intent of showing that, far from being the Holy Virgin Mother of God celebrated in Christian devotion and doctrine, Mary the mother of Jesus was a prostitute and a sinner.[29] Beginning already with Byzantine writers, Western critics of Islam and of the Qur'ān, who dismissed the prophet as an unlettered camel driver with delusions of grandeur, seized on this passage to prove just how confused he was, mixing up two women who lived well over a millennium apart simply because they had the same name. It became the standard explanation of this verse to say that Muhammad had heard Jews speak about Miriam and Christians speak about Mary—both of them, presumably, identified as "Maryam"—and in his ignorance had made the two women into one. As the editor and translator of the most widely circulated translation of the Qur'ān into English has explained, however, "Muslim commentators deny the charge that there is confusion here between Miriam, Aaron's sister, and Maryam (Mary), mother of Jesus. 'Sister of Aaron,' they argue, simply means 'virtuous woman' in this context."[30] But the typological use of Hagar in the retelling of the story of Moses in the Qur'ān could be taken to suggest that even without following the high doctrine of biblical inspiration of the Qur'ān taught by Muslim orthodoxy, it would be possible to see in this identification something other than a simple mistake. For there was, already in post-biblical Judaism, widespread speculation and expectation not only of the return of Elijah, for whom a place was therefore set at the Seder table, but of the subsequent historical role of Moses. Christianity had picked up on this speculation, both by contrasting Moses and Christ in such passages as the formula, "The law was given by Moses, but grace and truth came by Jesus Christ,"[31] and by coordinating Moses and Christ (and Elijah) on the Mount of Transfiguration, where the two Old Testament figures appeared on either side of Jesus as he was transfigured.[32] Because it was the basic insistence—and, as seen by Islam, the basic corrective—of the Qur'ān to restore Jesus to the prophetic succession, before Muhammad and after Moses, the parallelism between Moses and Jesus was a central emphasis. It would therefore appear to be at least a plausible alternative to the standard Western diminution of Muhammad to see this phrase "sister of Aaron," addressed to Mary mother of Jesus, as another documentation of that parallelism.

34. *This was Jesus, son of Mary: A true account they contend about. 35. It does not behove God to have a son. Too immaculate is He! When He decrees a thing He has only to say: "Be," and it is. 36. [Jesus only said] "Surely God is my Lord and your Lord, so worship Him. This is the straight path." 37. Yet the sectarians differed among themselves.* This summation was clearly polemical. It explicitly asserted a disjunction where orthodox Christianity had taught a conjunction: "This was Jesus, son of Mary"—"It does not behove God to have a son. Too immaculate is He!" By the time of the coming of the prophet Muhammad, more than five hundred years of post–New Testament theology had passed, during which, in the words of the Qur'ān, "the sectarians differed among themselves"—and mightily. Five ecumenical councils had met and passed dogmatic decrees: Nicaea in 325, Constantinople I in 381, Ephesus in 431, Chalcedon in 451, Constantinople II in 553. Thus there was by this time a massive body of material in the orthodox Christian "deposit of the faith [*depositum fidei*]." And because the relation between the divine nature and the human nature in the one person of Jesus Christ was the burden of so many of those dogmatic decrees, Mary had figured prominently in them, as the title Theotokos, the Mother of God, documented: Jesus Christ was Son of God *and* son of Mary, and the problem was how to express that distinction without creating a division. Therefore the Muslim reaction against the course that orthodox dogmatics had taken in the Christian church, specifically with regard to the person of Jesus Christ, also had to follow the Christian development by focusing serious attention on Mary, not as Theotokos, Mother of God, here, but as Mother of Jesus. In these verses of sūrah 19, therefore, the counterpoint was between the two opening affirmations: "This was Jesus, son of Mary"—"It does not behove God to have a son." And as for Christian orthodoxy, so in a directly antithetical way also for Muslim orthodoxy, the key to the correct understanding both of who Jesus was and of what he did was Mary, his mother.

The portrait of Mary the Virgin Mother of Jesus in the Qur'ān not only occupied an important place in the Qur'ān itself, and therefore in the faith of Islam, but it carried "bridge-building" implications in several directions. One of these was certainly the implications of Mary for the relation between Judaism and Islam. It may be difficult for some to believe, but the portrait of Judaism in the Qur'ān represented at heart a profound affirmation. "The People of the Book" was the honorific title with which it referred to the people of Israel throughout, and even some of the less than flattering language in sūrah 17, Bani Isrā'il, "The Children of Israel," was chiefly a repetition of what the Lord God had said about the people of Israel over and over in the Hebrew Bible. A case can be made for the thesis that the Qur'ān was a large-scale effort to redress the balance after six centuries of Christian anti-Judaism. That became evident in a special way through the reclaiming of Abraham as the common ancestor and father in faith, as he was celebrated in sūrah 14: "All praise be to God who bestowed on me Ishmael and Isaac in old age," Abraham prayed there,[33] linking the two sons of Abraham, and therefore the two peoples descended from those two sons, in coordination with each other, rather than in a subordination of Ishmael to Isaac. In the light of the subsequent importance of Egypt in Islamic culture and politics, it is amusing to note that the history of the patriarch Joseph, as elaborated in later rabbinical traditions, was retold in sūrah 12 from Israel's side, not from Egypt's side. And Moses emerged in the Qur'ān as the giver of the law and the predecessor of the prophet. But among these connections between Judaism and Islam, Mary occupied a special place. Because the Qur'ān could be read as the restoration of Jesus to the history of Israel, Mary had to be the decisive hinge in its campaign, for she was, also for Christians, the point of connection between Jesus and the history of Israel. And even in the negative language of the Qur'ān about Judaism she had to put in her appearance: "Cursed were disbelievers among the children of Israel by David and Jesus, son of Mary, because they rebelled and transgressed the bounds," God said through the prophet.[34]

Parallel to those implications of Mary for the relation between Judaism and Islam were the implications of Mary for the relation between Islam and Christianity. The portrait of the Virgin Mary in the Qur'ān was one of its most surprising features even to the earliest authors of Christian responses to Islam. One writer of anti-Muslim treatises, Bartholomew of Edessa, probably in the ninth century, declared: "In the entire Qur'ān there do not occur any praises of Muhammad or of his mother Aminah, such as are found about our Lord Jesus Christ and about the Holy Virgin Mary, the Theotokos."[35] For, as Norman Daniel has said, "There is nothing else in all the Qur'ān to parallel the warmth with which Christ and His mother are spoken of. Christ is presented as a unique being, but His mother's personality appears more vividly. The Qur'ān inspires a devotion to Mary of which Muslims might have made more."[36] One can only add that Christians, too, might have made more of it than they did. The two principal objections of Islam to the Christian attitude toward Mary were to the concept and title Theotokos and to her portrayal in icons. Because of its dedication to the transcendence and otherness of God, Islam found the title Theotokos offensive—"It does not behove God to have a son. Too immaculate is he!"[37]—and at least some Muslim apologists claimed that Christians were including Mary the Mother of God in the Godhead. In spite of disclaimers of this in Christian responses, especially Byzantine responses, the Muslim critique may well have reflected kinds of confusion about Mary at the level of folk religion that were making her into a goddess, a confusion not without parallels in Christian history, as other chapters of this book suggest. The special standing of her image among Byzantine and Slavic icons[38] singled her out for special attention also from the Muslim spokesmen who attacked the worship of icons as idolatry. Nevertheless, as the Christian responses sought to make clear, Christian faith did not place her alongside the Deity but exalted her as the supreme exemplar of what human nature could become—and what it had become in her by the very sovereign will and decree of God of which the angelic messenger spoke when he said to Mary in the Qur'ān: "Your Lord said: 'We shall make him a sign for men and a blessing from Us.' This is a thing already decreed.'"[39] For Islam this meant, as an earlier sūrah had insisted, that "the Christ, son of Mary, was but an apostle, and many apostles had [come and] gone before him; *and his mother was a woman of truth.*"[40]

But even beyond all of these implications were the implications of the picture of Mary in the Qur'ān for multicultural Christian understanding with Islam and beyond. The urgent need to find symbols and concepts in our several cultural traditions that can perform the function of a *pontifex*, the function of priestly mediation and bridge-building, suggests that there has probably been no symbol or concept in Christendom that has carried out this "pontifical" vocation of mediation with more success and more amplitude than Mary.[41] And a primary proof for that thesis was the picture of Mary in the Qur'ān, in which, according to the interpretation quoted from Daniel, her "personality appears more vividly" even than that of her son or of the prophet. But with apologies to Muslim iconoclasm, this thesis would have to be extended chiefly through attention to the sacred pictures of Mary in a variety of cultures.[42] It would apply as well to the feasts and festivals devoted to her and to the shrines that have sprung up in her honor at such places as Lourdes, Fátima, Marpingen, and Guadalupe.[43] And here an important contribution to what might be called the "multicultural Mary" came from a source discussed earlier, the words of the Bride from the Song of Songs: "Black am I and beautiful,"[44] together with the portraits of the Virgin Mary that have been grouped as "Black Madonnas."[45] As part of the same commentary in which he corrected the usual translation of those words, Marvin Pope, citing the most important art-historical monograph on the subject,[46] presented several hypotheses to explain the Black Madonnas, concluding that an origin in Asia Minor seemed "highly probable" and drawing significant parallels with the Black Demeter, Isis, and other black deities of paganism.[47] The early history of the veneration of the Virgin Mary in Africa anticipated these later developments.[48]

The title "Black Madonna" acquired special significance when it came to be applied to the celebrated icon of Mary at Jasna Góra in the Polish city of Częstochowa, attributed to Saint Luke the icon painter, which is the most revered sacred image in Central Europe and the object of countless pilgrimages (see p. viii, above).[49] Prince Ladislaus Opolszyk brought it to Częstochowa in 1382, and Prince Jagiełło built the church for the shrine of the icon after his marriage to Queen Jadwiga of Poland

and his coronation in 1386. Out of a lifetime spent in the Polish culture of which she was the primary symbol, Henryk Górecki in 1976 composed his Opus 36, *Symfonia pieśni żałosnych* [Symphony of songs of complaint], which stands with Benjamin Britten's *War Requiem* and the *Leningrad Symphony* of Dmitry Shostakovich as a memorial to the victims of the Second World War. But it also stands as the expression, especially in its soprano arias, of what the Polish tradition has seen in the face of the Black Madonna of Częstochowa.[50] The blackened face of the Virgin in that icon was the result of smoke, but it has nevertheless had the salutary effect of stimulating and sanctioning the process of what Pope John Paul II, a special devotee of the Virgin of Częstochowa, has called "acculturation," particularly liturgical and artistic acculturation. Yet by an irony that is not without many historical parallels, the most forceful statement ever made of the case for these multicultural images came from a source that denounced all images, the Holy Qur'ān of Islam.

Johannes Vermeer, *Allegory of Faith*, c. 1671–74. The Metropolitan Museum of Art, New York, The Friedsam Collection, Bequest of Michael Friedsam, 1931.

6 The Handmaid of the Lord
and the Woman of Valor

And Mary said,
Behold the handmaid of the Lord.
—Luke 1:38

A woman of valor who will find?
—Proverbs 31:10

I f historians of art or of the church were to follow the example of their colleagues in the natural sciences by compiling a "citation index," not of the articles, papers, and books of other scholars as scientists do, but of the themes that have captured the attention of painters and sculptors throughout history, and especially if they were to prepare such an index together, it seems clear that among all the scenes in the life of the Virgin Mary that have engaged the piety of the devout and the creativity of the artists, the annunciation has been predominant. The annunciation has been so prevalent, in fact, that the number of references to it in such an index would probably exceed the number of references to all other Marian themes combined. Each theme and chapter in this book could in one way or another have been illustrated by an artistic rendering of the annunciation.[1]

Depending on how one interprets them, at least three works of early Christian art in the Roman catacombs appear to have portrayed the annunciation: one from the Catacomba di Santa Priscilla, another from the Catacomba di Santi Marcellino e Pietro, and a third from the Catacomba di Via Latina, discovered only in 1956.[2] The annunciation became a theme for altarpieces and other paintings in the Western Middle Ages, becoming especially frequent in the later Middle Ages, as David Robb has shown.[3] In the Byzantine East, the annunciation constituted one of the twelve feasts of the church year. Eventually the annunciation became the subject of many icons in the East, including two Byzantine cameos that have been dated by some art historians to as early as the sixth century; these are preserved in the collections of the Hermitage Museum in Saint Petersburg.[4] More grandly, the annunciation often appeared on the "royal portal" of the iconostasis in a Byzantine church. At the "great entrance" of the priest through the iconostasis in the course of the *Byzantine Liturgy of Saint Basil*, he recited the several "comings" of God and Christ in the course of the history of salvation, including above all the coming that took place through the incarnation at the event of the annunciation to Mary.[5] So also the annunciation painted on that portal represented the supreme coming of God the Logos in the flesh that he received from the Virgin Mary.

As these artistic representations suggest, the primary importance of the annunciation was believed to lie in the miracle of the incarnation.[6] In the dramaturgic structure of the first chapter of the Gospel of Luke, the annunciation constituted the narrative counterpart to the climax of the first chapter of the Gospel of John: "And the Word was made flesh."[7] It was the central meaning of the annunciation, and of Christian faith and teaching about the doctrine of the incarnation, that, as these words of John's Gospel confessed (which were recited as part of the Angelus), "*Verbum caro factum est*, The Word was made flesh,"[8] and that this had happened when, in the words of the Epistle of Paul to the Galatians, "God sent forth his Son, made of a woman."[9] Throughout history the attention to the person of Jesus Christ was, as in the words just quoted, closely linked with attention to his Mother. What the Gospel of John stated in the language of theology and of Hellenistic philosophy when it said "The Word [Logos] was made flesh," the Gospel of Luke described in the language of drama and dialogue, in the form of an exchange between Mary as the chosen one of God and the angel Gabriel as the emissary of

God. This annunciation, as well as the earlier one to Zechariah, father of John the Baptist, followed a set outline and stylized form.[10]

At the same time, the annunciation represented for Christian thought the supreme example and paradigm for pondering the mysterious question that had occupied so much attention in both the history of philosophy and the history of theology and that had engaged the major attention of thinkers not only in the Christian tradition but in the Jewish and Muslim traditions as well: the relation between necessity and free will or between divine sovereignty and human freedom. This was one of the most difficult of all Christian controversies to explain to Jewish thinkers, who saw no need of choosing between the freedom of God and the freedom of the human will. Throughout history Mary was seen as, on one hand, the "handmaid of the Lord," as she called herself in Luke,[11] the one who became the instrument of the divine plan. In every century she served as the model of patience, indeed of quietistic passivity and unquestioning obedience. When the prophet Isaiah asked, "Shall the clay say to him that fashioned it, What makest thou?" and again affirmed, "We are the clay, and thou our potter"; or when the apostle Paul, echoing these words of the Hebrew Bible, asked, "Hath not the potter power over the clay, of the same lump to make one vessel unto honor, and another unto dishonor?"[12]—that was an affirmation of the unknowable and unquestionable authority of God, in relation to which the human race and the individual person had to be viewed as submissive, even as inert matter. The word of the angel of the annunciation, "With God shall nothing be impossible," became the basis for seeing Mary, by her own self-designation of Handmaid (*Ancilla* in the Vulgate), as proof that when the sovereign authority and almighty will of God prevailed, as they always had and always would eventually, the outcome was one that had to be be acknowledged as good and wise altogether, even though it had been veiled in obscurity for the eyes of mortals at the time. It added to this definition of Mary the Handmaid that she was a woman and was therefore supposedly cast, by a deadly combination of nature and creation and fall, in the role of the passive and submissive one, the vessel that received. Therefore she could be held up to women as a model of how they ought to behave, in submissive obedience to God, to their husbands, and to the clergy and hierarchy of the church.

But throughout most of the history of reflection on the events of the annunciation and on the participation of the person of Mary in those events, this portrait was only half the picture. For it has often been noted that an obedience that is open to the future should be defined as supreme activity, not passivity. On closer inspection, therefore, the title Handmaid of the Lord was significantly more complex than many of its interpreters had supposed. The Greek term was *doulē kyriou*, literally, woman slave of the Lord. It was the feminine form of the much more familiar and more frequent phrase in the masculine, *doulos Iēsou Christou*, slave of Jesus Christ,[13] which became, in the New Testament, almost a technical term for the apostles. It went on to become the more elaborate and more complete title "slave of the slaves of God [*servus servorum Dei*]": Augustine, for example, had styled himself "slave of Christ and slave of the slaves of Christ [*servus Christi servorumque Christi*]," but beginning with Pope Gregory the Great *servus servorum Dei* was added to the panoply of the standard titles of the bishop of Rome.[14] It would be difficult, on the basis of studying the pontificate of Gregory I, to conclude that the term *servus* provided a justification for passivity or quietism. At its foundation, the term was a reference to the paradox of Christ as being both in "the form of God [*morphē theou*]" and in the "form of a slave [*morphē doulou*]."[15] The masculine title *doulos* and the feminine title *doulē* appeared together in the New Testament only once, in a quotation from the Greek of the Septuagint in the second chapter of the Book of Acts: "And on my servants and on my handmaidens [*epi tous doulous mou kai epi tas doulas mou*] I will pour out in those days my Spirit." And then the quotation added the portentous promise: "and they shall prophesy."[16] In the case of the male slaves, the *douloi*, the fulfillment of that promise was the history of the apostolic church as described in the following twenty-six chapters of the Book of the Acts of the Apostles and its continuation through the ages. But for the fulfillment of the promise of the prophet Joel in the case of the female slaves, the first and the preeminent place to look, as her association with the apostles in the first chapter of the Book of Acts suggested,[17] was the one who had identified herself in the story of the annunciation as doulē kyriou; and the content of her first prophesying was to be found in her responses to Gabriel, and then in the revolutionary cadences of the Magnificat. That certainly did not sound very "passive" or quietistic.

For, as the dual title of this chapter suggests, she was throughout the centuries the Handmaid of the Lord and the Woman of Valor, and neither of these without the other. Thus in a time far later than the subject matter of the present chapter, the period of slavery in the United States, "masters taught their slaves Christianity in order to inculcate obedience, but spirituals like 'Oh, Mary,' 'Go Down, Moses,' and others indicate that some slaves identified with those Biblical heroes who had challenged slavery in ancient times."[18] The Greek word for annunciation was euangelismos, which indicated the function of the annunciation story as the prime exemplar of "evangelization," as this was depicted in the icons of the event and as it was expounded in the commentaries of the Greek Christian tradition on the narrative. That function became evident in the formulations of the fourth-century philosophical theologian Gregory of Nyssa, as he commented on the words of the annunciation from the Gospel of Luke:

At once, with the coming upon her of the Holy Spirit and
with her being overshadowed by the power of the Most High,
the human nature in Mary (where Wisdom built her house)
[Prov. 9:1], though naturally part of our sensuous compound
[of flesh and spirit], became that which that overshadowing
power in essence was; for "without contradiction the less is
blessed of the better" [Heb. 7:7]. Seeing, then, that the power
of the Godhead is an immense and immeasurable thing, while
man is a weak atom, at the moment when the Holy Spirit
came upon the Virgin and the power of the Most High overshadowed her, the tabernacle formed by such an impulse was
not clothed with anything of human corruption; but, just as it
was first constituted, so it remained, even though it was man,
spirit nevertheless, and grace, and power. And the special attri-

butes of our humanity derived luster from this abundance of divine power.[19]

For in spite of the extraordinary, indeed unique, character of the event of the incarnation of the Logos in the man Jesus Christ, these thinkers took it also as a model of how the "gospel [euangelion]" functioned everywhere and at all times, and therefore it was as well for them the defining example of the full meaning of human freedom. It was, they maintained, a narrow and crabbed conception of freedom to equate it with anarchy and permissiveness and thus to define it as having the right to do whatever one pleased, no matter how destructive to self or to others; for in its fullest and deepest sense it included supremely, as the twentieth-century French man of letters Paul Claudel said and described it, the "liberty to obey."[20] For if the human creature, having been endowed by the Creator with free will as well as with the inalienable right to employ that freedom, was to employ freedom to attain authentic selfhood and authentic humanity, such a liberty to obey implied, as Hans Urs von Balthasar said, that "no finite freedom can be freer from restrictions than when giving its consent to infinite freedom."[21] And the supreme illustration for von Balthasar, as for such Greek theologians as Maximus Confessor whom von Balthasar had interpreted so brilliantly, was the consent of the "finite freedom" of the Virgin Mary to the "infinite freedom" of God in the annunciation.

In the annunciation to Mary, the word of God was communicated through a created messenger (and "angel" originally meant "messenger" in Greek, as the equivalent term had in Hebrew), the angel Gabriel. But unlike the "angel of the Lord" who in one night had slain 185,000 Assyrian soldiers from the armies of Sennacherib,[22] Gabriel brought the word of God to Mary in order to evoke a response from her that was free and unconstrained. In Greek Christian thought, Mary was predestined to be the Mother of Christ; she was the chosen one of the Almighty. And the will of the Almighty was law, for, once again in a formula of Gregory of Nyssa, "the power of the divine will is a sufficient cause for the things that are and for their coming into existence out of nothing."[23] Yet these Greek

Christian thinkers insisted at the same time that it was only when Mary said, and of her own free will, "Behold, the handmaid of the Lord: be it done to me according to thy word,"[24] that the will of the Almighty was carried out. And, they argued, if that was true of the most shattering intervention into human life and history ever launched by God, it had to be true of how the grace of God always operated, respecting human freedom and integrity and therefore, as in the defining case of Adam and Eve, risking disobedience.

As Irenaeus had put it, in the contrast between Eve and Mary discussed earlier,[25] "just as the former was led astray by the word of an angel, so that she fled from God when she had transgressed His word; so did the latter, by an angelic communication, receive the glad tidings that she should be the bearer of [portaret] God, being obedient to His word. And if the former did disobey God, yet the latter was persuaded [suasa est] to be obedient to God, in order that the Virgin Mary might become the patroness [advocata] of the virgin Eve."[26] She was "persuaded," not coerced, to yield an obedience that was no less voluntary in its affirmation than the disobedience of Eve had been in its negation. As free will could not be taken away from Eve in order to say that she was not accountable for her actions, so it could not be taken away from Mary either, in a misguided attempt to make the grace of God seem greater by minimizing or denying human free will. It was a differentiating characteristic of Byzantine philosophy and theology, and one that often provoked puzzlement or exasperation in the West, that in its views of the relation of grace and free will it did not work with the alternatives developed in the time of Augustine. When Pelagius, Augustine's arch-opponent in the controversy on grace, free will, and predestination, was summoned in 415 to a gathering of Greek theologians and bishops at Lydda-Diospolis in Palestine, he explained his teaching about the relation between grace and free will to the synod in such a way that he was pronounced orthodox— much to Augustine's consternation.[27] Augustine's defensive account of these proceedings, On the Proceedings of Pelagius, was one of the few works of his to be translated into Greek, perhaps during his lifetime, and was included in the Bibliotheca of the ninth-century scholar and patriarch of

Constantinople Photius. From a comparison of the decree, Augustine's reaction, and Photius's treatment, it is evident that for Eastern Christian thought the Augustinian formulation of the antithesis of grace and freedom, or even of nature and grace, represented a wrong question, to which any answer would have to be wrong.

In the West, the supreme paradigm for the relation between nature and grace, and hence between freedom and grace, was the apostle Paul. His experience of the violent intervention of God when he was thrown to the ground and blinded on the road to Damascus, which was recounted three separate times in the Book of Acts and rather differently in his self-defense at the beginning of the Epistle to the Galatians, was an experience of radical discontinuity between what he had been and what he became.[28] This radical discontinuity compelled him to look for continuity; hence, in the ninth, tenth, and eleventh chapters of the Epistle to the Romans he affirmed both his identification with his past and his drastic break with that past.[29] That Pauline model of conversion was at work in the thought of Augustine. When, in the famous scene in the garden, Augustine heard the voice saying "*Tolle, lege* [Pick it up, read it]," what he read was a passage from Paul on the theme of discontinuity with the past.[30] Paul had admonished the Romans, and was now admonishing Augustine: "Not in rioting and drunkenness, not in chambering and wantonness, not in strife and envying. But put ye on the Lord Jesus Christ, and make not provision for the flesh to fulfil the lusts thereof."[31] And, as Augustine had said somewhat earlier, "with great eagerness, then, I fastened upon the venerable writings of thy Spirit and principally upon the apostle Paul."[32] Again in the thought of Martin Luther, Paul and a passage from his Epistle to the Romans set the pattern: "The justice of God is revealed in the gospel from faith to faith [*Iustitia enim Dei in eo revelatur ex fide in fidem*]."[33] As he described in the autobiographical foreword to his collected Latin works, an *apologia pro vita sua* written in 1545, the year before his death, Luther as a monk and novice exegete had struggled over the meaning of this passage because he assumed that "the justice of God" referred, as he thought it did throughout Scripture, to the quality of the divine nature by which God was just and by which therefore God condemned sin. All of that changed, and as he said "I felt that I . . . had entered paradise itself through open gates," when he perceived that Paul was speaking instead about the justice with which God endowed the sinner in justification. It came, not as the consummation of the human quest, but as the intervention of the divine initiative.[34] Luther's doctrine of nature and grace, then, while significantly different from Augustine's, did emphasize discontinuity. And when, in 1525, he carried on his famous controversy with Erasmus and wrote The Bondage of the Will, he believed himself to be expounding the teaching of Paul as he denied to the human will before conversion any positive functioning toward the grace of God and as he put the whole action on the sovereign will of God.

Thinkers of the Eastern tradition, in contrast, characteristically substituted a complementarity for this antithesis. This does not mean that they in the slightest diminished the miracle of the grace of God, which they extolled in prose and poetry, praying as though everything depended on divine grace but acting as though everything depended on human works. But they interpreted grace simultaneously as a totally unearned divine gift and as an affirmation of continuity with nature and creation—and therefore with freedom. In the paradoxical formula of a leading seventh-century Byzantine thinker, Maximus Confessor, God "grants a reward as a gift to those who have believed him, namely, eternal deification."[35] Apparently "reward" and "gift" were not mutually exclusive but complementary concepts that together produced salvation as "deification."[36] One scholar pointed out, in commenting on such passages as this, that it was "possible for Maximus to say, on the one hand, that there is no power inherent in human nature which is able to deify man, and yet, on the other, that God becomes man insofar as man has deified himself."[37]

That characteristically Eastern emphasis on continuity came to voice in a highly personal letter written by Basil of Caesarea, probably in the year 375:

The teaching about God which I had received as a boy from my blessed mother and my grandmother Macrina, I have ever held with increased conviction. On my coming to ripe years of reason I did not shift my opinions from one to another, but carried out the principles delivered to me by my parents. Just as the seed when it grows is first tiny and then gets bigger but *always preserves its identity, not changed in kind though gradually perfected in growth*, so I reckon the same doctrine to have grown in my case through gradually advancing stages. What I hold now has not replaced what I held at the beginning.[38]

Significantly, what Basil said there about the continuity of his maturation in the context of Christian nurture he even applied, with significant and appropriate modifications, to the relation between Christianity and Classical culture, especially in his famous letter-essay, known in English as *Exhortation to Youths as to How They Shall Best Profit by the Writings of Pagan Authors*, in which he urged his nephews to plumb the depths of the classical Greek tradition and to learn from it lessons for their Christian faith and life.[39] And in the thought of his brother, Gregory of Nyssa, quoted earlier, that affirmation of continuity and that insistence on freedom even in relation to divine grace came to new depths of insight.[40]

But in support of that characteristically Byzantine emphasis on the active role of free will as it accepted the word and grace freely given by God, the active response of the Mother of God in the annunciation as she accepted the word and grace of God was a key incident. As the Eastern thinkers interpreted it, when she became the paradigm, the incarnation both in all its novelty and in its profound continuity with everything that she had been until then could be affirmed. Therefore she was "full of grace [*kecharitōmenē*]," as the angel Gabriel had said in saluting her.[41] For "the entire treasure of grace" dwelt in her,[42] but even though it was the grace of the Almighty, it dwelt in her by her own free will. Her free response to the will and grace of God made her, in a unique sense, a colaborer with God—as the apostle Paul said to the Corinthians, "We, then, as workers together [*synergoi*] with him"[43]—and therefore also an exemplar of freedom. In many of the centuries of thought and reflection about Mary, that role as exemplar may have been overshadowed by a cramped rendition of her words "Behold the handmaid of the Lord," so that the full dynamism was lost. But repeatedly the power of the annunciation narrative managed to reassert itself in all its vigor: "For he hath regarded the low estate of his handmaiden: for, behold, from henceforth all generations shall call me blessed."[44]

As if to refute, or at least to counterbalance by a preemptive linguistic strike, the quietistic interpretation that would be imposed on this portrait of Mary as, in her own words, *Ancilla Domini*, the Handmaid of the Lord, the Medieval portrayal of the Virgin also applied to her the words: "A woman of valor who will find?"[45] celebrating her as *Mulier Fortis*, the Woman of Valor. Whatever the original Hebrew term ḥāyil may have meant in the context of the closing chapter of the Book of Proverbs—several modern translations of the Bible into English seem to agree on the rendering "capable" here—the Hebrew vocable did allow for the meaning "valor"; and both the Greek translation in the Septuagint, *andreia* (this being the word for the classical virtue of "fortitude"), and the Latin translation in the Vulgate, *fortis*, understood it that way. Woman of Valor thus became a striking formula for the motif and metaphor of Mary as warrior and champion, as conqueror and leader.

The most influential expression of that motif, at any rate in Western Christendom, was the eventual Latin translation of the words of punishment addressed by God to the serpent after the fall of Adam and Eve, to read: "I shall put enmity between you and the woman, and between your seed and her seed; she will crush your head, and you will bruise her heel [*Inimicitias ponam inter te et mulierem, et semen tuum et semen illius; ipsa conteret caput tuum, et tu insidiaberis calcaneo eius*]."[46] There is clear evidence that this was not how Jerome translated the text; for as a Hebrew scholar, he knew that the pronoun should not be rendered with "she," and one of the earliest manuscripts of his translation, as well as an early use of it by Pope Leo I, carried the reading *ipse*, not *ipsa*.[47] Nevertheless, the reading eventually became *ipsa*, for reasons that are not clear. Yet even when it did, early interpreters of the feminine pronoun applied it to the church as the one who had crushed, and was continuing to crush, the head of Satan.[48] In his commentary on Genesis the Venerable Bede, in whose Anglo-Saxon

England the cult of Mary was flourishing,[49] quoted the passage with the feminine pronoun but declared that "the woman crushes the head of the serpent when the holy church dispels the snares and venomous lures of the devil";[50] and another eighth-century monk, Ambrosius Autpertus, celebrating "the daily victory of Christ in the church," saw this victory prefigured in the words spoken to the serpent in Paradise, that ipsa, the woman, would crush his head.[51] But it was already standard practice to identify the church with Mary, as the first one to have believed in the incarnation and, between Good Friday and Easter, the only one to have believed in the resurrection. By far the dominant Medieval interpretation of the feminine pronoun in this passage, therefore, was the Mariological one.[52] Having already applied to Mary the first half of the statement to the serpent, "I shall put enmity between you and the woman," Bernard of Clairvaux continued, "And if you still doubt that he has spoken of Mary, listen to what follows: 'She will crush your head.' For whom was this victory reserved except for Mary? Beyond doubt it was she who crushed the venomous head."[53]

Both biographically and iconographically, there would appear to be some possibility of connecting this first so-called messianic prophecy with the complex symbolism in Johannes Vermeer's late painting of circa 1671–74, Allegory of [the] Faith. "Only in Allegory of Faith," writes Arthur K. Wheelock, Jr., "does he explicitly incorporate abstract theological concepts into a visual vocabulary similar to his other paintings."[54] Vermeer was an adult convert to Roman Catholicism.[55] His conversion was reflected in a number of his paintings, including Christ in the House of Mary and Martha, which is often read as a depiction of the Medieval interpretation of the two sisters as representative of the relation between the contemplative and the active life. Scholars have identified the female figure in his Woman Holding a Balance as the Virgin Mary, the Mediatrix standing between the human race and divine judgment.[56] That judgment was depicted not only by the balance on which, as the words of Isaiah had said, "the nations are as a drop of a bucket, and are counted as the small dust of the balance,"[57] but by the painting of the last judgment on the wall behind her.

Because, as the Second Vatican Council was to put it in its decree *Lumen Gentium,* "Mary in a certain way unites and mirrors within herself the central truths of the faith [*maxima fidei placita in se quodammodo unit et reverberat*],"[58] a painting bearing the title *Allegory of Faith* (or Allegory of the Faith) could well concentrate on her. In the foreground, in a direct allusion to the narrative of the fall of Adam and Eve and the words of Genesis, was the bleeding carcass of a serpent, its head crushed by a stone, and next to it an apple; over it stood the victorious form of a woman, with her foot on a globe of the world. The painting on the wall, which as in *Woman Holding a Balance* seems to have been intended as a commentary on the action in the painting, portrayed the crucifixion, where the serpent did bruise the heel of the Mother and of the Son but was himself vanquished; in addition, as if to make sure that the viewer did not miss the point, there was a crucifix on the wall. There does not seem to be any way, even with a magnifying glass, to identify the title of the open book, much less its specific words. If it was a Bible, in Dutch or perhaps more likely in Latin, the text seems to have been near the end. Could that perhaps have been the vision of the Woman Clothed with the Sun from the Book of Revelation?[59] Or would it be completely far-fetched to speculate that the book might have been a Hebrew Bible, which was easily available in seventeenth-century Holland, and therefore have been open near the beginning rather than near the end—and specifically at the words of the Lord to the serpent, but interpreted in accordance with the accepted Latin translation and graphically documented by that venomous but now harmless serpent's head?

Another of the ways in which Mary showed herself to be the woman of valor spoken of in Proverbs was her role as lodestar and guide of mariners, "Mary, the star of the sea [*Maria maris stella*]," a name that was said to have been given her from on high.[60] The name was thought to have been prophesied in the oracle, "A star shall come forth out of Jacob."[61] Because "this class of [nautical] metaphor is extraordinarily widespread throughout the Middle Ages,"[62] the image of Mary as the star guiding the ship of faith was especially attractive, even though it depended at least in part on a trick of language. Its origins seem to lie in

Jerome's etymology for the name "Mary" as "a drop of water from the sea [*stilla maris*]," which he preferred to other explanations. This etymology was taken over by Isidore of Seville, but in the process "drop [*stilla*]" had become "star [*stella*]." On that basis, apparently in the ninth century, an unknown poet composed an influential hymn, hailing Mary as the Star of the Sea, the nourishing Mother of God, the Ever-Virgin, the Gate of Heaven:

> Ave, maris stella,
> Dei mater alma
> atque semper virgo,
> felix caeli porta.[65]

Soon the title became a part of the homiletical language about the Virgin, as well as of theological literature; but it was especially in poetry that the symbol of the courageous Mary as the lodestar of voyagers through life found expression. As Lodestar, she was seen as continuing to overcome the enemies and the storms, and therefore as continuing to be the Woman of Valor who was the Handmaid of the Lord.

Icon of the Virgin, Egypt, Byzantine period, sixth century. © The Cleveland Museum of Art, 1996, Leonard C. Hanna, Jr., Bequest 1967.144.

7 The Adornment of Worship
and the Leader of the Heavenly Choir

And Miriam the prophetess, the sister of Aaron, took a timbrel in her hand;
and all the women went out after her with timbrels and with dances.
And Miriam answered them, Sing ye to the Lord, for he hath triumphed gloriously;
the horse and his rider hath he thrown into the sea.
—Exodus 15:20–21

The identification of Mary, mother of Jesus, with Miriam, sister of Moses, was not only a theme of the Qur'ān[1] but had long before been a theme of Christian typology. Commenting on the words of the psalm "Among them were the damsels playing with timbrels [in medio iuvenculae tympanistriae],"[2] Augustine identified the Virgin Mary as "nostra tympanistria," because, like Miriam before the children of Israel, she led the people of God and the angels of heaven in the praise of the Almighty.[3] And thousands of English-speaking Protestant congregations in this century—most of them without realizing that they were carrying on this typology of Miriam and Mary, and many without realizing that they were addressing Mary at all—have attributed to her a role as the adornment of worship and leader of the heavenly choir, in the words of John A. L. Riley's hymn of 1906, "Ye Watchers and Ye Holy Ones":

O higher than the cherubim,
More glorious than the seraphim,
Lead their praises, Alleluia!

Thou Bearer of th' eternal Word,

Most gracious, magnify the Lord, Alleluia!

which was to say that when the angels of heaven, the cherubim and seraphim, praised God, they were led by one whom the Archangel Gabriel had hailed as "most gracious" and who had begun her own hymn with the words "My soul doth magnify the Lord," the one who, being the Theotokos, was the Bearer of the eternal Word of God, the Logos-made-flesh. Such sentiments about her, of course, would probably have been harder to voice from the pulpits of such congregations than from the hymnals in their pews.

Even in congregations where the association of the Virgin Mary with worship came naturally, moreover, she figured much more prominently outside the official public liturgy than within it. In the liturgy, the prayers of the Eastern *Liturgy of Saint Basil* and *Liturgy of Saint John Chrysostom* invariably invoked her intercessions.[4] Above all, the hymn *Akathistos* (whose title meant "not sitting down")[5] multiplied its celebration of her as "unwed bride" and object of the church's praises, and it was in turn reflected in the visual arts.[6] In the Western liturgy of the Mass, too, the recitation of the saints above who were joined with the church on earth in petition, praise, and thanksgiving accorded her pride of place. Nevertheless, two of the most widespread and popular devotions to Mary in the Western tradition were nonliturgical in character. The first was usually associated in its origins with the Dominican Order and the second with the Franciscan Order, although both of them became well-nigh universal throughout Roman Catholicism. The practice of the rosary was probably not originated by Saint Dominic, as conventional wisdom supposed on the basis of the unsubstantiated legends recounted by Alan de la Roche in his narrative of revelations. Nevertheless, the rosary did have special ties with the Order of Preachers.[7] Following a devotional practice that appeared also outside Christianity, for example in Hinduism, Buddhism, and Islam, the rosary was a string of beads to be used as a mnemonic device for the recitation of prayers. In fact, the very word *bead* in English came from the universal Germanic word for "to pray," as in the modern German *beten* and the modern English word *bid*; and, as the *Oxford English Dictionary* explained, "the name was transferred from 'prayer' to the small globular bodies used for 'telling beads,' i.e., counting prayers said, from which the other senses naturally followed."[8] With some variations from one tradition of observance to another, the prayers of the rosary consisted of 15 recitations of the *Pater Noster*, 15 sets of 10 recitations of the *Ave Maria*, and 15 recitations of the *Gloria Patri*, each of the sets of fifteen prayers being concentrated on one of the mysteries of the redemption; thus a full cycle of the rosary included 150 prayings of the *Ave Maria*.[9]

The *Angelus*, by contrast, was connected with the admonition issued in 1269 by Bonaventure, as minister general of the Order of Friars Minor, that Franciscan friars imitate Francis of Assisi by reciting *Ave Marias* in response to the ringing of the evening bell for prayer. This was expanded, apparently during the fourteenth century, into an *Angelus* in the morning (first noted at Parma in 1317–18), at noon (Prague in 1386), and in the evening (Rome in 1327, elsewhere even earlier).[10] It also achieved wide circulation among the laity; and it was, for example, incorporated into the first act of Puccini's *Tosca*, in the prayer of the sacristan, as was the *Te Deum Laudamus* into the mighty chords of the closing scene of that act. The *Angelus* took its name from the words of the Gospel of Luke: "Angelus Domini ad Mariam, Ave gratia plena, . . . "[11] Through these two extraliturgical forms of worship as well as through various components of the liturgy itself, the history of Mary embedded itself in the language and the spirituality of countless believers throughout the Western world.

But the area of worship in which Mary performed as leader most effectively was in the adornment of icons.[12] For in the eighth, ninth, and tenth centuries the political, religious, and artistic future of the Byzantine empire and of Byzantine culture was at stake in a struggle for its very identity, during the several successive attacks of Iconoclasm on the use of images in Christian worship. The argument against images, and eventually the argument for them as well, came to be based on the question of whether one could portray the divine-human person of Christ in an icon. But the argument also involved in a special way the person of the Virgin, just as the founding of Byzantium had.[13] According to their opponents, the Iconoclasts attacked not only the worship of icons generally but the orthodox devotion to Mary specifically.[14] They were also reported to have rejected the orthodox belief in the special intercession of Mary on behalf of the church.[15]

In response to such attacks, orthodox theologians—such as John of Damascus, who argued that "the honor paid to an image was meant not for the depiction but for the person depicted"[16]—felt compelled to define how the various forms of "worship [proskynēsis]" that Christians were permitted to render to creatures were to be differentiated from the "adoration [latreia]" that could be addressed only to God the Creator, not to any creature.[17] If paid to idols, such worship was (in the original term) "idololatry [eidōlolatreia],"[18] although the Iconodules insisted that this term did not apply at all to their worship of icons. But by "God the Creator" orthodox theology since the Council of Nicaea and even much earlier had meant God the Holy Trinity, Father, Son, and Holy Spirit, to each of whom it was legitimate to pay a "worship [proskynēsis]" that was "adoration [latreia]," exclusively restricted to the true God. Such "adoration [latreia]," moreover, was addressed, as it had been since the New Testament, to the person of Jesus Christ: whereas Christ had said on the cross, according to Luke, "Father, into thy hands I commend my spirit,"[19] Stephen, the first Christian martyr, had, also according to Luke, called out "Lord Jesus, receive my spirit,"[20] thus moving with evident ease from a prayer that had been addressed to the Father to the same prayer that was now addressed to the Son. For "at the name of Jesus," the apostle Paul declared, "every knee should bow, of things in heaven, and things in earth, and things under the earth, and every tongue should confess that Jesus Christ is Lord, to the glory of God the Father."[21] To Christian orthodoxy, this "bowing the knee" and "worship [proskynēsis]" was genuine and complete "adoration [latreia]," and it included as its proper object the entire person of the Son of God incarnate—not his divine nature alone, since his divine nature was not alone after the incarnation but was united, permanently and "inseparably [achōristōs]" (as the Council of Chalcedon had declared in 451),[22] to the human nature, which could not be the object of "adoration [latreia]" in and of itself, being a creature, but which could and should be adored in the undivided person of the God-man.

All other orthodox "worship [proskynēsis]," by contrast, was simple "reverence [douleia]," hence not a violation of the First Commandment. In at least some passages of his works, John of Damascus did distinguish between "adoration [latreia]" and "reverence [douleia]."[23] But by a curious turn of linguistic history, the best available documentation for this distinction was not in his writings, nor in those of any other Greek patristic or Byzantine thinkers at all, but in Latin Christian authors, above all Augustine of Hippo. Augustine wrote in his City of God:

> For this is the worship which is due to the Divinity, or, to speak more accurately, to the Deity; and to express this worship in a single word, as there does not occur to me any Latin term sufficiently exact, I shall avail myself, wherever necessary, of a Greek word. Latreia, whenever it occurs in Scripture, is rendered by the word "service." But that service which is due to men, and in reference to which the apostle writes that servants must be subject to their own masters [Eph. 6:5], is usually designated by another word in Greek [douleia], whereas the service which is paid to God alone by worship, is always, or almost always, called latreia in the usage of those who wrote from the divine oracles.[24]

This passage was among the first witnesses—or, at any rate, among the earliest preserved witnesses—to make the distinction specific.[25] It must be added that for Augustine to occupy that position in the history of Greek was somewhat ironic, in view of his repeated admissions about his unreliable knowledge of Greek: he had developed an intense dislike for the Greek language, even for the reading of Homer, as a schoolboy,[26] and then as a Catholic bishop defending the Nicene doctrine of the Trinity he had to confess that he did not fully grasp the terminological subtleties in the fundamental trinitarian distinctions made by Greek theologians during the preceding several generations.[27]

As Theotokos, Mary—and that included the Mary of the icons—
was the legitimate object of orthodox Christian "worship [proskynēsis]."
Such distinctions were all the more necessary because of the many
postures and gestures of respect toward many persons that were prescribed not only by Byzantine piety but by Byzantine social custom.
Already in classical Greek usage, all of these expressions of respect at all
levels could come under the category of "worship [proskynēsis]," which
therefore not only meant to "make obeisance to the gods or their
images, fall down and worship" but pertained especially to "the Oriental fashion of prostrating oneself before kings and superiors."[28] That
fashion was exaggerated still further by what Charles Diehl called "the
thousand refinements of the precise and somewhat childish etiquette
which regulated every act of the imperial life" in Constantinople.[29] In
this profusion of acts of "worship,"[30] there needed to be a special way
of speaking about the worship of God and about the worship of the
saints, and particularly about the worship of the Virgin Mary. Therefore
Medieval Latin theology, illustrated for example by Thomas Aquinas
(who used the Greek terms in their Latin form), found that the simple
distinction between "adoration [latreia]" and "reverence [douleia]," as it had
been drawn by John of Damascus, did not do full justice to the special
position of the Theotokos. For she was certainly less than God, but just
as certainly she was more than an ordinary human being and more than
any other saint; therefore she was not entitled to latria, yet she was
entitled to more than dulia.[31] For her cultus, then, the appropriate term
was hyperdulia.[32] After the Middle Ages, the Latin church was to find the
distinction between latria and dulia (including hyperdulia) additionally
useful when, in the aftermath of the Reformation, Protestant polemics
was regularly accusing the church of "Mariolatry."[33] "Mario-latry"
would have to be defined as a form of latria paid to Mary; and extravagant though the language of prayers and hymns addressed to her did
undoubtedly become also in the West, this distinction was intended to
stand as a barrier against "Mariolatry"—albeit a barrier that may sometimes have been all but invisible to the piety of ordinary believers,
whether Western or Eastern, in their prayers to her and to her icon.[34] As

even the defenders of the icons had to acknowledge, the relation between technical theology and the piety of ordinary believers was difficult to handle.[35]

Perhaps the most dramatic of all the traditional portrayals of the
Virgin Mary in Byzantine art was the so-called Deesis (from the Greek
word deēsis, entreaty or intercession).[36] This was the word regularly used
in classical Greek for an "entreaty" of one kind or another.[37] In Byzantine Greek it was employed for various secular petitions and supplica-
tions, such as those addressed to the emperor by his subjects.[38] But it
also became the standard term in patristic Greek, and then in Byzantine
Greek, for intercessory prayers: for those addressed by the church "not
only to God but also to holy men, though not to others"; for the prayer
which Christ as the eternal Mediator presented to the Father; and also
for the prayers that the saints, and especially the Mother of God, as
created mediators presented to Christ and to the Father on behalf of the
church.[39] The Deesis as an art form was divided into three sections or
panels. At the center was the figure of Christ as Lord. On either side of
Christ were, pleading with Christ on behalf of sinners, the Mother of
God and John the Baptist (often identified as "the Forerunner [ho Pro-
dromos]").[40] The Deesis could be presented in artistic creations of various sizes. On one tiny eleventh-century Byzantine reliquary, which is
just over three inches square when folded, the Deesis appears in cloi-
sonné, its two panels of Mary and John folding over the panel of the
central figure. By contrast, the uncovering of the mosaic of the Deesis
on a wall in Hagia Sophia in Istanbul shows this Byzantine motif on a
very large scale.

Historians of Byzantine art and architecture have exploited the significance of the Deesis with sensitivity and skill,[41] establishing the term
Deesis in English usage. Unfortunately, historians of Byzantine spirituality
and theology have not investigated the Deesis with equal thoroughness,
despite the profound and suggestive way it presented several of the
central motifs in the Eastern Christian understanding of the entire "dispensation [oikonomia]" of the history of salvation. The juxtaposition of
Mary and John the Baptist in the Deesis was a way of identifying the

two figures who, according to the Christian understanding of the history of salvation, stood on the border between the Old Testament and the New. According to the saying of Christ in the Gospel, the line of the Old Testament prophets had come only as far as John the Baptist.[42] This was taken by Justin Martyr in the second century to prove that after John there would no longer be any prophets among the people of Israel.[43] Zechariah, the Baptist's father, was a priest of the "tribe of Levi," who continued the sacerdotal mediation between God and the people going back to Aaron. John's parents were the recipients of an "annunciation [euangelismos]" by the angel Gabriel, analogous to that which came a few months later to the Virgin Mary, cousin of John's mother, Elizabeth.[44] According to Gregory of Nyssa, "the gift in him was pronounced by him who sees the secrets of a man to be greater than any prophet's."[45] For Christ himself had said about John the Baptist: "Never has there appeared on earth a mother's son greater than John the Baptist."[46]

No mother's *son* was greater than John the Baptist, but one mother's *daughter* was greater than any mother's son or daughter, namely, Mary the Mother of God, whom Gregory of Nyssa earlier in the same treatise called "Mary without stain [amiantos]."[47] Not only iconographically but theologically, she occupied a unique place in Eastern Christendom, which was, as we have seen, where both the devotion to her and the speculation about her had been concentrated throughout the early centuries of Christian history. The devotion to Mary had found its supreme expression in the Byzantine liturgy. From its sources in the Greek church fathers and in Byzantine Christianity, Eastern Mariology went on to exert a decisive influence on Western interpretations of Mary throughout the patristic and early Medieval periods, with church fathers like Ambrose of Milan functioning as transmitters of Greek Mariology to the Latin church.[48]

Behind the differences between the Latin and the Greek traditions lay an even more profound difference, identified by the teaching of Greek Christian theology that salvation conferred on its recipients nothing less than a transformation of their very humanity, by which they partake of the reality of the Divine. Anders Nygren saw the idea that "the human is raised up to the Divine" as one that the Greek church father Irenaeus shared "with Hellenistic piety generally."[49] And there were clear echoes of Hellenism in the Christian version of the doctrine.[50] But this idea of salvation as deification or theōsis[51] was not exclusively Greek; it appeared in various of the Latin fathers, including Augustine, and, as Nygren acknowledged, it was even occasionally echoed in the writings of the Protestant Reformers and their followers.[52] At almost the same time as the tapestry Icon of the Virgin, which illustrates this chapter, was created, a Latin Christian writer incorporated the idea of divinization into a work of philosophical reflection that achieved wide circulation in the Middle Ages: "Since that men are made blessed by the obtaining of blessedness, and blessedness is nothing else but divinity, it is manifest that men are made blessed by the obtaining of divinity. And as men are made just by the obtaining of justice, and wise by the obtaining of wisdom, so they who obtain divinity must needs in like manner become gods. Wherefore everyone that is blessed is a god, but by nature there is only one God; but there may be many by participation."[53] The idea could, moreover, lay claim to explicit biblical grounding. As it stood, "I have said, Ye are gods," was a mysterious Old Testament statement in the Book of Psalms, addressed to the rulers of this world.[54] But as quoted by Christ in the New Testament, this statement became proof that "he called them gods, unto whom the word of God came, and the scripture cannot be broken."[55] Because believers in Christ were preeminently "those unto whom the word of God came," and among them this was preeminently true of Mary, it followed, according to the Greek Christian tradition, that they—and above all she—were also preeminently those who should be called "gods." For this, too, was a "scripture that cannot be broken."

The Scripture that provided justification for the idea, and that therefore became the locus classicus cited in support of it especially in Byzantine theology, was the arresting New Testament formula: "Whereby are given unto us exceeding great and precious promises: that by these ye might be partakers of the divine nature [theias koinōnoi physeōs], having escaped the corruption that is in the world through lust."[56] Both the negative emphasis of the Greek church fathers on salvation as escape from "transiency, corruption [phthora]" and their positive emphasis on salvation as participation in the divine nature were articulated in this one New Testament passage. Thus the Greek word theōsis, deification or divinization, came to stand for a distinctive view of the meaning of salvation, summarized in the Eastern patristic formula, current already in the second and third centuries: "God became human so that man might become divine." This view had then been fundamental to the development of the doctrine of the Trinity; as Athanasius had put it, "By the participation of the Spirit, we are knit into the Godhead."[57] While striving to protect the biblical formula of participation in the divine nature from any trace of pantheism by emphasizing the inviolable transcendence of a God beyond language or thought or even being, the Greek fathers and their Byzantine pupils strove no less assiduously to give concrete content to its promise of a humanity made divine through the incarnation of the Logos of God in the person of Jesus Christ.

That concrete content found its supreme exemplar in the person of Mary the Theotokos, also in Russian Orthodox art.[58] The painters of the icons seem to have manifested no hesitation in portraying Mary as "divine," and the defenders of the icons often seemed to be almost insouciant in their manner of speaking about her "divine" qualities; for "divine" was indeed the right word for her as Theotokos. In its ultimate significance, salvation as deification, like every heavenly promise, was eschatological and could not be fully achieved by anyone here in this present life on earth. But Mary was proof positive that it could be achieved, truly though not fully, and in this world; her portrayal in icons was evidence of this fact, as was the Magnificat, which was sung as part of the Orthros, or Morning Office of the Greek church.[59]

Icons of Christ simultaneously presented both "the form of God" and "the form of a servant"[60] as they had been inseparably united in his person through the incarnation. Although his "divine nature" had not always been perceptible to his contemporaries behind "the nature of a slave," which they did see, in the transfiguration it had become visible already in this world and even before his resurrection. This was expressed in the earliest preserved mosaic of the transfiguration, whose iconographic interpretation William Loerke has skillfully connected to Maximus Confessor's theological interpretation of the event:

> About seventy-five to eighty years after the mosaic was set, Maximus the Confessor gave the Transfiguration an imaginative and profound interpretation. He saw Christ in this vision as a symbol of himself, a manifestation of the hidden in the visible, in which the luminous garments at once clothe the human nature and reveal the divine. The event was not a fixed image, but an unfolding drama. The brilliant garments of Christ, the changing tones of blue in the aureole, and the transparencies in the rays of light coming from the aureole, suggest a hidden force coming into view—the visual analogue of Maximus' interpretation.[61]

And the historical analogue for it, a reality that was at once the anticipation and the result of the miracle of the transfiguration of Christ, was Mary the Mother of God. She did not have a pre-existent divine nature, as Christ did, but was completely human in her origin, like all other human beings. Yet because she had been chosen by God to be the Theotokos, her completely human nature had been transfigured; and already in this earthly existence she had in a special way become a "partaker of the divine nature," as the Second Epistle of Peter had promised that all who believed in her divine Son would.

The ground for "deification" as a distinctively Eastern depiction of salvation was a distinctively Eastern depiction of the atonement. It was, according to Byzantine theology, necessary but not sufficient to speak of human salvation as the forgiveness of sins. The interpretation of the passion and crucifixion of Christ as the sacrifice for sin—an interpretation that came from Scripture and was therefore common to East and West—had a corollary image of *Christus Victor* as the distinctive way for the Christian East to speak about the mystery of the redemption. By his victory Christ as Second Adam had conquered sin and death, and through his transfiguration he had given humanity a glimpse of its eventual destiny; Mary as Second Eve had also manifested this destiny, because of her Son and because of the divine life that he had conferred—first on her, and then on all. Such a view of the human condition and of salvation sometimes came dangerously close to defining the sin of Adam and Eve as the consequence not of their having transgressed the commandments of God but merely of their being temporal and finite; such a definition of sin would then seem to have manifested greater affinities to Neoplatonism than to the New Testament. But the very concentration on Mary the Theotokos as the historical fulfillment of this promise of humanity made divine prevented this view from falling completely into the Neoplatonic teaching.

As the battle over iconizing Christ provided the grounds for defending the practice of iconizing his Mother, so her icon supplied the justification for the icons of all the other saints. The tapestry *Icon of the Virgin* offered striking documentation of that connection between Mary and the other saints: surrounding the imposing figures of the Theotokos and the archangels Michael and Gabriel were medallions of apostles and saints. Conversely, the defense of portraying the divine-human Christ led to a defense of portraying the human Mary who, through him and because she was chosen to give birth to him, had been made divine. And since the concept of deification was also the fundamental constituent of the Byzantine definition of sainthood, it was an obvious extrapolation from these Mariological discussions to affirm that the saints, too, were to be iconized. How, the Iconodules asked, was it possible to portray the supreme commander without portraying his troops?[62] For the life of Christ depicted in the icons was not merely the life he had lived while on earth during the first century. The resurrected Christ lived on in the life of his church—and in the lives of his saints. It would, they argued, be a disastrous foreshortening of perspective on his image if the portrayal of that life did not include portrayals of those in whom it had continued, and was continuing, to make sacred history. Yet the theology of icons could not stop even there. The Logos whose incarnate form it was legitimate to iconize was himself the living image of God and the one through whom heaven and earth and all that is therein had been created. The Mother of God whom it was permissible to depict on an icon was the Queen of Heaven. The saints whose lives were celebrated on the iconostasis and on individual icons were now in the presence of God in heaven. And standing by, not as recipients of salvation but nevertheless as participants in the drama, were the angels, who in the upper zone of this icon attended the exalted Christ and who in the lower zone stood on either side of his Mother. All of these images stood in relation to one another, in what Byzantine theology makes it necessary to call a "great chain of images."

Iconographically as well as theologically, the supreme person represented on this tapestry Icon of the Virgin was not the Virgin Mary but Christ. As Christ enthroned in glory, he occupied the higher of the two zones, which, though smaller, was certainly preeminent. In the lower zone, moreover, the Christ Child was still Christ the Lord, as he grasped the top of a scroll, probably the scroll of the law. Yet the most prominent figure in size, and in many ways the most striking in style, was the portrait of Mary the Mother of God seated on her throne, with an archangel on either side:

> On our tapestry the Virgin sits on an elaborately jewelled
> throne of Byzantine type with an enormous red cushion. She
> is clad in a simple purple *palla* and tunic and black shoes.
> One end of the *palla*—or *mataphorion*, to use its Greek name—
> is draped over her head as a veil; beneath it her hair is con-
> cealed by a little white cap on which is an "embroidered"
> gold cross. Her head is framed by a large yellow nimbus.
> The Christ Child, without a nimbus, is seated in her lap at
> the left. He is dressed in a golden-yellow tunic and *pallium*;
> purple *clavi* decorate the shoulders of the tunic. . . . The Vir-
> gin's costume is that of a woman of the ordinary classes in
> late antiquity. This is the costume in which she is universally
> represented on all pre-Iconoclastic Byzantine monuments. Al-

though never represented in the elaborate costume of an empress, as was frequently done in contemporary Roman art,
her simple garments are nevertheless consistently purple, the
color reserved for Byzantine royalty.[63]

Although the Icon of the Virgin is a tapestry rather than a painting, it does
appear iconographically necessary to associate its distinctive treatment
of the figure of Mary the Mother of God, including the throne, with the
history of the Byzantine liturgical and theological definition of Mary
as Theotokos, which would thereafter influence the way she was later
portrayed in the Christian art of the West no less than in that of the
East.[64]

Giotto di Bondone, *Marriage of the Virgin*, between 1304 and 1313. Scrovegni Chapel, Padua. (Alinari/Art Resource, N.Y.)

8 The Paragon of Chastity and the Blessed Mother

How shall this be, seeing I know not a man?
—Luke 1:34

The paradox of Mary as Virgin Mother not only effectively illustrated but decisively shaped the fundamental paradox of the Orthodox and Catholic view of sexuality, which was epitomized by the glorification of virginity over matrimony—and by the celebration of matrimony, but not of virginity, as a sacrament. For as Virgin she served as the unique and sublime paragon of chastity. At the same time as Mother she was uniquely "blessed among women," as Elizabeth called her and as the words of the *Ave Maria* saluted her, not because she was Virgin but specifically because she was, as Elizabeth went on to say, "the Mother of my Lord."[1] The tensions represented by that paradox ran through much of subsequent Christian history, and especially through the history of the effort to define the meaning of morality and the Christian life. For this history, too, the person of Mary was a major force.

Christian asceticism certainly predated Christianity. The world early Christianity entered was experiencing a series of vigorous movements dedicated to the denial of the claims of the physical life and to the cultivation of the disciplines of self-restraint in relation to food, drink, bodily comfort, and above all sexuality.[2] The classical Greek word *askēsis*, which referred in general to practice and discipline, came to be applied specifically to these practices of self-restraint and self-denial.[3] The language of military discipline and of athletic training was applied to the moral realm to explain the need for abstinence in the interest of some greater goal, in this life or in the life to come. As Marcus Aurelius said, applying the military metaphor, "life a warfare, a brief sojourning in an alien land; and after repute, oblivion. Where, then, can man find the power to guide and guard his steps? In one thing and one alone— Philosophy. To be a philosopher is to keep unsullied and unscathed the divine spirit within him, so that it may transcend all pleasure and all pain."[4] The writings bearing the name of the apostle Paul also invoked military language to describe Christian discipline.[5] But Paul's most vivid metaphor for ascetic discipline came from athletics, as practiced in the Hellenistic world: "Know ye not that they which run in a race run all, but one receiveth the prize? So run, that ye may obtain. And every man that striveth for the mastery is temperate in all things. Now they do it to obtain a corruptible crown; but we an incorruptible [one]. I therefore so run, not as uncertainly; so fight I, not as one that beateth the air. But I keep my body and bring it into subjection: lest that by any means, when I have preached to others, I myself should be a castaway."[6] Keeping the body and bringing it under subjection, which clearly was a duty incumbent on all Christians, eventually became the special province of the professional ascetic.

Sometimes, though not necessarily, the ascetic impulse was rooted in a metaphysical dualism, whether or not it was Platonic in origin, a view of the world and of human nature according to which human appetites, and above all sexual desire, having come from a lower source in their creation and being shared with the lower animals, were in conflict with the imperatives of the spirit and of the higher nature in human beings, so that the only way to liberate the mind and spirit was to overcome these appetites through denial. Though not directly connected with such speculation, the institution of the vestal virgins in Rome obliged them to preserve their virginity for the duration of their service, normally five years but sometimes much longer, and subjected them to entombment alive if they violated it.[7]

It seems evident that at least in part the celebration of virginity and the cultivation of asceticism came about in revulsion against what were taken to be the excesses of sexual self-indulgence in Late Antiquity. Later moralists have been fond of quoting Roman satirists like Tacitus, Juvenal, and Martial on these excesses; even Edward Gibbon, with his ill-concealed scorn for monasticism and asceticism, followed Tacitus's "honest pleasure in the contrast of barbarian [German] virtue with the dissolute conduct of the Roman ladies," noting that "the most dangerous enemy [of chastity] is the softness of the mind."[8] As Peter Brown has shown, there was a widespread sense in the society of Late Antiquity that human life needed to be rescued from its tendency to allow the senses unfettered reign and that true holiness could be found in rejecting what Gibbon called "the softness of the mind" in favor of restraint.[9] And as this was true of the individual, so it could be true of society, which therefore needed within it the presence of full-time and permanent ascetics who could be a challenge and an example to those who lived an ordinary life of the appetites and the senses.

So pervasive was the ascetic impulse in Late Antiquity that even Judaism came under its spell in some places. In the institution of the Nazarites, described in the Book of Numbers, Israel had had a group who bound themselves by sacred vows to live in self-denial, "to separate themselves unto the Lord."[10] The best-known example was Samson, who at the annunciation by the angel of the Lord to his father, Manoah, was designated "a Nazarite unto God from the womb."[11] But the Jewish philosopher and theologian Philo of Alexandria, a contemporary of Jesus and Paul, in a treatise entitled *On the Contemplative Life*, described a further elaboration of Jewish asceticism in group he called "Therapeutae," men and women who lived in a monastic community in the Egyptian desert near Alexandria. Among these, Philo said, "the women also share . . . , the greater part of whom, though old, are virgins in respect of their purity (not indeed through necessity, as some of the priestesses among the Greeks are, who have been compelled to preserve their chastity more than they would have done of their own accord), but out of an admiration for and love of wisdom, with which they are desirous to pass their lives, on account of which they are indifferent to the pleasures of the body, desiring not a mortal but an immortal offspring."[12] The striking similarities between this community of Therapeutae in Hellenistic Judaism and early Christian monasticism persuaded Eusebius, the first historian of Christianity, that Philo had in fact been describing a Christian group; quoting this passage, he took such evidence to be "more striking examples, which are to be found nowhere else than in the evangelical religion of the Christians."[13] As the comments of Eusebius indicated, asceticism and monasticism were beginning to take firm hold in the church by the fourth century. The most important documentation of this comes from *The Life of Saint Antony* by Athanasius of Alexandria, once more the biography of a monk in the Egyptian desert, but this time of a Christian monk, who learned to "fortify his body with faith, prayers, and fasting" even when "the devil took upon himself the shape of a woman and imitated all her acts simply to beguile Antony."[14] Significantly, it was from a Latin translation of the life of Antony, perhaps prepared during Athanasius's lifetime on one of his Western exiles, that Augustine learned about Christian asceticism.[15]

As might have been expected, the apologists for Christian asceticism fixed on the Virgin Mary as a model of the life of virginity and self-denial. Athanasius did so in his *Letter to Virgins*, in which he described Mary in language intended to motivate the female ascetics to whom he was writing.[16] Also notable among such apologists for the monastic life was Jerome, whose influence reached many of his contemporaries. For example, his "long drawn out correspondence" with Augustine on a variety of subjects, Peter Brown has said, "is a unique document in the Early Church. For it shows two highly-civilized men conducting with studied courtesy, a singular rancorous correspondence."[17] Jerome's greatest importance in history is certainly his translation of the Bible into Latin, but he made other major contributions. Among these, two of the most far-reaching were his monastic foundations and his doctrine of Mary. Early in life, before his ordination into the priesthood, Jerome lived as a hermit in the Syrian desert at Chalcis, devoting himself to ascetic practices and to scholarly study, including the study of Hebrew, which was to stand him in such good stead as commentator and translator of the Jewish Scriptures. A public career followed, at Constantinople and then at Rome as secretary to Pope Damasus; but even then he was a vigorous proponent of the ascetic life, persuading a number of Roman aristocratic women, including Paula and her daughter, Eustochium, as well as Marcella and Melania, to give up their lives of privilege and position in the fashionable society of Rome and to enter monastic communities.

These communities were in Palestine, to which in 386 Jerome himself emigrated and established a monastery in Bethlehem. Observing that "in those days no highborn lady at Rome had made profession of the monastic life, or had ventured—so strange and ignominious did it then seem—publicly to call herself a nun," he credited Athanasius's *Life of Antony* for having inspired Marcella and other women to the ascetic life.[18] In a letter to Eustochium on her mother's death, which he "spent the labor of two nights in dictating"[19] and which amounted to a miniature biography, Jerome described Paula's asceticism and the monastic community of consecrated women that she had headed. "So strictly did Paula separate them from men," he explained, "that she would not allow even eunuchs to approach them, lest she should give occasion to slanderous tongues (always ready to cavil at the religious) to console themselves for their own misdoing."[20] In another letter, addressed to Gaudentius, which contained some of his most moving statements about the sack of Rome in 410,[21] he spoke about the vocation of virginity. Clearly specifying, "What I say I do not say as universally applicable," he nevertheless asked Gaudentius: "Are you a virgin? Why then do you find pleasure in the society of a woman?" And concerning a small girl whom her father had dedicated to a life of virginity from her infancy, he prescribed that she "should associate only with girls, she should know nothing of boys and should dread even playing with them."[22]

Jerome was at the same time one of the most influential interpreters in the early church of the life and person of the Virgin Mary. Writing against Jovinian, who though himself a monk had attacked what he regarded as an exaggerated view of virginity, Jerome composed a sharp polemic in which, as the standard English manual on early Christian literature has put it, "the exegesis proposed for 1 Cor. 7 along with the picturesque expressions drawn from pagan antifeminist literature provoked resentment."[23] His treatise *Against Helvidius*, written in 383, was a defense of the perpetual virginity of Mary, "to show that the mother of the Son [of God], who was a mother before she was a bride, continued a Virgin after her son was born."[24] He took advantage of his formidable rhetorical skills as a controversialist and his outstanding skills as a biblical scholar to prove that the references in the New Testament to Jesus as Mary's first-born son did not necessarily mean that there were any sons of Mary after him, because "every only-begotten son is a first-born son, but not every first-born is an only-begotten."[25] He also devoted lengthy and careful argumentation to the problem arising from the references in the Gospels that spoke of the "brethren" of Jesus.[26] To resolve the problem, Jerome maintained "that the sons of Mary, the sister of our Lord's mother, who though not formerly believers afterwards did believe, can be called brethren of the Lord."[27] Jerome's defense of the perpetual virginity of Mary set down the standard arguments, which went on being used by subsequent expositors of this doctrine, even including Martin Luther. But after completing the portion of his treatise devoted to Mary, Jerome appended a discussion of the relative merits of virginity and matrimony, an issue that had been part of the treatise of Helvidius to which Jerome was writing an answer. "Are virgins better than Abraham, Isaac, and Jacob, who were married men?" Helvidius had argued. "Are not infants daily fashioned by the hands of God in the wombs of their mothers?" which seemed to Helvidius to imply necessarily that matrimony was at least as holy as virginity.[28]

Jerome's reply was to present himself as continuing the argumentation of the apostle Paul: "It is good for a man not to touch a woman. Nevertheless, to avoid fornication, let every man have his own wife, and let every woman have her own husband. So then he that giveth [a virgin] in matrimony doeth well; but he that giveth her not in matrimony doeth better."[29] This did not say that matrimony was evil: it was good, but the preservation of virginity was even better. On the basis of this New Testament authority Jerome felt qualified to say: "I beseech my readers not to suppose that in praising virginity I have in the least disparaged matrimony, and separated the saints of the Old Testament from those of the New, that is to say, those who had wives and those who altogether refrained from the embraces of women."[30] Nevertheless, Jerome did in fact go on to disparage matrimony—and women in general—as in the following vivid description, for which he summoned a rhetorical skill that had been honed on the writings of Cicero:

> The virgin's aim is to appear less comely; she will wrong herself so as to hide her natural attractions. The married woman has the paint laid on before her mirror, and, to the insult of her Maker, strives to acquire something more than her natural beauty. Then comes the prattling of infants, the noisy household, children watching for her word and waiting for her kiss, the reckoning up of expenses, the preparation to meet the outlay. . . . Meanwhile a message is delivered that the husband and his friends have arrived. The wife, like a swallow, flies all over the house. She has to see to everything. "Is the sofa smooth? Is the pavement swept? Are the flowers in the cups? Is the dinner ready?" Tell me, pray, where amid all this is there room for the thought of God? Are these happy homes?[31]

And in a sense, the best argument he could summon against the clear impression that such a description conveyed was to protest: "We do not condemn matrimony, for virginity itself is the fruit of matrimony."[32]

Missing in Jerome's presentations were, first, a more detailed consideration of Mary not only as Virgin but at the same time as Mother, and, second, a clearer statement of the sacramental definition of matrimony. The first of these was supplied by another of Augustine's associates, the man who brought him to the Christian gospel, Ambrose of Milan, who was, more than Augustine, a genuine *Doctor Marianus*, at least partly because of his strong dependence on the Greek Christian tradition.

Ambrose led the way in positing a "causal connection between the virginal conception and the sinlessness of Christ . . . , the combination of the ideas of the propagation of original sin through sexual union and of the sinlessness of Christ as a consequence of his virginal conception";[33] this would eventually force the Western Church to define the doctrine of the immaculate conception of Mary.[34] No less than Jerome, Ambrose insisted on the perpetual virginity of Mary, who, he said, "did not seek the consolation of being able to bear another son."[35] He also followed the words of Paul just quoted in recognizing that virginity was on a higher plane than matrimony, strongly rejecting those who claimed "that there is no merit in abstinence, no grace in a frugal life, none in virginity, that all are valued at one price."[36] Like Jerome, Ambrose devoted several writings to the theme of virginity, including the treatise *Concerning Virgins*. As the manual of early Christian literature quoted earlier on Jerome put it in speaking of Ambrose, "This composition, which is held to be the first organic treatise of spirituality and theology on the theme of virginity in Latin, maintains a balanced and positive judgment on matrimony."[37] In Book II of this treatise, having set forth for his sister, Marcellina, a description and commendation of the virginal estate, he drew the connection with Mary: "Let, then, the life of Mary be as it were virginity itself, set forth in a likeness, from which, as from a mirror, the appearance of chastity and the form of virtue is reflected. From this you may take your pattern of life, showing, as an example, the clear rules of virtue: what you have to correct, to effect, and to hold fast."[38]

Holding her up as a model of the Christian life, Ambrose described all kinds of virtues as having shone forth in Mary the Virgin, and specifically six virtues: "The secret of modesty, the banner of faith, the secret of devotion, the Virgin within the house, the companion for the ministry [of Christ], the Mother at the temple."[39] But the second of these two triads of virtue, "the Virgin within the house, the companion for the ministry [of Christ], the Mother at the temple," enabled Ambrose to go beyond the first triad, "the secret of modesty, the banner of faith, the secret of devotion," and thus to deepen his portrait well beyond Jerome's. The first triad characterized the Virgin in the privacy of her heart and in the mystery of her relation to God, whereas the second moved outward to her historic mission as the Mother of Christ. For "the Virgin within the house" was also "the Mother at the temple," and because she was not only Virgin but Mother she could be "the companion for the ministry of Christ." This put many of the stories in the Gospels into a new light, but it also tended to place even her virginity into the context of her divine maternity, as W. J. Dooley has made clear.[40] "Whatever she did was a lesson," Ambrose inferred from the Gospel story; for she "attended to everything as though she were warned by many, and fulfilled every obligation of virtue as though she were teaching rather than learning."[41] Therefore Ambrose also emphasized Mary's "abundance of services" and her being both "busy in private at home" and "accompanied by others abroad"[42]—which included being "busy" in the very ways that Jerome caricatured.

The metaphysical dualism mentioned earlier as a frequent corollary of asceticism in Late Antiquity did not disappear with the coming of Christianity but took up a place also in Christian thought, above all in the thought of those many Christian theologians who combined their Christianity with Neo-Platonism. When that happened, Christian asceticism expressed itself in a rejection of the body that appeared to deny that God had created it, and therefore in a revulsion at sexuality that equated it with immorality. Because most writers on the subject were men, and unmarried men at that, the revulsion easily became a misogynous contempt for women as the devil's snare to corrupt the *vita angelica* of the ascetic or celibate man. A second need, therefore, was the identification of matrimony as a sacrament of the church, which was a lengthy and complex process. Curiously, matrimony was the only one of the eventual list of seven sacraments to be identified in the New Testament as a *mystērion* or *sacramentum*.[43] Although these words were not originally used in Greek and Latin in the technical sense of the word *sacrament*, they contributed to the definition of matrimony as a sacrament.[44]

The role of the doctrine of Mary in this development of the doctrine of matrimony was somewhat obscure, as became evident, for example, in Giotto's painting *The Marriage of the Virgin*, in the Arena Chapel in Padua, by which John Ruskin was so captivated.[45] Superficially this might be taken to be just another depiction of a wedding, with the bride and groom dressed in finery and the guests supporting them with love and prayers. But there was something unique about this wedding and about this couple, specifically about the bride, who, having taken a prior vow of chastity, was and yet was not involved in the proceedings. In viewing this painting, one cannot but be reminded of the portrayal of *Saint Francis Being Married to Poverty*, celebrated also in Canto XI of Dante's *Paradiso*, in which the Franciscan renunciation of worldly goods was consecrated in an allegorical ceremony that was ordinarily the occasion for conferring worldly goods.[46] Here, too, the wedding was authentic, yet it had a singular quality because of the Bride. She was, as the Greek hymn *Akathistos* had called her, "the unwed Bride [nymphos anymphētos]."

For on one hand, both theologians and canon lawyers defended the thesis that the matrimony of Mary and Joseph was a true marriage even though it was not sexually consummated, on the basis of the principle that "it is consent, not sexual intercourse, that makes a marriage [consensus, non concubitus, facit connubium]." Therefore "a marriage in which both spouses voluntarily and for supernatural motives follow the precedent of Mary and Joseph in practicing total abstinence, either from the beginning or only later" is identified as a *Josephsehe* and has standing as a valid union.[47] But on the other hand, it proved to be difficult to deduce, on the basis of the mystical view of Mary as archetype of the church, and of the church in turn as the spouse of Christ, clear implications for the sacramental nature of human matrimony, which was not instituted by Christ during his ministry on earth (not even at the wedding in Cana of Galilee)[48] but by the Creator of Adam and Eve in the Garden of Eden before the fall into sin. Nevertheless, as the portrait of Mary as the Virgin combatted the perceived excesses of sexuality in Late Antiquity, so the portrait of Mary as the Mother likewise combatted the perceived excesses of asceticism. And the truth was seen to lie in the paradox.

Michelangelo Buonarroti, *Pietà*, 1498–99 / 1500. Saint Peter's Basilica, Vatican State.
(Alinari / Art Resource, N.Y.)

9 The Mater Dolorosa
and the Mediatrix

Yea, a sword shall pierce through thy own soul also.
—Luke 2:35

During the High Middle Ages of the twelfth and thirteenth centuries, which in a special way combined what Ernst Robert Curtius has called "the essential message of medieval thought," defined by him as "the spirit in which it restated tradition,"[1] with what Charles Homer Haskins has called a genuine "Renaissance of the twelfth century,"[2] that combination of tradition and innovation was nowhere more dramatically in evidence than in its portrayal of Mary as the Mater Dolorosa, Mother of Sorrows, and its correlative doctrine of Mary as the Mediatrix. The sheer number of references to her in poetry and prose, together with her ever-deepening prominence in the visual arts, would make it difficult not to agree with Otto von Simson's judgment that "the age was indeed the age of the Virgin."[3] In the Czech art of the Gothic period, for example, she was a dominant figure.[4]

If the systematic clarification of the title Mediatrix was the principal objective expression of Mariology and the chief theological contribution to the Christian teaching about Mary during this period, this must be seen also in creative tension with the growth of its most important subjective expression, the literary form and devotional motif of the Mater Dolorosa: Mary had simultaneously lamented the death of Christ because he was her Son and welcomed it because he was her Savior and the Savior of the world. The prophecy of Simeon in the Gospel, that "a sword will pierce your own soul also [*et tuam ipsius animam pertransiet gladius*],"[5] had long been taken as a reference to the experience through which Mary would have to pass as simultaneously the most important and the most involved spectator at the crucifixion, as well as a reference to her own death.[6] The description accompanying the third word from the cross, "Woman, behold thy son!" and "Behold thy mother!"—that "there stood by the cross of Jesus, his mother"[7]—although it came from the Gospel of John, seemed clearly to be the fulfillment of Simeon's warning in the Gospel of Luke. The combination of these two pictures, the Mother standing at the foot of the cross and the Mother with her groaning, sorrowing, and grieving soul pierced by a sword, produced the evocative verses of the *Stabat Mater Dolorosa*:

> Stabat mater dolorosa
> iuxta crucem lacrimosa
> dum pendebat filius;
> cuius animam gementem
> contristantem et dolentem
> pertransivit gladius.[8]

This anonymous poem may have been set to music soon after it was composed or may even have been written to be sung; but it remained an attractive text for composers until the nineteenth and twentieth centuries, drawing the attention of such widely different masters as Giovanni Pierluigi Palestrina, Franz Joseph Haydn, Giovanni Pergolesi, Franz Schubert, Giuseppe Verdi, and Krzysztof Penderecki.[9] The contrast between the renderings of the poem by Gioacchino Rossini and his younger contemporary Antonín Dvořák is instructive for understanding not only the differences between these two composers but the range of subjective emotion that could be expressed in the *Stabat Mater*. Dvořák's reading was meditative, looking inward into the anguished soul of the Virgin and then into the anguished soul of the pious believer and pondering the meaning of the awesome event on the cross. Rossini's, by contrast, was irresistibly operatic, at times almost exuberant, as in his dramatic setting for solo tenor voice of the words from Simeon's prophecy, "Cujus animam gementem pertransivit gladius." It was a free adaptation in German of the Latin text of the *Stabat Mater* when Johann Wolfgang von Goethe in his *Faust* had Gretchen in her hour of crisis pray to the Mater Dolorosa, "Incline thy countenance graciously to my need, thou who art abounding in pain. With the sword in thy heart and with a thousand pains thou dost look up at the death of thy Son. Thou dost look to the Father and send sighs upward for [thy Son's] trial and for thine own,"[10] thus giving sublime poetic expression to authentic folk piety toward the Virgin Mary—and, more important for his eventual poetic purpose, preparing the way for the supreme exaltation of the Mater Gloriosa.[11] Similarly paraphrasing the words of the *Stabat Mater* without quoting them, the Symphony no. 3 of Henryk Górecki used an exchange between Christ and his Mother to expand the scope of the sorrows of the Mater Dolorosa by embracing all the suffering and the fallen of the Second World War:

> Where has he gone,
> My dearest Son?
> Perhaps during the uprising
> The cruel enemy killed him.
> [*Kajze mi sie podziol*
> *mój synocek miły?*
> *Pewnie go w powstaniu*
> *złe wrogi zabiły*].[12]

But those were relatively restrained versions of the *planctus Mariae* or *Marienklagen*, the poetry of the complaints of Mary in this and later periods.[13] As those titles for the genre in Latin and German suggest, the Mater Dolorosa became a well-known Marian theme particularly in the Western church. But thanks to recent studies by Margaret Alexiou and Gregory W. Dobrov, it is now possible to draw the lines of development back from this Western version to the Byzantine poetry of the Lamenting Virgin, and back even from that to the classical threnody of the lamenting woman.[14] Thus in the Kontakion of Romanos Melodos, Mary complained:

> I am vanquished by loving grief, child, vanquished
> And cannot bear the thought of being in my chambers while you
>   are on the cross;
> I, at home while you are in the tomb.
> Let me come with you! The sight of you soothes my pain.

To which Christ replied:

> Lay aside your grief, mother, lay it aside.
> Lamentation does not befit you who have been called "Blessed."
> Do not obscure your calling with weeping.
> Do not liken yourself to those who lack understanding, all-wise
>   maiden.
> You are in the midst of my bridal chamber.

As Dobrov has put it, "This, of course, alludes to the Virgin's exalted status whereby she, as second in rank only to the Godhead, absorbs much of Christ's function as intermediary between God and man."[15]

What the poetry of the Middle Ages in both West and East was describing in its moving verses, the visual arts in both West and East also portrayed.[16] It would be possible for this purpose to examine the many statues, altarpieces, and woodcuts in which the Virgin was being pierced by the sword. But Michelangelo's Pietà was certainly the best-known attempt, in statuary or in painting, to capture the depth of the Virgin's grief as she held the broken body of her crucified Son.[17] It only added to the poignancy that, as has often been noted, Michelangelo presented Mary as a young woman who, because of her unique position as the Virgin full of grace, had not been subject to the ravages of age, just as in death her body would not be subject to the ravages of corruption.[18] On her face, for all its youthful beauty, sorrow and serenity are mingled: these, her most tragic hours, in which her Son had cried, "My God, my God, why hast thou forsaken me?"[19] were at the same time the hours of her fulfillment, and of the fulfillment of the words of the Lord concern-

Vault of the Cubiculum of the Annunciation, fresco, fourth century. Catacomb of Priscilla, Rome. (Scala / Art Resource, N.Y.)

Annunciation and Visitation, Coptic Christian textile, sixth century. Victoria & Albert Museum, London. (Victoria & Albert Museum / Art Resource, N.Y.)

Annunciation and Visitation, ivory sculpture book cover, late eighth century. Musées Royaux d'Art et d'Histoire, Brussels.

12

Annunciation from an Armenian manuscript of the Gospels, c. 1280. Yerevan, Armenia.
(© Edimedia)

Simone Martini, *The Annunciation*, detail, 1333. Galleria degli Uffizi, Florence. (Eric Lessing / Art Resource, N.Y.)

Annunciation at the Fountain, tapestry, early fourteenth century. Ikonenmuseum, Museen der Stadt Recklinghausen. (© Giraudon)

Andrea della Robbia, *Annunciation*, glazed terracotta, sixteenth century. La Verna, Santuario. (Scala / Art Resource, N.Y.)

Facing page: Fra Angelico, *The Annunciation*, illuminated initial from Missal, c. 1430. MS 558, f.33v., Museo di San Marco, Florence. (Nicolo Orsi Battaglini / Art Resource, N.Y.)

rlo di Giovanni Braccesco, *Annunciation*, late fifteenth century. Musée du Louvre. (Erich
sing / Art Resource, N.Y.)

ious page: Carlo Crivelli, *The Annunciation, with Saint Emidius*, 1486. National Gallery,
idon.

El Greco, *The Annunciation*. Museum of Fine Arts (Szepmuveszeti Muzeum), Budapest. (Erich Lessing / Art Resource, N.Y.)

Previous page: Matthias Grünewald, *Annunciation*, detail, Isenheim Altarpiece, c. 1510–15. Musée Unterlinden, Colmar. (Giraudon / Art Resource, N.Y.)

Pierre-Auguste Pichon, *The Annunciation*, 1859. Basilique Notre-Dame, Clery-Saint-André. Giraudon / Art Resource, N.Y.)

Orazio Gentileschi, *Annunciation*, c. 1623. Galleria Sabauda, Turin. (Scala/Art Resource, N.Y.)

Annunciation from an Ethiopian wood-carved box with panel paintings, eighteenth or nineteenth century. Musées Royaux d'Art et d'Histoire, Brussels.

Dante Gabriel Rossetti, *Ecce Ancilla Domini! (The Annunciation)*, 1849–50. Tate Gallery, London. (Tate Gallery, London/Art Resource, N.Y.)

Henry Ossawa Tanner, *Annunciation*, 1898. Philadelphia Museum of Art, The W. P. Wilstach Collection.

Salvador Dali, *The Annunciation*, 1947. Private collection. (Edimedia © ADAGP 1996)

ing her in the vision to Joseph: "And she shall bring forth a son, and thou shalt call his name Jesus: for he shall save his people from their sins."[20]

This theme—that, in the words of one of the most profound of twentieth-century Roman Catholic theologians, Hans Urs von Balthasar, "She suffers along with her Son, and in her spirit, she experiences His death"[21]—was by no means restricted to art, poetry, and sacred song. Repeatedly during the Middle Ages, the Mater Dolorosa provided the content of Marian visions,[22] in various periods and in places as widely separated as Sweden and Spain. Thus in the first book of the *Revelations* of Saint Birgitta of Sweden, Jesus said to his mother: "You are like the precious gold that has been beaten on the iron anvil, for you have been tried with countless tribulations. Through my suffering, you have suffered more than anyone else."[23] Elsewhere Birgitta paraphrased the account of the crucifixion in the Gospels as Mary might have narrated it (in the antique language of a non-Latin manuscript of Birgitta's visions): "I, his moest sorowful moder . . . for sorrow y myght unneth stonde. And my sonne, seying me and his frendis weping without comffort from the jntret of his breat . . . weping and crying out unto the fader, he said: 'Fader and my Godde, why haest thou for-saken me?' as yf he had said: 'There is none that must haue mercy on me but thou fader.' . . . for he said it more mevid out of my compassion than his owne."[24] And at the other end of the north-south axis of Medieval Europe, Saint Teresa of Avila, whom Pope Paul VI in 1970 decorated with the title Doctor of the Church, described a vision in which "the Lord . . . laid Himself in my arms in the way depicted in the 'Fifth Anguish' of Our Lady. . . . 'Be not afraid of this,' He said to me, 'for the union of My Father with thy soul is incomparably greater than this.'" As the editor of Teresa notes, the "Fifth Anguish (more properly the Sixth) represents Mary with the dead body of her Son in Her arms."[25]

The author of the most influential theological treatise ever written about Christ as Mediator, *Why God Became Man*, Anselm of Canterbury at the end of the eleventh century, also wrote a treatise *On the Virginal Conception and on Original Sin*, as well as fervent prayers addressed to the Virgin as Mediatrix.[26] As Anselm himself pointed out, the two treatises were closely connected, because consideration of Christ the Mediator provoked the question of "how it was that God assumed a man from the sinful mass of the human race without sin," which was also a question about Mary.[27] In Christian iconography as well as in Christian literature, there was a new attention to the significance of Mary: a painting of Ildefonsus of Toledo in the seventh century, who had been celebrated for his devotion to her, constituted "one of the oldest expressions of the cult of the Virgin, which was then beginning to pervade Christian piety."[28] Mary was also seen as the woman who conquered worldly wisdom through the miracle of the virgin birth, as well as the one who conquered the false teachings of the heretics and resisted the incursions of the barbarians.

Her uniqueness was the subject of titles that were bestowed on her. As in the East so also in the West, poets and theologians vied with one another in elaborating distinctive appellations for the Virgin. For she was "the standard-bearer of piety,"[29] whose life of prayer the faithful imitated in their own. She was a model to them because she was "courageous in her resolution, temperate in her silence, prudent in her questioning and righteous in her confession."[30] As "the Queen of Angels, the ruling Lady of the world, and the Mother of him who purifies the world," she could acquire such titles as these: Mother of Truth; Mother and Daughter of Humility; Mother of Christians; Mother of Peace; My Most Merciful Lady. She was also called, in a term reminiscent of Augustine, the City of God. The paradox that a creature had become the mother of her Creator justified such names as "the fountain from which the living fountain flows, the origin of the beginning." Therefore she was "the woman who uniquely deserves to be venerated, the one to be admired more than all other women," in fact, "the radiant glory of the world, the purest maid of earth." Thus she excelled all others, "more beautiful than all of them, more lovable than all of them, supersplendid, supergracious, superglorious." The glory of her name had filled the world.

Most of this could have been—and had been—said centuries earlier. What set the devotion and thought of this period apart from what preceded it was the growing emphasis on the office of Mary as Mediatrix. The title itself seems to have appeared first in Eastern theology, where she was addressed as "the Mediatrix of law and of grace." Whether from such Eastern sources or from Western reflection, the term came into Latin usage, apparently near the end of the eighth century. It was, however, in the eleventh and twelfth centuries that it achieved widespread acceptance. The title was a means of summarizing what had come to be seen as her twofold function: she was "the way by which the Savior came" to humanity in the incarnation and the redemption, and she was also the one "through whom we ascend to him who descended through her to us . . . , through [whom] we have access to the Son . . . , so that through [her] he who through [her] was given to us might take us up to himself." The term Mediatrix referred to both of these aspects of Mary's mediatorial position.

In the first instance, it was a way of speaking about her active role in the incarnation and the redemption. There seemed to be a direct and irrefutable inference from the universally accepted thesis that "it would have been impossible for the redemption of the human race to take place unless the Son of God had been born of a Virgin" to the corollary thesis that "it was likewise necessary that the Virgin, of whom the Logos was to be made flesh, should herself have been born." Thus she had become "the gate of Paradise, which restored God to the world and opened heaven to us." By her participation in redemption she had filled heaven with the saved and had emptied hell of those who would have been condemned except for her. Her assent to the word and will of God had made the incarnation and therefore the redemption possible. "O woman marvelously unique and uniquely marvelous," Anselm prayed, "through whom the elements are renewed, hell is redeemed, the demons are trampled under foot, humanity is saved, and angels are restored!" The reference to Mary's restoration of the angels was an allusion to the idea that the number of the elect would make up for the number of the angels who had fallen; Mary was seen as the one through whom "not only a life once lost is returned to humanity, but also the beatitude of angelic sublimity is increased," because through her participation in salvation the hosts of angels regained their full strength. In the same sense she wrought reparation for what Adam and Eve had done, and she brought life to all their posterity. Through her, then, the royal priesthood spoken of in the New Testament[31] had truly come into being in the Christian church. All of this made her "the minister and cooperator of this dispensation, who gave us the salvation of the world."

Mary's cooperation in the plan of salvation helped to explain the puzzling circumstance in the Gospel narratives, that after his resurrection Christ had not appeared first to his mother: "Why should he have appeared to her when she undoubtedly knew about the resurrection even before he suffered and rose?" She was the virginal human being of whom was born the divine human being who was to save the sinful human being. She was "the sanctuary of the universal propitiation, the cause of the general reconciliation, the vessel and the temple of the life and the salvation of all." Such praises as these by Anselm of the Virgin's place in the history of salvation, voiced in the setting of prayers, as so much of the language about her was, could only mean, in the words of Bernard of Clairvaux, that "she is our Mediatrix, she is the one through whom we have received thy mercy, O God, she is the one through whom we, too, have welcomed the Lord Jesus into our homes." Or, as Thomas Aquinas put it in the thirteenth century, "She was so full of grace that it overflows on to all mankind. It is indeed, a great thing that any one saint has so much grace that it conduces the salvation of many; but most wondrous is it to have so much as to suffice for the salvation of all mankind; and thus it is in Christ and in the Blessed Virgin. Thus in every danger thou canst find a refuge in this same glorious Virgin. . . . [Mary says] 'In me is all hope of life and of virtue.'"[32]

This title Mediatrix, however, applied not only to Mary's place in the history of salvation but also to her continuing position as intercessor between Christ and humanity, as the one whose "virginity we praise and whose humility we admire; but thy mercy tastes even sweeter, and it is thy mercy that we embrace even more fondly, think of even more often, and invoke even more frequently." The remembrance of Mary's "ancient mercies" aroused in a believer the hope and confidence to "return to thee [Mary], and through thee to God the Father and to thy only Son," so that it was possible to "demand salvation of thee [Mary]." The consummation of the believer's glory was the awareness that Mary stood as the Mediatrix between him and her Son; in fact, God had chosen her for the specific task of pleading the cause of humanity before her Son. And so she was "the Mother of the kingdom of heaven, Mary, the Mother of God, my only refuge in every need." Mary was addressed as the one who could bring cleansing and healing to the sinner and as the one who would give succor against the temptations of the devil; but she did this by mediating between Christ and humanity. "By thy pious prayer, make thy Son propitious to us," one could plead; or again: "Our Lady, Our Mediatrix, Our Advocate, reconcile us to thy Son, commend us to thy Son, represent us to thy Son. Do this, O Blessed One, through the grace that thou hast found [before God], through the prerogative that thou hast merited, through the mercy to which thou hast given birth."

"As we make a practice of rejoicing in the nativity of Christ," one preacher exhorted, "so we should rejoice no less at the nativity of the mother of Christ." For it was a basic rule that "whatever we set forth in praise of the Mother pertains to the Son, and on the other hand when we honor the Son we are not drawing back from our glory to the Mother." Christ was pleased when praise was offered to the Virgin Mary; conversely, an offense against either the Son or the Mother was an offense against the other as well. It was particularly the intercessory implication of the title Mediatrix that could be interpreted as taking something away from Christ, who was "the High Priest so that he might offer the vows of the people to God." The countervailing force against what the Protestant Reformation was to construe as Mariolatry and as a diminution of the glory of Christ, the sole Mediator,[33] was the recognition that she had been "exalted through thy omnipotent Son, for the sake of thy glorious Son, by thy blessed Son," as Anselm put it in one of his prayers. It was, moreover, a consensus that Mary had been saved by Christ, a consensus that had a decisive effect on the eventual formulation of the Western doctrine that by her immaculate conception she had been the great exception to the universality of original sin.[34] Extravagances of devotion and rhetoric were curbed by the principle that "the royal Virgin has no need of any false honor."

It was perceived as an appropriate honor and an authentic expression of her position in the divine order when Mary was acclaimed as second in dignity only to God himself, who had taken up habitation in her. The ground of this dignity was the part she had taken in the redemption, more important than that of any other ordinary human being. Through her Son she had been exalted "above all creatures" and was worthy of their veneration. This applied to all earthly creatures, but it included all other creatures as well, so that "there is nothing in heaven that is not subject to the Virgin through her Son." Echoing the language of the *Te Deum* about the praise of God, as other Marian hymns were to do later in the Middle Ages, a poem of Peter Damian proclaimed: "The blessed chorus of angels, the order of prophets and apostles affirm thee to be exalted over them and second only to the Deity." For none of them— "neither the chorus of the patriarchs for all their excellence, nor the company of the prophets for all their powers of foretelling the future, nor the senate of the apostles for all their judicial authority"—deserved to be compared with the Virgin. Because she was the one who held first place among the entire celestial host, whether human or angelic, she, next to God himself, should receive the praises of the whole world. There was, in short, "nothing equal to Mary and nothing but God greater than Mary." As the greatness of God could be defined in the famous formula of Anselm's ontological argument for the existence of God as "that than which nothing greater can be thought," so the purity of the Virgin could be defined, again by Anselm, as "that than which, under God, nothing greater can be thought." Among all that could be called holy, save God, Mary possessed a holiness that was unique.

Therefore it was also fitting that veneration and prayer should be addressed to her. Although there had long been such worship of the Virgin, as we have seen in previous chapters, various leaders of the church during these centuries systematically encouraged and nourished her cult. In a revealing autobiographical memoir, one Benedictine abbot, Guibert of Nogent, described how, when his mother was in great pain at his birth, "this vow was made . . . that if a male child should be born, he would be given over to the service of God and . . . offered to her who is

Queen of all next to God." Another Benedictine abbot, Bernard of Reichenau, made it a practice to refer to himself as "the slave of the Mother
of God." And yet another Benedictine abbot, Anselm, who went on to
become archbishop of Canterbury, commonly addressed prayers simultaneously to "my good Lord and my good Lady," saying to them: "I
appeal to you both, devoted Son and devoted Mother." What has been
called "the glowing reverence for Mary" in Bernard of Reichenau was
characteristic of the age. Prayers to Mary were cited as support for admo-
nitions and arguments on behalf of her cult, and it was urged that such
prayers would gain the succor of "the Mother of the Judge in the day of
need." The very day of the Sabbath was said to have been dedicated to
Mary, and those who appealed to her as "the Gate of Heaven, the Window
of Paradise" when they were plagued by the guilt of their sins received
full absolution.

It was no exaggeration of the importance of Mary in the devotion and
worship of the church when the festival of her nativity, said to have been
announced to her mother by an angel just as the nativity of Christ from
her was to be announced to her (although the New Testament was silent
about the first of these annunciations), was celebrated and asserted to be
"the beginning of all the festivals of the New Testament . . . , the origin of
all the other festivals." As was inevitable with any saint, and a fortiori
with her, it became a standard expression of piety to attribute to Mary the
performance of various miracles. A few of these may have taken place
during her earthly life, but others were continuing to take place long
afterward, up to the very present; moreover, the number of such miracles
ascribed to Mary would increase after the Middle Ages, reaching something of an apex in the nineteenth and twentieth centuries.[35] A special
form of the devotion to her miracles was the cultivation of her relics. In
her case this was made much more complicated than in that of any other
saint by the widely held belief that no parts of her body had remained on
earth, because at her death she had been assumed bodily into heaven, a
belief that was finally promulgated as a dogma by Pope Pius XII in
1950.[36] At Chartres, for example, according to one writer, "the name
and the relics of the Mother of God are venerated through almost all the

Latin world"; he was referring above all to her "sacred tunic." Yet when a particular church claimed to possess such relics, the same writer responded that if "she, through the same Spirit by whom she conceived, knew that he to whom she gave birth by faith was to fill the entire world," she would not have kept such mementos of his childhood as his baby teeth or her own mother's milk. A more appropriate way of celebrating her memory was the commemoration of her nativity or the recitation of the *Ave Maria*, whose cultic repetition became characteristic of piety during this period and whose exposition eventually provided a basis for the articulation of her special place in the history of salvation. Clearly there was a close correlation between the subjectivity of the devotion to Mary as the Mater Dolorosa and the objectivity of the doctrine of Mary as the Mediatrix. It was not the correlation of paradox, as was the celebration of her under the rubrics of the Paragon of Chastity and the Blessed Mother,[37] but the correlation of complementarity, at least until, in the modern era, the denial of her objective transcendence by many would deprive her of the title of Mediatrix even though the simultaneous rise of subjectivism would continue to find symbolic, if sometimes sentimental, expression in the Mater Dolorosa.

Quinten Massys, *The Virgin and Child Enthroned, with Four Angels*, c. 1490–95. National Gallery, London.

10 The Face That Most Resembles Christ's

Behold thy mother!
—John 19:27

One of the most sublime moments in the history of devotion to Mary came in the closing cantos of Dante's *Divine Comedy*, in which Bernard of Clairvaux gives praise to the Blessed Virgin Mary.[1] These praises were in great measure derived from Bernard's many writings about Mary.[2] For, as Steven Botterill has said, Bernard was "*helped* by the fact that his thinking is not on the cutting edge of academic theology: his writings about Mary are filled with an intense and intensely personal devotion to the Virgin, and aim as much to stir his audience's hearts as to provoke activity in their minds."[3] As Bernard instructed Dante, pointing to a family resemblance that has been caught, for example, by the Antwerp painter Massys (d. 1530):

> Look now upon the face that is most like
> the face of Christ, for only through its brightness
> can you prepare your vision to see Him.[4]

The privilege of beholding Mary, which had been granted in special measure to Bernard and which then Dante proceeded to share with

Bernard, was a transforming vision and quite literally an indescribable one. Yet this vision prepared for an infinitely grander one and pointed beyond itself to the vision of Christ as "the exalted Son of God and of Mary,"[5] and to the beatific vision of God. This "canto of apotheosis,"[6] beginning with the paradox, "Virgin mother, daughter of your Son, / more humble and sublime than any creature,"[7] stood as a summation and as a goal of the entire Divine Comedy—and of the entire history described in the preceding chapters of this book—as well as an anticipation of much of the history that was to follow. For it was Mary, as the "Gentle Lady" in heaven, by whose intercession the "stern judgment up above is shattered," who, near the beginning of the poem, commanded Beatrice to go to the assistance of the poet, "who loves you so / that—for your sake—he's left the vulgar crowd," thus setting the whole itinerary of Dante the pilgrim in motion.[8] And at the conclusion of the poem, Mary was to Dante not only "Our Lady [nostra donna]"[9] but "Our Queen [nostra regina],"[10] "the Queen of Heaven,"[11] and "the Empress [Agusta],"[12] the fulfillment of the promise of Paradise and the archetype of all who were saved. For "by virtue of being closer to the human plane, she is more approachable by those who have reason to fear, or who cannot comprehend, the ineffable mystery of God or the stern authority of Christ."[13]

It would be easy for the reader to be caught up by the rhapsodic, almost dithyrambic ecstasy of Bernard's poem and by the vision of a transcendent Virgin Mary that it celebrated, and in the process to forget that for Dante and for Bernard of Clairvaux, as for the entire Medieval tradition, Mary stood in continuity with the human race, the same human race to which the poet and his readers belonged. Therefore the glory with which she was crowned was a special form—different in degree, but finally not different in kind—of the glory in which all the saved participated, a glory that was communicated to her, as to them, by the grace and merit of Christ. She was, in the paradox of the incarnation, the Daughter of her Son, who had redeemed her, an emphasis that was, already among the Franciscans of Dante's time, an important component of the developing doctrine of the immaculate conception.[14] Early in the

Paradiso, in response to Dante's unspoken question about the relative degrees of merit and hence of salvation, Beatrice had to explain:

> Neither the Seraph closest unto God,
> nor Moses, Samuel, nor either John—
> whichever one you will—not *Mary* has,
> I say, their place in any other heaven
> than that which houses those souls you just saw,
> nor will their blessedness last any longer.[15]

Degrees of salvation there were, and therefore circles of Paradise, "in ways diverse" and "from stage to stage," as Beatrice had explained even earlier;[16] and Mary occupied the highest of these. Without such degrees of salvation there would not be perfect justice on the basis of merit, which varied from one to another and which therefore had to be rewarded by differing degrees of glory; and, for that matter, without these degrees of salvation and of damnation there would have been no *Divine Comedy.* The justice of God was a mystery that remained "past understanding,"[17] also when it brought about the damnation of pagans who had never had the opportunity to hear the gospel. Nevertheless, those who were destined to dwell eternally in the lower degrees of Paradise affirmed that "in His will is our peace"; for "every place / in heaven is in Paradise, though grace / does not rain equally from the High Good,"[18] because these were all degrees of the same heaven and of the one Paradise, as Mary was the culminating point of the one humanity, still in the one heaven.

As the culminating point, Mary was the new "Mother of all living," as Eve had been, according to the Bible, "mother of all living."[19] Mary therefore stood in a typological relation to Eve.[20] This relation of Eve and Mary, which I described in chapter 3 on the basis of Irenaeus of Lyons, was, significantly, the theme with which Bernard began his discourse about the Virgin Mary in the canto preceding his apostrophe to her:

> The wound that Mary closed and then
> anointed was the wound that Eve—so lovely
> at Mary's feet—had opened and had pierced.[21]

And now, in Bernard's explanation and Dante's vision, Mother Eve was seated at the feet of Mother Mary—and in a higher place than Rachel or even Beatrice.[22] None of this would have comported with the scheme of salvation as Dante was expounding it unless Mary as the Second Eve had been genuinely and completely a member of the human race. When Cacciaguida in Paradise spoke of how his mother invoked Mary "in pains of birth";[23] or when Buoconte still in Purgatory described having lapsed into a coma after being wounded in battle, just as he "had finished uttering the name of Mary [nel nome di Maria fini]";[24] or when Piccarda Donati, after recounting her quite remarkable life story,

> began to sing "Ave
> Maria" and, while singing, vanished as
> a weighty thing will vanish in deep water—[25]

the one whom all three were invoking in extremis was one who, though their Mediatrix, was also their fellow human being, who in fact could not have been truly their Mediatrix unless she had been their fellow human being.

She was at the same time the personal embodiment of the supreme virtues of which humanity was made capable through the gift of grace: in her, as Bernard said, "is every goodness found in any creature."[26] Yet in this connection there was a curious circumstance in the Divine Comedy, and one whose explanation is by no means obvious: much of the most explicit consideration of the specific virtues of Mary appeared in the Purgatorio rather than in the Paradiso. The hymn of Bernard in the Paradiso did laud her as "the noonday torch of charity" for those already in heaven and as "a living spring of hope" for those still on earth.[27] Therefore she not only manifested great faith, which was implicit throughout,[28] but she was likewise the exemplar of both hope and charity. In short, she embodied all three virtues celebrated in 1 Corinthians 13: "faith, hope, charity, these three."[29] It was on these three virtues that, in Cantos XXIV–XXVI, Dante was examined by the three apostles, or "doves,"[30] Peter, James, and John, a trio who had already been anticipated in the closing cantos of the Purgatorio[31] and who formed the inner circle of the twelve apostles.[32] Yet the virtues that stood out were the ones for which Mary was being singled out in the *Purgatorio*, rather than those that were identified with her in the *Paradiso*. Perhaps part of the reason was that the souls in Paradise were already enjoying the fruits of virtue, which they shared (though in lesser measure) with Mary, whereas those in Purgatory, who still had to attain to Paradise, stood in need of the grace that was merited and communicated through the virtues of Mary, which therefore needed a more complete description.

The attack on "arrogant Christians" in Canto X of the *Purgatorio* thus had as its foil the humility of the Virgin Mary, who at the annunciation had called herself "the handmaid of God."[33] Similarly, when the pilgrim came to the place where "the sin of envy / is scourged within this circle," what he heard arising from those who were being cleansed of such envy was "the cry of, 'Mary pray for us.'"[34] Further on, as he saw "people whom the fire of wrath / had kindled," they were contrasted with "the gentle manner" of the Virgin's reproof to her twelve-year-old son when she found him in the temple at Jerusalem: "Son, why hast thou thus dealt with us? behold, thy father and I have sought thee sorrowing."[35] The terrace of those who had been guilty of "sloth and negligence" was one where it was no longer Mary's "gentle manner" but her "haste" and her zeal that were being celebrated.[36] The sin of avarice, whose "hungering is deep and never-ending," caused its victims here in Purgatory to lament "Sweet Mary [*Dolce Maria*]!"[37] Those "whose appetite was gluttonous" stood in the sharpest possible contrast with Mary, who while on earth had not concerned herself with satisfying her own hunger.[38] And those who were in Purgatory to burn away the fires of lust had to cry aloud the words of the Virgin Mary in her chastity.[39] The tour through Purgatory thereby became at the same time a catalog of the virtues of the Blessed Virgin.

For Dante's view of the empirical church and its need for reform, the debates of the thirteenth and fourteenth centuries over poverty and property carried great importance. The discourse of Thomas Aquinas about Francis of Assisi in Canto XI of the *Paradiso* described the spiritual marriage between Francis and Lady Poverty, who had been "deprived of her first husband," Christ, and who had thereafter remained without a suitor for "eleven hundred years and more," until the coming of Francis.[40] But one

of the questions being debated in the Franciscan controversies over poverty during Dante's time was whether, like Christ, Mary, too, had taken a
vow of absolute poverty and, if she had, what she had done, for example,
with all that gold, frankincense, and myrrh that the Wise Men from the
East had brought to her and to her Child.[41] Dante's answer to the question
of the poverty of Mary seemed unequivocal: "Sweet Mary!" Dante heard
a voice say in Purgatory,

> In that hostel where
> you had set down your holy burden, there
> one can discover just how poor you were.[42]

The chastity of the Virgin Mary, who was, as Bernard said in the two
opening words of his song, unique among women in being simultaneously Virgin and Mother,[43] was contrasted in the *Purgatorio* not only
with "the force of Venus' poison," the extramarital unchastity of others,
but even with the marital chastity of virtuous wedlock: "Virum non
cognosco, I know not a man," as Mary had said, in Latin, to the angel of
the annunciation.[44] And when Dante confronted in Purgatory those souls
who had been guilty of the sins of gluttony and drunkenness in this life,
he was reminded once more of the contrast with the virtue of Mary,
manifested at the wedding feast in Cana of Galilee, and of her role as
Mediatrix both at Cana and now in Purgatory. As a voice explained,

> Mary's care was for the marriage-
> feast's being seemly and complete, not for
> her mouth (which now would intercede for you),[45]

continuing in heaven the intercession that she had articulated while on
earth.

It was likewise in the *Purgatorio* that Dante the poet first described the
relation Mary bore to the angels. The two guardian angels dressed in
green whom Dante the pilgrim saw, with their flaming swords shortened
but their faces blinding for sheer brilliance, "both come from Mary's
bosom," Sordello told him, "to serve as the custodians of the valley / against the serpent that will soon appear."[46] The other reference in

the Purgatorio to Mary's relation with the angels appeared two cantos later. The pilgrim was contemplating an amazingly beautiful wall of white marble, adorned with carvings that put to shame not only the greatest of human sculptors but nature itself.[47] Carved on the marble wall was the figure of the angel Gabriel:

> The angel who reached earth with the decree
> of that peace which, for many years, had been
> invoked with tears, the peace that opened heaven
> after long interdict, appeared before us,
> his gracious action carved with such precision—
> he did not seem to be a silent image.
> One would have sworn that he was saying, "Ave";
> for in that scene there was the effigy
> of one who turned the key that had unlocked
> the highest love; and in her stance there were
> impressed these words, "Ecce ancilla Dei,"
> precisely like a figure stamped in wax.[48]

Already in Purgatory, therefore, the divinely decreed mission of the Virgin Mary to "turn the key" and become the human means for the incarnation and thereby for salvation was being announced to the souls that awaited release into Paradise; and already in Purgatory the angels were making it evident that they stood ready to serve her, and through her both her divine Son and the humanity he came to save.

Yet it was in Paradise that the special relation between Mary and the angels was disclosed in all its glory. Once again, the angel Gabriel,

> the angelic love who had descended
> earlier, now spread his wings before her,
> singing "Ave Maria, gratia plena."[49]

But this time it was not, as it had been in Purgatory, in a mere physical representation on cold marble, which was beautiful but was not living, but in the spiritual reality of heaven itself that Gabriel continued forever the salutation with which the history of salvation had begun[50]—not any longer in the "modest voice" of his original greeting but in full-throated praise.[51] It was from this event of the annunciation, rather than from the nativity of Christ itself, that Dante, who followed the Florentine custom, dated the beginning of the new era through the incarnation, so that the new year began on 25 March.[52] Gabriel was joined in his salutation and praise by all the angelic hosts of heaven. Dante the pilgrim saw and heard the heavenly "brightnesses" as they expressed "the deep affection each possessed for Mary" and as they sang the *Regina Coeli* so sweetly, Dante the poet added, "that my delight in that has never left me" even now as he wrote.[53] It was a song in praise of Mary in which the angels were joined by the church triumphant of the saved who had already come to Paradise.[54] As "the greatest flame,"[55] Mary, Lady of Heaven, was the object of this angelic paean:

> I am angelic love who wheel around
> that high gladness inspired by the womb
> that was the dwelling place of our Desire;
> so shall I circle, Lady of Heaven, until
> you, following your Son, have made that sphere
> supreme, still more divine by entering it.[56]

This "ineffable vision,"[57] which attributed to Mary the ability to make the glories of the supreme sphere of heaven "still more divine" through her presence, prepared Dante for the sublimely ineffable vision of Mary and the angels that wold come to him as the occasion for Bernard's discourse about the Blessed Virgin.

It was that vision that was described in the concluding tercets of Canto XXXI of the *Paradiso*. As his awe had deepened, the pilgrim had been reluctant to contemplate the full power and glory before him. Therefore, "son of grace" that he was, he had nevertheless to be admonished:

> You will not come to know this joyous state
> if your eyes only look down at the base;
> but look upon the circles, look at those
> that sit in a position more remote,

until you see upon her seat the Queen
to whom this realm is subject and devoted.[58]

The souls of the saints who had already come to heaven, including in particular "the Hebrew women,"[59] were part of the celestial realm, and Mary was their archetype. But the angels, those dread and powerful spirits who did God's bidding day and night, had been its citizens all along, and there they had remained even after their rebellious fellow angels had been cast into the Inferno, where, as the pilgrim learned, the demons had now become as foul as they once had been fair.[60] And since Mary was indeed the Queen of Heaven, she was Queen of Angels, too.

Lifting his eyes in response to the admonition, the "son of grace," in language reminiscent of the apocalyptic visions of Ezekiel, Daniel, and Saint John the Divine,

. . . as, at morning,
the eastern side of the horizon shows
more splendor than the side where the sun sets,
so, as if climbing with my eyes from valley
to summit, I saw one part of the farthest
rank of the Rose more bright than all the rest.[61]

Before the transcendent light of the glorified Queen of Heaven, the angels gathered—not an indiscriminate mob, but as distinct individuals, since, as Thomas Aquinas taught, "it is impossible for two angels to be of one species," but each had to be a species unto itself.[62] The poet described what he saw:

I saw, around that midpoint, festive angels—
more than a thousand—with their wings outspread;
each was distinct in splendor and in skill.[63]

The "midpoint" and the object of their sportive celebration was the ineffable beauty of Mary, who ruled over a realm in which both saints and angels had their place. That special place of Mary among the saints in heaven became the theme for the altarpiece that Giovanni Bellini was to create for the church of San Giobbe in Venice, *Madonna Enthroned with the Saints*, sometime in the 1480s.[64] Bellini, like Dante, was a devotee of Francis of Assisi, who was represented on the altarpiece.[65] In his portrayal of the Virgin, Bellini put into living color the very qualities of Mary that Dante described:

> And there I saw a loveliness that when
> it smiled at the angelic songs and games
> made glad the eyes of all the other saints.

Here it became the task of poetic language about transcendent reality not to describe the object but to describe its own incapacity to describe the object:

> And even if my speech were rich as my
> imagination is, I should not try
> to tell the very least of her delights.[66]

That sentence needs to be parsed with some care. As his treatises on literature and language attested, Dante was honest enough to know that he had a skill with words, and it would have been the most hypocritical kind of false modesty for him to pretend otherwise. Moreover, here he recognized in himself a "wealth of imaginative power," and he found that it in turn far exceeded all of this verbal power. Yet even if it had not, he was saying, if word could truly have been matched to imagination in some simple one-to-one correlation, that would have been inadequate for describing Mary—indeed, inadequate for describing not her regal and transcendent position in the cosmos but "the very least of her delights."

It would be easy to read all of this extravagant language about the Virgin Mary as what Protestant polemics against Medieval Catholicism came to call "Mariolatry."[67] It would be easy, but it would be superficial and mistaken. For, as Henry Osborn Taylor put it, "One may say that the *Commedia* begins and ends with the Virgin. It was she who sent Beatrice into the gates of Hell to move Virgil—meaning human reason—to go to Dante's aid. The prayer which obtains her benediction, and the vision following, close the *Paradiso*." But, he warned, "no more with Dante than with other mediaeval men is she the end of worship and devotion. Her eyes are turned to God. So are those of Beatrice, of Rachel, and of all the saints in Paradise."[68] Mary could not have been the archetype of the saved unless she herself had been saved. She had been saved in a special manner, as by now almost all the theologians of the church affirmed, although it did not become official and binding until 1854—that is, by being preserved from original sin rather than, as everyone else was, rescued from it—but saved by the same divine grace and through the same divine Redeemer as the rest of humanity.[69] Dante's attitude toward this explanation of Mary's holiness was not altogether clear, but in Canto XIII he had Thomas Aquinas declare,

> I do approve of the opinion
> you hold, that human nature never was
> nor shall be what it was in those two persons,

namely, in Adam and in Christ.[70] This does seem to justify the conclusion drawn by Alexandre Masseron: "Dante affirms that Christ and Adam are the only ones who were created perfect," the explicit position of Bernard of Clairvaux, who rejected the doctrine of the immaculate conception.[71] Such was as well the teaching of Saint Thomas Aquinas.[72] That in turn makes it necessary to consider the question of the relation of Mary to Christ in Dante's theology.[73]

Whatever may have been Dante's doctrine about the special privilege of the immaculate conception at the beginning of the life of the Blessed Virgin, he clearly did teach, as did Bernard, that at the end of her life Mary was granted the privilege of the assumption, through the grace of Christ.[74] Therefore Saint John explained very carefully concerning himself that (*pace* some legends about him) he had not received this privilege of being assumed into heaven:

> On earth my body now is earth and shall
> be there together with the rest until
> our number equals the eternal purpose.

But then John added the significant stipulation, speaking of Mary and of Christ: "Only those two lights that ascended wear/their double garment in this blessed cloister,"[75] the "double garment" being the body and the soul, not only the soul. The two were Christ, through the ascension narrated in the New Testament and confessed in the creed, and then Mary through the assumption celebrated throughout the liturgy of the Medieval church but not officially promulgated as a dogma of the church until 1950. When Dante, bidden by Beatrice, lifted his eyes to behold Mary in heaven as "the Rose in which the Word of God became/flesh,"[76] he celebrated the ascension of Christ as an event intended "to grant scope to the eyes there that had not strength for Thee," and immediately went on to recognize that through her bodily assumption into heaven Mary shared in that exaltation, becoming not only "the fair flower which I always invoke morning and evening" on earth but "the greatest of the fires" in the Empyrean.[77] Therefore it was to Mary assumed into heaven that Bernard addressed his petition on Dante's behalf, to "curb his mortal passions" and to "disperse all the clouds of his mortality," so that Dante might receive the vision of the "Eternal Light" and so "that the Highest Joy might be his to see."[78]

Seeing that "Eternal Light" was the content of the vision of God. And in the final hundred lines of the final canto of the Paradiso, Dante celebrated the vision of the Trinity of three divine Persons in one divine Substance:

> In the deep and bright
> essence of that exalted Light, three circles
> appeared to me; they had three different colors,
> but all of them were of the same dimension;
> one circle seemed reflected by the second,
> as rainbow is by rainbow, and the third
> seemed fire breathed equally by those two circles.[79]

Therefore it must not be forgotten that a canto opening with the celebration of the Virgin Mary by Bernard of Clairvaux went on—through her and not around her, but nevertheless beyond her—to the celebration of the Eternal Light and Eternal "Love that moves the sun and the other stars,"[80] including Mary as the sun from which "the morning star draws beauty"[81] and Mary as *Stella Maris*, the Star of the Sea and the Queen of Heaven.[82] Hence there was not, in those final hundred lines, a single explicit reference to her; or perhaps it was all a reference to her, as the fellow creature (as Bernard explicitly described her)[83] who had pioneered in this vision. And that would have been in keeping with her role throughout the poem, as the heavenly Muse whose intervention, as it had been described by Beatrice already in Canto II of the *Inferno*,[84] had made it all possible. Thus "Maria" was for Dante "the name of that fair flower which I always / invoke, at morning and at evening";[85] singing the *Salve Regina* to her already while traveling through Purgatory,[86] but becoming her most eloquent troubadour in the *Paradiso* and above all in its final cantos.

Lucas van Leyden, *The Virgin with Two Angels*, 1523. Yale University Art Gallery, Stephan Carlton Clark, B.A. 1903, Fund.

11 The Model of Faith
in the Word of God

And Mary said,
Be it unto me according to thy word.
—Luke 1:38

W hen a great faith disappears, Gilbert Chesterton once observed, its sublime aspects go first: the Puritans rejected the worship of the Virgin Mary but went on burning witches.[1] Like so many of Chesterton's aphorisms, this one managed to be both true and false, as a closer examination of the attitude (or, rather, the several attitudes) of the sixteenth-century Reformation toward Mary would reveal. For the Protestant Reformers contended that just as their critique of what they regarded as Medieval sacramental magic had raised and restored the Lord's Supper to its divinely instituted place, so taking from Mary the false honors with which she had been burdened in the Middle Ages was in fact a liberation of her to be a supreme model of faith in the word of God.[2] And Mary as model of faith has also been an integral element of the Mariology of Western Catholicism; for "faith as lived by Mary is total, trusting self-surrender of mind and body to God."[3] The most obvious characteristic of the picture of Mary in the Protestant Reformation was its critique and rejection of what it took to be the excesses of Medieval devotion and teaching. Taking up the familiar Latin translation of Genesis 3:15, "She

[Ipsa] will crush his head,"[4] in his *Lectures on Genesis*, which occupied him during the final ten years of his life, Luther found it "amazing" and "damnable" that "Satan has managed to apply this passage, which in fullest measure abounds in the comfort of the Son of God, to the Virgin Mary. For in all the Latin Bibles the pronoun appears in the feminine gender: 'And *she* will crush.' "[5] At its most radical, particularly in Switzerland, this rejection of Medieval Mariology took the form of a new iconoclasm, what Lee Palmer Wandel has called "a conception of the 'Reformed' Church in which there were no images."[6] In Charles Garside's chilling description of "the war against the idols,"

> The committee as a body went into every church in Zurich. Once inside, they locked the doors behind them, and then, free from all disturbance from the curious crowds without, began to dismantle the church. . . . Every standing statue was removed from its niche or its base and, together with the base, taken out of the church. It was then either broken up by the masons, if made of stone or plaster, or burned, if made of wood. Every painting was taken down from the altars and burned outside. All murals were chipped away or scraped off the walls. The altars were stripped of all images and vessels, all votive lamps were let down and melted outside, and all crucifixes were removed.[7]

And many of the most prominent victims of this zeal were representations of the Virgin. But even such Reformers as Martin Luther, who in 1525 protested vigorously against this iconoclasm,[8] protested no less vigorously against what Luther called the "abominable idolatry [*grewliche Abgötterey*]" of Medieval Mariology, an idolatry that was, he said, "not praising Mary, but slandering her in the extreme and making an idol of her."[9]

The context of that Reformation critique was a fundamental reconsideration of the practice of invoking the saints. Articles XIX and XX of Ulrich Zwingli's *Sixty-Seven Articles* of 1523 declared that because "Christ is the only Mediator between God and us," it followed "that we do not need any mediator beyond this life but him."[10] For, in the words of the *Heidelberg Catechism*, "He is our Mediator."[11] Also quoting the words of the New Testament, "There is one mediator between God and men, the man Christ Jesus,"[12] Article XXI of the *Augsburg Confession* of 1530, written by Luther's colleague Philip Melanchthon, entitled "The Cult of the Saints," reinforced this polemic by defining Christ as "the only highpriest, advocate, and intercessor before God. He alone has promised to hear our prayers."[13] Although Melanchthon's *Apology of the Augsburg Confession* did "grant that the saints in heaven pray for the church in general, as they prayed for the church universal while they were on earth,"[14] that did not justify the practice of invoking them for particular needs. Not even the highest of the saints, the Virgin Mary, therefore, could infringe on the sole mediatorship of Christ. For with varying degrees of severity, the Protestant Reformers were using their slogan of *solus Christus* to attack what John Henry Newman was to call the system of "created mediation,"[15] the principle that, under the sovereignty of the unique uncreated mediation of Christ, there was an entire chain of mediating powers—the sacraments, the church, the saints, and Mary—which, though created, conveyed the power of the uncreated mediation of Christ to believers.

In part this critique of the Medieval cult of Mary was the application to her cult of the far-reaching Reformation insistence on their slogan of *sola Scriptura*, the sole authority of Scripture over tradition—not simply the *supreme* authority, which almost everyone would accept, but the *sole* authority of the Bible. Thus the *Thirty-Nine Articles* of the Church of England of 1571 listed the "inuocation of Saintes" as the last in a list of "Romishe Doctrines" that were "a fonde [foolish] thing, vainly inuented, and grounded vpon no warrantie of Scripture, but rather repugnant to the worde of God."[16] Or, at greater length, Calvin in his dissertation on the idea asked: "Then who, whether angel or demon, ever revealed to any man even a syllable of the kind of saints' intervention they invent? For there is nothing about it in Scripture. What reason, then, did they have to invent it? Surely, when human wit is always seeking after assistance for which we have no support in God's Word, it clearly reveals its own faithlessness."[17] The application of the exclusionary principle of *sola*

Scriptura was directed not only against the doctrine of the intercession of Mary and the saints but against the Medieval proliferation of stories about Mary and the saints for which there was no biblical basis. Contrasting the stark simplicity and credibility of the biblical account of Sarah with such stories, Luther asserted, "The legends or accounts of the saints which we had under the papacy were not written according to the pattern of Holy Scripture."[18] And elsewhere he expressed the wish: "Would to God that I had the time to cleanse the legends and examples, or that somebody else with a higher spirit would venture to do it; they are full, full of lies and deception."[19] Particularly deceptive, of course, were legends about biblical saints, and above all about Mary, for they crowded out the testimony of Scripture about the very qualities that had made them saints in the first place.

At the same time, the doctrine of Mary during the Reformation underwent a revival of various early theologies that had been denounced as heresy, including some of the heretical theories about Mary examined in earlier chapters of this book. As the leading historian of the Radical Reformation, George Huntston Williams, has pointed out, the Mariology of Caspar Schwenckfeld issued in

> the glorification of the human nature of Christ and his scriptural discernment of Mary as indeed unique among women in the very words of Elizabeth after she was filled with the Holy Spirit: "Blessed art thou, Mary, among women and blessed is the fruit of thy womb," for she in Schwenckfeld's own words "received from the Holy Spirit natural flesh," whereby she, unique among women[,] fulfilled the prophecy of Jer. 3:22: "a new thing, a woman will encompass a man," that is, says Schwenckfeld, it was foreseen that Mary, "impregnated through the Holy Spirit, would carry and give birth to God's and her son, a son of such glory that his flesh could see no decomposition."[20]

But some Radical Reformers went even further, as when Orbe Philips, rejecting the idea that "the body of Christ had been made by Mary (as the

world thinks and says with such want of understanding regarding it),"
asserted instead that "God, the Heavenly Father, prepared for Jesus Christ,
his only begotten Son, a body [Heb. 10:5], but not of corrupt human
seed [Luke 1:35], rather of his incorruptible seed." For, he continued, "it
is impossible for the flesh of Christ to be formed of the seed of Mary; for
neither the seed of Mary, nor that of any earthly creature can by any
means be the true living bread that came down from heaven [John 6:31–
35], or be so called."[21]

In response to such speculations among the Radical Reformers, the
Anglican, Lutheran, and Reformed confessions of faith reaffirmed the
traditional doctrine of Eastern and Western orthodoxy, which had originally been formulated in opposition to Gnosticism, that the entire human
nature of Christ, body and soul, was a creature, was derived from the
created and human body of the Virgin Mary, and was not in any sense
pre-existent. Therefore the Lutheran *Formula of Concord* of 1577, which
devoted a major part of its discussion to differentiating the Lutheran
Reformation from the Calvinist Reformation on such issues of doctrine as
the relation of the two natures in the person of Christ, the real presence in
the Eucharist, and double predestination, was in this case speaking also
for its Calvinist adversaries when it rejected the teaching "that Christ did
not assume his flesh and blood from the Virgin Mary but brought it along
from heaven."[22] In this way Mary once more became, also for the mainline Reformers, what she had always been: guarantee of the reality of the
incarnation and of the human nature of Christ.[23]

But it would be a mistake, and one into which many interpretations
of the Reformation both friendly and hostile have all too easily fallen, to
emphasize these negative and polemical aspects of its Mariology at the
expense of the positive place the Protestant Reformers assigned to her in
their theology.[24] They repeated—and in many cases used their superior
grasp of the original languages of the Bible to reinforce—the central
content of the orthodox confession of the first five centuries of Christian
history.[25] For despite the constantly repeated accusations that the doctrinal principles of the Reformation, consistently carried out, would and
did lead to a repudiation of historic Christian and Catholic orthodoxy,

especially of the dogmas of the Trinity as confessed by the Council of Nicaea in 325 and the person of Christ as confessed by the Council of Chalcedon in 451, Luther and Calvin and their colleagues indignantly insisted that, in the opening words of the *Augsburg Confession*, "we unanimously hold and teach, in accordance with the decree of the Council of Nicaea."[26] The same words could have been applied to the decree of the Council of Chalcedon, and to Reformed, Calvinist teaching, as Thomas F. Torrance has argued in pointing out that "care was taken to repudiate and avoid all the classical errors in Christology on both sides of the Chalcedonian fence."[27] The texts on which Torrance was commenting with that observation, namely, the authorized catechisms of the Reformed church in Scotland, were evidence, moreover, that this adherence to the orthodox teaching of the church was not a mere formality or political ploy by the Reformers but what was being believed, taught, and confessed in the concrete life of the churches. Thus the *Larger Catechism* of 1648 taught: "Christ the Son of God became man, by taking to Himself a true body, and a reasonable soul, being conceived by the power of the Holy Spirit in the womb of the Virgin Mary, of her substance, and born of her, yet without sin."[28]

It was thus possible for Walter Tappolet in 1962 to compile a remarkable collection of texts from Luther, Calvin, Zwingli, and Bullinger under the title "The Reformers in Praise of Mary."[29] Drawing on sermons and devotional material as well as on theological treatises, he documented, first of all, this continuing orthodoxy of the Mariology of the Reformers. Zwingli, for example, called Mary "the highest of creatures next to her Son" and "Mother of God," and Balthasar Hubmaier asserted her perpetual virginity.[30] Luther did the same—and not only in his private writings and sermons, as when he described Mary as "in childbirth and after childbirth, as she was a Virgin before childbirth, so she remained."[31] Even in the only confessional statement of faith by him that was officially adopted by the Lutheran church and incorporated into the official collection of the *Book of Concord* of 1580—as distinct from his *Small Catechism* and *Large Catechism*, which were also included but were not, strictly speaking, confessions—the *Smalcald Articles* of 1537, the Latin text contained the words (which did not, however, appear in the German version): "from Mary, pure, holy, and Ever-Virgin [*ex Maria pura, sancta, Semper Virgine*]."[32] But beyond the orthodoxy of their language and teaching about Mary, the Protestant Reformers one after another spoke of her with warmth and dedication, as when Luther in 1521, the year of his excommunication by Pope Leo X, could close his *Commentary on the Magnificat* with the words: "May Christ grant us this through the intercession and for the sake of His dear Mother Mary! Amen."[33] Such sentiments, which could easily be duplicated, belied the impression, which the Protestant Reformers themselves sometimes gave and which their opponents often magnified, that they were sweeping aside the entire accumulation of Christian devotion to Mary in the name of restoring the primitive Christianity of the apostolic church.

More than either of these principles, *sola gratia*, "by grace alone," or *sola Scriptura*, "by Scripture alone," however, the Reformation slogan that epitomized Mary's positive position in the Reformation was *sola fide*, "by faith alone." For in the theology of the Reformers she was the model of faith, as the Reformation redefined it.

A favorite passage of the Reformers was Paul's statement, "Faith cometh by hearing, and hearing by the word of God,"[34] which provided the title for an important twentieth-century study of Reformation theology by Ernst Bizer.[35] That connection between faith and the hearing of the word of God had, of course, been a component of the definition of faith all along. As one of the triad of faith, hope, and love set forth by the apostle Paul,[36] faith, and consequently the function of the word of God as the means by which faith was aroused and sustained, had always received its share of attention: "Since, therefore, faith comes by hearing, and hearing by the word of God [*Cum ergo fides sit ex auditu, auditus autem per verbum Christi*]," Thomas Aquinas could argue in his *Commentary on the Sentences*.[37] But the Reformers, beginning with Luther, taught that authentic Christian love was dependent on faith and therefore, despite the identification of love as "the greatest of these,"[38] assigned to faith the central position in that triad and therefore assigned to the word of God what must be called a sacramental function: as the sacraments were, in a formula that the Reformation took over from Augustine, a "visible word,"[39] so the preaching and teaching of the word of God could have been called an audible sacrament. Thus Calvin, in a carefully crafted discussion, defined "faith to be a knowledge of God's will toward us, perceived from his Word."[40]

Mary became the obvious case study of this for Luther, as the opening words of Mary's Magnificat showed him that "holiness of spirit . . . consists in nothing else than in faith pure and simple." In a characteristic summary of the Reformation doctrine of justification by faith and not by works, he insisted on the basis of Mary's faith "that works breed nothing but discrimination, sin, and discord, while faith alone makes men pious, united, and peaceable." Therefore "faith and the Gospel . . . are the highest goods . . . which no one should let go."[41] For when Mary said to the angel Gabriel (in Luther's German), "Let it happen to me as you have said [Mir geschehe, wie du gesagt hast],"[42] this was above all an expression of her faith. And "through such faith alone she was saved and freed from sin."[43]

In a bold definition of faith—which was in some ways an anticipation of Blaise Pascal's famous argument du pari, "One has to wager . . . and calculate the gain and loss of wagering whether or not God exists"—Luther asserted in 1522: "Faith does not require information, knowledge, or certainty, but a free surrender and a joyful bet on his unfelt, untried, and unknown goodness."[44] In his Commentary on Galatians, by contrast, Luther spoke more positively about the quest for certainty: "This is the reason why our theology is certain: it snatches us away from ourselves and places us outside ourselves, so that we do not depend on our own strength, conscience, experience, person, or works, but depend on that which is outside ourselves, that is, on the promise and truth of God, which cannot deceive."[45] For both of these definitions, Luther, like the apostle Paul, took Abraham as the biblical figure who especially exemplified this characteristic of faith; and in his lengthy portrait of Abraham as part of the Lectures on Genesis of 1535—45 he dwelt above all on Abraham's faith, which "was counted to him for righteousness."[46] But the faith of Abraham, which caused him to forsake Ur of the Chaldees and venture forth into the unknown in obedience to the word and promise of God and then to be willing to offer up his only son, was matched by the faith of the Virgin Mary, who also offered up her only Son. Even in the context of an attack on those who "exalt the Virgin Mary too highly and praise her for having known everything," therefore, Luther could speak of her as "blessed and endowed with every kind of grace [*gebenedeyet und hoch begnadet mit allerley gnaden*]" and describe how "God led her in such a way that he concealed many things from her," which he took as a reminder that "in Christendom nothing should be preached but the pure word of God."[47]

A particularly fascinating aspect of the relation between the Protestant Reformation and the cult of the Mary as Virgin and Queen was the cult of Elizabeth I as Virgin and Queen, as Gloriana. As Roy Strong has suggested, "The cult of Gloriana was skillfully created to buttress public order, and even more, deliberately to replace the pre-reformation externals of religion, the cult of the Virgin and saints with their attendant images, processions, ceremonies and secular rejoicing."[48] Although it has been brought into question by some scholars, who have seen it as a later theory,[49] there are at least some indications that Elizabeth consciously invoked the parallel. For example, the "Virgin Queen of Walsingham" was the name of the most widely venerated image of Mary in pre-Reformation England. Although it had been destroyed before the reign of Elizabeth, it was widely venerated into the sixteenth century;[50] and Elizabeth's title of "Virgin Queen" would seem to have been borrowed from it. Edmund Spenser did seem to be invoking the parallel, consciously and frequently, as in *The Shepheardes Calender*:

> Of fayre *Elisa* be your silver song,
> that blessed wight:
> The flowre of Virgins, may shee florish long,
> In princely plight.
> For she is *Syrinx* daughter without spotte,
> Which *Pan* the shepheards God of her begot:
> So sprong her grace

Of heavenly race,

No mortall blemishe may her blotte,[51]

those final three lines sounding unmistakably like an echo of Medieval Mariology. And near the beginning of *The Faerie Queene* he addressed Queen Elizabeth in similar language:

And with them eke, ô Goddesse heauenly bright,

Mirrour of grace and Maiestie diuine,

Great Lady of the greatest Isle, whose light

Like *Phœbus* lampe throughout the world doth shine,

Shed thy faire beames into my feeble eyne,

And raise my thoughts too humble and too vile,

To thinke of that true glorious type of thine,

The argument of mine afflicted stile:

The which to heare, vouchsafe, ô dearest dred a-while.[52]

Just as in his *Paradise Lost*, John Milton could not avoid attention to Eve, but also to Mary as the Second Eve,[53] so likewise in his *Paradise Regained* Mary had to have a place, as when he had Christ explain:

These growing thoughts my Mother soon perceiving

By words at times cast forth, inly rejoiced,

And said to me apart: High are thy thoughts

O Son, but nourish them and let them soar

To what height sacred virtue and true worth

Can raise them, though above example high.[54]

Thus a special case of "Protestant Mariology" was the place of Mary in sacred poetry, hymnody, worship, and devotion, which perpetuated some of these patterns of the Reformation into modern times, as I noted in an earlier chapter on the basis of John A. L. Riley's hymn of 1906, "Ye Watchers and Ye Holy Ones."[55] Again, in the hymn "Crown Him with Many Crowns," originally by Matthew Bridges but with additions and supplements by others,[56] Christ was saluted as "Fruit of the mystic Rose, / As of that Rose the stem," making Mary in Protestantism the

Mystic Rose that she had been in the piety of the Middle Ages and the Counter-Reformation.

In art as well as in poetry, Mary continued to claim a place in the affections of those who on doctrinal grounds did not share the traditional reverence for her. So it was that, as Owen Chadwick has suggested, "*The Annunciation* by Fra Angelico, for a cell of the Dominican priory of San Marco in Florence, [was] one of the two or three pictures which most helped Protestants, as well as Catholics, to remember St. Mary with affection."[57] The relation of the art of Albrecht Dürer to the Reformation continues to be the object of serious investigation.[58] Most pertinent to our theme here was his cycle of woodcuts, *The Life of Mary*.[59] A colleague and in some ways a pupil of Dürer, and even an artistic subject of his, was Lucas van Leyden.[60] Whatever his own complex relation to the Reformation may have been, his woodcut of *The Virgin with Two Angels*, dated 1523, epitomized the Reformation tension being discussed here: between a retention of the Dantean, and universally Medieval, depiction of the Virgin Mary as Queen of Angels (and therefore, at least by implication, Queen of Heaven), and a reinterpretation of her in the light of the Reformation principles of *sola Scriptura, sola gratia,* and above all *sola fide* as the totally human Maid of Nazareth, a peasant girl snatched by the initiative of God from her ordinary life to take her great and historic part in the drama of salvation.

Paolo and Giovanni Veneziano, *The Coronation of the Virgin*, 1358. Copyright The Frick Collection, New York.

12 The Mater Gloriosa
and the Eternal Feminine

Mary hath chosen the better part,
which shall not be taken away from her.
—Luke 10:38–42

When truly archetypal motifs and figures of tradition cease to be the objects of the devotion to which they have been attached for many centuries, the afterglow can sometimes seem even brighter than the glow. So it has been true in a preeminent sense of the figure of Jesus that, by a phenomenon that could be labeled Christocentric agnosticism, "as respect for the organized church has declined, reverence for Jesus has grown."[1] And so it has been with his Mother. In the Romantic poetry of many countries during the nineteenth century, therefore, Mary came to glow with a halo that was in some respects no less resplendent than the one with which the unsophisticated piety of the people, the speculations of the theologians, and the liturgy of the church had adorned her. For if, with René Wellek, Romanticism is defined as "that attempt, apparently doomed to failure and abandoned by our own time, to identify subject and object, to reconcile man and nature, consciousness and unconsciousness by poetry which is 'the first and last of all knowledge,'"[2] then William Wordsworth, the poet from whose preface to the 1800 edition of *Lyrical Ballads* the closing words of that definition were taken, well illustrated the situation. Wordsworth's early "radical Protestantism," as Geoffrey Hartman has called it,[3] continued to manifest itself even in his later and more conservative *Ecclesiastical Sonnets*. As a Protestant, he seems to have been quite sure, as he said there, that "From false assumption rose, and fondly hailed/By superstition, spread the Papal power."[4] Nevertheless, he was able to address the Virgin Mary this way:

> Mother! whose virgin bosom was uncrost
> With the least shade of thought to sin allied;
> Woman! above all women glorified,
> *Our tainted nature's solitary boast;*
> Purer than foam on central ocean tost;
> Brighter than eastern skies at daybreak strewn
> With fancied roses, than the unblemished moon
> Before her wane begins on heaven's blue coast;
> Thy Image falls to earth. Yet some, I ween,
> Not unforgiven the suppliant knee might bend,
> As to a visible Power, in which did blend
> All that was mixed and reconciled in Thee
> Of mother's love with maiden purity,
> Of high with low, celestial with terrene![5]

For if Mary truly was "celestial" as well as "terrene," that seemed to come close to calling her Queen of Heaven. Here Wordsworth echoed the portrayal of "the coronation of the Virgin," which became a standard part of the iconography of Mary during the twelfth century, regularly depicted her as sitting at Christ's right hand, and it was a continuation of this understanding when later painters showed Christ or God the Father or the entire Trinity investing her with the crown.[6]

Similarly, Mary Ann Evans, as the anonymous translator into English of the radical *Life of Jesus* by David Friedrich Strauss, knew very well that it had relegated the Virgin Mary and the virgin birth to the realm of myth, for she had translated the section about this, which was entitled (in her translation) "History of the Conception of Jesus Viewed as a Mythus."[7] But later in her life, writing as George Eliot, in perhaps her greatest novel, she had Tertius Lydgate, the discredited physician, exclaim about the protagonist of the novel, Dorothea Brooke Casaubon: "This young creature has a heart large enough for the Virgin Mary. She evidently thinks nothing of her own future, and would pledge away half her income at once, as if she wanted nothing for herself but a chair to sit in from which she can look down with those clear eyes at the mortals who pray to her. She seems to have what I never saw in any woman before—a fountain of friendship towards men"; and a little later Dorothea was described as having "the pale cheeks and pink eyelids of a *mater dolorosa*" (which, for late twentieth-century American readers, the editor of *Middlemarch* felt obliged to explain in a footnote as "a title of the Virgin Mary").[8]

Similar passages could easily be added from Romantic poets of the several national literatures, because, as a German poet said,

> I see thee, Mary, beautifully depicted
> in a thousand pictures;
> Yet none of them can portray thee
> As my soul perceives thee.
>
> I only know that ever since then
> The tumult of the world has vanished like a dream,
> And a heaven, ineffably sweet,
> Abides eternally in my heart.
>
> [Ich sehe dich in tausend Bildern
> Maria lieblich ausgedrückt;
> Doch keins von allen kann dich schildern,
> Wie meine Seele dich erblickt.
>
> Ich weiß nur, daß der Welt Getümmel
> Seitdam mir wie ein Traum verweht,
> Und ein unnennbar süßer Himmel
> Mir ewig im Gemüte steht];[9]

and those thousand pictures came into view throughout the poetry, music, and painting of the Romantic century. It will not, however, be on that German poet, but on his more celebrated countryman, Johann Wolfgang von Goethe, that this chapter will concentrate, and specifically on Goethe's *Faust* as the supreme example of the Virgin Mary as an enduring archetype.[10] Goethe's relation to historic Christianity, too, was a complex one. In the *Conversations with Goethe in the Last Years of His Life* recorded by Johann Peter Eckermann, Goethe was reported as having said on 11 March 1832, just eleven days before his death: "Beyond the grandeur and the moral elevation of Christianity, as it sparkles and shines in the Gospels, the human mind will not advance." But the context of that declaration made it clear that he was doing anything but affirming the orthodox and catholic faith of the church.[11] Nevertheless, like Wordsworth, Goethe was profoundly fascinated by the mystical figure of the Virgin Mary, and especially by her exalted status as Mater Gloriosa and the Eternal Feminine [*das Ewig-Weibliche*]. For like Dante's *Divine Comedy*, and apparently in a conscious echoing of it, Goethe's *Faust* began in the setting of Holy Week and ended in Paradise with the vision of Mary and the Eternal Feminine. But before Mary manifested herself as the Mater Gloriosa in the closing scene of *Faust*, she had first been seen as the Mater Dolorosa.[12] In her despair, Gretchen prayed to her, in a fervent petition to the Virgin Mary inspired by the *Stabat Mater Dolorosa*.[13] As the drama turned out, then, "the young woman who is at first the object of Faust's purely sensual passion, inspired by Mephisto—Gretchen—becomes in fact Mephisto's victorious rival in the battle for Faust's soul."[14] For she was told that it was her elevation to "higher spheres" of glory that would become the means for Faust to attain to those spheres of glory, too.[15]

Those words were addressed to the Woman Penitent, Formerly Called Gretchen by the Mater Gloriosa, seen as the special refuge for those who, like Gretchen, had been "easy to seduce" and were "hard to save" but who were now "penitent women, in need of grace."[16] The Chorus of Penitents addressed the Mater Gloriosa with the praise, "Thou dost soar to the heights of the everlasting kingdoms," and with the petition, "Receive our pleading, thou incomparable one, who art full of grace!"[17] She was "full of grace," as she had been addressed by the angel of the annunciation, "Ave, gratia plena, Dominus tecum."[18] The penitents were "in need of grace," and through her grace and purity their impurity was healed. But the Mater Gloriosa did not represent the healing only of their individual lusts, nor only of Faust's conflicts; as has been said about such theological terms in this scene, "it is, of course, contrary to the sense to interpret them according to the strict sense of the terminology of the church, but it would be forcing things to exclude echoes of this completely."[19] Not only was it the case that "the several persons of Margarete-Galatea-Helen are now subsumed in the one person of Mary Mother of God";[20] but through these "echoes" of themes that had been sounding throughout the rest of the work, the several titles with which she was identified here in the closing scene may be said to have achieved a new synthesis of disparate elements, not by negating them but by exalting them to the level of the sublime, in what one scholar called "that loving fusion of pagan and Christian convictions in which Goethe . . . found his own final religious peace."[21]

Those titles were brought together by Doctor Marianus, whose importance for the outcome of the drama has been well summarized in this sensitive observation by Cyrus Hamlin: "As a sublime counter-figure to Doctor Faustus in his study at the outset of the drama, this mystical devotee of the Virgin represents the highest level of spiritual perfection attainable within the human sphere. Thematically he may be compared with Nereus in his devotion to Galatea in the final scene of the 'Classical Walpurgis Night.' Through Doctor Marianus the theme of the Eternal Feminine is re-introduced to *Faust* in its highest traditional form."[22] Doctor Marianus brought the titles together in the final two lines of the worshipful ode with which he introduced the transcendent closing hymn. The ode was spoken first to the penitents: "Look upwards to this saving look, all who have been made tender through repentance, in order to transform yourselves thankfully into your blessed destiny." Then Doctor Marianus turned to the Mater Gloriosa herself: "Let every higher sense be placed at thy service. *Virgin, Mother, Queen, Goddess:* continue to grant grace!"[23] Such a heaping up of titles was a familiar device from earlier passages in the drama.[24] These four titles had been anticipated in the other ode of Doctor Marianus, shortly preceding this one: "The Glorious One in the center, in her wreath of stars, the Queen of Heaven. I can tell from her splendor. She is the Supreme Ruler in the world!"[25] And again: "Virgin, pure in the most beautiful sense, Mother worthy of honor, our chosen Queen, equal in birth to the gods."[26] He implored her to "grant approval to that which earnestly and tenderly moves this man's breast and which with a holy passion of love he bears to thee."[27] He prayed, "Let every higher sense be placed at thy service."[28] By such petitions, the various yearnings and intuitions in "this man's breast," every "passion of love," including even Faust's original "coarse passion of love,"[29] and "every higher sense," as these had manifested themselves in Faust's development throughout the work, were being raised to the exalted plane of the Virgin Mary, and thus of Christ her Son, and thus of God the Father in heaven (where this entire "postlude in heaven parallel to the 'Prologue in Heaven'"[30] was being played, with no action in heaven between these two scenes).

"In the soteriology, as in the ethics, of Goethe's play," one commentator has suggested, "love, not egoism, is both the principal instrument of Grace and the highest value."[31] The saving power of that love through each of the three occupants of that exalted plane—Mary, her Son Jesus Christ, and God the Father—had already been explicitly adumbrated by the Woman Penitent Formerly Called Gretchen while she was still alive on earth, in her penitential sighs for grace before the "devotional image of the Mater Dolorosa," as she prayed a paraphrase of the Medieval Stabat Mater Dolorosa: "Incline thy countenance graciously to my need, thou who art abounding in pain. With the sword in thy heart [Luke 2:35] and with a thousand pains thou dost look up at the death of thy Son. Thou dost look to the Father and send sighs upward for [thy Son's] trial and for thine own."[32] Now at the end, having become a participant in the grace and glory of heaven, she prayed to Mary once more. Her prayer "is transposed into a radiant major key,"[33] and it was no longer addressed to the Mater Dolorosa but to the Mater Gloriosa: "Incline, oh incline, thy countenance graciously to my happiness, thou incomparable one, thou radiant one! The one whom I first loved, now no longer troubled, is coming back."[34] The sharp contrast, and yet the special bond, between Gretchen as the fallen woman, whom her own brother had called "a whore," and Mary as the "Virgin, pure in the most beautiful sense,"[35] became the subject of prayers to the Virgin on Gretchen's behalf by the three Women Penitents of this closing scene, with a devotional version of the logical argument *a maiori ad minus,* from the greater to the lesser: "Thou who dost not deny thy presence to women who have sinned greatly and dost elevate a repentant recovery to the level of eternity [which was how all three of them had been treated, despite the magnitude of their sins], grant also to this good soul, who forgot herself only once and who did not know that she was doing wrong, thy fitting forgiveness!"[36] If even they had not been denied the grace of forgiveness, so the prayers argued, she certainly ought to receive it.

It was significant for this special bond that the prayer of each of the three Penitents to Mary on behalf of Gretchen, and much earlier Faust's lamentation over Gretchen, should have contained the most detailed references anywhere in the drama to the redemptive work of Christ, who nevertheless, "significantly, does not appear and is not invoked" directly as such even here.[37] When Mephistopheles sneered about Gretchen, "She is not the first," this was apparently a verbatim quotation from the accounts of an actual case that occurred in Frankfurt in 1771, as reported by Goethe.[38] But Faust's reaction to the sneer was to explode, with its reference to "rendering satisfaction for guilt" apparently intended as an allusion to the atoning death of Christ: "Not the first! How utterly miserable! No human soul can comprehend that more than one creature has descended to the depths of this misery, that the death-agony of the first was not enough to render satisfaction for the guilt of all the others in the eyes of the One who pardons eternally!"[39] Mephistopheles always had the typical devil's horror of the cross.[40] In their original hostile encounter, Faust confronted Mephistopheles-as-poodle with the crucifix and with the death of Christ, whom he described as "the never-begotten One, the ineffable One, who was poured out through all the heavens and was blasphemously pierced" on the cross.[41] And now, before Mary as Mater Gloriosa, each of the three penitents in her turn intoned the litany, by referring to the person of Christ and citing the authority of some aspect of his life and death.[42]

The first was the Mulier Peccatrix.[43] In the exegetical tradition, though not in the text of the Gospel itself, she had been identified with Mary Magdalene[44] and was the Mary of whom the Dies Irae, sung at the Requiem Mass for Gretchen's mother, prayed: "Thou who didst absolve Mary, and listen to the petition of the thief, thou hast also granted hope to me." But it was striking that this petition, with its confident reference to divine forgiveness, was omitted from the Dies Irae in that scene in Part One, though it was echoed here in Part Two. Paraphrasing the Gospel, the Magdalene based her petition on Christ's statement that "Her sins, which are many, are forgiven; for she loved much,"[45] and addressed it to the Virgin Mary: "By the love that made tears flow as balsam on the feet of thy divinely transfigured Son, despite the scorn of the Pharisees; by the jar that so richly poured out its incense; by the locks of hair that so gently dried the sacred limbs."[46] The second was the Mulier Samaritana, who encountered Christ at the well.[47] She now made "the well to which Abraham once brought his flocks to be watered" and at which "the cup was permitted to touch and cool the Savior's lips" into an allegory of the "superabundant, eternally clear fountain" of grace "that flows from there through all the worlds."[48] And the third was Maria Aegyptica, whose life was recorded not in the New Testament but in the Acta Sanctorum, including her conversion while on a pilgrimage to the Holy Sepulcher in Jerusalem, "the consecrated place where the Lord was laid to rest," and then her forty-seven years of penance as a hermit in the desert east of Jordan.[49] Although it does seem "that according to the earliest conception of the closing scenes it was to be Christ who would free Faust's soul from hell after his victory over Lucifer,"[50] Christ himself did not appear directly and was not prayed to directly in these petitions. Rather, all of these references to the history of Christ were invoked in a prayer to Mary in support of the petition for Gretchen—a reminiscence of the closing cantos of Dante's *Paradiso*, with the description of the Virgin Mary by Bernard of Clairvaux as "the one whose face most resembles that of Christ."[51]

But she was called "Virgin"—and then "Mother." This can be taken as an echo of the "pantheistic" symbol of the Mothers in Part Two, for the theme of Nature as the All did resound here in the closing scene of *Faust*. Thus the content of redemption was defined as "being saved in the company of the All."[52] That "company of the All" was one of the very things which "earnestly and tenderly moves this man's breast and which with a holy passion of love he bears" to the Virgin Mother.[53] In keeping with this "holy passion of love," the mighty forces of Nature, according to the Pater Profundus, "are messengers of love, they proclaim that which surrounds us in eternal creativity."[54] It does not seem to be an exaggeration to conclude that "this transfigured Nature becomes a metaphor of love. It is the only theme at the conclusion of Part Two of *Faust*."[55] And just as those forces of a transfigured Nature surged everywhere and yet provided continuity and stability, "so it is almighty love that shapes and cares for the All,"[56] apparently yet another echo of Dante's *Paradiso*, this time of the closing line of its Marian vision about "the love that moves the sun and all the other stars,"[57] as well as of the words of God to the angels in the Prologue in Heaven about being "embraced by that which is becoming, which works and lives eternally, with the chaste bonds of love," and of Faust's reminiscence of his youthful sense of "the love of heaven."[58] Immediately preceding the prayer of the Pater Profundus, however, came that of the Pater Ecstaticus, which opened by calling God "the eternal torch of joy, the glowing bond of love,"[59] and closed with another reference to the theme of the All, but to a way of transcending it in eternal love, "until everything worthless is put to flight and what continues to shine is the star, the core of everlasting love."[60] That transcending even of the All in the Eternal was the fulfillment of the aspirations of Faust's science and his pantheism, for which "everything transitory is only a parable" of what abides;[61] and it was this in Mary, not only as Virgin but as Mother and as the Eternal Feminine.[62]

Yet, in the words immediately preceding these, the Eternal Feminine who was Virgin and Mother was called Queen and Goddess as well[63] and was thus the fulfillment also of the aspirations of Faust's poetic polytheism, and specifically of the typology represented in the figures of Leda, Galatea, and above all Helen of Troy. Leda had appeared in a vision as Queen.[64] Helen was repeatedly hailed simply with the title Queen,[65] even when she was being identified as the sacrificial victim.[66] Elsewhere she was labeled as "the high Queen."[67] Faust expanded on the title, speaking to her as the Queen whose arrow had found its mark in him[68] and as "the Ruler who, the moment she appeared, assumed the throne."[69] She also used the title Queen in referring to herself. The title Goddess, applied at the end of the drama to Mary, was also used earlier for various deities: the Sun, the Moon, Nike, Galatea, and the Mothers.[70] Yet to Faust, Helen was the preeminent holder of that title, too. His incredulous exclamation at the initial vision of her, calling her "the sum total of the content of all the heavens" and asking, "Is it possible that something like this can be found on earth?"[71] already put her into that realm.

But when she appeared to him in person, coming back to life out of the mists of Classical Antiquity, he told her: "To you I owe the springs of every action and the quintessence of passion. I devote myself to you in affection, love, worship, yes in madness."[72] The Poet, speaking for Faust and for all those present, proceeded to express that "worship" as, watching her kiss Faust for the first time, he described her as the Goddess. When she embraced Faust for the last time and disappeared, leaving her garment behind, the Phorcyad told him to keep the garment, because although "it is not the Goddess any more" and he had lost her, the garment was still "divine."[73] The vision of "godlike" feminine figures that Faust then experienced—followed immediately by a vision of "my most youthful summum bonum, of which I have been deprived for very long," which seems to have been an obvious reference to Gretchen—may be seen as a precognition of the closing scene: "Yes, my eyes do not deceive me! I see it, on a sunlit couch, gloriously stretched out, but truly gigantic—the godlike form of a woman! It resembles Juno, Leda, Helen. With what majestic loveliness it shimmers before my eyes!"[74] For to Faust, Helen was "the sole object of my yearning," but she was more: "The eternal being, equal in birth to the gods, as great as she is tender, as majestic as she is lovable!"[75] And "equal in birth to the gods" was the epithet used again here in the closing scene by Doctor Marianus for Mary the Virgin.[76] Under the titles Queen and Goddess, then, the Virgin was the sublime fulfillment of Faust's vision of a "the godlike form of a woman that resembles Juno, Leda, Helen" at the beginning of Act IV of Part Two, just as she was, under the title Mother, the fulfillment of his vision of Nature as Mother at the beginning of Part One and elsewhere throughout the drama, and at his visit to the Mothers. The title addressed to her by Doctor Marianus, when "in mystical rapture" he called her Supreme Sovereign of the World, likewise seemed to bring these two motifs together.[77] In a sublimely ironic way, therefore, this fulfilled eschatologically the prediction of Mephistopheles after the potion in the Witch's Kitchen that Faust would now "see Helen in every woman," except that what he now saw was not Helen, but Mary, as he traveled "from Gretchen and Helen through Sophia, which brings with it the best of our inner life, higher to Mary, who alone, as the supreme center of humanity, lifts the upward look into the miracle of the mystery."[78]

Thus the final salvation of Faust was assured as, like the Boy Souls, he was invited to "rise upward to a higher circle and go on growing imperceptibly."[79] These words, "rise upward," pointed in the same upward direction as the final words of the drama, which celebrated the Ultimate Reality in its relation to that which floated in shifting appearances, as the transcendent vision of Mary made the quest sublime. For "all that is transitory is only a parable. Here the inadequate becomes an event. Here the indescribable is accomplished. The Eternal Feminine leads us upward."[80]

The Apparition to Juan Diego, engraving from the 1685 edition of Luis Becerra Tanco, *Felicidad de Mexico en el Principio, y Milagroso Origen, que Tubo el Santuario de la Virgen Maria N. Señora de Guadalupe.* (Courtesy of the Special Collections, University of Arizona Library, Tucson)

13 The Woman Clothed with the Sun

And it shall come to pass in the last days, saith God,
I will pour out my Spirit on all flesh:
and your sons and your daughters shall prophesy,
and your young men shall see visions,
and your old men shall dream dreams.
—*Acts 2:17, Joel 2:28*

Although African-American spirituals, with their profound and powerful identification between the slave experience in North America and the history of Israel, contained relatively few references to Mary, probably because the churches of most of the slaves were Evangelical and Protestant rather than Roman Catholic, it is striking to find, in one of these spirituals, Mary designated as "that woman clothe' with the sun, moon under her feet."[1] For the application to the Virgin Mary of that title from the words of the Book of Revelation, "And there appeared a great wonder in heaven: a woman clothed with the sun [*mulier amicta sole*], and the moon under her feet, and upon her head a crown of twelve stars," was characteristic of the Roman Catholic rather than the Protestant tradition of New Testament interpretation.[2] More specifically, it has been used in that tradition to justify and validate the apparition, not only to the seer of the Apocalypse but to later visionaries, of that same "wonder in heaven" and of Mary as the Woman Clothed with the Sun. Literally thousands of such apparitions of the Virgin have been reported through the centuries, beginning with this one in the Book of Revelation. One of the earliest came in the fourth century, as reported by the philosophical theologian and mystic Gregory of Nyssa, in a sermon in his biography of Gregory the Wonder-Worker.[3]

In spite of the eminence of the saint and theologian who reported it, that early apparition never received official approval by responsible church authorities. In fact, although the impression has been widespread among critics that the church fosters such apparitions, along with other superstitions, in order to hawk its wares to the gullible,[4] the history of their reception clearly shows that, to the contrary, "the Church is very prudent with regard to apparitions, and accords them a low status because they are signs which reach us through our senses and are subject to the illusions of subjectivity."[5] So observed René Laurentin, the leading authority on the history of Marian apparitions, whose critical edition of the documents surrounding and following the appearances at Lourdes in 1858 is an indispensable repository of historical source material for the entire history of Marian apparitions.[6] A catalog published in 1962 of the Marian apparitions that had been ecclesiastically acknowledged to be worthy of pious belief, out of the innumerable accounts reported by individuals and groups, produces the following list of ten, in chronological order of their happening (which did not always correspond to the chronological order of their official acknowledgment):[7]

9–12 December 1531: at Guadalupe, Mexico, to Juan Diego;[8]

17 November 1830: at Paris, to Sister Catherine Labouré;[9]

19 September 1846: at La Salette in the French Alps near Grenoble, to Maximin Giraud and Mélanie Calvat;[10]

11 February–16 July 1858: at Lourdes, France, to Bernadette Soubiroux;[11]

12–13 January 1866: at Filippsdorf (Philippsdorf), now in the Czech Republic, to Magdalena Kade;

17 January 1871: at Pontmain in Brittany;

8 July 1876: at Pompeii, Italy;

13 May–13 October 1917: at Fátima, Portugal, to three children, Lucia, Francisco, and Jacinta;[12]

29 November 1932–3 January 1933: at Beauraing, Belgium;[13] and
15 January–2 February 1933: at Banneux, Belgium, to Mariette
   Beco.[14]

Of these ten, the three most celebrated, and the ones we shall chiefly
discuss here, were Guadalupe, Lourdes, and Fátima. Of those that failed
to achieve ecclesiastical recognition, the most celebrated was probably
the series of apparitions that began on 3 July 1876, at Marpingen, Germany, to five young girls: Katharina Hubertus and her sister, Lischen
Hubertus, Susanna Leist, Margaretha Kunz, and Anna Meisberger.[15]

For our purposes, several features were common to most of these
modern apparitions. In the course of his study of Marpingen, historian
David Blackbourn identified "all the elements of the classic modern
apparition" as they had "fused" at Lourdes: "The simplicity of the humble visionary, the delivery of a message, the initial scepticism of the parish
priest, the hostile reaction of the civil authorities, claims of miraculous
cures, and finally the purposive creation of an official cult by the
church"[16]—the last of these having, of course, been absent in the case of
the Marpingen visions of 1876.

It would appear that the vast majority of those to whom the Virgin
appeared during what deserves to be called the great century of Marian
apparitions—the hundred years from the 1830s to the 1930s[17]—were
not members of the elites but laypeople and peasants.[18] This has been
seen as fulfilling her proclamation and prophecy in the Magnificat, "He
hath scattered the proud in the imagination of their hearts. He hath put
down the mighty from their seats, and exalted them of low degree. He
hath filled the hungry with good things and the rich he hath sent empty
away."[19] That contrasted with many of the earlier instances in the Middle
Ages, when she manifested herself to religious professionals, and professional religious (as was also true, in the present list, of the apparition to
Sister Catherine Labouré in 1830); among these, some, such as for example Saint Birgitta of Sweden, came from the upper classes. But when, on
13 May 1946, more than 700,000 pilgrims, almost a tenth of the population of Portugal, gathered at Fátima in honor of Mary as Queen of Peace to

give thanks to her for the end of the Second World War, it was, as it had been for the thirty years preceding in the devotion to this particular Marian apparition, "scrubwomen, waiters, young and old, rich and poor, all sorts of people (but most of them humble, most of them barefoot, most of them workers and their families)," who paid tribute to the Virgin.[20] Whether the explanation for this privileging of the poor and humble was, as critics such as Emile Zola charged,[21] the manipulative power of the church over the invincible ignorance of the unenlightened masses, which would be dissipated when science and schooling prevailed, or whether it was, as defenders maintained, the predilection of the Virgin for those who were like herself,[22] both the initial reaction to the visions and the subsequent controversy over them sometimes reflected an almost textbook case of the "class struggle," in the interpretation of which its most influential advocate, though anything but a proletarian himself, took the side of the proletariat even as he scorned such manifestations of lower-class spirituality as "the opium of the masses."

The events associated with the appearance of the Virgin at Guadalupe in 1531 attached themselves to tensions that were evidence not only of class struggle but of racial struggle, as well as of struggle over religious syncretism.[23] For Juan Diego was an Indian, and those who initially refused to accept the reliability of his account were Caucasian.[24] In the difference of opinion over *Nuestra Señora de Guadalupe*, therefore, as one account inspired by twentieth-century liberation theology has put it, "it is the Indian's work or mission that the white man must acknowledge. It is the Indian's word that is at stake, and it is his mission to struggle to be recognized by the whites. In this struggle the Indian is certain that he has absolute backing from the Virgin."[25] Examination of the rise of the cult of the Virgin of Guadalupe by anthropologists has suggested many close connections with the condition of the native Indian population under Spanish colonial domination.[26] She has likewise been seen as a vindication not only of Indians' self-conscious resistance to the transformation of their homeland into "New Spain" but of "the female self-image" in resistance to the patriarchal dominance represented by the Spanish conquistadores—and by the Spanish missionaries.[27] Evidently at work in the struggle was also the identification of the site of the apparition with a native female deity, whom the Spanish Christian missionaries had sought to expel but who now seemed to them to have returned to their Indian converts in the borrowed guise of the Mother of God.[28] Yet even that situation was not without its special ironies. The very name "Guadalupe," now so closely identified with the Indian cause in Mexico that she has been called, in words quoted earlier, "the unofficial, the private flag of Mexicans,"[29] was not an Indian word but was of Spanish origin, having been the name of the Marian shrine in the province of Cáceres in Spain long before Juan Diego ever saw *Nuestra Señora de Guadalupe*; the continuing prominence of the Virgin in Spain during this period is documented by her many apparitions there in the Medieval and Early Modern periods and is well illustrated by Baroque statues of her.[30] But by her identification with the native population and with the downtrodden there and everywhere, Mary the Virgin of Guadalupe became, as the poet Octavio Paz has said, "the mother of Mexico,"[31] and, as more than one writer has called her, a "Mexican national symbol."[32] Thus the dual title of an exhibit devoted to her, "Mother of God, Mother of the Americas,"[33] summarized well the dual role she has come to occupy. And in the poetry devoted to her all these themes have been sounded.[34]

Sometimes, when the Virgin appeared, she remained silent, even enigmatically so. But more usually she communicated a message, first to the visionaries in their private devotion but then also to the church and the world. Occasionally, as in the celebrated "third message" of the Lady of Fátima,[35] that message was conveyed in secret, to be disclosed at some future time when it would be needed most; this has generally been followed by tantalizing speculations about what the secret message might contain and when it might become public. The political messages delivered by the Virgin have drawn by far the most attention, both in the popular press and in the scholarly literature. Our Lady of Guadalupe, by the sheer fact of her having singled out an Indian native rather than a Spanish conqueror as the object of her attentions, became a Mexican national symbol and has become decisive in "the formation of Mexican national consciousness."[36] But our other prime case studies, Lourdes and

Fátima, as well as Marpingen, also represented the Virgin's explicit inter-vention into the political affairs of the time with a message. At Lourdes, therefore, "Mary, refuge of the sick and sinners, could also be Mary the refuge of Catholic France. In her Immaculate Conception, she van-quished not only Satan but also his Republican legions and materialist ideas. Queen of heaven, she was also Queen of France, or at least the symbol of the 'true France.' Yet in her youth and simple clothes she could also be identified with the young, poor, and the humble. Mary was truly a unifying symbol that could help French people overcome their class, regional, and local differences."[37]

Similarly, when, on the twenty-fifth anniversary of the Virgin's ap-pearance at Fátima, Pope Pius XII addressed the Portuguese people in 1942, which in the event turned out to be the midpoint of World War II, he made a direct connection between her appearance in 1917, the nadir of World War I, and the crisis of their own time during another world war: "The greater the mercies for which today you thank Our Lady of Fatima, the more assured the confidence you place in Her for the future, the nearer you feel Her to be, protecting you under Her mantle of light, the more tragic appears, by contrast, the fate of so many nations torn to pieces by the greatest calamity in history. . . . Now more than ever, only confidence in God can be of avail; voiced before the Divine Throne, by a Mediatrix such as She."[38] But for many who had passed through the fiery trial of both world wars, including the church that had passed through many wars during its history, the outcome of World War II was a fiery trial no less threatening. The domination of Eastern Europe, including not only such Eastern Orthodox lands as Russia, Serbia, and Bulgaria but also such Roman Catholic lands as Poland, Croatia, and Lithuania, by a mili-tary power and political ideology even more hostile to Christianity and all religion than the French Revolution had been was very much on the mind of Roman Catholic leaders. And it was seen as having been on the mind of the Lady of Fátima when she put in her appearance in the very year of the Russian Revolution. When Pope Paul VI came to pay his devotion to her at Fátima for the fiftieth anniversary of the apparition in 1967, therefore, he declared: "The whole world is in danger. For this reason we have come to the feet of the Queen of Peace to ask her for the gift of God which supposes his intervention, divine, good, merciful and mysterious."[39]

Concentration on the political messages of the Virgin has, however, sometimes led secular-minded journalists and historians to a reductionism that ignores the role she has assumed also in the doctrinal development of the church's message. Above all, she has been seen as intervening in support of that doctrinal development when the doctrine at issue has dealt specifically with her own person. In the next two chapters I shall turn to two of the three most important "new" doctrines to have been defined by the Roman Catholic church in the entire modern era: the dogma of the immaculate conception of the Virgin Mary in 1854 and the dogma of the bodily assumption of the Virgin Mary in 1950. (The third was the dogma of the infallibility of the pope, promulgated by the First Vatican Council in 1870, at least partly to vindicate the action of Pius IX in 1854.) It was especially to reinforce the first of these that the Virgin appeared only a few years later at Lourdes; for the mysterious Lady said to Bernadette Soubiroux (in her own native dialect): "I am the Immaculate Conception."

In the light of the conservatism of both the political and the religious messages that the Virgin has conveyed when she appeared, it may seem surprising that the official reaction at all levels has not been instantly enthusiastic. In fact, the church has at all levels proceeded with great caution in dealing with such phenomena, developing over the years a set of doctrinal and pastoral criteria for distinguishing the genuine from the illusory.[40] What Blackbourn identifies as "the initial scepticism of the parish priest [and] the hostile reaction of the civil authorities"[41] has been a commonplace of the apparition narratives.[42] Particularly impressive in one account of Marian apparitions after another, including both that of Juan Diego and that of Bernadette, has been the persistently negative reaction attributed to the local parish priest and to local magistrates.

Such reactions from the clergy and local authorities betoken the profound ambiguity of the very phenomenon of the Marian apparition as a two-edged sword. For it did serve as a weapon in the sometimes rearguard battle of the church against its modern enemies. The France of Voltaire and Diderot may have been seen by all sides at the end of the eighteenth century as the seedbed of rationalism and the stronghold of atheism; but it was to rationalistic, atheistic France that the Virgin repeatedly granted her presence during the following century, to Sister Catherine Labouré on 17 November 1830 in Paris, to Maximin Giraud and Mélanie Mathieu on 19 September 1846 in La Salette, and above all to Bernadette Soubiroux on 11 February–16 July 1858 in Lourdes. There is good reason to believe that neither the intellectual defense of Christian revelation by the apologetic enterprise in nineteenth-century Roman Catholic theology, including the revival of Thomistic philosophical apologetics, nor the political defense of the institutional church and its prerogatives against the anticlericalism of that time was as effective a campaign, particularly among the common people, as the one that the Virgin Mary waged. For it has been well said that "Rome is the head of the Church but Lourdes is its heart."[43] But therein also lay much of the ambiguity of the Marian apparitions. The authority of the parish priest in the confessional and even the solemnity of his celebration of the Mass before the local altar seemed to pale into insignificance when compared with the dramatic appeal of a personal appearance by none less than the Mother of God and her continued activity in the grotto at Lourdes. As in the period of the Reformation the peddling of papal indulgences by itinerant preachers threatened to undercut the administration of the sacrament of penance at the parish level, so a struggling parish pastor in nineteenth-century France could well resent the interference in his ministry by the "delusions" of these children that they had sighted the Blessed Virgin.

For many of the Marian shrines called into being by the apparitions, the most prominent dimension has been the miraculous, together with the mass movement of pilgrims who have been attracted primarily by the miraculous element. In the first instance, that miraculous quality applied to the visions themselves, which were attributable only to a capacity that exceeded normal sight, whether the root cause was to be ascribed to supernatural forces or to neurosis. An apparition of Mary or of Christ was in its own right a transcendent event, whose credibility would usually seem to depend on the prior credibility of miracles of any kind. Conversely, once accepted or "verified" (whatever that process of verification may have entailed), its miraculous power extended itself to the person of the visionaries or to the site of the vision or to some physical feature of the site even when, as in the case of the wonder-working water of Lourdes, it has been carried far away from the original venue of the apparition. Always, however, at least in theory, the miracles and the credit for them still belonged to the person of the Virgin, not to some magic thought to be intrinsic to the places or inherent in the things that she had touched and transformed by her presence. The frequently noted reversal over time in the role of miracles—from the ancient view of both pagans and Christians that miracles were actions that proved the authority of the miracle worker to the modern view of the Enlightenment that purported miracles depended for any credibility they might have on the already accepted authority of the holy person—does not completely apply here; for the miracles of Lourdes or Fátima have functioned both ways.

The statistics of miraculous cures, particularly in the case of Lourdes, have been variously perceived.[44] It has sometimes been estimated, whether accurately or not, that Lourdes has, in something less than a century and a half, attracted twice as many pilgrims as has Mecca in more than thirteen centuries.[45] Undoubtedly some of those who have come were sightseers or curiosity-seekers, and many others came only to pray. But tens of thousands, and perhaps millions, have made the pilgrimage to Lourdes to seek a miraculous cure for ills of body and spirit. The miraculous powers of the Virgin of Lourdes and the Virgin of Fátima have received certification at the highest level of authority. The entire civilized world, Roman Catholic or not, was shocked when Pope John Paul II was shot and gravely wounded in Saint Peter's Square on 13 May 1981 and gratified when he survived. The pope himself left no doubt regarding his view of how and why he was spared: "And again I have become indebted to the Blessed Virgin. . . . Could I forget that the event in Saint Peter's Square took place on the day and at the hour when the first appearance of the Mother of Christ to the poor little peasants has been remembered for over sixty years at Fátima in Portugal? That day . . . I felt that extraordinary motherly protection, which turned out to be stronger than the deadly bullet."[46] Pius XII on the twenty-fifth anniversary, Paul VI by his visit to the shrine on the fiftieth anniversary, and John Paul II after the attempted assassination—all three called special attention to Our Lady of Fátima, as they and other twentieth-century popes also lent their authority to the cult of Our Lady of Lourdes.

For the counterpart to the "initial scepticism" of which Blackbourn speaks as a characteristic of the history of Marian apparitions has been what he goes on to call "the purposive creation of an official cult by the church," of which Lourdes is for him the outstanding instance (and Marpingen an outstanding exception).[47] Because, as Barbara Pope has said, "Rome . . . had an interest in shoring up traditional faith within the country that it considered to be the seedbed of modern revolutions . . . . the combined motives of faith and political sensitivity moved the papacy to confirm the French Catholics' belief that they had been chosen by Mary."[48] As that description implies, the belief of French Catholics in the apparition and in their having been "chosen by Mary" took hold first on the local, regional, and national levels, from which it went on to gain papal approbation. Similarly, it was the action of the "ordinary," the responsible bishop of Leiria, in 1930, "(1) to declare worthy of credence the visions of the shepherds at the Cova da Iria, in the parish of Fátima of this diocese, on the 13th day of the months from May to October 1917 and (2) to give official permission for the cult of Our Lady of Fátima."[49] Far from being imposed on a reluctant laity by an authoritarian regime, as hostile interpreters assumed, belief in Marian apparitions has, as often as not, been imposed from below on the ecclesiastical authorities by what is in some sense a democratic process. As John Henry Newman once described the process, speaking not about the doctrine of Mary in the nineteenth century but about the doctrine of the Trinity in the fourth, it was "the orthodoxy of the faithful" that prevailed over the speculations of the theologians.[50] More realistically (or more cynically), the granting of ecclesiastical approbation and the systematic encouragement of an official cult may be seen as the effort to restrain in the legions of the

Marian faithful the excesses to which Marian devotion has been especially subject. Indeed, as one scholar judges, "Lourdes, because of its careful guardianship by the Church since its inception, is perhaps the most tightly controlled and orchestrated, at the levels of both meaning and practice of all the pilgrimage cults,"[51] although it needs to be added that in at least some respects both Guadalupe and Fátima do not seem to have lagged far behind. It does seem safe to say that for many millions of people no form of Marian devotion or doctrine has carried more momentous significance than her miraculous apparitions.

Diego Velázquez, *The Virgin of the Immaculate Conception*, c. 1618. National Gallery, London.

14 The Great Exception, Immaculately Conceived

Behold, I was shapen in iniquity,
and in sin did my mother conceive me.
—Psalms 51:5

As we have seen in the early chapters of this book, much of the venue for the development of both devotion and doctrine connected to the Virgin Mary was the Christian East—Syriac, Coptic, Armenian, and Greek—rather than the Latin West, to which the results came from the East. To be sure, that was also true of other doctrines, such as the doctrine of the person of Christ, though it was not by any means true of all of them. To the doctrine of the Trinity, for example, Latin writers such as Tertullian in North Africa made substantial contributions, including the word *trinitas*; and at the Council of Nicaea in 325, a Western bishop, Ossius of Cordova, not only presided over the council but was a principal theological adviser to the emperor Constantine and, it seems, the source of the formula adopted by the council, that the Son of God was "one in being [*homoousios*] with the Father." But even that formula, with its origins in earlier heresies, was in Greek, and so were such formulas for Mary as Theotokos.

One issue in the historical development of the doctrine of Mary, however, was in great measure confined to the Latin West: the dogma of the immaculate conception.[1] The reason was the form that the doctrine of original sin had taken in the West, which was itself closely tied to the interpretation of Mary.[2] The assertion of the virgin birth of Jesus Christ—or, more precisely, of his virginal conception—originated in the New Testament, being found in the Gospels of Matthew and Luke but nowhere else.[3] In the first of these, as Krister Stendahl has put it, "the Virgin Birth story is theologically mute, no christological argument or insight is deduced from this great divine intervention."[4] The narrative in Luke was somewhat more specific in identifying the significance of the intervention, for the angel said to Mary: "The Holy Ghost shall come upon thee, and the power of the Highest shall overshadow thee: therefore also that holy thing which shall be born of thee shall be called the Son of God."[5] The word "therefore [dioti]" indicated that "the inference is self-evident"[6] and thus that the holiness and the divine sonship of the child had some connection, perhaps even a causal one, with the special circumstances of his conception; but it fell far short of specifying just what that connection might be.

As noted earlier, Ambrose of Milan, who in turn became the mentor of Augustine on these matters, was probably responsible for the definitive establishment of a firm "causal connection between the virginal conception and the sinlessness of Christ . . . , the combination of the ideas of the propagation of original sin through sexual union and of the sinlessness of Christ as a consequence of his virginal conception."[7] To be free from sin, Christ had to be free from the normal mode of conception; this was the conclusion Ambrose seemed to draw from the words of the prophet: "Who will tell the story of [enarrabit] his having been begotten [generationem]?"[8] As he continued the argument, his chief proof text was likewise from the Old Testament: "Behold, I was shapen in iniquity; and in sin did my mother conceive me."[9] According to the superscription of the psalm, these words were spoken by "David, when Nathan the prophet came unto him, after he had gone in to Bathsheba." As Ambrose put it, David "was regarded as righteous beyond others." If Christ was to be called truly righteous, it had to be "for no other reason than that, as one who was born of a virgin, he was not bound in any way by the ordinances against a guilty mode of having been begotten."[10] Therefore Ambrose summarized the relation between original sin and the virgin birth of Christ this way: "Even though he assumed the natural substance of this very flesh, he was not conceived in iniquity nor born in sin—he who was not born of blood nor of the will of the flesh nor of the will of a man, but of the Holy Spirit from a virgin."[11] (It bears noting in those words that Ambrose was quoting the Latin variant noted earlier, by which the words of John 1:13 were taken in the singular and applied to the birth of Christ.)[12] This doctrine of original sin was established in Western teaching through the thought of Augustine of Hippo, which in turn made necessary a special treatment of the place of Mary in the schema of sin and salvation.[13]

For where did that leave the Virgin? She had conceived without sin, but how had she in turn *been* conceived? In a famous and controversial passage of On Nature and Grace, one of the most important treatises that he devoted to the defense of the doctrine of original sin, Augustine had listed the great saints of the Old and New Testaments, who had nevertheless been sinners. Then he continued: "We must make an exception of the holy Virgin Mary, concerning whom I wish to raise no question when it touches the subject of sins, out of honor to the Lord. For from him we know what abundance of grace for overcoming sin in every particular [*ad vincendum omni ex parte peccatum*] was conferred upon her who had the merit to conceive and bear him who undoubtedly had no sin."[14] When he made such a statement, Augustine was being more faithful to the Greek tradition in his doctrine of Mary than he was in his doctrine of human nature. As suggested in chapter 6, the East and the West took significantly divergent directions in their handling of the distinction between nature and grace—perhaps more divergent from each other than were, for example, Thomas Aquinas and Martin Luther. In spite of these differences between Augustine's theory of original sin and the definitions of "ancestral sin [*propatrikon hamartēma*]" in the Greek fathers, however, they were agreed about the Theotokos, as this quotation from On Nature and Grace indicated. But Augustine did not explain this great exception, leaving it to the doctrinal development of the West over the next fourteen centuries to clarify it.

One of the earliest and most important thinkers in the Latin West to move that development along was a ninth-century Benedictine monk at Corbie, Paschasius Radbertus.[15] He is best remembered for having raised the doctrine of the real presence of the body and blood of Christ in the Eucharist to a new level of discussion and for having in significant ways anticipated the form that the doctrine was eventually to take with the adoption of the concept of transubstantiation at the Fourth Lateran Council in 1215. But Radbertus was at the same time a pioneer in Marian doctrine, with a treatise on how Mary gave birth. Radbertus is also, by almost universal consent, regarded as the author of a treatise entitled *Cogitis me* ("You compel me"), which was, however, written under the name of Jerome, who had lived more than four centuries earlier. *Cogitis me* was devoted to the question of whether it was appropriate to celebrate a festival commemorating the nativity of the Virgin Mary, not the day of her death, or "dormition,"[16] which could be celebrated as the victorious climax of her life, but the day of her physical birth. Inevitably, a consideration of that question raised the question not only of her birth but of her conception, specifically whether, like the rest of humanity, she had been conceived and born in original sin or whether she deserved to be regarded as another "great exception" to that universal rule, her Son, Jesus Christ, having been the primary exception. The treatise of Radbertus raised the question but left it unsettled.

During the High Middle Ages no one spoke more articulately or eloquently about Mary than one of the great preachers of Christian history, Bernard of Clairvaux.[17] As mentioned earlier, Dante put his praise of the Virgin at the conclusion of the *Divine Comedy* into the mouth of Bernard and in so doing quoted extensively from his writings.[18] But when it came to this question of what is being called here "the great exception," Bernard was adamant. In his famous *Epistle 174*, addressed to the canons of the cathedral of Lyons, he insisted: "If it is appropriate to say what the church believes and if what she believes is true, then I say that the glorious [Virgin] conceived by the Holy Spirit, but was not also herself conceived this way. I say that she gave birth as a virgin, but not that she was born of a virgin. For otherwise what would be the prerogative of the Mother of God?"[19] It was widely believed that the "special novelty of grace" by which Mary had given birth to Christ did not affect in any way the manner by which she herself had been born, which did not differ from the usual method of conception and birth. Yet, the virgin birth of Christ from one who had herself been conceived and born in sin did not seem to resolve the question of how he could be sinless in his birth if his mother was not. Sometimes, in the eyes of its critics and even of its supporters, such argumentation seemed to lead to the notion of an infinite regress of sinless ancestors, going back presumably to Adam and Eve, all of whom had been preserved free from sin in order to guarantee the sinlessness of Christ and of Mary. A certain kind of "superfluous curiosity" could then begin to inquire into Mary's parentage as a means of explaining how she had given birth through how she herself had been born. For if, as was by now universally assumed, Augustine's doctrine was correct in declaring those who were conceived and born in the usual way were infected by original sin, then Mary must have been unique in some way. It remained to be determined "how it was that the Virgin was purified before the conception" of Christ; this could not have been "otherwise than by him" to whom she gave birth, because he was pure and she was not. There was unanimity that Mary had been saved by Christ, so that, although she lamented his death because he was her Son, she welcomed it because he was her Savior.[20] A feast devoted to the commemoration of her conception or nativity, which was adopted from time to time in one place or another, therefore, was not appropriate, because it was not how she had been conceived but how she herself had conceived that set her apart. But Bernard also added the important stipulation that he was prepared to defer to the judgment of Rome on the entire question, both of the doctrine of the immaculate conception itself and of the commemoration of a feast of the nativity of Mary.

The iconographic tradition, like the theological one, had had a two-fold development, with the two parts not clearly harmonized. One was the pattern of emphasizing the humanity of the Virgin, therefore also her relation to her parents, Anna and Joachim. Various paintings and panels devoted to "the childhood of the Virgin" represented the legends about her life, and especially about her early life, that had been growing, such as her early vow of chastity.[21] The almost naturalistic depiction of her childhood was evident in Peter Paul Rubens's *Anna Teaching Mary*, which could be taken to be the picture of a normal bourgeois family, with the mother teaching and the daughter learning. But as it has done with the doctrine of Mary throughout history, Christian art often anticipated the development of dogma, which eventually caught up with the iconography. In a variety of artistic forms, the immaculate conception was shown both directly and indirectly, and an elaborate schema of symbols was created for it.[22] Several of those symbols, notably the moon as a symbol for the immaculate conception of the Virgin, have been woven into the early painting of Diego Velázquez, *The Virgin of the Immaculate Conception*. Although various commentators on this painting have commented on the absence of idealization in it, they have also noted its dramatic use of light as an expression of the mystery in this "great exception."

As the controversy over the immaculate conception developed already in the thirteenth and fourteenth centuries,[23] it became customary to put into juxtaposition these two passages from teachers of massive authority in the Latin West: Augustine's identification of Mary as in some way or other an "exception," and Bernard's *Epistle* 174 to the canons of Lyons, opposing the immaculate conception. When they were lined up that way, depending on the viewpoint, the author would proceed to explain one of them on the basis of the other. Gregory of Rimini, citing other passages from Augustine that made Christ the only exception to the universality of original sin, explained that in the passage under discussion he must have been referring only to actual sin, from which everyone, including Bernard, agreed that Mary was free. But this explanation could not satisfy those who interpreted Augustine's phrase "overcoming sin in every particular [*ad vincendum omni ex parte peccatum*]" as comprehending both actual and original sin, so that she alone among all the saints did not have to pray the words of the Lord's Prayer: "Forgive us our debts."

The controversial letter of Bernard was all the more troublesome because of his standing as "bearer of the flame" for the Virgin. For example, all but one of the *Sermons on the Festivals of the Glorious Virgin Mary* of Gabriel Biel, a vigorous Franciscan supporter of the immaculate conception, included at least one quotation from Bernard, just as his exposition of the doxology to Mary in the Mass quoted Bernard in every paragraph; and it was to Bernard that he turned for the doctrine of her position as Mediatrix. In the face of such eminent authority, a head-on refutation of Bernard's letter, point by point, was a difficult tactic, but some ventured to undertake it. Others found an extenuation in the large number of Patristic and Medieval doctors who had shared Bernard's ideas—they were certainly in the majority over those who had taught something like the theory of the immaculate conception—or they argued that both of the conditions stipulated by Bernard for accepting the doctrine (a feast of Mary's conception as an official day of the church year, and a pronouncement by the see of Rome on the doctrine) had now been fulfilled. There arose a legend not long after his death that Bernard had a black mark placed on his breast by God as punishment for "writing what ought not to be written about the conception of Our Lady" and that he was undergoing the cleansing punishments of purgatory for this. The legend was even used to discredit his doctrine of Mary generally, although that did seem to be going too far.

The most formidable argument that Bernard of Clairvaux and then Thomas Aquinas, as well as their later followers, had directed against the immaculate conception of Mary was the charge that if she had been conceived without original sin, she did not need redemption—which would detract from "the dignity of Christ as the Universal Savior of all." If Christ died for those who were dead, then his having died for the Virgin necessarily implied that she, too, had been dead in original sin. On the basis especially of the verse quoted earlier, "Behold, I was shapen in iniquity; and in sin did my mother conceive me,"[24] Augustine had declared the universal need of humanity for the redemption wrought by Christ. If Mary was to be included as part of humanity, albeit a very special part, did that universal statement apply to her, and if not, why not? To this specific objection it was possible to reply that she was exempt from other universal statements of Scripture, such as "All men are liars."[25]

But the fundamental reply to this entire line of reasoning was, as Heiko Oberman has put it, "the great invention of Scotus, [who] was to use this precise argument to *defend* the doctrine under discussion."[26] This was a speculative tour de force with few if any equals for sheer brilliance in the history of Christian thought.[27] Duns Scotus considered the question of Mary on the basis of a theological method that has been called "maximalism." It was, he said, possible for God (1) to preserve her from original sin or (2) to rescue her from it within an instant of her conception (as Thomas Aquinas taught), so that, though conceived in sin, she was born pure of sin, or (3) to purify her of it at the end of a period of time. "Which of these three . . . it was that was done," he continued, "God knows," because neither Scripture nor tradition had spoken unequivocally about it. "But," he went on, "if it does not contradict the authority of Scripture or the authority of the church, it seems preferable to attribute greater rather than lesser excellence to Mary." Or, as a later thinker put it, "I would rather err on the side of superabundance by attributing some prerogative to her than on the side of inadequacy by taking away from her some excellence that she had": better to believe and teach too much than too little. Another component of this method was the oft-repeated formula: "Whatever was both possible and eminently fitting for God to do, that he did [*potuit, decuit, fecit*]." The defenders of the formula conceded that it seemed to be indispensable to the doctrine of the immaculate conception, and its critics objected that the issue was "not whether it was possible for her to be conceived without [original] sin, but whether in fact she was conceived without it." On the basis precisely of "the excellence of her Son as Redeemer," Scotus insisted that the most perfect of Redeemers must have had "the most perfect possible degree of mediation with respect to *one* creature" and that the most fitting candidate for this honor was, obviously enough, his mother. The most perfect method of redemption, moreover, was to preserve her from original sin rather than to rescue her from it. As in the case of others "the rescuing grace of redemption does away with original sin," so in the case of Mary "*preserving grace* does not do away with original sin, but prevents [it]."[28] In this sense it was even possible for Scotus to assert that "Mary needed Christ as Redeemer more than anyone did," for she needed the suffering of Christ, "not on account of the sin that was present in her, but on account of the sin that would have been present if that very Son of hers had not preserved her through faith." She was immaculately conceived because what nature had not given to her, the special grace of God had accomplished in her. In spite of the counterargument that then the most perfect method of all would have been to preserve everyone from original sin, it was in her case alone that this method of redemption-by-preservation was adjudged "the most fitting," and therefore her "restoration was not an act of supplying what had been lost, but an act of increasing what [she] already had."

Contributing to the eventual resolution of the issue and of the controversy was the belief that a basic reason for the difference between Mary and all of humanity was that there was never any actual sin in her—an exemption from the universal rule that everyone had to grant, regardless of views about whether she had been conceived in original sin. The paradox of that exemption evoked from Pierre D'Ailly such an affirmation as this, addressed to Mary: "It was not by thy righteousness, but by divine grace that thou didst merit to be the only one without the woe of venial and mortal guilt, and, as is devoutly believed, without the woe of original guilt as well." His disciple Jean Gerson took the affirmation the rest of the way, paraphrasing the Apostles' Creed in Middle French: "I believe that in the sacrament of baptism God grants, to every creature who is worthy of receiving it, pardon from original sin, in which every person born of a mother has been conceived, with the sole exceptions of our Savior Jesus Christ and his glorious Virgin Mother." This was not, he explained in response to the standard objection, tantamount to putting her on the same level as Christ. In the case of Christ sinlessness was "by right," in the case of Mary it was "by privilege." Another paradox, and one that Bernard had already noted, appeared in the Gospel account of the annunciation, in which the angel had saluted Mary as "full of grace [gratia plena, in the Latin]" and thus presumably not in need of further grace, but then had gone on to explain to her,

"The Holy Spirit shall come upon thee," the Holy Ghost being the divine agent of sanctifying grace.[29] It could well be asked whether the Virgin required sanctification or, more precisely, when she had received it. Sometimes the doctrine of the immaculate conception could, and did, lead to such "superfluous" extremes as the theory that from the beginning of creation God had set aside a special portion of "prime matter" that was predestined to be eventually present in Mary at the time of the conception of the flesh of Christ, or the theory that Mary, being free of original sin, was also free of all its possible consequences, including physical weariness. Even some who favored the doctrine warned that there were certain gifts and privileges, as for example a total knowledge of the future, that Christ could have given his mother but did not. Nevertheless, the method prevailed, and by the sixteenth century even the heirs of Thomas Aquinas were using it to substantiate the immaculate conception.

The thirty-sixth session of the Council of Basel, on 18 December 1439, decreed that the immaculate conception was "a pious doctrine, in conformity with the worship of the church, the Catholic faith, right reason, and Holy Scripture." It prescribed that the doctrine "be approved, held, and professed by all Catholics," and it forbade any preaching or teaching contrary to it. That might have seemed to settle the matter, and was probably intended to do just that—except that by the time of this session Basel was itself under a cloud because of its statements and actions on the relation of the authority of the pope to that of a general council, which were subsequently condemned and which therefore made these later sessions of the Council of Basel invalid and not entitled to the designation of "ecumenical council." Therefore the decree on the immaculate conception was not canonically binding. Nevertheless, defenders of the immaculate conception in the fifteenth century used this decree to assert that although there may have been an earlier time when it was permissible to question the immaculate conception, the church had now spoken out definitively on the question, and it was "foolish and impudent" to continue to oppose it. By the end of the fifteenth century, with or without the authority of the Council of

Basel, the doctrine had become generally accepted in Western Christendom, believed by the faithful and taught by the doctors of the church.

At the Council of Trent, which was held from 1545 to 1563 at least partly in response to the attacks of the Protestant Reformation on Catholic doctrine, including the doctrine of the immaculate conception as well as other supposedly postbiblical doctrines about Mary, the extensive debates over original sin led to a consideration of the immaculate conception as an unavoidable implication.[30] When one of the draft decrees for the seventh session of the Council of Trent spoke of original sin as transmitted "to the entire human race in accordance with its universal law," the implications of this statement for the doctrine of Mary led to its deletion and, eventually at the fourteenth session, to a new paragraph at the end of the decree, specifying that it was not the council's intention to include Mary in its assertion of the universality of original sin and citing the constitutions on the Virgin promulgated by Pope Sixtus IV in 1477 and 1483 but still stopping short of defining the immaculate conception as a dogma binding, as an article of faith, on the entire church. That would not come until 8 December 1854, with the bull *Ineffabilis Deus* of Pope Pius IX, which declared: "The doctrine which holds that the Most Blessed Virgin Mary was preserved from all stain of original sin in the first instant of her conception, by a singular grace and privilege of Almighty God, in consideration of the merits of Jesus Christ, Savior of the human race, has been revealed by God and must, therefore, firmly and constantly be believed by all the faithful."[32] And less than four years later, on 25 March 1858, at the French village of Lourdes in the Pyrenees, a "lovely lady" appeared to the peasant girl, Bernadette Soubiroux, and announced, in the vernacular dialect: "I am the Immaculate Conception."[32]

The specific content of the promulgation of the dogma of the immaculate conception by Pius IX evoked controversy and polemics from both Eastern Orthodoxy and Western Protestantism; for as Marina Warner has said, "Although the Greeks led the way to the doctrine of the Immaculate Virgin by their cult of her miraculous birth, they opposed veneration of her as anything but the mother of the Redeemer, and were followed in this belief by the Reformed Churches."[33] But the doctrine of Mary was in some ways overshadowed by the procedural and juridical question of the authority of the pope on his own to define a dogma for the entire church, the doctrine of papal infallibility, which so dominated the agenda of the First Vatican Council in 1869–70 that further elaboration of the doctrine of Mary was largely deferred. It was a fascinating irony in the history of Western thought, therefore, that much of the weight of authority for the Augustinian doctrine of original sin had come from the teaching about the "privilege" of Mary by which Jesus Christ had been born of a Virgin and therefore was free of original sin, but that this very teaching about her "privilege" went on in later centuries to make it necessary for Augustine's Western heirs to develop an elaborate explanation of her "privilege" of being holy in a special sense. And once again, the doctrine of Mary proved to be one of the most important places to observe and test the processes by which great ideas have developed.

15 The Queen of Heaven, Her Dormition and Her Assumption

Death is swallowed up in victory.
—Isaiah 25:8, 1 Corinthians 15:54

hroughout this book, in discussing the themes and doctrines dealing with the Virgin Mary I have deliberately eschewed the many debates about her, cultural as well as theological, that have broken out during the twentieth century.[1] Rather, I merely mentioned them briefly in the Introduction, as a foil for the review that followed, which dealt only with the earlier centuries; or in some cases I have mentioned them only in order to take the account of an earlier development into its subsequent stages.[2] Nevertheless, one event in the history of Mary at the precise middle of the twentieth century, together with its aftermath, demands inclusion as the final—or, at any rate, the most recent—stage in that history: the issuance, on 1 November 1950, of the papal bull *Munificentissimus Deus*.[3] In this solemn proclamation, which presumably carried the stamp of the papal infallibility decreed by the First Vatican Council, the belief in the bodily assumption of the Virgin Mary, long held to be true both among the faithful and by theologians, was promulgated as a dogma of the Roman Catholic church by Pope Pius XII: "that the immaculate Mother of God, Mary *Semper Virgo*, when the course of her earthly

The Winchester Psalter, *The Death of the Virgin* and *The Virgin as Queen of Heaven*, MS. Cotton Nero V.IV, folios 29 and 30, c. 1145–55. London, The British Library.

life was run, was assumed *in body and soul* to heavenly glory."[4] Thus it became obligatory in 1950 for Roman Catholics to believe and teach that, as the Spanish Marian mystic Sister María de Jesús de Agreda had said in her *Life of the Virgin Mary* already in 1670, Mary "was elevated to the right hand of her Son and the true God, and situated at the same royal throne of the Most Blessed Trinity, whither neither men nor angels nor seraphs have before attained, nor will ever attain for all eternity. This is the highest and the most excellent privilege of our Queen and Lady: to be at the same throne as the divine Persons and to have a place in it, as Empress, when all the rest of humanity are only servants or ministers of the supreme King."[5]

Not at all surprisingly, the issuance of *Munificentissimus Deus* caused an uproar among Protestant theologians and clergy, both over its doctrinal content and over its dogmatic authority.[6] It was seen as sharply and confrontationally divisive, and all the more tragic because it came just when the painfully slow deepening of ecumenical awareness had begun to show signs of healing the ancient conflicts between the Eastern and the Western churches and even between Protestantism and Roman Catholicism. On the authority of Scripture and the doctrine of justification by faith, the two central doctrinal issues of the Reformation—central enough to have been identified during the nineteenth century as, respectively, the "formal principle" and the "material principle" of Reformation Protestantism—the Roman Catholic and the Protestant positions had been converging over a period of time. Roman Catholic theologians were increasingly emphasizing, significantly more than many of their sixteenth-century predecessors had in the polemical atmosphere of the Reformation and the Counter-Reformation, that the authority of Scripture, and in the original languages, established the legitimacy of a Christian doctrine (*sola Scriptura*, at least in some sense), even as Protestant theologians were paying more respect than they once did to the claims of tradition and to the role that tradition had played in the formation of Scripture. Similarly, the primacy of the initiative taken by the divine gift of grace (*sola gratia*) and the centrality of justifying faith (*sola fide*, once more only in some sense) had become a standard concern of Roman Catholic theology, just as the inseparability of good works from justifying faith was occupying a more central position in Protestant teaching. Almost as if to find new reasons to perpetuate the schism now that some of these earlier points of disagreement had at least begun to yield on both sides of the conflict, the Marian doctrines of the immaculate conception in 1854 and the assumption in 1950 came along to counter this trend. Even a well-disposed Protestant response felt constrained to warn in 1950: "While today the majority of churches with tears of penitence confess before God that they share in the guilt of a divided Body of Christ, and in common prayer and serious scholarly effort seek to diminish the area of disagreement and increase the area of agreement . . . the Roman Church would increase the area of disagreement by a dogma of the Assumption. Creation of a dogma of the Assumption would be interpreted today in the midst of the efforts at closer relationships between the churches as a fundamental veto on the part of the Roman Church."[7] For the New Testament and the early centuries of the church had been silent about "when [and how] the course of her earthly life was run," so this argument ran, although many traditions and various pious opinions about it had sprung up in subsequent centuries.[8] But to take these traditions and opinions and now to elevate them to the status of an official doctrine, binding on the entire church *de fide* and laying claim to the same authority as the doctrine of the Trinity, seemed to be completely presumptuous and utterly without biblical warrant.

By contrast with that reaction, the influential twentieth-century psychologist Carl Gustav Jung addressed the significance of Mary in a striking and controversial book originally published in German in 1952, entitled *Answer to Job* [*Antwort auf Hiob*].[9] The year of its original publication is relevant, for the book contained Jung's response to the bull of Pius XII. Carl Jung was the descendant of a long line of Swiss Protestant ministers and an associate and eventually an opponent of Sigmund Freud. But in his *Answer to Job* he basically defended the papal doctrine. The Book of Job, with its climax in the voice of God out of the whirlwind, "Who is this that darkeneth counsel by words without knowledge?"[10] had pushed the concept of divine transcendence just about as far as it could go in the direction of what Martin Luther would later call the *Deus absconditus*, the hidden God. But by its doctrine of the incarnation, and then even more effectively by its picture of the Virgin Mary, Catholic Christianity had mollified the austerity of this transcendence, rendering the Deity gentler and more accessible, "even as a hen gathereth her chickens under her wings."[11]

Already at the time of the promulgation of the dogma of the immaculate conception in 1854, there was widespread support in many quarters of the Roman Catholic church for a corresponding definition of the doctrine of the assumption, with 195 of the council fathers in attendance at the First Vatican Council of 1869–70 urging it. The political and ecclesiastical turmoil surrounding that council precluded the possibility of such a definition; but the doctrine of the assumption of the Virgin, though it would not become a dogma until 1950, and then only in Catholicism, did have far better support and more ancient attestation in the tradition than, for example, the doctrine of the immaculate conception had had before its definition.[12] There was a specific feast in the church year, fixed during the Middle Ages at 15 August.[13] That feast commemorated "the day when she was assumed from the world and entered into heaven," as it was called by Bernard of Clairvaux in the very epistle in which he challenged the observance of a feast of the immaculate conception.[14] By her presence, he said elsewhere, in a set of brilliant sermons on the assumption, not only the entire world but even "the heavenly fatherland shines more brightly because it is illumined by the glow of her virginal lamp."[15] Her assumption had elevated her above all the angels and archangels, and even all the merits of the saints were surpassed by those of this one woman. The assumption of the Virgin meant that human nature had been raised to a position superior to that of all the immortal spirits.

Eastern Christendom did not participate in the dogmatic definition of the assumption.[16] But that did not mean that the issue had been left without consideration in the development of doctrine in Byzantium.[17] There was a tradition repeated by the Council of Ephesus in 431, that when, in obedience to the word of Christ from the cross, "Woman, behold thy son!" and "Behold thy mother!" the disciple John "took her unto his own home,"[18] they lived in Ephesus, and that she died there; a later and quite unreliable tradition even went on to identify the House of the Virgin at Ephesus. The hour of her death or, as it was usually termed, her falling asleep or "dormition [*koimēsis*],"[19] was the subject of many icons. Those icons reflected the Christian art of very early times.[20] Because of its prominence in the iconographic tradition,[21] the defenders of the icons also had occasion to speak about the dormition. Theodore the Studite, for example, described it as an "ineffable" mystery, at which the twelve apostles, together with the Old Testament figures of Enoch and Elijah (both of whom had been assumed bodily into heaven),[22] attended the Theotokos at the end of her earthly life.[23] There was a homily on the subject of the dormition attributed to the seventh-century patriarch of Jerusalem, Modestos.[24] On the basis of internal evidence, however, the date of the homily has been moved forward to a century or so after Modestos, but many of the Mariological themes celebrated in it were, of course, much older.[25] For, as a later Byzantine historian reported, around the end of the sixth century the festival celebrating the dormition had, by imperial decree, been appointed for 15 August (which, as we have noted, also became the date in the Western Church for the Feast of the Assumption of the Blessed Virgin Mary).[26] Thus it eventually became one of the twelve feasts observed in the Eastern Church. It is likewise to that period that the earliest iconographic treatments of it by Byzantine artists are traced. Although an ivory plaque of the dormition came from a later period in the history of Byzantine art (perhaps as late as the twelfth century), it was an especially comprehensive treatment of the theme: the Theotokos was surrounded by the figures of the twelve apostles, in addition to two others with their faces covered (perhaps Enoch and Elijah, for the reasons indicated earlier); angels hovered overhead, hands extended to receive her into heaven.[27] At the center of the plaque—in a striking reversal of the roles they took in the conventional icons of Mother and Child—was Christ in Majesty with the infant Mary in his arms. And the adult Mary reposed in tranquility, as she was about to be received into heaven—apparently in body as well as in soul, as the East and eventually the West came to affirm—where the process by which her humanity was made divine would be completed.

In the art of the West, the dormition of the Virgin often at least implied her assumption, for example, in Caravaggio's *Death of the Virgin*.[28] A particularly dramatic depiction of the connection and the contrast between the dormition and the assumption appeared in two portrayals from the Winchester Psalter, dated "before 1161," *Death of the Virgin and Queen of Heaven*.[29] Angels were in attendance for both events, and once again Christ was holding the infant Mary in the moment of her dormition. But the point of the juxtaposition between the two was that the figure who was in repose at the dormition, according to the superscription of the second portrait, *Ici est faite Reine del Ciel*, "has now become Queen of Heaven." Now the angels on either side of her held banners of victory, to show that she, having vanquished the enemy and having crushed the head of the serpent as, according to the Vulgate, God had promised already in the Garden of Eden that "she [*ipsa*]" would do,[30] now participated in the victory that was accomplished not only by the passion and death of Christ but also by the resurrection of Christ. As Pope Pius XII declared in *Munificentissimus Deus*, employing in his Latin the Greek word for the resurrection, *anastasis*, "just as the glorious resurrection of Christ [*gloriosa Christi anastasis*] was an essential part and the ultimate trophy of this victory, so the struggle that the Blessed Virgin had shared in common with her Son was to be concluded with the 'glorification' of her virginal body. As the apostle says [1 Cor. 15:54, Isa.25:8], 'When . . . this mortal shall have put on immortality, then shall be brought to pass the saying that is written, Death is swallowed up in victory.'"[31]

As was evident from the pope's reference to 1 Corinthians and through it to Isaiah, "Death is swallowed up in victory," one question raised by the doctrine of the assumption had been whether Mary had ever died or whether she had, like Enoch and Elijah, been taken up alive into heaven.[32] The prophecy of Simeon to her, considered earlier as a theme of Mary the Mater Dolorosa, "Yes, a sword shall pierce through thy own soul also,"[33] seemed to imply that she would die, just as her divine and sinless Son would. As it stood, the prophecy spoke only of "sorrow, not the martyrdom of death." But this was not an adequate ground to "arouse doubt concerning her death," because she was by nature mortal. The prophecy did, moreover, appear to disprove the pious feeling of some that she who had given birth without pain should also have died without pain; for "by what authority can one suppose that she did not suffer pain in her body? . . . But whether at her death she did not feel pain, which God could grant, or whether she did feel it, which God could permit," the conclusion seemed to be that "the Blessed Virgin did undergo the vexation of the flesh by dying." Mitigating this conclusion was the widely held belief of "Christian piety" that her death had been followed immediately by a resurrection, which in turn was followed by her assumption; for she was "the firstfruits of [human] incorruptibility." Yet it was also recognized that "we do not dare to affirm that the resurrection of her body has already taken place, since we know that this has not been declared by the holy fathers." Although it was "wicked to believe that the chosen vessel" of Mary's body had been subject to corruption, still "we do not dare to say that she was raised, for no other reason than that we cannot assert it on the basis of evident proof."

The defenders and exponents of the dogma of the assumption have emphasized its consistency both with the larger body of Christian teaching and with the Mariological development that had preceded it.[34] In her function as the representative of the human race, as noted earlier, she had uniquely documented the subtle relation between divine grace and human freedom when, by her voluntary assent to God's plan of redemption through her Son, "Be it unto me according to thy word,"[35] she had set in motion the series of events that would lead to the redemption of humanity and its victory over sin and death through the death and resurrection of Christ. Her victory over all sin, original and actual, had been achieved through the unique gift, conferred on her as a consequence of the merits of Jesus Christ, of being spared the burden of original sin through her immaculate conception. It was only logical, so it could be argued, that when, as Isaiah had prophesied and Paul had proclaimed, "Death is swallowed up in victory,"[36] her death, too, should participate in that victory by Christ as an anticipation of the full participation of all the saved through the general resurrection at the end of human history. There had, after all, been such an anticipation when, at the time of the crucifixion of Christ, "the graves were opened; and many bodies of the saints which slept arose, and came out of the graves after his resurrection, and went into the holy city, and appeared unto many."[37] She was eminently more worthy of such an honor than any of these saints.

Considerations like these have made the dogma of the assumption of the Virgin perhaps the most provocative illustration of the position of Mariology in its entirety as the most controversial case study of the problems represented by "development of doctrine" as a historical phenomenon and as an ecumenical issue.[38] To those who harbored fundamental misgivings about the very idea of development of doctrine, or about the notion that the Virgin Mary should be the subject of a "doctrine" in her own right rather than be discussed as part of the doctrine of Christ or the doctrine of the church (or about both of these questions), the evolution of the assumption over a period spanning so many centuries, from a pious practice and a liturgical observance to a speculative theological theory to a dogma that was finally made official only at the middle of the twentieth century, simply proved that development of doctrine was pernicious both in theory and in fact. And even those Protestant theologians who were prepared to come to terms with the idea of development as, in the words of the Dominican scholar Yves Congar, "an inner dimension to that of tradition,"[39] balked at the assumption. One reason in the case of some of them was, undoubtedly, a basic aversion to the phenomenon of lay piety, out of which, as we have seen throughout this book, so much of the history of the development of Mariology, including the assumption, had emerged. On such aversion, the observations of a leading Protestant commentator on Roman Catholicism who was highly critical of its doctrine and its structure deserve to be quoted in full:

The worship of God "in spirit and in truth" [John 4:24] is an ideal that is only seldom attained in its entirety. Only certain individuals, as for example the great mystics, have been capable of it. Basically, all popular piety is a compromise. Only a few people grasp the idea that we can approach God only through pictures and symbols. But it would be cruel to deprive the great mass of simple souls of such pictures and symbols, for this would cut them off from any access to the being of God itself. Why should God not hear even a prayer addressed to Mary if it rises from a simple, pious heart? To use a figure, God must smile at our more spiritual forms of devotion and our high theological skill, just as we adults kindly recognize the serious purpose manifest in the games of children. . . . Many a Protestant fanatic, who flies into a rage when he sees a votive tablet with the motto "Mary has helped me," does not realize at all how petty his own basic idea of God is. Perhaps this same fanatic regards it as his sacred duty to tie God's salvation to some particular dogmatic formula. . . . No, naïve and unconscious paganism is not the real evil in Marian piety.[40]

It bears remarking that those words were written only a few years after the dogma of the assumption has been promulgated but a few years before the Second Vatican Council had been convoked.

On the eve of the Second Vatican Council it appeared reasonable to suggest that ecumenical understanding would come if Roman Catholics could recognize what made the Reformation necessary and Protestants what made it possible. On no issue of doctrine was that paradox more strikingly appropriate than on the doctrine of Mary.[41] There were observers, both hostile and friendly, who expected—or feared—that the "new" dogma of 1950 would lead a decade later to further Mariological development and to the definition of additional "new" doctrines.[42] To them, the Second Vatican Council came as a disappointment,[43] just as the issuance of the papal bull *Ineffabilis Deus* by Pope Pius IX on 8 December 1854 had been obliged to yield center stage to the First Council of the Vatican fifteen years later. For although, as Avery Dulles has said, "a separate document on the Blessed Virgin was contemplated, and was presented in draft form by the Theological Commission at the first session in 1962," the council went on to incorporate the doctrine of Mary into its first decree, the Dogmatic Constitution on the Church, *Lumen Gentium.*[44] "The Fathers," Dulles continues, "saw a danger in treating Mariology too much in isolation; they preferred to link her role more closely with the main theme of the Council, the Church."[45] They also wanted it to be seen, as they themselves put it, that they "carefully and equally avoid the falsity of exaggeration on the one hand, and the excess of narrow-mindedness on the other,"[46] partly on ecumenical grounds and partly to come to terms with the new biblical and historical scholarship within Roman Catholic circles that had inspired so many of the council's actions. What emerged from this process was no new doctrine at all but a balanced and evenhanded summary, dated 21 November 1964, of the principal themes of the entire historical development of the doctrine of Mary.

The five major headings, which the council itself supplied for its text, read:

I.   *The Role of the Blessed Virgin Mary, Mother of God, in the Mystery of Christ and the Church,* according to which "because of this gift of sublime grace she far surpasses all other creatures, both in heaven and on earth"; and yet "at the same time, however, because she belongs to the offspring of Adam she is one with all human beings in their need for salvation." Nevertheless, "the Synod does not, however, have it in mind to give a complete doctrine on Mary [*completam de Maria proponere doctrinam*], nor does it wish to decide those questions which have not yet been fully illuminated by the work of theologians."

II. *The Role of the Blessed Virgin in the Economy of Salvation,* including the way "the books of the Old Testament . . . , as they are read in the Church and are understood in the light of a further and full revelation, bring the figure of the woman, Mother of the Redeemer, into a gradually sharper focus" [Gen. 3:15, Isa. 7:14]. Through the entire history of the Bible, "the Blessed Virgin advanced in her pilgrimage of faith, and loyally persevered in her union with her Son unto the cross."

III. *The Blessed Virgin and the Church*, in which "the Blessed Virgin was eternally predestined, in conjunction with the incarnation of the divine Word, to be the Mother of God," so that "Mary figured profoundly in the history of salvation and in a certain way unites and mirrors within herself the central truths of the faith [*in historiam salutis intime ingressa, maxima fidei placita in se quodammodo unit et reverberat*]."

IV. *Devotion to the Blessed Virgin in the Church*, with the directive "that practices and exercises of devotion toward her [*praxes et exercitias pietatis erga Eam*] be treasured as recommended by the teaching authority of the Church in the course of centuries," but with the warning "that true devotion consists neither in fruitless and passing emotion, nor in a certain vain credulity [*neque in sterili et transitorio affectu, neque in vana quadam credulitate*]."

V. *Mary, a Sign of Sure Hope and of Solace for God's People in Pilgrimage*, because "in the bodily and spiritual glory which she possesses in heaven, the Mother of Jesus continues in this present world as the image and first flowering of the Church [*imago et initium Ecclesiae*]."[47]

Many of these guiding principles were almost (if not quite) formulated in the terms that have been employed here, in the preceding chapters of this book, and that are summarized in the chapter to follow.

Master of the Saint Lucy Legend, *Mary, Queen of Heaven*, c. 1485. © 1996 Board of Trustees, National Gallery of Art, Washington. Samuel H. Kress Collection.

16 The Woman for All Seasons—
And All Reasons

For, behold, from henceforth all generations shall call me blessed.
—Luke 1:48

During nearly twenty centuries, these words of the Magnificat have come true over and over, and only the most churlish have dared to be an exception to them. Retrospective consideration of the many topics and themes of this book suggests various areas of history for which the centrality of the person of the Virgin Mary is an indispensable interpretive key. Her importance as such a key does not depend on the belief or unbelief of the observer; for even those who do not, or cannot, have faith need to grasp the faith of other ages in order to understand them.

It is impossible to understand the history of Western spirituality and devotion without paying attention to the place of the Virgin Mary. The "social history" of various ages and various places has been engaging the attention of many of the most important and productive historians during the past generation or two. Ours is, therefore, a time of great interest in the history of everyday life and therefore also in "popular religion." Scholars have zealously sought a methodology that would get beyond the dominance of "high culture" to discover the beliefs and practices of simple and illiterate people. Such a methodology has, on closer scrutiny, proven to be a far subtler problem than it might have appeared at first. How does one read the surviving evidence, much of it literary in form, in order to probe the hidden (or even concealed) material it contains about the lower classes and the other members of the silent majority? How, for example, should the social historian read the legislation of other eras? Does the repetition of prohibitions directed against certain practices necessarily imply that those practices held on among the common people, or could the repetition be evidence of the inherent tendency of laws to be left standing on the books long after the need for them has passed and the reason for them has been forgotten? Because, in the case of the church, a major component in the history of its legislation has taken the form of liturgy, creed, and dogma, should the historian in a later age automatically assume, as orthodox theologians and historians have sometimes tended to do, that what the councils of the church legislated as dogma and liturgy was what the common people actually believed? Or conversely, is the frequent and no less automatic assumption among modern secularizing historians any more plausible, that what the common people actually believed was undoubtedly quite different from dogma and creed and that the "real meaning" of popular religion is to be sought in the categories of race or class or gender or anywhere else except in creed and liturgy? It would also seem to be an essential assignment specifically for such social history to ask, and if possible to answer at least in part, questions about the movement of ideas and practices in the opposite direction, from the faith of the common people into liturgy, creed, and dogma, rather than the other way around.

At least within the history of Christianity, it is difficult to think of a more fitting theme to explore for its bearing on these issues than the Virgin Mary. Why has she maintained her hold on most of the Western world even in a secular age and even in the face of anti-religious propaganda and downright persecution during the Communist era in Eastern and Central Europe? It was not primarily because she has been the subject of solemn pronouncements of doctrine and creed since the councils of the early Christian centuries and was in fact the subject of the most recent official promulgation of a dogma by a pope, on 1 November 1950. A far more important explanation is that she has been, to paraphrase the famous words of "Light-Horse Harry" Lee about George Washington in 1799, "first in the hearts of her countrymen." Historians and comparativists, not to mention such propagandists and persecutors, have frequently remarked on the continuity and tenacity of religious devotion from one period to another, including the persistence of external devotional observance long after the death of the devotion itself. Nor would it be sound to ignore the subtle but profound changes that can take place in the meaning of words and actions across such continuities, for which, as we have seen, devotion to Mary provides many striking examples.

A special form of devotion to the Virgin Mary has been Marian mysticism. We may leave aside for the moment the highly mooted question of whether the mystical form of devotion and language has a legitimate place in the Christian faith. But if it does, it has found some of its most profound expressions in the prayers and poetry addressed to the Virgin. As it is the ambition of the mystic to rise through the visible to the Invisible and through the things of earth to the things of heaven, so these prayers to Mary take their start from her simple historical person and her humble earthly life to rise toward her special place in the kingdom of God and her unique role in the universe. This mystical vision of the Virgin, moreover, is not intended merely for passive enjoyment but has been said to carry a transforming power, as those who have had the privilege of beholding the Queen of Heaven have dedicated their lives to her service. Thus in his powerful poem, "The Blessed Virgin Compared to the Air We Breathe," Gerard Manley Hopkins spoke about

New Nazareths in us,
Where she shall yet conceive
Him, morning, noon, and eve,
New Bethlems, and he born
There, evening, noon, and morn—
Bethlem or Nazareth,
Men here may draw like breath
More Christ and baffle death;

Who, born so, comes to be
New self and nobler me
In each one and each one
More makes, when all is done,
Both God's and Mary's Son. [1]

Here the union with Christ of which the apostle Paul spoke when he said, "I am crucified with Christ: nevertheless I live; yet not I, but Christ liveth in me," [2] was expanded into a union also with his Mother, yet in a highly Christocentric form. Because of the reliance on trendy "psychobabble" that seems to have gained such currency also among academics, it does perhaps need to be added that this Marian mysticism has by no means been confined to celibate men such as Gerard Manley Hopkins, but has been widely cultivated among both men and women, married as well as celibate.

That observation may be the appropriate context in which to consider the psychological significance of Mary. And in the first instance that pertains above all to her significance for women. As clergy of all denominations have noted, the women were the first to render service to Christ on Easter Sunday morning—and that, they have often been tempted to add, is the way it has been on most Sunday mornings ever since. Many of the mighty women of the history of the Middle Ages, for example, are known to us chiefly or even solely through the medium of what men wrote down from them or about them. It has been pointed out earlier that the visions of Birgitta of Sweden were transmitted chiefly in Latin, and in a version intended to demonstrate her credentials as a candidate for sainthood. Or, to mention two examples from the fourth century who deserve to be compared in Plutarchian "parallel lives": Saint Macrina, sister of two of the most important theologians of the Greek East, Saint Basil of Caesarea and Saint Gregory of Nyssa, who was celebrated by the latter of these as *adelphē kai didaskalos*, "our sister and our teacher" in philosophy and theology; and Saint Monica, mother of Saint Augustine, who taught him and bore with him through the trials of his stormy youth, until Saint Ambrose of Milan, who eventually was to baptize

Augustine, told her that the child of such tears could not be lost. If we could enable the silent millions among Medieval women to recover their voices, the evidence that we do have from those relatively few who did leave a written record strongly suggests that it was with the figure of Mary that many of them identified themselves—with her humility, yes, but also with her defiance and with her victory: "*Deposuit potentes de sedibus suis, et exaltavit humiles; esurientes implevit bonis, et divites dimisit inanes*—He hath put down the mighty from their seats and exalted them of low degree; he hath filled the hungry with good things, and the rich he hath sent empty away." And he could do it again.

Because of that role that she has been playing for the history of the past twenty centuries, the Virgin Mary has been the subject of more thought and discussion about what it means to be a woman than any other woman in Western history. To an extent that many have chosen to ignore, explanations about Mary or portraits of her in words or in pictures can tell us much about how "the feminine" has been perceived. Together with Eve, with whom she has often been contrasted as the Second Eve, she has provided the subject matter for some of the best and some of the worst in that checkered history. A highly one-sided and prejudiced account of this history has been permitted to engage in a drastic kind of oversimplification that would be attacked, and rightly, if it were arguing on the opposite side. Because Mary is the Woman par excellence for most of Western history, the subtleties and complexities in the interpretation of her person and work are at the same time central to the study of the place of women in history, which has begun to claim its proper share both of scholarly and of popular attention. But some extremely valuable resources for that history are being neglected.

Another important part of this psychological significance of Mary has been her function as the symbol of those qualities, in a God who is beyond all gender, that have traditionally found expression through the feminine. Although it is fashionable today to speak about Judaism and Christianity as "patriarchal" not only in their ethics and way of life but in their picture of God, the most serious reflection of Jewish and Christian thought has transcended any such easy identification. For "the divine power," as Gregory of Nyssa wrote, "though it is exalted far above our nature and inaccessible to all approach, like a tender mother who joins in the inarticulate utterances of her babe, gives to our human nature what it is capable of receiving; and thus in the various manifestations of God to humanity, God both adapts to humanity and speaks in human language."[3] And an important bearer of this dimension in the relation of God to humanity has been the person of Mary. That has made her prominent also in the relation between Christianity and other religions. As Christianity confronted religions in which not only gods but goddesses were central, it had in Mary a way of simultaneously affirming and yet correcting what those goddesses symbolized. The most striking symbol of how she did this is probably to be found in the city of Ephesus, as noted earlier.[4] According to the Book of Acts, the preaching of the apostle Paul there posed a threat to the silversmiths of the city, who made their livelihood by fashioning silver shrines to the goddess Artemis. To combat the threat of this new deity without a face, they stirred up a riot among the people with the cry "Great is Diana of the Ephesians!"[5] And it was in that same city of Ephesus, slightly less than four centuries later, that the Third Ecumenical Council of the church in 431 solemnly decreed that Mary was to be called Mother of God, Theotokos.

Yet another dimension of her psychological significance has been pedagogical. Throughout most of the history of Christian education, at least until the Reformation, the lives of the saints served as patterns of character, and among these the life of Mary occupied a unique position, corresponding to the unique position she had occupied in the plan of God. Each of the special Christian virtues—or, as they were often designated, "theological virtues"—defined in the New Testament, "faith, hope, and charity, these three,"[6] but also each of the four classical virtues—or, as they were often designated, "cardinal virtues"—defined by Plato and then incorporated into the deuterocanonical Wisdom of Solomon, "temperance and prudence, justice and fortitude,"[7] found a special embodiment in her. Taken together, these seven virtues were fundamental to moral teaching. But in the saints, and to a special degree in the person of the Virgin Mary, these virtues were there not only to be admired and cherished but to be imitated. Individual incidents from the Gospels in which she was sometimes little more than a bit player nevertheless lent themselves to elaboration as guides to God-pleasing behavior. Above all, she served as a model of the fundamental Christian—and particularly monastic—virtue of humility. "Quia respexit humilitatem ancillae suae" was how the Latin Vulgate translated, or really mistranslated, her words in the Magnificat,[8] which are more accurately rendered, for example, in the New Revised Standard Version with "For he has looked with favor on the lowliness of his servant." Mistranslation or not, however, this humilitatem in the Vulgate became the occasion for some of the most profound explorations of the concept of humility—not in the sense in which Uriah Heep of Charles Dickens's David Copperfield could say, "I am well aware that I am the 'umblest person going. . . . My mother is likewise a very numble person. We live in a numble abode," but in the sense in which Augustine could say, "All strength is in humility, because all pride is fragile. The humble are like a rock: the rock seems to lie downwards, but nevertheless it is firm."[9]

Nor has it been only for morality and life that Mary has been important. By one of the most dramatic reversals in the history of ideas, this humble peasant girl from Nazareth has been made the subject of some of the most sublime and even extravagant theological speculation ever thought up, considerable portions of which have been occupying these pages. It is a fascinating question to ask just why and how a particular subject "becomes a doctrine." It cannot be simply because it is spoken of in the Bible: there are hundreds of references to "mountains" in the Bible, and many hundreds to the flora and fauna of the Near East; yet no one has ever seriously suggested that there be a "doctrine" of birds or trees or hills. One decisive criterion has probably been the connection of a particular topic with the central themes of the biblical message. Thus angels qualified as a doctrine not simply because angels were mentioned in the Bible or because they were identified as creatures of God but because, from the angel who was posted at the gate of the Garden of Eden after the fall to the angel who came to strengthen Christ in the Garden of Gethsemane on the night before his death,[10] angels were not only messengers but actors, dramatis personae, on the biblical stage; the two gardens, of Eden and of Gethsemane, in contrast, were only part of the scenery in the drama.

The explicit references in the New Testament to Mary the mother of Jesus were few in number, and most were quite brief. Even when, by typology or allegory, various statements were applied to her that were taken from earlier biblical books, relatively little amplification was supplied. From this sparse evidence, however, Christian thought almost from the beginning was moved to reflect on its hidden and deeper meanings and on its potential implications. The methods of such reflection were many and various, but at their core they constituted an effort to find and to formulate her place within the themes of the biblical message. Concerning no other merely human being, none of the prophets or apostles or saints, has there been even a small fraction of the profound theological reflection that has been called forth by the person of the Blessed Virgin Mary. It has been a continuing question as we have looked at "Mary through the centuries" just why this should have been so, and just how the bits of information about her provided by the Bible of both Testaments could have been expanded into a full-blown Mariology. Conversely, it also bears asking what has happened in those theological systems, such as those of Protestantism since the Reformation, in which, without any denial of the uniqueness of the Virgin Birth of Christ, the person of his Mother as such has not been accorded special significance. For in a curious way these systems, too, are part of the unbreakable hold that she has continued to have on the imagination of the West.

That imagination has expressed itself above all, of course, through the place of the Virgin in the history of the arts, as this is symbolically depicted in the serenade of the angelic orchestra amusingly and profoundly portrayed by the fifteenth-century Flemish Master of the Saint Lucy Legend. From the many that have been cited or alluded to earlier, let just three examples suffice now in conclusion. Among the hundreds of lovely settings of the *Ave Maria*, that of Franz Schubert may be the most familiar and the most beloved. The paintings of Madonna and Child have been so frequent that it would be possible to write a history of the idea of children on the basis of them. And one of the great churches of the West is Rome's Santa Maria Maggiore, constructed in direct response to the proclamation by the Council of Ephesus in 431 that she was to be called Theotokos. Even more universally than Goethe might have meant it, then, "the Eternal Feminine leads us upward."[11]

Bibliographic Note

The bibliography about the Virgin Mary is truly enormous. The on-line catalog of the Yale University Library at the end of 1995 listed 2,424 books on the subject (a few of them duplicates), and that did not include either articles or most works from before this century. Among books about her, some should be listed here, because they could have been cited in every chapter: Juniper Carol, ed., *Mariology*, 3 vols. (Milwaukee: Bruce, 1955–61); Carol Graef, *Mary: A History of Doctrine and Devotion*, 2 vols. (New York: Sheed and Ward, 1963–65); Walter Delius, *Geschichte der Marienverehrung* (Munich: Ernst Reinhardt Verlag, 1963); the 1,042-page encyclopedic dictionary by Wolfgang Beinert and Heinrich Petri, *Handbuch der Marienkunde* (Regensburg: F. Pustet, 1984); and the massive festschrift to René Laurentin, *Kecharitōmenē: Mélanges René Laurentin* (Paris: Desclée, 1990).

The subject of Mary has been engaging me as scholar and author for more than four decades. As Herman Kogan has described in *The Great EB*, my long and fruitful association with *Encyclopaedia Britannica* began in the 1950s, when I was called in for crisis management after several successive drafts for the article MARY by various authors had been rejected by one or another outside reviewer. That article continues to appear in the set to the present; and thirty years later, employing its basic structure, I wrote an essay that appeared, in German in 1985 and in English in 1986, on "Mary—Exemplar of the Development of Christian Doctrine" as part of Jaroslav Pelikan, David Flusser, and Justin Lang, *Mary: Images of the Mother of Jesus in Jewish and Christian Perspective*, published in the United States by Fortress Press. My *Riddle of Roman Catholicism*, written on the eve of the Second Vatican Council and honored with the Abingdon Award in 1959, contained a chapter entitled "Ave Maria." The publication of the English translation of Otto Semmelroth, *Mary, Archetype of the Church* (New York: Sheed and Ward, 1963), gave me the opportunity to prepare a brief essay as a foreword entitled "The Basic Marian Idea." In the Thomas More Lectures, published by Yale University Press in 1965, *Development of Christian Doctrine: Some Historical Prolegomena*, I had analyzed "Athanasius on Mary," especially his idea of the Theotokos. The Mason Gross Lectures at Rutgers University, which I delivered in 1989 and which were published in 1990 by Rutgers University Press as *Eternal Feminines: Three Theological Allegories in Dante's "Paradiso"*, included a chapter on Dante's vision of the Virgin Mary. The Andrew W. Mellon Lectures at the National Gallery of Art, delivered for the twelve-hundredth anniversary of the Second Council of Nicaea in 1987 and published by Princeton University Press also in 1990 as *Imago Dei*, contained a discussion of early Byzantine iconography of Mary and of its theological justification. *Faust the Theologian*, my Willson Lectures at Southwestern University published by Yale University Press in 1995, climaxed, as does Goethe's *Faust*, with the picture of Mary as the Mater Gloriosa and the Eternal Feminine. Moreover, throughout the five volumes of *The Christian Tradition*, which appeared at the University of Chicago Press between 1971 and 1989, the doctrines of Mary from various periods repeatedly came in for close attention.

All of these previous treatments of Mary have made their contribution to this book, and I am grateful for the opportunity (and, where appropriate, the permission) to recycle them here for the first time in a full-length and connected historical account; simple references to the books, as distinct from such passages, are introduced with "See." In the documentation for all these books, and above all for the last one cited, the hundreds of citations from primary sources underlying the historical narrative have also been identified in full, and it did seem supererogatory to repeat most of them here.

Abbreviations

ADB   *Anchor Dictionary of the Bible.* Edited by David Noel Freedman et al. 6 vols. New York: Doubleday, 1992.

Bauer-Gingrich   Bauer, Walter, F. Wilbur Gingrich, et al., eds. *A Greek-English Lexicon of the New Testament and Other Early Christian Literature.* 2d ed. Chicago: University of Chicago Press, 1979.

Deferrari-Barry   Deferrari, Roy J., and Inviolata M. Barry, eds. *A Lexicon of St. Thomas Aquinas Based on the "Summa Theologica" and Selected Passages of His Other Works.* Washington, D.C.: Catholic University of America Press, 1948.

Denzinger   Denzinger, Henricus, and Adolfus Schönmetzer, eds. *Enchiridion symbolorum editionum et declarationum de rebus fidei et morum.* 36th ed. Freiburg and Rome: Herder, 1976.

DTC   *Dictionnaire de théologié catholique.* 15 vols. and indexes. Paris: Letouzey et Ané, 1909–72.

Lampe   Lampe, Geoffrey W. H., ed. *A Patristic Greek Lexicon.* Oxford: Clarendon Press, 1961.

Liddell-Scott-Jones   Liddell, Henry George, Robert Scott, and Henry Stuart Jones, eds. *A Greek-English Lexicon*. 9th ed. Oxford: Clarendon Press, 1940.

OED   *The Oxford English Dictionary*. 16 vols. Oxford: Oxford University Press, 1933–86.

PG   *Patrologia Graeca*. 162 vols. Paris: J. P. Migne, 1857–66.

PL   *Patrologia Latina*. 221 vols. Paris: J. P. Migne, 1844–64.

Schaff   Schaff, Philip, ed. *Creeds of Christendom, with a History and Critical Notes*. 3 vols. 6th ed. Reprint edition. Grand Rapids, Mich.: Baker Book House, 1990.

Sophocles   Sophocles, E. A., ed. *Greek Lexicon of the Roman and Byzantine Periods*. Boston: Little, Brown and Company, 1870.

Tanner   Tanner, Norman P., ed. *Decrees of the Ecumenical Councils*. 2 vols. Washington, D.C.: Georgetown University Press, 1990.

Notes

Introduction

1. Jaroslav Pelikan, *Jesus Through the Centuries: His Place in the History of Culture* (New Haven and London: Yale University Press, 1985), 1.

2. James Arnold Hepokoski, *Otello* (Cambridge: Cambridge University Press, 1987), 71–75. I am indebted for this reference to Philip Gossett.

3. William Shakespeare, *Othello*, V.ii.25.

4. Alexandra to Aleksandr Syroboiarsky, 29 November 1917, in Mark D. Steinberg and Vladimir M. Khrustalëv, eds., *The Fall of the Romanovs* (New Haven and London: Yale University Press, 1995), 206. Her letters, as well as those of the czar, are replete with such references to the Virgin Mary.

5. CBS News, 23 January 1995 (the day after her death at the age of 104).

6. Richard Rodriguez, *Days of Obligation: An Argument with My Mexican Father* (New York: Penguin Books, 1993), 16–20.

7. William F. Maestri, *Mary Model of Justice: Reflections on the Magnificat* (New York: Alba House, 1987), xi.

8. See, e.g., Isabel Bettwy, *I Am the Guardian of the Faith: Reported Apparitions of the Mother of God in Ecuador* (Steubenville, Ohio: Franciscan University Press, 1991); see also chapter 13, below.

9. Richard Foley, *The Drama of Medjugorje* (Dublin: Veritas, 1992); Medjugorje is located within the context of the nineteenth-century apparitions by Sandra L. Zimdars-Swartz, *Encountering Mary: From La Salette to Medjugorje* (Princeton, N.J.: Princeton University Press, 1991).

10. Elizabeth Rubin, "Souvenir Miracles: Going to See the Virgin in Western Herzegovina," *Harper's*, February 1995, 63–70.

11. See the recent study of Jill Dubisch, In a Different Place: Pilgrimage, Gender, and Politics at a Greek Island Shrine (Princeton, N.J.: Princeton University Press, 1995).

12. F. Adeney Walpole, Women of the New Testament (London: James Nisbet, 1901), 835.

13. Wolfhart Schlichting, Maria: Die Mutter Jesu in Bibel, Tradition und Feminismus (Wuppertal: R. Brockhaus, 1989).

14. Alvin John Schmidt, Veiled and Silenced: How Culture Shaped Sexist Theology (Macon, Ga.: Mercer University Press, 1989), 95.

15. Simone de Beauvoir, The Second Sex, tr. H. M. Parshley (New York: Alfred A. Knopf, 1971), 171.

16. Els Maeckelberghe, Desperately Seeking Mary: A Feminist Appropriation of a Traditional Religious Symbol (Kampen, The Netherlands: Pharos, 1991).

17. Maurice Hamington, Hail Mary? The Struggle for Ultimate Womanhood in Catholicism (New York: Routledge, 1995).

18. Elizabeth Schüssler Fiorenza, "Feminist Theology as a Critical Theology of Liberation," in Churches in Struggle: Liberation Theologies and Social Change in North America, ed. William K. Tabb (New York: Monthly Review Press, 1986), 57, 59.

19. Paul Evdokimov, Woman and the Salvation of the World: A Christian Anthropology on the Charisms of Women, tr. Anthony P. Gythiel (Crestwood, N.Y.: St. Vladimir's Seminary Press, 1994).

20. J. Gresham Machen, The Virgin Birth of Christ (New York: Harper and Brothers, 1930).

21. See Pelikan, Flusser, and Lang, Mary; Hans Küng and Jürgen Moltmann, eds., Mary in the Churches (New York: Concilium, 1983).

22. Hans Urs von Balthasar, Theodrama: Theological Dramatic Theory, tr. Graham Harrison (San Francisco: Ignatius Press, 1992), 3:293.

Chapter 1   Miriam of Nazareth

1. Louis Ginzberg, Legends of the Bible (New York: Simon and Schuster, 1956), xxi.

2. The Catholic Encyclopedia, 15:464E.

3. Bauer-Gingrich, 491.

4. See chapters 11 and 15, below.

5. Raymond E. Brown, Karl P. Donfried, Joseph A. Fitzmyer, and John Reumann, eds., Mary in the New Testament: A Collaborative Assessment by Protestant and Roman Catholic Scholars (Philadelphia and New York: Fortress Press and Paulist Press, 1978), 28–29.

6. Matt. 28:18–19.

7. Denzinger, 125.

8. John Courtney Murray, The Problem of God Yesterday and Today (New Haven and London: Yale University Press, 1964), 55.

9. Matt. 26:26–28; Mark 14:22–25; Luke 22:19–20; 1 Cor. 11:23–25.

10. Tanner, 230–31, 695.

11. Matt. 16:18.

12. Denzinger, 875.

13. Jaroslav Pelikan, "Canonica Regula: The Trinitarian Hermeneutics of Augustine," in Proceedings of the PMR Conference 12/13 (1987–88): 17–30; Collectanea Augustiniana, vol. 1: Augustine: "Second Founder of the Faith," ed. Joseph C. Schnaubelt and Frederick Van Fleteren (New York: Peter Lang), 329–43.

14. Matt. 28:19; John 1:1.

15. John 1:1, 14:28.

16. Matt. 1:18; Luke 1:34–35.
17. John 1:14.
18. John 1:12–13.
19. *The New Jerusalem Bible* (Garden City, N.Y.: Doubleday, 1985), 1745.
20. See chapter 2, below.
21. Schaff, 2:53.
22. Luke 1:28 (Vg).
23. Bauer-Gingrich, 877–78; Lampe, 1514–18.
24. See chapter 15, below.
25. *LTK* 1:1141, with bibliography (Josef Andreas Jungmann).
26. Luke 1:28, 42.
27. Gal. 4:4.
28. Job 14:1.
29. William Shakespeare, *Macbeth*, V.viii.12–16.
30. Rom. 5:19.
31. Luke 3:15.
32. John 1:29; 27.
33. Luke 1:42–43.
34. Cf. Luke 1:36.
35. Ferdinand Hahn, *Christologische Hoheitstitel: Ihre Geschichte im frühen Christentum* (Göttingen: Vandenhoeck und Ruprecht, 1963).
36. Deut. 6:4; Mark 12:29.
37. Luke 1:26–27.
38. See Jean Pétrin, *Le sens de l'oeuvre de Saint Luc et le mystère marial* (Ottawa: Séminaire Saint-Paul, 1979).
39. See Joseph Fischer, *Die davidische Abkunft der Mutter Jesu* (Vienna: A. Opitz Nachfolger, 1910).
40. Luke 2:3.
41. Matt. 1:23; Isa. 7:14.
42. Luke 1:1–3.
43. *ADB* 4:398–402 (Eckhard Plümacher).
44. Col. 4:14; 1 Cor. 15:8.
45. Gisela Kraut, *Lukas malt die Madonna: Zeugnisse zum künstlerischen Selbstverständnis in der Malerei* (Worms: Wernersche Verlagsgesellschaft, 1986); see *Imago Dei*, pl. 22.
46. *LTK* 6:618–19 (Karl Hermann Schelke).
47. John 19:26–27.
48. Origen *Commentary on John* I.6.
49. Luke 2:35.
50. Heb. 11:38, 1.
51. Rom. 10:17, 1:5, 16:26.
52. Rom. 3:28; James 2:24.
53. Heb. 11:8–12; Rom. 4:1; James 2:21–23.
54. Rom. 4:11.
55. Gen. 3:20.
56. Luke 1:38.
57. Luke 1:48.
58. Matt. 26:13.

Chapter 2   The Daughter of Zion

1. *The Catholic Encyclopedia*, 15:464E.
2. The definitive study of this issue is Henri de Lubac, *Exégèse médiévale: Les quatre sens de l'écriture*, 2 vols. in 4 (Paris: Aubier, 1959–64).
3. Brown et al., *Mary in the New Testament*, 29.
4. Luke 2:4.
5. Matt. 1:1–17; Luke 3:23–38.
6. Luke 3:23.
7. Song of Songs 1:5 (Vg; AV).
8. Rodriguez, *Days of Obligation*, 16–20.
9. Gen. 3:15.
10. Irenaeus *Against Heresies* V.xxi.1–3.
11. Tibor Gallus, *Die "Frau" in Gen 3,15* (Klagenfurt: Carinthia, 1979).
12. See, e.g., Vermeer's *Allegory of [the] Faith*, at chapter 6, below.
13. Prov. 31:10 (Vg).
14. L. N. Tolstoy, *War and Peace*, Book I, ch. 22 (tr. Ann Dunnigan).
15. Edwin Hatch and Henry A. Redpath, eds., *A Concordance to the Septuagint*, 3 vols. (Oxford: Clarendon Press, 1897–1906), 3:108.
16. Ex. 15:20–21.
17. Isa. 7:14; Matt. 1:22–23.
18. Luke 1:34.
19. Matt. 12:46; Matt. 13:55; Mark 3:31; John 2:12; John 7:3, 5.
20. 1 Cor. 9:5; Gal. 1:19.
21. Song of Songs 4:12 (AV; Vg).
22. Jerome *Against Jovinian* I.31.
23. Matt. 27:60; Luke 23:53; John 19:41.
24. Gen. 2:7 (LXX).
25. 1 Cor. 13:12.
26. Num. 6:24–26.
27. 2 Cor. 4:6.
28. Ps. 27:8.
29. Gen. 22:12.
30. Murray, *Problem of God*, 5.
31. Ex. 3:2, 14.
32. Isa. 6:1, 21:2.
33. Amos 1:1; Obad. 1; Nah. 1:1.
34. Ezek. 11:24, 12:27, 37:2, 47:1; Dan. 8:1.
35. Luke 3:2; John 1:14; Matt. 11:13.
36. Acts 2:17; Joel 2:28.
37. Acts 10:9–16.
38. Acts 16:9, 18:9–10, 26:19.
39. Luke 10:18.
40. Luke 22:43.
41. Matt. 1:20, 2:12, 19.
42. Rev. 1:13.
43. Rev. 12:1.

44. Brown et al., *Mary in the New Testament*, 339.
45. Rev. 14:6-7.
46. See *The Christian Tradition*, 3:223-29.
47. Ps. 51:5.
48. Luke 24:27.
49. Isa. 25:8; 1 Cor. 15:54.
50. Theodore the Studite *Orations* V.2-3 (*PG* 99:721-724); see chapter 15, below.
51. Gen. 5:24; 2 Kings 2:11-12.
52. *ADB* 2:508-26 (Richard S. Hess, George W. E. Nickelsburg, Francis I. Andersen).
53. *ADB* 2:465-69 (Siegfried S. Johnson, Orval S. Wintermute).
54. Matt. 17:3.
55. Luke 10:38-42.
56. Ps. 68:18; Eph. 4:8.
57. John 12:26.

Chapter 3   The Second Eve

1. See the exhaustive collection of source material for this and subsequent chapters in Sergio Alvarez Campo, ed., *Corpus Marianum Patristicum*, 5 vols. (Burgos: Aldecoa, 1970-81).
2. Plato *Laws* 709B (tr. Benjamin Jowett).
3. Constantine Despotopoulos, *Philosophy of History in Ancient Greece* (Athens: Academy of Athens, 1991), 78-80.
4. See Norma Thompson, *Herodotus and the Origins of the Political Community* (New Haven and London: Yale University Press, 1996).
5. Ex. 3.
6. John 1:1, 14.
7. James 1:17.
8. Marcus Aurelius *Meditations* XII.14 (tr. Maxwell Staniforth).
9. Lino Cignelli, *Maria nuova Eva nella patristica greca, sec. II-!V* (Assisi: Studio teologico Porziuncola, 1966).
10. Gen. 3:5.
11. Matt. 4:2-3.
12. Rom. 5:12, 15.
13. 1 Cor. 15:45, 47.
14. Irenaeus *Proof of the Apostolic Preaching* 33 (tr. Joseph P. Smith, revised).
15. In Brown et al., *Mary in the New Testament*, 257 (italics added).
16. See *The Christian Tradition*, 1:108-20.
17. Gen. 3:20.
18. See chapter 6, below.
19. Mary Christopher Pecheux, "The Concept of the Second Eve in *Paradise Lost*," *PMLA* 75 (1960): 359.
20. John Milton *Paradise Lost* V.385-87.
21. Milton *Paradise Lost* XII.379-81.
22. See *The Christian Tradition*, 1:141-46.
23. Isaiah Berlin, "The Hedgehog and the Fox," in *Russian Thinkers*, ed. Henry Hardy and Aileen Kelly (New York: Penguin Books, 1979), 22-81.
24. Tolstoy, *War and Peace*, Second Epilogue, ch. 12 (tr. Aylmer and Louise Maude).

25. Charles Norris Cochrane, *Christianity and Classical Culture* (Oxford: Clarendon Press, 1944), 483–84, summarizing the argument in Book XII of Augustine's *City of God*.

26. Irenaeus *Proof of the Apostolic Preaching* 33 (ET Joseph P. Smith, revised).

27. 1 Cor. 15:45, 47.

28. Ginzberg, *Legends of the Bible*, xxi.

29. H. R. Smid, *Protevangelium Jacobi: A Commentary* (Assen: Van Gorcum, 1975), is useful and balanced.

30. Brown et al., *Mary in the New Testament*, 248–49.

31. *Protevangel of James* 19:3–20, 17:20, 9:2.

32. Irenaeus *Against Heresies* I.vii.2, III.xi.3.

33. Gregor Martin Lechner, *Maria Gravida: Zum Schwangerschaftsmotiv in der bildenden Kunst* (Munich: Schnell und Steiner, 1981).

34. Adolf von Harnack, [*Grundrisz der*] *Dogmengeschicht*, 4th ed. (Tübingen: J. C. B. Mohr [Paul Siebeck], 1905), 192.

35. See chapter 4, below.

36. Matt. 4:3, 6.

37. Ignatius *Epistle to the Trallians* 9.

38. A useful corrective on standard interpretations of Mozart's relation to religious faith is Hans Küng, *Mozart: Traces of Transcendence*, tr. John Bowden (London: SCM Press, 1992).

39. Jaroslav Pelikan, *Christianity and Classical Culture: The Metamorphosis of Natural Theology in the Christian Encounter with Hellenism* (New Haven and London: Yale University Press, 1993), 328.

40. Luke 23:26.

41. ap.Irenaeus *Against Heresies* I.xxiv.4.

42. Virginia Corwin, *St. Ignatius and Christianity in Antioch* (New Haven: Yale University Press, 1960), 170.

43. See the table in Schaff, 1:53.

44. Schaff, 1:53.

45. ap.Irenaeus *Against Heresies* I.vii.2.

46. Tertullian *Against Marcion* III.xi.

47. Richard Crashaw, "The Shepherds' Hymn," in *The New Oxford Book of English Verse, 1250–1950*, ed. Helen Gardner (Oxford: Oxford University Press, 1972), 314.

48. *Imago Dei*, 129, 71.

49. Gregory of Nyssa *Against Eunomius* IV.3 (PG 45:637).

50. See the discussion of these views in William P. Haugaard, "Arius: Twice a Heretic? Arius and the Human Soul of Christ," *Church History* 29 (1960): 251–63.

51. Quoted by Irenaeus *Against Heresies* III.xxxi.1.

52. John of Damascus *On Heresies* 31 (PG 94:697).

53. Peter Robert Lamont Brown, *The Body and Society: Men, Women, and Sexual Renunciation in Early Christianity* (New York: Columbia University Press, 1988), 111–14.

54. Ignatius *Epistle to the Trallians* ix.1.

55. Gal. 4:4; see chapter 1, above.

56. Gen. 3:20 (LXX).

Chapter 4   The Theotokos

1. *Imago Dei*, 134–38.

2. Liddell-Scott-Jones, 792, cites no pre-Christian instance of it.

3. Athanasius *Orations Against the Arians* III.29 (PG 26:385).

4. Guido Müller, ed., *Lexicon Athanasianum* (Berlin: Walter de Gruyter, 1952), 650.

5. Julian *Against the Galileans* 262.

6. Theodora Jenny-Kappers, *Muttergöttin und Gottesmutter in Ephesos: Von Artemis zu Maria* (Zurich: Daimon, 1986).

7. Acts 19:23–41.

8. Council of Ephesus (Tanner, 59).

9. Carlo Pietrangeli, *Santa Maria Maggiore a Roma* (Florence: Nardini, 1988).

10. John of Damascus *The Orthodox Faith* III.12 (PG 94:1029–32).

11. John of Damascus *Orations on the Holy Icons* II.11 (PG 94:1293–96).

12. Theodore the Studite *On the Images* 1 (PG 99:489); see chapter 7, below.

13. *Development of Christian Doctrine: Some Historical Prolegomena*, 105–19.

14. Hugo Rahner, "Hippolyt von Rom als Zeuge für den Ausdruck Theotokos," *Zeitschrift für katholische Theologie* 59 (1935): 73–81. See the discussion and bibliography in Walter Burghardt, "Mary in Eastern Patristic Thought," in Carol, ed., *Mariology*, 2:117, n. 147.

15. John Henry Newman, *An Essay on the Development of Christian Doctrine*, 6th ed., Foreword by Ian Kerr (Notre Dame, Ind.: University of Notre Dame Press, 1989), 145.

16. Alexander of Alexandria *Epistle to Alexander of Constantinople* 12 (PG 18:568).

17. See, e.g., Arnold J. Toynbee, *A Study of History*, 12 vols. (Oxford: Oxford University Press, 1934–61), 7-B:717.

18. Burghardt, "Mary in Eastern Patristic Thought," in Carol, ed., *Mariology*, 2:120.

19. Athanasius *Orations Against the Arians* III.29 (PG 26:385).

20. The controversy is well summarized in Aloys Grillmeier, *Christ in Christian Thought: From the Apostolic Age to Chalcedon (451)*, tr. J. S. Bowden (New York, 1965), 193–219, where most of the recent literature is discussed.

21. DTC 7-I:595–602 (Anton Michel).

22. 1 John 1:7; Acts 20:28.

23. Grillmeier, *Christ in Christian Thought*, 357.

24. Phil. 2:5–7.

25. Athanasius *Orations Against the Arians* I.42 (PG 26:100).

26. Athanasius *Orations Against the Arians* III.29 (PG 26:385).

27. John Henry Newman, "The Orthodoxy of the Body of the Faithful during the Supremacy of Arianism," Note V to *The Arians of the Fourth Century*, 3d ed. (London: E. Lumley, 1871), 454–72; the note originally appeared as a separate article in 1859.

28. Bernard Capelle, "Autorité de la liturgie chez les Pères," *Recherches de théologie ancienne et médiévale* 22 (1954): 5–22.

29. Cf. Georg Ludwig, *Athanasii epistula ad Epictetum* (Jena: Pohle, 1911), a careful textual analysis; on the role of the epistle to Epictetus at Ephesus and Chalcedon, 22–25. Ludwig's textual observations are supplemented by Hans-Georg Opitz, *Untersuchungen zur Überlieferung der Schriften des Athanasius* (Berlin: Walter de Gruyter, 1935), 173–74.

30. Cf. Grillmeier, *Christ in Christian Thought*, 204–5, 214–17, on the significance of the *Epistle to Epictetus*.

31. Athanasius *Epistle to Epictetus* 9 (PG 26:1064).

32. Athanasius *Epistle to Epictetus* 4 (PG 26:1056–57).

33. Athanasius *Epistle to Maximus the Philosopher* 3 (PG 26:1088).

34. See chapter 3, above.

35. In 2 Peter 1:15, *tēn toutōn mnēmēn poieisthai* is translated "to recall these things."

36. Basil *Epistles* 93 (PG 32:484).

37. See chapter 15, below.

38. Martin Jugie, "La première fête mariale en Orient et en Occident: L'Avent primitif," *Echos d'Orient* 22 (1923):129-52.

39. Martin Jugie, *La mort et l'assomption de la Sainte Vierge: Etude historico-doctrinale* (Vatican City: Studi e Testi, 1944), 172-212.

40. Graef, *Mary*, 1:133-38.

41. Athanasius *Orations Against the Arians* III.29 (PG 26:385).

42. Athanasius *Epistle to Epictetus* 12 (PG 26:1069).

43. Henry Melville Gwatkin, *Studies of Arianism* (Cambridge: Cambridge University Press, 1881), 265.

44. Quoted in Athanasius *Orations Against the Arians* I.5 (PG 26:20).

45. Gwatkin, *Studies of Arianism*, 134-35, n. 3.

46. Quoted in Athanasius *On the Councils of Ariminum and Seleucia* 16 (PG 26:709).

47. Athanasius *Defense of the Nicene Council* 9 (PG 25:432).

48. But see William P. Hauggard, "Arius: Twice a Heretic? Arius and the Human Soul of Jesus Christ," *Church History* 29 (1960): 251-63.

49. Athanasius *On the Councils of Ariminum and Seleucia* 26 (PG 26:729).

50. Quoted in Theodoret *Ecclesiastical History* I.12-13.

51. Athanasius *Orations Against the Arians* I.43 (PG 26:100).

52. Athanasius *On the Incarnation of the Word* 54 (PG 25:192); cf. Jaroslav Pelikan, *The Light of the World: A Basic Image in Early Christian Thought* (New York: Harper and Brothers, 1962), 120, nn. 18-21.

53. Newman, *Essay on the Development of Christian Doctrine*, 138-39, contains certain suggestions of this line of development.

54. Adolf von Harnack, *Lehrbuch der Dogmengeschichte*, 5th ed., 3 vols. (Tübingen: J. C. B. Mohr [Paul Siebeck], 1931), 2:477.

55. Athanasius *Letter to the Virgins*.

56. Maurice Gordillo, *Mariologia Orientalis* (Rome: Pontifical Institute of Oriental Studies, 1954), 7-8, n. 56; Gérard Gilles Meersseman, *Der Hymnos Akathistos im Abendland* (Freiburg in der Schweiz: Universitäts-Verlag, 1958), 1:14-15.

Chapter 5   The Heroine of the Qur'ān

1. LTK 8:613 (Max Bierbaum).

2. See chapter 8, below.

3. Elisabeth Ott, *Thomas Merton, Grenzgänger zwischen Christentum und Buddhismus: Über das Verhältnis von Selbsterfahrung und Gottesbegegnung* (Würzburg: Echter Verlag, 1977).

4. This sentence and the balance of the paragraph are adapted from my "Introduction" to the Qur'ān in Jaroslav Pelikan, ed., *Sacred Writings*, 6 vols., with companion volume, *On Searching the Scriptures—Your Own or Someone Else's* (New York: Book of the Month Club, 1992), 3:xiv.

5. Qur'ān 21:107-8.

6. I am, throughout this chapter, following the translation of the Qur'ān by the late Pakistani poet and scholar Ahmed Ali, which I had the privilege of incorporating into the collection *Sacred Writings*.

7. Gen. 3:20.

8. Yvonne Y. Haddad and Jane I. Smith, "The Virgin Mary in Islamic Tradition and Commentary," *Muslim World* 79 (1989): 162.

9. See chapter 1, above.

10. Ludwig Hagemann, *Maria, die Mutter Jesu, in Bibel und Koran* (Würzburg: Echter Verlag, 1992).

11. Neal Robinson, "Jesus and Mary in the Qur'an: Some Neglected Affinities," *Religion* 20 (1990): 169–71.

12. Qur'ān 66:12.

13. See also Nilo Geagea, *Mary of the Koran*, tr. Lawrence T. Farnes (New York: Philosophical Library, 1984); C. H. Becker, *Christianity and Islam*, tr. H. J. Chytor (New York: Burt Franklin Reprints, 1974), 22.

14. *ADB* 3:889 (Paul W. Hollenbach).

15. Qur'ān 19:12.

16. Gen. 21:18.

17. Qur'ān 3:42–43.

18. Luke 1:32–33.

19. Qur'ān 3:45–46.

20. Norman Cohn, *The Pursuit of the Millennium* (New York: Academy Library, 1969).

21. Luke 1:34.

22. Gen. 4:1, 25.

23. Qur'ān 3:47.

24. Luke 1:37.

25. Luke 1:35.

26. Gen. 16:6, 21:9–21.

27. See chapter 3, above.

28. Qur'ān 19:16, 41, 51.

29. R. Travers Herford, *Christianity in Talmud and Midrash* (New York: Ktav Publishing House, 1975), 358.

30. N. J. Dawood, ed. and tr., *The Koran*, 5th ed. rev. (London: Penguin Books, 1995), 215, n. 1.

31. John 1:17.

32. Matt. 17:3.

33. Qur'ān 14:39.

34. Qur'ān 5:78.

35. Bartholomew of Edessa *Refutation of the Hagarene* (PG 104:1397).

36. Norman Daniel, *Islam and the West: The Making of an Image* (Edinburgh: Edinburgh University Press, 1960), 175.

37. Qur'ān 19:35.

38. See chapter 6, below.

39. Qur'ān 19:21.

40. Qur'ān 5:75.

41. Placid J. Podipara, *Mariology of the East* (Kerala, India: Oriental Institute of Religious Studies, 1985).

42. See, e.g., Charles Belmonte, *Aba ginoong Maria: The Virgin Mary in Philippine Art* (Manila: Aba Ginoong Maria Foundation, 1990).

43. See chapter 13, below.

44. Song of Songs 1:5 (tr. Marvin Pope); see also chapter 2, above.

45. See the massive illustrated study of Stanisław Chojnacki, *Major Themes in Ethiopian Painting: Indigenous Developments, the Influence of Foreign Models, and Their Adaptation from the Thirteenth to the Nineteenth Century* (Wiesbaden: F. Steiner, 1983).

46. Marie Durand-Lefèbvre, *Etude sur l'origine des Vierges noires* (Paris: G. Durassié, 1937).

47. Marvin H. Pope, *Song of Songs: A New Translation with Introduction and Commentary* (New York: Doubleday, 1977), 307–18.

48. A. J. Delattre, *Le culte de la Sainte Vierge en Afrique: d'après les monuments archéologiques* (Paris: Société St-Augustin, 1907).

49. Maria Tarnawska, *Poland the Kingdom of Mary*, tr. Rosamund Batchelor (Lower Bullingham, Hereford: Zgromazdenie księży Marianow, 1982).

50. See also chapter 9, below.

Chapter 6   The Handmaid of the Lord

1. A specialized study in art history, which on closer examination turns out not to be so specialized after all, is Don Denny, *The Annunciation from the Right: From Early Christian Times to the Sixteenth Century* (New York: Garland, 1977).

2. *Imago Dei*, 131–34.

3. David Metheny Robb, "The Iconography of the Annunciation in the Fourteenth and Fifteenth Century," *Art Bulletin* 18 (1936): 480–526.

4. See the comments and bibliography in Alice Bank, *Byzantine Art in the Collections of Soviet Museums*, tr. Lenina Sorokina, 2d ed. (Leningrad: Aurora Art Publishers, 1985), 289.

5. Frank Edward Brightman, ed., *Liturgies Eastern and Western*, vol. 1: *Eastern Liturgies* (Oxford: Clarendon Press, 1896), 318–320.

6. On its place in the Gospel tradition, see Lucien Legrand, *L'Annonce à Marie (Lc 1, 26–38): Une apocalypse aux origines de l'Evangile* (Paris: Cerf, 1981).

7. John 1:14.

8. John 1:14 (Vg).

9. Gal. 4:4.

10. Xavier Léon-Dufour, "L'Annonce à Joseph," in *Etudes d'évangile* (Paris: Seuil, 1965), 65–81.

11. Luke 1:38.

12. Isa. 45:9, 64:8; Rom. 9:21.

13. E.g., Rom. 1:1.

14. *LTK* 9:695–96 (Remigius Bäumer).

15. Phil. 2:6–7.

16. Joel 3:2; Acts 2:18.

17. Acts 1:14.

18. Sterling Stuckey, "Through the Prism of Folklore: The Black Ethos in Slavery," in *America's Black Past*, ed. Eric Foner (New York: Harper and Row, 1970), 79.

19. Gregory of Nyssa *Epistles* 3 (PG 46:1021).

20. Richard Griffiths, ed., *Claudel: A Reappraisal* (London: Rapp and Whiting, 1968), 5.

21. Hans Urs von Balthasar, *Theodrama: Theological Dramatic Theory*, tr. Graham Harrison (San Francisco: Ignatius Press, 1992), 300.

22. 2 Kings 19:35.

23. Gregory of Nyssa *On the Making of Man* 23 (PG 44:212).

24. Luke 1:38.

25. See chapter 3, above.

26. Irenaeus *Against Heresies* V.xix.1. Although written in Greek, this treatise is preserved in its entirety only in a Latin translation; hence the Latin terms in this quotation.

27. Augustine *On the Proceedings of Pelagius* 20.44.

28. Acts 9:1–31, 22:1–16, 26:9–23; Gal. 1:11–24.

29. Krister Stendahl, *Paul among Jews and Gentiles* (Philadelphia: Fortress Press, 1976).

30. Augustine *Confessions* VIII.xii.29.

31. Rom. 13:13–14.

32. Augustine *Confessions* VII.xxi.27.

33. Rom. 1:17 (Vg).

34. *Luther's Works: The American Edition*, ed. Jaroslav Pelikan and Helmut Lehmann, 55 vols. (Saint Louis and Philadelphia: Concordia Publishing House and Fortress Press, 1955–), 34:337.

35. Maximus Confessor *Questions to Thalassius* 61 (PG 90:637).

36. On this concept, see chapter 7, below.

37. Lars Thunberg, *Microcosm and Mediator: The Theological Anthropology of Maximus the Confessor* (Lund: C. W. K. Gleerup, 1965), 457–458; italics his.

38. Basil *Epistles* 223.3.

39. PG 31:563–90.

40. Pelikan, *Christianity and Classical Culture*.

41. Luke 1:28.

42. Lampe, 1519.

43. 2 Cor. 6:1.

44. Luke 1:48.

45. Prov. 31:10 (Vg).

46. Gen. 3:15 (Vg).

47. E. F. Sutcliffe, "Jerome," in *The Cambridge History of the Bible: The West from the Fathers to the Reformation* (Cambridge: Cambridge University Press, 1969), 98–99.

48. *The Christian Tradition*, 3:71, 166.

49. Mary Clayton, *The Cult of the Virgin Mary in Anglo-Saxon England* (Cambridge: Cambridge University Press, 1990).

50. Bede *Commentary on Genesis* 1.

51. Ambrosius Autpertus *Commentary on the Apocalypse* 2.

52. Its evolution has been described and documented by Franz [Leander] Drewniak, *Die mariologische Deutung von Gen. 3:15 in der Väterzeit* (Breslau: R. Nischowsky, 1934); see also Nicholas Perry and Loreto Echeverría, *Under the Heel of Mary* (London: Routledge, 1988).

53. Bernard of Clairvaux *In Laud of the Virgin Mother* 2.4.

54. Arthur K. Wheelock, Jr., and Ben Broos, "The Catalogue," *Johannes Vermeer* (Washington, D.C., and New Haven: National Gallery of Art and Yale University Press, 1996), 190.

55. John Michael Montias, *Vermeer and His Milieu: A Web of Social History* (Princeton, N.J.: Princeton University Press, 1989), 129.

56. See Eugene R. Cunnar, "The Viewer's Share: Three Sectarian Readings of Vermeer's *Woman Holding a Balance*," *Exemplaria* 2 (1990): 501–36.

57. Isa. 40:15.

58. *The Documents of Vatican II*, ed. Walter M. Abbott (New York: Guild Press, 1966), 85–96.

59. See chapter 13, below.

60. *The Christian Tradition*, 3:162.

61. Num. 24:17.
62. Ernst Robert Curtius, *European Literature and the Latin Middle Ages*, tr. Willard R. Trask (Princeton, N.J.: Princeton University Press, 1953), 129.
63. F. J. E. Raby, ed., *The Oxford Book of Medieval Latin Verse* (Oxford: Clarendon Press, 1959), 94.

Chapter 7   The Adornment of Worship

1. See chapter 6, above.
2. Ps. 68:25.
3. Augustine *Expositions on the Book of Psalms* 67.26.
4. Louis Bouyer, "Le culte de Marie dans la liturgie byzantine," *Maison-Dieu* 38 (1954): 122–35.
5. Lampe, 57.
6. Alexandra Pätzold, *Der Akathistos-hymnos: Die Bilderzyklen in der byzantinischen Wandmalerei des 14. Jahrhunderts* (Stuttgart: F. Steiner, 1989).
7. Maxime Gorce, *Le Rosaire et ses antécédents historiques* (Paris: Editions à Picard, 1931).
8. OED "B" 724, with many examples.
9. LTK 9:45–49 (Günter Lanczkowski, Angelus Walz, Ekkart Sauer, and Konrad Hofmann).
10. DTC 1:1273–77 (Ursmer Berlière).
11. Luke 1:26–28.
12. *Imago Dei*, 137–45.
13. Vasiliki Limberis, *Divine Heiress: The Virgin Mary and the Creation of Christian Constantinople* (London: Routledge, 1994).
14. Nicephorus *Refutation* II.4 (PG 100:341).
15. Nicephorus *Refutation* I.9 (PG 100:216).
16. Warren Treadgold, *The Byzantine Revival* (Stanford, Calif.: Stanford University Press, 1988), 88.
17. John of Damascus *Orations on the Holy Icons* I.14, III.27–28 (PG 94:1244, 1348–49).
18. Lampe, 408 (including cognates).
19. Luke 23:46.
20. Acts 7:59.
21. Phil. 2:10–11.
22. Denzinger, 301.
23. John of Damascus *Orations on the Holy Icons* III.27–28 (PG 94:1348–49).
24. Augustine *City of God* X.1.
25. Lampe, 384, 793.
26. Augustine *Confessions* I.xiii.20–xiv.23.
27. Augustine *On the Trinity* VII.vi.11.
28. Liddell-Scott-Jones, 1518.
29. Charles Diehl, "Byzantine Civilization," in *The Cambridge Medieval History*, vol. 4 (Cambridge: Cambridge University Press, 1936), 755.
30. The ambiguity appears also in earlier English usage, for example in the Authorized Version of Luke 14:10: "Then shalt thou have *worship* in the presence of them that sit at meat with thee."
31. DTC 3:2404–27, esp. 2406–9 (Jean-Arthur Chollet).
32. Deferrari-Barry, 346, 627–28, 494.
33. See chapter 11, below.

34. Demosthenes Savramis, "Der abergläubliche Mißbrauch der Bilder in Byzanz," *Ost-kirchliche Studien* 9 (1960): 174–92.

35. Theodore the Studite *Orations* XI.iv.24 (PG 99:828).

36. Christopher Walter, "Two Notes on the Deesis," *Revue des études byzantines* 26 (1968): 326–36.

37. Liddell-Scott-Jones, 372.

38. Sophocles, 347.

39. Lampe, 334.

40. Lampe, 1144.

41. See Cyril Mango, *Materials for the Study of the Mosaics of St. Sophia at Istanbul* (Washington, D.C.: Dumbarton Oaks, 1962), 29.

42. Matt. 11:13.

43. Justin Martyr *Dialogue with Trypho* 51 (PG 6:589).

44. Therefore the Greek term was used in patristic Greek both for the annunciation to Zechariah (Luke 1:8–23) and for the annunciation to Mary (Luke 1:26–38): Lampe, 559.

45. Gregory of Nyssa *On Virginity* 6.

46. Matt. 11:11; Luke 7:28 (NEB).

47. Gregory of Nyssa *On Virginity* 2 (PG 46:324).

48. See chapter 8, below.

49. Anders Nygren, *Agape and Eros*, tr. Philip S. Watson (Philadelphia: Westminster Press, 1953), 412.

50. L. Bieler, *Theios anēr: Das Bild des "göttlichen Menschen" in Spätantike und Frühchristentum*, 2 vols. (Vienna: O. Höfels, 1935–36).

51. Lampe, 649–50.

52. Nygren, *Agape and Eros*, 734.

53. Boethius *The Consolation of Philosophy* III.pr.x.23–25.

54. Ps. 82:6.

55. John 10:35.

56. 2 Peter 1:4.

57. Athanasius *Orations Against the Arians* III.24 (PG 26:373).

58. Ioann B. Sirota, *Die Ikonographie der Gottesmutter in der Russischen Orthodoxen Kirche: Versuch einer Systematisierung* (Würzburg: Der Christliche Osten, 1992).

59. James Mearns, *The Canticles of the Christian Church Eastern and Western in Early and Medieval Times* (Cambridge: Cambridge University Press, 1914).

60. Phil. 2:6–7.

61. William Loerke, "'Real Presence' in Early Christian Art," *Monasticism and the Arts*, ed. Timothy George Verdon (Syracuse, N.Y.: Syracuse University Press, 1984), 47.

62. John of Damascus *Orations on the Holy Icons* II.15 (PG 94:1301).

63. Dorothy G. Shepherd, "An Icon of the Virgin: A Sixth-Century Tapestry Panel from Egypt," *Bulletin of the Cleveland Museum of Art* 56 (March 1969): 93.

64. James H. Stubblebine, "Two Byzantine Madonnas from Calahorra, Spain," *Art Bulletin* 48 (1966): 379–81.

Chapter 8   The Paragon of Chastity

1. Luke 1:42.

2. Bernhard Lohse, *Askese und Mönchtum in der Antike und in der alten Kirche* (Munich: R. Oldenbourg, 1969).

3. Lampe, 244.

4. Marcus Aurelius *Meditations* II.17 (tr. Maxwell Staniforth).

5. Above all, Eph. 6:10–17; but also 1 Tim. 6:12 and 2 Tim. 4:7, and other places.

6. 1 Cor. 9:24–27.

7. Plutarch *Parallel Lives, Numa,* 10.

8. Jaroslav Pelikan, *The Excellent Empire: The Fall of Rome and the Triumph of the Church* (New York: Harper and Row, 1987), 59.

9. Peter Robert Lamont Brown, *The Body and Society: Men, Women, and Sexual Renunciation in Early Christianity* (New York: Columbia University Press, 1988).

10. Num. 6:2.

11. Judges 13:5.

12. Philo *On the Contemplative Life* 68 (tr. C. D. Yonge).

13. Eusebius *Ecclesiastical History* II.xvii.18–19 (tr. Arthur Cushman McGiffert, Sr.).

14. Athanasius *Life of Antony* 5.

15. Augustine *Confessions* VIII.vi.14–15.

16. *Development of Christian Doctrine: Some Historical Prolegomena,* 100–104.

17. Peter Brown, *Augustine of Hippo* (London: Faber, 1969), 274.

18. Jerome *Epistles* 127.5.

19. Jerome *Epistles* 108.33.

20. Jerome *Epistles* 108.20.

21. See Pelikan, *Excellent Empire,* 43–52.

22. Jerome *Epistles* 128.3.

23. Johannes Quasten, *Patrology,* 4 vols. (Westminster, Md.: Newman Press and Christian Classics, 1951–86), 4:239; the treatise appears PL 23:211–338.

24. Jerome *Against Helvidius* 2.

25. Jerome *Against Helvidius* 12.

26. See chapter 2, above.

27. Jerome *Against Helvidius* 16.

28. ap.Jerome *Against Helvidius* 20.

29. 1 Cor. 7:1–2, 38.

30. Jerome *Against Helvidius* 22.

31. Jerome *Against Helvidius* 22.

32. Jerome *Against Helvidius* 21.

33. Joseph Huhn, *Das Geheimnis der Jungfrau-Mutter Maria nach dem Kirchenvater Ambrosius* (Würzburg: Echter Verlag, 1954), 79–80.

34. See chapter 14, below.

35. Ambrose *Epistles* 63.111.

36. Ambrose *Epistles* 63.7.

37. Quasten, *Patrology,* 4:167.

38. Ambrose *Concerning Virgins* II.ii.6.

39. Ambrose *Concerning Virgins* II.ii.15.

40. W. J. Dooley, *Marriage According to St. Ambrose* (Washington, D.C.: Catholic University of America, 1948).

41. Ambrose *De virginibus* II.ii.9.

42. Ambrose *De virginibus* II.ii.8–9.

43. Eph. 5:32.

44. See *The Christian Tradition,* 3:211–12.

45. John Ruskin, *Giotto and His Works in Padua: Being an Explanatory Notice of the Series of Woodcuts Executed for the Arundel Society After the Frescoes in the Arena Chapel* (London: Arundel Society, 1854).

46. See chapter 10, below.

47. *LTK* 5:1140–41 (Joseph Wenner).

48. John 2:1–11.

Chapter 9   The Mater Dolorosa

1. Ernst Robert Curtius, *European Literature and the Latin Middle Ages*, tr. Willard R. Trask (Princeton, N.J.: Princeton University Press, 1953), 598.

2. Charles Homer Haskins, *The Renaissance of the Twelfth Century* (New York: Meridian Books, 1957).

3. Otto von Simson, *The Gothic Cathedral: Origins of Gothic Architecture and the Medieval Concept of Order* (New York: Pantheon Books, 1956), 172.

4. M. Kotrbová, *České gotické madony*, photographs by V. Fyman (Prague: Charita, 1985).

5. Luke 2:35.

6. See also chapter 15, below.

7. John 19:25–26.

8. Raby, *Oxford Book of Medieval Latin Verse*, 435.

9. Avery Thomas Sharp, "A Descriptive Catalog of Selected, Published Eighteenth-through Twentieth-Century Stabat Mater Settings for Mixed Voices, with a Discussion of the History of the Text" (Ph.D. diss., University of Iowa, 1978).

10. Johann Wolfgang von Goethe, *Faust*, 3588–95.

11. See chapter 12, below.

12. See also chapter 5, above.

13. Sandro Sticca, *The "Planctus Mariae" in the Dramatic Tradition of the Middle Ages*, tr. Joseph R. Berrigan (Athens: University of Georgia Press, 1988).

14. Margaret Alexiou, *The Ritual Lament in Greek Tradition* (Cambridge: Cambridge University Press, 1974); Gregory W. Dobrov, "A Dialogue with Death: Ritual Lament and the thrēnos Theotokou of Romanos Melodos," *Greek, Roman, and Byzantine Studies* 35 (1994): 385–405.

15. Dobrov, "Dialogue with Death," 393–97.

16. Jutta Barbara Desel, *"Vom Leiden Christi oder von dem schmertzlichen Mitleyden Marie": Die vielfigurige Beweinung Christi im Kontext thüringischer Schnitzretabel der Spätgotik* (Alfter: VDG—Verlag und Datenbank für Geisteswissenschaften, 1994).

17. Gerda Panofsky-Soergel, *Michelangelos "Christus" und sein römischer Auftraggeber* (Worms: Wernersche Verlagsgesellschaft, 1991).

18. On the relation of Michelangelo's Pietà to other depictions of the scene, see the collection of photographs in Paolo Monti, *La Pietà: A Rondini di Michelangelo Buonarroti* (Milan: P. Battaglini, 1977).

19. Matt. 27:46.

20. Matt. 1:21.

21. Hans Urs von Balthasar, *The Threefold Garland: The World's Salvation in Mary's Prayer*, tr. Erasmo Leiva-Merikakis (San Francisco: Ignatius Press, 1982), 102.

22. This theme will occupy us again in chapter 13, below.

23. Aron Anderson, ed., *The Mother of God and St Birgitta: An Anthology* (Rome: Vatican Polyglot Press, 1983), 33.

24. Domenico Pezzini, "'The Meditacion of oure Lordis Passyon' and Other Bridgettine Texts in MS Lambeth 432," *Studies in Birgitta and the Brigittine Order,* ed. James Hogg (Lewiston, N.Y.: Edwin Mellen Press, 1993), 1:293.

25. Teresa of Avila, *Spiritual Relations,* in *Complete Works of Saint Teresa of Jesus,* tr. and ed. E. Alison Peers, 3 vols. (London: Sheed and Ward, 1950), 1:363–64.

26. *The Christian Tradition,* 3:160–74.

27. Anselm *On the Virginal Conception and on Original Sin,* preface, *Sancti Anselmi opera omnia,* ed. F. S. Schmitt (Edinburgh: Thomas Nelson, 1938–61), 2:139.

28. Meyer Schapiro, *The Parma Ildefonsus: A Romanesque Illuminated Manuscript from Cluny, and Related Works* (New York: College Art Association, 1964), 71.

29. Guibert of Nogent *On His Own Life* 1.16 (PL 156:871).

30. Bernard of Clairvaux *Sermons on Diverse Topics* 52, *Sancti Bernardi Opera,* ed. Jean Leclercq and Henri Rochais, 8 vols. (Rome: Editiones Cistercienses, 1957–77), 6-I:276.

31. 1 Peter 2:5; Rev. 1:6.

32. Thomas Aquinas, *The Three Greatest Prayers: Commentaries on the Our Father, the Hail Mary and the Apostles' Creed,* tr. Laurence Shapcote (Westminster, Md.: Newman Press, 1956), 32–33.

33. See chapter 11, below.

34. See chapter 14, below.

35. See chapter 13, below.

36. See chapter 15, below.

37. See chapter 8, above.

Chapter 10   The Face That Most Resembles Christ's

1. *Eternal Feminines,* 101–19.

2. H. Barré, "Saint Bernard, docteur marial," *Saint Bernard théologien* (Rome: Analecta Sacri Ordinis Cisterciensis, 1953), 92–113.

3. Steven Botterill, *Dante and the Mystical Tradition: Bernard of Clairvaux in the "Commedia"* (Cambridge: Cambridge University Press, 1994), 167.

4. Par.XXXII.85–87. Here and throughout this chapter, I have employed the translation in blank verse by Allen Mandelbaum, and I have therefore also printed it as verse, by contrast with my own prose translations of verse in chapter 12, below.

5. Par.XXIII.136–37.

6. Alexandre Masseron, *Dante et Saint Bernard* (Paris: A. Michel, 1953), 82.

7. Par.XXXIII.1–2.

8. Inf.II.95–105.

9. Par.XXI.123.

10. Par.XXXII.104.

11. Par.XXIII.128.

12. Par.XXXII.119.

13. Botterill, *Dante and the Mystical Tradition,* 169.

14. Par.XXXIII.1; see chapter 14, below.

15. Par.IV.28–33.

16. Par.II.118, 122.

17. Par.XIX.98.

18. Par.III.85, 88–90.

19. Gen. 3:20.

20. Barbara Newman, *Sister of Wisdom: St. Hildegard's Theology of the Feminine* (Berkeley: University of California Press, 1987), 89–120.

21. Par.XXXII.4–6.

22. Par.XXXII.7–9.

23. Par.XV.133.

24. Purg.V.101.

25. Par.III.121–23.

26. Par.XXXIII.21.

27. Par.XXXIII.10–12.

28. So, e.g., Par.XXXII.37–39, where she would seem to be the supreme example of the faith that is spoken of.

29. 1 Cor. 13:13.

30. Manfred Bambeck, *Studien zu Dantes "Paradiso"* (Wiesbaden: Steiner, 1979), 147–54.

31. Purg.XXXII.73.

32. Peter, James, and John were the only ones present at the raising of the daughter of Jairus (Mark 5:37), on the Mount of Transfiguration (Matt. 17:1–9), and in the Garden of Gethsemane (Matt. 26:36–37).

33. Purg.X.121, 44; Luke 1:38.

34. Purg.XIII.37–38, 50.

35. Purg.XV.106, 88–89; Luke 2:48.

36. Purg.XVIII.107, 100.

37. Purg.XX.14, 19.

38. Purg.XXIII.65, XXII.142–44.

39. Purg.XXV.121–28.

40. Par.XI.58–66.

41. Matt. 2:11.

42. Purg.XX.19–24; Luke 2:7.

43. Par.XXXIII.1.

44. Purg.XXV.128–35, quoting Luke 1:34 (Vg).

45. Purg.XXII.142–44, citing John 2:3.

46. Purg.VIII.25–39.

47. Purg.X.31–33.

48. Purg.X.34–45.

49. Par.XXXII.94–96.

50. Par.XVI.34.

51. Par.XIV.36.

52. Par.XVI.34–39.

53. Par.XXIII.124–29.

54. Par.XXIII.130–32.

55. Par.XXIII.90.

56. Par.XXIII.103–8.

57. Masseron, *Dante et Saint Bernard*, 82–83.

58. Par.XXXI.112–17.

59. Giuseppe C. Di Scipio, *The Symbolic Rose in Dante's "Paradiso"* (Ravenna: Longo, 1984), 57–85.

60. Inf.XXXIV.34.

61. Par.XXXI.118–23.

62. *Summa Theologica* I.50.4.

63. Par.XXXI.130–32.

64. Rona Goffen, *Giovanni Bellini* (New Haven and London: Yale University Press, 1989), 143–60.

65. His relation to Franciscan theology is carefully analyzed in John V. Fleming, *From Bonaventure to Bellini: An Essay in Franciscan Exegesis* (Princeton, N.J.: Princeton University Press, 1982).

66. Par.XXXI.133–38.

67. OED "M," 6-II:165; see chapter 11, below.

68. Henry Osborn Taylor, *The Mediaeval Mind*, 2 vols., 4th ed. (London: Macmillan, 1938), 2:581–82.

69. See chapter 14, below.

70. Par.XIII.85–87.

71. Masseron, *Dante et Saint Bernard*, 139–41.

72. S.T.III.27.2.

73. The entire discussion "The Mother of God" in Newman, *Sister of Wisdom*, 156–95, bears on the subject of this chapter.

74. See chapter 15, below.

75. Par.XXV.127–28.

76. Par.XXIII.73–74.

77. Par.XXIII.86–90.

78. Par.XXXIII.31–43.

79. Par.XXXIII.115–20.

80. Par.XXXIII.145.

81. Par.XXXII.107–8.

82. See chapter 6, above.

83. Par.XXXIII.21.

84. Inf.II.85–114.

85. Par.XXIII.88–89.

86. Purg.VII.82.

Chapter 11   The Model of Faith

1. G. K. Chesterton, "Introduction" to Everyman Library edition of Charles Dickens, Oliver Twist.

2. See the discussion of Horst Gorski, *Die Niedrigkeit seiner Magd: Darstellung und theologische Analyse der Mariologie Martin Luthers als Beitrag zum gegenwärtigen lutherisch-römisch katholischen Gespräch* (Frankfurt: Peter Lang, 1987).

3. John Paul II, *Mary: God's Yes to Man*, commentary by Hans Urs von Balthasar (San Francisco: Ignatius Press, 1988), 168.

4. See chapter 6, above.

5. Martin Luther, *Lectures on Genesis*, in *Luther's Works*, ed. Pelikan and Lehmann, 1:191.

6. Lee Palmer Wandel, *Voracious Idols and Violent Hands: Iconoclasm in Reformation Zurich, Strasbourg, and Basel* (Cambridge: Cambridge University Press, 1995), 21–22.

7. Charles Garside, *Zwingli and the Arts* (New Haven: Yale University Press, 1966), 159.

8. *Luther's Works*, ed. Pelikan and Lehmann, 40:84.

9. Martin Luther, *House Postil*, in *Luthers Werke: Kritische Gesamtausgabe*, 57 vols. (Weimar: Hans Böhlau, 1883–), 52:689.

10. Schaff, 3:200.

11. *Heidelberg Catechism*, question 36 (Schaff, 3:319).

12. 1 Tim. 2:5.

13. *Augsburg Confession* XXI.2 (tr. Theodore Tappert), *The Book of Concord* (Philadelphia: Fortress Press, 1959), 47.

14. *Apology* XXI.9 (tr. Jaroslav Pelikan), *Book of Concord*, 230.

15. Newman, *Essay on the Development of Christian Doctrine*, 138–39.

16. *Thirty-Nine Articles*, XXII (Schaff, 3:501).

17. John Calvin, *Institutes of the Christian Religion*, III.xx.21, ed. John T. McNeill (Philadelphia: Westminster Press, 1960), 879.

18. Martin Luther, *Lectures on Genesis* (16:4), in *Luther's Works*, ed. Pelikan and Lehmann, 3:51.

19. Martin Luther, *The Misuse of the Mass*, in *Luther's Works*, ed. Pelikan and Lehmann, 36:195.

20. George Huntston Williams, *The Radical Reformation*, 3d ed. (Kirksville, Mo.: Sixteenth Century Essays and Studies, 1992), 797–98.

21. Orbe Philips in George Huntston Williams, ed. *Spiritual and Anabaptist Writers* (Philadelphia: Westminster Press, 1957), 238–39n.

22. *Formula of Concord*, Solid Declaration, XII.25, *Book of Concord*, 635.

23. See chapter 3, above.

24. For contemporary efforts at a restatement of this positive place, see Heiko Augustinus Oberman, *The Virgin Mary in Evangelical Perspective* (Philadelphia: Fortress Press, 1971); and David Wright, *Chosen by God: Mary in Evangelical Perspective* (London: Marshall Pickering, 1989).

25. A splendid and learned summary, which like so many of his studies, could have become a full-length book, is the work of my late colleague and friend, Arthur Carl Piepkorn, "Mary's Place within the People of God according to Non-Roman Catholics," *Marian Studies* 18 (1967): 46–83.

26. *Augsburg Confession*, I.1, *Book of Concord*, 27.

27. Thomas F. Torrance, "Introduction" to *The School of Faith: The Catechisms of the Reformed Church* (New York: Harper and Brothers, 1959), lxxx.

28. *Larger Catechism*, question 37, in *School of Faith*, 191.

29. Walter Tappolet, ed., *Das Marienlob der Reformatoren* (Tübingen: Katzmann Verlag, 1962).

30. See *The Christian Tradition*, 4:261.

31. Luther, "Sermon on the Presentation of Christ in the Temple," in *Luthers Werke*, 52:688–99.

32. *Smalcald Articles*, I.4, in *Die Bekenntnisschriften der evangelisch-lutherischen Kirche* (Göttingen: Vandenhoeck und Ruprecht, 1952), 414.

33. Martin Luther, *Commentary on the Magnificat*, in *Luther's Works*, ed. Pelikan and Lehmann, 21:355.

34. Rom. 10:17.

35. Ernst Bizer, *Fides ex auditu: Eine Untersuchung über die Entdeckung der Gerechtigkeit Gottes durch Martin Luther* (Neukirchen Kreis Moers: Verlag der Buchhandlung des Erziehungsvereins, 1958).

36. 1 Cor. 13:13.

37. Thomas Aquinas *Commentary on the Sentences* IV.vi.2.2.1a.

38. 1 Cor. 13:13.

39. This concept is carefully examined by Joseph C. McLelland, *The Visible Words of God: An*

Exposition of the Sacramental Theology of Peter Martyr Vermigli, A.D. 1500–1562 (Grand Rapids, Mich.: Wm. B. Eerdmans, 1957).

40. Calvin Institutes III.ii.6. McNeill ed., 549.
41. Martin Luther, Commentary on the Magnificat, in Luther's Works, ed. Pelikan and Lehmann, 21:304, 305, 338.
42. Luke 1:38.
43. Martin Luther, House Postil, in Luthers Werke, 52:624–34.
44. Martin Luther, Sermon for 25.vii.1522, in Luthers Werke, 10-III:239.
45. Martin Luther, Commentary on Galatians, in Luther's Works, ed. Pelikan and Lehmann, 26:387.
46. Gen. 15:6; Rom. 4:3; Gal. 3:6.
47. Martin Luther, "Sermon on Luke 2:41–52," in Luthers Werke, 12:409–19.
48. Roy Strong, The Cult of Elizabeth: Elizabethan Portraiture and Pageantry (London: Thames and Hudson, 1977), 16.
49. The most thorough investigation of the supposed parallels, Helen Hackett, Virgin Mother, Maiden Queen: Elizabeth I and the Cult of the Virgin Mary (Houndmills: Macmillan, 1995), questions the existence of a direct connection, attributing the idea more to the twentieth century than to the seventeenth.
50. Margaret Aston, Lollards and Reformers: Images and Literacy in Late Medieval Religion (London: Hambledon Press, 1984), 325n.
51. The Yale Edition of the Shorter Poems of Edmund Spenser, ed. William A. Oram et al. (New Haven and London: Yale University Press, 1989), 72.
52. Edmund Spenser, The Faerie Queene, I, 4, ed. Thomas P. Roche, Jr. (New Haven and London: Yale University Press, 1981), 40.
53. Milton, Paradise Lost, V.385–87; see chapter 3, above.
54. Milton, Paradise Regained, I.227–32.
55. See chapter 7, above.
56. John Julian, Dictionary of Hymnology, reprint ed. (New York: Dover Publications, 1957), 270.
57. Owen Chadwick, A History of Christianity (New York: St. Martin's Press, 1996), 166.
58. David Price, "Albrecht Dürer's Representations of Faith: The Church, Lay Devotion and Veneration in the Apocalypse," Zeitschrift für Kunstgeschichte 57 (1994): 688–96.
59. Albrecht Dürer, Das Marienleben (Leipzig: Insel-Verlag, 1936).
60. LTK 6:1169 (Wolfgang Braunfels).

Chapter 12   The Mater Gloriosa

1. Pelikan, Jesus Through the Centuries, 232.
2. René Wellek, Concepts of Criticism (New Haven: Yale University Press, 1963), 221.
3. See Geoffrey H. Hartman, Wordsworth's Poetry, 1787–1814 (New Haven and London: Yale University Press, 1971), 273.
4. William Wordsworth, Ecclesiastical Sonnets, Part II, Sonnet ii, The Poems, 2 vols. (New Haven and London: Yale University Press, 1977), 2:464.
5. Wordsworth, Ecclesiastical Sonnets, Sonnet xxv, 2:474; italics added.
6. Emile Mâle, The Gothic Image: Religious Art in France of the Thirteenth Century, tr. Dora Nussey, reprint ed. (New York: Harper, 1958), 254–58.
7. David Friedrich Strauss, The Life of Jesus Critically Examined, tr. George Eliot, 5th ed. (London: Swan Sonnenschein, 1906), 140–43.

8. George Eliot, *Middlemarch*, ed. Bert G. Hornback (New York: W. W. Norton, 1977), 530, 544.

9. Novalis, *Werke und Briefe [von] Novalis*, ed. Alfred Kelletat (Munich: Winkler-Verlag, [1962]), 102.

10. *Faust the Theologian*, 115–28.

11. Johann Peter Eckermann, *Gespräche mit Goethe in den letzten Jahren seines Lebens*, ed. Fritz Bergemann, 3d ed. (Baden-Baden: Insel Verlag, 1955), 716–20. Translations throughout this chapter are my own.

12. See chapter 9, above.

13. Johann Wolfgang von Goethe, *Faust*, 3588–95; although in chapter 10 I have, in quoting Mandelbaum's translation of Dante into blank verse, printed the quotations in verse forms, these translations into prose, which are my own, have been woven into the text.

14. Reinhard Buchwald, *Führer durch Goethes Faustdichtung: Erklärung des Werkes und Geschichte seiner Entstehung*, 7th ed. (Stuttgart: Alfred Kröner, 1964), 59.

15. *Faust*, 12094–95.

16. *Faust*, 12013–19.

17. *Faust*, 12032–36.

18. Luke 1:28 (Vg).

19. Günther Müller, "Die organische Seele im Faust," *Euphorion* 34 (1933): 161n.

20. Stuart Atkins, *Goethe's Faust: A Literary Analysis* (Cambridge, Mass.: Harvard University Press, 1958), 172.

21. Harold Stein Jantz, *The Form of Goethe's "Faust"* (Baltimore, Md.: Johns Hopkins University Press, 1978), 48.

22. Cyrus Hamlin, ed., Johann Wolfgang von Goethe, *Faust, A Tragedy: Backgrounds and Sources*, ed. Cyrus Hamlin, tr. Walter Arndt (New York: W. W. Norton, 1976), 304 n. 9. On the meaning of the title "Doctor Marianus," see Ann White, *Names and Nomenclature in Goethe's "Faust"* (London: University of London Institute of Germanic Studies, 1980), 37–38.

23. *Faust*, 12096–103. On the Mater Gloriosa and these titles, Gerhard Möbus, *Die Christus-Frage in Goethes Leben und Werk* (Osnabrück: A. Fromm, 1964), 291–95, urges that these lines not be read as Christian and Catholic.

24. For example, *Faust*, 1334, 9028–30, 9364.

25. *Faust*, 11993–97.

26. *Faust*, 12009–12.

27. *Faust*, 12001–4.

28. *Faust*, 12100–12101.

29. *Faust*, 1114.

30. Jantz, *Form of Goethe's "Faust,"* 101.

31. Robert E. Dye, "The Easter Cantata and the Idea of Mediation in Goethe's *Faust*," *PMLA*, 92:974.

32. *Faust*, 3588–95; see also chapter 9, above.

33. Hermann Fähnrich, "Goethes Musikanschauung in seiner Fausttragödie—die Erfüllung und Vollendung seiner Opernreform," *Goethe: Neue Folge des Jahrbuchs der Goethe-Gesellschaft* 25 (1963): 257.

34. *Faust*, 12069–75. See the comments of Max Kommerell, *Geist und Buchstabe der Dichtung*, 3d ed. (Frankfurt: Vittorio Klostermann), 125–26.

35. *Faust*, 3730, 12009.

36. *Faust*, 12061–68.

37. Wilhelm Emrich, *Die Symbolik des Faust II*, 2d ed. (Bonn: Athenäum-Verlag 1957), 418–19.

38. *Faust*, "Trüber Tag," 15.

39. *Faust*, "Trüber Tag."

40. *Faust*, 10703–9.

41. *Faust*, 1298–1309.

42. *Faust*, 12037–60.

43. Luke 7:36–50.

44. *ADB* 4:579–81 (Raymond F. Collins).

45. Luke 7:47.

46. *Faust*, 12037–44.

47. John 4:4–26.

48. *Faust*, 12045–52.

49. *Faust*, 12053–60.

50. Ernst Grumach, "Prolog und Epilog im Faustplan von 1797," *Goethe: Neue Folge des Jahrbuchs der Goethe-Gesellschaft* ¹⁴/₁₅ (¹⁹⁵²/₅₃): 63–107.

51. See chapter 10, above.

52. *Faust*, 11807–8.

53. *Faust*, 12001–4.

54. *Faust*, 11882–83.

55. Heinz Schlaffer, *Faust zweiter Teil: Die Allegorie des 19. Jahrhunderts* (Stuttgart: Metzler, 1981), 163.

56. *Faust*, 11872–73.

57. Par.XXXIII.145.

58. *Faust*, 346–47, 771.

59. *Faust*, 11854–55.

60. *Faust*, 11862–65.

61. *Faust*, 12104–5.

62. *Faust*, 12102, 12110.

63. *Faust*, 12102–3.

64. *Faust*, 6914.

65. *Faust*, 8592, 8640, 8904.

66. *Faust*, 8924, 8947, 8954.

67. *Faust*, 7294.

68. *Faust*, 9258–59.

69. *Faust*, 9270–73.

70. *Faust*, 1084; 7915, 8289; 5450; 8147; 6213, 6218.

71. *Faust*, 2439–40.

72. *Faust*, 6498–6500.

73. *Faust*, 6510, 9948–50.

74. *Faust*, 10055–66, 10047–51.

75. *Faust*, 7412, 7440–41.

76. *Faust*, 12012.

77. *Faust*, 11997.

78. *Faust*, 2603–4; Hans Urs von Balthasar, *Prometheus: Studien zur Geschichte des deutschen Idealismus*, 2d ed. (Heidelberg: F. H. Kerle Verlag, 1947), 514.

79. *Faust*, 11918–25.
80. *Faust*, 12104–11.

Chapter 13   The Woman Clothed with the Sun

1. "Wasn' That a Wonder," *Slave Songs of the Georgia Sea Islands*, ed. Lydia Parrish (New York: Creative Age Press, 1942), 139.
2. Rev. 12:1; see Altfrid Th. Kassing, *Die Kirche und Maria: Ihr Verhältnis im 12. Kapitel der Apokalypse* (Düsseldorf: Patmos-Verlog, 1958).
3. *PG* 46:909–13.
4. See Edmond Paris, *Les mystères de Lourdes, La Salette, Fatima: Les marchands du temple, mercantilisme religieux, marché d'illusions* (La Chaux-de-Fonds: Union de défense protestante suisse, 1971).
5. René Laurentin and René Lejeune, *Messages and Teachings of Mary at Medjugorje* (Milford, Ohio: Riehle Foundation, 1988), 15.
6. René Laurentin, ed., *Lourdes: Documents authentiques* (Paris: L. Lethielleux, 1966).
7. *LTK* 7:64–65 (Hermann Lais).
8. Rubén Vargas Ugarte, *Historia del culto de María en Ibero-américa y de sus Imágenes y Santuarios más celebrados*, 2 vols., 3d ed. (Madrid: Talleres Gráficos Jura, 1956), 1:163–207; the vast literature is cataloged in the bilingual work of Gloria Grajales and Ernest J. Burrus, eds., *Guadalupan Bibliography* (Washington, D.C.: Georgetown University Press, 1986).
9. Edmond Carpez, *La Vénérable Catherine Labouré, fille de la Charité de Saint Vincent de Paul (1806–1876)*, 6th ed. (Paris: Lecoffre, 1913).
10. Sandra L. Zimdars-Swartz, *Encountering Mary: From La Salette to Medjugorje* (Princeton, N.J.: Princeton University Press, 1991).
11. René Laurentin, *Lourdes: Histoire authentique des apparitions*, 6 vols. (Paris: Lethielleux, 1961–64); more recent is Stéphane Baumont, *Histoire de Lourdes* (Toulouse: Editions Privat, 1993).
12. Cyril C. Martindale, *The Message of Fatima* (London: Burns, Oates, and Washbourne, 1950).
13. Beinert and Petri, *Handbuch der Marienkunde*, 533 (René Laurentin); a critical psychological examination of these two visisons in Belgium is that of Gerd Schallenberg, *Visionäre Erlebnisse* (Augsburg: Pattloch Verlag, 1990), 83–95.
14. Since the publication of this list of ten apparitions, two additional ones have been "approved": Akita in Japan and Betania in Venezuela.
15. See now David Blackbourn, *Marpingen: Apparitions of the Virgin Mary in Nineteenth-Century Germany* (New York: Alfred A. Knopf, 1994).
16. Blackbourn, *Marpingen*, 5. Because this roster of elements corresponds so closely to the one I had formulated in the first draft of this chapter, before reading (and reviewing) Blackbourn's study, I am gratefully adapting it here to my rather different historical purposes.
17. On the significance of this proliferation in the modern era, see René Laurentin, *Multiplication des apparitions de la Vierge aujourd'hui: est-ce elle? Que veut-elle dire?* 3d ed. (Paris: Fayard, 1991).
18. See, in general, Werner Freitag, *Volks- und Elitenfrömmigkeit in der frühen Neuzeit: Marienwallfahrten im Fürstbistum Münster* (Paderborn: F. Schöningh, 1991).
19. Luke 1:51–53.
20. William Thomas Walsh, *Our Lady of Fatima* (New York: Macmillan, 1947), 214, 140.

21. Emile Zola, *Lourdes*, tr. Ernest Alfred Vizatelly (Dover, N.H.: A. Sutton, 1993).

22. Antonio González Dorado, *Mariología popular latinoamericana: De la María conquistadora a la María liberadora* (Asunción, Paraguay: Ediciones Loyola, 1985).

23. Anna Gradowska, *Magna Mater: El sincretismo hispanoamericano en algunas imágenes marianas* (Caracas: Museo de Bellas Artes, 1992).

24. Christopher Rengers, *Mary of the Americas: Our Lady of Guadalupe* (New York: Alba House, 1989).

25. Ivone Gebara and Maria Clara Bingemer, *Mary, Mother of God, Mother of the Poor* (Maryknoll, N.Y.: Orbis Books, 1989), 152.

26. William B. Taylor, "The Virgin of Guadalupe in New Spain: An Inquiry into the Social History of Marian Devotion," *American Ethnologist* 14 (1987): 9–25.

27. Ena Campbell, "The Virgin of Guadalupe and the Female Self-Image: A Mexican Case History," *Mother Worship*, ed. James J. Preston (Chapel Hill: University of North Carolina Press, 1982), 5–24.

28. Adela Fernandez, *Dioses prehispánicos de Mexico: Mitos y deidades de panteón Nahuatl* (Mexico, D.F.: Panorama Editorial, 1983), 108–12.

29. Rodriguez, *Days of Obligation*, 16–20.

30. William A. Christian, Jr., *Apparitions in Late Medieval and Renaissance Spain* (Princeton, N.J.: Princeton University Press, 1981); María Dolores Díaz Vaquero, *La Virgen en la escultura cordobesa del barocco* (Cordova: Monte de Piedad y Caja de Ahorros de Córdoba, 1987).

31. Octavio Paz, *The Labyrinth of Solitude*, tr. Lysander Kemp (New York: Grove Press, 1965), 85.

32. Eric R. Wolf, "The Virgin of Guadalupe: A Mexican National Symbol," *Journal of American Folklore* 71 (1958): 34–38; Stafford Poole, *Our Lady of Guadalupe: The Origins and Sources of a Mexican National Symbol, 1531–1797* (Tucson: University of Arizona Press, 1995).

33. Edwin Eduard Sylvest, ed., *Nuestra Señora de Guadalupe: Mother of God, Mother of the Americas* (Dallas, Tex.: Bridwell Library, 1992).

34. Joaquín Antonio Peñalosa, ed., *Poesía guadalupana: siglo XIX* (Mexico City: Editorial Jus, 1985).

35. Peter Laszlo, *La troisième secret de Fatima enfin connu* (Montreal: Guérin, 1987).

36. Jacques Lafaye, *Quetzalcóatl and Guadalupe: The Formation of Mexican National Consciousness, 1531–1813* (Chicago: University of Chicago Press, 1974), 211–57.

37. Barbara Pope, "Immaculate and Powerful: The Marian Revival in the Nineteenth Century," in *Immaculate and Powerful: The Female in Sacred Image and Social Reality*, ed. Clarissa W. Atkinson, Constance H. Buchanan, and Margaret R. Miles (Boston: Beacon Press, 1985), 173, 183–84, 189.

38. Finbar Ryan, *Our Lady of Fatima* (Dublin: Brown and Nolan, 1942), 228–29.

39. Paul VI, *Pilgrimage to Fatima—Addresses* (Washington, D.C.: United States Catholic Conference, 1968), 6.

40. These criteria were systematically formulated by the Sacred Congregation for the Doctrine of the Faith (the Holy Office) on 25 February 1978.

41. Blackbourn, *Marpingen*, 5.

42. See, e.g., Cornelia Göksu, *Heroldsbach: Eine verbotene Wallfahrt* (Würzburg: Echter Verlag, 1991).

43. Andrea Dahlberg, "The Body as a Principle of Holism, Three Pilgrimages to Lourdes," *Contesting the Sacred: The Anthropology of Christian Pilgrimage*, ed. John Eade and Michael J. Sallnow (New York: Routledge, 1991), 35.

44. An early attempt at an assessment was A. Marchand, *The Facts of Lourdes: And the Medical Bureau*, tr. Francis Izard (London: Burns, Oates, and Washbourne, 1924).

45. B. Pope, "Immaculate and Powerful," 173.

46. *L'Osservatore Romano*, 12 October 1981.

47. Blackbourn, *Marpingen*, 5.

48. B. Pope, "Immaculate and Powerful," 183–84.

49. Joseph A. Pelletier, *The Sun Danced at Fatima* (New York: Doubleday Image Books, 1983), 146–47.

50. John Henry Newman, "The Orthodoxy of the Body of the Faithful during the Supremacy of Arianism," Note V to *The Arians of the Fourth Century*, 3d ed. (London, E. Lumley, 1871), 454–72.

51. Dahlberg, "The Body as a Principle of Holism," 10–11.

Chapter 14   The Great Exception

1. Edward Dennis O'Connor, *The Dogma of the Immaculate Conception: History and Significance* (Notre Dame, Ind.: University of Notre Dame Press, 1958), contains important historical and iconographic materials on this dogma.

2. *The Christian Tradition*, 1:286–90.

3. Matt. 1:18; Luke 1:34. See chapter 8, above.

4. Krister Stendahl, "Quis et unde? An Analysis of Mt 1–2," in *Judentum Urchristentum Kirche: Festschrift für Joachim Jeremias*, ed. Walter Eltester (Berlin: Alfred Töpelmann, 1960), 103.

5. Luke 1:35.

6. Bauer-Gingrich, 197.

7. Huhn, *Das Geheimnis der Jungfrau-Mutter Maria nach dem Kirchenvater Ambrosius*, 79–80.

8. Isa. 53:8 (Vg).

9. Ps. 51:5.

10. ap.Augustine *Against Two Epistles of the Pelagians* IV.xi.29.

11. Ambrose *Commentary on Psalm 37* 5.

12. See chapter 1, above.

13. Brunero Gherardini, *Dignitas terrae: Note di mariologia agostiniana* (Casale Monferrato: Piemme, 1992).

14. Augustine *On Nature and Grace* xxxvi.42.

15. *The Christian Tradition*, 3:71–74.

16. See chapter 15, below.

17. *The Christian Tradition*, 3:171.

18. See chapter 10, above.

19. Bernard of Clairvaux *Epistles* 174.7.

20. *The Christian Tradition*, 3:169.

21. A splendid collection, pertinent to this chapter and to this entire book, is Jacqueline Lafontaine-Dosogne, *Iconographie de l'enfance de la Vierge dans l'Empire byzantin et en Occident* (Brussels: Académie royale, 1992).

22. Mirella Levi D'Acona, *The Iconography of the Immaculate Conception in the Middle Ages and Early Renaissance* (New York: College Art Association, 1957).

23. *The Christian Tradition*, 4:38–50.

24. Ps. 51:5.

25. Ps. 116:11.

26. Heiko A. Oberman, *The Harvest of Medieval Theology* (Cambridge, Mass.: Harvard University Press, 1963), 289.

27. Roberto Zavalloni and Eliodoro Mariani, *La dottrina mariologica di Giovanni Duns Scoto* (Rome: Antonianum, 1987).

28. Carolus Balić, *De debito peccati originalis in B. Virgine Maria: Investigationes de doctrina quam tenuit Ioannes Duns Scotus* (Rome: Officium Libri Catholici, 1941), 84.

29. Luke 1:28, 35 (Vg).

30. *The Christian Tradition*, 4:302–3.

31. Denzinger, 2803–4.

32. See chapter 13, above.

33. Marina Warner, *Alone of All Her Sex: The Myth and Cult of the Virgin Mary* (New York: Alfred A. Knopf, 1976), 251.

Chapter 15   The Queen of Heaven

1. See Jan Radkiewicz, *Auf der Suche nach einem mariologischen Grundprinzip: Eine historisch-systematische Untersuchung über die letzten hundert Jahre* (Constance: Hartung-Gorre, 1990).

2. See the brief summary of Edward Schillebeecks and Catharina Halkes, *Mary: Yesterday, Today, Tomorrow* (New York: Crossroad, 1993).

3. It will be evident how much the following presentation owes to the trenchant essay of Karl Rahner, "The Interpretation of the Dogma of the Assumption," in *Theological Investigations*, tr. Cornelius Ernst (Baltimore: Helicon Press, 1961), 215–27.

4. Denzinger, 3903.

5. María de Agreda, *Vida de la Virgen María según la Venerable Sor María de Jesús de Agreda* [Madrid, 1670] (Barcelona: Montaner y Simón, 1899), 365; translation adapted from Nanci Gracía.

6. A sympathetic but still critical account was that of Raymond Winch and Victor Bennett, *The Assumption of Our Lady and Catholic Theology* (London: Macmillan, 1950).

7. Edmund Schlink et al., "An Evangelical Opinion on the Proclamation of the Dogma of the Bodily Assumption of Mary," tr. Conrad Bergendoff, *Lutheran Quarterly* 3 (1951): 138.

8. On the silence, O. Faller, *De priorum saeculorum silentio circa Assumptionem Beatae Mariae Virginis* (Rome: Gregorian University, 1946).

9. Carl G. Jung, *Answer to Job*, tr. R. F. C. Hull (Princeton, N.J.: Princeton University Press, 1969).

10. Job 38:2.

11. Matt. 23:37.

12. *The Christian Tradition*, 3:172–73.

13. See the studies collected in Michel van Esbroeck, *Aux origines de la Dormition de la Vierge* (Aldershot: Variorum, 1995).

14. Bernard of Clairvaux *Epistle* 174.3.

15. Bernard of Clairvaux *Sermons on the Assumption* 1.1.

16. *Imago Dei*, 145–50.

17. Antoine Wenger, *L'Assomption de la trés sainte Vierge dans la tradition byzantine du VIe au Xe siècle* (Paris: Institut Français d'Etudes Byzantines, 1955).

18. John 19:26–27.

19. Lampe, 760.

20. Christa Schaffer, *Aufgenommen ist Maria in den Himmel: Vom Heimgang der Gottesmutter in Legende, Theologie und liturgischer Kunst der Frühzeit* (Regensburg: F. Pustet, 1985).

21. See chapter 7, above.

22. Gen. 5:24; 2 Kings 2:11.

23. Theodore the Studite Orations V.2–3 (PG 99:721–24).

24. Modestos On the Dormition of the Blessed Virgin Mary (PG 86:3277–312).

25. Jugie, La mort et l'assomption de la Sainte Vierge, 214–24.

26. Nicephorus Callistus Ecclesiastical History XVII.28 (PG 147:292).

27. See Imago Dei, pl. 41.

28. Pamela Askew, Caravaggio's "Death of the Virgin" (Princeton, N.J.: Princeton University Press, 1990).

29. C. R. Dodwell, The Pictorial Arts of the West (New Haven and London: Yale University Press, 1993), 360–61.

30. Gen. 3:15 (Vg); see chapter 6, above.

31. Denzinger, 3901.

32. See the helpful study of Walter J. Burghardt, "The Testimony of the Patristic Age Concerning Mary's Death," Marian Studies 8 (1957): 58–99, together with the articles that follow in the same issue of that journal, by J. M. Egan on the Middle Ages (100–124) and by T. W. Coyle on the present status of the question (143–66).

33. Luke 2:35; see chapter 9, above.

34. LTK 1:1068–72 (Michael Schmaus).

35. Luke 1:38.

36. Isa. 25:8; 1 Cor. 15:54.

37. Matt. 27:52–53.

38. See chapter 1, above.

39. Yves M.-J. Congar, Tradition and Traditions: An Historical and a Theological Essay, tr. Michael Naseby and Thomas Rainborough (New York: Macmillan, 1966), 211.

40. Walther von Loewenich, Der moderne Katholizismus, 2d ed. (Witten: Luther-Verlag, 1956), 276–77.

41. See The Riddle of Roman Catholicism, 128–42.

42. See the analysis of Ina Eggemann, Die "Ekklesiologische Wende" in der Mariologie des II. Vatikanums und "Konziliare Perspektiven" als neue Horizonte für das Verständnis der Mittlerschaft Marias (Altenberge: Oros Verlag, 1993).

43. The evolution of the Dogmatic Constitution on the Church as it dealt with the doctrine of Mary is well summarized in Gérard Philips, "Die Geschichte der dogmatischen Konstitution über die Kirche 'Lumen Gentium,'" in Das Zweite Vatikanische Konzil, ed. Herbert Vorgrimler, 3 vols. (Freiburg: Herder, 1966–68), 1:153–55.

44. The close theologial connection between the doctrine of Mary and the doctrine of the church has been set forth in Yves M.-J. Congar, Christ, Our Lady, and the Church, tr. Henry St. John (Westminster, Md.: Newman Press, 1957); and in Otto Semmelroth, Mary, Archetype of the Church, Foreword by Jaroslav Pelikan (New York: Sheed and Ward, 1963).

45. Avery Dulles, "Introduction" to Lumen Gentium, in The Documents of Vatican II, ed. Walter M. Abbott (New York: Guild Press, 1966), 13.

46. Lumen Gentium 67.

47. Abbot, Documents, 85–96.

Chapter 16   The Woman for All Seasons

1. W. H. Gardner, ed., Poems of Gerard Manley Hopkins, 3d ed. (New York: Oxford University Press, 1948), 101.

2. Gal. 2:20.

3. Gregory of Nyssa *Against Eunomium* II.419.

4. Theodora Jenny-Kappers, *Muttergöttin und Gottesmutter in Ephesos: Von Artemis zu Maria* (Zurich: Daimon, 1986).

5. Acts 19:23–41.

6. 1 Cor. 13:13.

7. Wis. 8:7; Plato *Laws* I.631C.

8. Luke 1:48 (Vg).

9. Augustine *Expositions on the Book of Psalms* XCII.3.

10. Gen. 3:24; Luke 23:43.

11. *Faust*, 12104–11.

Index of Proper Names

Index of Biblical References